READINGS
IN
ECONOMIC GEOGRAPHY

The Location of Economic Activity

READINGS
IN
ECONOMIC GEOGRAPHY

The Location of Economic Activity

Edited by

Robert H. T. Smith
University of Wisconsin

Edward J. Taaffe
The Ohio State University

Leslie J. King
The Ohio State University

RAND McNALLY & COMPANY • CHICAGO

Rand McNally Geography Series

Edward B. Espenshade, Jr., ADVISORY EDITOR

Alexander, *World Political Patterns*, 2nd Edition
de Blij, *A Geography of Subsaharan Africa*
Espenshade, ed., *Goode's World Atlas*, 12th Edition
Espenshade, ed., *Rand McNally Regional Atlas*, 2nd Edition
Highsmith, Jensen, Rudd, *Conservation in the United States*
Murphey, *An Introduction to Geography*, 2nd Edition
Smith, Taaffe, King, *Readings in Economic Geography*

AAG MONOGRAPH SERIES

1. Hartshorne, *Perspective on the Nature of Geography*
2. Meinig, *On the Margins of the Good Earth*
3. Alexander, *Offshore Geography of Northwestern Europe*
4. Thrower, *Original Survey and Land Subdivision*

PREFACE

This joint venture was conceived almost three years ago, when the editors were involved in teaching economic geography courses at three different universities. It was felt that such a book of readings would serve to identify further the locational analysis approach to the study of economic geography which the editors, along with many other geographers, continue to pursue. In this regard also, the book would make more widely available some excellent studies concerned with locational analysis.

This selection of readings has been used by the editors in both introductory and more advanced economic geography courses. The selections contained in the Introduction, Part One, and Part Two are already familiar to most students of economic geography and will provide very useful supplementary readings for introductory and intermediate level courses. Parts Three and Four present materials that may not be so widely known or used in economic geography courses at present. However, it is the editors' experience that careful reading of these selections, along with some of the other expository statements referenced in these sections of the book, is not beyond the capability of students in intermediate and advanced courses and in seminars in economic geography. Increasingly, serious students of economic geography are completing work in economics, particularly regional economics and quantitative analysis; and their ability to handle the types of materials presented in the final sections is increasing. Resulting new insights into locational analysis would seem worthy of encouragement.

Although most of the articles in this book were written by geographers, studies by economists and regional scientists also are included, reflecting the editors' view that locational analysis in economic geography is a field in which interdisciplinary communication is most rewarding. Of the 31 selections in the book, 21 are authored by geographers, seven by economists, and three by regional scientists; almost two-thirds of the selections are drawn from the literature of geography.

The editors gratefully acknowledge the cooperation accorded by the contributors to this volume. The suggestions and comments concerning the project which were forthcoming from many colleagues and friends proved invaluable.

R.H.T.S.
E.J.T.
L.J.K.

January, 1967

TABLE OF CONTENTS

Part Three   RESTATEMENTS OF THEORY

READINGS
IN
ECONOMIC GEOGRAPHY

The Location of Economic Activity

INTRODUCTION: LOCATIONAL ANALYSIS
IN ECONOMIC GEOGRAPHY

The location of economic activity has been of continuing concern in the development of economic geography. The economic geographer has long questioned why economic activities are located where they are. This locational approach to economic geography is emphasized here, although the editors are quite aware that there are other approaches to the large and diverse subject of economic geography.

The critical examination of the location of economic activities has been approached by economic geographers in a number of ways, including comparison of a series of mapped distributions and examination of the effects of particular location factors. There also have been attempts to generalize locational tendencies into theoretical statements which could be tested on empirical distributions. Studies in economic geography have emphasized one or another of these approaches and occasionally have contained all of them in varying proportions.

The role of theory in the analysis of locational patterns is of particular concern in this volume. The term theory frequently is used loosely in geographic literature and some clarification of what is meant is appropriate. At least three different but related viewpoints can be identified. These consist of, "(1) a concise, often mathematical, statement (more often called a model) bringing together the critical elements of a set of propositions into hypotheses; (2) the whole of an analysis including assumptions, model, hypotheses, and tests; and (3) a body of generalized propositions relating to a broad class of phenomena."[1] The studies in this book illustrate all three approaches to theory.

Theories of why economic activities are located where they are have proven useful to the geographer in his attempts to "provide scientific description of the earth as the world of man,"[2] or to deal with "perceived

---

[1] G. Wunderlich and W. L. Gibson, "Selection of Analytical Procedures," in J. Ackerman, M. Clawson, and M. Harris (eds.), *Land Economics Research* (Baltimore: The Johns Hopkins Press, 1962), p. 212.

[2] R. Hartshorne, *Perspective on the Nature of Geography* (Chicago: Rand McNally and Co., 1959), p. 172.

similarities and differences between areas, perceived in the first instance rather vaguely and in the end given a more precise definition, quantitative in some cases."[3] These theories provide condensed statements of general locational tendencies which have at least partial applicability in many specific situations. An awareness of these general tendencies is useful in empirical geographical study, not only of particular spatial distributions, but also of specific places in that they represent statements of similarities among areas. In turn, careful identification of similarities is essential in defining differences between areas.

Precise conformity to theories in any social science, including geography, is neither to be sought nor expected, and many of the empirical studies in this book include extended interpretations of discrepancies between deductions from a particular theory and observed patterns in reality.

An attempt is made to identify some articles primarily as statements of theory and others as empirical studies which present partial verification of theory. This organizational convenience should by no means obscure the editors' conviction that the theoretical and empirical studies are closely interrelated and that sharp distinctions between theoretical or deductive studies on the one hand, and empirical or inductive studies on the other, can be misleading. The development of theory in economic geography, as in most fields of knowledge, has been accompanied by an interplay between inductive and deductive approaches. For example, early studies such as those of Aurousseau and others concerning the spatial distribution of cities were largely inductive.[4] However, these studies pointed up certain spatial regularities and made possible some generalized statements concerning the distribution of settlements of varying sizes. Christaller incorporated a number of these statements into a general theory of the location of tertiary activity.[5] Although subsequent applications of this theory to the study of particular distributions showed some conformity, invariably there were obvious deviations as is illustrated in Brush's work on settlement patterns in southwestern Wisconsin.[6] The deviations often suggest, in an essentially inductive fashion, additional hypotheses about the distribution of settlements. These in turn might be incorporated into the original theory and a new cycle of deduction and verification would then commence. This recycling is apparent in much of the recent central place analysis.[7]

Since the central theme of this book is locational analysis in economic

[3]R. S. Platt, "Determinism in Geography," *Annals,* Association of American Geographers, Vol. 38, No. 2, 1948, p. 132.

[4]M. Aurousseau, "The Arrangement of Rural Population," *Geographical Review,* Vol. 10, No. 4, 1920, pp. 223-240.

[5]See W. Christaller, *Central Places in Southern Germany.* Trans. by C. W. Baskin (Englewood Cliffs: Prentice-Hall, Inc., 1966).

[6]See this study by Brush included in Part Two of this volume.

[7]Some of this recent work is summarized in the selection by Berry and Barnum in Part Three of this volume.

geography, the selection of readings is introduced by two classic articles dealing with this general field of inquiry. In themselves these two studies are indicative of the long-standing concern over locational analysis in geography. McCarty, in attempting to clarify the general problem of human location in modern geography, emphasizes the structural and locational interdependence of economic activities. In this respect his work provides a useful backdrop against which more recent analytical work can be viewed. Hartshorne's work is among the earlier attempts by geographers to identify the elements in the location decision and to emphasize the importance of relative location in the distribution of economic activities.

The remaining articles are divided into four broad groupings. The first section includes articles dealing with classical location theory as represented by the work of Von Thünen and Haig on land-use patterns, Weber on manufacturing location, and Christaller and Lösch on the location of tertiary activity. The term classical is used in reference to these contributions in the sense that they represent the earliest and most comprehensive attempts to deductively structure location theories for different economic activities.

Then follows a set of empirical studies which relate in some way to classical location theory. The selection includes studies of land-use patterns, distribution of manufacturing, and tertiary activity locations. In some the reference to theory is quite explicit, in others only implicit.

The third group of articles focuses on restatements of location theory. In contrast to classical location theory, there are more explicit statements of the assumptions and hypotheses. Further, the models are structured in the mathematics of equilibrium analysis, linear programming, or multivariate statistical analysis. These articles do not exhaust the range of recent theoretical work on locational analysis, as is noted in the introductory note to this third section. Rather, the selections are suggestive of certain lines of theoretical work which appear relevant to economic geography.

Finally, the fourth section consists of geographic articles in which some of the mathematical models introduced in section three are used in empirical studies of location patterns. In addition, some of these studies introduce alternative approaches to locational analysis, for example, by way of behavior theory and simulation. In this respect, the studies are suggestive of the interplay between empirical analysis and theory building.

Harold H. McCarty

A FUNCTIONAL ANALYSIS OF POPULATION DISTRIBUTION

Despite the central position of the problem of human location in modern geography, no attempt seems to have been made to set down in systematic form the general principles underlying this phase of human activity. The following statement is an effort to explore the field rather than to provide an exhaustive list of the factors governing population distribution.

Maximum Real Income

Any attempt to consider the problems of human occupance must be couched in terms of a particular culture situation. In primitive cultures marked by a maximum emphasis on individual or household self-sufficiency and a corresponding minimum of social intercourse, the most desirable places of residence are those providing the best facilities for food, clothing, shelter, and protection from enemies. In the more complicated community economies the area of self-sufficiency is shifted from the family to a larger community group. Labor becomes specialized, and the number of factors that must be considered in choosing a place of residence is reduced. The provision of protection and other essentials is transferred to specialists within the community, and each may choose his location with reference to conditions that apply only to his particular type of production. As the primitive community is, by definition, a closed economy, it is guided as a unit by much the same principles as those governing the choice of locations in the household economy. Within the community, however, individuals have greater freedom of choice.

In general, the number of factors that influence individual location decreases proportionately with increases in specialization. As the scope of the economy is broadened to include larger areas and larger numbers of people, opportunities for specialization become greater, and the number of factors influencing the individual's choice of location is diminished. The modern commercial economy is marked by many cases of settlement in areas having a small variety of resources. We are familiar with desert mining camps to which even the drinking water must be transported and with fishing settlements that prosper in cold areas the environment of which provides adequate supplies of neither building materials nor fuel. In a commercial economy, a wide variety of environmental deficiencies may be ignored by individual producers if facilities are present to produce commodities that may be exchanged for needed items not available locally. It seems that in the modern exchange economy the most attractive locations for human settlement are likely to be those which promise to provide the individual with the maximum real income.[1]

In placing the desire for maximum income first in the list of motives influencing the choice of locations, we must not lose sight of the assumptions involved in this line of reasoning. The statement implies freedom of choice on the part of the individual and assumes that all satisfactions can be measured quantitatively as income. There are also the assumptions that men are in possession of

Reprinted with the permission of the author and publisher from the *Geographical Review*, Vol. 32, No. 2, 1942, pp. 282–93. Dr. McCarty is Professor of Geography at the State University of Iowa, Iowa City.

[1] "Real income" is defined as income expressed in quantities of want satisfactions.

adequate information concerning employment opportunities and that they will make rational choices based on this information. Such assumptions restrict the applicability of the principle, but they do not radically impair its significance as a statement of the major factor in human settlement. The first task is to trace the implications of the income motive as a factor in location.

The Service Industries

In the analysis of production and income it is customary to distinguish sharply between goods and services. Economics defines production as *either* making goods more useful (by changing their form or the time or place of their availability) *or* rendering human services that satisfy human wants directly. Individual incomes, which represent payments for production, are thus derived from two very different types of effort: the manipulation or handling of goods, and the rendering of human services. This distinction is basic to any analysis of the location problem.

In general, the production of human services must be carried on near the market. This statement applies particularly to services that are administered frequently and directly to individuals. Doctors find it advantageous to locate near their patients, and barbers near their customers. Such occupations are followed by a fairly constant percentage of the population of all sections of the United States. A service of this type is analogous to an extremely perishable commodity that must be transmitted directly and instantaneously from the producer to the consumer. The point of production is identical in both time and space with the point of consumption.

A slightly different type of market exists for the various types of emergency and repair services, but the locational results are similar. It is not economical to be compelled to wait long for the fire department if one's house is afire, or for a welder to repair a broken machine that has stopped operations in a factory. Similar considerations prompt the decentralization of police services and automobile repair shops.

In fact, the attractiveness of the market is the ruling force in the location of nearly all types of service industries. The force is diminished considerably, however, by three sets of circumstances. In the first place, we must consider the most efficient size for the establishment. Many service enterprises are one-man concerns, but in others an association of individuals is desirable in the interests of economy and efficiency. The "economies of the firm" may be great enough to offset the disadvantage of being farther from customers.[2] In the second place, we must recognize differences in the intensity of the demand for various types of service. Thus we should expect to find physicians in every community but brain surgeons only in the larger cities. Finally, the ease and speed of transportation tend to diminish the attractiveness of the market for all types of service industries. Every development that permits the service occupations to establish contact with their customers more cheaply or more quickly makes it possible for them to choose locations farther from those customers without diminishing the quality of the service. We have witnessed the migration of many service establishments from rural villages to larger towns as a consequence of the coming of the automobile and improved roads. In all these cases, however, no considerable deviation from the principle that service occupations seek locations near their markets has been noted. These businesses may migrate from the village to the small city, or from the small city to the large one, but they never move far enough to lose contact with their customers. As a rule, the location of service occupations is *consequent* to the location of other types of productive activity. The reasons for agglomerations of population are seldom found in an analysis of the service occupations. These producers have settled in an area primarily to be near other types of productive activity.

The Production of Commodities

In turning from the service industries to the production of commodities, we encounter a new set of location factors. In contrast with most types of services, the great majority of goods can be stored and transported and therefore can be produced at some distance from the market. This distinction, however, is not all-inclusive. Certain types of commodities are characterized by large

---

[2]Important examples of this trend toward large-scale service establishments are the offices of the central governments and the colleges and universities. Even in these institutions, however, it has not been considered desirable to choose locations great distances from the people who are to be served.

applications of individualized personal service, and others are so perishable that the time consumed in transportation causes rapid deterioration of the product. Together, these custom-made and perishable products constitute only a small fraction of the aggregate production of goods of all types, but they are of sufficient importance to merit consideration.

The production of custom-made goods tends to be carried on near the market, for the obvious reason that the workman must fashion the goods according to the specifications of his customer. Custom-made articles have become relatively rare in the United States, and it is difficult to realize that they constituted the bulk of industrial production as recently as seventy-five years ago. The industrial history of the United States is largely the story of the decline of custom industries in the face of competition from standardized, factory-made products. The largest remaining industry of this type is the construction industry; others include tailor shops and photography.[3]

Despite improvements in transportation, communication, refrigeration, and packaging, many types of perishable commodities are most advantageously produced near the market. We refuse to buy stale bread or yesterday's newspapers even if bread and newspapers can be produced more cheaply in distant factories than in local plants. In agriculture, the production of market vegetables and fluid milk follows similar trends. Nearly every urban center has market gardeners and dairy farmers as its nearest rural neighbors.

The antithesis of the perishable-goods industry is the one whose materials are perishable but are made imperishable in the manufacturing process. This type of production seeks a location near the source of its materials unless other cost considerations offset this advantage.

Beyond these classes of goods lie most of our commodities—those that are standardized and nonperishable. This category includes practically all types of farm products except market vegetables and fluid milk, as well as the products of forests, fisheries, and mines, and nearly all types of manufacturing establishments. In these industries the problem is to select the location that will permit

producing the goods and delivering them to the market at the least cost. Holmes[4] indicates that, in selecting a site for a new manufacturing plant, an industrialist should add together all the costs of procuring the materials, manufacturing the products, and delivering them to the customers from each of the various sites under consideration. The site offering the lowest delivered-to-customer cost presumably will be selected as the new location. The same principle may be applied to the production of all types of nonperishable, standardized goods. In agriculture, the cost of raw materials is relatively low and the main emphasis is on the cost of land and machinery and delivery to the markets. But in agriculture as well as in mining or lumbering the critical figure is the delivered-to-customer cost.

Inasmuch as the elements of delivered-to-customer cost vary from one type of production to another, the criterion cannot be applied to individual industries without a knowledge of their cost elements. Weber[5] has shown that in an area of uniform transport facilities and uniform ton-mile transportation charges the choice between a location near the materials and one near the markets would be governed by the saving in weight accomplished by the manufacturing process. In general, those industries in which the products weigh less than the materials seek locations near the materials, and those in which the products weigh more than the materials choose locations near the markets. In interpreting this theory it must be remembered that most industries use materials drawn from a variety of sources and that some materials (such as water) are available almost universally—at the market as well as elsewhere. Weber's theory offers a satisfactory explanation of the reason why, in America, the manufacture of commodities such as carbonated beverages is definitely market-oriented, whereas other industries, such as the smelting of ores of the nonferrous metals, are nearly always carried on near the source of materials. The theory is difficult to apply to American conditions, however, because of its assumption of uniform ton-mile transportation rates. But if the freight tariffs actually in force are used instead of tons and miles, the computations become fairly accurate. Weber's

---

[3]Products may be custom-made to the specifications of the individual consumer or upon order for dealers. In a later section of this article the women's garment industry, an excellent example of the latter type, is shown to be market-oriented.

[4]W. G. Holmes: Plant Location (McGraw-Hill Industrial Management Ser.), New York, 1930. "Delivered-to-customer cost" is Holmes's term.

[5]C. J. Friedrich, edit.: Alfred Weber's Theory of the Location of Industries, Chicago, 1929.

theory is based on the simple truism that producers will not pay transportation costs on those portions of the product that cannot be sold, if they can avoid doing so. It serves the useful purpose of pointing out which types of industry are likeliest to be located near their markets and which ones are likeliest to seek locations near the sources of materials.[6]

The Occupational Pyramid

Reviewing the various factors, we arrive at a conception of occupational arrangement that may be applied to any productive area, large or small. It is a statement of the number and types of occupations that would be represented in the area if all types of economic forces were given an opportunity to exert their full effect. This occupational structure assumes the shape of a pyramid. The base of the pyramid consists of that group of occupations whose presence in the area is not predicated on the existence of other types of production. These basic industries will include most types of agriculture as well as mining, fishing, lumbering, and those types of manufacturing not tied to sources of materials or to local markets. Occasionally the base will include centralized service institutions such as governmental agencies, insurance companies, and universities. In general, however, the basic industries will be concerned with goods rather than services.

The base of the pyramid dictates the pattern of the remainder of the structure. Frequently there must be some types of manufacturing to prepare goods for shipment to distant markets. The basic industries may also require tools and other equipment and supplies, some of which can best be produced locally. On the other hand, the workers in basic industries are not self-sufficing individuals, and the local economic organization must provide them with many types of goods and services, including merchandising establishments. Transportation facilities for both incoming and outgoing goods as well as for the movement of persons must be provided. A variety of both business and personal services must be made available. Each of these

groups, in turn, requires workers to care for its needs, and thus the occupational pyramid is created. But the key to its structure is to be found in the basic industries that form its foundation.

With these relationships as a guide it is quite possible to construct a hypothetical occupational structure for any area for which data concerning the basic industries are known. The research student may compare this hypothetical structure with the existing distribution of occupations in the area and concentrate his analysis on those cases in which the greatest differences appear and which may therefore offer clues to local economic and social maladjustments. Or, to cite a problem of the moment, he may be able to predict with fair accuracy the size and nature of the occupational structure that will result from the addition of a new basic industry (such as a munitions plant) in an area. The same technique may be applied to ascertain what shrinkages must be anticipated in the occupational structure if a basic industry is removed from an area. Reasonably accurate estimates of this character would be of great value to both the business world and public planning agencies.

In accounting for the location of basic industries, the investigator is on more familiar ground.[7] Primary attention must be given to local natural resources and a comparison of the costs of producing commodities in the given area and competing areas. In the long run, we may expect most types of agricultural, mining, timber-products, fishing, and manufacturing industries to seek locations promising the lowest aggregate cost of obtaining the materials, producing the products, and delivering them to the customers.

Before we promise too much, however, it is well to recognize the problem common to all types of investigations dealing with social behavior. Essentially, this is the problem of attempting to fit a long-run principle to a short-run situation. The principles of human location, like other principles of human behavior, assume either instantaneous reaction to new situations or a long period of time in which the factors remain unchanged and human

---

[6]Fuel and power are not treated separately in this discussion because their behavior as locational influences is similar to that of a material. In a few industries fuel and power are of sufficient cost importance to attract plants to their sources. For most industries they are minor locational factors.

[7]Inasmuch as the factors in the location of the industries that produce goods are well presented in the general literature of economic geography, they are not elaborated here. For a review of recent textbooks in the field see J. O. M. Broek: Discourse on Economic Geography, *Geogr. Rev.*, Vol. 31, 1941, pp. 663–674. An excellent functional classification of cities is presented by M. Aurousseau in "The Distribution of Population: A Constructive Problem," *ibid.*, Vol. II, 1921, pp. 563–592.

reactions are given an opportunity to work themselves out.

In practice, a concrete social situation must always be considered dynamic. A number of forces are exerting their influence, and the social structure is being brought into alignment. If these forces were to remain unchanged over a period of years, a logical social arrangement would appear that would exhibit the impact of the various forces. But the factors that influence social behavior vary from time to time, and each variation brings about changes in the social structure. The alacrity with which producers are willing and able to respond to locational forces varies greatly from one type of occupation to another. Thus the occupational structure of an area presents the appearance of always approaching an equilibrium that it never reaches because new factors are entering the situation. The various types of friction that prevent the rapid rearrangement of an occupational structure in response to changed conditions must be recognized in any consideration of the problem of human location.

Anomalies in Distribution

The restrictive factors in social adjustment are brought to light most clearly when one attempts to discover the reasons for differences between an actual situation and a theoretical situation. Let us suppose that the occupational structure of an area is under investigation in response to the age-old query "Why does this community exist?" In the course of the investigation the basic industries are discovered and their cost positions with respect to competing areas are computed. The investigator is very likely to encounter certain establishments whose existence is difficult to justify on purely competitive grounds. Among the consequent occupations, he again is almost certain to find groups that are too large or too small to conform with the theoretical norms between these groups and the basic groups. In which types of occupations are these abnormal distributions most likely to appear, and what are the reasons for such situations?

The reasons why an industry remains in an area when another location seems to be more profitable are practically synonymous with the factors that discourage mobility among productive enterprises. They may be economic, social, or political.

On the economic level a major bar to the free migration of productive enterprises is the presence of types of capital that cannot be moved from one location to another without financial loss. Factories can be dismantled and moved only at great cost, and the statement applies equally to many other types of enterprise. Laborers, on the other hand, are rather highly mobile, and so are most of the service occupations. Even among these groups, however, there is likely to be a considerable ownership of immobile capital, such as houses and lots, which it is difficult or impossible to transfer to a new location. In any case, the superior attractiveness of the new location must be sufficient to offset the loss to be incurred in moving from the old. Translated into local terms, this statement means that the tendency for an established industry to remain in a locality rather than seek a more profitable location elsewhere varies directly with the percentage of its net worth that is represented by loss involved in moving to the new location. In general, the types of production that are most resistant to migration are those that involve the largest use of immobile capital. Such industries often remain in a community long after the hope of getting a reasonable return on their entire investment has been abandoned.

Numerous other economic considerations would appear in any cost analysis, but they are likely to be overlooked in a general inquiry. It is evident, for example, that the precision with which individual enterprises select locations will be affected by the nature of the market, the efficiency of various sizes of productive units, and the degree of monopoly possessed by such establishments. In certain industries nominally oriented to the market, it is possible that the most efficient size of plant is so large, and the market for the product so small, that one establishment serves an entire nation or group of nations. If the market is not only small but also scattered, the industry has considerable latitude in its choice of location. If, on the other hand, the market is extensive and production can be carried on in relatively small plants, the industry is impelled to seek locations correlated rather precisely with the market. In most cases, the precision with which a market-oriented industry selects market locations represents a compromise between the savings to be gained from operating larger and more efficient plants on the one hand and the increased costs of marketing the product from central locations on the other.

In connection with the analysis of markets, it is well to remind ourselves that the concept of market is not identical with the idea of consumption. Most types of services and many types of goods are marketed direct to the consumer, but the great majority of goods are sold through a more complicated distributive system involving wholesalers and retailers. Thus it is perfectly proper to speak of the manufacture of women's clothing as a market-oriented industry, despite the fact that it is highly centralized in New York City. More than two-thirds of the wholesale purchases of women's clothing are made in that city. In other words, the garment industry has chosen locations near *its* market; and if we want to know why the market is centralized, we must undertake a new problem, involving sales geography. In America there is a decided tendency for the wholesale sales of shopping goods (in which comparison precedes purchases) to be centralized in a few large cities. As these goods commonly are not standardized, manufacturing plants seek locations near those city markets.[8]

The concept of the most efficient size of plant also requires some elaboration. The term "plant" as used here is defined as the institution or group of institutions required to turn out a product (or service) in salable form. In many lines of production the productive operation is not carried on by a single industry but by a group of industries that coöperate in a single area to create a salable product. In the cotton-textiles industries, for example, it is customary for certain plants to specialize in spinning and weaving while other plants concentrate on bleaching, dyeing, and finishing. The two other types of operations really constitute a single process; neither of them is complete without the other. A greater complication of specialized subsidiary activities characterizes other types of pro-

ductive activity. Although it is generally possible to discover the basic industry in any such agglomeration, we must not lose sight of the significance of the subsidiary activities involved. In pondering the problem of seeking a new location, the individual producer is often severely restricted in his choice by the question whether a complex group of supporting industries is available, or can be made available, in the area under consideration. In such cases the "plant" essentially includes a number of supporting firms.

Another group of frictional elements that serve to delay the migration of industries to more profitable locations involves the conditions of monopoly. Although we must not forget that business is carried on primarily for profit, and that in the long run monopolists will seek the most profitable locations as surely as producers in competitive industries do, the monopolist does possess advantages that enable him to delay the time of migration longer than if competition prevailed. In essence, "monopoly" may be defined as control over supply sufficient to control price. Thus the monopolist may consider it desirable to maintain his price high enough to justify a relatively unprofitable location for a long enough time to permit the liquidation of his local investments in an orderly manner. In a competitive industry, on the other hand, a price reduction becomes the handwriting on the wall. Many times it is not a choice between high profits and low profits, but between profits and losses. In the long run, identical adjustments would be reached, but in the short run, monopolistic industries are apt to respond more slowly than competitive industries to migrational influences. In agriculture, those that produce for a protected local market are likely to shift to other types of farming more slowly than those that produce for a competitive general market. Among the human services, the most highly specialized producers are apt to be the least mobile.

Noneconomic Factors

Finally we come to a group of factors that tend to delay or prevent the adjustment of occupational structures to purely economic changes. This group of factors may be described as noneconomic or, more precisely, as factors the sig-

---

[8]In the interests of brevity, this problem is not pursued to its logical conclusion. It seems, however, that the prestige factor is very important in determining why retail merchants prefer to have their buyers purchase women's apparel in the New York market. The garment industry is essentially a job-order industry in which orders are made up to individual buyers' specifications after samples have been displayed. None of these trends in the location of either sales or manufacturing are observable in the apparel industries that produce standardized garments such as hosiery and men's shirt. Such products are ordinarily manufactured considerable distances from the market.

nificance of which cannot readily be measured in pecuniary terms. Because many of these factors are broadly social, they are, in a sense, more nearly fundamental than the economic factors that commonly receive the principal emphasis in occupational analysis.

There is no way of evaluating the relative strength of different types of human motives except as we are able to impute an evaluation from human behavior. Despite the general acceptance of the principle that persons seek locations promising the maximum real income, all of us know of establishments whose locations cannot be explained solely in terms of the profit motive. Other types of values must be recognized in explaining such cases. Some of these values are purely esthetic and include such intangibles as the beauty of the scenery. Others are more directly biological and are of great importance in explaining, for example, the residence of hay-fever sufferers in the north woods and of retired Iowans in southern California. In addition, the qualities of the human environment often exert strong locational pressure. The desire to be near one's relatives and friends has real importance as a locational factor. These personal relationships should be differentiated from a similar set of social relationships. There is genuine satisfaction in being a member of certain social groups. These groups may range in type from a Saturday-night poker club to a highly institutionalized religious organization. We are familiar with cases in which people did not remain in a new location because they "didn't like the people" or "didn't feel at home."

It seems that business organizations as well as individuals are affected by noneconomic values. Factory owners prefer to remain in the cities in which their factories have become accepted social institutions. To them, there is an element of predictability in the behavior of local townspeople that does not attach to residents of other areas. The feeling that he understands local labor, the bankers, the chamber of commerce, and the railroad interests has made many a factory owner reluctant to migrate to a new location.

The capstone of social control lies in the realm of government. Here are established the formalized procedures and organizations by means of which individual behavior is kept within bounds established by the group. The government provides many types of services and goods and maintains establishments for their production. Its establish-ments are similar to business establishments, but, because they are not located in response to the profit motive, their locations cannot be analyzed strictly in accordance with the procedures used for business enterprises. It seems likely, however, that when once established, they may well be subjected to the same locational criteria as those that apply to private businesses. In other words, no amount of economic reasoning can be expected to explain the location of a national capital or a monastery, but such locations may be evaluated according to how well they are situated to render the services for which they were established. Governmental establishments constitute a major sector in the basic industries of the various national and state capitals. These concentrations of workers, plus the consequent occupational groups that they attract, have created population agglomerations of the first magnitude in every modern nation.

Another important function of government is to guide and direct the course of certain types of private enterprise. In capitalistic societies these aspects of public policy are accomplished largely by a variety of taxes and subsidies that discourage or encourage certain types of industries. In the United States the protective tariff has long been used to stimulate various types of manufacturing. More recently, a variety of subsidy payments have been used to direct the course of agriculture. No analysis of the Great Plains wheat industry, the Florida cigar industry, or the Baltimore steel industry could proceed without reference to the locational effects of government planning, implemented by tariffs and subsidies.

Thus it seems that the forces of society and government, like the forces of economics, may serve as positive factors in the location of basic industries, or they may provide frictional elements that serve to delay the accommodation of an occupational structure to existing locational factors. Because such delays constitute an important element in every occupational situation, the study of historical backgrounds becomes an essential feature of any functional appraisal of population distribution.

Richard Hartshorne

LOCATION AS A FACTOR IN GEOGRAPHY[1]

Introduction

The subject discussed in this paper developed out of previous studies presented in brief to this association.[2] In the study of the distribution of the iron and steel industry, and the study of the lake traffic of Chicago, it was found that relative location in its various aspects was the most important factor. Relief, soil, drainage, and even climate were of minor importance; the lake traffic of Chicago exists largely in spite of the nature of those factors at Chicago, and the distribution of steel plants is only locally affected by them.

Similiar though more superficial studies of other manufacturing and transportation activities lead to much the same conclusion. In contrast with relative location, other factors—even such as climate in the cotton industry—are of very minor importance. In general, just as climate, relief, and soil are the major factors in agricultural geography; natural vegetation in pastoral geography and in forest geography; and the mineral resources in mining geography; so in the geography of manufacturing and transportation, relative location is the all-important factor.

Such studies of manufacturing have indicated a need for a general method by which we may determine the importance of the various factors which have influenced the location of manufacturing plants in particular places or districts where they are found—and which should determine the location of new plants. Consultation with economists and a brief survey of the literature in economics indicate that this task has been left to someone else—I have presumed, to the geographer.[3]

To avoid the confusion already perhaps apparent, due to different uses of the same word, the term "location" is used hereafter to indicate simply the act of placing a factory, or the fact that it is placed, at a certain point; situation in reference to other places—variously called relative location, geographic location, vicinal location, et cetera—will be referred to as *"locus."*

Optimim Location

Since most factories were formerly located without any *a priori* consideration of the advantages of different locations, some have accepted the obvious inference that there was no logic in their present distribution; in other words there could be no such thing as a science of industrial geography. But the same conclusion would appear even more justified in agricultural geography, whereas Baker and others have shown that experience teaches even ignorant farmers to plant, not whatever occurs to them, but those crops which make the most profitable adjustment. Similarly in manufacturing: iron smelting was started, at one time or another, in every one of the Atlantic states, but to-day is concentrated, not where it first started, but where the optimum location is found; much the same, as

Reprinted with the permission of the author and publisher from the *Annals*, Association of American Geographers, Vol. 17, No. 2, 1927, pp. 92–99. Dr. Hartshorne is Professor of Geography at the University of Wisconsin, Madison.

[1]Read at the Philadelphia Meeting of the Association of American Geographers, Dec. 29–31, 1926.

[2]A much longer and more detailed treatment of this subject was written by the author for a different purpose and from a different point of view, and published in *Annals of Real Estate Practice, 1926, Vol. VII, Industrial Property,* (National Association of Real Estate Boards, Chicago, 1926), pp. 40–76.

[3]Studies of certain individual industries are to be found in Keir: *Manufacturing Industries of the United States,* but no general method is given.

Keir has shown, is true of the cotton industry, and it could be shown for many others. However in certain types of manufacturing the so-called "advantage of an early start" is admittedly of major importance.

How is the optimum location for any industry to be ascertained? First, it is to be determined primarily on the basis of cost. Other elements, such as the marketing advantages resulting from the concentration of an industry in a restricted district, and the advertising value of the prestige of certain places, indicated by the significance of such terms as "Grand Rapids furniture," "Minneapolis flour," "Swedish steel," and the "made in Germany" label, these are today of minor and decreasing importance. We are concerned almost entirely with the *costs* of translating raw materials in the place of production into finished products in the place of consumption. The optimum location is that in which the total of these costs is less than the selling price obtainable by the maximum amount.

Analyzing Costs of Production

It is convenient to divide these costs loosely into direct, or operating, costs, and indirect, or overhead, costs. The direct costs include those connected with raw materials, marketing, power and fuel, labor, water supply, and waste disposal. The indirect costs include those of land; fixed equipment (including buildings); machinery, tools and auxiliary equipment; taxes; maintenance of heat, light, and moisture; administration; advertising; liquid or free capital; and others.

Each of these factors has been studied in detail to determine to what extent they may vary with different locations, and how important such variations may be. The conclusions can be given only in summarized form.

The direct or operating costs are of course the most important in practically all kinds of manufacturing (in contrast, it might be noted, with agriculture or railroad transportation). Consequently plant location should depend chiefly on the factors of direct costs, and if changing conditions in these factors make the location disadvantageous, the inertia of fixed investment in land, buildings, and others is seldom sufficient to prevent, for more than a short time, the shift of the industry to some other location.

Many cost factors are of very minor or neg-

ligible significance in the location of modern industries, either because they constitute such a small part of the total costs, or because they are usually but slightly affected by differences in location, or for both reasons. These are the factors of administration; advertising; capital; fixed equipment, including buildings; tools and auxiliary equipment; and maintenance of heat and light.

The factors of taxes, machinery, and the maintenance of moisture conditions are normally as of little significance to plant location as those of the first group, but for certain industries, or in special locations, may be of very considerable importance.

Factors that show far greater variations in local conditions within limited districts than in general conditions in large regions may be of great significance in determining local sites for plants, but have little effect on the general location. The factor of land is always important in this connection and, for industries requiring them, water supply and waste disposal may be most important.

Finally there are four major factors of direct cost which usually vary most with location and are therefore most important in determining plant location, namely the factors of raw material, power and fuel, marketing, and labor.

Geographic Conditions Affecting Costs

It will be observed that, with the partial exception of the labor factor, all these factors, major and minor, vary from one location to another, largely because of differences in the locus with relation to other areas or places. Special exceptions can always be noted; climate in the maintenance of heat and light in all industries, and moisture in the textile industries; relief, surface waters, soil, and climate in the cost of land improvements, buildings, waterways, etc.; surface waters and relief in the cost of water power, water supply and waste disposal; but for the most part these are of minor importance, either because the factors are themselves small in amount, or because suitable conditions are generally available.

Ultimately, in the great majority of cases the problem of plant location may be reduced to differences in labor costs and locus in reference to three sets of places or areas—those of raw material production, those of power and fuel resources, and those of consuming markets.

Granted that those are the four principal

factors concerned, we need some method of measuring their relative importance in different industries,—other than the inductive method of studying the present distribution of plants of particular industries and correlating the relations found thereby. The method used in the study of the iron and steel industry, which was based on the amount and character of the materials involved—raw materials, fuel, and finished goods, is generally applicable in the case of three of the four major factors. In all industries, differences resulting from different locations in the cost of raw materials at the plant and the cost of shipping the finished products to the markets, are clearly dependent on the amounts of the materials involved and the costs of transporting them. Power and fuel, whether used for power, for heating, or for chemical reduction, may be derived in practically all industries, from coal, and hence the requirements are always measurable in terms of tons of coal.

The relative importance of these three factors in influencing factory location is to be measured in terms of four variables: (1) the quantities of the commodities handled, (2) their perishability, (3) the unit costs of transporting them and (4) the extent of concentration of the producing or consuming areas. A few examples will have to suffice to illustrate these.

Some Typical Industries

Industries which convert raw materials into a much smaller quantity of finished products, the residue being essentially waste or of very low value, will tend to be located close to or within the areas producing the raw materials rather than the market areas, (e.g., saw-milling, ore-reduction, and sugar-milling).

In certain industries such as nitrogen-fixation, or the manufacture of aluminum, the amount of power used is so great that the power factor, as measured in tons of coal, overshadows all other factors; since the cheapest sources of power are large water power resources, these industries tend to concentrate at the large water power sites. (e.g., Niagara Falls; Shawinigan Falls, Quebec; Muscle Shoals.)

A slightly more complex situation is found in the wood-pulp industry: one hundred tons of pulpwood produce less than thirty tons of pulp, but the power required is the equivalent of about 120 tons of coal, hence the location of so many pulp mills at convenient power sites close to the forest area.

If either the raw materials or the finished products are highly perishable, focus with reference to the areas producing or consuming the perishable commodities is clearly the major factor. Consequently we find dairy factories, and canneries of vegetables, fruits, and fish within or close to the region of raw material production; while bakeries, ice cream factories, and newsprinting establishments are found in the centers of consumption. Where both groups of commodities are somewhat perishable, as in the meat packing industry, their relative importance is indicated by the special handling costs—refrigeration, depreciation, etc.

Importance of Transportation Costs

The unit transportation costs are usually higher on finished goods than on raw materials, so that when the manufacturing process involves little or no loss in weight, and the raw material is non-perishable, locus with reference to markets is more important than that with reference to raw materials. It might be noted that this conclusion conflicts with the serious error not infrequently heard in the argument that the finished goods, being more valuable, are "better able to bear the cost of transportation." Transportation costs of coal are always less than those on finished products and usually less than those on raw materials; consequently that factor is less important, in proportion to amount handled, than the others.

Where either the sources of raw materials or the market for an industry is concentrated in a small district, the influence of that factor is not only more readily determinable but is greatly enhanced. As this feature is usually least characteristic of the markets, the importance of that factor is in many cases much less than would otherwise be expected. On the other hand, it is just this feature which gives such importance to the presence of a large local market in the immediate neighborhood of a plant, even though that constitutes less than half of the total market for its products. (e.g., the clothing industries in large cities.)

A contrasted situation is found in the manufacture of cotton. Since nearly all American cotton mills use a variety of raw cottons obtained from different parts of the South, a cotton mill at Atlanta may have little or no advantage of locus with reference to raw cotton over a mill at New Bedford, because of coastwise transportation from southern ports.

The high degree of concentration of the sources of power and fuel, whether from water power or coal, is nearly always to be counted on as increasing the relative importance of that factor.

In view of the dependence on transportation elements of these three of the four major factors affecting location, the intimate and all-important relation of transportation to the location of industries is clear. This is the three-fold advantage of seaboard districts as compared with interior districts in the development of a large number of industries; likewise it helps to explain the concentration in interior regions of manufacturing around the larger rail centers. In addition to the primary advantages of routes to and from many areas of production and consumption, such centers have the resultant advantages both of special transportation privileges and rates, and of more abundant and cheaper labor, capital, machinery and other materials. The special advantage of location at points of necessary transshipment—e.g., lake ports and ocean ports—which permits the saving of one handling, is obvious.

Labor as a Factor in Location

Evaluating the influence of the labor factor is more difficult, but not impracticable. From the point of view of economic geography, labor may conveniently be divided into three classes: unskilled laborers, skilled workers (including in both these classes only adult male workers), and the so-called "parasitic" labor, consisting of the dependents, women and children, of the adult male workers in other industries and including both skilled and unskilled, both factory workers and "home workers."[4] The following generalizations are significant to the geographer: unskilled labor is found in naturally increasing numbers in all population centers, may readily be drawn from other industries—including agriculture—and is readily transferred from other regions or countries; workers skilled in a particular industry are to be

found in large numbers only in districts where that industry or allied industries are well established, is developed in new areas only at great expense, and is extremely difficult to transfer from other districts; "parasitic" labor is found chiefly in large cities and in permanent mining communities, and is extremely difficult, if not impossible, to move more than commuting distance.

Aside from the cost of transferring labor to new places, labor costs depend on a great variety of factors including: labor unions and labor laws—usually more important in older areas and for skilled workers; the cost of living, which gives a permanent advantage to location near surplus agricultural areas; and the efficiency of the labor, which is affected by its community training, racial characteristics, labor unionism, living conditions, and climate. (The determination of importance of this last factor, climate, is too difficult a problem for discussion here.)

Whatever the elements involved in the labor factor, their total effect may be measured in terms of cost of each class of labor, per ton of raw material, fuel, or finished product. In case this cost for the skilled labor class or the parasitic class is very high, the labor factor may be the dominant factor in plant location—as it clearly is in the manufacture of jewelry, silverware, and other articles of exceptional value. The presence of labor skilled in such industries is the most important element in the concept of "advantage of an early start."

This means of measuring the importance of the labor factor may be illustrated by two contrasting examples, the textile industries, and the flour-milling industry. Using census figures for the United States in 1919 we find that in the textile industries the cost of labor, consisting largely of the immobile classes, per ton of raw material was $270 in the cotton industry, $688 in the woolen industry, and $4,500 in the silk industry. The same costs per ton of coal that would be required to generate all the power used were roughly $48, $47.50 and $89 respectively. An increase of as much as ten per cent in these labor costs which a new location might necessitate, would off-set very great advantages in freight rates due to closer proximity to raw materials, markets or power. On the other hand, in the flour-milling industry a total labor cost of $2.10 per ton of grain, on which freight rates vary by more than a dollar for a difference of only a hundred miles, indicates that the labor factor is

---

[4] A special class, seasonal labor, is of such minor importance in most types of manufacturing as to be disregarded here.

negligible in determining the location of the industry.

When the labor cost is high, but consists chiefly of wages for unskilled male laborers, the mobility of this type of labor will prevent this factor from being of major importance, excepting in discouraging location in areas of notably high cost of living.

Conclusion

This paper has attempted to outline a method by which we may study the geography of any manufacturing industry to determine the importance of the different factors affecting the distribution of its plants. In general it is found that locus,—i.e., relative location with reference to specific areas— is the all important element; that locus with reference to areas of raw materials, power or fuel, and markets, together with the labor factor are the four major factors influencing factory location; other minor factors have been touched on; the important relation of transportation to factory location has been analyzed, so that it can be properly evaluated in any particular case; a concrete means of measuring the quantitative importance of each factor has been described and illustrated. This method should provide not merely a basis for correlating present and past situations with natural and economic conditions, but also a basis for making predictions or recommendations for the future.

Certain important questions naturally arise however in regard to the factor discussed as all-important—i.e., locus or relative location. Geographers are by no means in agreement with regard to this factor. Its name, its exact definition or even general meaning, the manner of describing or measuring it, and its position among the other factors, natural and social, with which geographers deal—on all these points few geographers would agree, though all must recognize the great importance of the factor, not merely in manufacturing, but in other activities. The analytical study of the cultural landscape in a market gardening belt, or a dairy district, or a wheat farm is essentially incomplete if this factor be left out. The same is obviously true of every commercial enterprise in agriculture, mining or lumbering.

Considerable thought and study have been devoted to this question, the results of which will require a separate paper, to present a definite concept of this important factor on which agreement may be possible, and which will permit of definite classification and more or less definite measurement.

Part One

CLASSICAL LOCATION THEORY

Introductory Note

In locational analysis, a distinction is often made between the approach emphasizing the theory of the firm and that which views locations as a system of spatial relations.[1] The first approach considers the decisions which the individual firm or entrepreneur has to make in relation to the location of his production unit. These decisions may be influenced in real-world situations by industry-wide considerations such as agglomeration economies and competitive policies, but the theoretical analysis typically has been pursued as if the individual firm existed in a free market. In contrast, the second approach considers the problem at a more aggregative level and emphasizes the patterns of land use, spatial interaction, and market areas that result from the competition of a number of different economic activities, firms, or industries.

This distinction between an individual firm approach and a more aggregative analysis obviously is not clearcut. For one thing, the agricultural location problem can be considered from the point of view of the individual farmer (firm), choosing among alternative uses for the land at his disposal. It can also be viewed as a problem in spatial relations, and land-use patterns can be analyzed at a macro level. Similarly, the distinction is blurred with regard to location of tertiary activities in a rural region. Individual retail and service establishments (firms) choose to locate in particular urban places in response to levels of demand existing not only in the urban places themselves but also in the surrounding areas. Thus there develops a system of market areas and associated patterns of spatial interaction.

---

[1]See for example J. Friedmann and W. Alonso (eds.), *Regional Development and Planning* (Cambridge: The M.I.T. Press, 1964), pp. 704–706.

Nevertheless, the distinction between the two approaches in locational analysis is worth keeping in mind; also it shows up in the statements of classical location theory included in this section. The first three articles for example, deal essentially with the spatial relations of agricultural and urban land uses. In the chapter from Chisholm's book there is first a review of the classical Ricardian theory of land-rent which viewed rent differentials as a function of land quality. Von Thünen's contribution then is seen as an alternative explanation of rent differentials in terms of location with respect to the market. As distance from the market increases, the rent-yielding abilities of different farm activities decrease but at varying rates. The result is the development of a concentric pattern of land-use zones around the market located at the center of the isolated state. Chisholm notes the empirical basis of Von Thünen's work.

The short selection from Hoover's book further develops the concept of rent gradients over distance. First, the relationship between the rent gradient and the structure of transfer costs is noted. Second, differences in the gradients for different products are explained in terms of the "amount and transferability of the product produced per unit of land." Finally, Hoover introduces a system of markets and notes the implications of market competition upon both the rent gradients and the pattern of land-uses.

The hypothesis of accessibility to market as the allocative force for agricultural land uses has a parallel in Haig's study of urban land use. The city-center is the most desirable location by virtue of its high accessibility to the rest of the city; hence charges for the use of the land (site-rents) will be higher there than elsewhere in the city. Away from the center, accessibility decreases, distribution costs to the remainder of the city are correspondingly higher, and site-rents are lower. The cost of locating any activity in the city then involves two elements, a site-rent and a transportation cost. These two elements clearly are complementary; Haig refers to their sum as the "cost of friction." One other element in the urban location problem is the existence of "packets of functions" for which strong locational linkages are important.

Weber's analysis of the manufacturing location problem, some aspects of which are outlined in the selection by Daggett, is formulated in terms of the individual firm approach. The major elements in the location decision, namely the weight-losing properties of the material inputs, the factor of agglomeration, and the desire to minimize transportation costs are summarized. The Weberian model stimulated a great deal of later work and is referred to often in more recent classic studies, particularly those of Isard.[2] An English translation of Weber is available,[3] and the serious stu-

---

[2] W. Isard, *Location and Space Economy* (New York: John Wiley and Sons, Inc., 1956).
[3] A. Weber, *Theory of the Location of Industries*. Trans. by C. J. Friedrich (Chicago: University of Chicago Press, 1928).

dent of economic geography should supplement the brief summary by Daggett with a reading of this more complete work.

The concept of a system of market areas is developed at some length in the works reviewed by Berry and Pred, and Valavanis. The first selection gives a very concise summary of Christaller's attempt to explain the size, number, and distribution of urban places in a region. The basic definitions of centrality, central places, central goods and services, complementary region, and the range of a good are discussed. Then follows a brief review of the three principles upon which different systems of market areas were developed by Christaller. Of these systems the hexagonal pattern associated with the marketing principle is best known. Valavanis in reviewing Lösch's work, notes how this scholar presented a more formal discussion of the hexagonal market area in terms of demand cones.[4] Furthermore, in Lösch's work Christaller's system of market areas, which is organized according to the principle of threes, appears as but a special case of a more general spatial system.

Again the selections included in this volume relating to the work of Christaller and Lösch are intended only as signposts and in both cases there are English translations available which should be consulted by those interested in the topic's.[5] This is especially so with regard to Lösch's work which appears rich in ideas and hypotheses that remain untested.[6]

---

[4]A more recent discussion of this same point is E. S. Mills and M. R. Lav, "A Model of Market Areas with Free Entry," *The Journal of Political Economy*, Vol. LXXII, No. 3, 1964, pp. 278-288.

[5]A. Losch, *The Economics of Location*. Trans. by W. H. Woglom and W. F. Stolper (New Haven: Yale University Press, 1954). W. Christaller, *Central Places in Southern Germany*. Trans. by C. W. Baskin (Englewood Cliffs: Prentice-Hall, Inc., 1966).

[6]A recent study that examines some Loschian notions on city-development is E. Smolensky and D. Ratajczak, "The Conception of Cities," *Explorations in Entrepreneurial History*, Vol. 2, No. 2, 1965, pp. 90–131.

Michael Chisholm

JOHANN HEINRICH VON THÜNEN

A point of fundamental importance to the understanding of what follows in this chapter is the fact that the ideas developed and expounded by von Thünen do *not* constitute a theory of location. They amount to a method of analysis which may be applied to any situation in any time or place, and von Thünen himself was at pains to make it clear that his particular findings had no claim to universality. But, he claimed, the method by which these results were obtained could be applied generally. It is the failure to grasp this basic point that has caused many writers to reject von Thünen's ideas as of historical interest only, having no application to modern situations. It is from this initial proposition, that it is the method and not the particular finding which counts, that the character of this chapter derives; an essay in *a priori* reasoning.

Von Thünen published his major work, *The Isolated State*, in 1826,[1] with the avowed aim of discovering the laws which govern the prices of agricultural products and the laws by which price variations are translated into patterns of land use. His was the approach of a practical farming man,

for he owned and very successfully operated the estate of Tellow, near Rostock; a point of considerable interest to him was to discover the financially most rewarding system for conducting his enterprise.

His argument started from the premise that the areal distribution of crops and livestock and of types of farming depends upon competition between products and farming systems for the use of any particular plot of land. On any specified piece of land, the enterprise which yields the highest net return will be conducted and competing enterprises will be relegated to other plots where it is they which yield the highest return. Von Thünen was, then, concerned with two points in particular: 1. the monetary return over and above the monetary expenses incurred by different types of agriculture; 2. such net returns pertaining to a unit area of land and not to a unit of product. For example, if a comparison is being made between potatoes and wheat, we will not be concerned with the financial return obtained per ton of product but with the return which may be expected from a hectare of land in either crop. Thus, at certain locations wheat may be less profitable than potatoes because, although the return per ton on wheat is higher than on potatoes, the latter yield perhaps three times the weight of crop to a hectare of land. In this case, potatoes will occupy the land.

Economic Rent

The actual process of competition for the use of land is more complicated than is suggested in the last paragraph and in order to analyse the matter von Thünen introduced the concept of Econom-

Reprinted with the permission of the author and publisher from *Rural Settlement and Land Use* (London: Hutchinson University Library, 1962), pp. 21-35. Mr. Chisholm is Reader in Economic Geography at Bristol University, England.

[1] J. H. von Thünen, *Der isolierte Staat in Beziehung auf Landwirtschaft und Nationalökonomie*, Rostock, 1826. There have been subsequent editions, including an expurgated version edited by W. Braeuer, 1951. [An English translation appeared in 1966 as *von Thünen's Isolated State*, edited by Peter Hall.]

For brief (and not always complete) accounts, see: *Encyclopaedia of Social Sciences*; C. Ponsard, 1955 and 1958, supra (Chap. 1); R. Krymowski, 'Graphical Presentation of Thünen's Theory of Intensity', *Journal of Farm Economics*, 1928, pp. 461-82; O. Jonasson, 'Agricultural Regions of Europe', *Economic Geography*, 1925, pp. 284-6; R. L. Cohen, *The Economics of Agriculture*, reprinted 1957; A. Grotewold, 'Von Thünen in Retrospect', *Economic Geography*, 1959, pp. 346-55.

For important elaborations, see: E. T. Benedict (editor), *Theodor Brinkmann's Economics of the Farm Business*, 1935; E. S. Dunn, Jr., *The Location of Agricultural Production*, 1954.

ic Rent, a concept which had been propounded by Ricardo a few years previously. At the time of preparing his first draft, von Thünen was unaware of Ricardo's work, though by the time the first edition of *The Isolated State* was completed he had read Ricardo. Von Thünen had therefore arrived at the same idea quite independently. Economic Rent, it must be stated at once, is not the same concept as the term rent in ordinary usage, rent denoting the payment which a tenant makes for the right to occupy a farm or dwelling or other property. It is unfortunate that the two terms are widely used: as they both have common currency, some explanation of the concept of Economic Rent is essential to the exposition.

The Ricardian argument regarding the nature of Economic Rent may be recapitulated in the following manner. Imagine a town which has a certain demand for wheat, requirement which can be met by cultivating only the best quality of land in the vicinity. This, we will say, yields 2 metric tons per hectare per annum. Suppose that the population of the city grows, with a consequential rise in the demand for wheat. All the best farmland is already in use and it is necessary to press into service terrain of a lower fertility, yielding only 1½ tons per hectare. We will assume that the cultivation costs of grade A land are the same as for grade B irrespective of the differing yields. We now have the situation in which farmers occupying grade A land get a ½ ton of wheat more than their neighbours on each hectare they farm, and for no greater outlay. Now it would be worth the while of a farmer on grade B land to offer a farmer on grade A soil anything up to a ½ ton of wheat a year for the right to cultivate this better land. This ½ ton represents the 'surplus' which the farmer operating the better land obtains through applying his labour there rather than on the poorer land. Let us now suppose that all the land belongs to one landlord. Farmer Y on the B quality land may go to him offering to pay ¼ ton a hectare for the land currently farmed by X on the better land. At the time Y goes to the landlord, nobody pays him anything for the use of the land they cultivate. If the landlord accepts the offer, Y will now obtain 2 tons from each hectare but will have the additional expense of the ¼ ton given to the landlord; this will leave him better off by as much as a ¼ ton. On the other hand, farmer X will now have to cultivate some of the poorer soil, from which he will obtain only 1½

tons per hectare; he will be worse off by ½ a ton. It would therefore be to the advantage of farmer X to offer the landlord somewhat more than a ¼ ton in order to retain the use of his A quality land. If farmer Y offered more, it would be worth the while of X to raise his own bid as high as a ½ ton, which is the highest figure to which Y could go. At this figure, both farmers would be getting the same return and the 'surplus' which accrues to the better land would be taken by the landlord.

In the imaginary case cited above, Economic Rent is a ½ ton a hectare on the better land and nothing on the poorer. It is equivalent to the surplus production which can be obtained from the use of the better soil above the return which could be obtained by applying the same resources of labour etc. to the poorer land. As there is plenty of grade B soil, some of which is not used, this gives no Economic Rent. However, if the urban population grows still further, it may that all the grade B land is cultivated and that the next poorer soil, grade C, must also be utilized, the latter yielding only 1 ton of wheat per hectare. If we assume that the cultivation costs of this inferior land are the same as on the superior grades, a simple repetition of the steps of the above argument will show that the best land now has an Economic Rent of 1 ton per hectare while the middle grade now has an Economic Rent of a ½ ton. In other words, the Economic Rent of a particular piece of land is the return which can be obtained above that which can be got from the land which is at the margin of economic cultivation. The position illustrated in Figure 1.

In the above exposition, the idea of tenants paying landlords for the use of land has been employed, yet previously a distinction was drawn between Economic Rent and the rental payments which people actually make. This need not be confusing if it is remembered that the Ricardian exposition assumes a perfect degree of adjustment in all parts of the economy at all times. Under such circumstances, the rental payment which farmer X would make for the use of grade A land would equal the Economic Rent and this would be a ½ ton per hectare when only the B quality soil was being used in addition and 1 ton when grade C land was also cultivated. In practice, there are innumerable imperfections in the way the economy works so that it is usually accidental if the actual rental payments equal the Economic Rent. But it is the level of Economic Rent which in the long

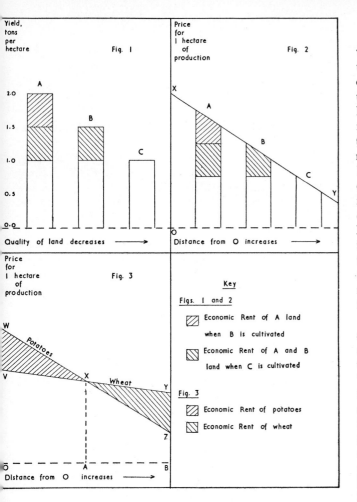

FIGURES 1—3. The Nature of Economic Rent.

run tends to determine what will be paid for the use of any parcel of land. The kind of hindrance which occurs in practice may be illustrated by two closely related examples. Until recently, the rentals of certain classes of residential property in Great Britain were controlled at levels which in some cases were the ruling levels of pre-1914; thereby, the rentals which many persons actually paid were much depressed compared with what they would have been in the absence of the controls. By contrast, the post-1945 regulation of land use has restricted the amount of land available for residential building, whereby prices have become much inflated. A third example is that the rents of many farms in the Netherlands are controlled at levels which are nominal.

It is, therefore, the concept of Economic Rent

which underlies all questions of competition for the use of land and provides the means whereby this competition is resolved to provide patterns of land use. But the above account sketches only the outlines of the concept. Those who wish to pursue the matter further are referred to any of the standard textbooks on economics. It will be sufficient to notice here that the above argument has been based on the notion of the surplus which can be obtained by the employment of labour (or other inputs) on one particular piece of land instead of on a plot at the *extensive* margin of cultivation. Economic Rent also arises with respect to the *intensive* margin of land use, and also with respect to additional doses of labour (or other inputs, such as fertilizers) on the same piece of land. There is not the space here to explore these avenues, nor is it necessary to do so for the purpose in hand.

Von Thünen observed that Ricardo based his argument about the nature of Economic Rent on differences in the inherent fertility of the soil, but that exactly the same phenomenon arises if the 'quality' of the soil varies not with respect to fertility but with respect to location. The point will be seen quite readily by comparing Figure 1 with Figure 2. In the latter, three locations, A, B and C, are shown, situated at increasing distances from the consuming city at O. The vertical axis shows the price that can be obtained for the produce of one hectare of land under wheat. At O, this price is OX, but as the distance from O increases the price declines on account of the cost of transport to the market, this declining price being shown by the sloping line XY. (It is assumed that the yield per hectare is constant at all locations.) The shaded portions of the columns represent the level of Economic Rent at A and B if the next poorer location is cultivated. These shaded sections represent the limiting amount it would be worth the while of a farmer to pay as a rental in order to retain the use of the land he farms, under conditions of perfect adjustment throughout the economy.

It is but a short step to Figure 3, in which the Economic Rent of wheat and potatoes at various locations is compared. The shaded portion VWX represents the Economic Rent yielded by potatoes with respect to wheat and the portion XYZ the amount of Economic Rent of wheat in relation to potatoes. Under these circumstances, potatoes will be grown between OA and wheat between AB. If we imagine the same sequence of crops being found in all directions about the central city, we have an inner belt of potato cultivation and an outer one of wheat production.

A fundamental element of this analysis is the facility with which a commodity can be transported. Potatoes yield a large bulk per hectare, much greater than does wheat. If a hectare of land is at a certain distance from the market, the cost of transport per *hectare* would be considerably greater for potatoes than for wheat. It is, therefore, advantageous if potatoes are grown nearer the market than wheat. This is doubly so when it is remembered that potatoes command a lower price per unit weight than does wheat. The other important aspect of this matter is the perishability or otherwise of the produce. Where deterioration is rapid, there is a great gain from being near the market because spoliation is reduced or eliminated. Consequently, perishable goods yield an Economic Rent which declines very sharply as the distance from the market increases, much more sharply than for other products; therefore, they tend to be located near the consuming centre.

So far, we have considered only the substitution of products as distance from the market increases. An alternative adjustment is to grow the same crop in a different manner, which will have the effect of altering production costs. Under any particular system of farming, it is possible to vary the level of inputs—such as fertilizers—to a considerable extent. By the 'law' of diminishing returns, each successive increase of inputs yields a smaller increment of production than the last. Under these conditions, if we move towards the market from a distant place, it becomes worth while to intensify production, in so far that savings in transport costs compensate for higher production costs. There will come a point when the advantages to be had from intensifying further the particular system of farming are more than offset by the gain which could be had from an altogether different system. This may be illustrated quite simply. Arable farming with a rotation of cash crops and no livestock is normally an unintensive system of farming compared with an economy based on a rotation of cash crops and grass, the latter being fed to livestock. Both systems can be more or less intensive, but the latter offers much greater scope for raising the output per hectare. In Figure 3, substitute for wheat rotation arable farming without livestock and for potatoes ley farming with live-

stock. There is, therefore, a spatial distribution of farming systems as well as of products. Generally —but not exclusively—those systems which have large inputs of manure, labour etc. are found near the market and the extensive ones further away. The exceptions are of two kinds: 1. when the production from a hectare is very large despite small inputs, and of small value, as in the case of forestry at the time von Thünen wrote (see p. 000); 2. a large quantity of inputs yields a small bulk of valuable end-product, as with butter. The former may be situated near the market, the latter at a considerable remove.

The Isolated State

In order to develop these ideas, von Thünen conceived the idea of a state which had no trade connections with any other nation and was therefore surrounded by an uncultivated wilderness. Within the confines of this imaginary state, the soil was of uniform fertility and there was a single city located centrally, all other habitations being rural. No lines of improved communications crossed the level plain, all goods transport being by horse-drawn carts. Von Thünen then proceeded to examine data collected over a five-year period from his own estate pertaining to the costs of production of various goods, the yields obtained, the costs of transport to market and the ruling market prices. On this basis, he calculated the Economic Rent accruing to each type of land use at various distances from the central city and thereby obtained an ideal distribution of production as a series of concentric circles arranged about the central city. His findings are illustrated in Figure 4.

A point which many writers have seized upon is the fact that von Thünen put forestry as the land use occupying the zone second from the central city, whereas certain types of agriculture were put at greater distances. This arrangement accords so ill with the reality of location patterns in the developed parts of the world in the mid-twentieth century that people are often tempted to reject the whole analysis. A few explanatory words are therefore in place. At the time von Thünen wrote, forest products were in great demand for building and, more particularly, for fuel. Large quantities of timber were required for these purposes, and consumers were not willing to pay high prices. A hectare

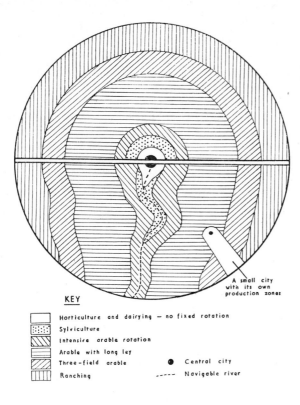

A small city
with its own
production zones

KEY

	Horticulture and dairying — no fixed rotation
	Sylviculture
	Intensive arable rotation
	Arable with long ley
	Three-field arable
	Ranching

● Central city

----- Navigable river

FIGURE 4   Von Thünen's System of Land Use.

of land produced a very large quantity of lumber, even though few inputs were applied; the bulky material incurred high transport costs. Thus, the advantages of proximity to the market were such that all other types of agricultural use, except the innermost zone of intensive production, were displaced by forestry; it produced a higher Economic Rent than any other product in the second zone. For the time at which he wrote, this arrangement was entirely logical. Since then, technical conditions have changed and forestry has been ousted from much of the land near the urban centres. This does not undermine the method by which von Thünen arrived at his circles.

In the first part of his work, von Thünen presented the model of his 'isolated state' for which he postulated ideal conditions. He then proceeded to use this model as a tool by which he could examine the effects of other variables, to see how they modify the 'ideal' pattern of rural land use. He was keenly aware that there is a host of other factors which all have their influence on the loca-

tion of agricultural production. The 'isolated state' was never meant to be something that could really exist; indeed, he originally planned to call the work *Der Ideale Staat*, the *Ideal* or *Imaginary State*. Once the ideal had been established, deviations from it could be analysed.

There are first of all three points concerned directly with production costs. In his analysis, von Thünen included as a part of production costs the remuneration of the farmer, or that income of the farmer which ensures a 'normal' living wage. In imagination, we may consider this to be the wage which the farmer pays himself for his own labour, equivalent to what he would have had to pay a labourer to do this work. Von Thünen expressed wages in terms of agricultural products, so that as distance from the central city increased and prices generally tended to decline, monetary wages also fell: but the standard of living remained constant in all parts of the 'isolated state.' This opens up the possibility that the symmetry of his circles will be disturbed if in fact farmers in one part of the country have different ideas regarding their just reward from those inhabiting other regions. For example, farmers living near the margin of cultivation may accept a lower standard of living than those nearer the central city; this will depress the cost of production in the marginal areas and enable cultivation to be pushed further into the remoter areas than otherwise would be the case. An example of this is provided by inhabitants of the Appalachian Mountains in the United States who have a very meagre standard of living compared with that in most other parts of the country. This can only happen in an economy which is not perfectly adjusted.

The second point in connection with production costs was the observation that many inputs vary in price from one place to another, especially in the case of those which originate from the central city. The item which von Thünen particularly had in mind was manure. At that time, urban transport depended upon horses; these yielded a plentiful supply of fertilizer which was evacuated to the surrounding countryside. Because of the cost of transport, this manure became progressively more costly as distance from the city increased, until the point was reached at which it ceased to be profitable to purchase manure. This factor, combined with the bulk and perishability of the articles produced, determined the limit of the inner zone of agriculture. However, other kinds of input were included, such as the medical and legal services which all citizens require, the costs of which vary in space.

Third, the soil is not of uniform fertility, and therefore production costs vary substantially. Von Thünen showed that the variability of soil fertility has as big an effect on the location of production as the factor distance. He also noticed the importance of climate in this context, affecting as it does the costs of plant and animal production in various locations. Implicit in this point—and in the others also—is the possibility that where large differences in these factors occur they may be the determining factor in crop distributions. However, this does not negate his analysis: it merely means that the question of distance which he analysed operates in conjunction with other factors; a *complete* explanation of a particular situation must include this factor of distance, even though in particular cases it be largely obscured by other considerations.

In his initial formulation, von Thünen assumed that the cost of transport was proportional to distance. He later relaxed this assumption somewhat, examining the situation which arises when an improved means of transport is introduced, such as a navigable river or canal, by which transport costs are less than by overland cart. Although the cost of transport along such a route was assumed to be proportional to distance, a journey which used two or more means of transport could involve different costs for the same distance; the actual cost would depend on the proportionate distance travelled by each medium. This line of better communications was assumed to run through the city (see Figure 4). The zones of production expanded along the line of the river, while contracting elsewhere. He also considered the effects of such things as mountain barriers and import duties upon the costs of moving goods. Thus distance must be thought of as economic distance, not merely physical distance; it is the cost incurred and not the distance in so many kilometers which matters.

Von Thünen also abandoned the assumption that there is a single city. He introduced into his analysis a subsidiary city and discussed the manner in which the zones of production are modified. Though he did not press the matter, the idea of a secondary city opens up the possibility of numerous towns of roughly equal importance with production zones which mingle and mutually modify each other. The result, which is common in the real world, is a pattern of extreme complexity, but the difficulty in unravelling the details does not destroy the underlying principle. . . .

Finally, a number of other factors was explored by von Thünen as modifications to his general scheme, notably the role of trade restrictions, subsidies and taxes. All of these, to a greater or lesser extent, impinge upon the prices of products and hence upon locations of production.

Subsequent workers have taken up the ideas of von Thünen and have sought to introduce improvements. These have not affected the fundamental principles but have attempted to add precision to their formulation and to bring some of the assumptions more nearly into line with reality. We need not concern ourselves with these refinements, for, while important in some respects, they do not add to an understanding of the underlying idea and are not necessary for the arguments of the succeeding chapters. The reader who wishes to pursue the matter further is referred to *The Economics of Location* by A. Lösch and *The Location of Agricultural Production* by E. S. Dunn.

There is one aspect of von Thünen's work which has received but scant attention. The above account has been couched in terms of the best manner in which to conduct the farm as a whole, given its location, and the pattern of agricultural zones which arises as a consequence. He explicitly observed that exactly the same argument applies to the distribution of cropping etc. *within* the farm or estate, and devoted much space to an examination of the problem at this scale. The farmer knows the price of any particular product at his farm gate (the market price less the cost of transporting the commodity to market). This, then, is the local price at the farm buildings, which form the centre of operations for the farm. The fields which lie far away from these buildings incur higher costs of operation than do the nearer plots, on account of the greater amount of time spent in travelling back and forth. If the distance is sufficiently great, there will be no profit in cultivating a particular crop on the more distant lands; at a certain distance from the farmstead, the cultivation of that crop will cease. Alternatively, the returns to be had from some other crop will, at a particular distance from the farmstead, become greater: it might be that potatoes are grown on the hither fields and wheat on the further ones. Furthermore, the intensity with which each crop is grown will decline as the distance from the farmstead increases: the farming system will vary from one part of the farm to another. There will thus be a zoning of land use within the farm which repeats certain aspects of the zoning found at larger scales.

Four consequences were noted by von Thünen. First, anyone conducting a farm or estate should look to the costs of cultivating each field and the returns obtained from it and try to arrange the pattern of cropping so that the net return obtained from each field is maximized. Second—a closely related point—for any particular type of farming system there is an optimum areal extent of holding: farm size is therefore closely related to location, this being one of the determinants of farming systems. Third, the distance from the central city at which a particular crop ceases to be grown is affected by the distance within the farm from the farmstead at which it is grown. For example, near the central city, wheat may be grown on the furthest fields of the farms. At greater distances from the city, the Economic Rent yielded by wheat will be less, but farmers may choose to compensate for this by reducing their production costs. This they could do by growing the wheat nearer the farmstead on fields which, because they are closer, require lower costs of cultivation. In this way the belt of wheat production could be extended somewhat beyond the limits it would otherwise have. Fourth, there is a consequence important to the question of reorganizing farm holdings. Over much of the world, farms are fragmented, with numerous parcels lying at different distances from the farmsteads. A particular parcel may be far removed from the farmstead from which it is operated, yielding a low or even negative Economic Rent. If this parcel lies near to some other farmstead, it possesses a higher potential Economic Rent for this second farmer. If some exchange can be effected which reduces the average distance of the parcels from their respective farmsteads, then the economy of the two farms will be improved and the country as a whole will be slightly better off. This is an important benefit of farm consolidation schemes which springs straight from location principles. . . .

Edgar M. Hoover

LAND-USE COMPETITION

. . . with increasing distance from a market there is a rather consistent decline of the ceiling rents payable by any one type of land use. Since increased distribution costs reduce the net receipts of the producer, such producers can afford less rent if they are farther from the market and finally none at all at a point beyond which it would no longer pay to use the land for that purpose even if rent free.

There is such a "rent gradient," or progression of ceiling rents, for each kind of use, and no two such gradients are identical. What determines their shape?

The level of transfer costs naturally influences the slope of rent gradients. When transfer is costly, the ceiling rent for any given kind of use drops off rapidly with increasing distance; but along a route of cheap transfer, the corresponding rent gradient is relatively flat.

The structure of transfer costs influences the shape of rent gradients. It has already been noted that the characteristic long-haul economy of transfer is reflected in an accentuated concavity of the gradients; i.e., ceiling rents fall off rapidly with distance from market as long as the distance is short but less and less rapidly as longer hauls are involved. Over any stretch of distance for which the rate is uniform, the gradient will be horizontal, except as influenced by considerations other than freight cost. Thus the steplike characteristic of transport-rate progressions may be reflected by steps in the gradient of land use return as well.

As between different products, the slope of the

gradient will differ according to the *amount and transferability of the product produced per unit of land*. This is not at all the same thing as the intensity. Intensity of use is measured by the input of capital and labor per unit of land; what is in question here is the cost of delivering the products of a unit of land. Some very intensive uses, like diamond mines, yield compact and easily transferable products; some uses of low intensity, like city parking lots, are forced by transfer considerations to be very close to their markets. Within any single kind of use, however, larger output per unit of land (of a given intrinsic quality) is directly dependent on increased intensity.

Regardless of relative intensity of land use, processes that yield a large volume of output per unit of land, particularly if the product is expensive to distribute, have relatively steep rent gradients. This is because each addition to distance adds a relatively large amount to the expense of distributing the products of an acre and thus makes a relatively large reduction in the rent earnable on an acre.

The ultimate extreme in this direction is the production of direct personal services, such as shoe shining. Where the potential customers pass, i.e., on main shopping streets, the use of space for a shoe-shining establishment may justify paying a high rent; a short distance away on a side street it may be impossible to earn enough to pay any rent at all. In other words, the rent gradient in this kind of use is so steep as to be almost vertical. It is limited by the extent to which the customers themselves are wiling to detour in order to get the service, and in the case of small-scale "convenience" transactions this is a very short distance indeed. At the other extreme are land uses producing small

Reprinted with the permission of the author and publisher from *The Location of Economic Activity* (New York: McGraw-Hill Book Company, Inc., 1948), pp. 93-97. Dr. Hoover is Professor of Economics at the University of Pittsburgh.

amounts of easily transferable products per unit of land. Sheep grazing, for example, is profitably practiced thousands of miles from the market for wool and mutton.

Evidently the gradients and patterns of ceiling rents will show different characteristic forms for different land uses even in the absence of any intrinsic-quality differentiation in the land itself. Some kinds of use can afford to pay more than others for the occupance of sites convenient to markets.

The same can be said with reference to the effect of procurement costs on the location of different industries around material-supply points. That case, however, is far less significant. It is rare for a number of industries, requiring considerable space, to be competing for sites as close as possible to a single materials source. On the other hand, nearly all types of industry find a *market* in towns and cities, and for many of them the ease of access to that market is the dominant locational factor.

Characteristic Patterns of Land Uses Around Markets

The way in which the different slopes of rent gradients around a market produce an orderly sequence of land uses is illustrated schematically in Fig. 6.1. Four representative types of use are included, with the rent gradient for each rising to a peak in the market city, since that would be the optimum location for each use from the standpoint of distribution costs alone. The rent gradients fall at different rates, so that each use in turn appears as the highest bidder.[5] The resulting idealized pattern of land uses—a series of four concentric zones—is indicated mapwise in the lower part of the figure.

In the actual world it is rare to find so neat a pattern. One reason for this is the irregularity with which transfer costs correspond to distance. Another reason is that each product or kind of land use has its own geographic pattern of supply areas and market centers.

In Fig. 6.1 the influence of only a single market center is shown. But some products (such as fluid milk) have a primarily local sale, whereas

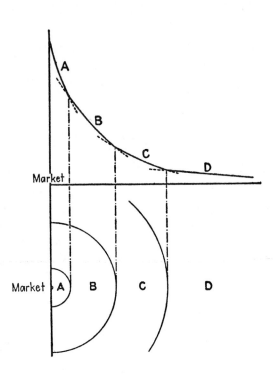

FIGURE 6.1 Rent Gradients and Zones of Land Use Tributary to a Single Market Center. The upper part of the diagram shows the relation between distance from a market and rent in four different types of land use A, B, C, and D. Each of the four rent gradients is drawn as a solid line over the interval in which the corresponding land use is the highest rent use. The lower part of the diagram is a map of the resulting pattern of land-use zones.

others (such as wheat) are produced largely for national or even world markets, and their whole geographic price structures are based on the prices quoted at a few major market centers. A more complete picture, which takes account of this diversity of patterns, is shown in Fig. 6.2. The flatter rent gradients of the more easily transferable products are intermittently penetrated by the more closely spaced peaks of the steeper local gradients.

The over-all pattern of land uses shows broad regions of supply for the most easily transferable products, interrupted occasionally by smaller enclosed supply areas for less easily transferable products, which are, in turn, interrupted frequently by the very small enclosed supply areas of the least transferable products. The rather complex pattern

[5] The composite gradient of actual rents, as determined by the sequence of "highest bidder" uses, must be even more concave than the gradients for individual uses. Figure 6.1 adequately demonstrates this.

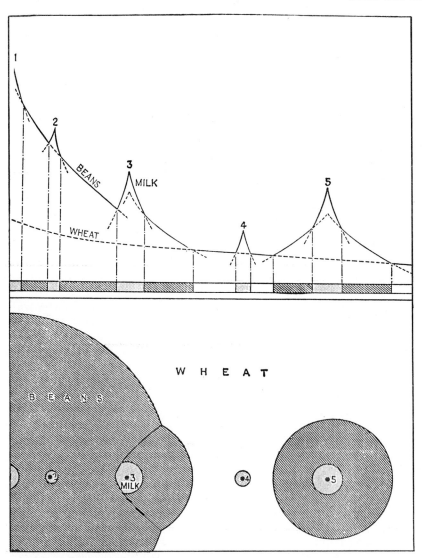

FIGURE 6.2 Rent Gradients and Zones of Land Use Tributary to Five Market Centers, 1,2,3,4, and 5. Three types of land use are involved: milk, beans, and wheat production. It is assumed that a market for milk exists at each of the five market centers, that markets for beans exist at market centers 1, 3, and 5 only, and that a market for wheat exists only at market center 1.

The upper part of the diagram shows the rent gradients for the three types of use, each rent gradient being drawn as a solid line over the interval in which the corresponding land use is the highest rent use.

The resulting progression of land uses along the route running through the five market centers is shown by the shadings on the strip near the middle of the figure: Strippled stretches on territory are devoted to milk production; shaded stretches to bean production; and white areas to wheat production.

The lower part of the diagram is a map of the resulting pattern of land use zones. Dots represent the five market centers. Stippled areas are devoted to milk production; shaded areas to bean production; and white areas to wheat production. The bean-supply areas of market centers 1 and 3 meet along the boundary that curves around market center 3.

of land-use areas derived in Fig. 6.2 for only three products under highly simplified assumptions should make it clear why in the much more com-plicated actual world, with many rival products and sets of markets, we see a patchwork that some-times appears utterly unsystematic.

Robert Murray Haig

TOWARD AN UNDERSTANDING OF THE METROPOLIS

The Assignment of Activities to Areas in Urban Regions

In the preceding paper[1] dealing with the factors affecting the general "pattern" of population distribution, it was suggested that the urban areas are apparently the most economical points at which to supply people with the varied assortments of goods and services in effective demand at the present state of the world's development; that, assuming a given state of the arts and a given distribution of natural resources, the relative importance of rival urban areas is determined fundamentally by relative transportation advantages; and that the entire "foot-free" population (all persons not required to man the natural resources, the "portability-producing" industries, the "supplementary" industries, the transportation system, and the necessary services such persons with their consumption assortments) is tending to locate in urban areas. Attention will now be directed to the urban areas themselves. What are the forces that determine the several uses of urban land?

At first glance, land utilization in an urban area such as New York and its environs appears to be without rhyme or reason, a confused and baffling welter of anomalies and paradoxes. The land is being used, most of it, very intensively indeed. Nine million people eat and sleep, work and play in the area. But the assignment of the land to the various uses seems to the superficial observer to have been made by the Mad Hatter at Alice's tea party. Some of poorest people live in conveniently located slums on high-priced land. On patrician

Reprinted by permission of the publishers from Robert Murray Haig, *The Quarterly Journal of Economics*, Cambridge, Mass.: Harvard University Press, 1926.
[1]Quarterly Journal of Economics, February, 1926, pp. 179-208.

Fifth Avenue, Tiffany and Woolworth, cheek by jowl, offer jewels and jimcracks from substantially identical sites. Childs restaurants thrive and multiply where Delmonico's withered and died. A stone's throw from the stock exchange, the air is filled with the aroma of roasting coffee; a few hundred feet from Times Square, with the stench of slaughter-houses. In the very heart of this "commercial" city, on Manhattan Island south of 59th Street, the inspectors in 1922 found nearly 420,000 workers employed in factories. Such a situation outrages one's sense of order. Everything seems misplaced. One yearns to rearrange the hodgepodge and to put things where they belong. The confusion, of course, is more apparent than real. The deeper one delves into the reasons underlying the present layout, the more distrustful he becomes of sweeping indictments of its soundness and efficiency. Most of the apparent anomalies and paradoxes dissolve into commonplaces when subjected to serious study and detailed examination.

Where do things "belong" in an urban area? What is the test of the fitness of an activity to occupy a given part of the area? By what standard can an activity be said to be misplaced? Is there a perfect economic design or pattern of layout which the planner should strive to approximate? Is it possible to construct a defensible order of precedence among the activities clamoring for space? Is there a valid distinction between "primary" and "ancillary" activities? On what basis can the conflict of claims be reconciled? Is there a scientific foundation for the exercise of collective control through zoning? These are questions which are troubling the more thoughtful leaders in the city-planning movement.

True it is that answers to these questions and, in general, an understanding of the principles which determine the assignment of activities to areas in urban centers, are essential if city planning is to proceed intelligently. "One of the most stupendous dreams of the social control of civilization concerns the remaking of cities," says Douglas.[2] "It is proposed to decentralize them deliberately. By removing obstacles, or interposing deflecting factors, the decentralization which is actually going on may be guided, accelerated and focussed. This is the meaning of modern city planning. In the process of deliberate decentralization, science is ultimately to decide what elements in the present city ought to remain and what ought to go."

Unfortunately one finds little in the literature of social science upon which to base a definite prescription as to what functions should be decentralized. The sociologists, it is true, have recently begun to discuss what they call the "ecology"[3] of the city, but their analysis has not yet proceeded to the point where it can offer a substantial contribution to the solution of this particular problem.[4] And when one turns to the economists, it appears that surprisingly little attention has been given to the problem. In the standard texts, urban site rent is commonly dismissed with a brief observation regarding its resemblance or lack of resemblance to the rent of agricultural land. Professor Taussig[5] is one of the few writers who has made a real effort to shed light upon this problem. In a separate chapter devoted to the topic, he points out that urban rent "results from the differential advantages of certain plots." "The application of capital and labor on some sites yields greater returns than on others," and "the possibilities of production on the better sites are limited." However, in discussing "the cause and the extent of the differential advantages of urban land," he is forced to content himself with suggesting, in a few examples, what the cause may be. There is little consideration as to precisely what it is about one type of use which enables it to outbid another type of use for the privilege of utilizing a choice site. Professor Ely, in his recent series of monographs on "land economics," contributes the following toward a solution: "The 'center of the city' is merely the point of greatest concentration of people in a market. The size of this market depends upon the population of the city and upon its wealth. To be situated at the center of this market is to occupy the most advantageous place, hence men will bid high for the ownership or the privilege of occupying this favored space."[6] He quotes the following sentence from Thünen: "If we investigate the reasons why the site rent increases steadily toward the center of the city, we shall find it in the labor saving, the greater convenience and the reduction of the loss of time in connection with the pursuit of business."[7] This is very suggestive, but falls far short of supplying a scientific guide for a policy of deliberate decentralization. All can agree with Professor Ely's observation that "perhaps no one has sufficiently developed the law of urban rent."

The interests at stake in decentralizing cities are sufficiently great to justify considerable effort to learn where, in a soundly-conceived economic plan, things "belong." The committee on the Regional Plan of New York decided to attack the problem in a realistic manner by making a series of studies of trends and tendencies in the location of the chief economic activities in the area. It was hoped that, by observing what is actually happening in the competitive struggle for urban sites, it might be possible to glimpse the outlines of an economically ideal pattern or plan; that, by examining what was being crowded out of the choice central locations and what was doing the crowding, it might be possible to infer where "things belonged."

The results of these studies of trends and tendencies in urban land utilization are too voluminous to be presented here.[8] However, some of the aggregate figures are shown in the table on page

---

[2]The Suburban Trend, pp. 272-274.

[3]They point out that "the city has an internal organization which may be termed an ecological organization, by which we mean the spatial distribution of population and institutions and the temporal sequence of structure and function following from the operation of selective, distributive, and competitive forces tending to produce typical results wherever they are at work." Park and Burgess, The City, p. 187.

[4]They assert that "in the process of community growth there is a development from the simple to the complex, from the general to the specialized; first to increasing centralization and later to a decentralization process." Ibid., p. 73. "There is a struggle among utilities for the vantage points of poistion. . . . As competition for advantageous sites becomes keener with the growth of population, the first and economically weaker types of utilities are forced out to less accessible and lower-priced areas." Ibid., p. 74. But what are these "economically weaker" types and precisely wherein does the weakness consist? They observe further that "land values are the chief determining influenc in the segregation of local areas and in the determination of the uses to which an area is to be put." Ibid., p. 203. But is it not the uses which determine the land values rather than vice versa?

[5]Principles of Economics, Revised Edition, ii, 77.

[6]Characteristics and Classification of Land, p. 143.

[7]Der isolierte Statt, pp. 212-213.

[8]The studies are being published in a series of monographs by the Regional Plan of New York, 130 East 22d Street, New York City. In this paper, citations of these studies are made to the number of the monograph in the Economic Series.

47, and some of the general conclusions will be briefly summarized. In this article, however, the primary purpose is not to exhibit the evidence in detail, but to outline and submit for criticism certain tentative hypotheses regarding the assignment of activities to areas in urban areas which have been suggested by these special studies. For most of the supporting data the reader must be referred to the published monographs.

In some respects New York is a peculiarly good place to study the problem outlined above. Its size and complexity, which at first glance appear to be such serious obstacles, prove upon examination to carry with them great advantages. The magnitude of the metropolis not only minimizes the influence of "sport" cases, but it also operates, like a Bunsen flame under a test-tube, to produce phenomena which do not become explicit in small places where the pressure for space is not great. Again, the complexity of New York implies a wide range and a high degree of segregation of economic activities, and consequently an opportunity to observe and to distinguish among many rather than a few economic functions struggling for the more convenient locations.

When the city planners speak of decentralization, they usually have prominently in mind the decentralization of factories. Manufacturing seems to them one thing which certainly does not "belong" in the center of the metropolis. Consequently it is interesting to examine the figures in the table on page 47 to see how far decentralization of factories is taking place under the lash of the competition for space. Zone I, Manhattan south of 59th Street, consists roughly of the southern third of the island, the heart of the city. The other two zones, together, stretch approximately to the commuting limits of the metropolis.[9]

In the first place, while many more people worked in factories in the center of the city in 1922 than in 1900, fewer worked there than in 1917.[1] The rate of increase in the center, when one compares 1900 with 1922, was 44.8 per cent. For the rest of New York and its environs the increase was 114 per cent. The population of the entire area increased, betwen 1900 and 1920, 66.8 per cent.

These figures appear to furnish grounds for the belief that the peak of manufacturing in the center of the city was reached about ten years ago and that a process of decentralization is already under way.

When the figures are broken into the ten industrial groups shown in the table on page 47, other significant facts emerge. Thus, between 1900 and 1912, the wood-products groups was the only group in Zone I which actually declined in numbers. Between 1912 and 1917, metals, textiles, and tobacco also went into decline. Between 1917 and 1922, the textiles group gained slightly; but the chemical, the men's and women's clothing, and the food groups joined the ranks of those that were losing their hold in the center of the city. Printing is the only group showing a consistent record of gain in the central zone throughout the twenty-two-year period.

As the result of these developments, the industrial complexion of the center of the city has changed. In 1900 a representative group of 100 factory hands employed in the center of the city would have contained 33 clothing workers; in 1912 and in 1917 the group would have contained 43 clothing workers, and in 1922, 40.[2]

Moreover, in spite of their relative strength in the center of the city, both the men's and the women's clothing groups have grown more rapidly in Zone II than in Zone I. As a result, while approximately two thirds of the men's-clothing workers were in the center in 1900, only one half were there in 1922. Even with women's clothing, in 1900 only about one seventh of the workers were employed outside the center, whereas in 1922 one fifth were outside.

These general figures seem to indicate, then, that, on the whole, manufacturing is certainly not more than holding its own in the center of the city and has probably already begun to be crowded out. Moreover, the figures give evidence of considerable variability in the degree of persistence with which the different industries cling to the choice central locations.

When the industries are broken still further into smaller sub-groups, as is done in the table on page 48 for the years 1900 and 1922 in the center

---

[9]For maps showing the precise boundaries of the zones, see the published monographs of the Economic Series.

[1]This decline is not to be attributed to the business depression of 1922, as appears to be shown by the fact that between 1917 and 1922 the region as a whole gained materially in number of factory employees.

---

[2]These include only those employees who are grouped under the heading of men's clothing and women's clothing. If the needle-workers included in the "all others" group were added, the 1922 figure of 40 becomes 56.

TABLE I Employees of Inspected Factories Classified by Industries and by Zones in New York and its Environs in 1900, 1912, 1917, and 1922, with Per Cent of Increase of 1922 over 1900*

Industry	Number of Employees				Per cent increase 1922 over 1900
	1900	1912	1917	1922	
ZONE I—MANHATTAN SOUTH OF 59TH STREET					
Chemicals	5,400	6,262	7,775	7,523	39.3
Men's clothing	35,471	63,189	70,119	52,670	48.5
Women's clothing	59,181	112,756	128,108	114,061	92.7
Metals	37,623	44,940	42,870	42,065	11.8
Printing	35,946	50,648	52,868	53,873	49.9
Food	22,361	25,393	27,457	24,197	8.2
Textiles	9,774	11,437	10,325	11,417	16.8
Wood	21,701	20,774	17,058	14,872	—31.5
Tobacco	10,515	11,740	6,658	5,423	—48.4
All others	51,931	62,996	97,225	93,683	80.4
Total	289,903	410,135	460,463	419,784	44.8
ZONE II—TWENTY-MILE INDUSTRIAL ZONE					
Chemicals	21,336	36,560	38,914	56,882	166.6
Men's clothing	10,045	37,024	36,516	43,110	329.2
Women's clothing	6,911	20,510	26,364	28,210	308.2
Metals	89,200	147,973	164,161	182,814	104.9
Printing	5,374	9,871	13,233	16,601	208.9
Food	23,201†	39,553	38,516	53,177	129.2†
Textiles	55,255	87,520	82,940	96,420	74.5
Wood	18,804	40,731	31,280	36,393	93.5
Tobacco	12,319	17,595	13,147	19,946	61.9
All others	59,301	106,255	94,488	128,407	116.5
Total	301,746	543,592	539,559	661,960	119.4
ZONE III—OUTLYING AREA					
Chemicals	1,284	2,185	15,722	6,096	374.8
Men's clothing	4,580	7,015	8,545	12,119	164.6
Women's clothing	4,220	3,931	7,662	7,924	87.8
Metals	23,638	36,177	63,881	44,200	87.0
Printing	983	1,738	2,132	2,870	191.4
Food	2,760†	2,586	3,899	5,098	84.7†
Textiles	8,380	11,672	12,944	15,924	90.0
Wood	2,494	2,469	2,773	4,298	72.3
Tobacco	1,005	1,010	1,486	1,126	12.0
All others	15,994	35,737	24,593	24,724	54.6
Total	65,338	104,520	143,637	124,379	90.3

* The total figures for all three zones will be found in the table on page 190, Quarterly Journal of Economics, February, 1926.
† A comparison of the factory inspection figures for New Jersey in 1900 with fragmentary figures from the census indicates that perhaps as many as 2000 workers in food plants were omitted from Zone II, and as many as 600 from Zone III.

of the city, it is found that the aggregate figures conceal marked variations in the growth and decay of branches of the various industries. While the aggregate figures for the printing industry, for example, show a strong and steady growth in Zone I, amounting to about 50 per cent in the 22 years, the more detailed figures for the sub-groups show that photo-engraving quadrupled in this area, newspaper printing nearly trebled, book- and job-printing increased approximately the normal 50 per cent, lithography was practically static, and bookbinding declined 20 per cent. Again, while in the aggregate women's clothing about doubled in this central area, one branch, dresses and waists, trebled, and yet another branch, neckwear, lost more than half its employees. In the aggregate, the metal-products industry almost stood still in Zone I; but one branch, technical instruments, more than doubled, and another branch, heavy machinery, declined to less than half its former size. Equally striking statements can be made for practically all the other industries.

Turning from manufacturing to the other activities that are competing for choice central sites, serious difficulties are encountered because of scanty statistical data. The space-demands of housing may, however, be roughly gauged by using the census figures of population. In 1900, 1,149,226 people were reported as living south of 59th Street. This number increased to 1,252,893 in 1910, but dropped to 1,063,962 in 1920, a decline of 168,931. Moreover, it is the very poor who are abandoning the center as a place to live. A study of the 58 sanitary districts south of 14th Street show that, in the 27 districts which may fairly be classed as slums, there was a decrease in population between 1910 and 1920 of 158,632, a loss nearly large enough in itself to account for the entire population decline in Zone I.[3] Apparently the well-to-do are not being crowded out; they may be doing some of the crowding.

The following fragmentary information regarding marketing, financial, and professional activities in downtown New York may be considered in connection with the fact, mentioned above, that factory employees in Manhattan south of 59th Street increased approximately 45 per cent between 1900 and 1922.

The number of investment bankers (firms and

TABLE II Employees of Inspected Factories in Manhattan South of 59th Street Classified by Branches of Industry in 1900 and 1922, with Per Cent Increase

	1900	1922	Per cent increase or decrease
Photo-engraving	447	2,202	392.6
Men's furnishings	1,103	5,133	365.4
Knit goods	779	2,827	262.9
Embroidery	3,365	11,494	241.6
Dresses and waists	16,302	50,598	210.4
Millinery	7,383	21,353	189.2
Newspaper printing	3,511	9,354	166.4
Soap and toilet preparations	1,371	3,484	154.1
Corsets	954	2,268	137.7
Technical instruments	5,438	11,772	116.5
Fur, leather, and rubber	15,667	30,963	97.6
Textile finishing	871	1,637	87.9
Children's wear	4,659	8,653	85.7
Textile small wares	2,616	4,574	74.8
Miscellaneous clothing	3,363	5,876	74.7
All others	2,750	4,722	71.7
Women's cloaks and suits	23,167	38,013	64.1
Men's clothing	24,776	38,568	55.7
Cigarettes and miscellaneous tobacco	1,577	2,447	55.2
Book and job printing	19,742	30,324	53.6
Housedresses and kimonas	2,774	4,218	52.1
Light metal products, etc.	10,872	15,937	46.6
Women's underwear	5,274	7,358	39.5
Paints, dyes, and inks	942	1,243	32.0
Paper and paper goods	9,206	11,505	25.0
Jewelry and precious metals	6,130	7,537	22.9
Miscellaneous wood products	2,025	2,453	21.1
Laundry, cleaning, and dyeing	3,535	4,177	18.2
Miscellaneous printing	3,670	4,136	12.7
Lithography	3,394	3,685	8.6
Food	22,361	24,197	8.2
Men's hats and caps	5,531	5,463	—1.2
Miscellaneous chemicals	749	707	—5.6
Pianos and other musical instruments	3,645	3,406	—6.6
Fine chemicals	2,338	2,089	—10.7
Men's shirts	4,061	3,506	—13.7
Silk goods	1,511	1,274	—15.7
Bookbinding	5,182	4,172	—19.5
Furniture and cabinet work	9,072	6,290	—30.7
Stone products	5,305	3,211	—39.5
Pencils, pipes, and cork	2,127	1,244	—41.5
Women's neckwear	6,051	2,953	—51.2
Heavy machinery, etc.	15,183	6,819	—55.1
Cigars	8,938	2,976	—66.7
Lumber and planing mill products	4,465	1,427	—68.0
Power	1,357	382	—71.9
Miscellaneous textile products	3,997	1,105	—72.3
Cooperage	367	52	—85.8
	289,903	419,784	44.8

[3]From an unpublished study made by Miss Celia Lesser.

individuals) in New York City increased from 204 in 1902 to 372 in 1922, or 58 per cent.[4]

The number of insurance brokers south of 59th Street increased from 3474 in 1912 to 6613 in 1923, or 90 per cent.[5]

The number of accounting firms south of 59th Street increased from 43 in 1900 to 726 in 1922, or 1588 per cent.[6]

The number of corporations listed in Moody's Manual as having offices in New York south of 59th Street increased from 69 in 1912 to 570 in 1922, or 726 per cent.

The number of custom brokers and forwarding agents south of Fulton Street increased from 110 in 1900 to 370 in 1922, or 236 per cent.[7]

The number of lawyers south of 59th Street increased from 6135 in 1900 to 12,769 in 1922, or 108 per cent.[8]

The floor space occupied by the large department stores[9] south of 60th Street increased from 4,101,000 square feet in 1902 to 7,083,000 square feet in 1922, an increase of 73 per cent.[1] In 1912 the corresponding figure was 7,272,000 square feet, there being a marked decline between 1912 and 1916.

The number of middlemen (including commission merchants, converters, brokers, jobbers, selling agents, factors, New York buyers for out-of-town jobbers, New York sales offices of out-of-town manufacturers, etc.) in the wholesale cotton, silk, and knit-goods markets south of 59th Street increased from 733 in 1900 to 3924 in 1922, or 435 per cent.[2]

The number of jewelry jobbers and wholesalers south of 59th Street increased from 387 in 1900 to 1025 in 1923, or 165 per cent.[3]

Such data as these furnish a very rough and approximate answer to the questions what is being crowded out of the center of the city and what is doing the crowding. However, this answer, tho realistic in form and to some degree helpful in solving the practical problem of the planner, is cast in terms which do not greatly advance the search

toward an understanding of the phenomena. It is only when inquiry is made regarding the detailed reasons for growth and decline of the various activities that the study begins to yield the stuff out of which an explanation can be constructed.

Several of the extreme cases are easily explained on the special ground of the fluctuating fortunes of the industry as a whole. Cooperage has almost disappeared as a down-town industry. But cooperage throughout the country is on the decline, the prohibition amendment and the scarcity of white oak being among the contributing causes.[4] Again, photo-engraving, the most rapidly growing industry in the table on page 48, was in its technical swaddling-clothes in 1900, and has grown to manhood during the period under review, hand in hand with the art of photography. The high rate in the growth of toilet preparations is traceable in large part to the success which has recently crowned the struggle of the lip-stick for respectability. Further, the gain of one branch of an industry is sometimes at the expense of another branch. The popularity of cigarettes has retarded growth in the manufacture of cigars. The high rate of growth of the dress industry is partly the cause of the relatively low rate of growth of the cloak and suit industry. In other words, the rate of growth or decline in the center of the city is not a sure indication of the degree of fitness of a particular industry to compete for choice sites. Men's hats and caps, an old industry whose rate of growth was practically zero, may "belong" in the center quite as much as "knitted outerwear," a new industry, which grew nearly four-fold.

When one begins to seek the reasons for growth and decline in the center, he is immediately impressed by the inadequacy of the terminology ordinarily used in discussing the problem. Broad terms such as "industry," "manufacture," "commerce," and "trade" are not well adapted to the task in hand. If, for example, a silk mill, formerly located on Manhattan, moves to Pennsylvania but keeps its head office and salesroom in New York, it is not accurate to say that this "industry" has left New York. What has actually happened is that there has been a territorial subdivision of functions which were formerly united in the same place, certain activities being sent to Pennsylvania and

[4]Williams and Company's Directory of Brokers.
[5]Lists of Insurance Department of State of New York.
[6]Trow's Business Directory and Donnelly's Red Book.
[7]Custom-House Guide Book.
[8]Bender's Legal Directory.
[9]Those having a gross floor space of 25,000 square feet or more.
[1]Real Estate Atlases of Manhattan.
[2]Davison's Directory.
[3]List of National Jewelers, Board of Trade.

[4]Cooperage, of course, also requires large space. See Mills, Economic Series, Monograph Number Four, p. 45.

certain others kept in the metropolis. Fabrication and certain other functions have gone, but selling and many of the other functions remain. Fourth Avenue is full of establishments bearing the names of manufacturing plants, but no fabrication is in evidence. Tho it is the center of the silk industry, not a loom is to be found there. Nor is the situation changed fundamentally if the establishment, instead of retaining its New York office, delegates its selling to a jobber or agent operating in New York under his own name. The significant thing is the amount and the character of the activity which leaves, and the amount and the character of the activity which remains. If a Fifth Avenue merchant sends his buyer to open an office in Paris, transfers his reserve stocks to a warehouse on the waterfront, and places his alteration shop in Long Island City, it is misleading to say merely that the "merchant" is located on Fifth Avenue. He has scattered his activities to many places. If the fact that his sign still graces the Avenue is accepted as the sole test of his location, significant facts will be entirely over-looked. Every business is a packet of functions, and within limits these functions can be separated and located at different places.

The pressure for space in the center of New York has stimulated a great deal of relocation of functions which is difficult to catch in any statistical net. A Fifth Avenue merchant testifies that he has found it profitable in recent years to rent extensive accommodations in bonded warehouses instead of storing his imported goods in his own establishment, as was formerly his practice. Many Wall Street lawyers, finding their office space too expensive at four dollars per square foot to use for storage purposes, have sent their old files to Brooklyn, where special facilities have been established to perform this function at relatively low cost. The New York Telephone Company has tried the plan of reducing its commercial offices to mere counter-space and sending its clerical staff to low-rent quarters. A large silk manufacturer, who now uses most of his large building on Fourth Avenue as a stock-room, states that upon the completion of the new vehicular tunnel his New York building will become strictly a sample-room and his stock-room will be in New Jersey. Even in Newark, one of New York's Jersey satellites, the pressure for space in the shopping center has caused one large department store to establish a "service station" on cheap land, where the orders are assembled and the deliveries routed.

The extent to which a business may with profit separate physically certain of its functions from the others varies greatly. In some cases the packet of functions is loosely tied and in others is tied tightly. Obviously the difficulties of coördination and control increase as the disintegration progresses. The scale of the business is a factor of importance in this connection. In a very small business the option of moving part of the functions simply may not exist. It may be a case of moving all or none. A little cigar factory may market its entire output over a small counter in the front of the room and fabricate it with a force of a half-dozen workers in the rear. The proprietor in such a case supervises the entire process and does much of the work. He buys the materials, "bosses" the men, makes cigars, and conducts the sales. To separate the functions of fabrication and selling in such a case would increase the costs of management more than would be saved by using the back of the store for some other purpose than for the making of cigars. The little factory must, therefore, stand or fall in competition with the big factory, which can separate its functions at a smaller increase in costs of management, on the basis of some special advantage. In most cases this advantage is found in specializing the product so as to meet the demands of a particular clientele. Perhaps the persistence with which clothing fabrication clings to Manhattan is to be partly explained by the fact that the small size of the shop prevents the physical separation of functions. There is a tendency, then, finding its root in increased costs of management, to resist the separation of functions which derive advantages from close physical proximity. But as, in a game of chess, a pawn is sacrificed to gain a king, management costs are increased when by so doing site rentals can be decreased by a larger amount.

Certain advantages also flow from a cohesion of functions in a given district, and the result is a number of specialized centers with definite unities of interest rather than a single diversified center. The efficiency of the financial district would be materially lessened if it were scattered over a wider area, as it would necessarily be if it were mixed up with the shopping center. The shopper gains real advantages from a consolidated area of shops. Broadly speaking, the financial district contains only such shops as minister to the immediate convenience of the workers in that district. The students at Columbia University do not go to Wall

Street to buy their hats or their cigarettes. In the shopping districts, on the other hand, are found only such banks and brokers' offices as minister to the immediate convenience of the shops and their customers. The same factor operates to bring the wholesale silk houses into a fairly well-defined cluster. With factories also there are often material advantages in placing like with like.

Thinking of the economic activities, then, as packets of functions, it becomes a matter of interest to inquire regarding the advantages which accrue from performing groups of functions in the center of the urban area. The competition for space is a competition among these packets; but, since the constituent functions in the packets are constantly shuffled and the packets themselves constantly moved about, there is a possibility that prolonged observation and study may eventually yield an order of precedence among the functions themselves with respect to their ability to utilize choice urban sites economically. In other words, the answer to the question where things belong in an urban area seems most likely to be found, if it is ever found in a realistic and usable form, through an analysis of the business and a weighting of the functions according to their position in a scale of precedence. When the city planner of the future is asked whether a button factory belongs on Fifth Avenue, it may be possible to reply somewhat as follows: "This activity consists of 70 per cent fabrication, 15 per cent storage, 10 per cent price establishment, and 5 per cent miscellaneous functions, giving it a rating of 2.7[5] points. Land on Fifth Avenue of this degree of accessibility may not be utilized economically by any activity with a rating of less than 9.3. The proper location for activities rating from 2.6 to 2.8 is in Zone Q. The button factory should locate, say, in Rahway, New Jersey, or in Stamford, Connecticut." If this be fantastic, the notion that "in the process of deliberate decentralization, science is ultimately to decide what elements in the present city ought to remain and what ought to go" is also fantastic. At the present time the button factory, perhaps after several trials and errors, goes to the outskirts because it cannot pay the downtown rents. The formula of the future, if sound, will send the factory out for the same reason. Not so simply, but perhaps with fewer trials

and errors, it will show what activities can and what cannot pay down-town rents. It will supply a scientific basis for zoning.

The construction of a weighted scale and a precise order of precedence for functions is a task for the distant future. A study of the available data, however, yields a number of interesting clues which, if followed up, may lead to a more complete understanding of "the cause and extent of the differential advantages of urban land." A study of the functions performed by those activities which thrive and those which die in the urban center should show why "the application of capital and labor on some sites yields greater returns than on others."[6]

Ignore, for the time being, the physical conformation of the area and the unevenness of its present equipment of transportation facilities. One then has a circular plane whose center is, of course, the point most easily reached from all the points within its circumference. The essential quality which the center possesses is physical proximity, or accessibility, to all parts of the area. Obviously all activities with concentric circles of influence coinciding with this center will find the center most convenient as a location. If physical relationship to the surrounding territory is of any importance at all, all such activities would prefer, in the absence of obstructing forces, to be located at the center. But these activities differ in the degree to which they can make effective use of the quality of physical proximity or accessibility possessed by the center—that is, in the degree that they can turn accessibility into profits.[7] An order of precedence of activities is worked out by competitive bidding, the relative size of the bids being determined fundamentally by the degree to which the various activities can profitably utilize sites.

The term accessibility, as used in the preceding paragraph, really means ease of contact—contact with relatively little friction. The friction of space may be overcome by means of transportation; but transportation involves costs. Rent appears as the charge which the owner of a relatively accessible site can impose because of the saving in transportation costs which the use of his site makes possible. The activities which can "stand" high rents are those in which large savings in transportation costs may be realized by locating on central sites where accessibility is great. The complemen-

---

[5]The figure of 2.7 is, of course, purely arbitrary. The suggestion of *weighted functions* should not be confused with the plan of *weighted factors* used by many engineers in analyzing location problems.

[6]See page 49.
[7]The term profits is here used to include site rent.

tary character of these two things—site rents and transportation costs—is imperfectly recognized, and in view of its vital relationship to sound regional planning, deserves elaboration.

Transportation is in essence a method of overcoming the friction of space, and so long as transportation is imperfect (and it can never become instantaneous or effortless), the movement of people, goods, or intelligence from one spot to another spot on the earth's surface is a costly process. The center is the point at which transportation costs can be reduced to a minimum. Since there is insufficient space at the center to accommodate all the activities which would derive advantages from location there, the most central sites are assigned, for a rental, to those activities which can best utilize the advantages, and the others take the less accessible locations. Site rents and transportation costs are vitally connected through their relationship to the friction of space. Transportation is the means of reducing that friction, at the cost of time and money. Site rentals are charges which can be made for sites where accessibility may be had with comparatively low transportation costs. While transportation overcomes friction, site rentals plus transportation costs represent the social cost of what friction remains. Obviously an improvement in transportation, other things remaining the same, will mean a reduction in friction and, consequently, the diminution of the aggregate sum of site rentals. The two elements, transportation costs and site rentals, are thus seen to be complementary. Together they may be termed the "costs of friction."[8]

It is these costs of friction which the city planner must seek to reduce to the lowest possible level. Of two cities, otherwise alike, the better planned, from the economic point of view, is the one in which the costs of friction are less. This will mean that the aggregate site rents are less or that the transportation system is superior—or both. It may be suggested as an hypothesis that the layout of a metropolis—the assignment of activities to areas —tends to be determined by a principle which may be termed the minimizing of the costs of friction.

An economic activity in seeking a location finds that, as it approaches the center, site rents increase and transportation costs decline. As it retreats from the center, site rents decline and transportation costs increase.[9] The sum of the two items, the costs of friction, is not constant, however. On the contrary, it varies with the site. The theoretically perfect site for the activity is that which furnishes the desired degree of accessibility at the lowest costs of friction.

If the economic activity seeking a site happens to be housing, is not the problem worked out in this fashion? In choosing a residence purely as a consumption proposition, one buys accessibility precisely as one buys clothes or food. He considers how much he wants the contacts furnished by the central location, weighing the "costs of friction" involved—the various possible combinations of site rent, time value, and transportation costs; he compares this want with his other desires and his resources, and he fits it into his scale of consumption, and buys. When, as is usually the case, the choice of a residence is not merely a consumption problem but a production problem as well, is it not probable that, to the extent that added accessibility is required for business purposes, the business pays the cost? The negro chauffeur in Harlem often pays a rent which would stagger a small-town banker in the middle west.

If the economic activity seeking a site is a factory in one of the sub-groups shown in the table on page 48, the question is again fundamentally one of minimizing the costs of friction: will a central location save more than it costs?

It is now possible to make some observations regarding the varying tenacity with which these factories cling to the central locations. Does not this tenacity vary directly in proportion to the advantages, in reduced costs of friction, derived from

[8]The considerations stated above suggest the possibility of stating in general terms the sound limit of expenditure for transportation facilities in any community. Such expenditure for transportation facilities should proceed to the point where the cost of further improvement will be greater than the time and money saved by the improvement. That is, in the case of a rapid-transit installation, for example, the cost of the improvement should not exceed the value of the time saved the passengers plus the reductions in fares plus the reductions in rents, which would accrue as the result of the improvements. The implications of this principle for the financing of improvements are important. That changes in transportation facilities affect site rentals and land values has long been recognized. But the use of transportation to reduce the site rentals of a community is a somewhat novel conception. The assessment of costs of rapid transit against property owners clearly involves careful discrimination to determine true beneficiaries.

[9]In the field of periodical printing, for example, two concerns which sent their printing away from down-town New York report that "railroad fares, express, freight, telephone, telegraph, and hotel expenses all show heavy increase." Hinrichs, Economic Series, Monograph Number Six, p. 31.

location on the more accessible sites? It may be granted that, in these packets of functions, fabrication is an important element, and that in the struggle for sites fabrication itself ranks very low in competitive power. In the clothing trades, for example, the mere change in the form of the wool from a bolt of cloth into a suit of clothes is neither facilitated nor retarded by the fact that the fabrication is accomplished in the center of New York rather than in some remote village. The fact remains, nevertheless, that in the packet there are other functions, such as that of assembly. For example, in this fluctuating seasonal industry large numbers of workers must be gathered daily to the factory and returned to their homes. With the present radial system of transportation in New York, the performance of this function is greatly facilitated by a central location. Other functions in the packet of this "style" industry are price establishment, and selling on the basis of a comparison of varieties and qualities, for which a central location is highly important. Moreover, space can be very intensively used by this industry. It is estimated that a modern twelve-story loft building may contain one clothing worker for every 120 square inches of land area! Finally, with a high degree of cohesion of functions, traceable not only to the small scale of many of the establishments but also to the desirability of protecting styles from "piracy," the tenacity shown by the clothing trades is understandable. Ten of the twenty-two groups[1] that show a higher rate of growth than the average are clothing groups.

A functional analysis of the various branches of the printing industry may serve to test the principle still further. It has already been suggested that the extremely high rate of growth in photo-engraving may be explained, in part at least, by the fact that it is a new industry. But it is also a service industry; that is, its product is used by the printers, and convenient access to the printers is of great importance. The time which is saved by its being in a readily accessible location is worth the cost. Newspaper printing, another branch of the printing industry with a high rate of growth in Zone I, occupies the most expensive land of any of the branches. It clings to choice central locations because, for at least one of its functions, time is

all-important. The printing process itself does not gain by being performed on a high-priced site. But a central location is convenient from the point of view of the assembly of the news. Moreover, there must be the closest possible contact between the copy desk and the mechanical departments. Finally, and perhaps most important, the papers must be made available to the readers with the least possible loss of time. Time saved is also the explanation for the persistence of job printing in the center. The work that can wait tends to go to outside shops. Work that is "rush" is done down-town. In periodical printing also there is a direct correlation between central location and the time-limits within which the work must be done. In a sample of twenty-two periodicals, edited in New York, with a margin of four days or less between the time of closing the last form and release, eighteen were printed in Manhattan itself and only two were printed on sites more than two hours distant from Manhattan. As the time-margin increases, the per cent printed outside increases. In the case of bookbinding, where time is less important, the trade is rapidly abandoning central locations. In the printing industry, then, fabrication by itself ranks low in competitive power to command choice sites, but the other functions tied up in the printing packet rank high.

A similar analysis of the other industries would merely reinforce the explanation outlined in the cases of clothing and printing. Fabrication as a function by itself gains nothing from being located on high-priced land. But in the industrial packet there are other functions in varying proportions, which do gain materially because of the contacts afforded by the central sites. The industries that are leaving Manhattan are those in whose packets these other functions are relatively unimportant.

Illustrations already given suggest that storage may deserve classification with fabrication, as a function with little capacity to utilize effectively the contacts offered by central locations. In the packets of functions performed by most merchandising establishments, both wholesale and retail, storage plays an important rôle. A detailed study of twenty wholesale markets in New York City reveals a distinct tendency to scatter throughout the area, rather than to cluster in the center, on the part of merchants who, like wholesalers of groceries and meats, have a serious problem of storage, because of the bulky character of the products handled. If, however, the function of price establishment is present to an important extent, as in the case of the fruit and produce markets, they tend to remain clustered in the center. Warehouses offering space to rent were formerly grouped for the most part in a belt along the Manhattan waterfront. The new warehouses now being built are largely in a new belt along the shore line opposite Manhattan.

The highest land values in the city are in the Wall Street and the 42d Street sections. The Wall Street district, filled with high buildings, is dedicated to "finance." The 42d Street section is primarily a retail merchandising section, altho it has recently developed considerable importance as a miscellaneous office center. "Finance," as here used, includes the exchanges, the banks, the insurance offices, as well as various professional groups, such as lawyers and accountants. Largely through the control of loanable funds, there is centralized here the function of coördinating the business activities of a very wide area.

The exercise of this managerial function of coördination and control is at first glance singularly independent of transportation. It does not require the transfer of huge quantities of materials. It deals almost exclusively with information. What is all-important is transportation of intelligence. The mail, the cable, the telegraph, and the telephone bring in its raw material and carry out its finished product. Internally easy contact of man with man is essential. The telephone is prodigally used, of course, but the personal conference remains, after all, the method by which most of the important work is done. Conferences with corporation officers, with bankers, with lawyers and accountants, with partners, with fellow directors, fill the day. The work is facilitated when the time of the men whose time is most valuable is conserved. The district must be conveniently accessible and must be at the heart of the system of communication. It must be arranged so as to give the greatest possible ease of contact among men whose presence is desired in arriving at decisions. The financial district is in effect one big structure; the streets, practically cleared of all except pedestrian traffic, are little more than corridors and air-shafts. The corner of Wall and Broad on a busy morning is much more quiet than many a suburban business corner. The geometrical proposition that the contents of two

spheres are to each other as the cubes of their diameters has sent sky-scrapers up into the air. This was the economical way to produce accessibility in the center.[2]

The closely interrelated and interdependent group in Wall Street find their functions sufficiently facilitated by a central location to make it worth their while to outbid all others for the spot they want. It may be observed that this group of activities in the financial district is concerned, for the most part, with matters of great import, not with petty transactions. A decision as to whether the Kingdom of Norway shall be loaned $25,000,000 of American capital and whether the rate shall be five or six per cent, is obviously more important than a decision as to whether a neighborhood haberdasher shall be granted a loan of $250 and at what interest rate. One transaction may require no more physical space than the other and about the same amount of time, but the Norway decision will be made by a man whose time may be worth more per hour than the branch-bank manager earns in a month. A change to a more convenient location, which would save the large bankers one hour per day, might justify an increase in site rental of $30,000 per year (300 hours at $100 per hour). A similar change in the case of the branch-bank manager would justify an additional site rental of only $300 (300 hours at $1 per hour).

Selling in the 42d Street area is for the most part of two kinds. One type is the trade of quality —the sale of the rare, the exclusive, the unstandardized: rich jewels, rare paintings, fashionable clothing, articles beyond the reach of the masses of men. The limited number of potential customers in the United States of America is at present most easily accessible in the neighborhood of Fifth Avenue and 42d Street, near the hotels and the choicest residential district. These are people who can and will pay to have their time saved and their convenience served. The saving in the aggregate is sufficiently large to make it possible for these shops to outbid competing activities for the sites.

The second type may be called the trade of selection, the sale of the required assortment of mis-

[2]"The skyscraper facilitates personal contacts in a way never possible before. From my office on the twenty-eighth floor of a building in the Times Square district, I can get to practically every person of importance in the architectural and business field in fifteen minutes' time." Harvey Wiley Corbett, "New Stones for Old," Saturday Evening Post, March 27, 1926.

cellaneous goods. The modern department store, catering not to the extremely wealthy, but to those of moderate and low incomes, is here the typical agency, altho a conveniently grouped assortment of specialty shops under independent ownership sometimes performs the same function. The peculiar function of the great store is to provide an assortment. A woman may more conveniently buy a yard of blue taffeta in the little store on the main street of her suburban home town. But if she wishes to make her selection from twenty shades of a single quality of an identical fabric, she must go to the central shopping district, to the department store, or to several department stores. Much more must she go there if during the same morning she must buy, after a certain amount of prayerful consideration and comparison, a new hat, a pair of silk stockings to match the blue taffeta, and a new set of dishes. Her time is not worth $100 per hour. She need not be greeted by a dozen wonderfully gowned saleswomen in a cathedral-like edifice; but she appreciates fairly prompt and efficient service, and must catch the 11.50 train back to Yonkers. The convenience of the thousands of such persons is sufficient to offset the convenience of the hundreds of de-luxe shoppers, with the result that the department store can compete for Fifth Avenue sites on practically even terms with the exclusive shop.

It has already been pointed out that the small scale of some businesses tends to prevent the division and separate location of functions. There are many other special circumstances which also operate to distort the outlines of the ideal urban layout or to retard conformity to it. Ignorance, inertia, chance, and personal idiosyncrasies, all play a part. The physical characteristics of the terrain and the peculiarities of the transportation system are important factors influencing the pattern. Conditions of land tenure may retard or facilitate conformity to it. Similarly, the absence of competitive pressure is responsible for much bad location. Several of the most striking cases of misplaced plants in New York are factories making patented articles. Nor is it necessary that the monopoly be complete for an effect to be felt. In some cases, the low competitive pressure is traceable simply to the relative insignificance of the factor of site rentals, as compared with the other factors of cost. Perhaps most important of all the distorting factors is the obsolete

building. A surprisingly large number of concerns are the beneficiaries of bargains in rents offered by owners of run-down real estate.

Some writers have urged that a distinction should be drawn between "primary" and "ancillary" activities: that primary activities be given precedence in the city plan and that ancillary activities be zoned out. It seems impossible to draw any sharp line between primary and ancillary activities. Certainly a division on the ground that certain activities supply the primary wants of food, shelter, and clothing, while other activities supply luxuries and superfluities, would not be defensible for the purpose in hand. No one could seriously urge complete provision for such primary activities before providing for those which would be thus classed as ancillary. It would be a tragic waste to turn Times Square into a potato patch. The sound procedure is not to divide board classes of activities into primary and ancillary groups, but rather to develop an accurate scale of functions, in which scale ranking will depend upon ability to make profitable use (all costs considered) of the accessibilty of central sites. The present uses of land are not so irrational as they sometimes seem to be. In a very real sense the people of a community decide for themselves by their expenditures how they desire the land to be used. It is important to establish a sufficient degree of social control over land utilization to make sure that the decisions on points of precedence are socially sound—that all the costs properly chargeable to an activity are assumed by it, and that no activity shall be given the decision on the basis of accounts which fail to include, as costs, the losses suffered by neighbors or the community as a whole. Such social control may be exercised through wise methods of zoning and public finance.

While a general survey of trends and tendencies does demonstrate the need for collective intelligence in coordinating and controlling, to some extent at least, the uses of land in the metropolitan area, it also impresses the student with the need for caution. A hasty and superficial examination of the situation has often led an observer to conclusions which are found upon careful analysis to be entirely unsound. It is not always easy to differentiate the permanent from the ephemeral in a highly dynamic situation such as that in New York. Often a plot which is clearly destined ultimately for a high use is not quite "ripe" for such a use, and during the process of ripening may offer a temporary home for some lower use. To express it in a different way, every growing function has its reserved territory for future expansion, but these reserves are not allowed to lie idle. There is every reason for utilizing them, provided their use is properly controlled. It enables them to be productive of some revenue during the period of ripening. It enables the lower use to take advantage of a more convenient site for the time being, and results in getting the community's work accomplished with less effort than if such uses were prevented. But intelligent control is necessary. Temporary uses should not be permitted to interfere with the proper functioning of the permanent uses which are destined ultimately to supplant them, and should not be permitted to demand facilities (such as transit, for example) which will not be necessary after the temporary uses have passed away, beyond the ability of the temporary use to finance such facilities on the assumption that their life is conditioned upon the length of temporary use.

To illustrate, let it be assumed that the manufacture of men's clothing is an activity which is destined to give way to other activities on Manhattan Island. Even tho it were clearly recognized that the industry was destined to give way ultimately, it might be unwise to attempt to zone the clothing manufactures off the island immediately. They should be encouraged to use the land not now needed for the higher functions, under certain limitations. Obviously, the clothing industry should not be permitted to spoil the character of the choice shopping district by flooding the shopping streets with throngs of non-buying pedestrians. Again, it should not be permitted to block the avenues leading to the shopping district with vehicles which prevent the flow of merchandise and shoppers into the shopping center. Further, it should not be permitted to preëmpt the transit facilities to the detriment of the shoppers and the employees of merchandising establishments. If the centering of the clothing industry on the island means special transit facilities, the cost of such facilities should be a charge on the industry, to be written off during the life of the function in this location. If the trucks of woolens, of empty boxes, and of outgoing products block the streets which otherwise would be adequate to the needs of the island, in their efforts to serve temporary occupants of obsolete buildings,

the streets should be cleared and made usable for all at the expense of the clothing industry, perhaps by insisting that buildings whose tenants require such services provide suitable loading facilities behind the building line.[3]

An ordering of functions according to their permanence and importance has clear implications for those who are responsible for problems of traffic and transit. The street system and the rapid-transit system are designed, not for the uses of the coming twelve months, but for the uses of the coming decades. Their life is longer than a year, and they should be designed for the uses which promise to persist during a period long enough to offset their costs.

To state the same thing in a different way— the forces of competition do tend to approximate the ideal layout, and the trends actually in operation are the surest indication as to what is economically sound. However, the trends are the result of the individual decisions of persons in search of a dollar of profit.

It so happens that unless social control is exercised, unless zoning is fully and skillfully applied, it is entirely possible for an individual to make for himself a dollar of profit but at the same time cause a loss of many dollars to his neighbors and to the community as a whole, so that the social result is a net loss. A glue factory on the corner of Park Avenue and 50th Street might show a net profit, considered by itself and ignoring the losses of its neighbors. The truth is that an individual simply by buying title to a single lot should not be given the right to use it as he chooses, whenever by merely buying a lot he does not meet his full site costs. Zoning finds its economic justification in that it is a useful device for ensuring an approximately just distribution of costs, of forcing each individual to bear his own expenses. Regional planning, based upon economic analysis and operating through zoning restrictions, is the intelligent method of bringing about a truly sound economic layout of the metropolis.

This, then, is the type of control needed: that which will ensure the fullest use of the space facilities available consistent with the proper functioning and future development of the entire area, which will allocate to each activity its real costs,

---

[3]This is done in some of the new buildings constructed for the women's garment industry.

and will prevent the parasitic encroachment of lower functions upon the facilities of the higher functions. Planning consists not merely of beautiful pictures of civic centers or interesting projects for pleasure boulevards. It includes also the designation of the uses of areas and the equipment of those areas with means of access. It seeks to achieve its ends by both voluntary coöperation and legal compulsion. Voluntary coöperation from individual business men may be expected to be greatly facilitated if the business men are assured that the plan is economically sound and in conformity with the true values of the community. Moreover, if this assurance can be given, legal compulsion, through zoning and similar methods, can be carried very much further than would otherwise be feasible.

Stuart Daggett

THE SYSTEM OF ALFRED WEBER

In von Thünen's illustration there was but one city upon the plain. His interest was in the changes in crops and in methods of cultivation which occurred as distance from this city increased. But let us suppose that several cities exist upon the plain, that each of these cities may engage in manufacturing operations for the benefit of whatever consumers may be persuaded to buy its wares, and that the raw materials for manufacturing processes as well as fuel or other sources of power are obtainable from many, though fixed, points. Where, under these assumptions, will production—primarily manufacturing production—occur, and also from what parts of the plain will the raw materials of industry be drawn? These are the questions which occupied Alfred Weber.

Terms and Assumptions Used by Weber

Weber was a German economist, born at Erfurt in 1868. He taught at the University of Prague from 1904 to 1907 and at the University of Heidelberg from 1907 to 1933. In 1909 he published a treatise upon the location of industry which is still the standard reference for certain aspects of the subject. The treatise laid great emphasis upon the factor of transportation.[13]

In order to understand Weber's analysis we need to familiarize ourselves with the assumptions upon which his argument is based and with the meaning of certain terms which he employs. The formal assumptions are as follows:

1. Weber postulates a single country, with uniform climate and technique, inhabited by a population of a single race.

2. He proposes to deal with a single product, or at least to consider a single product at a time. Goods of different quality, though of similar type, are treated as different products.

3. The position of sources of raw material is stated, and is assumed to be known.

4. The position of points of consumption is stated, and is assumed to be known.

5. Labor is geographically fixed. Weber assumes that there exists a number of places where labor at definite, predetermined wages can be had in unlimited quantities.[14]

6. Transportation costs are a function of weight and distance. Differences in topography are allowed for by appropriate additions to distance and differences in transportability by additions to actual weight.

Among the terms which Weber uses are the following:

1. *Ubiquities.* These are materials available practically everywhere, and presumably at the same price everywhere.

2. *Localized materials.* These are materials obtainable only in geographically well-defined localities.

3. *Pure materials.* These are localized materials which enter to the extent of their full weight

---

Reprinted by permission of Harper & Row, Publishers from pp. 434-41, 449-51, PRINCIPLES OF INLAND TRANSPORTATION by Stuart Daggett. Copyright 1928, 1934, 1941, 1955 by Harper & Brothers.

[13]Alfred Weber, *Über den Standort der Industrien,* Erster Teil, *Reine Theorie des Standorts,* Tübingen, Mohr, 1909. An English translation was published by the University of Chicago in 1929. See Alfred Weber, *Theory of the Location of Industries,* Chicago, University of Chicago, 1929 (English translation by C. J. Friedrich). Prior to Weber a German mathematician named Launhardt anticipated some of the conclusions at which Weber arrived.

[14]Tord Palander, *Beiträge zur Standortstheorie,* Uppsala, Almquist & Wiksells, 1935, p. 173.

into the finished product. Thread to be woven into cloth is perhaps an example of this category.

4. *Gross materials.* Under this head are assembled localized materials which impart only a portion or none of their weight to the finished product. Fuel is the extreme type of gross material, for none of its weight enters into the product.

5. *Material index.* Such an index indicates the proportion which the weight of localized materials bears to the weight of the finished product. A productive process which uses pure material has an index of 1.[15]

6. *Locational weight.* This is the total weight to be moved per unit of product. An article made out of ubiquities would have a locational weight of 1 because only the product itself would be moved; if it were made from pure material the locational weight would be 2 because transportation of both the product an equivalent weight of materials would be required.

7. *Isodapane.* This is the locus of points of equal transportation cost. The meaning of the term will appear more clearly in the discussion.

Working with these assumptions, employing these terms, and seeking in the first instance to measure the effect of transportation upon location, Weber now imagines certain cases and announces the conclusions at which he arrives.

Case I. One Market and One Source of Raw Materials

The first case supposes a raw material to be produced at A and the finished product made out of the material to be consumed at B. The problem in the case illustrated by the diagram is to determine where the manufacture or processing is to take place. Weber states that four possibilities exist:

A ——————————————— B

FIGURE 53 Alfred Weber—Case I.

1. If ubiquities only are used, the processing will occur at point of consumption B, because the selection of B will make transportation unnecessary.

2. If one pure material is used, processing may occur at A, at B, or at any point between A and B. This conclusion is based upon the fact that the weight to be transported and the distance to be covered is the same in all instances. It has been pointed out in criticism of Weber's statement that manufacture at an intermediate point will require an extra handling of the goods, and that the through rate from A to B may be less than the sum of the rail or motor rate from A to the intermediate point and from that point to B. The first of these difficulties Weber disregards, and the second is probably eliminated by the sixth of the assumptions that we have earlier set down.[16]

3. If pure material plus ubiquities is used the processing will occur at the point of consumption B, because the pure material will be without influence, and the ubiquities will govern.

4. If one weight-losing material is used, processing will occur at point of production, because if this decision is made the weight which is lost will not have to be transported.

Case II. One Market and Two Sources of Materials

Weber's second case supposes raw materials which are available at two places, A and B, at equal prices. The finished product is to be consumed at C and the problem as before is to determine where manufacture or processing is to take place. Three possibilities are now considered:

1. If ubiquities alone are used, manufacture will occur at the point of consumption for the same reasons which governed when only two points were involved.

2. If several pure materials are employed, manufacture will also take place at point of consumption. On this supposition the weight of materials exactly equals the weight of the product. All

---

[15]The distinction between pure and weight-losing materials is now fully recognized in discussions of location, although Weber's names are not always used, and Weber's writings may not be responsible. It must always have been made in practical operation. It was not, apparently, understood by writers of many of the older books.

[16]Ohlin says that if the product which may be processed at A is also shipped to other places than B, then B cannot be as favorable a point for its manufacture as A. But (1) this suggestion is contrary to Weber's hypothesis that the entire product is consumed at B; and (2) it assumes advantages of large-scale production which are outside the field of discussion at this point.

weights, whether in the form of materials or in the form of product, have to be moved from their deposits to the place of consumption. They should not deviate unnecessarily; therefore each material will proceed along the straight line which leads from the place of its origin to the point of its consumption. Unless the way of one should lead by chance through the deposit of another, all of these ways will meet for the first time in the place of consumption. Since the assembly of all materials at one spot is the necessary first condition of manufacture, the place of consumption is the location where manufacturing will be carried on; a productive enterprise, using several pure materials alone, will always locate at the place where its products are consumed.

3. The conclusion is different if several localized weight-losing materials are used. In analyzing this case Weber sets up what he calls a "locational figure," which is a triangle in the simpler illustrations with which we are concerned. Let us suppose a process which uses two weight-losing materials produced at A and at B, and let us suppose that the product is to be consumed at C. Manufacture will not take place at C because it is undesirable to transport from A and B to C the material weight which does not enter into the weight of the finished product. It will not, according to Weber, occur at A or at B unless the importance of one material happens to be so great as to overcome the influence of all other elements.

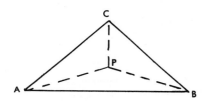

FIGURE 54   Alfred Weber—Case II.

It will, usually, be found somewhere within the triangle—as at point P. To this point the raw material will be brought, there it will be manufactured, and from P the finished product will be sent on. Let us imagine, says Weber, a process of production which uses two localized materials, ¾ ton of one and ½ ton of another being necessary in order to produce one ton of the product. These weights will represent the force by which the corners of the lo-

cational figure will draw the location toward themselves. Suppose a frame to be set up, with corners placed at the corners of the locational figure. Over these corners run threads, the threads being loaded with weights proportional to the amounts indicated. In the inner part of the figure these threads are connected at some point. Where this connecting point comes to a rest, there will be the location. It will be the place which, if selected, will cause the industry to be burdened with the smallest number of ton-miles.[17]

Introduction of the Labor Factor. The Isodapane

An isodapane, as Weber uses the term, is a line which is the locus of points of equal, though not of minimum transportation cost. The essential result of the part of Weber's location theory which we have so far described is that it indicates where, upon a plain, intelligent businessmen will manufacture an article whose market and sources of raw material have been stated, when they are influenced only by conditions of transportation. For any commodity at any time the decision will fix upon a point. Manufacture at any other location than this point will involve an increase in total transportation costs. How much this increase will be will depend upon the position of the alternative location. It should be possible to list all points at which aggregate transportation costs in connection with a given volume of output will exceed aggregate transportation costs at the ideal location by 1; in another list may be placed all points at which the excess is 2; in still another the points at which the excess is 3, and so on. If all the plus-1 points are indicated upon a map and there joined together by a line, the line will unite points of equal transportation costs. It will, therefore, be called an isodapane. A second isodapane may unite the plus-2 points, and a third, the plus-3 points. Every point of optimum location from the point of transportation alone may be surrounded by a series of isodapanes by which the increase of transportation cost may be measured which deviation from the optimum will produce.

---

[17]Weber considers the possibilities of using localized pure materials with ubiquities, localized weight-losing materials with ubiquities, and localized weight-losing materials with pure materials, but these combinations introduce no new principles.

The accompanying illustration, adapted from Palander,[18] will show the method of constructing an isodapane. Let us suppose a raw material to be available at a point in the diagram indicated by the letter M. The product made from this raw material is to be consumed at N. The circles surrounding N measure the cost of shipping a single unit of the finished product. It is assumed that the necessary raw material weighs twice as much as the product, and to show this fact upon the diagram the successive circles concentric to M are drawn close together and those concentric to N are drawn relatively far apart. According to Weber's rule, the optimum point for manufacture under these circumstances — transportation conditions alone being taken into account, and rates for material and finished product being the same per pound—is M, and the truth of this principle under the assumptions with which we work can be demonstrated by a little calculation.

It is, however, possible to manufacture at other places. If the processing is done at M, the finished product can be shipped to N at a cost of 8 and there will be no cost for shipment of material. If the point B is selected, the cost of forwarding the finished product will be the same, but there will be an expense of 4 incurred in the course of assembling material at B. The total transportation expense will be 12. If the point D is chosen, the cost of forwarding the finished product will be 6 and the cost of assembling raw material also 6, or again a total of 12. The same total will result if manufacture occurs at A, B, C, E, or F. A line drawn through these various points—an isodapane —will connect points of like shipping costs, in all cases in excess of the minimum possible by the amount of 4.

So long as transportation conditions alone determine the location of manufacturing activity isodapanes supply no useful information. But if labor or other costs are different in different locations the entrepreneur may sometimes find it advisable to abandon the spot which is most suitable from the point of view of transport in favor of a site where labor is less expensive. Whether he will do so will depend upon the amount which he will lose by such action and upon the amount which he will gain. If the labor advantage at a given site is to be measured by the figure 4 he will profit by a shift if the new point lies within the area bounded by the isodapane which indicates a transportation disadvantage of 4. If it lies without this area he will lose. The isodapane of 4 in this case will be called the "critical isodapane." Weber's use of isodapanes adds nothing to our knowledge of the effect of labor upon industrial location. The material assembled in the preparation of "factor lists" is much more informative in this regard. But it provides a technique for the systematic introduction of a new variable into a theoretic scheme which the extreme complexity of the data considered seems to demand.[19]

Weber's Generalizations

Although Weber did not invent the locational triangle, it forms the basis of much of his exposition and by the use of this device, along with the concept of pure materials, weight-losing materials, and ubiquities, he threw light upon questions of location which some authors of factor lists never understood. He also drew, out of his abstract discussion, a number of conclusions, also abstract. These included the following:

1. The orientation of industry is independent of the general level of transport costs. This conclusion properly emphasizes the relative character of problems of location. Critics have pointed out, however, changes in the general level of transport costs may cause new sources of material to be employed and old ones to be abandoned; these changes may also affect location by altering the relative importance of transport and other costs.

2. Pure materials can never bind production to the place where pure materials are produced. This is logical, but only on Weber's assumption that transport cost varies strictly with weight and distance and that interruption of movement is not expensive.

3. Weight-losing materials draw industries toward the sources of production. Production will be located at any source if the weight of a given material is equal to or greater than the sum of other materials plus the weight of the product. The concept of weight-losing materials is important.

[18]Tord Palander, *Beiträge zur Standortstheorie,* Uppsala, Almquist & Wiksells, 1935, p. 312.

[19]Weber also allows for a second variable, which he calls "agglomeration." . . . [See note on "Agglomeration," page 63 of this volume.]

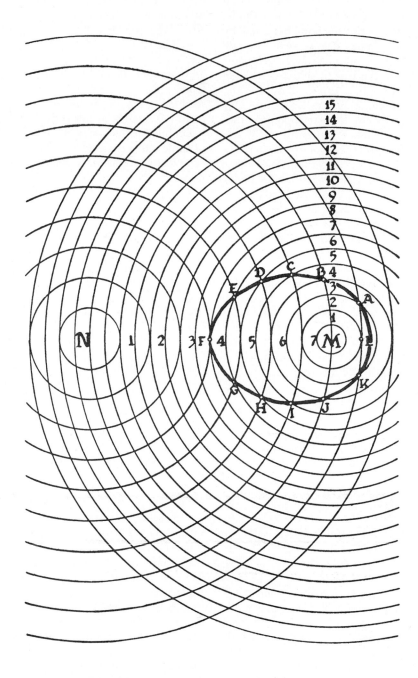

FIGURE 55 Construction of an Isodapane.

4. Industries with a high material index are drawn toward the source of supply of raw material; these with low material index are drawn toward the place of consumption. As stated, this appears to be true.

5. Given a single market and two weight-losing materials located at different points the place of production will be found in a triangle the lines of which connect the market and the material sources. The exact location will depend upon the relations of the weight components to each other. It will be near a given corner if the weight component of that corner is high. This is again true under the assumptions which Weber makes. But Hoover later reasoned that the resultant calculation will place the processing point at the market or at one of the other corners of the triangle in more cases than Weber seems to have supposed . . .

Note on "Agglomeration"

Agglomeration is a word used by Alfred Weber to cover three distinct situations. There is, first the case of simple enlargement of plant, bringing into existence the advantages of large scale production. There is, second, the local association of several plants, presumably in the same industry, which encourages the development of technical equipment and facilitates the sale of finished product. And there is, third, the case in which the mere aggregation of manufacturing activities, of unrelated as well as of related types, leads to conditions which are on the whole more favorable than any single plant or group of related plants could develop for itself.

Points for agglomeration differ from locations where sources of raw materials or supplies of capable labor are to be found in that they depend for their existence upon the decision of the undertakings which agree to create them. A competent prior survey will reveal deposits of coal and iron. Proper inquiry will bring to light efficient groups of laborers. Weber assumes that labor is geographically fixed. But an agglomeration point is merely a place to which a number of persons engaged in industry decide to resort. Without the decision, it does not exist; after the decision, it is there. Looked at from another point of view, a point for agglomeration is not one to which it is to the advantage of any single producer to transfer his plant. While it may be to the advantage of two producers to come together, neither will gain unless the other also acts. It is in spite of these conditions that the location of industry is influenced by advantages arising out of the association of manufacturing enterprises.

Weber takes four steps in absorbing the factor "agglomeration" into his conceptual scheme. In the first place, he puts aside for the moment variations resulting from geographical differences in the supply of labor. We start again from locations determined by transportation conditions alone. Secondly, he assumes a gain which is to result from agglomeration. This gain may be progressive, increasing with the extent of agglomeration, or it may be fixed, emerging when a definite amount of concentration has been attained. In our explanation of Weber's theory we shall restrict ourselves to the latter, more simple case. A third assumption is that an enterprise which shifts from the best available location, from the point of view of transportation, incurs a loss which has to be balanced by gains from agglomeration. And lastly, there is recognition of the fact that there can be no gain from concentration unless the opportunity for association is presented to several enterprises at once.

Figure 60 shows how these suppositions are applied.

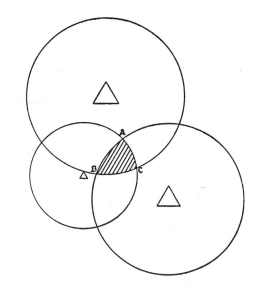

FIGURE 60   Diagram Illustrating "Agglomeration."

Let us suppose three locational triangles within each of which there is a manufacturing point. We are already familiar with the method by which such points are selected. Around the optimum points in each triangle let us draw isodapanes. Let us imagine a fixed gain from agglomeration measured by the figure 5, and let the isodapanes upon the chart, on the other hand, connect the points where manufacture is more costly than at the optimum, in terms of transportation expense, by the amount of 4. On these assumptions it may be profitable to move an enterprise, in order to obtain the advantages connected with agglomeration, from any optimum location within a triangle to another location within the area bounded by the encircling critical isodapane. Actually to induce movement there must be an area which is within the critical isodapanes encircling two or more producing points, for the advantages of agglomeration appear only when two or more points are involved. Such an area is the shaded figure ABC. Industries will locate within this space, rather than at points within the various locational triangles, if their directors are alert to seek the most favorable positions for their enterprises. There have been some criticisms of this analysis but the method used is consistent with that which Weber elsewhere employed . . .

Brian J. L. Berry and Allan Pred

WALTER CHRISTALLER'S *DIE ZENTRALEN ORTE IN SUDDEUTSCHLAND*—ABSTRACT OF THEORETICAL PARTS

Christaller, W., *Die zentralen Orte in Süddeutschland: Eine ökonomisch-geographische Untersuchung über die Gesetzmässigkeit der Verbreitung und Entwicklung der Siedlungen mit städtischen Funktionen.* Jena: Gustav Fischer Verlag, 1933.

This work contains the classic statement of central place theory, developed as a "general purely deductive theory" to explain the "size, number, and distribution of towns" in the belief that "there is some ordering principle governing the distribution." Christaller considered that his theories "could also be designated as the theory of location of urban trades and institutions" to be placed beside Thünen's theory of the location of agricultural production and the theory of location of industries developed by Weber and Engländer.

The crystallization of mass about a nucleus is part of the elementary order of things. Centralistic principles are similarly basic to human community life. In this sense the town is a center of a regional community and the mediator of that community's commerce; it functions, then, as the central place of the community.

Central places vary in importance. Those of higher order dominate larger regions than those of lesser order, exercise more central functions, and therefore have greater centrality. For all, however, "the sum of the distances which rural residents travel to the central place is the smallest conceivable sum."

Reprinted with the permission of the authors and publisher from *Central Place Studies—A Bibliography of Theory and Applications* (Philadelphia: Regional Science Research Institute, Bibliography Series No. 1, 1961), pp. 15-18. Dr. Berry is Professor of Geography at the University of Chicago; Dr. Pred is Associate Professor of Geography at the University of California, Berkeley.

The goods and services provided by the central place because it is central are known as central goods and services. Higher order goods are offered at central places of higher order, and lower order goods at places of both higher and lower order.

The region for which a central place is the center should be called the complementary region; it includes relationships in both directions—town to country and country to town. Complementary regions are likewise of higher and lower order. They are hard to determine because they differ for different types of goods, undergo periodic and seasonal variation, and consistently overlap neighboring complementary regions at the periphery. Distance plays a vital role in any determination of complementary regions, especially "economic distance," measured in time and cost. The range of a good is the farthest distance a dispersed population is willing to go in order to buy a good offered at a place. This range will take on a lower limit if there is competition from another center.

A decisive fact in the development of central places is the net income which inhabitants earn. There is a functional relationship between the size of a central place on the one hand and the sizes of the complementary region, its population and income on the other.

Central goods offered at a larger place have a larger range than those offered at smaller, and the fact that a central place is larger or smaller has an immediate influence on the range of a central good because more types of central goods are offered at a center of higher order. The possibility that on a single trip several types of goods may be offered simultaneously has the same effect as a general price decline in goods offered by larger towns.

Every type of good has its special range, which differs at different central places and is not the same in all directions from the same center, but varies according to objective and subjective economic distance. More basically, range is determined by (1) the size and importance of the center and the spatial distribution of population, (2) the price-willingness of purchasers, (3) subjective economic distance, and (4) quantity and price of the good at the central place. The range is actually a ring with an upper limit beyond which a good can no longer be obtained from a center, and a lower limit which is determined by the minimum amount of consumption which is necessary before production or offering the central good will pay.

There is a system of central places comprising several size-types, determined in general by the spatial effects of the upper and lower limits to the range of central goods. According to this *marketing or supply principle*, if the assumption of a homogeneous plain with equal access in all directions is made, complementary regions become hexagonal, and lower order centers and their complementary regions "nest" within those of larger centers according to a rule of threes. In this system the relations between size, spacing, functions and hierarchical interdependence in the system of central places are determined precisely. Seven levels to the hierarchy are postulated from the level of hamlet to world-city, based upon south German evidence. This strict mathematical scheme is, of course, as imperfect as the simplifying assumption, and reality may be approached by recognizing price differences, differences in population distribution, etc. Note the strong parallel between size and frequency of central places and intensity of traffic, but it is the former which determine the latter, and not vice-versa.

The system of central places developed on the basis of range of central goods used the assumption that all areas were able to be served from a minimum of central places; therefore the principle on which the system was developed can be called the *marketing or supply principle*. But there are other factors. *The principles of traffic* say that the distribution of central places is at an optimum where as many important places as possible lie on one traffic route between larger towns, the route being established as cheaply as possible. Complementary regions then "nest" according to a rule of fours. Principles of traffic are fundamentally linear, those

of marketing spatial. *The political-social (administrative) principles* are based upon ideas of separation of complementary regions for purposes of protection, or of distinction which implies clear-cut administrative control. In this case "nesting" follows a rule of sevens. Figure 1 depicts the patterns that result from the operation of each of the three principles.

The three principles determine, each according to its own laws, the system of central places. Two of them are economic and one is political. Under certain circumstances one or the other principle may dominate, but mostly they have to fight for predominance, a predominance which depends upon the operation of dynamic processes—of short-run, periodic, and seasonal fluctuations, and longer-run secular changes.

Summary of Empirical Evalution

Christaller then discusses the central place systems of southern Germany dominated respectively by München, Nuremberg, Stuttgart, Strasburg, and Frankfurt. On the basis of this discussion he evaluates his theory; we return to his evaluation.

We may call (the three principles) laws of distribution of central places, or laws of settlement, which fundamentally determine the location of a central place with astonishing exactness.

The chief and uncontested range of the principle of marketing lies in the prevalent agricultural provinces. Dominance of the principles of traffic *per se*, depends upon orientation to real traffic flows not related to the marketing of goods; in many cases pseudo-traffic orientation may also be found, as along valleys or on the margins of mountains. Dominance of the socio-political or administrative-separation principle is hard to prove; it can only be established by historical study. But wherever two low order places lie close together in a place where we might predict a higher order center to be, the probability exists that the separation principle is operative. Generally, both the latter principles must operate together with that of marketing; the marketing principle is the chief law, and the transport and administrative principles are secondary laws of deviation.

Many deviations not explainable by any of the principles are nevertheless explainable by economics: (a) a whole system may be raised to a

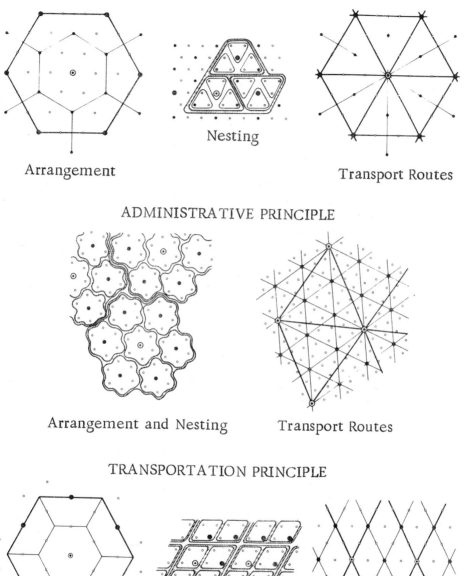

MARKETING PRINCIPLE

Arrangement   Nesting   Transport Routes

ADMINISTRATIVE PRINCIPLE

Arrangement and Nesting   Transport Routes

TRANSPORTATION PRINCIPLE

Arrangement   Nesting   Transport Routes

higher or lower level with general wealth and a dense population or general poverty and a sparse population; (b) spacing may be enlarged or compressed by the relative strength of any one system and adjacent systems; (c) depending upon the economic base of the area in question, there may be more or less of centers of any order.

Deviations from population: centrality ratios may be of a local nature, viz: spas, mining towns, dormitory suburbs etc. Similarly, local price dif-ferences, international borders, etc., may result in differences in the subjective evaluation of the importance of distance.

Other deviations are not explainable by economics. One class must be explained historically, for example in the foundations of sovereign nobility or of religious sites or of industrial towns. Another class depends upon circumstances of physical geography. Yet another class is of a military character. And so on.

Stefan Valavanis

LÖSCH ON LOCATION

The Economics of Location[1] belongs to that class of works, of which each generation produces very few, that both introduce a new subject and exhaust it. As with the *Theory of Games,* or Keynes' *General Theory,* the main ideas are few and appear utterly simple once popularized. They are *fortunate* ideas; that is, they have many consequences that matter and that are not obvious.

My task is to sift and present simply Lösch's key ideas and results, to point out which of them have and which have not analogues elsewhere in economics, and to show which areas of economics are affected by his contribution.

Even if the earth's surface were perfectly homogeneous, it would become differentiated into farms, cities and roads for purely economic reasons. Economic activities would arrange themselves into honeycombs of regular hexagons. Regions would emerge with characteristic prices and wages, and would trade their characteristic products.

The purely economic reasons for spatial differentiation in the absence of historical or geographical accidents are three: economies of scale, transport costs and agriculture's need for space. With economies of scale and no transport costs whatever, all production would be concentrated in

one, or a few, optimum-sized plants located at random. With transport costs and no economies of scale, a little of every product would be produced on every square inch of the earth's surface. With both economies of scale and transport costs, the result is intermediate: several production sites at definite distances compromise between mass production and freight costs. This is what happens if space as such is not an ingredient of production, as is approximately true in industry. In agriculture, however, acreage itself is an input. This fact alone, if there were no economies of scale or transport costs, would squeeze non-agricultural production into small sites.

Unquestionably, spatial differentiation will develop. What will it look like?

Price Funnels and Demand Cones

Let population be equally dense everywhere and let all people have like tastes. If *d,* in Figure 1, is an individual demand curve for beer, and *OP* is the price at the brewery, which is at *P,* those living there will buy *PQ* bottles of beer. Farther away the price is higher by the amount of the freight, and the quantity demanded consequently smaller. At *F* no beer can be sold at all. Total sales are equal to the volume of the cone produced by rotating triangle *PQF* (Figure 1) around *PQ.* The brewery is surrounded by a *demand cone* (Figure 2) and by a *price funnel* (Figure 3) which is steeper the higher the freight per mile. The brewery's *sale area* is a circle of radius ρ. Likewise, its *supply areas* of barley, hops, and labor are circles of various sizes around *P.*

Reprinted with the permission of the publisher from the *American Economic Review,* Vol. 45, 1955, pp. 637-44.

[1] August Lösch, *The Economics of Location,* translated from the second revised edition by William H. Woglom with the assistance of Wolfgang F. Stolper (New Haven: Yale University Press, 1954). The German title is *Die räumliche Ordnung der Wirtscaft; eine Untersuchung über Standort, Wirtschaftsgebiete und internationalen Handel* (Jena: Fischer, 1943). The Yale University Press has kindly given permission for the reproduction of Figures 20 (p. 106), 26 (p. 117), 28 and 29 (p. 125), and Table 7 (p. 119) in the book, which here appear as Figures 1, 5, 7 and 8, and Table I. Figure 2 is adapted from Figure 21 (p. 106) in the book.

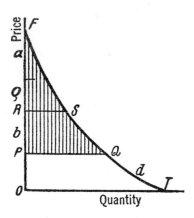

FIGURE 1   Demand.

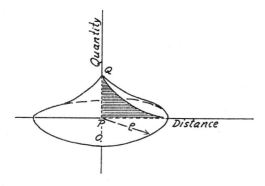

FIGURE 2   Demand Cone.

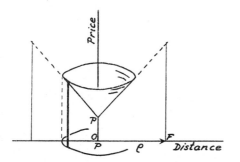

FIGURE 3   Price Funnel.

As long as profits are made, new breweries are established. Competition squeezes together the round sales areas into equal regular hexagons until both brewery profits and beerless areas have disappeared. Of all regular patterns that can fill up the space, the honeycomb of hexagons minimizes total transport costs. This is true for every commodity. On the other hand, the size of the hexagons depends solely on the individual demand for beer, and on freights for beer and its raw materials.

This proves too much. If the criterion is minimum transport costs, why are they not eliminated altogether by people living right at the breweries? It is true that the optimum distance between breweries may not be optimum for bakeries or laundries, so that some transport costs would persist. However a best average distance could be found and people would group together in equally spaced identical settlements, each having a brewery, bakery and laundry.

Duality Between Agriculture and Industry

Now we appreciate the full force of Lösch's distinction between agriculture and industry. Agricultural production is areal, industrial production is punctiform. The best location for the consumption of industrial goods is the city, whereas the best one for consumption of food implies an even distribution of the people. As long as products of the soil are an important item of demand, population will be scattered, if not continuously at least evenly, like polka dots, over the land.

Punctiform industry selling to areally spaced customers is characterized by *price funnels*. Conversely, areal agriculture selling to a punctiform city is characterized by *crop* gradients—the continuous counterpart of Thünen's rings. This easy result, based on the duality between agriculture and industry, illustrates again Lösch's Midas touch.

Discontinuous Settlement

There are two reasons why population should be scattered like sparse polka dots: (1) It is the best compromise between proximity to food and proximity to industrial production. (2) It is best for certain aspects of agricultural production. Shelter for cattle, the farm house, the well, are not areal

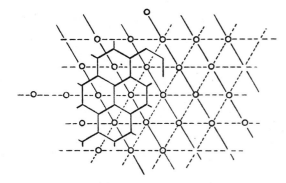

FIGURE 4 Sixty-Degree Lattice.

but punctiform, and some farm operations resemble those of the brewery. Hexagonal farms are best.[2] Farm houses will then be laid out on a 60-degree lattice (Figure 4).

Market Sizes

Discontinuous settlement restricts the possible market sizes. If I publish a rural newspaper, I do not care how far from the printer's is the nearest or the remotest corner of my subscribers' farms, because the newsboy has to deliver to the house.[3] If a circulation of 7 copies is economical each newspaper serves an area like Figure 5. If a circulation of 9 is indispensable, my sales area (Figure 6) will include the seven original customers at N, H_1 to H_6 plus one-third of the six farms J_1 to J_6 of the next ring. The other two-thirds read rival newspapers like N_1. Circulation of 7½, 8, or 8½ and a hexagon intermediate between Figure 5 and Figure 6 is impossible, not because of discontinuity in the number of copies that can be produced, but because of discontinuity in the number of customers that can be found for them.[4]

Now a few definitions, yielding a jackpot of results:

n the number of *equivalent customers*. If a customer, like J_3, is on a boundary, he is

divided up equally by the number of suppliers on whose areas he verges. In Figure 6, each J-customer is divided by 3. The J's then add up to 2 equivalent customers for supplier N, who has altogether 9 equivalent customers.

b the distance between towns that produce rival products.

a the distance between original settlements.
Results:

(1) $b = a\sqrt{n}$; that is, the distance between two like enterprises is proportional to the square root of the number of equivalent customers.

(2) The size of a market area is always $a^2 n \sqrt{3/2}$.

(3) The number of equivalent customers increases by jumps according to the law

(3.1) $n = (k\sqrt{3})^2 + j^2$

(3.2) $n = [(k + \frac{1}{2})\sqrt{3}]^2 + (j + \frac{1}{2})^2$

where j runs the integers from 0 to k first according to (3.1) and then according to (3.2), and where k runs the integers from 1 to infinity. Thus the seventeen smallest market areas have 3, 4, 7, 9, 12, 13, 16, 19, 21, 25, 27, 28, 31, 36, 37, 39, and 43 equivalent customers. (See Table I.)

TABLE I The Fifteen Smallest Market Sizes

Area No.	n	Area No.	n
1	$(1\sqrt{3})^2 + 0^2 = 3$	3	$(1\frac{1}{2}\sqrt{3})^2 + (\frac{1}{2})^2 = 7$
2	$(1\sqrt{3})^2 + 1^2 = 4$	4	$(1\frac{1}{2}\sqrt{3})^2 + (1\frac{1}{2})^2 = 9$
5	$(2\sqrt{3})^2 + 0^2 = 12$	8	$(2\frac{1}{2}\sqrt{3})^2 + (\frac{1}{2})^2 = 19$
6	$(2\sqrt{3})^2 + 1^2 = 13$	9	$(2\frac{1}{2}\sqrt{3})^2 + (1\frac{1}{2})^2 = 21$
7	$(2\sqrt{3})^2 + 2^2 = 16$	10	$(2\frac{1}{2}\sqrt{3})^2 + (2\frac{1}{2})^2 = 25$
11	$(3\sqrt{3})^2 + 0^2 = 27$	15	$(3\frac{1}{2}\sqrt{3})^2 + (\frac{1}{2})^2 = 37$

Systems of Networks

With uniformly distributed population (continuous or not) each industry has its characteristic size of hexagon and divides space with a honeycomb of such hexagons. Now if two or more honeycomb-shaped nets are thrown on a table at random, thread-density is neither uniform nor random.

---

[2] Lösch's treatment here is incomplete. See page 115, note 12 [of Lösch, *op. cit.*].

[3] Or the mailbox, which is also on a 60-degree lattice of mailboxes.

[4] Lösch does not notice that the tendency toward discontinuity of area sizes is helped from the input side. A brewery gets its barley and hops from barns at H_1, ... H_6 and not from all over the farm. Barley grown at A (Figure 6) goes to N_2, while barley grown at B (which is farther than A) goes to N.

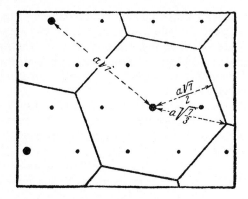

FIGURE 5   Market Area n = 7.

There are local bunchings of thread, and because of the regularity of the several nets, equally complex bunchings form logical patterns on the table. The same is true of the hexagons' centers. They bunch into regular patterns. Now and then in a small neighborhood we find both a brewery and a bakery, or both a bakery and a laundry. More rarely a neighborhood contains all three industries. Industrial centers, in other words, emerge in spite of continuous and uniform population.

Now suppose that hexagon nets randomly thrown together are no longer of continuously varying diameters, but come in a few assorted sizes. Bunchings and patterns of bunchings become more likely, because now the few assorted diameters have lowest common multiples, which was

not true before. When farm houses are laid out as in Figure 4, the tendency for industrial concentration, low prices, high wages, and much commuting is intensified.

Urban Cogwheels

We now lay honeycomb nets of the possible sizes together so that they have at least one point, the metropolis, in common (Figure 7). We rotate the nets so as to get a cogwheel pattern of six sectors with few and six with many production sites (Figure 8). With this arrangement (1) the

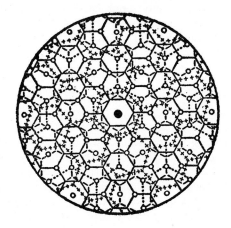

FIGURE 7   System of Networks.

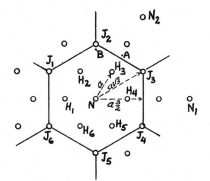

FIGURE 6   Market Area with n = 9 Equivalent Customers.

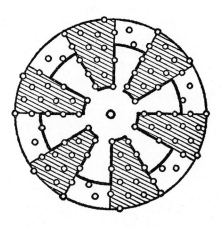

FIGURE 8   Cogwheel.

greatest number of locations coincide, and a maximum of purchases can be made locally, (2) sums of minimum distances between industrial locations are least, and consequently shipments, transport costs and highways are minimized, (3) a very deep price funnel around the metropolis is surrounded by a ring of quite deep funnels around regional centers, and in between are rings of rings of less deep funnels.

These results have two very important consequences for traditional theory.[5] First, it is clear that the notion of an economic region is derivable and not primary. International trade theory can now explain rather than assume local cost differences on a homogeneous globe. Second, price funnels break up the landscape so completely as to make meaningless the concept of local price levels; no simple deductions can be made therefore about comparative advantage, migration of factors, or purchasing power parity.

Interregional Equilibrium

When uniform natural endowments are assumed, men, goods, and places are mutually determined. Every worker carries with him his individual demands. Every good requires certain inputs and a market area of a certain size. Every location, by its prices and rents, attracts or repels industries and dictates to men how they will spend their incomes.

Other things being equal, the following questions can be answered, one at a time, by means of marginal analysis: (1) What does a given person produce? (2) Who works at the production of a given good? (3) Where does a given person reside? (4) Who lives in a certain locality? (5) What does a given locality produce? (6) Where is a given good produced? That all six answers can be determined simultaneously is no surprise to the economist. Demands, freight costs, balance equations and marginal conditions are just enough to determine a solution.

How is this equilibrium restored if disturbed? In the short run, prices change and goods are transferred. Long-run disturbances lead to change

of jobs or migration of industries. In fact all six relations play a part according to their price, time and space elasticities.

Price Waves

Lösch devotes much space[6] to short-run disturbances and the transfer problem. I summarize this here only to present one last main idea, that of price waves.

Suppose a foreign firm suddenly orders from Paris 1,000 marks' worth of shoes instead of buying them, as it had formerly, in Berlin. In Paris, the price of shoes will rise; their market area will shrink but hides and nails will have to be bought farther afield. Workers will be attracted from other industries, and rents will rise. Neighboring shoe factories faced with shortage of materials and labor will raise the price of their shoes and bid up hides in their own supply areas. Paris will become the focus of inflationary price waves that ever expand in area, but ever diminish in intensity. This is so because the impact is divided among more and more establishments and other kinds of goods. Berlin would be the focus of deflationary waves.

Waves diminish because they divide. Their total volume, however, remains constant, unless, sooner or later, *compensatory absorption* occurs. To illustrate, Luxembourg with its new income may want to buy precisely what Leipzig had to give up.[7] This will wipe out the wave, not just divide and divert it. Compensatory transfer of goods may occur anywhere, in the Saar, on the Rhine, or in Mongolia. It does not have to take place on the Franco-German border.

Lösch's analysis uses tools of traditional economics, like maximization, pure competition, partial equilibrium, and simultaneous equilibrium. Conceptual analogies are less obvious.

The downward sloping demand of Figure 1 is analogous to that of imperfect competition. Localization of production corresponds to product differentiation. Space is to agriculture as time is to capital theory, an essential new ingredient. As the Walrasian system determines relative and not

---

[5]Strangely enough, nothing in economic history or economic geography is invalidated. This is because Lösch's main results have abstracted completely from historical and geographical accidents.

[6]Pages 265-304.

[7]Compensatory absorption may occur on the major arc of the great circle through Paris and Berlin, say with Bordeaux absorbing what Königsberg had to give up, or it may occur off the great circle entirely.

absolute prices, so in Lösch the metropolis itself can be anywhere. The flattening of price waves is deceptively like the dying out of the multiplier. Compensatory transfer is a little like the Pigou effect.

Ideas with no analogues in ordinary economics, like the discontinuity of hexagon sizes (Table I), and the rotation of hexagonal networks (Figure 8) I find very rare. The persistence of rent differences in spite of homogeneous endowments is *not* due to any novel assumption.

That familiar concepts should generate startling results more than any other thing attests to the genius of August Lösch.

Part Two

SELECTED EMPIRICAL STUDIES

Introductory Note

The empirical studies in this section incorporate, either explicitly or implicitly, elements of classical location theory. In some cases hypotheses derived from the theory are submitted to careful examination; in others the connections with theory are not so clearly spelled out but there is an obvious concern for the same factors mentioned in the theory.

The first two selections are concerned with land-use patterns. In the first study, dealing with locational change in the Kentish hop industry, Harvey emphasizes the general tendency for the intensity of this particular agricultural activity to decrease away from a core area. This distance decay in agricultural intensity is of course consistent with the Von Thünen model. In seeking an explanation for the patterns of locational change over time, Harvey refers to the factors of agglomeration, cumulative change, and the economics of diminishing returns. His overall stress on locational *change* rather than on the factors governing the initial location patterns accords well with a general feature of location theory. This theory is concerned more with locational tendencies over space and through time than with detailed patterns of distribution in all their layered historical complexities.

Yeate's study attempts a more explicit link-up with location theory, in this case the theory of urban land use as stated by Haig. The hypothesis that land values decrease away from the city center is examined for a number of different years, and Yeates concludes that in Chicago this relationship has weakened steadily over the period 1910 to 1960.

Of the following six articles concerned with manufacturing location, the four by Smith, Lindberg, Kennelly, and Pred can be related specifically to the Weberian model. Smith critically examines the use of the "material index" in analyzing the location patterns of British industries. In Lindberg's article the question of transportation costs is emphasized and isodapane analysis employed in an examination of the location of the Swedish paper industry. There is an attempt to handle production areas rather than simply production points. Kennelly in his study of the Mexican steel industry, using modifications related to the work of Launhardt and Palander, presents one of the few examples of a detailed Weberian analysis. The possibility of interplay between empirical analysis and theory is illustrated in Kennelly's attempt to move from the "uniform transport surface" assumed in these models to the actual Mexican transportation system. Finally, Pred examines the hypothesis suggested by Weber's treatment of agglomeration factors, that high-value-added industries should be concentrated in the American Manufacturing Belt. Pred's study suggests how models can be used to provide "norms," even in an essentially historical approach to questions of locational analysis.

Two other articles in this section are concerned with questions of manufacturing location. In neither the Isard and Cumberland article nor the Harris study is there any explicit reference to location theory, but the lines of analysis suggested in these two studies have proven useful in much subsequent locational research. Isard and Cumberland undertake a comparative cost analysis related to the possibility of locating an integrated iron and steel works in New England. Comparative cost analysis in this context might be viewed as an operational form of the Weberian model. In a similar way, Harris attempts to measure directly the "market-pull" which is incorporated unsatisfactorily in Weber's location theory. The "potential" concept discussed in this selection is developed further in a number of other geographic studies, particularly those of Warntz,[1] and has influenced certain lines of analysis in the field of transportation geography.[2]

The final two articles in this section are concerned with the relative location of urban places as centers of tertiary activity and with the associated systems of market areas. Brush's study is a classic application of the Christaller model to the pattern of "central places" in southwestern Wisconsin, with an attempt to account for some of the deviations between model and reality. A modification of the theoretical system of market areas suggested by Brush's findings is presented in Godlund's article. In the latter an alternative model for the system of market areas is outlined and some questions concerning the dynamics of such a system are considered. Godlund's formulation relies heavily upon a concept of market-pull or attraction which is very similar to that in Harris' study.

---

[1]See W. Warntz, *Towards a Geography of Price* (Philadelphia: University of Pennsylvania Press, 1959). _____, "Macrogeography and Income Fronts," *Regional Science Research Institute Monograph Series*, No. 3, 1965.

[2]See for example E. J. Taaffe, "The Urban Hierarchy: An Air Passenger Definition," *Economic Geography*, Vol. 38, No. 1, 1962, pp. 1–14; R. H. T. Smith, "Toward A Measure of Complementarity," *Economic Geography*, Vol. 40, No. 1, 1964, pp. 1–8.

D. W. Harvey

LOCATIONAL CHANGE IN THE KENTISH HOP INDUSTRY AND THE ANALYSIS OF LAND USE PATTERNS

Human geographers are invariably concerned with the analysis of patterns of economic activity. But these patterns are rarely a simple function of modern conditions, so that location studies should differentiate between the factors that govern the initial location of a particular form of production and the factors that govern the shift from a pre-existing to a new pattern. In a 'mature' economy such as that of Great Britian, the process of locational change may well be more important to the explanation of present distributions than the factors that governed initial location. Yet, in spite of this, geographers have tended to ignore the problem of exactly how a shift from one geographical pattern to another is accomplished. The lack of study focused directly on the processes of locational change stems, largely, from methodological problems of dealing with space and time in the same context. Thus, although the processes of locational change have not been entirely ignored, the complexities involved have often been wrapped up in general terms such as 'inertia' or 'historical momentum.' Unless these terms are broken down into more meaningful concepts, the analysis of location will inevitably lack penetration.

This paper is concerned with an examination of some of the processes that govern the evolution of land-use patterns. In particular it is concerned with the trend towards regional concentration of hop production in Kent during the nineteenth century, and with the three processes that appear to have accounted for this trend.

The Problem Isolated

Locational change in the Kentish hop industry was very complex and its explanation is even more so. It is not intended here to examine every aspect of change, but rather to isolate the tendency towards regional concentration and to discuss the factors that governed it.[1]

During the nineteenth century there were rapid changes in demand for hops which, together with technical adjustments in the hop industry, resulted in long-term fluctuations in the hop acreage (Fig. 1). The general trend was one of rising acreage from 1815 to 1861. After this date the repeal of the duty on hops, coupled with a rapid expansion of output in the brewing industry, led to a sharp rise in the hop acreage, which reached a maximum in the period 1878-85. After 1885 the acreage contracted rapidly so that by 1900 it had declined to approximately its 1860 level. This decline was mainly due to foreign competition, to technical change in the brewing industry, and to rising productivity in the hop industry.

These general trends were modified in the Kentish case by two further factors. First, there were sharp cyclical fluctuations in the hop acreage connected, before 1878, with the 'major cycles' of growth in the British economy as a whole.[2] This makes any analysis of changing location very difficult since at no period in the century was the

the University of Bristol, England. The author is indebted to the Colston Fund in the University of Bristol for a grant towards the cost of illustrations.

[1]For a full account see D. W. Harvey, *Aspects of agricultural and rural change in Kent, 1800-1900*, unpublished Ph.D. dissertation, University of Cambridge (1961).

[2]Ibid., appendix 2.

distribution of the hop acreage anywhere near stable. Second, there was a persistent tendency throughout the century for hop production to become concentrated in Kent and Sussex at the expense of other producing areas. Between 1810 and 1878 the proportion of the national acreage located in Kent rose from 43 per cent to 65 per cent. It is not, however, the purpose of this article to explain either the cyclical fluctuations in acreage, or the shift of production towards Kent. These facts must, rather, be regarded as the given base against which locational change in the Kentish hop industry can be analysed.

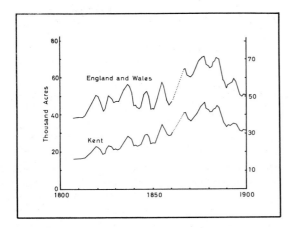

FIGURE 1   Fluctuations in the Hop Acreage 1807-1900.

The location of the hop acreage at any particular date between 1807 and 1861 can be ascertained from the returns to the Hop Excise. From 1867 until the end of the century the agricultural statistics provide the necessary data. The individual parish statistics are, in both cases, often suspect, and are difficult to use for comparative purposes. But the general pattern of distribution of hop cultivation can be fairly accurately illustrated from both sources.[3]

Figure 2 indicates the distribution of the hop acreage in Kent at selected dates throughout the

nineteenth century. It illustrates, in a general way, the regional reaction within Kent to the basic changes in hop acreage shown in Figure 1. It suggests the existence of two core areas of hop production—one centred near Canterbury in east Kent, and one centred on Maidstone in central Kent. The east Kent district was less important, concentrated on a very high quality product and was, thus, susceptible to change in one sector of the market only. During the phase of depression after 1885, for example, the demand for high quality hops remained unimpaired, so that the hop acreage in east Kent remained fairly constant, while the acreage declined rapidly in the rest of Kent. Because it was affected by such special circumstances, the east Kent industry will not be considered here. Attention will be focused on that part of Kent roughly defined by the rim of the chalk scarp, the county boundary and Romney Marsh (Fig. 3).

Within this district the maps indicate that the hop acreage tended to be located in zones of declining density ranged around a central core area. Using a 'gravity model'[4] the centre of hop cultivation was determined for 1837 and 1855, and in both cases the centre determined was the parish of Wateringbury. To determine how density varied with distance, successive zones two miles in width were circumscribed around this centre (Fig. 4), and the average density of hop cultivation in each zone was calculated. Parishes which lay more or less equally divided between zones were counted in both zones in averaging out the parish statistics. The regular decline of density with distance is illustrated in Figure 5.

This regular distribution of the hop acreage according to distance from the main centre of cultivation appears to have little respect for differing soil conditions.

The hop plant is tolerant of a wide variety of soil conditions for it will 'grow and crop even in extreme adversity as far as its soil is concerned'.[5]

[3]Ibid., appendix 1. Generally speaking the acreages recorded by the Hop Excise are accurate, but the published parish statistics (contained in yearly volumes of the British Parliamentary Papers 1822-62) must be treated with care since acreages often appear to 'float' from one parish to the next. There are other minor errors in compilation and printing that make detailed use of the statistics difficult. But the general accuracy of the returns need not be doubted. For a critique of the agricultural statistics see J. T. Coppock, 'The statistical assessment of British agriculture', Agricultural History Review, 4 (1956), 4-21 and 66-79.

[4]For a full account of these models see W. Isard, Methods of regional analysis (1960), chapter 11. In this case the gravity model adopted was given by the formula

$$g = \Sigma \frac{p}{d}$$

where
 p is the density of hops in any parish
 d is its distance away.
When the value for g has been ascertained for the parishes in and around the centre of hop cultivation, the parish with the highest g value was then designated the 'centre of gravity' of hop cultivation.
[5]B. S. Furneaux, 'Soils for hop growing, Journal of the Southeastern Agricultural College, Wye, 44 (1939), 30-6.

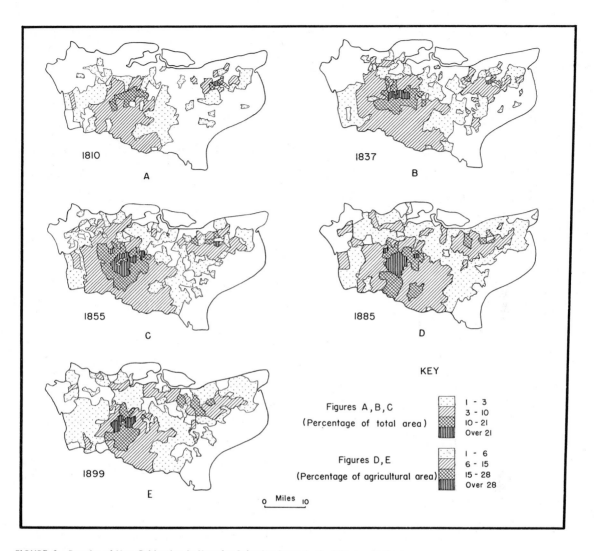

FIGURE 2 Density of Hop Cultivation in Kent for Selection Dates in the Nineteenth Century.
(*Source:* Hop Excise and Ministry of Agriculture.)

Yet despite this the commercial production of hops is profoundly influenced by physical conditions and many studies have suggested that there is a close connection between hop yields and both soil drainage and soil texture.[6]

In the absence of detailed soil surveys, a definitive analysis of the relationship between hop cultivation and soil conditions is impossible. Generally speaking, however, soil conditions in the Wealden area are closely related to underlying geology. Using this as a basic guide (Fig. 3), certain interim conclusion may be reached.

There are certain soil groups which were completely negative for hop cultivation: namely, soils developed over open chalk, where drainage was far too rapid, and soils where drainage was impeded. The chalk soils are well distributed along the North Downs, so that although hop cultivation was carried on (nearly always on the clay-with-flint deposits) the North Downs tended to form a major negative area for hop growing. The high water-table soils are limited to the alluvium of the river

[6]A. D. Hall and E. J. Russell, *A report on the agriculture and soils of Kent, Surrey and Sussex* (1911).

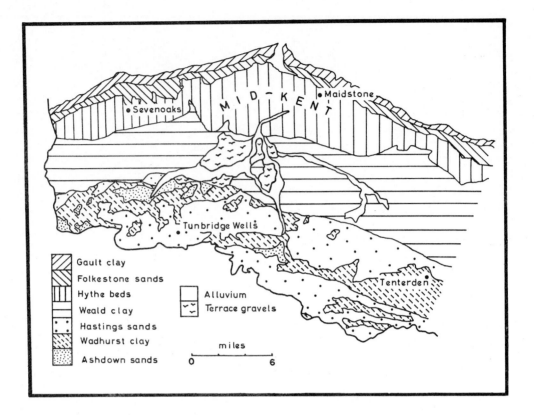

FIGURE 3 The Kentish Weald: generalized geology.

flood-plains, but Romney Marsh formed a major negative area for hop cultivation because of its physical characteristics.

At the other extreme, there are certain soil groups of limited distribution that were ideally suited to hop cultivation. Most favourable of all were the well-drained loams developed over the Hythe Beds. An analysis of these soils distinguished thirteen soil series: five of these were very localized in distribution, two were derived from lime-free sand and were poorly drained and acidic, while the remaining six were derived from the 'ragstone' and were deep, loamy and well drained. These latter soils, together with those derived from Pleistocene valley gravels, predominated around Maidstone and this district—termed Mid-Kent—formed the highly favoured core area of hop cultivation.[7]

There are soils elsewhere that were reasonably suited to hop cultivation. Some of the terrace gravels spread over the Wealden clays to the south of

Mid-Kent were in this category. Some of the soils developed over the Hastings Beds in the High Weald were also favourable, although soil conditions are so varied here that N. B. Bagenall and B. S. Furneaux found hardly a single field with a uniform soil series throughout. They distinguished sixteen series; six were well drained and covered 41.5 per cent of the area they surveyed and undoubtedly some of these were suited to hop cultivation.[8]

But most of the soils throughout the district were neither absolutely negative to hop cultivation, nor particularly favourable. Most could be used, however, given the right economic conditions. The heavy, poorly drained soils associated with the

[7] W. A. Bane and G. H. G. Jones, 'Fruit growing areas on the Lower Greensand in Kent', *Ministry of Agriculture, Bulletin* No. 80 (1934).

[8] N. B. Bagenal and B. S. Furneaux, 'Fruit growing areas on the Hastings Beds in Kent', *Ministry of Agriculture, Bulletin* No. 141 (1949).

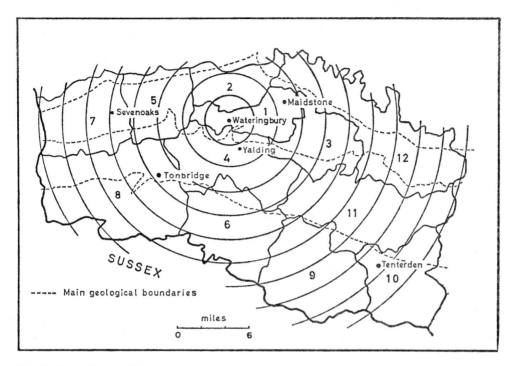

FIGURE 4 The Kentish Weald: showing the parish groupings used in Table I and the zones of equal distance constructed around Wateringbury.

Weald and Wadhurst Clays were probably the most marginal, although in many places they were ameliorated—the Weald Clay, for example, by beds of Paludina limestone or by river gravels. The soils developed over the Folkestone Sands were often not sufficiently retentive of moisture, while some of the sandy soils of the High Weald suffered from a similar disadvantage. The Gault Clay soils, on the other hand, tended to be too heavy for the cultivation of good quality hops. But none of these defects were sufficiently crippling to prevent hop cultivation completely.

The location of the core area of hop cultivation in Mid-Kent was, thus, closely defined by the excellence of the soils. But outside of this core area soil conditions appear to have played little part in determining the pattern of hop densities, for there was very little relationship between the zoning of the hop acreage around the centre and the distribution of suitable soil types. Only the totally unsuitable soils were avoided. This indiscriminate cultivation of hops over such varied soil conditions in Kent puzzled many contemporary writers. W.

Topley, for instance, could see no clear reason why hops were not cultivated in other parts of England if they could be so easily cultivated in Kent.[9] Clearly, therefore, causes other than physical ones must be sought if this pattern of hop location is to be explained.

The relationship between acreage distribution and distance from Mid-Kent was not simply a static one. The maps suggest that expanding demand resulted in either an increase in density in the central area or in a spread outward of acreage around the centre. The actual details of regional change are, however, rather complex. By dividing the district as a whole into twelve parish groups (Fig. 4) the regional reaction to the general trends of acreage change can be analysed in greater detail.

The density of the hop acreage for each region has been calculated for selected years throughout the century. The years chosen are those that cor-

---

[9]W. Topley, 'On the comparative agriculture of England and Wales', *Journal of the Royal Agricultural Society*, Second series, 7 (1871), 269-84; and 'On the agricultural geology of the Weald', *Journal of the Royal Agricultural Society*, Second series, 8 (1872), 241-67.

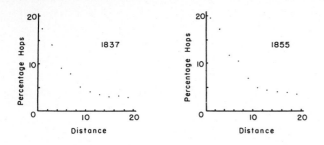

FIGURE 5 Decline of Density of Hop Cultivation with Miles Distance from Wateringbury.
(*Source*: Hop Excise)

respond to the peak and trough dates in the cyclical fluctuations of the acreage. Table I thus indicates the main regional changes in Kent in relation to national trends.

Between 1810 and 1819 there was a phase of rapid adjustment in agriculture as a whole to meet rapidly changing price conditions. Hop cultivation remained one of the few profitable forms of agriculture after 1815 and the hop acreage tended to increase rapidly in many areas of Kent. After 1819, however, the importance of distance from Mid-Kent as a factor in hop acreage change can be more clearly demonstrated.

The general trend in the three parish groupings comprising Mid-Kent was one of expanding acreage in response to the overall rise in demand between 1819 and 1826. After this date two of the parish groups (1 and 2) tended to decline while the group to the south-east of Maidstone (group 3) continued to expand over the cyclical fluctuation culminating in 1837. All three groups remained

static during the 1840s and expansion was only renewed after 1850 to culminate in the high densities of 1878—but even in 1878 the density was not very much higher than it had been in 1826, except to the south-east of Maidstone (group 3). The problem here is to explain why this favourably placed core area should have failed to expand its hop acreage between 1826 and 1846 when the general trend in demand for hops was upward.

After 1837 expansion was most rapid in those areas closest to the core area without actually being in it (groups 4, 5 and 6). These groups expanded very little before 1826, but after this date expansion was very rapid indeed until 1878. Farther away from the core area the expansion was not so marked, although the parish groups in the western Weald (groups 7 and 8) and in the eastern Weald (groups 11 and 12) expanded fairly steadily after 1826. But in the districts farthest from the centre (groups 9 and 10) the pattern of growth was rather different, for here the highest densities were almost reached in 1819; after this date the tendency was for the hop acreage to remain steady or to contract slightly.

There were thus three distinctive phases in the pattern of regional expansion in the hop acreage before 1878. The first phase from 1819 to 1826 saw the rapid growth of the central nucleus, while the other districts experienced little or no acreage change. The second phase, from 1826 to 1846, was characterized by stagnation in the core area, accompanied by a rapid expansion in the areas near-

TABLE I Percentage of Total Area under Hops by Parish Groups shown in Figure 4

Date	Parish groups											
	1	2	3	4	5	6	7	8	9	10	11	12
1810	13.2	4.2	5.8	8.0	2.0	4.7	2.0	1.4	4.8	0.9	2.8	1.3
1819	17.9	6.1	6.7	11.6	3.9	5.7	2.2	2.2	7.2	2.8	3.2	1.6
1823	16.2	5.7	6.0	11.0	4.0	5.2	2.0	1.9	5.3	2.1	2.3	1.4
1826	22.5	7.2	8.0	11.1	3.9	5.0	2.1	2.4	6.3	2.4	2.8	1.5
1831	17.3	5.5	8.6	10.9	4.0	5.0	2.2	2.0	6.4	1.6	2.2	1.7
1837	19.4	6.4	10.1	13.2	5.3	6.2	3.3	3.0	8.0	3.1	3.8	2.2
1840	11.3	5.0	9.9	9.4	4.8	4.8	3.1	2.5	6.6	2.8	3.2	2.0
1846	16.4	6.4	9.9	14.1	7.2	7.3	3.4	3.0	6.6	3.0	3.9	2.5
1849	14.9	5.6	8.5	12.0	6.9	5.9	2.6	2.8	4.9	2.5	2.5	2.0
1855	19.8	7.3	11.6	17.5	8.3	9.2	4.1	4.0	7.7	3.7	4.4	2.6
1859	19.6	6.7	10.2	14.9	7.2	7.2	3.3	2.8	5.4	2.5	3.2	2.0
1878	23.9	10.2	15.8	20.0	7.4	11.3	4.1	4.4	8.8	4.3	7.2	4.0
1885	22.0	9.2	13.6	19.5	6.1	12.1	4.0	4.3	9.2	5.0	8.0	4.6
1899	14.2	4.9	7.7	15.8	3.0	9.5	2.6	3.0	5.8	2.1	4.8	2.5

(*Source*: Hop Excise 1810-59, Ministry of Agriculture 1878-99.)

est to the core and a slight decline in the more remote districts. After 1846 there was a third phase of all-round expansion most marked at the centre and in the areas nearest to it.

Thus, even though the central area of Mid-Kent tended to stagnate at certain periods, there was a persistent tendency for the hop acreage to increase most in the parishes in, or near to, Mid-Kent. This tendency can be illustrated statistically by plotting the percentage change in the hop acreage for certain parishes against their distance from the centre of hop cultivation. This was done for one period of expansion and one period of contraction of acreage for each parish across the High and Low Weald (parish groups 4, 5 and 8 to 11 in Fig. 4). The statistical 'centre of gravity' varied throughout the century between Wateringbury and Yalding and since the latter parish lay within the area under consideration it was chosen as the central point.

During the phase of expansion from 1829-35 to 1856-61 a negative correlation coefficient (r) of −0.52 was obtained (Fig. 6, A), which indicates that there was a tendency for the percentage increase in the hop acreage to be more marked near the centre than farther away. The r^2 value of 0.27 indicates, however, that only 27 per cent of the variance in percentage change can be explained by the factor of distance from the centre. Thus, although the trend is significant it is not a full explanation.

The period of contraction of acreage from 1885 to 1889 (Fig. 6, B) shows a far closer relationship with a clear tendency for the percentage decline to become more marked with increasing distance from the centre. In this case the r^2 value of 0.50 indicates that 50 per cent of the variance is the result of distance. The figures in this case are in every way more reliable, especially as they may be expressed in relation to the agricultural land of each parish rather than in absolute terms. But both examples indicate that the factor of distance from the centre of cultivation was a significant one in accounting for the regional rate of expansion or contraction of the hop acreage during the nineteenth century.

The details of locational change were, of course, far more complex than the simplified account given here would suggest. But it has been shown that there was a persistent tendency throughout the century for the distribution of the

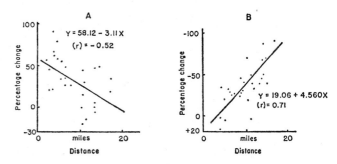

FIGURE 6 Relationship Between Hop Acreage Change and Distance from Yalding for 28 Parishes in the Kentish High and Low Weald.
A. Absolute change 1829/35 to 1856/61.
(Source: Hop Excise)
B. Percentage change 1885 to 1899 in relation to agricultural area.
(Source: Ministry of Agriculture)

hop acreage to be related to distance from the centre of production. A recognition of this tendency is essential to both the study of changing location and the understanding of the location of hop cultivation at any one particular time. This tendency, however, poses three specific problems. First, why did hop cultivation tend to concentrate in Mid-Kent? Second, what were the limits set to this concentration? Third, why, once these limits were reached, did the industry spread out and around Mid-Kent in a way more consistent with distance than with soil conditions?

The Problem Explained

The problems posed above can best be answered in terms of three specific processes—agglomeration, cumulative change, and diminishing returns. These three processes need detailed consideration.

AGGLOMERATION

The process of agglomeration has been studied often in relation to industrial structures, but it has been largely ignored in an agricultural context.[10] There were, however, certain economics to be gained from establishing any new hop acreage in or near the existing locations. Economies of scale operated within the individual farm unit. Hop cultivation demanded the use of specialized equip-

---

[10]W. Isard, *Location and space economy* (1954), chapter 8.

ment—oast houses, special implements, hop poles and so on—and it was in the grower's own interest to make an optimum use of all this equipment. The oast house was the most important item. It was scarcely economic to build one for less than ten acres of hops, while thirty acres was generally considered necessary to keep a well-designed oast house fully employed at mid-century. Other buildings and items of technical equipment also encouraged the grower to keep up a certain minimum area under hops, since their inefficient use meant a higher cost per unit of output.

But the tendency towards concentration can only be fully explained in terms of the external economies of scale which accured from establishing new acreage in the existing locations. Mid-Kent, for example, had long been the commercial centre of hop cultivation and possessed marked physical advantages. But by 1800 a whole range of capital assets had been built up which increased the attraction of the district from the point of view of hop cultivation.

Many of the Mid-Kent planters, for example, had accumulated quite impressive capital resources. Hop cultivation was, by nineteenth-century standards, an extremely expensive form of cultivation. The initial investment was heavy—anything between £60 and £100 per acre—and the annual costs of cultivation were also high—usually between £25 and £40 per acre. The accounts for one farm between 1838 and 1846 indicate an annual expenditure of £35 per acre on the hop land compared with £5 12s. on the arable.[11] The total capital requirements for successful hop cultivation were thus considerable; one agent stated that he would not accept a tenant unless he possessed at least £125 working capital per acre of hop land compared to £10 or £12 per acre of arable land.[12] At the same time there was a high element of risk involved in cultivating a crop with so unreliable a yield.[13]

High costs of cultivation were met, however, by a high turnover per acre. It was, thus, far easier for a farmer already cultivating hops successfully to finance further expansion than it was for the ordinary arable farmer, with a low turnover, to develop an initial acreage. Similarly, the successful hop farmer was able to build up capital reserves over a period of years and so he was better able to face the fluctuations in yield and market price so characteristic of hop cultivation. Thus the accumulation of capital resources from any years of successful hop cultivation created the capital by which further expansion could be financed. In this respect nothing, apparently, quite succeeded like success.

But the financial resources essential to hop cultivation were not entirely provided from within the industry. Much of the capital was provided by the country bankers and, more often, the hop factors and merchants of Southwark. For traditional reasons, specialized financial facilities—extended credit, advances, capital loans and so on—were far easier to obtain in the established locations than elsewhere.

Successful hop cultivation also required considerable skill, for it was 'too hazardous to be attempted where not well understood.' The skills were not only those of the planter who had to deal with complicated production and marketing arrangements, but also extended to the agricultural labourers of the district who were 'eminently skilled and with fair education.' The development of these skills further enhanced the position of Mid-Kent as the centre of hop cultivation, for 'the importance of having every man, woman and child already trained . . . instead of having to train them is inappreciable.'[14] Hop cultivation also required a very large casual labour force at picking time; the development of a regular seasonal migration from London and elsewhere into this part of Kent gave another specific advantage to this district.[15]

One of the most important subsidiary facilities essential to hop cultivation was the supply of hop poles. Before the introduction of creosote in the 1860s and of wirework in the 1870s, the demand was very heavy; 3000 to 4000 poles were required to establish an acre of hops and 500 to 600 of these had to be replaced every year.[16] By

---

[11]Lord Amherst, 'An account of Hall Farm, Sevenoaks', *Journal of the Royal Agricultural Society*, 8 (1848), 33-46. For a general summary of expenses see H. H. Parker, *The hop industry* (1934), chapter 2 and appendix 2.

[12]'Report of the Select Committee on the operation of excise and customs duties on hops', *British Parliamentary Papers* (1857, session 2, volume 14), qq. 3753-4.

[13]P. Mathias, *The brewing industry in England 1700-1830* (1959), 477; A. Young, 'A fortnight's tour in Kent and Essex', *Annals of Agriculture*, 2 (1784), 70-7; and C. Whitehead, 'On recent improvements in the cultivation and management of hops', *Journal of the Royal Agricultural Society*, Second series, 6 (1870), 336-66.

[14]*Maidstone Gazette*, editorial of 14 April 1846.

[15]J. Y. Stratton, *Hops and hop pickers* (1884).

[16]H. H. Parker, op. cit., 64.

1800 much of the woodland along the North Downs and in the Weald, together with all available space in Mid-Kent, had been converted to the systematic production of hop poles. The development of a tradition of woodland management, designed for the production of hop poles, further encouraged expansion in and around the existing locations.

Hop cultivation also demanded enormous quantities of manure and fertilizer. The trade in manure and fodder was already developed by 1800 and it expanded rapidly during the century. By 1846 G. Buckland could write that the cost of 'oil cake and artificial manures considerably exceeds the rental.'[17] Accounts indicate that lime, dung, rags, sprats and ashes were also used.[18] In obtaining these Mid-Kent had the tremendous advantage of proximity to navigable water, but the building up of the trade in fodder and fertilizer was a further asset for the Mid-Kent hop grower.

Agglomerative advantages also existed in the process of hop marketing. The Southwark hop market, which dominated the hop trade, was one of the most unreliable of the London commodity markets. Prices shifted rapidly from day to day, and it was essential for the grower to sell his hops at exactly the right moment if he were to maximize his profit. Marketing thus required special facilities in warehousing and transport, adequate market information, and close contact between grower and factor. Once these facilities and contacts had been developed they could easily be expanded.

Prejudice in the hop trade also played its part. The parish 'mark' was very important, for every bag of hops was legally bound to have its parish of origin marked on it. Hops grown in a parish with a good reputation often sold more easily than hops from another parish irrespective of their intrinsic quality. Most Mid-Kent parishes carried a mark of high repute and this again meant a competitive advantage for the industry here. The hop market was far from operating under conditions of pure competition. The prejudices and imperfections contained within the marketing structure almost always operated in favour of the established locations.[19] Since external financial aid

came mainly from the hop market, similar prejudices may also have guided decisions regarding loans and credit.

The structure of land-holding, farm occupance and landlord policy were also important. Hop cultivation generally required some outlay on the part of the landlord as well as the tenant, while some security was also essential for the tenant's capital outlay. This latter problem was largely overcome by the valuation system common to Kent, Surrey and Sussex whereby the incoming 'tenant paid for all manures and hop poles (the two most important items of outlay for the tenant.)[20] But it was usual in the hop districts for long leases of up to 21 years to be granted. Undoubtedly the landlords in Kent pursued a policy of active encouragement to hop cultivation based on the higher rental that such cultivation yielded and the 'addition it made to the value of their woodland.'[21] Landlords who understood the special demands which hop cultivation made and who were favourably inclined towards it may well have been essential for the expansion of the hop acreage.

The advantages that have been listed here illustrate the marked economies to be had from locating new acreage in or near the traditional areas of hop cultivation. Some of these factors making for agglomeration were localized in distribution to the central area of Mid-Kent, but most were partially mobile in the sense that they could be utilized in districts close to Mid-Kent without too much extra cost. It is thus hardly surprising that the hop acreage tended to be zoned around a central core area since the costs of production were clearly affected by proximity to Mid-Kent. Economies of agglomeration would be more or less available according to distance from the centre and this factor may explain much of the peculiar locational pattern of hop cultivation within Kent. A. Lösch has summarized this tendency when commenting on the land-use structures that will emerge around centres of market activity:

Other things being equal, profits decrease with distance from these centers, either because all shipments pass through them, or because with increasing distance their facilities can be en-

---

[17]G. Buckland, 'On the farming of Kent', *Journal of the Royal Agricultural Society*, 6 (1846), 273.

[18]Details of this trade are given in the Medway navigation accounts, Kent Archives Office, S/MN, A21.

[19]'Report of the Select Committee on . . . hops', op. cit. (1857), qq. 1162, 2168 et seq.

[20]'Report of the Select Committee on agricultural customs', *British Parliamentary Papers*, (1847-48, volume 7), q. 6607; and T. B. Grainger and L. Kennedy, *The present state of the tenancy of land in Great Britain* (1828), 249-51.

[21]'Report of the Select Committee on . . . hops', op. cit. (1857), q. 2621.

joyed only with correspondingly greater difficulty.[22]

Although the factor of agglomeration was perhaps vital, it would be wrong to assume that it always operated with the same strength. Throughout most of the century it was a static factor that directed where an increase in demand could best be met, or where a decline in demand would result in contraction of acreage. But as the organization of the hop trade became more complex, as technical development brought increasing dependence upon subsidiary services, and as the transport system became focused on nodal points in the rail network, so the agglomerative pull around one specific nucleus became more important. This factor may well account for the persistent tendency for the areas in or close to Mid-Kent to grow at a more rapid rate than the more remote districts in the Weald.

Agglomeration was thus a vital factor affecting the distribution and development of the hop industry. Its main effect was one of concentrating the hop acreage in and around a central nucleus in Mid-Kent—but it was not the only process operating towards this end.

CUMULATIVE CHANGE

One of the most difficult problems associated with the study of locational change is that of determining how far the process of change is self-sustained. As G. Myrdal has pointed out:

> In the normal case a change does not call forth countervailing changes but, instead, supporting changes, which move the system in the same direction as the first change but much further. Because of such circular causation a social process tends to become cumulative and often to gather speed at an accelerating rate.[23]

This process of cumulative change appears to have been important to the development of the hop acreage. The development of hop cultivation in Kent had a profound effect upon social and economic structures; these changes in social and economic factors led, in turn, to the further expansion of hop cultivation. The tendency can be illustrated most readily by considering two basic elements in the farmer's costs—rent and wages.

The relationship between rent per acre and land use is a complex one. But all contemporary observers agreed that hop cultivation bore a higher rent per acre than any other form of land use apart from intensive market gardening and some forms of fruit cultivation.[24] There were, however, considerable variations in the value of hop land—a survey of rental values in Mid-Kent for 1867 indicated that the rent of hop land varied between 44s. and 105s. per acre.[25] Generally speaking, however, the greater the area under hops in any particular parish the higher was the average rent per acre likely to be. This can be illustrated by comparing the density of hops, as given by the tithe awards c. 1840, with the assessment of rent per acre on lands given in 1843.[26] The relationship is a fairly convincing one and yields a positive correlation coefficient of 0.80 (Fig. 7).

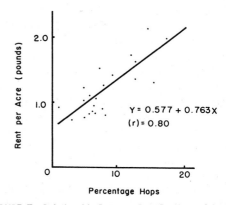

FIGURE 7   Relationship Between Rent Per Acre of Agricultural Land and Percentage of Agricultural Area Under Hops for a Block of 22 Parishes in Mid-Kent c. 1840.
(*Source: Land use and agricultural area from tithe awards; rent figures from British Parliamentary Papers, 1845, volume 38.*)

Once it was shown, however, that the hop land could bear a higher rent than other forms of land use, and that a particular district, such as Mid-Kent was particularly suited to that form of production, then there was a tendency for an all-around rise in rental values to take place. The value of the

[22]A. Lösch, *The economics of location* (1954), 87.
[23]G. Myrdal, *Economic theory and underdeveloped regions* (1957), 13.

[24]A. Young, op. cit., 94; B. Buckland, op. cit., 279.
[25]R. W. Tootell, 'Hop cultivation', *Transactions of the Royal Institute of Surveyors*, 11 (1879), 296.
[26]For the use of these returns see D. B. Grigg, 'Changing regional values during the agricultural revolution in south Lincolnshire', *Transactions and Papers*, Institute of British Geographers, 30 (1962), 91-104.

land was not simply assessed by what the land actually produced, but by what the valuer thought it could produce under the most advantageous system of management. No Mid-Kent landlord, for example, would tolerate a low rental because a farmer preferred to produce corn rather than hops. There were often instances of landlords deliberately raising the rent since, they argued, the tenant could easily produce more hops. The net result was that rents tended to increase on all classes of land independent of their form of cultivation.

A similar process is evident with regard to wages. These varied from district to district according to the form of land use, among other things.[27] In areas of high-quality hop production, such as Mid-Kent, day wages were higher than in the arable districts. The opportunities for remunerative piece-work were also far greater in the hop districts than they were elsewhere, so that the best labourers in the hop districts were invariably drawn into hop cultivation by the high wages offered. But the wages paid out and the competition for the best labourers varied from district to district rather than from farm to farm. Thus labour costs tended to be far higher in the hop districts than elsewhere independent of the sort of land use the individual farmer adopted. But there were other, more subtle pressures. Hop cultivation required more labourers per acre than other forms of cultivation. The net results of this was that the hop districts were faced with high social costs—cottage accommodation, provision of services, support of the poor, and so on. These social costs were often spread over a parish as a whole rather than over the hop growers only, so that parish rates and local taxes also tended to be higher in the hop districts than elsewhere.[28]

The effect of hop cultivation on the farming structure is more difficult to assess. There was undoubtedly a fairly close association between owner-occupancy and hop cultivation. Figure 8 indicates the relationship between density of hop cultivation and percentage of land under owner-occupancy for twenty Mid-Kent parishes c. 1840. The correlation is fairly close and gives a coefficient of 0.78. How far this relationship is evidence of a cumulative trend is difficult to assess, but undoubtedly the owner-occupiers were better able to adjust their acreage to changing demand conditions than were

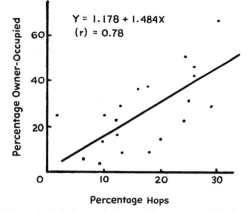

FIGURE 8 Relationship Between Percentage of Agricultural Land Under Hops and Percentage of Land Farmed by Owner-Occupiers for 20 Mid-Kent Parishes c. 1840. (Source: Tithe Awards)

the tenant farmers who had to await a landlord's decision. At the same time, the existence of so many owner-occupiers could also be explained by hop cultivation since this was one of the few forms of cultivation which would allow the accumulation of sufficient capital reserves for the farmer to buy his own land. So that although there are sound historical reasons for the development of owner-occupancy in Kent (especially related to the prevailing law of gavelkind), it is very difficult to decide how far there is a one-way causal connection between this feature and the development of the hop acreage. It seems reasonable to atribute a certain cumulative element to both features.

The development of hop production undoubtedly influenced social and economic features. The net effect of these changes was the evolution of a distinctive pattern of overhead farming costs. The farmer in the hop districts was faced with a high rental, high wage costs, and high social costs irrespective of his farming system. These extra costs made his competitive position in ordinary forms of cultivation rather unsatisfactory. This provided an extra incentive to expand hop cultivation, provided economic conditions were favourable, in the already established locations which, once completed, further influenced the pattern of overhead costs. This process could continue until some sort of conformity of land use was established. Conformity, however, does not necessarily mean uniformity, for there may be more than one system of management that meets a particular pattern of

[27]D. W. Harvey, op. cit., chapter 5.
[28]Ibid., 257.

overhead costs. In Mid-Kent, for example, the fruit industry formed an adequate alternative to hop cultivation.

Cumulative change was, thus, a further process that encouraged the concentration of hop cultivation into one district, by eliminating many of the alternative forms of land use. This pressure was a dynamic one, that inevitably led to conformity of land use within any particular district. Whether or not the farmer yielded to these pressures was a matter of individual choice; but the economics of the situation are clear. The net result was to reinforce the tendency towards concentration already determined by agglomerative processes.

DIMINISHING RETURNS

The concentration of hop cultivation was limited, however, by the rate of diminishing returns. Thus the process of spread outward from a central core area can be partially interpreted as 'the centrifugal effects of diminishing returns.'[29]

The tendency for overhead costs to rise with the development of hop cultivation has already been examined, but as the hop acreage expanded so the cost of many other factors of production varied. At first the cost per unit of output declined with scale of output, but after a certain limit these costs tended to increase. Some elements in the cost structure of hop farming in the central core area were thus more expensive than they were elsewhere—the rent of land and the cost of hop poles were two important examples at mid-century. The result was that the hop industry tended to be located elsewhere in order to avert these diseconomies; but the agglomerative pull meant that this relocation always took place with reference to distance from the centre. The interaction between the processes governing concentration and the centrifugal effects of diminishing returns can thus be regarded as the key explanation of the zoned distribution of the hop acreage. But this explanation depends very much upon ascertaining the point at which diminishing returns proved a serious barrier to an extension of the hop acreage.

The ultimate limit to hop cultivation was, clearly, a situation of monoculture where the entire agricultural area was given over to hop cultivation. But the statistics indicate that hops rarely accounted for more than 35 per cent of cultivated area, while 15 per cent was more normal. Simple percentage figures conceal much, however.

Sir Charles Middleton's account of his farm at Teston in the late eighteenth century indicates an interesting situation. Only 40 out of the 260 acres were under hops, yet the whole farm was oriented to the needs of hop-growing. The hop ground made very heavy demands upon manure and fertilizer, and the account outlines how much of the farm was given over to the production of fodder crops:

> this year, I take it for granted, I shall be out of pocket by fatting stock more than two hundred pounds . . . yet with all these losses attending feeding in this way, I find it answers on the whole; and without such expenses I could not possibly keep up the quantity of hop ground, in the state it now is. We look, in general, to hops for profit; and most farmers in this neighbourhood think themselves well off, if they do not lose by their arable.[30]

Because of the heavy manure requirements, 15 per cent of the farm was capable of dominating the rest. Under the Mid-Kent system, the bulk of the farm was a fertilizer factory which 'nothing but the all-receiving and frequently all-paying hop-garden would justify.'[31]

These heavy demands for manure could partially be met by bringing onto the farm either manure or cattle fodder, but these alternatives tended to be rather expensive and to increase costs of unit ouput. Thus the farmer could cultivate 10 to 15 per cent of his land under hops without depending too heavily on external supplies of manure and fodder. But beyond this limit the farmer could only increase the hop acreage provided that dependence upon external supplies of manure and fodder did not result in increasing unit costs. When hop prices were high and fodder prices low, the farmer could obviously afford to cultivate a higher density of hops on his farm—in this respect the optimum density of hop cultivation fluctuated with prices and demand. But technical considerations were also important. The cost of obtaining fertilizer and fodder varied regionally, so that higher densities were achieved in Mid-Kent—with its access to

---

[29]W. Isard, op. cit. (1954), 4.

[30]Sir Charles Middleton, 'Queries relative to the farm at Teston, Kent', *Communications to the Board of Agriculture*, 2 (1800), 119-27.

[31]G. Buckland, op. cit., 273.

cheap water transport—than in the remoter parts of the Weald. These costs also varied with time, so that with the cheapening of freight rates after 1850 and the development of a national trade in artificial fertilizer and cattle feeds, higher densities became possible.

There was thus some sort of optimum economic level for the density of hop cultivation. Empirical definition of this level is impossible because of the many variables involved. In the latter part of the century some farms had 80 per cent or more of their acreage under hops, but the large quantities of manure and fodder required clearly made this system expensive to operate. In general the farmer kept the proportion of hops down to the level where most of the fertilizer requirements could be provided from within the farm. This was true even on the smaller farms and there was surprisingly little variation in the proportion of the land under hops in different farm size groups (Table II). It can be assumed that 10 to 15 per cent of the agricultural area could be cultivated without difficulty, but at some point above this level, rising costs tended to check any increase in acreage. The evidence of actual densities suggests that this level lay somewhere between 15 and 35 per cent of the agricultural area throughout most of the century; it is impossible to pin it down more closely than that.

But in spite of its vagueness, this concept has considerable importance. In particular it serves to explain the changing fortunes of the Mid-Kent industry, for by 1826 the hop acreage appears to have reached an optimum level so that further expansion would have certainly meant rising costs per unit of output. This may account for the lack of expansion in Mid-Kent between 1830 and 1850. After 1850, however, declining costs of obtaining

fertilizer and fodder in conjunction with a phase of very remunerative prices entailed a renewed expansion of hop cultivation in the core area. The development of the Mid-Kent acreage before 1878 may thus be interpreted as a function of fluctuations in the economic and technological conditions which determined the optimum density of hop cultivation.

SUMMARY

There were three basic processes governing the tendency for the hop acreage to be ranged in zones of declining density around a specific centre of production. First, agglomeration of production allowed the grower to benefit from economies of scale in or near the established locations. The traditional centre of hop cultivation, Mid-Kent, accordingly exercised a powerful influence over the subsequent spread of the hop acreage. Second, the development of hop cultivation engendered strong cumulative pressures that tended to eliminate most rival forms of cultivation by imposing a specific pattern of overhead costs. Agglomeration meant economies of scale in the established locations, cumulative change meant cost diseconomies for rival forms of land use. The net result was a tendency towards concentration which was only effectively limited by diminishing returns after an optimum acreage density had been reached. The relative strengths of these three processes were by no means constant, however, and the fluctuating development of the hop acreage around the Mid-Kent core may be explained by the fluctuating importance of each process as economic and technological conditions changed.

Conclusions

This article has illustrated how two specific processes—agglomeration and cumulative change—can lead to concentration of production. It has also illustrated how diminishing returns, operating in the face of expanding demand, can lead to a spread of a particular form of production out into areas which possess no inherent advantages for that form, apart from proximity to an initial production centre.

It is unfortunately impossible in the remaining space to attempt any general survey of how these processes have, or might, influence forms of agri-

TABLE II Hop Cultivation and Land Occupance in Seven Mid-Kent Parishes, c. 1840

Farm size group	Percentage of agricultural land in group	Percentage of hop acreage in group	Mean percentage of hops on each farm in group
1—10	3.0	5.6	29.7
10—50	9.9	13.0	21.0
50—150	20.7	17.6	13.5
150—300	28.3	25.7	14.5
300—600	38.0	38.1	15.9
Owner-occupied	30.2	32.5	18.3

(*Source:* Tithe commutation awards for East and West Barming, Mereworth Teston, Wateringbury and East and West Farleigh)

culture other than hop cultivation. In this there would be a major difficulty because of the lack of empirical knowledge on the subject; even such an important feature as the operation of internal and external economies of scale, with which the process of agglomeration is closely allied, has been given very scant attention in the literature.[32] But nevertheless some theoretical points can be made about these processes.

The importance of diminishing returns in agriculture has long been recognized. In the face of expanding demand the finite factor of land yields at a diminishing rate as its use is intensified, until it proves cheaper to move production to an alternative location, providing, of course, that land is available elsewhere. If all the factors of production (skill, technical knowledge, capital, labour, and so on) are completely mobile, then the alternative site chosen would obviously be determined by optimum physical considerations. But these factors are only partially mobile and the friction of distance acts in such a way as to make the spread out of cultivation partially a function of distance from the initial centre. This sort of process has been discussed in the greatest detail in terms of the diffusion of innovations and the evolution of settlement patterns, while gravity and potential models of economic activity may also have some relevance.[33] In fact it is not uncommon for agricultural distributions to be ranged around a series of nodal centres in declining zones of intensity; the location of fruit growing in either Kent or Worcestershire is one such example, while Lösch has noticed a similar feature in the pattern of cotton production in the U.S.A.[34] Further evidence is certainly worth looking for.

The case of cumulative change, however, is difficult. Any particular farmer should decide which crop or combination of crops to cultivate in terms of the demand (price) for each commodity and his relevant costs of factor inputs. But the cost of factor inputs will vary with the cumulative decisions of all the farmers in any particular district. This can have two diametrically opposed effects.

The first would be declining costs in one form of production through economies of scale, and rising costs in all other forms of production because of the creation of a specific pattern of overhead costs. This will lead to concentration of production. The second effect could be a decline in factor costs for several lines of production through a fuller use of all factor inputs; one form of production may employ labour fully for certain limited periods only, and it will therefore benefit the farmer to adopt some complementary form of production to use up this unused factor at a time of the year when it is under-employed. This second tendency leads to diversification of production.[35] For most ordinary forms of production a modest degree of diversity is probably the most desirable situation, but for highly specialized forms of production—hops, fruit, market gardening, and so on—the cumulative tendency is probably dominant. The cumulative process which was demonstrated by reference to the hop industry, probably only applies, therefore, to highly specialized forms of agriculture which create very marked patterns of overhead cost.

The process of agglomeration also depends upon the variation in factor costs with the cumulative decisions of many farmers in any district. But in this context we are dealing with the problem of competition between different agricultural regions in producing the same crop, rather than with the factors that influence the choice from a variety of alternative crops within any one district. Agglomeration in agriculture is simply an example of those 'economies of specialization' which form a basic tenet of international trade theory. The pattern of international trade in agricultural produce is as much a result of these economies as is trade in industrial products; the Danish dairy industry and the Canadian wheat industry are typical examples where economies of scale and specialization result from the adoption by numerous producing units of similar forms of production. But, as B. Ohlin and subsequent writers have pointed out, trade theory does not cease to apply below national units; it can also be applied to inter-regional patterns of trade within any country.[36] The logic behind economies of scale through agglomeration of agricultural production into regional specialisms is just

[32]For this approach see E. O. Heady, *Economics of agricultural production and resource use* (1952), 360-3.

[33]T. Hägerstrand, "The propagation of innovation waves,' *Lund Studies in Geography*, Series B, 4 (1952); E. Bylund, 'Theoretical considerations regarding the distribution of settlement in inner north Sweden,' *Geografiska Annaler*, 42 (1960), 225-31.

[34]K. M. Buchanan, *Report of the Land Utilization Survey of Britain*, Part 68, *Worcestershire* (1944) (especially the maps on pp. 636, 648 and 649); and L. Dudley Stamp, ibid., Part 85, *Kent* (1943), 581. Also A. Lösch, op. cit., 87.

[35]For a full analysis of this process see T. Brinkmann, *The economics of the farm business* (English edition 1935), 62-71.

[36]B. Ohlin, *Interregional and international trade* (1933); and W. Isard (1960), op. cit., chapter 8.

as strong as it is for inter-regional trade theory as a whole. In determining which region specializes on which crop or combination of crops, it is comparative advantage rather than absolute advantage which matters.[37] It may be, for example, that Mid-Kent has an absolute advantage over East Anglia in both hop and sugar-beet production, but it is nevertheless mutually advantageous for each district to specialize on one crop.

The difficulty that arises here, of course, is to differentiate between the economic and physical factors involved in regional specialization. The sort of situation that could arise may be demonstrated in the following way.

If we assume two crops making equal demands upon factors of soil and climate, and assume two separate districts of equal physical capacity and position relative to the market, then there is no physical reason why each district should not split its productive capacity equally between the two crops. If the two crops are not complementary, and there are no economies of integration, then economies of specialization will lead to agglomeration and each district will concentrate on one crop only. Which district concentrates on which crop may be determined by chance. If we now drop the assumption of equal physical conditions, and assume a situation where there are minor differences in the productive capacity between the two districts, then regional specialization will still occur provided that the mutual economies of specialization are greater than the diseconomies of cultivating one crop under inferior conditions. Again, which district specializes on which crop may be determined by chance. Two districts of slightly different physical capacity are now cultivated under completely different cropping systems, but it is impossible to argue in this case that the cause of the difference is the difference in physical capacity even though there is a coincidence between the two distributions. It is, thus, dangerous to argue about agricultural distributions and physical capacity in a way that assumes that coincidence between the two is proof of causal connection.

The sort of confusion that may arise is illustrated by two recent articles on dairying in Great Britain. In an article on Cheshire, E. S. Simpson illustrates the stability of land use in the face of rapidly changing technology and economic conditions. Because stability exists, and because it is a

district of certain physical characteristics, Simpson concludes that the stability 'gives some measure of the strength of the contribution of the physical environment to the agricultural economy.'[38] A similar feature of stability in the face of changing price support policy was noted by F. A. Barnes in an article on the Anglesey dairy industry. But the conclusion in this case is that 'events in Anglesey are demonstrating that once capital has been fixed in the necessary buildings, equipment and herds in an area of small farms such as this, dairying is strongly resistant to change.'[39]

Physical factors may well be a fundamental cause of stability in the Cheshire and Anglesey cases, but there are also good economic reasons for stability—as R. O. Buchanan has pointed out, 'the specialized area . . . will fight to the last ditch rather than accept a change of specialization.'[40] The explanation of stability is undoubtedly very complex, but land-use systems grow and develop and the factors that govern evolution are so very complex that there is an inherent danger that physical coincidence will be read as physical causation.

The initial location of a particular form of production in an empty area may be 'explained' (so far as it is rationally explicable) by a relatively simple interaction between demand factors and innate physical capacity assessed in terms of current technology. But once an initial location pattern has been developed, the factors that govern its subsequent evolution multiply in complexity. Fundamental changes in agricultural technology, transport technology, consumer taste, and so on, may alter the whole context of resources, distance and demand. But it is clear also that there are systematic economic factors that also govern the 'where' and 'how' of agricultural development. The factors of agglomeration, cumulative change and diminishing returns are only three elements in a complex matrix of causal interconnections. But their operation is surely worth consideration in any final analysis of the logic of locational patterns in agriculture.

---

[37]E. O. Heady, op. cit.

[38]E. S. Simpson, 'The Cheshire grass-dairying region', *Transactions and Papers*, Institute of British Geographers, 23 (1957), 162.

[39]F. A. Barnes, 'Dairying in Anglesey', *Transactions and Papers*, Institute of British Geographers, 21 (1955), 137-56.

[40]R. O. Buchanan, 'Some reflections on agricultural geography', *Geography*, 44 (1959), 12.

Maurice H. Yeates

SOME FACTORS AFFECTING THE SPATIAL DISTRIBUTION OF CHICAGO LAND VALUES, 1910 – 1960 *

It is the purpose of this paper to examine the spatial distribution of Chicago land values during the last fifty years in the light of certain theoretical concepts. The classical body of land value theory, developed by such writers as Haig, Ely, Doreau, Ratcliff, and, more recently, Wendt,[1] provides the urban geographer with a number of insights concerning the spatial distribution of urban land values.

Discussion of Hypotheses

An assumption basic in classical theory and implicit in the work of Alonso[2] is that land values decline with distance from the center of the city. In this study the center of the city is defined as the peak land value intersection of State Street and Madison Avenue. This point, in Chicago, is close to the geographic center of the Central Business District, which is commonly defined as that area surrounded by the rapid transit elevated railroad, known locally as the "Loop." The peak value intersection has arisen because transport routes converge at the center of the city making that location the point of minimum aggregate travel costs. Locations away from the center incur greater transport costs, and thus land values decline reflecting decreasing accessibility,[3] smaller market hinterlands, and lower net returns.

However, the Central Business District is but one, although it is the largest, of a number of commercial areas in the city. If land values rise toward the peak value intersection of the Central Business District, they should also rise toward the highest value intersections of the smaller commercial areas. Recognizing this, both Knos[4] and Marble[5] attempted to relate land values to distance from major business centers as well as the Central Business District. The evidence from these studies is somewhat contradictory, for in the former the assumptions were substantiated and in the latter rejected.[6] As a consequence these ideas will be

Reprinted with the permission of the author and publisher from *Economic Geography*, Vol. 41, No. 1, 1965, pp. 57-70. Dr. Yeates is Assistant Professor of Geography at Queens University, Kingston, Ontario.

A grateful acknowledgment is due the Computing Center at Northwestern University, and the National Science Foundation whose funds helped in the establishment of the Center, for allowing the writer computing time under project number UG 3946-0295.

*The oral form of this paper won an Association of American Geographers 20th International Geographical Congress Participation Award.

[1]R. M. Haig: Regional Survey of New York and Its Environs; Major Economic Factors in Metropolitan Growth and Arrangement, Vol. 1 (Regional Plan Association of New York, 1927); R. T. Ely and E. W. Morehouse: Elements of Land Economics (New York, 1924); H. B. Doreau and A. G. Hinman: Urban Land Economics (New York, 1928); R. V. Ratcliff, Urban Land Economics (New York, 1949); P. F. Wendt: Theory of Urban Land Values, *Land Econs.*, Vol. 33, 1957, pp. 228-240.

[2]W. Alonso: A Theory of the Urban Land Market, *Papers and Proceedings of the Regional Science Association*, Vol. 6, 1960, pp. 149-157.

[3]W. C. Pendleton: The Valuation of Accessibility (Ph.D. dissertation, University of Chicago, 1962).

[4]D. S. Knos: Distribution of Land Values in Topeka, Kansas (Center for Research in Business, the University of Kansas, May, 1962).

[5]W. L. Garrison, D. F. Marble, et al.: Studies of Highway Improvement and Geographic Change (Seattle, 1959).

[6]These differences in results may well be related to the surrogate for land value used. Knos used assessed evaluations while Marble used the average value for single family dwelling units in a block, which contains not only the value of the land but the improvements, that is, the buildings as well. Land value data on a front-foot basis can be obtained from *Olcott's Land Values Blue Book of Chicago* compiled and published by George C. Olcott and Co. annually. The earliest volume was published in 1907 and referred to the situation in 1906.

reexamined in the Chicago area, at decennial intervals since 1910, in relation to the Central Business District (the Loop) and regional shopping centers.[7]

The city, however, presents an ever-changing pattern of accessibility. These varying patterns are a result of physical changes in the structure of internal linkages, such as the construction or widening of highways, and technological changes in transport media, such as the development of faster and more efficient rapid transit, or the introduction of small, low-cost automobiles. Physical improvements, in particular, tend to make one area more accessible, and therefore more desirable, than another that does not have the same facilities. This is because increases in accessibility tend to reduce transport costs, and therefore not only provide additional funds that can be used for the purchase of land[8] but also increase the number of potential users and range of use for that particular area. Evidence from the Chicago suburbs, for example, indicates that there are relatively lower land values in areas without commuter rail service or at some distance from such a service.[9]

Since the turn of the present century the City of Chicago has witnessed the extension and decline of such a physical transport improvement. The elevated-subway system reached its maximum coverage in 1930 and has subsequently decreased in total mileage.[10] This is a reflection of the primacy of public transport in the first three decades of the century, and its replacement by the automobile during the last three decades. Thus one would expect the physical location of rapid transit facilities to reach its maximum importance as a determinant of land values in 1930 and to decline thereafter.

But this decline in physical extent and coverage of rapid transit cannot be divorced from social and economic changes in society that have occurred during the period under discussion. Just as it is everywhere evident that the automobile is replacing public transit as the chief mover of people in the city, so it is becoming increasingly evident that people as such are changing their location preferences. These changes in location preferences are evidenced by the general decline of population densities in the city and the spreading out of population[11] beyond the political limits of the city into the suburbs and interstitial areas. The factors that have permitted this movement are many and interactive. Not the least of them are: the universal use of the automobile, the construction of highways and expressways, the shorter working week, increasing wages, and increased leisure.

The net impact of such changes as far as land values are concerned should appear to be a more rapid growth of land values at the periphery of the city and in areas offering certain amenity advantages. Thus, throughout the period under discussion, the postulated negative relationship between land values and distance from the center of the city should weaken. This situation may be modified in the case of Chicago because of the truncated nature of the city. The Central Business District is located adjacent to Lake Michigan and the city has grown to the north and the south. The lake shore today exhibits the geographic juxtaposition of a number of factors, such as the Outer Drive (a high speed limited access highway), and part of the elevated-subway system, as well as being an amenity and prestige location. All these factors would seem to suggest that land values should decline with distance from Lake Michigan.

Changing location preferences can be further examined by analyzing the relationship between land values and population densities. If there is a negative relationship between land values and distance from the center of the city, and if population densities decrease with distance from the center of the city, then land values and population densities should be positively related. However, this relationship may be becoming more and more affected by changing characteristics of the urban population. For example, the proportion of the city classified as nonwhite (which in reality means Negro)

[7]The location of the regional centers used in the analysis was based on a map entitled "Chicago's Outlying Business Centers," which was compiled under the direction of B. J. L. Berry, University of Chicago, and obtained from the Chicago Community Renewal Program. The Community Renewal Program recognizes four classes of centers: "Major Regional Centers, Smaller Shopping Goods Centers, Community Centers, and Larger Neighborhood Centers." In this paper the first two groups have been combined and given the name "regional centers."

[8]For a discussion of the impact of highway improvements see H. D. Mohring and M. Harwitz: Highway Benefits: An Analytic Framework (Evanston, Illinois, 1962).

[9]C. R. Hayes: Suburban Residential Land Values Along the C. B. & Q. Railroad, Land Econs., Vol. 33, 1957, pp. 177-181.

[10]R. L. Abrams: The Story of Rapid Transit in Chicago, Bull. of the National Rwy. Histor. Soc., Vol. 26, No. 2, pp. 18-28, and No. 3, pp. 14-31.

[11]For an illuminating discussion of this see B. J. L. Berry, J. W. Simmons, and R. J. Tennant: Urban Population Densities: Structure and Change, Geogr. Rev., Vol. 53, 1963, pp. 389-405.

has increased enormously during the past few decades. In nineteen forty, 8.3 per cent of the total population of the City of Chicago was classified as nonwhite. By 1950 this proportion had increased to 14.1 per cent and by 1960 reached 24.1 per cent. The highly clustered nature of the distribution of these nonwhite persons makes the net effect of this movement difficult to determine.

Land Value Maps

The land value maps (Figs. 1 and 2) were constructed from a disproportionate stratified random sample of 484 points[12] (Table I), for which average front-foot land values could be obtained on a block basis, located within the 1960 city limits of Chicago. Preliminary analysis of the arrayed land value data suggested a sharp positive skewness at each time period. In order to facilitate later statistical analysis the data were logarithmically transformed, and in order to facilitate comparison of the land value maps between time periods the transformed data were converted into normal standard deviates. The isoline interval chosen for each map is one standard deviation; therefore each map can be compared because the intervals are comparable and related to their respective means.

A visual analysis of the maps (Figs. 1 and 2) yields some interesting observations. Throughout the whole time period the highest land values are found within and adjacent to the Central Business District (the center being the peak-value intersection at State and Madison), and from this area there is a sharp decline in all directions. This decline was logarithmically fairly uniform in 1910, but by 1960 it does not exhibit the same consistency. The contraction of the mean isoline and general reduction of land values on the south side of the Central Business District is marked by the presence of residual outliers which indicate the position of regional business and shopping centers. Therefore, it could be suggested that the effect of distance from, and consequently access to, the Central Business District on land values appears to have diminished in importance during the past 50 years, while the front-foot value of locations in the vicinity of outlying regional service centers has increased.

TABLE I Sampling Ratios and Number of Points Sampled by Zones

Zone[a]	Percentage of total area in city	Sampling ratio	Number of sample points
A(0 —1.5 mls.)	2	3:1	30
B(1.5—3.0 mls.)	7	2:1	70
C(3.0—4.5 mls.)	10	12:10	60
D(rest of city)	81	8:10	324

[a] The zones are rings centered on the peak-value intersection of State Street and Madison Avenue, Chicago.

A further locational factor that appears to influence the general spatial distribution of land values is Lake Michigan, for relatively higher land values are found close to the lake shore. The 1950 and 1960 maps, however, suggest that land values within the vicinity of Lake Michigan on the north side of the city are generally increasing and higher than those on the south side where values are declining. This is possibly a reflection of the nonwhite, low-income nature of the southern area which discourages "high rise" apartment speculation.

Land at the periphery of the city appears to be becoming relatively more valuable than land in the middle of the city.[13] In the 1960 map this tendency is much more strongly developed in the north than in the southwest, and hardly present at all in the west. The great rise in land values at the periphery of the city in the north is probably a reflection of the high-income nature of this area. The absence of any rise to the west is a result of the political boundary on the west being closer to the center of the city than the boundary to the

---

[12]There are many types of sample and an infinite number of sampling ratios that could be used. For example, the number of points dropped in each zone could be equal to the proportion of the city's total land value found in that zone. The ratios used in this sample were determined by trial and error. A number of disproportionate stratified random samples were mapped and the one that seemed best for operational purposes was chosen. In the case of equal proportion of points to equal proportion of land value, for example, Zone A had so many sample points that they overlapped each other, and as a consequence would have been very difficult to identify in later mapping and plotting. The sample chosen represents approximately a 3 per cent sample of all blocks in the city. For a discussion and description of stratified random sampling see W. G. Cochran: Sampling Techniques (New York, 1962), pp. 65-110.

[13]The descriptive term "middle of the city" refers to the area between the peripheral zone and the Central Business District and the fringe (Zone A in this analysis). For a diagrammatic presentation of this concept see E. J. Taaffe, B. J. Garner, and M. H. Yeates: The Peripheral Journey to Work (Evanston, Illinois, 1963), p. 6.

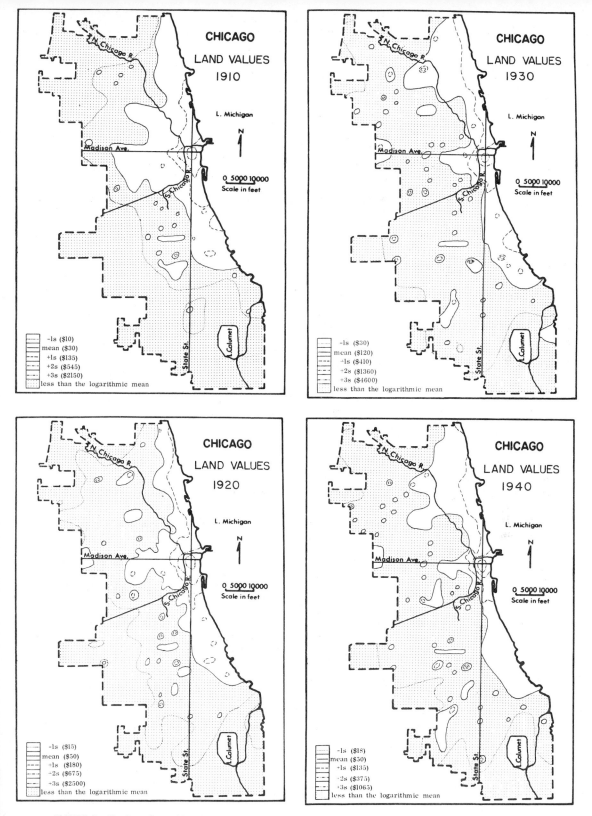

FIGURE 1 The Transformed Land Value Maps, Chicago, 1910—1940.
(Source: Olcott's Land Values Blue Book of Chicago, 1911, 1921, 1931, 1941. Each book refers to the situation in the previous year.)

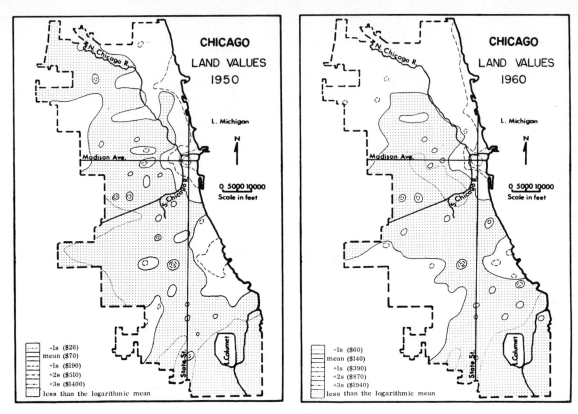

FIGURE 2 The Transformed Land Value Maps, Chicago, 1950—1960. (*Source:* See Figure 1.)

north or south, and thus peripheral developments which are within the city on the north or south are absent in that area.

Regional, or sectoral, variations can be discerned particularly from the 1960 land value map. The area within, and adjacent to, the Central Business District has exhibited the highest land values throughout the whole time period. To the north, land values are, and have been, consistently high within the area bordering Lake Michigan, and in the past two decades have increased markedly throughout the whole northwestern part of the city. West of the Central Business District land values appear to have become relatively much lower during the past 30 years. Land values in the southern part of the city have generally been low throughout the whole time period. An exception to this is seen in a small area in the southwest where there has been a relative rise.

The discussion of the land value maps would, therefore, seem to support a number of the hypotheses discussed in the previous section. Furthermore, the visual analysis suggests that the development of sectoral variations should also be exam-

ined. All the hypotheses can be incorporated into a statistical model as accessibility can be simulated in terms of distance, and the population data can be numerically determined from census tract records.

Application of A Multiple Regression Model

The following model was examined decennially for the years 1910-1960 using the Chicago data:

$$V'_i = a + b_1 C'_i + b_2 R'_i + b_3 M'_i + b_4 E'_i + b_5 P'_i + b_6 N_i + e;$$

where

$V'_i =$ logarithm of front-foot land value at the ith place;

$C'_i =$ logarithm of distance (in hundreds of feet) of the ith place from the Central Business District;

R'_i = logarithm of distance (in hundreds of feet) of the ith place from the nearest regional shopping center;

M'_i = logarithm of distance (in hundreds of feet) of the ith place from Lake Michigan;

E'_i = logarithm of distance (in hundreds of feet) of the ith place from the nearest elevated-subway system;

P'_i = logarithm of population density at the ith place (by census tract);

N_i = the per cent nonwhite at the ith place (by census tract);

and a, b_1 . . ., b_6 are empirically derived constants, $i = 1, 2, . . ., 484$, and e is the error term.

The application of the above hypothesized model at each one of the time periods yields some interesting results. In 1910 and 1920 the model fits the actual structure of land values extremely well, but in 1930 the explanation drops appreciably, and by 1950 and 1960 the "explanation" is extremely low (Table II). This may well be a reflection of the decline in importance of a number of variables in the model. For example, an examination of Table III suggests that the regression coefficient pertaining to the variable distance from the Central Business District has declined in magnitude considerably throughout the whole time period even though it tests as being significantly different from zero in 1960. The regression coefficient pertaining to the variable distance from the nearest elevated-subway system fails, however, to test as being significantly different from zero in 1960. These changes in magnitude and statistical significance may well be a result of actual changes through time in how these variables affect land values, or the result of inadequate transformations chosen for the individual variables, which for all variables, except percentage nonwhite, has been presumed to be logarithmic. The distribution of the individual variables was tested at each time period and a logarithmic transformation appeared to be most appropriate to assure normality.

Thus it would seem tenable that the decline in coefficient of determination through time may well be a result of the decline in importance of certain variables. One way of investigating this would be to make a comparison of the regression coefficient (or slope) between each independent variable (all other independent variables held constant) and the dependent variable. In this particular case the regression coefficients are not complete because the independent variables are expressed in different units. Comparability can be achieved, however, if the dependent and independent variables are expressed in standardized form. The regression coefficients are then called standard regression coefficients.[14]

The regression coefficients have been standardized for each year, and on the basis of comparison of slopes a ranking can be made of the importance of each variable at each time period in this particular model. A comparison of these rankings (Table IV) indicates that the distance measures have been particularly important, especially those related to the Central Business District, the elevated-subway system, and Lake Michigan. All these are distance variables; they measure airline distance to important facilities, such as transport and recreational amenities. Of these the distance measure concerning the Central Business District has been interesting in that the decline in importance of this variable has been largely responsible for the great decline in power of the model. The sign of the coefficient indicates that on the whole land values do decline with distance from the Central Business District, but the standardized slope of this variable has declined by some 60 per cent in the last 40 years, illustrating a decline in attractive power of the Central Business District. Not only has there been a decline in absolute magnitude of the Central Business District standard regression coefficient but also a decline in its relative position among the other variables.

Along with the decline in importance of proximity to the Central Business District has been the marked decline in the ranking and absolute magnitude of the standard regression coefficient related to distance from the nearest elevated-subway.[15] The theoretical discussion suggested that this vari-

---

[14] For a discussion of the computation of standard regression coefficients see F. C. Mills: Statistical Methods (New York, 1956), pp. 643-645.

[15] This association is in part due to the high intercorrelation between these two variables at every time period (simple correlation coefficient usually about .66), the magnitude of which was increased by the type of sample used. In this study the sampling intensity increased zonally toward the Central Business District. The elevated-subway system radiates from the Loop, and as a consequence a disproportionate number of points are located close to rapid transit facilities and the Central Business District. This results in a disproportionate number of points having similar values for both variables and hence a higher intercorrelation than would be obtained with a purely random sample.

TABLE II Results of Multiple Correlation Analysis, 1910—1960

	1910	1920	1930	1940	1950	1960
Multiple correlation coefficient........(R)	.8784	.8070	.6089	.5846	.4885	.4216
Coefficient of determination.....(R^2)	77%	65%	37%	34%	24%	18%
"F" test............(F^a)	222.3	145.0	45.9	25.2	24.4	16.8
Sample size [b]	402	473	474	474	475	475

[a] The least highly significant value of F(0.01) with 6 and 400 degrees of freedom is 2.85. For a discussion of the computation and use of the analysis of variance test in multiple correlation analysis see Frederick C. Mills, *Statistical Methods* (New York, 1955), pp. 627-629.

[b] Of the 484 points sampled in 1960, 475 fell in a part of the city where a discernible land value was recorded. The great reduction in 1910 is a result of incomplete coverage of Olcott's estimates for the whole city.

TABLE III Constants and Regression Coefficients for Multiple Regression Analysis, 1910—1960

	a	C'	R'	M'	E'	P'	N
1910	4.745	—0.837[a]	—0.038	—0.450[a]	—0.248[a]	+0.105[a]	+0.005[a]
1920	4.826	—0.673[a]	—0.122[a]	—0.414[a]	—0.240[a]	—0.008	+0.001
1930	4.107	—0.268[a]	—0.156[a]	—0.367[a]	—0.214[a]	+0.039	—0.003[a]
1940	3.387	—0.275[a]	—0.134[a]	—0.285[a]	—0.140[a]	+0.044	—0.002[a]
1950	3.562	—0.268[a]	—0.081	—0.227[a]	—0.152[a]	—0.116[a]	—0.002[a]
1960	3.356	—0.173[a]	—0.092[a]	—0.146[a]	—0.050	—0.137[a]	—0.002[a]

[a] Significantly different from zero at t(.05). For a discussion of the computation and use of "t" see H. M. Walker and J. Lev: *Statistical Inference* (New York 1953), pp. 337-339.

able should reach maximum importance in 1930 and decline thereafter. The rankings indicate that this was only partially true (Table IV), for this variable ranked second in 1930, but first in 1950. The tendency for a decline after 1940 was, perhaps, delayed by the special circumstances of the 1940-1950 period which emphasized the importance of mass transit. This recent great decline may have been accentuated by the great increase in peripheral employment opportunities and the recent construction of Loop oriented expressways. Hoch[16] used Olcott's land values to examine the relationship between new expressway facilities and the value of adjoining land, taking the case of Edens Expressway from Foster Avenue to just north of Lake-Cook Road. Only a portion of the survey was within the City of Chicago, and although land values tended to rise toward Edens, the lowest increases were recorded in that portion of the study in the city. Thus it would appear that although transport improvements result in an increase in land values the greatest increases are occurring beyond the city boundaries, and those within the city hardly result in increases at all.

The great rise, both relative and absolute, in importance of the standard regression coefficient related to the nonwhite variable has occurred during the past decade. The interpretation, for the city as a whole, must be that as the percentage nonwhite in an area increases, land values decrease.

TABLE IV Comparison of Banking of Standard Regression Coefficients

Rank	1910	1920	1930	1940	1950	1960
1	C'	C'	M'	M'	E'	N
2	M'	M'	E'	C'	M'	M'
3	E'	E'	C'	N	C'	C'
4	P'	R'	N	E'	N	P'
5	N	N	R'	R'	P'	R'
6	R'	P'	P'	P'	R'	E'

It must be remembered, however, that this variable is quite closely associated with income.[17] The statistical analysis, therefore, supports the map analysis which suggested that lower land values in the City of Chicago were generally associated with low income nonwhite areas.

[16]I. Hoch: Rising Land Values Found Along Edens, *Cook County Highways*, Vol. 4, 1957, p. 4.

[17]The simple correlation coefficient for median income and per cent nonwhite, by census tract (using the same sample of 475 points), for 1950 was —.60 and 1960 —.55

In the multiple regression model the influence of Lake Michigan on the spatial distribution of land values also supported the conclusions of the map analysis. The regression coefficient pertaining to this variable tested as being significantly different from zero throughout the whole time period and the sign was, as expected, negative (Table III). Furthermore, the table of rankings (Table IV) indicates that this variable has maintained a high relative importance throughout the whole time period. This supports the presumption that the geographic juxtaposition of the Outer Drive, part of the elevated-subway system, and the amenity and prestige advantages of the lake shore have all combined to maintain the important influence of this variable on land values.

The general influence of regional centers did not, however, prove to be as important as the visual analysis of the land value maps suggested. Although the regression coefficient tested as being significantly different from zero in four out of the six time periods, and the sign supported the hypotheses that land values decline with distance from regional centers, the value of the standard regresion coefficient ranked very low among the other variables. A reason for this may well be that the influence of regional centers on land values is spatially extremely local, resulting in a very tight peaking of land values. Also, the regional centers over the whole city exhibit a variation in stage of growth. It could be expected that relatively higher values would be found in regional centers of recent growth and lower values in the older and declining centers.

The interpretation of the results obtained from the analysis of the relationship between land values and population density is rather more complex than the initial theoretical discussion suggested. It will be recalled that the theoretical discussion suggested that "if there is a negative relationship between land values and distance from the center of the city, and if population densities decrease with distance from the center of the city, then land values and population densities should be positively related." The analysis, so far, as indicated that land values and distance from the Central Business District are inversely related, but that this relationship has declined during the past 40 years. With this modification one would expect the hypothesized positive relationship between land values and population density to weaken through

time. Examining the second part of the argument, it appears that, over the whole city, there has been a distinct decline in the negative relationship between population density and distance from the Central Business District Table V) which would further emphasize the decline in the positive relationship between land values and population density.

TABLE V Simple Correlation Coefficients (R): Population Density (P') and Distance from the CBD (C')

	1910	1920	1930	1940	1950	1960
R	—.63	—.56	—.23	—.13	—.20	+.04

The multiple regression analysis supports this hypothesis modification. In 1910 the regression coefficient pertaining to this variable supported the hypothesis of a positive relationship. For the next three time periods the regression coefficient did not test as being significantly different from zero, and in 1950 and 1960 there was a statistically significant negative relationship. That is, over the whole city, land values increased as population density decreased. The reasons for this are threefold: first, the general flattening of the population density curve through time; second, declining central densities and the outward movement of the inflexion point of the population density curve (which is the result of a number of sample points located in the commercial center of the city having both very high land values and very low population densities); and, third, increasing land values at the periphery of the city.

Sectoral Variations

The discussion of the population density variable illustrates rather clearly the emerging importance of sectoral variations, a possibility that was suggested at the conclusion of the visual analysis of the land value maps (Figs. 1 and 2). The broad areas of land values above and below the logarithmic mean suggest a number of sectors that are largely conformant to those used by Breese,[18] with one addition and one boundary alteration. Figure 3 shows the location of these sectors, which are:

  i. The Central Business District and vicinity

---

[18] G. W. Breese: The Daytime Population of the Central Business District of Chicago (Chicago, 1949).

(Zone A): This zone is an addition to Breese's sectors, and includes all points within 1.5 miles of the intersection of State and Madison, thus conforming with Zone A in which the sampling ratio was the highest. It is an area largely dominated by commerical buildings, hence population densities are extremely low.

ii. The North Sector: This includes an area of high land values bordering Lake Michigan with a steep decline in the land value surface to the west. It is a sector of generally high income (median family income by census tract above $7,000), and excellent Central Business District oriented transit facilities.

iii. The Northwest Sector: The Northwest sector also demarcates an area of values greater than the logarithmic mean, where land values related to housing have exhibited the most recent growth. This sector is larger than that defined by Breese for it includes part of his West sector.

iv. The West Sector: The West sector has developed as an area of consistent, low land values characterized by the most recent and rapid extension of nonwhite neighborhoods. This area is well served by transit and expressway facilities.

v. The Southwest Sector: This represents an area of most recent growth in land values related to semisuburban developments. The sector has always been remote from rapid transit facilities.

vi. The South-southeast Sector: The South-southeast sector displays a number of important characteristics. Much of the northern part of the area has been well served by rapid transit since the turn of the century. Also, it has been the location of well-established nonwhite communities for four decades. Along the margin of Lake Michigan there exist pockets of high income (for example, around Jackson Park). Finally, in the far southeast around Lake Calumet, there is a broad area of heavy industrialization. This whole sector embraces a large area of land values less than the logarithmic mean of the land value distribution in 1960, with pockets of higher values demarcating the high income areas bordering Lake Michigan.

These sectoral variations can be built into the regression equation by the use of dummy and interaction variables[19] so that the regression equation is enlarged to become:

$$
\begin{aligned}
V_i' = a + (b_1 \quad &+ d_1 S_{1i} + d_2 S_{2i} + d_3 S_{3i} \\
&+ d_4 S_{4i} + d_5 S_{5i}) C_i' \\
+ (b_2 \quad &+ d_6 S_{1i} + d_7 S_{2i} + d_8 S_{3i} \\
&+ d_9 S_{4i} + d_{10} S_{5i}) R_i' \\
+ (b_3 \quad &+ d_{11} S_{1i} + d_{12} S_{2i} + d_{13} S_{3i} \\
&+ d_{14} S_{4i} + d_{15} S_{5i}) M_i' \\
+ (b_4 \quad &+ d_{16} S_{1i} + d_{17} S_{2i} + d_{18} S_{3i} \\
&+ d_{19} S_{4i} + d_{20} S_{5i}) E_i' \\
+ (b_5 \quad &+ d_{21} S_{1i} + d_{22} S_{2i} + d_{23} S_{3i} \\
&+ d_{24} S_{4i} + d_{25} S_{5i}) P_i' \\
+ (b_6 \quad &+ d_{26} S_{1i} + d_{27} S_{2i} + d_{28} S_{3i} \\
&+ d_{29} S_{4i} + d_{30} S_{5i}) N_i' \\
+ (b_7 S_{1i} &+ b_8 S_{2i} + b_9 S_{3i} + b_{10} S_{4i} \\
&+ b_{11} S_{5i} + e,
\end{aligned}
$$

where

S_{1i} = a nominal variable delimiting the North sector;

S_{2i} = a nominal variable delimiting the Northwest sector;

S_{3i} = a nominal variable delimiting the West sector;

S_{4i} = a nominal variable delimiting the Southwest sector;

S_{5i} = a nominal variable delimiting the South sector;

and a, b_1, . . ., b_{11}, d_1 . . ., d_{30}, are empirically derived constants, and e is the error term. Solution of the above equation for the 1960 data resulted in an estimate of the parameters for the variables within each of the six sectors (the signs of the regression coefficients are listed in Table VI), and a coefficient of determination of 51 per cent. Thus the hypothesized model, which was expanded to incorporate the concept of "within-city" sectoral variations, resulted in an increase in "explanation" of about 33 per cent. Therefore, it could be suggested that given the variables and the basic model, sectoral variations, arising out of differing stages of historical growth and differing spatial characteristics, are beginning to account for a highly significant proportion of the variation of urban land values in Chicago.

---

[19]D. B. Suits: Use of Dummy Variables in Regression Equations, *Journ. of Amer. Statis. Assn.*, Vol. 52, December, 1957, pp. 548-551; D. S. Knos, *op cit.*, pp. 26-27.

102

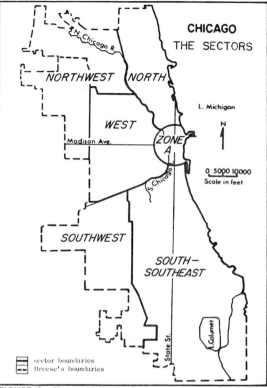

FIGURE 3 Sectors in the Analysis.

An examination of the signs of the regression coefficients (Table VI) provides support for a number of conclusions reached in the previous section, and illuminates the relationship between land values and population densities. In only one sector in 1960 was the population density coefficient significantly different from zero and that was in the South sector, where there did appear to be a positive relationship. Furthermore, examination of the population density and per cent nonwhite variables in the West and Southwest sectors reveals that land values and percentage nonwhite are negatively related (conformant with the theoretical concepts), but that population density is insignificant. However, the South sector, which has been the recipient of Negro urban immigration since the turn of the century, shows no significant decline in land values as the per cent nonwhite in an area increases. This may be related to the "piling-up" process mentioned by Duncan.[20] In areas of recent nonwhite incursion and estab-

[20]O. D. Duncan, and B. Duncan: The Negro Population of Chicago (Chicago, 1957), p. 142.

lishment land values drop, but as the number of people increase in the neighborhood land values may become stable and increase as the population density increases. The area of greatest "piling-up" is in the South sector; and the idea is given some credence by the fact that this was the only sector where there was a significant positive relationship between land values and population density.

TABLE VI Comparison of Sign of Regression Coefficients by Sector: 1960

Sector	C'	R'	M'	E'	P'	N
North	+[a]	—	—[a]	—	—	—
Northwest	+[a]	—[a]	—	—[a]	+	+
West	—	+[a]	—	—	—	—[a]
Southwest	+	—	+[a]	—	+	—[a]
South	+[a]	—	—[a]	—[a]	+[a]	—
Zone A	—[a]	—	—	—	+	—
Whole city	—[a]	—[a]	—[a]	—	—[a]	—[a]

[a] Significantly different from zero at t(.05).

As far as the other variables are concerned, this analysis by sector suggests that although the influence of the elevated-subway may be declining over the whole city, it still has a significant effect on land values in two sectors. Lake Michigan influences, as would be expected, those sectors adjacent to it. The positive relationship in the Southwest can be dismissed, as here the variable has little meaning except as a measure of proximity to the periphery. Land values rise toward regional shopping centers in the newer Northwest, but decline in the vicinity of such centers in the older and more industrialized West.

The regression coefficients substantiate quite adequately conclusions already reached concerning the influence of proximity to the Central Business District. In three sectors there proved to be a significant rise in land values with distance from the center of the city. Only in Zone A (demarcating an area within 1.5 miles of the Central Business District) did land values decline with distance from the intersection of State and Madison.

Conclusion

A mathematical model for 1910, expressed in multiple regression format, "explained" 77 per cent of the variation in Chicago land values. However, there was a continuous decline in "explanation" derived from a multiple regression model of the same form applied during ensuing time periods. For 1960 this "explanation" had dropped to 18 per cent. This decline in power of the model can be related in particular to the decline in influence of the Central Business District and the increase in importance of sectoral variations. Addition of sectors raised the "explanation" in 1960 to 51 per cent, which seems to suggest that sectoral differences at this period accounted for a further 33 per cent of the variation in land values.

The hypothesis that land values decline with distance from the Central Business District was substantiated for the whole city at each time period, though there appeared to be a continuous decline in strength of the association. The sectoral analysis in 1960 suggested some important spatial modifications. At this time period land values in the North, Northwest, and South sectors appeared to increase toward the periphery, thus refuting the hypothesis when applied to these sectors individually. The hypothesis was clearly substantiated only in the area within 1.5 miles of the intersection of State and Madison (Zone A in the analysis).

The statistical analysis did not prove the influence of regional service centers to be as important as the visual analysis of the maps suggested. The results indicate that land values will diminish with distance from regional centers in the newer and more rapidly expanding, relatively high-income, areas of white population. Regional centers, however, will be detrimental to land values in old areas of manufacturing and commerce, which in Chicago are occupied by a very large number of low-income nonwhite persons.

The influence of recreational and physical amenities on land values, taken in this study as meaning distance from Lake Michigan, appears to have increased in relative importance during the past 50 years. This may be due to the fact that proximity to the lake, in the case of Chicago, measures not only accessibility to amenities and a pleasant situation, but also accessibility to the Lake Shore Drive and rapid transit facilities, which parallel the lake for much of its distance.

The importance of this geographic juxtaposition is emphasized further in the analysis of land values with respect to rapid transit facilities. The evidence indicates that rapid transit, representing a system of relatively low transport costs, appears to have declined markedly since 1930 as a determinant of land values. In 1960 only the South sector showed any decrease in land values away from the elevated-subway, reflecting the larger, low-income, labor pool which relies on the continuing existence of rapid transit in this area. Evidence has also been presented indicating that although land values appear to rise toward new automobile expressways the greatest increases were observed beyond the city limits, and very minor increases just within the city. Therefore, it could be suggested that within the city high-speed low-cost transport facilities are no longer such important determinants of land values as in times past.

The population density and nonwhite variables proved to be inter-related. In the early years of this century higher land values were associated with high population densities. During later time periods, however, this concept was unsubstantiated, except in the South sector in 1960 where land values and population density were positively related. This appears to be related to Negro migration into urban areas such as the South sector of Chicago, a movement which has accelerated in recent decades. The analysis of both of these factors suggests that as percentage nonwhite in an area increase, land values decrease, until such time as the population density begins to rise (due to "piling-up" in overcrowded ghettos), at which time land values start to rise as a result of intense subdivision of property and competition for living space.

The analysis of some simplistic concepts, formulated as variables in a descriptive model, would, therefore, seem to indicate that in the City of Chicago there is an upward trend of land values at the periphery. This is possibly one side of a ridge of higher values,[21] which is complemented by a developing pocket of lower values in the area between the periphery and the Central Business District. This suggests that the one focus, the Central Business District, toward which land values used to rise, and around which population densities were the greatest, will soon be complemented by a number of other foci. These foci lie on and beyond the political limits of Chicago, and though they may never be as concentrated as in the Central Business District, their combined influence on the land value structure may equal that of the core in the past.

[21] Taaffe, et al., *op. cit.*, p. 120.

Wilfred Smith

THE LOCATION OF INDUSTRY

In this address I want, first, to place the study of the location of industry in its general geographical context; second, to discuss the value of Alfred Weber's loss-of-weight hypothesis in the analysis of industrial location; and third, to map out the area within which industry is located by the provenance of raw materials and beyond which it is located by conditions other than those presented by raw materials.

I

The location of industry is a problem amenable to methods of geographical analysis. Analysis of the map and analysis in the field are as essential as in geomorphology. The industrial distribution map, like the population distribution map, displays pattern and texture, and a geographer is as much concerned with pattern and texture as is a painter or a musician. The distribution map brought to life by the skilled geographer has, indeed, the same symphonic quality as the musical score brought to life by a first-class orchestra. To be adequate, a distribution map must be a map in relief and depth and not merely flat and two-dimensional, showing, for example, size of factory or scale of output as well as simple position, clustering and dispersion as well as regional quantity. Whatever our particular interests in the subject may be, we have all seen a map grow and come to life before our eyes as we have worked on it, and this creation of a map out of bits and pieces is of the very stuff of craftsmanship. To be complete, a distribution map must also embody those other distributions which are relevant to the analysis of the particular distribution under examination. In order to discover what is relevant, the map is the geographer's experimental tool as well as the canvas on which he presents his finished picture. But distribution maps by themselves are not enough. They present problems and suggest solutions, just as does a geomorphological map, but the solution of these problems is possible only after work in the field. This is dissection, the separate examination of the single case, and it is by the examination of a whole population of single cases that conclusions are built up. Work in the field involves examination of the qualities of each industrial site on the ground; it involves inquiries from each firm of the qualities of the site *vis-à-vis* other alternative sites as known at the time when the site was selected; it involves inquiries of the requirements and sources of materials and of power, of labour and of markets; and it involves a discussion with the management of the problem of scale and of internal and external economies on that site and in that district. Further, the economic geographer needs theoretical analysis to clarify his mind, to define his problem and to strip it of irrelevancies; but in order to arrive at solutions theoretical analysis must run in harness with the examination of evidence collected from an accumulation of particular cases. Only by the marriage of theory with concrete fact can the principles of industrial location be formulated. If I pay more attention to the presentation of my conclusions in tabular than in cartographical form, it is that this paper attempts to deal with the full range of manufacturing industry in a country

Reprinted with the permission of the publisher. TAKEN FROM I.B.G. TRANSACTIONS No. 21, 1955, pp. 1-18, by courtesy of the Institute of British Geographers (Copyright reserved).

The author acknowledges the financial help given by the University of Liverpool towards the cost of the illustrations.

where industrial plants jostle each other closely on the ground. I shall present a few maps of individual industries, for they are cartographically manageable, but I shall not attempt any of industry in the total sense.

II

I come now to the core of my paper. I propose to consider the location of manufacturing industries alone and to ignore the service industries. The latter were once regarded as outside the geographer's field. When physical was equated with geographical this was natural enough, but the development of urban geography has created a very genuine interest among geographers in the location and character of service industries and I would regard them as indubitably of geographical interest. It is indeed very difficult to draw the line between manufacturing and service industries for some, like baking, present characteristics of both. I shall draw the line empirically and consider only those where the manufacturing aspect dominates the service aspect.

In their work on the rationale of the location of manufacturing industry, it is natural for geographers to turn first to location by materials. Materials are physical substances which provide concrete data and which are capable of being mapped. I propose to follow tradition and to adopt location by materials as the starting point of geographical analysis; as the starting point but not as the terminus. I shall show that not all manufacturing industries are in fact located by materials. It would be as false to dismiss these as outside the interest of the geographer as to dismiss those industries located by materials as outside the interest of the economist. Both geographers and economists, in my opinion, are entitled to work in this field of the location of industry for, approaching the problem by different routes, they have each something different to contribute.

In 1909 there appeared Alfred Weber's theory of the location of industry.[1] He endeavoured to formulate it as a 'pure' theory argued out from stated assumptions, hoping at a later stage to relate it to the actual facts of location and by the adjustments thus necessitated to formulate a 'realistic' theory. The theory has been criticized as incomplete, for industrial location is too rich and too varied to fit into Weber's formalized economic box and competition is not perfect but imperfect, but I do not propose to embark on any critical evaluation of the theory as such. What I do propose to do is to pick out one of his propositions and see what relevance it possesses to the interpretation of the observed facts of location in Great Britain today. This is the relatively simple proposition that industries whose product weighs less than the materials from which it is made (in which, in other words, there is a loss of weight in the course of manufacture) are tied in location to their raw materials. It is then cheaper to manufacture at the site of materials than at the market, other things being equal, for the cost of transporting the smaller weight of product is less than the cost of transporting the larger weight of materials. Weber was well aware that the structure of transport rates, being not infrequently higher per ton-mile for the product than for the material, may distort the shape of the location figure, to use the economist's expression when dealing with the location of a single plant, and the shape of the distribution pattern, to use the geographer's expression when dealing with the location of a congregation of plants. And he was well aware that this hypothesis alone could not furnish a complete theory in itself. For the purposes of his proposition Weber defined materials as including coal and as consisting only of localized materials, that is, excluding ubiquitous materials such as water. I shall have occasion later to criticize this definition but I will accept it for the time being in order to discover what relevance Weber's proposition has to the observed facts of location in Great Britain today. If we are discussing his hypothesis it must be discussed in the terms in which he defines it.

Without question some industries fulfil Weber's requirements. The weight of the raw sugar extracted in a sugar beet factory is one-eighth of the weight of the materials (beet, coal and lime) used in the extractive process; the weight of the butter, cheese and manufactured milk products is in the aggregate one-sixth of the weight of materials used in the milk factory; the weight of pig iron is between one-fourth and one-third of the blast furnace charge. In Weber's terminology they have a material index of 8, 6 and 3-4 respectively.

[1] A. Weber, *Über den Standort der Industrien* (Tubingen, 1909). Translated by C. J. Friedrich as *Alfred Weber's theory of the location of industries* (Chicago, 1929).

The watershed which Weber adopts between industries orientated to materials and industries orientated to markets is a material index of one, that is, in which weight of product equals weight of materials. The sugar beet factories are in the midst of the beet-growing districts, though a few are peripheral (Figure 1); the blast furnaces are on ore-field or coalfield, with the single exception of the Ford plant at Dagenham; the milk processing factories are in the midst of dairying districts, with the exception of those urban plants manufacturing waste milk surplus to urban consumption (Figure 2). Each of these industries displays a large loss of weight of the main product during manufacture and each is located close to supplies of raw material. The few plants located elsewhere are capable of rational, if not always of economic, explanation. Two points arise immediately out of these examples. The first is that they can all be described as primary industries, the initial handling of a material direct from mining or from farming. It is in this initial processing of a material that large losses of weight arise. I will return to this point shortly. The second is that these large losses of weight occur in respect of the main product and that in arriving at them by-products and waste have been ignored. In each of these industries there are by-products of some importance: beet pulp for stock feeding from sugar extraction, basic slag for fertilizers from iron smelting, whey and butter-milk for stock feeding from cheese and butter making. These by-products are bulky, are very much lower in value than the main product, and for precisely these reasons are most extensively used within a relatively short distance of the processing plant. They do not invalidate the conclusion that such plants must be located close to their raw materials.

There are many other industries whose raw materials lose in weight during manufacture but not to this extent. The loss in grain milling varies with the extraction rate which itself varies with the kind of flour it is intended to produce: for white flour the loss is 30 per cent, not including coal. In fish curing it is 31 per cent for herrings and more for other fish; in mineral oil refining 22 per cent. These are also primary industries in the sense that they handle materials for the first time though not necessarily at the site of primary production. It is not an accident that they are port industries processing materials imported by sea, though there is some milling and tanning from

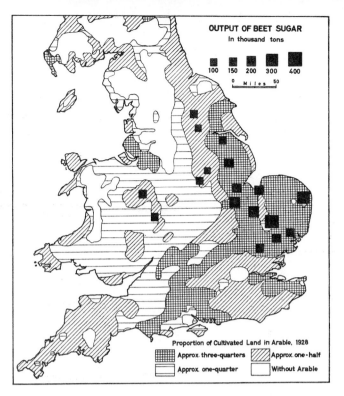

FIGURE 1 Distribution of Sugar Beet Factories in Relation to Arable Land.

home resources and in inland districts. The weight loss from these imported materials is very much less than in beet sugar, pig iron, and milk product manufacture which handle only (or largely) home resources. If loss were as high in this second group as in the first, then the initial processing would be at the site of the raw material abroad, as it is, for example, in cane sugar, in which loss of weight during the extraction of the sugar juice is of the same order of magnitude as in sugar beet. The extraction of sugar from the sugar cane, therefore, is an industry of the sugar plantations and only the refining of raw cane-sugar is a British industry. It is significant that the loss of weight in leather tanning is 34 per cent from British hides coming fresh from slaughter-houses with fat and hair still attached, but only 10 per cent from imported wet salted hides from which such waste material has been removed before shipment. It is also significant that the weight of pig iron as a proportion of the blast furnace charge, while one-fifth for home ores, is one-third for imported ores, for only the richer ores are brought in from abroad.

These examples have been selected in order

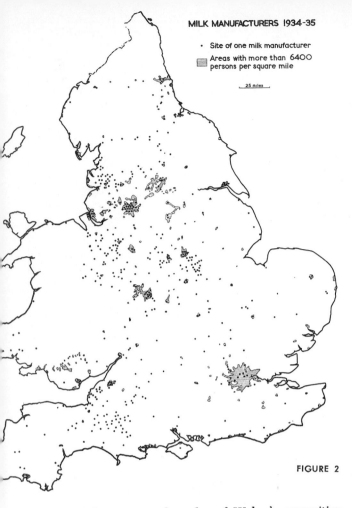

· Site of one milk manufacturer

Areas with more than 6400
persons per square mile

25 miles

FIGURE 2

tries no weights whatever are given for production and weights are given for only a fraction of the materials. In tailoring and dressmaking, for example, production is recorded only in terms of values and of number of articles, and materials are recorded only in terms of square yards. No estimation is possible for production but some estimation is possible for materials: nevertheless, it can be no more than rough approximation for cloth varies considerably in weight per square yard. The employment of the returns of the Census of Production for the examination of Weber's thesis, therefore, is full of difficulty. Should the weight of the unrecorded items be estimated on the assumption that the ratio of weight to value is the same for the unrecorded as for the recorded items? I have attempted estimation along these lines for every industry for which it is at all possible, but I am convinced that the estimations are of little value for the purpose of testing Weber's hypothesis. Rough approximations are valueless: order of magnitude is not enough, for the problem involves not single quantities but the relation of two quantities to each other. Moreover, the premise that the ratio of weight to value is the same for the unrecorded as for the recorded items is inaccurate, for it is usually the items whose weights are substantial for which weights are actually recorded and the items for which weights are unrecorded are usually those relatively higher in value in proportion to weight. This is not always true, but whether such methods overestimate or underestimate weight' it is clear that at best they can only be approximate and that at worst they may distort the ratio completely. I have been compelled, therefore, to ignore those industries for which a substantial proportion of their materials or of their production is recorded only in terms of values or of quantities of such a kind that calculation of weights is impossible. Some others cannot be included as they are merged in the census classification with other trades of different character: thus, butter and cheese making is combined with milk bottling. Sixty-five industries remain. They range widely from those whose product is less than 20 per cent of weight of materials (including coal) to those whose product is more than twice the weight of materials (including coal).

They have been tabulated in Table I and classified by observation of each industry in turn whether in fact they display location at materials, such as blast furnaces, whether in fact they display

to demonstrate the value of Weber's proposition that weight-losing industries are drawn to their raw materials and they also serve to demonstrate that the strength of the tie varies with the amount of the loss. It is one thing, however, to observe its operation in certain selected cases and an entirely different thing to dignify it as a universal law. I propose now to turn to the full range of British industry and to examine Weber's hypothesis in this wider context. I shall draw my data from the 1948 Census of Production, the most recent full census, later censuses being partial and of sample particulars only. Values of materials and of production have been recorded in every census, but the first census which required weights was that of 1935. The 1948 Census records these weights more fully than the 1935 Census. But, while virtually complete for many industries, the particulars of weight are incomplete for many others. Even for industries as well documented statistically as iron and steel some weights are unrecorded. For other indus-

108

partial location at materials and partial location independent of materials, such as leather tanning, or whether in fact they display location entirely independent of localized materials, such as bread baking or beer brewing. It will be recalled that Weber regards water as ubiquitous and, therefore, not a localized material. The tabulation shows that all industries located at materials have a value below 100, that is a material index of more than one. Those industries with a value over 100 and, therefore, with a material index of less than one are located either wholly or partly independently of materials. Weber's watershed has some validity. But industries located at materials are dispersed along the entire range of values below 100 and industries located independently of materials are likewise dispersed along the entire range of values below 100 with the single exception of that below 20. It may be inferred that the material index provides us with a tool of analysis but that it is a blunt tool and is effective only at the very extremities of the classification. For industries within the very wide range from a material index of one to a material index of five this index offers no certain guide to whether an industry is or is not located at its materials. This middle range comprises no less than 49 out of 65 industries and of these 20 are located at materials, 20 independently of materials and 9 partly at materials. It classifies together, for example, blast furnaces and cotton spinning, the one located firmly at the source of ore and coal and

the other located with complete independence of the source of raw cotton. This is inclusive of coal in all cases.

Weber's inclusion of coal with industrial raw materials, however, confuses the issue for all industries except those, like blast furnaces and briquette plants, for which coal is a raw material in the real sense and not only a source of power. A high coal index, in fact, indicates tie to coalfield and not tie to raw materials as such. For the geographer the distinction is of great importance. The textile industries, for example, use considerably greater quantities of coal than of textile raw materials; they may be located on coalfields, but they are certainly not tied to their sources of wool, or cotton, or raw silk. In view of this I have recalculated loss of weight for each of the same sixty-five industries by excluding coal from materials (Table II). The material index of one does not appear to have the same validity as when coal is included, but the two industries located at materials and yet with an index below one are both capable of rational explanation. One is the preserving and bottling of fruit and vegetables which, even if there be a gain in weight, must be located where such fruit and vegetables can be handled in fresh condition, and the other is oils and greases which should perhaps have been omitted from consideration as the weight of its raw materials is under-recorded. This second tabulation narrows the middle ranges and increases the range of effectiveness of the tool at the

TABLE I   Loss of Weight During Manufacture

Industries	Weight of product as per cent of weight of material (including coal)												Totals
	10-19	20-29	30-39	40-49	50-59	60-69	70-79	80-89	90-99	100-109	110-199	200+	
Located at materials	2	2	1	1	2	3	3	5	3				22
Located partly at materials		2		2	2	1	1	1		3			12
Not located at materials		3	3	2	1	6	2	2	1	3	3	5	31
Totals	2	7	4	5	5	10	6	8	4	6	3	5	65

TABLE II   Loss of Weight During Manufacture

Industries	Weight of product as per cent of weight of material (excluding coal)										Totals
	Under 30	30-59	60-69	70-79	80-89	90-99	100-109	110-119	120-199	200+	
Located at materials	2	1	3	4	5	5	2				22
Located partly at materials		1	1	1	1	3	1	3	1		12
Not located at materials		1	1	4	6	3	2	3	4	7	31
Totals	2	3	5	9	12	11	5	6	5	7	65

extremities. Of the industries with a material index of over 1.4 (that is, with weight of product less than 70 per cent of weight of localized material) most are located at materials, 6 wholly so, and only 2 are independent of materials. Of the industries with a material index of under 1.0 (that is, with weight of product more than weight of localized material) most are located independently of materials, 16 wholly so, and only 2 are located at materials. But the middle ranges (even when defined thus less rigidly than in the interpretation of Table I) still include half of the industries in the table, and of these 14 are located at materials, 13 independently of materials and 5 partly at materials. In these middle ranges the material index jostles with other conditions to determine location.

III

I come now to the third part of my paper. Is it possible to devise other tests of the location of industry on the site of its materials in addition to loss of weight during the course of manufacture and, in particular, is it possible to sort out industries in the middle ranges of the loss-of-weight classification for which that classification gives us so little help? Industries may have the same percentage loss of weight during manufacture, but may employ very different aggregate weights of materials. The test I wish to consider is the weight of materials per operative,[2] and the data I shall use are those of the 1948 Census of Production. The weight of materials processed by each industry varies, of course, with the size of the industry and it is essential, if one industry is to be compared with another on a common list, to relate them to some common denominator. The number of operatives has been used for this purpose. Numbers of operatives returned are not, of course, strictly comparable, for there is the difference between adult and juvenile, male and female, good worker and

poor worker, mechanized industry and handicraft industry. But they are at least fully recorded.

The industries in the middle ranges of the classification according to loss of weight have been tabulated according to weight of material per operative (Table III). They display wide range in weight per operative per annum from 1450 tons in class A to 3 tons in class M.[3] These were then classified as previously according to whether by observation they display location at materials, location partly at materials, or location independent of materials. The result is striking, for these industries in the middle ranges of rank are arranged into two groups with little overlap. Those with high weights per operative are located at materials, those with low weights per operative are not located at materials. The break between them comes at 30-40 tons of material per operative per annum. This is exclusive of coal.

If weight of material per operative is so effective a tool in sorting out these industries of the middle ranges of the loss-of-weight classification with regard to the observed facts of location at materials, may it be equally effective over the whole range of industry? I have examined it for the 65 industries which have been considered previously for the operation of loss of weight (Table IV). I have examined it also for the 125 industries for which there are records adequate for the purpose (Table V). It is an effective tool in both cases, though the amount of overlap is greater than for the smaller sample. The boundaries between the two groups, those located at materials and those not located at materials, are blurred, but the area of uncertainty is very much narrower and more sparsely populated than in the classification according to loss of weight. The area of overlap is, of course, greatest for those industries located partly at materials and partly independent of materials, like the tanning of sole leathers, at materials, and of upper leathers, independent of materials, or like earthenware and refractories, at materials, and china, independent of materials.

It would thus appear that weight of material per operative is a sharper tool than loss of weight

---

[2]I have employed this before in 'Mobility in the location of industry in Great Britain', *The Advancement of Science*, 6 (1949-50), 115-7 and in Appendix C of *An economic geography of Great Britain* (2nd edn., 1953). It has been pointed out to me by Mr. Brian Law that Weber's labour coefficient is not unlike my weight of materials per operative, except that it refers to costs of labour and not to quantity of labour irrespective of cost. This paper does not include an examination of costs of materials, of value of product or of labour costs of conversion. I have considered costs of materials and value of product in the two papers listed above, but have not yet examined labour costs of conversion. This paper confines its attention to weight: the analysis of costs must be left for a further occasion.

[3]The classification into sixteen classes (A-P) is the same in Table III as in Tables IV and V. The three tables can thus be directly compared. There are eight industries in each of the sixteen classes. Table V embodies the full list of 128 industries, less three whose particulars are too incomplete for inclusion. Weight of material per operative is greatest in class A and least in class P.

TABLE III Weight of Material per Operative

Industries																

Classification according to weight of material (excluding coal) per operative, greatest at A, least at P

Industries	A	B	C	D	E	F	G	H	I	J	K	L	M	N	O	P	Totals
Located at materials	4	3	2	3	1					1							14
Located partly at materials						1	2		1		1						5
Not located at materials						1	1	2		3	2		2	2			13
Totals	4	3	2	3	2	2	4	0	4	3	1	2	2	0	0	0	32

These industries are those in the middle ranges of the classification according to loss of weight (cf. Tables I and II).

TABLE IV Weight of Materials per Operative

Classification according to weight of materials (excluding coal) per operative, greatest at A, least at P

Industries	A	B	C	D	E	F	G	H	I	J	K	L	M	N	O	P	Totals
Located at Materials	6	3	5	4	1		1			2							22
Located partly at materials		1	1		2	1	2	2	1		2						12
Not located at materials					2	3	3	3	5	4	2	3	4	1	1		31
Totals	6	4	6	4	5	4	6	5	6	6	4	3	4	1	1	0	65

These industries are those which appear in Tables I and II.

TABLE V Weight of Materials per Operative

Classification according to weight of material (excluding coal) per operative, greatest at A, least at P

Industries	A	B	C	D	E	F	G	H	I	J	K	L	M	N	O	P	Totals
Located at materials	7	6	6	7	2		1			2							31
Located partly at materials	1	2	1	1	2	2	2	3	1		2						17
Not located at materials			1		4	4	5	5	7	6	6	8	8	8	8	7	77
Totals	8	8	8	8	8	6	8	8	8	8	8	8	8	8	8	7	125

All industries for which information is available.

during manufacture for sorting out industries into that group located by materials and into that group located independently of materials. It is a sharper instrument partly for mechanical reasons, the nature of the returns of the Census of Production and the greater spread of values. But there is a more fundamental reason. Loss of weight has significant locational effects only when it is combined with large weight per operative, for variation in transport costs are substantial enough to affect location only if weights handled are large. A combination of large loss of weight and large amount of material per operative ties an industry in location to its raw materials: a combination of large gain in weight and small amount of material per operative frees an industry from location at its raw materials: where the two conflict, as in many engineering trades which produce large quantities of metal scrap and which therefore display substantial loss of weight during manufacture but which handle only small weight of material per operative, it is the weight of material per operative which is the more significant in its effects on locational ties to material. Engineering industries in the mass are now by no means tied to material.

IV

The analysis has been of contemporary conditions using contemporary data. There is reason to believe that particular industries have changed in the strength of their locational ties to materials with the course of time. There is a large number of industries not now tied to materials but which seem originally to have been tied to materials often on the same sites which they now occupy. Examples are the older finished iron trades, such as chains and hardware, tools and cutlery; the mechanical engineering trades, such as textile machinery and locomotive building; and the textile trades, although the particular textile material may have changed. These all employ only relatively small weights of material per operative per annum, much smaller than is commonly realized, fifteen tons for chains, nails and screws, less than one ton for cutlery, five tons for textile machinery, six tons for locomotive shops, three tons for cotton, two and a half tons each for wool and for linen, less than one ton for hosiery. Each of these has a well-defined regional distribution but their materials are no longer drawn wholly locally, if indeed they are drawn locally at all. Some would doubtless argue that they present examples of industrial inertia. The phrase is not an apt one if by inertia is implied maladjustment to present conditions. There is no alternative site within Britain where they would be better placed. Even small weights of material per operative were significant when transport was rudimentary and expensive, but they are not significant today. The small weights of materials which they use can now be drawn in readily from elsewhere by the present transport system. It is, indeed, open to question whether some of these industries, particularly the textile, were ever as firmly located by raw materials as is commonly supposed. They have now a very solid balance of advantages in their present location, established labour skills, external economies as a result of the aggregation of like with like, and, although both materials and markets are now distant, there the industries remain and they move only if the solid advantages which have kept them so long begin to evaporate. The shortage of labour in the West Riding has led some wool textile firms to migrate to districts where labour is available, even if it is raw and untrained. While some industries are less tied to raw material than formerly there are some others, fewer in number, whose tie to raw materials is now stronger than previously. Grain milling, newsprint, tailoring and dressmaking are examples; they have become concentrated in the ports and in the textile districts respectively. In these instances the condition responsible for the change is the greater weight of material per opera-

tive as a result of more intense mechanization, thus strengthening the tie to materials.

There is another set of industries whose location pattern with regard to materials is subject to change. Large loss of weight ties industry to raw material provided it be linked with large weight of material per operative, and this large loss of weight is due to the production of large quantities of waste material for which no economic use can be found. When an economic use opens up for these waste products the most economic site may be changed thereby. In some cases the economic use is at too low a value to carry any locational significance. Thus sugar-beet pulp, even when prepared for sale, is only a third of the value of the unrefined sugar; and basic slag, even when ground, is only a fourteenth of the value of pig iron. But in a few cases it is sufficiently high to be significant. When coke was made wholly in beehive ovens and the coke-oven gas ran to waste, then the pit head was the most suitable site for coking plant for there was a substantial loss of weight in a bulky material. But when coke-oven gas proved to be usable for heating in steel plant, then there was advantage to be gained by locating coking plant adjacent to steel works. As coke is used in greater quantities in blast furnaces than in steel works, it was at integrated plants with both blast furnaces and steel mills that such coking plant was set up. Coke plants are now, therefore, located not only at pit head but also at integrated blast furnace-steel plants: some of the former pass their waste gas into town mains (Figure 3).

V

I come now to coal as a location factor. I have already pointed out that coal and materials should be distinguished. We are all familiar with the powerful locational influence of coal during the first half of the nineteenth century when steam-power, generated by coal-fired boilers, created a seething mass of industrial plants on the coalfields. Coalfield and factory industry were coincident. The metalworking, mechanical engineering and textile industries, the last using larger quantities of coal than of materials, congregated on the coal-fields and there were relatively few plants of these kinds elsewhere. As boiler efficiency was low, the amount of coal consumed per operative was higher than it is today, and transport of coal away from the coalfield was then both expensive and troublesome. The coalfield monopoly of factory industry has subsequently been infringed. This has been due not so much to the emigration of these industries from the coalfields, though some blast furnaces and steel plants have thus moved, as to the creation of new industries on new types of site as the British economy has become diversified. The railway made it possible to move coal more readily about the country and it became possible for industrial plants to be set up away from the coalfields, whether they were run by steam-power or by electricity. At first, electricity was generated expensively by coal in small plants in consuming districts, for transmission of electric current was only over short distances. Transfer to electric power was thus retarded. The completion of the Grid, permitting current to be transmitted across country, has accelerated such transfer, and acceleration is likely to be increased still further by the concentration of output which is now in progress on low-cost sites in gigantic plants located on the Trent near to the largest and most cheaply worked coalfield in the country.

Weight of coal per operative has been plotted against weight of material per operative in terms of rank in each case and expressed in tabular form in Table VI. In many industries there is a reasonable degree of agreement in rank. There is absolute agreement in 17 per cent and little divergence in another 29 per cent of industries. The metal and engineering trades are examples of close agreement in rank, whether they be of high rank, as blast furnaces, of middle rank, as foundries or mechanical engineering, or of low rank, as electrical engineering. But there is substantial divergence in half the examples and the two classifications are often widely at variance. For 29 per cent they are a full quartile removed. Some with a high rank in weight of material per operative use little power of any kind, such as fish curing or textile converting and some, if they use power in quantity, employ mainly electricity, such as saw-milling. They are located by materials but are not at all attracted to the coalfields. Others with a low rank in weight of material per operative have a conspicuously higher rank in weight of coal per operative. The textile industries are almost wholly of this kind. They use small quantities of material per operative, as I have shown, but they subject that material to a succes-

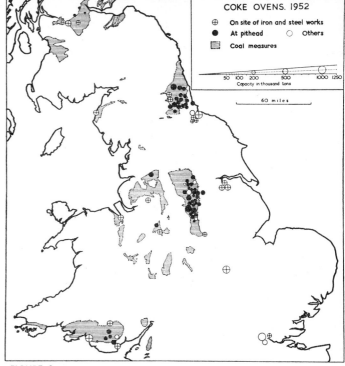

FIGURE 3

sion of mechanical processes which require substantial quantities of power, and that power is still steam-power generated from coal on the mill site. The tie of these textile industries to a coalfield, however, is relative and not absolute, for the coal they use still places them only in the middle rank and their coalfield site is largely a relic of the early nineteenth century. For the tie to a coalfield to be absolute the quantities of coal must be large and they must exceed the quantities of the raw materials, unless those raw materials are themselves located in the coalfield. Few industries fulfil these conditions today. It is primarily those industries processing coal in large quantities as a raw material which are tied to a coalfield. I do not wish to be misunderstood. Many industries derive positive advantage from location on a coalfield, but these advantages, it is necessary to repeat, are relative and not absolute.

VI

In conclusion and by way of summary I will endeavor to demonstrate the validity of the conclusions of this paper by reference to the location pattern of a particular sequence of industries ma-

113

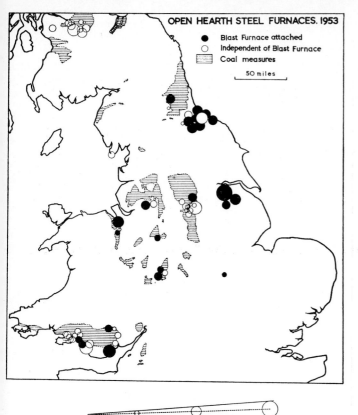

OPEN HEARTH STEEL FURNACES. 1953

- ● Blast Furnace attached
- ○ Independent of Blast Furnace
- ▨ Coal measures

50 miles

Furnace capacity per heat (in tons)
0   100   500   1000   1500   2000   2750

FIGURE 4

nipulating a particular material in a more and more elaborate form. The sequence is, first, blast furnaces; second, steel mills; third, tube mills; fourth, chain, nail and screw mills; fifth, textile machine shops; sixth, motor vehicle manufacturing shops. The weight of the finished product as a percentage of the weight of materials is for blast furnaces 27 per cent, for steel mills 81 per cent, for tube mills 84 per cent, for chain, nail and screw mills 74 per cent, for textile machine shops probably no more than 50 per cent, but for motor vehicle shops it is not possible to make a calculation owing to inadequacy of evidence. For the first three items in the sequence there is less and less loss in weight as the material becomes more highly manufactured, but then loss of weight increases again owing to the production of scrap in machine shops. The weight of material per operative is for blast furnaces 1447 tons, for steel mills 117 tons, for tube mills 38 tons, for chain, nail and screw mills 15 tons, for textile machine shops 5 tons, and for motor vehicle manufacturing shops 7 tons. There is a consistent decrease in weight of material per operative as the material becomes more highly manufactured. The increase in motor vehicle shops over textile machine shops is due to methods of line assembly and to prefabrication elsewhere, both of which have increased weight of material per operative in the assembly shops themselves. Weight of coal per operative varies in the same sequence and more

TABLE VI Weight of Material per Operative and Weight of Coal per Operative

Classification according to weight of material per operative	Classification according to weight of coal and coke per operative, greatest at A, least at P																
	A	B	C	D	E	F	G	H	I	J	K	L	M	N	O	P	Totals
A	3	2		2								1					8
B	1	1	3	1	2												8
C	3	3		1	1												8
D		1	1			1	1					1	1		2		8
E			1			1	1		2		1	1					8
F	1		1	2	1			1		1					1		8
G			2			1	1	1	2	1							8
H		1		1	1		2			1			1	1			8
I						1	1			3		2				1	8
J			1	1		1	1	1	1	2							8
K						1		1	1	1	1			1	1	1	8
L				1	1		1			1	1	1	1				8
M						3	1	1			1		2				8
N												1	1	4	2		8
O							1				1	1	1	2	1	1	8
P									1			1		1	2	3	8
Totals	8	8	8	8	8	8	8	8	7	9	7	9	7	9	9	7	128

114

regularly, for coal per operative is less in the motor vehicle shops than in the textile machine shops. As these quantities change, so also does the nature of the location pattern. Blast furnaces are tied to sources of ore or coal, being mainly at the source of ore: steel mills are partly at the site of blast furnaces and partly elsewhere, being mainly on the coalfield (Figures 4 and 5); textile machine shops are in textile districts: and motor vehicle manufacturing shops are in the English Plain removed from blast furnaces and steel works altogether, with the single exception of the Ford works at Dagenham.[4] The distribution of steel works overlaps the distribution of blast furnaces; the distribution of rolling mills overlaps the distribution of iron works and steel works: the distribution of engineering shops overlaps the distribution of rolling mills. But no two of these distributions coincide. Each stage overlaps the preceding, but the terminal points, smelting and engineering, are only rarely associated in the same firm on the same site. The more and more elaborately manufactured a material becomes, the more completely do the mills or shops which manipulate it become divorced in location from the plants which handle the original raw material. A sequence of this kind displays the full range of locational shift from a location tied to raw material to a location wholly independent of raw material.

This paper does not pretend to be a complete study of the location of industry. I have limited myself to location by materials and have discussed only the evidence relating to weight of materials. I have endeavoured to discover the area within which industry is tied to materials and I have endeavoured to discover some of those features which distinguish industries located by materials from those which are located independently of materials. There remains a vast sector of manufacturing industry and, of course, service industry which is not tied to materials at all. Some industries are tied firmly to a local market, though

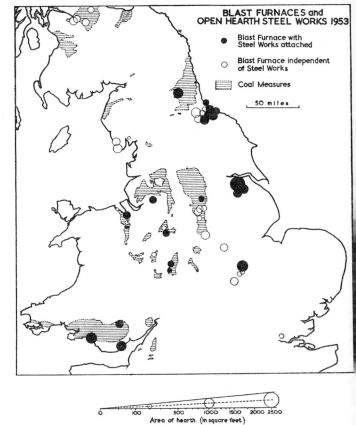

Area of hearth (in square feet)

FIGURE 5

improvements in transport services have greatly expanded the range of distribution and the size of that local market; but some have a market covering the entire country. Some are tied, relatively or absolutely, to areas where the labour skills they require are present; but others migrate readily to areas where labour is cheaper, if less skilled. In this sector, technological advance, internal economies through scale of plant, external economies through the association of like with like, all display their effects. They may even in the particular case compensate for a poor site with regard to materials. Some industries, indeed, are tied to no specific set of conditions, provided that labour and transport, power and water are obtainable. This concourse of industries not located by materials presents a field of inquiry which requires a new set of analytical tools, more rather than less difficult to fashion than those with which I have worked in this paper.

Olof Lindberg

AN ECONOMIC-GEOGRAPHICAL STUDY OF THE LOCALISATION OF THE SWEDISH PAPER INDUSTRY[1]

This study attempts to analyse the transport costs of certain Swedish paper and pulp mills. The method used has been an adaptation to a geographical foundation of the theory of location as it appears in economic works at the present time.

In this investigation, the most important way of illustrating the conditions imposed by location makes use of the concepts *isovecture* and *isodapane*. An isovecture is a line joining points with equal transport costs for a certain commodity to a certain place. Isodapane is the name given to a line joining points with the same total transport costs for all the commodities entering into the production process. The relation between isovectures and isodapanes is illustrated in Fig. 1. The point B in that figure indicates a raw-material locality (for example, iron ore), and point A a consumption locality or harbour

for shipping the finished good. Two tons of ore are taken to be necessary for the production of one ton of iron, consequently, around B, the lines for transport costs (isovectures) are drawn twice as close together as they are around A. The total cost of the transport of ore and iron may be read off at the points of intersection of the two systems of isovectures. The oval lines which join these points of intersection are the above-mentioned isodapanes.

The construction in Fig. 1 indicates the relation between isovectures and isodapanes when the raw material is supposed to come from a *point*. But if it is gathered from an *area*, the relations are somewhat different. The shaded area in Fig. 2 denotes a bounded area where a raw material is produced. The figure shows four different consumption localities: *a, b* and *c* within the "harvest"

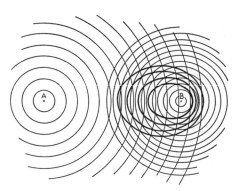

FIGURE 1   Construction of Isodapanes.

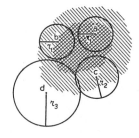

FIGURE 2   Harvest Circles at Areal Consumption.

Reprinted with the permission of the author and publisher from *Geografiska Annaler,* Vol. 35, No. 1, 1953, pp. 28-40. Dr. Lindberg is Associate Professor in the Geografiska Institutionen, Umeå Universitet, Sweden.

[1]Summary of: Studier över pappersindustriens lokalisering. Geographica Nr 23. Uppsala 1951.

area, and d outside it. If the amount of consumption remains constant, at a and b a circular area of radius r_1 may be harvested. If c is the consumption locality, the harvest circle must be greater (radius r_2), and at point d outside the harvest area the radius of the harvest circle must be increased to r_3. Since the radius of the circle increases, the transport costs also increase. The more peripheral the consumption locality with respect to the harvest area, the higher the transport costs when the amount of consumption is constant. In the central parts of the harvest area the location of the consumption locality is of no importance. The cross-shaded area in Fig. 2 is an "area of ubiquity," within which the harvest circle is everywhere of radius r_1.

The increase in transport costs is illustrated in Fig. 3. For the sake of simplicity, the harvest area is taken to be circular. The variable consumption locality is taken to require a surrounding circular area of radius r_1. The average costs for transport within this area have been abstracted in the upper half of the diagram in the figure. We suppose that these costs are 8 units everywhere within the area of ubiquity, and the isovecture for this value passes through the point r_1. If the locality is moved outside the area of ubiquity, the transport costs rise, as is shown in the figure, for instance. When the distance to the harvest area is great, the variations of costs are similar to those for production at a point. The isovectures, which are widely spaced in the beginning, become closer as the distance from the harvest area increases. Ultimately, the distance between them becomes constant, as in Fig. 1.

The scale of consumption in Figs. 2 and 3 has been taken to be constant. The consequence of any variation would be that the area of the harvest circle would increase or decrease, and the transport costs to the consumption locality would thereby be altered. Unlike the situation when consumption is *at a point* (Fig. 1), when consumption is *over an area*, not only the position, but also the amount of consumption, affects the transport costs. The effect is illustrated in Fig. 4, which shows how transport costs increase with increasing consumption. The different curves indicate different positions of the consumption locality within the harvest area. If this latter is taken to be circular, and the consumption locality is taken to be situated at its centre, the greatest possible harvest yield at the lowest possible transport cost is obtained, since

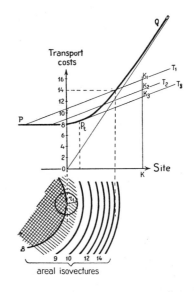

FIGURE 3   Increase of Transport Costs at Areal Consumption.

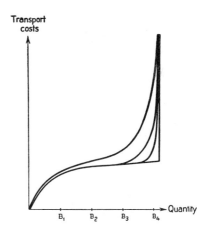

FIGURE 4   Increase of Transport Costs at Different Scale of Consumption.

the harvest area and the harvest circle coincide. There cannot then be any further increase of the harvest, however, because the curve for transport costs rises vertically.

The reasoning from the theory of location

117

which has been used in connection with Figs. 2, 3 and 4 is applicable to every branch of industry for which the raw material is harvested. However, in the case of the paper industry, the production process is often divided up into the manufacture of paper-pulp and the further treatment of this pulp to make the finished paper. The location circumstances for such non-integrated production may be illustrated by the upper part of Fig. 3. If the consumption locality is taken to be K, the total transport costs there may be obtained by adding the areal transport costs (the curve PQ) to the linear transport costs T_1, T_2 etc.).

When the total cost is K_1 the production locality is situated at one of the points of intersection of the line T_1 and the curve PQ. If the production locality is on the left-hand part of the curve, the total transport costs are higher because of the heavy freight charges to K for the paper. But if it is on the steeper part of the curve to the right, the total transport costs will be high because the cost of raw material increases with the distance from the place where it is obtained. The costs are lowest at K if the production locality is situated at P_t, that is, the linear transport costs touch the curve PQ.

If we suppose that there is a paper mill at K, the costs for the linear transport are equal to zero, but on the other hand the cost of raw material is very high. In such a case, the costs may be diminished by separating the pulp manufactory from the paper mill. The pulp mill ought to be at P_t, and the pulp manufactured there transported to K. If we

neglect the differences which arise because of freight charges for the transport of pulp and paper, and the extra expenditure on the production process necessitated by increased drying and the like, and if we suppose that a ton of paper is obtained from a ton of pulp, the cost at K should also be K_3 in this case.

For those paper mills which lie to the right of P_t, integration with the pulp mill is not advantageous. On the other hand, to the left of P_t, it is more profitable to combine the pulp and paper mills than it is to transport the pulp from separate pulp mills. P_t is a boundary point for profitable integration.

Since the preceding investigation has dealt with a "harvesting" industry, the concept of isovectures has been used both for points and for areas when the conditions imposed by the location of various places has been described. The isovectures have also been used to describe the development of conditions during different periods, as will be seen from Figs. 5–7.

These figures show a region at three stages of the development of its location. The towns A and H lie on the river a, A being a central place with a relatively large need for paper and H is a seaport dealing with imports and exports. There are water-falls on the tributaries b and c, and the suffices of their symbols indicate the order of their capacities. Near to the river a is the agricultural land, and farther away is the thinly populated forest region marked with forest symbols.

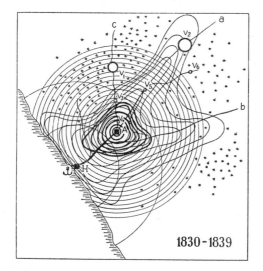

FIGURE 5 Handmill Period.

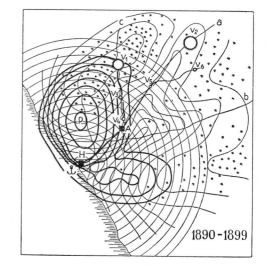

FIGURE 6 Groundwood Period.

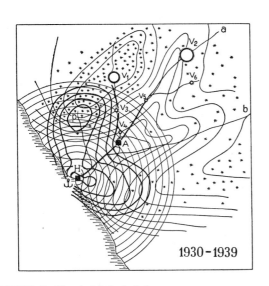

FIGURE 7   Chemical Pulp Period.

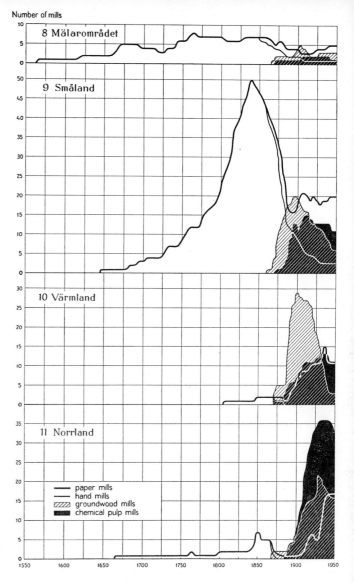

FIGURE 8—11   The Evolution of Paper Industry in Four Regions of Sweden.

Fig. 5 shows an example of the conditions imposed by localisation during the first half of the nineteenth century. The raw material, straw and rags, was brought from the densely populated areas at that time. The region nearest to the river *a* may be regarded as an area of ubiquity but farther away the cost of transport for the raw material is much higher, and this is apparent in the increasing closeness of the areal isovectures. As far as the transport of finished paper is concerned, this must be greater the farther one goes from the main consumption locality A. It is assumed that only insignificant amounts are shipped from H, so that the point system of isovectures around A is considerably tighter around A than around H. As in Fig. 1, the total costs are given by isodapanes (the heavy lines in Fig. 5). They are almost coincident with the point isovectures around A. Not until the distance from the consumption locality is large do the isovectures for the raw material begin to have an effect on the system of isodapanes.

So the optimum place as far as transport costs are concerned is certainly at A. But during the nineteenth century it was impossible to have a paper mill there, since there was no waterfall. The paper mill had to be built at the nearest waterfall—V_4—which is taken to be capable of driving a hand-mill.

Fig. 6 shows the same region as before, but the date is now the end of the nineteenth century, and the conditions imposed by the localisation of the paper industry are now quite different. The raw material is now no longer straw and rags, but wood, and consequently the isovectures for the raw material are close together in the more densely populated areas which are free of forest, and thinly distributed in the forest land near these areas. The area of ubiquity is now in the forest instead of the agricultural land. For the point isovectures, the seaport H has increased in importance; export has come to be of some importance, and there is also some importation of coal for instance. The hand-mill has now been replaced by machinery, and the paper industry now requires greater power. However, the most important power is water-power.

119

The mechanical methods for the production of pulp made particularly large demands on cheap and abundant water-power. At that time it was not possible to transport power from the waterfall, and it was therefore necessary to build the paper mill by the waterfall. So, in Fig. 6 it is not p, the best place from the point of view of transport costs, which is chosen as the site of the mill, but the most favourably situated large waterfall, V_1.

Fig. 7, which shows the conditions at the present time, is not much different from Fig. 6. The configuration of the isovectures is much the same as at the end of the nineteenth century. What is different is that the large waterfalls V_1 and V_2 have been harnessed to power stations, and since technical development at the beginning of the twentieth century made it possible to carry electric power for long distances, the paper mill need no longer be at the waterfall, but can be sited at p, the optimum place from the point of view of transport costs.

In order to find out the extent to which the development of the theoretical conditions has actually been in accordance with the localisation which occurred, the development of paper mills in different parts of the country has been studied. The result has been illustrated in the diagrams Figs. 8—11 and in the circle-cartograms Figs. 12—14. The investigation shows that certain forest regions

in Southern Sweden (Småland) had a surprisingly large number of paper mills during the first half of the nineteenth century, which does not agree with what was to be expected from the reasoning based on location which has been advanced. The reason for the rise of the paper industry in Småland at that time seems to have been the need to find outlets for the productive capacity of these poor and somewhat overpopulated districts.

However, the expansion of the paper industry in Småland was brought to a hasty stop at the end of the nineteenth century, when the machine produced pulp began to replace rags as the raw material. The outlying forest regions west of Lake Vänern then became the main area for the paper industry. There was water-power and forest, as well as relatively good communications with the seaport of Gothenburg. Mechanical pulpmills especially flourished there just before the end of the century. Then the transmission of electric power made it possible to choose a locality independent of water-power, and the remoteness of the forest sites became a considerable disadvantage for many of the firms in this region, and the day of the Värmland groundwood mills came to an end as abruptly as had the period of the hand-mills in Småland (cf. Figs. 9 and 10).

So, as regards the earlier localisation of the paper industry, it may be said that the so-called

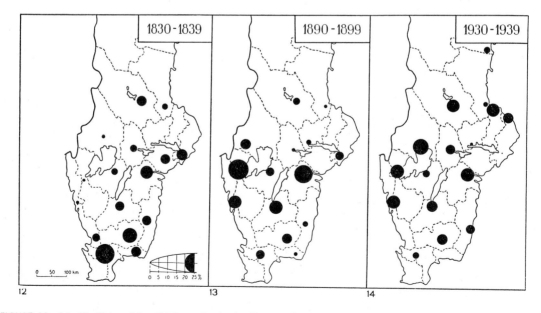

FIGURE 12—14   The Value of Swedish Paper Production Percentually for each County.

hand-mill period was hardly at all dependent on factors concerned with transport economy. In the heyday of the *mechanical pulp-mills* the agreement of theory and reality was better, but even here in many cases other factors were of importance in determining the site of the mill. The present-day paper industry bears traces of earlier localisation, but the tendency to fit the locality to considerations of transport economy is fully apparent at the present time.

How, then, is the present transport situation of the paper industry to be measured? In the first place, in order to give some estimate of the situation with regard to raw material, it is necessary to know the productivity of forest land in terms of wood for paper in different regions, and to be able to estimate the freight charges for different means of transport.

The first element of the analysis, the forest, is given in Fig. 15. This map has been based on a calculation of the lumber yield, which was made by the Ingeniörsvetenskapsakademi (The Academy of Engineering Science) in 1939, and the figures which were obtained from that investigation were proportioned with the help of map information from Riksskogstaxeringen (National Forest Taxation) 1923–32. The map is drawn according to the "absolute dot"-method, and each dot represents a lumber capacity of 200 m³ solid measure of spruce.

The second element, transport costs, has been illustrated by point isovectures for each firm investigated. Road transport has been taken to be upon a uniform transport surface. Where it has been possible to include rail or water freight charges, these means of transport have caused anomalies in the circular system for road transport. Fig. 16 shows an example of such isovecture maps. The distance from one isovecture to another, called "zone" here, has been calculated from available figures on freight charges. In general the railways do not give rise to big irregularities in the form of the isovectures, but water transport and ways for floating may lead to patterns which are quite complicated.

The above-mentioned elements have been combined by superimposing the isovecture map for a firm on the forest map, and the dots of the latter have been counted within each "zone." In this way we get a measurement of the amount of wood which is theoretically at the disposal of the mill, at a certain transport price. The figures used

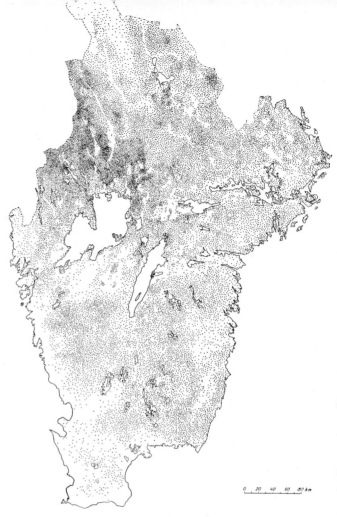

FIGURE 15   Potential Production of Pulp Wood (spruce). Each dot represents a production capacity of 200 m³ (solid measure).

have been dealt with in such a way that the average transport costs have been computed for various magnitudes of supply. If the relation between quantity and transport costs is illustrated in a diagram in this way, the rise in costs may be given by a curve like that in Fig. 4. Since these curves give a comprehensive picture of the raw material situation at each place investigated, they have been called *characteristics*.

Usually, characteristics of two sorts have been shown, A and B curves. The A curves have been so drawn that they refer only to road transport. The isovecture map which has been used in this case has been entirely regular and made up of rings, similar for every place investigated. Thus the A curves are only different from one another in that there are local differences in the potential of the

121

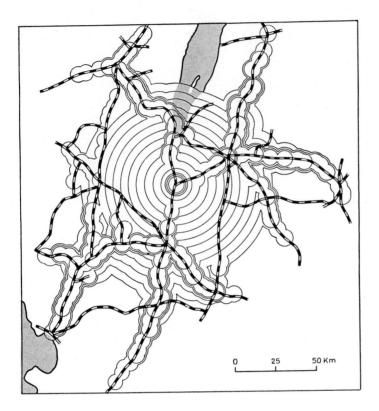

FIGURE 16 Isovectures for the Vaggeryd Mill in Southern Sweden. Each isovecture represents an increase of the transport costs with 20 öre/m³ pulp wood.

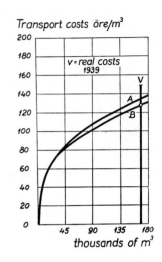

FIGURE 17 Characteristics for the Vaggeryd Mill.

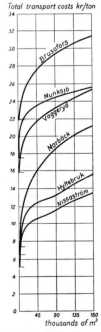

FIGURE 18 Comparative Diagram for the Total Transport Costs of some Paper Mills in the Counties of Jönköping and Halland.

forest. The B curves show the influence which cheap transport might be supposed to have on the situation. So the difference between the A and B curves at a place is an indication of the importance of floatage ways, railways, etc., with respect to the supply of wood to the firm (Fig. 17).

Since the transport costs of the paper industry do not depend only on the raw material, but also on the transport of coal, sulphur and limestone, as well as the finished paper, the transport costs for each firm examined with respect to these materials have also been computed. These costs per ton do not change with the scale of production, and the total transport costs are therefore the costs for the transport of the raw material (from the characteristics) together with the total costs for the materials just mentioned (Fig. 18).

The analysis which has been carried out for some fifty paper and pulp mills in the way de-

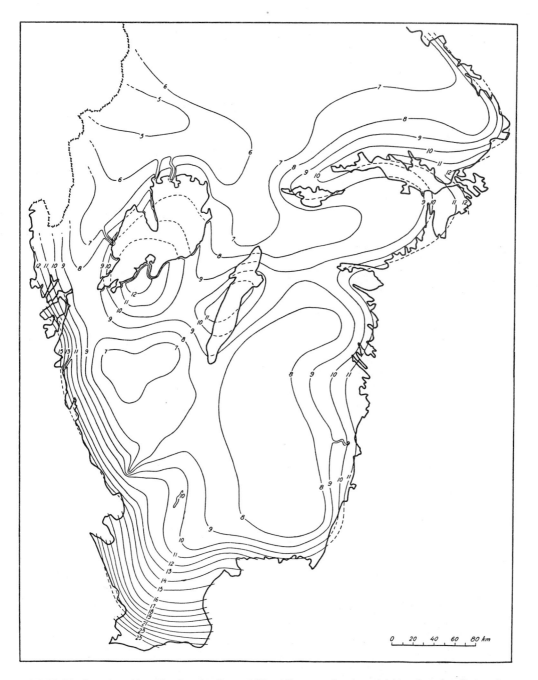

FIGURE 19 Isovecture Map Showing the Costs of Wood Transport for Assumed Manufacturing Centres in Various Parts of the Country. Only the "A-situation" is considered, corrections having been made for certain big floating-ways but not for sea-floating. The lines connect places with the same average costs of pulp wood transport in kronor per unit of production, the yearly consumption being 120 000 m³. The units of production 1 ton of paper equals a consumption of 7 m³ of pulp wood.

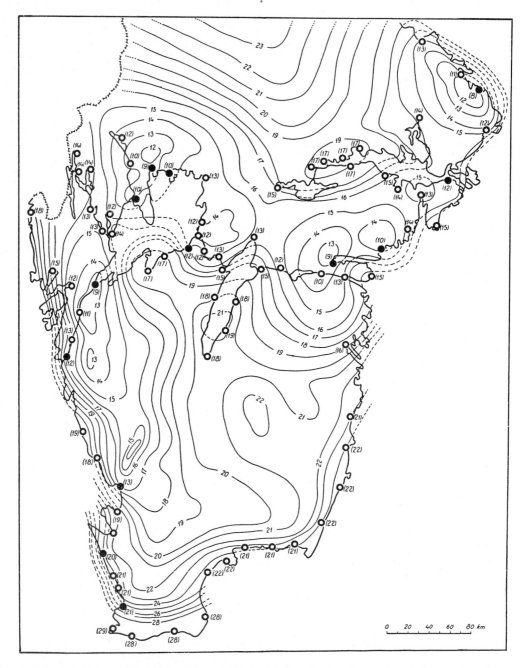

FIGURE 20 Isodapane Map Showing the Total Costs of Transport with Reference to Assumed Manufacturing Centres. The ports included in the calculation are indicated by circles—open ones only for import harbors and filled ones for both export and import harbours. The transport costs for factories if situated in the ports are indicated by figures in brackets.

scribed above shows that there are considerable differences with regard to the transport costs for factories in different parts of the country. Since the paper produced is mostly exported, the inland mills often have a disadvantageous position compared with those which are near the coast. The differences with regard to raw material have not in general signified so much as the differences with regard to the possibilities for easy and cheap communications for export.

Thus, for Sweden, the generally accepted idea that the paper industry is mainly dependent on its raw material does not apply. Previous opinion in this respect seems to have been based on Weber's theories on the location of industry. But since the paper industry is a "harvesting" industry, Weber's ideas are not entirely applicable to it. The raw material—wood—is ubiquitous to such a great extent that its localising effect is small, despite its low material index (3 tons of wood to one ton of paper).

In order to describe the localisation conditions for such an industry as the paper industry it is necessary to apply the same method as has already been described in connection with Figs. 5, 6 and 7. The areal isovectures in Fig. 19 have been drawn in such a way that the transport costs have been computed for a large number of points, and those with the same transport costs have been joined by isovectures.

To these areal isovectures have been added point isovectures originating from the seaports, which are marked by small circles. Some ports have only been taken as import ports (open circles), while others are counted as both import and export ports (filled circles). The result of this combination of point isovectures and areal isovectures is the *isodapanes,* which have been constructed in Fig. 20. These isodapanes give a picture of the conditions of localisation of the Swedish paper industry at the present time.

Robert Andrew Kennelly

THE LOCATION OF THE MEXICAN STEEL INDUSTRY

. . .

The analysis of the location will be based principally upon transportation costs incurred in the assembly of the significant transported materials and delivery of the finished product to the market, since we have eliminated other factors in previous discussion. It has been shown that material supplies are generally available throughout the country at the same market prices, leaving cost of transportation of the materials to the production point as the major variable in material costs. Labor supplies and regional variations in wage rates have been largely discounted as locational factors. F.O.B. pricing policies on steel in Mexico give significance to the location of the plant relative to the market. Though the cost of transportation of the finished product is actually paid by the consumer, the concept of delivered-to-customer cost will allow us to speak of it as if it were incurred by the production center. We can assume the same level of efficiency for all plants since any variation in production cost on this point would be attributable to technical factors which are not dependent upon location.

The first part of the location analysis will be concerned only with the two existing plants and the actual conditions of their operations, taking material supplies and markets as known for each plant. A comparison will be made of transportation expense and the factors contributing to this expense.

An analysis will then be made on a more general basis, using average figures and a more general supply pattern for the industry. An attempt will be made to determine the point of minimum transportation cost for this supply-market pattern. This will first be done on a hypothetical basis, limiting consideration to the two major factors of weight and distance, while assuming uniform transportation facilities for all points. This hypothetical situation will then be modified by removing the assumption of uniform transportation facilities and considering the effect of the actual transportation network upon the location of the minimum transportation point (MTP). As a third step, actual freight costs will be introduced and their effect upon the location of the MTP, in terms of money costs, will be noted.

To find transportation costs it will first be necessary to determine the amount of each material consumed per ton of finished steel produced and then to apportion these materials to their supply points.

ANALYSIS OF THE TWO PRIMARY STEEL LOCATIONS

Consumption of significant transported materials per ton of finished steel for both primary steel producers is shown in Table XI.

For the Fundidora plant, for which data are generally more adequate, the amounts of material obtained from each source are known for the three major transported materials, iron ore, coke and oil. These account for about 95 per cent of the total weight of materials. The sources of market scrap, however, must be estimated. In view of sources of scrap for Altos Hornos and the smaller companies, it may be reasonable to assume that one-half comes

Excerpted and reprinted with the permission of the author and publisher from *Revista Geografica*, Tomo XV, No. 41, 1954, pp. 109-129; Tomo XVI, No. 42, 1955, pp. 199-213; Tomo XVII, No. 43, 1955, pp. 60-77. Dr. Kennelly is Professor of Geography at California State College at Long Beach.

from the United States, one-fourth from Monterrey and one-fourth from Mexico City as these are the centers of the principal supplies. As only about 5 per cent of the transported weight is represented by market scrap, any error in the above estimate will have small effect.

For Altos Hornos, the amounts from each source of iron ore and coke are also known. As for oil, however, only the sources and the total amount of oil consumed are known. Division of the total amount between sources must therefore be estimated. For the purposes of this problem, Reynosa and Tampico will each be assumed to supply one-half of the oil.

Market scrap supplies for Altos Hornos come from the same sources and in the same proportions as for Fundidora.

Fundidora sales are divided about equally between Mexico City and Monterrey, while those of Altos Hornos may be divided about 80 per cent Mexico City and 20 per cent Monterrey.

The freight rates applying to the various materials and the finished products are shown in Figure 4.

The supply and market position of the primary steel plants, along with the transportation expense incurred, may be summarized in tabular form as in Table XII. It may be noted that Fundidora has a locational advantage over Altos Hornos. In the assembly of materials and delivery of steel to the market, Fundidora moves 2,141 ton-kilometers, paying freight costs of 109.94 pesos; Altos Hornos moves 2,740 ton-km. and pays 148.83 pesos.

Considering the various items entering the

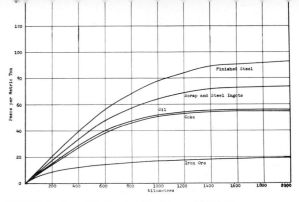

FIGURE 4   Freight Rates on Materials and Products.
(*Source: Ferrocarriles Nacionales de Mexico.*)

situation, we find that there is only a minor difference between the two plants on transportation cost of iron ore. While Fundidora consumes about 250 kg. more ore per ton of finished steel than Altos Hornos, part of its ore supply comes from nearer sources, cancelling the disadvantage of higher consumption. The freight rate on iron ore is very low and, after about 400 km., adds very little to the cost of shipment, which minimizes the effect of differences in amount of ore used or the distance it is carried.

With regard to coke consumption and location relative to the coke supply, Fundidora is at a disadvantage. This plant consumes 1,400 kg. per ton of finished steel compared to 1,059 kg. at Altos Hornos. Moreover, it is located 340 km. from the coke supply, while Altos Hornos is only 122 km., so the higher freight rate on coke, as may be seen in Figure 4, magnifies the difference in transportation cost on this material. Fundidora spends 31.57 pesos on transportation of coke per ton of steel produced while Altos Hornos spends only 8.63.

TABLE XI   Consumption of Principal Materials per Ton of Finished Steel, 1950

COMPANY	Finished steel production M.T.	IRON ORE		COKE		OIL		MARKET SCRAP	
		Total Con-sumption M.T.	Con-sumption per ton of finished steel K.g.	Total Con-sumption M.T.	Con-sumption per ton of finished steel K.g.	Total Con-sumption M.T.	Con-sumption per ton of finished steel K.g.	Total Con-sumption M.T.	Con-sumption per ton of finished steel K.g.
Fundidora	110,000	213,389	1,940	153,900	1,400	29,000 107,000*	263 974*	22,000	200
Altos Hornos	102,000	172,500	1,691	108,000	1,059	95,000	931	33,000	323
TOTAL	212,600	385,889		261,980		202,000		55,000	
Weighted average			1,820		1,235		953		259

* Assuming oil to be the only fuel used at Fundidora.

An important advantage enjoyed by the Fundidora plant is found in consumption of fuel in processes beyond the blast furnace stage. Monterrey is served by an industrial gas pipeline from Texas which supplies about three-fourths of Fundidora's fuel needs. This makes the plant less dependent upon oil, with consequent reduction in freight costs. Only 263 kg. of oil are used per ton of steel, incurring transportation expense of 9.42 pesos. Altos Hornos, using oil for all heating, uses 931 kg. per ton of steel and pays 36.17 pesos for transportation. The freight rate on oil, which is slightly higher than that on coke, serves to accentuate this difference.

Transportation costs of market scrap are comparatively minor for both plants. Fundidora uses less scrap than does Altos Hornos and, in addition, is located at the source of some of the scrap supply. As a result, it pays only 5.65 pesos freight on scrap while Altos Hornos pays 10.09 pesos. However, greater scrap consumption by Altos Hornos results in a lower consumption of iron ore and coke, hence somewhat reducing freight costs for these categories.

Up to this point, the assembly of the major materials, Fundidora has only a minor advantage in freight costs, spending 70.79 pesos to 79.27 pesos for Altos Hornos. Fundidora's advantage in being free of transportation costs on much of its fuel is largely overcome by Altos Hornos' nearness to the coke supply. If Fundidora were wholly dependent upon oil, as is Altos Hornos, and obtained oil from the same sources, it would be at a disadvantage, spending 87.86 pesos on freight to 79.27 for Altos Hornos.

The most significant factor contributing to Fundidora's advantage with respect to freight costs is found in its location relative to its market. Consumption of Fundidora steel is divided about equally between Mexico City and Monterrey, leaving only 39.15 pesos freight cost on the portion going to Mexico City and no freight cost on the portion sold in the local market.

Altos Hornos, with no local market, sells about 80 per cent of its production in Mexico City, a distance of nearly 1,100 km., paying 64.92 pesos freight on this portion. The rest of its production goes largely to Monterrey, and incurs freight of 4.64 pesos, giving a total freight cost for a ton of finished steel of 69.56 pesos. While finished steel represents less than 25 per cent of the total weight moved for both plants, the high freight rate on steel products makes it much more important than

an equivalent weight of materials. For Fundidora, freight on steel amounts to 36 per cent of the total freight cost, while at Altos Hornos it amounts to 47 per cent.

ANALYSIS OF LOCATION BASED UPON A GENERALIZED SUPPLY PATTERN

While the above analysis is based upon the specific supply and market situation for each of the primary steel plants in Mexico, the detail involved would make the use of these specific patterns unwieldy in an attempt to determine the point of minimum transportation cost for the industry in general. For this reason, an attempt will be made to establish a general supply and market pattern. This pattern will differ only in details from the actual situation analyzed above and will retain all essential factors and relationships.

A simplification may be achieved in the case of iron ore by eliminating the numerous minor supplies and by assuming that all ore consumed comes from Durango. As the freight rate on iron ore is very low and total freight cost increases very little after about 400 km., little error results from this assumption. If it were applied to the Fundidora supply situation, it would result in a freight cost on ore of 27.74 pesos, while the actual cost is 24.15 pesos. For Altos Hornos freight would be 24.60 pesos instead of 24.38 pesos. As to the amount of ore consumed per ton of finished steel, a weighted average of consumption by the two plants may be used, which would amount to 1,820 kg. per ton of steel, as shown in Table XII.

No simplification is necessary with regard to coke. We shall assume consumption per ton of steel produced will be the weighted average of consumption by the two plants, or 1,235 kg. per ton of finished steel.

It is different in the case of oil. At Monterrey, with natural gas available, oil consumption is quite low. Use of the weighted average for oil consumption here would introduce an error because oil supplies only a part of heat required. Since gas is available only in Monterrey and several border towns and will probably not be available in other locations for some time, it would be wrong to assume a gas supply for all locations. As any location within Mexico other than Monterrey must depend upon oil for heat, the problem may be met by expressing the heat requirements of the Fundidora plant in terms of oil, as in Table XI. A weighted average of these figures would then be a reasonable figure for heat requirements for any locality and would assume their proper weight in analysis of transportation costs. The weighted average of oil consumption on this basis is 953 kg. per ton of finished steel. Since any plant would face the sulphur problem connected with Tampico oil, the sources of oil may be assumed to be equally divided between Reynosa and Tampico.

Market scrap supplies need no adjustment for the general pattern except to change the amount to a weighted average, giving 259 kg. per ton of finished steel. Nuevo Laredo will be taken as the origin of supplies imported from the United States, except for several locations which may be served more cheaply through Piedras Negras.

Since the general steel market is divided about 25 per cent Monterrey and 75 per cent Mexico City, we may use this division rather than the weighted averages for the two plants.

The general supply and market pattern may be summarized in tabular form as in Table XIII. The distribution and weights of the supply and market points are shown on Map 4.

Transportation cost may now be considered to be a function of weight and distance. At some place within or on the margins of the polygon formed by a line drawn between the supply-market points, there is a point at which transportation costs, or weight multiplied by distance, is at a minimum. We may conceive of each point on Map 4 as having a certain force or pull proportionate to the weight of materials originating at or sent to that point. If we assume a uniform transportation system which will allow movement in all directions, each point will exert its force in a straight line to the production point.

This minimum point may be located by calculating the ton-kilometers of transportation incurred at various possible production points. These may be chosen arbitrarily throughout the map, the distance measured from each to the supply and market points. This distance is then multiplied by the weight at each supply and market point, the sum of which gives the ton-km. for each point of possible production. After this sum has been calculated for several places, the direction in which the lowest value lies becomes evident. By choosing additional points of possible production in this direction and calculating their ton-km. values, it is possible, by dint of numerous calculations, to determine the MTP quite accurately.

This method was followed in the case of the Mexican industry, and the MTP was found on the northern border of the state of Zacatecas, about 165 km. southwest of Monterrey. This point, having a ton-kilometer value of 1,999, is designated as point P_1 on Map 4. A map of these values is presented in Figure 10.

As would be expected in this case where only weight and distance are considered, the production point tends to be nearer the larger weights, with the market exerting a comparatively minor influence.

A measure of the influence of the market may be obtained by changing the weighting of the points to exclude consideration of the market, finding the MTP for materials only, and noting the difference in the location of the production point. This point, determined in the manner outlined above, is marked as P_1', on Map 4. The difference between the locations of P_1 and P_1', may be ascribed to market influence. The removal of 750 kg. from

MAP 4 Distribution and Relative Weights of Supply-Market Points and Locations of the Minimum Transportation Points.

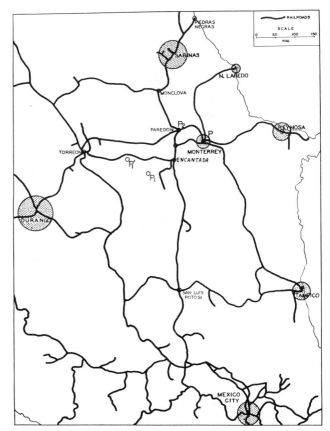

TABLE XII Sources of Materials, Amount from Each Source and Transportation Cost on Materials and Finished Product for Fundidora and Altos Hornos, 1950

IRON ORE

COMPANY	Consumption per metric ton of finished steel (Kg.)	Source, Amount, Distance to Plant and Freight Cost																					Freight cost per metric ton of finished steel (P.)
		Durango			Dinamita			Rinconada			Golondrinas			Castanos			Sol y Luna			Ciudad Guzman			
		Kg.	Km.	P.	Kg.	Km.	P.	Kg.	Km.	P.	Kg.	Km.	P.	Kg.	Km.	P.	Kg.	Km.	P.	Kg.	Km.	P.	
Fundidora	1,940	1,352	637	19.33	91	414	1.11	144	58	.50	165	120	1.07	37	200	.32	151	222	1.82				24.15
		1,940*	637	27.74																			27.74*
Altos Hornos	1,691	1,437	677	20.90	254	455	3.23													81	1,343	1.42	24.38
		1,691*	677	24.60																			24.60*

COKE

Consumption per metric ton of finished steel (Kg.)	Source, Amount, Distance to Plant and Freight Cost			Freight cost per metric ton on finished steel (P.)
	Sabinas			
	Kg.	Km.	P.	
1,400	1,400	340	31.57	31.57
1,059	1,059	122	8.63	8.63

OIL

Consumption per metric ton of finished steel (Kg.)	Source, Amount, Distance to Plant and Freight Cost						Freight cost per metric ton of finished steel (P.)
	Reynosa			Tampico			
	Kg.	Km.	P.	Kg.	Km.	P.	
263	0	247	0	263	521	9.422	9.42
973†	486	247	9.099	486	521	17.40	26.49
931	465	465	15.11	465	739	21.06	36.17

MARKET SCRAP

Consumption per metric ton of finished steel (Kg.)	Source, Amount, Distance to Plant and Freight Cost									Freight cost per metric ton of finished steel (P.)
	United States			Mexico City			Monterrey			
	Kg.	Km.	P.	Kg.	Km.	P.	Kg.	Km.	P.	
200	100	268	2.42	50	999	3.23	50	0	0	5.65
323	162	238	3.23	81	1,093	5.37	81	218	1.49	10.09

TABLE XII (Cont.)

FINISHED PRODUCT

Freight cost on materials	Steel to market	Consuming Center, Amount, Distance from Plant and Freight Cost						Freight cost per metric ton of finished steel	Total transported weight	Total transport cost per M.T. of finished steel	
		Mexico City			Monterrey						
P.	Kg.	Kg.	Km.	P.	Kg.	Km.	P.	P.	Kg.	T-Km.	P.
70.79	1,000	500	999	39.14	500	0	6	39.15	4,523	2,141	109.94
87.86†	1,000	800	1,093	64.92	200	218	4.64	69.56	5,517†	2,341x	127.01†
79.27									5,008	2,740	148.83

* Assuming Durango to be the source of all ore.
† Assuming oil to be only fuel used at Fundidora.

the Mexico City point and 250 kg. from Monterrey allows the minimum point to move away from these points toward the ore and the coke as these materials now represent a greater proportion of the total weight involved.

With the removal of the assumption of uniform transportation for all points and introducing in its place the existing railroad network, the MTP must be located by actual measurement of rail distances, multiplied by the weight of each supply and market point. The basic elements, weight and distance, are still the only factors considered, and the results remain a measure of purely economic costs of transportation.

Transportation costs were calculated for a number of possible production points on the railroads and the lowest ton-km. value was found at Paredón, a railroad junction about 90 km. west of Monterrey, at which the transportation incurred is only 2,618 ton-km. This is designated as P_2 on Map 4. From Paredón the ton-km. values increase in all directions, leaving only the central railroads from about Torreón to Monterrey and north to Monclova with ton-km. values below 3,000. The highest ton-km. value within the supply-market polygon is found at Mexico City, at which, although it is the major market center, the ton-km. of 5,090 is nearly twice that at Paredón. A map of these values is presented in Figure 12.

With respect to the hypothetical production point found in the idealized problem, point P_1, the minimum ton-km. point, is shifted about 140 km. to the north-east. This point is on the most direct route between ore and coke and, in general, centrally located with regard to most of the supply points. This shift is not to the nearest railroad line, however. The line from Torreón to Encantada is nearer to point P_1 but does not form as direct a connection between oil, scrap and Monterrey market on the one side and ore and coke on the other, as does the northern line through Paredón. With restriction of possible production points to locations on the railroads, the minimum ton-km. value is increased by 619 ton-km., an increase of 31 per cent over the idealized situation.

As would be expected, ton-km. values increase less rapidly in the direction of the major materials, iron ore and coke. As a result, Durango and Sabinas are only about 25 per cent higher on a ton-km. basis than Paredón, the minimum point. With distance

TABLE XIII Average Consumption and Sources of Principal Materials Per Ton of Finished Steel Production, 1950

IRON ORE		COKE		OIL			MARKET SCRAP				MARKET		
Con- sump- tion per ton	Durango	Con- sump- tion per ton	Sabinas	Con- sump- tion per ton	Reynosa	Tampico	Con- sump- tion per ton	United States	Mexico City	Mon- terrey	Mexico City	Mon- terrey	Total trans- ported weight
1,820	1,820	1,235	1,235	953	476	476	259	130	65	65	750	250	5,267

toward the minor materials and the market, ton-km. values increase more rapidly due to greater transportation of the iron ore and coke. Long distances to all supplies are reflected in the very high ton-km. value for Mexico City.

The use of actual freight rates, rather than the assumption that weight and distance are the only relevant factors in transportation cost, introduces differences in the cost of transporting different materials and takes account of savings resulting from long hauls. As a result, actual freight costs for each location give a slightly different pattern than that found on the basis of ton-km. only. The freight rates, which are different for each item, distort the pattern toward the sources of items having the higher rates.

The minimum point for actual costs is found at Monterrey, point P on Map 4. However, Monterrey is only slightly lower than Paredón, the minimum ton-km. point, and several other nearby locations. Beyond this small group of low-cost locations, all between 140 and 148 pesos, freight costs increase rapidly. Only one other point, Sabinas, the source of coke, has freight costs below 150 pesos. Details of these data are found in Figure 13.

Monterrey's favorable position with respect to actual freight costs is due to the existence of a portion of the market and some of the scrap supply at this location. There is no freight cost on 250 kg. of steel and 65 kg. of scrap. While only a small portion of the steel market is here, high freight rates apply to the steel and give this portion greater significance.

In contrast, locations near the source of iron ore, which had only moderately-high values on a ton-km. basis, lose this advantage due to the low freight rates on ore. Production here would effect only a minor money saving on ore shipment while making it necessary to transport all other materials and finished products, all of which have higher freight rates than iron ore.

Conversely, Mexico City is only moderately high on the basis of actual freight costs while it was one of the highest points in terms of ton-km. Since it is the center of most of the market, freight is saved on the highest-freight item, which counteracts to some extent the transportation of all materials for long distances.

The variation in freight costs between the minimum point within the supply-market polygon, Monterrey, and the highest point, Gualtero, southeast of Durango, is 73 pesos. This difference amounts to between 5 per cent and 8 per cent of the market price of steel mill products.

SUMMARY

In this chapter the locations of the two existing primary steel plants were analyzed on the basis of their individual supply and market patterns. The analysis showed the Monterrey plant to have a significant advantage in location largely because of its location at the market for one-half of its production upon which no freight cost was incurred. The availability of natural gas was also a significant advantage but was balanced by the Altos Hornos locational advantage with respect to coke.

The supply and market pattern set up for general analysis retained as far as possible the essential characteristics and weights of the individual-plant patterns. Using the general pattern, the MTP was determined for an idealized situation in which transportation facilities were assumed to be uniform at all points and in which weight and distance were considered to be the only significant factors in transport costs. The location of P_1 was definitely oriented towards the heavier raw materials.

The actual rail network was then imposed upon the general supply-market pattern and the ton-km. of transportation calculated for various possible reduction points. As a result, P_2 was found at Paredón, located at the most direct junction between the various supply and market points. At Paredón, the ton-km. value was 31 per cent greater than the minimum found in the idealized situation.

The railroad rate structure was then added to the problem, introducing actual money costs rather than purely economic costs. On this basis the minimum cost point again shifted, this time to Monterrey, point P, as the various freight rates in effect changed the weighting of the supply and market points. Monterrey's principal advantage over Paredón was derived from existence of part of the market at this point and consequent freedom from part of the freight cost on finished steel, the item with the highest freight costs.

Referring to location of the existing primary steel plants in Mexico, it may be concluded that the Fundidora plant at Monterrey is situated in a better competitive situation than would be possible with any other location. In the general analysis, which included several conditions less favorable to a Monterrey location than the actual conditions under which the plant operates, Monterrey had a slight cost advantage over all other points. However, several possible locations west of Monterrey had monetary costs very nearly as low as those at Monterrey. It is evident, then, that if a dispersed market were assumed rather than a concentrated market in which a significant part of production is consumed at Monterrey, other locations would be able to produce with lower transportation costs than at Monterrey.

The Altos Hornos plant at Monclova, on the other hand, must operate under a disadvantage under any of the conditions considered here. In actual operation, transportation costs for this plant are significantly higher than for Fundidora. In the general situation, Monclova is also at a disadvantage, although a less-pronounced one. Money costs on transportation are 14 per cent higher than at Monterrey, the lowest point. The difference is less pronounced on the basis of purely economic costs.

Analysis of the Location of the Secondary Steel Industry

Analysis of the location of the secondary steel plants in Mexico involves only three significant considerations, scrap, fuel and market, in contrast to the more complex pattern of the primary industry. All other materials are used in comparatively minor quantities and can be ignored.

Due to the several types of secondary plants, each having its own supply-market pattern, there is no overall pattern in the secondary industry in Mexico. These types must be considered separately. In both types of plants scrap is the major supply item.

THE OPEN–HEARTH PLANT

La Consolidada, due to its use of open-hearth furnaces and the separation of the steel-making and rolling operations, must be considered separately. Most of its crude steel is made at Piedras Negras while the rolling mills are located in Mexico City.

The entire scrap supply for the open hearth plant at Piedras Negras comes from the United States, as no home scrap is produced here. In 1950 the plant consumed about 73,300 metric tons of scrap to produce 60,550 tons of crude steel, or 1,210 kg. of scrap per ton.

The fuel used here is natural gas from Texas, leaving scrap and steel ingots as the only significant transported items. In this case, the processing plants of the same company at Mexico City must be considered as the market.

The choice of location for this type of operation is, then, whether to transport the scrap or the steel. In purely economic terms, the question is decided in favor of steel, the lighter item, as less ton-km. of transportation are incurred if only the steel is transported. With greater distance from the source of scrap, the ton-km. value increases, reaching its highest point at Mexico City (Figure 5).

In monetary terms, the choice of location will depend upon the relationship between the freight rates on the two items. In Mexico the freight rates

FIGURE 5 Transport Costs in Ton-Km. for Secondary Steel Production at Locations Between Piedras Negras and Mexico City.

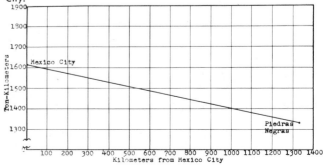

on scrap and crude steel are almost identical. Therefore the relative weights are not changed and it remains cheaper to ship the steel. Shipping one ton of ingots from Piedras Negras to Mexico City costs 70.55 pesos, while shipping the scrap necessary to make one ton of steel would cost 85.80 pesos. Locations between the two points would have a higher freight cost than either point because neither item would receive full benefit from the decrease in rates on long hauls, and, in addition, would occasion more handling. Vanegas, a location about midway between Piedras Negras and Mexico City, for example, would have freight costs of 113.50 pesos. Freight costs for these points and various locations between them are shown in Figure 6.

As locations other than border points such as Piedras Negras would have to use oil for heating, additional transportation costs would apply to these locations. An open-hearth plant, with no processing of the ingots, would probably consume about 120 kg. of oil per ton of steel produced.[1] This would have to be sulphur-free oil, hence Reynosa may be considered as the source. The supply-market pattern for this type of works would then be Piedras Negras, 1,210 kg. of scrap; Reynosa, 120 kg. of oil, and Mexico City, 1,000 kg. market.

Restricting consideration to weight and distance and assuming uniform transportation as was done with primary steel, calculation of the MTP for the three transported items shows that it is still at the source of scrap, Piedras Negras.

Introduction of the rail network in place of the assumption of uniform transportation will have no significant effect upon the location. While the ton-km. values are increased due to greater distance, the minimum point remains at Piedras Negras.

Introduction of railroad rates in place of the weight and distance calculations results in an increase of transportation cost due to the addition of oil but does not change the location of the minimum point. Recalling the earlier instance in which only scrap and market were considered, it was noted that Piedras Negras had transport costs which were 15 pesos lower per ton of steel than at any other point. The amount of oil needed per ton of steel may be sent to any point within the supply-market area for 6.50 pesos or less. Therefore Piedras Negras will retain an advantage of at least 8.50 pesos over any other point.

The Mexico City plants of La Consolidada are supplied with most of their crude steel by the Piedras Negras open-hearth works. As most of the Mexican steel market is here at Mexico City, this location in effect saves the difference in freight between crude steel and finished steel from Piedras Negras to Mexico City. On a ton-for-ton basis this would amount to only 17 pesos per ton, while in practice more than one ton of crude steel must be transported to produce a ton of finished steel. This would reduce the saving on freight costs. Counteracting this saving, however, is a probably higher fuel cost resulting from the division of operations as the rolling mills must begin with cold ingots rather than hot, as in an integrated plant.

The steel-making carried on by one of the Mexico City plants of La Consolidada does not present a difficult location problem. The two small electric furnaces here were installed expressly to use the scrap resulting from rolling operations and most of their scrap needs are met by this supply. The scrap supply coincides with the market and an electric power supply in the metropolitan area. This electric furnace production may be considered consequent to the other operations of this plant rather than basic to them.

ELECTRIC STEEL PLANTS

The electric steel plants, most important of which are Aceros Nacionales at Mexico City and Hojalata y Lámina at Monterrey, have the same general supply and market situation. Scrap and electric power are the principal items consumed.

About one-half of the scrap is obtained from the United States, while the other half is obtained locally or from plant operations. As the Mexican scrap coincides closely with the markets for steel, a greater weight originates at the market end of the line, making production uneconomical at any other location from a transport-cost viewpoint.

As an example we may take the operation of Aceros Nacionales in Mexico City. At this plant about 1,200 kg. of scrap are needed per ton of production. Of this amount 60 per cent, or 720 kg., comes from the United States, while the balance is obtained locally and from plant operations. The market, 1,000 kg., plus the local market scrap far outweighs the imported scrap and is the MTP.

Electric power is important in that it must be available in rather large amounts, but it is not a major cost item. Electric furnace consumption is

---

[1] J. M. Camp and C. B. Francis, *The Making, Shaping and Treating of Steel*, 6th ed., United States Steel Co., Pittsburgh, 1951, p. 190.

about 500 KWH per ton of crude steel. At Monterrey in 1946, industrial power cost from 5.2 to 10.4 centavos per KWH,[2] which would give a cost of 26 to 52 pesos per ton of crude steel production. This would amount to only 6 to 12 per cent of the cost of scrap.

As power use is intermittent rather than steady, it is desirable for these plants to obtain their electricity from large utility systems, which can absorb these variable demands for current. A private generating station would necessitate a large capital investment, which a small plant would find difficult to obtain in Mexico, and would be difficult to operate economically under these conditions of variable load. This, in effect, limits the electric steel plants to metropolitan locations.

SUMMARY

In this chapter the locations of the two principal types of secondary steel plants in Mexico have been considered. Analysis of their locations was based upon the three significant factors of scrap, fuel and market.

The open-hearth plant of La Consolidada was found to be located at the MTP under all the conditions considered. For its actual operation in which only United States scrap and the crude steel product are moved, the border proved to be the minimum point in both purely economic and monetary terms. Substitution of Mexican oil for Texas gas, which is available only along the border, in order to test the possibility of other locations did not affect the location of the minimum point in either way.

The electric steel plants were also found to be at their minimum transportation points. Importing only a part of their scrap needs, the market exerted the greatest pull on their location. The market pull was strengthened by market scrap supplies originating here and by the occurrence of adequate electric power.

Location Theory Applied to the Mexican Steel Industry

In the foregoing chapters we have described the steel industry of Mexico, determined the supply and market pattern and analyzed the location

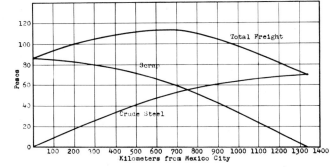

FIGURE 6 Transport Costs in Pesos for Secondary Steel Production at Locations Between Piedras Negras and Mexico City.

of both primary and secondary producers. The analysis of this industry will now be related to location theory. To this end we will survey, briefly, existing theories and discuss those which are relevant to the problem.

To aid in eliminating irrelevant material, we might, with Palander, divide all existing studies of location of industry into two principal classes, those of a descriptive and classificatory nature and those of theoretical nature.[1] The descriptive and classificatory studies on location of industry will not be of interest here because these works provide no theoretical explanation of the causes of location. Many of them have an explanation for location, though it is usually a rationalization rather than a theoretical structure. We will consider only those works which are of a theoretical character.

The theoretical studies can be divided into treatments of location of agricultural activity and those of industrial activity. Since agriculture is an areal production, in contrast to industrial production which occurs at points, its theoretical treatment, essentially based on Thünen, is not applicable to this problem.

The theories considering industrial location may be divided further into theories concerned with the location of individual industries and individual producers and theories treating the general location of all industries in an economy. The first of these we will, with Lösch, call the special theory and the latter, the general theory. They overlap, of course, and the establishment of one is difficult without the help of the other. In this case it seems clear that the problem at hand is that of the individual producer and the socio-economic aspects are present only by implication.

---

[2]*Wall Street Journal* (New York), May 14, 1946, p. 1.

[1]Tord Palander, *Beitraege zur Standertstheorie*, Almqvist och Witsells Boktryckeri-a.-b., Uppsala, 1935, p. 109.

Thünen will be mentioned here only because he was the first to attempt a theory of location and for his suggestion of a methodological approach which has become standard. His work, published in 1826,[2] was limited to agricultural production, however. In spite of the rapid development of economic theory in the 19th century, none of the classical economists or geographers took up the work left by Thünen. Many of them since the time of Adam Smith had been aware of the problem of location but did not include it in their considerations even though Thünen established location as a significant factor in land rent.[3]

Thünen's method of locating economic activities was applied to industry for the first time by Launhardt in 1882,[4] who developed several mathematical laws of location for certain types of transportation-oriented industries. His work was neglected until Weber, in 1909, developed a theory of location.[5] Again, this remained the only theoretical contribution on industrial location for another quarter century. Though there developed an extensive literature on Weber, either applying his ideas or criticizing them, there was no further theoretical development. Most of the literature remained descriptive or used Weber's concepts for classifications.

Palander, in his dissertation in 1935, examined Thünen, Launhardt and Weber and attempted to formulate a new theory of his own.[6] Palander was followed by Lösch in 1940 with a work that emphasized the general theory of location.[7]

Probably as a result of the lack of interest in theory of location in the English classical literature of economic theory, a similar neglect of the problem is shown by American literature. Friedrich tried to interest American geographers and economists in Weber by a translation and commentary on his work in 1929.[8] Before that time Weber was hardly known in America. After Friedrich, Hoover and Dean were evidently the only students attracted by the problem. Hoover's study of the shoe and leather industry in 1937, followed by his *Location of Economic Activity* in 1948, are the principal theoretical works by an American.[9] He uses much of the work of Palander, who had improved upon some of Weber's concepts, in a study of the shoe and leather industry, while his later book also includes much of the work of Lösch, along with Palander. Hoover must be given major credit for stimulating American thought on the theory of location. Dean's study in 1938, largely completed before Hoover's work was published, analyzes some aspects of Weber's work.[10]

All other American literature on the subject has been descriptive and classificatory. In 1896, Ross discussed the problem in respect to the factors of location.[11] Hall treated these factors more fully and concisely several years later. Writing in the United States Census of Manufactures in 1900, Hall analyzed United States industries and classified the factors influencing their locations.[12] His contribution remained on the classificatory level. It influenced substantially many later American publications. His classification appears in the studies by Keir, Jennings and Carver,[13] and in various textbooks on industrial management, business administration and production economics, such as

[2]J. E. von Thünen, *Der Isolierte Staat in Beziehung auf Landwirtschaft und Nationaloekonomie*, 3 vols., Hamburg and Rostock, 1826-1863. An outline of Thünen may be found in R. T. Ely and G. S. Wehrwein, *Land Economics*, Macmillan, New York, 1940.

[3]Discussion of the literature of location theory may be found in *Alfred Weber's Theory of the Location of Industries*. C. J. Friedrich, ed., University of Chicago Press, 1929, pp. xiii-xxxiii; Andreas Predohl, "The Theory of Location in its Relation to General Economics," *Journal of Political Economy*, Vol. 36, 1928, pp. 371-90; Witold Kryzanowski, "Review of the Literature of the Location of Industry," *Journal of Political Economy*, Vol. 35, 1927, pp. 278-91.

[4]Wilhelm Launhardt, "Die Bestimmung des Eweckmaessigsten Standortes einer gewerblichen Anlage," *Zeitschrift des Vereines Deutscher Ingenieure*, Vol. 26, 1882, pp. 106-115.

[5]Alfred Weber, *Ueber der Standort der Industrien*, Part I, *Reine Theorie des Standorts*, translated by C. J. Friedrich, *op. cit.*

[6]Palander, *op. cit.*

[7]August Losch, *Die raeumliche Ordnung der Wirtschaft*, Gustav Fisher Verlag, Jena, 1940.

[8]Friedrich, *op. cit.*

[9]E. M. Hoover, *Location Theory and the Shoe and Leather Industries*, Harvard Economic Studies, Vol. 55, Harvard University Press, 1937. . . . *The Location of Economic Activity*, McGraw Hill, 1948.

[10]W. H. Dean, *The Theory of the Geographic Location of Economic Activities*, (selections from Harvard doctoral dissertation), Edwards Bros., Ann Arbor, Mich., 1938.

[11]E. A. Ross, "The Location of Industries," *Quarterly Journal of Economics*, Vol. 10, 1896, pp. 247-268.

[12]F. S. Hall, "The Localization of Industries," *Twelfth Census of the United States*, 1900, Vol. VII, Manufactures, I, XXXIX, pp. cxc-ccxiv.

[13]Malcolm Keir, "Economic Factors in the Location of Industries," *Annals*, American Academy of Political and Social Science, Vol. 85, 1921, pp. 83-92; W. W. Jennings, *A History of Economic Progress in the United States*, Crowell Co., New York, 1926, pp. 444-45; F. B. Garver, F. M. Boddy and A. J. Nixon, "The Location of Manufactures in the United States, 1899-1929," *Bulletin*, University of Minnesota Employment Stabilization Research Institute, Vol. 2, No. 6, 1933, p. 10, University of Minnesota Press.

Diemer, Duncan, Marshall, Jones and Lansburgh.[14] A similar approach is found in all of these, with differences among them confined to details or to the emphasis placed on the various factors.

The National Resources Planning Board made a significant contribution to the problem of isolating and evaluating the factors of location by the publication in 1943 of its *Industrial Location and National Resources*.[15] This extensive study, to which Hoover contributed, includes a statistical analysis of United States industry and attempts to measure the importance of the various factors of location.

From this general approach there has developed a large number of studies of a practical nature dealing with the problems of plant location. The most important of the general works of this type is that of Holmes. His *Plant Location*,[16] published in 1930, is a practical handbook containing a wealth of empirical material and treating plant location problems as faced by the industrial engineer. Representative of minor studies of this type are those of Frederick, Piquet and Anderson.[17]

STEEL INDUSTRY STUDIES

The studies of the steel industry follow the same pattern as the general ones outlined above. Most of them consist of descriptive works of the industries of various regions, with some of the writings attempting to analyze the factors of location. In the United States, White has made a number of these studies, all of them descriptive and analytical

but, although he has evidently worked on the subject more than any other geographer, there is little of general applicability in these works and no attempt at theoretical development.[18] Many other Americans have worked along the same line.[19] The several studies of Mexican steel, either by Americans or Mexicans, have been descriptive.[20]

Of more general application are the works analyzing the locational factors of the industry. Hartshorne contributed the first significant study of this type in 1928, in which United States steel industry data were analyzed and an attempt made to evaluate the factors of location. He also suggested several hypotheses, based on transport advantage relative to ore, coal and market, to explain various situations that may be encountered.[21]

Isard, in 1948, paid more attention to the influences on the factors brought about by changing technology, markets and material reserves.[22]

---

[14]Hugo Diemer, *Industrial Organization and Management*, La Salle Extension University, Chicago, 1915, pp. 31-42; J. C. Duncan, *Principles of Industrial Management*, Appleton, New York, 1911, pp. 5-48; L. C. Marshall, *Business Administration*, University of Chicago Press, 1931, pp. 23-114; M. D. Jones, *Administration, of Industrial Enterprises*, Longmans Green, New York, 1925, pp. 44-68; H. H. Lansburgh, *Industrial Management*, Wiley, New York, pp. 101-10.

[15]National Resources Planning Board, *Industrial Location and National Resources*, Washington, Government Printing Office, 1943.

[16]W. C. Holmes, *Plant Location*, McGraw Hill, New York, 1930.

[17]J. G. Frederick, "Scientific Location of Manufacturing Plants," *Industrial Management*, Vol. 62, 1921, pp. 153-55; J. A. Piquet, "Scientific versus Haphazard Plant Location," *Industrial Management*, Vol. 69, 1925, pp. 330-335; A. G. Anderson, "Solving a Factory Location Problem," *Industrial Management*, Vol. 70, 1925, pp. 21-24; Many additional examples have been published in the various trade journals. References may be found in: D. M. McDonal, "A Select Bibliography on the Location of Industry," McGill University, *Social Research Bulletin No. 2*, McGill University Press, Montreal, 1937; J. H. Perry and C. W. Cuno, "New Bibliography on Plant Location," *Chemical and Metallurgical Engineering*, Vol. 41, 1934, pp. 439-42; "Plant Location Bibliography," *Chemical and Metallurgical Engineering*, Vol. 48, 1941, pp. 121-22.

[18]C. L. White, "The Iron and Steel Industry of the Pittsburgh District," *Economic Geography*, Vol. 4, 1928, pp. 115-39; "Location Factors in the Iron and Steel Industry of the Buffalo District, New York," *Denison University Bulletin, Journal of the Scientific Laboratories*, Vol. 24, 1929, pp. 81-95; "The Iron and Steel Industry of Youngstown, Ohio." *Denison University Bulletin, Journal of the Scientific Laboratories*, Vol. 25, 1930, pp. 125-46; "Geography's Part in the Plant Cost of Iron and Steel Production at Chicago, Pittsburgh and Birmingham," *Economic Geography*, Vol. 5, 1929, pp. 327-34; and E. J. Foscue, "The Iron and Steel Industry of Sparrows Point, Maryland," *Geographical Review* Vol. 21, 1931, pp. 244-58; "The Iron and Steel Industry of Wheeling, West Virginia," *Economic Geography*, vol. 8, 1932, pp. 274-281; and George Primmer, "The Iron and Steel Industry of Duluth; A Study of Locational Maladjustment," *Geographical Review*, Vol. 27, 1937, pp. 82-91.

[19]J. B. Appleton, "The Iron and Steel Industry of the Calumet District: A Study in Economic Geography," *University of Illinois Studies in the Social Sciences*, Vol. 13, No. 2, 1925, University of Illinois Press, Urbana; W. O. Blanchard, "The Iron and Steel Industry of Europe," *Journal of Geography*, Vol. 27, 1928, pp. 247-62; Richard Hartshorne, "The Iron and Steel Industry of the United States," *Journal of Geography*, Vol. 29, 1929, pp. 133-53; E. C. Eckel, "The Iron and Steel Industry of the South," *Annals, American Academy of Political and Social Science*, Vol. 153, Jan. 1931, pp. 54-62; A. B. Carlson and C. B. Gow, "Scrap Iron and Steel Industry," *Economic Geography*, Vol. 12, 1936, pp. 175-84; Muzaffer Erselcuk, "Iron and Steel Industry of Japan," *Economic Geography*, Vol. 23, 1946, pp. 105-129; J. E. Brush, "The Iron and Steel Industry of India," *Geographical Review*, Vol. 42, 1952, pp. 37-55.

[20]Ben F. Lemert and Rose V. Lemert, "Mexico, the Iron and Steel Industry," *Journal of Geography*, Vol. 35, 1936, pp. 199-202; J. B. Modelski, "The Production of Steel in Mexico," unpublished thesis, Mexico City College, Mexico City, March 1951; Oscar Realme Rodriguez, "La Industria Siderúrgica Nacional," unpublished thesis, Universidad Nacional Autonomia de México, Mexico City, 1946.

[21]Richard Hartshorne, "Location Factors in the Iron and Steel Industry," *Economic Geography*, Vol. 4, 1928, pp. 241-52.

[22]Walter Isard, "Some Locational Factors in the Iron and Steel Industry Since the Early 19th Century," *Journal of Political Economy*, Vol. 56, 1948, pp. 203-17; and W. M. Capron, "The Future Locational Pattern of Iron and Steel Production in the United States," *Journal of Political Economy*, Vol. 57, 1949, pp. 118-33.

He, too, gives greatest consideration to the matter of transportation advantages. An application of Isard's ideas is found in his most recent study relating to the possibility of establishing a steel industry in New England.[23]

While Hartshorne and Isard have probably done the most significant work in determining the factors in steel industry location, many others have contributed to the literature. All have been concerned with the isolation and evaluation of locational factors.[24]

In sum, the works on iron and steel are limited to description of the industry and to analysis and isolation of the locational factors. While some of these studies contribute to our knowledge of the industry, they do not furnish a theoretical structure which may be used to explain the location.

For these reasons, then, the existing body of location theory is German and, with Palander, Swedish. We shall limit the study here to the problem of examining this theory in relation to the location of the Mexican steel industry. Our work will be further limited to the theory applicable to individual enterprises, rather than the broader socioeconomic aspects of the theory. We will not be concerned here with the descriptive and classificatory writings.

VARIGNON'S FRAME

Of value to us in finding the minimum transportation point and in suggesting some principles of location is the mechanical arrangement of weights known as Varignon's frame. This mechanism was invented, according to Weber, by Pierre Varignon, an early eighteenth century mathematician, to demonstrate the parallelogram of forces. It was first mentioned in connection with the determination of the MTP by Launhardt[25] and by Weber[26], who used the basic principles of the mechanism by way of analogy in the problem of finding the MTP. From its operation Weber was able to draw certain inferences applicable to the location of the minimum point. As it demonstrates several basic features of the location problem, it will be considered first.

An adaptation of Varignon's frame was set up for use on the Mexican problem and its operation checked against the empirically-determined MTP. The adaptation employed consisted of a board with a map of Mexico mounted upon it. Holes were drilled through the map and board at the various supply and market points. Weights corresponding to the supply-market weights were suspended on strings running through the board and the strings joined in a knot above the board. This knot was then free to move in all directions. Friction was reduced by the use of glass bearings. A sketch of this model is shown in Figure 7-A.

It may be seen that this board is a mechanical means of vector addition that automatically determines the balance of forces, which we may identify as the MTP. The attractive forces of the supply-market points may be considered as vector forces. Vectors, however, by definition have both magnitude and direction. In the case of finding an MTP, only the weight is known and the model finds the directions in which the forces act.

There can be only one minimum point in any problem except in the case of two supply-market points with exactly equal weights. This can be shown, and the solution of the problem tested, by graphic addition of the vectors determined by the model. If a group of vectors represents a balance of forces, graphic addition of them will result in a closed polygon.[27] This is demonstrated by reference to the Mexican situation in Figure 7-B, 7-C. If the resulting polygon is not closed, a minimum point has not been located and the gap represents the distance and direction from the minimum point.

The minimum point found by the model may be accepted as the production point under certain

[23]Walter Isard and J. H. Cumberland, "New England as a Possible Location for an Integrated Iron and Steel Works," *Economic Geography*, Vol. 26, 1950, pp. 245-59.

[24]C. E. Wright, "The Geography of Steel; Factors Governing the Location of Main Producing Areas," *Annalist*, Vol. 49, 1937, pp. 766-67; H. W. McQuaid, "Small Steel Mills for Local Markets," *Iron Age*, Vol. 165, 1950, pp. 90-94; C. B. Fawcett, "Key Metals and the Location of Industry," *Nature*, Vol. 150, 1942, pp. 451-53; Allan Rodgers, "Industrial Inertia—A Major Factor in the Location of the Steel Industry in the United States," *Geographical Review*, Vol. 42, 1952, pp. 56-66; W. Trinks, "Automobile Steel and Geography," *Blast Furnace and Steel Plant*, Vol. 22, 1934, p. 587; H. M. Baker, "Steel Mills in Detroit Base Sales on Time Savings," *Automotive Industries*, Vol. 63, pp. 362-65.

[25]Wilhelm Launhardt, *op. cit.*, p. 107.

[26]*Alfred Weber's Theory of the Location of Industries*, C. J. Friedrich, ed., University of Chicago Press, 1929, p. 54, and Mathematical Appendix (by Georg Pick), pp. 228-29. Hereinafter, page references to Weber will be to Friedrich's translation.

[27]C. E. Weatherburn, *Elementary Vector Analysis*, G. Bell and Sons, London, 1942, p. 16, or most other texts on vector analysis.

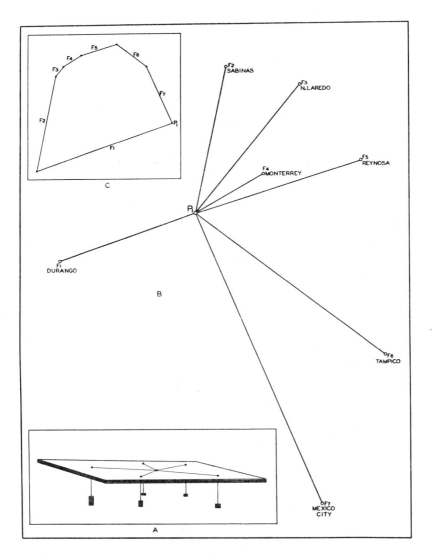

FIGURE 7 An Adaptation of Varignon's Frame and Its Application to Mexicon Primary Steel.

conditions. The first necessary condition is that weight and distance are the only significant factors in transportation cost. The second is that the area is a homogeneous plain allowing unimpeded movement in all directions from all points. Other factors affecting transportation costs must be considered as distorting influences on the ideal situation.

The model was set up to find the MTP for the Mexican steel location under the ideal conditions with the resulting minimum point, P_1, shown in Map 4. This is the same, of course, as the empiri-cally-determined P_1. Comparison with P, Monter-rey, shows the distortion attributable to the other factors. They are in this case the rail network and the rate structure.

Comparison of P_1 with P_2 on the rail lines, Paredón, shows them to be about 140 km. apart. The amount of transportation incurred on the rail network is about 30 per cent greater than in the ideal situation, due to the sparse railroad network which occasions roundabout movement of mate-rials and products. However, there seems to be

139

sufficient agreement for the suggestion that if there were a dense rail system in this area, the MTP found by the mechanical model might be reasonably close to the MTP on the railroads.

The influence of the railroad rate structure has been noted in the analysis, its effect having been to shift the MTP to Monterrey, 165 km. from the ideal MTP found by the model. Examination of the rates suggests the reason for this may be due to the higher freight on finished products and fuels and the lower freight on iron ore. Existence of a segment of the market at this point was also significant to the low freight costs here. The difference between P_2 and P could possibly be explained by agglomeration which might attract P to Monterrey and there share the gas supply. But since we have found earlier that if the fuel needs are translated into oil, Monterrey is still the MTP, this factor is obviously not relevant.

It is difficult to say anything about the general applicability of the model from this test on the Mexican problem. It is useful in our case since it indicates the general area of the MTP. An understanding of the principles of the model may then also permit some judgment as to the possible effect of additional factors, though the model cannot quantify them since it deals only with weights. Weber suggests means of considering these factors in terms of weight and distance which will be discussed later.

The mechanical solution for the MTP also permits certain inferences relating to its location. Weber points them out by reference to the model and to the mathematical determination of the MTP.[28] Firstly, it becomes apparent from the examination of the model that the minimum point must rest within or on the sides of the supply-market polygon. There is no force to move it beyond the margins of the figure. Secondly, if one weight is greater than the sum of the others, the minimum point must lie at the source of the largest weight. In the model this weight can not be pulled away from that point. Thirdly, one weight may be less than the sum of the others but its location may still be the MTP because of the direction from which the other weights pull.

Apart from these observations we may say that the mechanical model is easily used in cases involving more than the three supply-market points which are usually demonstrated in geometrical and graphic methods.

. . .

Launhardt's Mathematical Determination of the MTP

The first theoretical work on industrial location was published by Wilhelm Launhardt in 1882. This was a short paper limited to the problem of locating a plant with fixed supply and market points, in which he considered only the problem of finding the MTP, using weight and distance as the only variables, and did not attempt to treat other factors of location.[29] Though of limited scope, his work remains basic to the problem. It was used in its essentials by Weber and by Palander, the latter expanding Launhardt's ideas to apply to more general problems involving location of market areas.

Using the case of two material supplies and one market point, Launhardt sets up the situation shown in Figure 8-A in which A, B and C represent the weights of materials and product while a, b and c represent distances. Freight rates may be represented by the letter f. It may be seen then that production at A will incur transport costs of $(Bc + Cb)$ f; at B, costs will be $(Ca + Ac)$ f; at C, $(Ab + Ba)$ f. With the location of the production point, P, within the triangle and independent of the supply-market points (Fig. 8-B) the ton-kilometers of transportation cost may be stated as:

$$S = Ar + Bs + Ct \qquad (1)$$

Launhardt offers a mathematical solution of this equation based on Figures 8-B and 8-C. However, it was found inadequate and therefore we present Dr. Gustav Bergmann's solution in Appendix A. Launhardt's geometrical construction, which also follows from Dr. Bergmann's proof, is valid and permits more insight into the nature of the MTP.

In the geometrical treatment Launhardt employs construction 8-A in which A and B are material supply weights and C is the market weight.

---

[28]Weber, *op. cit.*, pp. 53–58.

[29]Launhardt, *op. cit.*

They are located in their proper relationship with a, b and c representing the distances separating them. When P is at the minimum point the angles α, β and γ around P to give the supplementary angles α, β, and γ, according to the theorem about angles at the circumference of a circle which states that opposite angles of a rectangle inscribed in a circle are supplementary. The angles α, β and γ, are formed by a triangle with side lengths proportionate to the weights A, B and C as in Figure 8-D, which we may call the weight triangle.

To determine the weight triangle and its supplementary angles α, β and γ, we may plot arcs with radii $\dfrac{B}{C}$c and $\dfrac{A}{C}$c from A and B respectively. Their intersection gives the apex 0, of the weight triangle with its base c, as in Figure 8-E. This weight triangle, it may be seen, has sides proportionate to the weights A, B and C because the ratios $\dfrac{B}{C}$ and $\dfrac{A}{C}$ are multiplied by the distance between the two supply points.

With this weight triangle proportionate to A, B and C and having the angles α, β and γ, the Point P, around which we must have the angles α, β and γ, will lie on the circumference of a circle drawn around ABC, according to the theorem about angles at the circumference of a circle. P must also lie on the circumference of a circle constructed on the other sides of the locational triangle. Hence the construction of two circles will give the location of P, as in Figure 8-F.

Launhardt, in addition, uses another procedure to determine P. With construction 8-F, he applies the theorem regarding angles at the circumference of a circle and draws a line from 0, which he terms the "pole," to C. As the location of the pole 0 is a function of the angles α, β and γ, the line CO must always intersect the arc ABO at P. Therefore the location of P is found with the construction of only one circle and the line CO (Fig. 8-G).

As the location of 0 is also determined by the factors A, B, C and c, its location is not dependent upon the locus of C but only upon its weight. From this we may draw the inference that, when C is outside the location circles and within the extensions of the pole lines $\dfrac{B}{C}$c and $\dfrac{A}{C}$c, P will always lie on the arc AB (Fig. 8-H). Pick, in his mathematical appendix to Weber,[30] also makes these observations regarding the location of P for various positions of C. However, he did not develop the idea as Palander did, showing its significance to the determination of market areas.

Launhardt draws another inference of general applicability from this construction by applying Ptolemy's theorem relating to quadrilaterals within a circle. According to it, the product of the diagonals of a quadrilateral within a circle is equal to the sum of the products of the opposite sides. Applying this to construction 8-G, we have the polygon APBO. Then, according to the theorem:

$$\overline{AP} - \overline{BO} + \overline{BP} - \overline{AO} = \overline{AB} + \overline{PO} \qquad (2)$$

In the terms of weight and distance in our construction then

$$r\left(\dfrac{A}{C}c\right) + s\left(\dfrac{B}{C}c\right) = c - \overline{PO} \qquad (3)$$

This may be simplified, giving

$$rA + sB = C - \overline{PO} \qquad (4)$$

As the total transport costs, above, were

$$S = Ar + Bs + Ct \qquad (1)$$

They may also be expressed in terms of formula (4) as

$$S = C - \overline{PO} + Ct \quad \text{or} \quad S = C - \overline{CO}$$

In other words, the total transportation costs at the minimum point are equivalent to transportation of the finished product from O to C. The pole not only expresses the total transport cost incurred, but also, by its determination of P, gives the direction of P from A and B.

Launhardt then uses the pole principle to infer certain characteristics of the location of P. While he suggested the application, it was left for Palander to develop it.[31] If a pole is constructed as in Figure 8-G and another pole, O', constructed on the opposite side of the line s, we obtain Figure 8-I. We may make several general statements about the location of P for any location of C, the market, if the weights A, B and C remain the same. As P, C and O all lie on the same line, movement of C will cause P to move along the arc AB, and as long as C remains within the extensions of the

[30]Weber, op. cit., p. 234.
[31]Palander, op. cit., Chapter III.

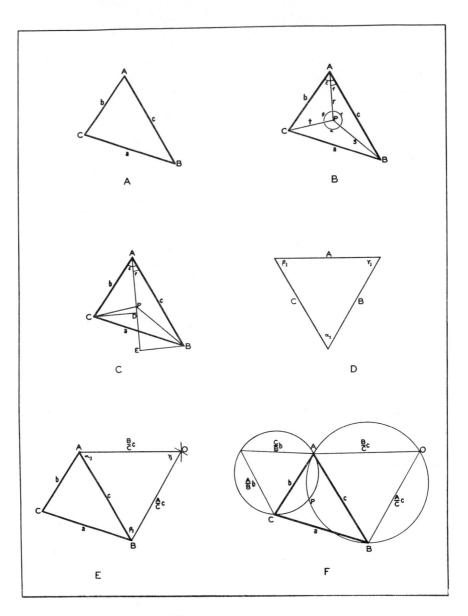

FIGURE 8   Laundardt's Determination of the MTP.

lines OA, OB and O'A, O'B and outside the respective location circle. If C lies within the angles DAF or EBG, then P will lie at A or B respectively, because movement of P beyond this point will place it outside the locational triangle with a consequent increase in the values of r, s and t. If C lies within the two arcs AB, P will lie at C. For other combinations of weights, the location of the pole O will change, giving different areas where C and P may

be located. Examples of this have been shown by Palander.[32]

Application of this method is limited to problems having only three supply-market points. Launhardt attempted to apply it to problems with more than three points but without success, as pointed

---

[32]*Ibid.*, pp. 149, 151.

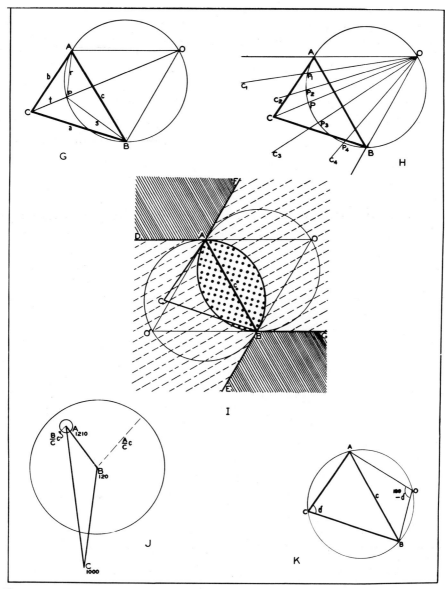

FIGURE 8 (Cont.)

out by Friedrich and proved by Palander.[33] From the discussion of the triangular case it may be seen that the construction of the pole rests on the application of the theorem regarding rectangles within a circle. Launhardt, using four supply-market points, attempted to apply the pole principle to two of the supply points and then to use the result-

ing pole as the third point for a triangular solution. This use of the pole does not agree with the premises of the triangular construction.

APPLICATION TO MEXICAN STEEL

Due to the above limitation, only one instance is found in the Mexican steel industry where we have the appropriate number of points. This is the case of the Piedras Negras plant of La Con-

[33]Friedrich, *op. cit.*, pp. 238-39; Palander, *op. cit.*, p. 146; Dean contends that a solution of other polygons is possible but does not supply proof, *op. cit.*, p. 17.

solidada where we assumed an oil supply from Reynosa, giving a supply-market pattern of 1,210 kg. of scrap for Piedras Negras, 120 kg. of oil at Reynosa and a market of 1,000 kg. at Mexico City. With A and B representing Piedras Negras and Reynosa, respectively, and C representing Mexico City, we obtain Figure 8-J. Here it is not possible to construct the pole O because $\frac{A}{C}$ and $\frac{B}{C}$ do not intersect, for we may note that it is not possible to construct a weight triangle with those weights. While Launhardt does not consider this variation, it is discussed by Pick.[34] Using Launhardt's method, the circle around one material point will be enclosed by the circle from the other material point in all cases in which one weight is greater than the sum of the other two. In the Piedras Negras example, then, production will be at A, the source of scrap.

This concept may be extended to include the other secondary steel producers in Mexico. For all of them, scrap and market are the significant considerations. As the market is also the source of part of their scrap supply, the market point has a much greater weight than the other scrap sources. While other factors, such as the freight rate structure, are present, they are nevertheless dominated by the weight factor. Hence we can apply this explanation to Aceros Nacionales at Mexico City which obtains part of its scrap there and part of it from the United States. In the case of Hojalata y Lámina at Monterrey, though the market and the sources of scrap are both divided, Monterrey remains the dominant point. The minor producers all show the same orientation with the exception of the Teziutlan Copper Company, in eastern Puebla. This is a special case because this company has turned to steel and ferroalloy production to utilize installations made for copper production in former years and since discontinued.

The Mexican primary steel supply-market pattern is rather complex for a test of this theoretical concept since it has more than three points. It would be interesting to attempt to apply the concept, nevertheless, but we must keep in mind that it would not constitute a test of Launhardt's method. On the other hand, we might get some special insight into the concept or into the location of Mexican steel, which encourages us to attempt the

application. To do so, we must make several assumptions which are not quite warranted. Firstly, we may safely ignore the market scrap as a minor item here as it represents only five per cent of the total weight involved. Secondly, let us consider Mexico City to be the location of the entire market, rather than only three-fourths of it. This reduces the pattern to five points, namely, Mexico City market; Durango iron ore, 1,820 kg.; Sabinas coke, 1,235 kg.; Reynosa and Tampico oil, each 476 kg. Thirdly, then, we may take the three fuel supplies as one supply point by determining their center of gravity and using this as the third point of our locational triangle. This center of gravity for fuels, 2,187 kg., is located about 75 km. northeast of Monterrey. Applying Launhardt's method to this problem, we obtain Figure 9 in which A represents Durango, B the center of gravity of fuels, and C, Mexico City.

The MTP in Figure 9 is located a short distance southwest of Monterrey. As this minimum point agrees quite well with the MTP we found empirically and with the mechanical model, we

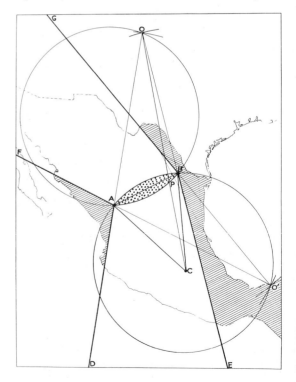

FIGURE 9 Launhardt's Method Applied to Mexican Primary Steel.

---

[34]Weber, *op. cit.*, p. 232.

may conclude that our simplifying assumptions have not distorted the pattern too badly. The corollary information offered by this construction, therefore, could also be reasonably accurate.

We may see then that production for any market point south of the lower arc AB will be located along this arc. Any Mexican steel plant using the present material supplies will be best located in the north from the viewpoint of transportation cost, even though the markets be as far south as Guatemala. Conversely, should sizable markets develop in northwestern Mexico, the production point would be located along the northern arc AB, regardless of the distance to the market. If C is located in the west, within the angle DAF, production would be at A, Durango, the source of iron ore. To the east of the line EBG production would be at B, the center of the gravity of the fuels. It may be noted that this is the largest angle included in any of the market areas corresponding to the heavier weight of the fuels. Only if C lies between the two arcs will P locate at the market.

While Launhardt's determination of the MTP is limited to the basic factors of weight and distance and does not attempt to include other factors of transportation cost, it has been helpful to us in giving some insight into the Mexican location. By it we can explain the location of Mexican secondary steel and in the case of primary steel we have been able to make some useful inferences regarding the location of production based on the present material supplies.

WEBER'S THEORY OF THE LOCATION OF INDUSTRIES

The first major attempt to formulate a theory of industrial location was published by Alfred Weber in 1909.[35] Basing his theory upon the concept of the minimum transportation point, although he arrived at it independently of Launhardt, according to Palander, Weber attempted to consider other significant factors in industrial location. He also considered elements of transportation cost in addition to the weight and distance factors treated by Launhardt. While his ideas have been improved upon by later writers, especially Palander, they remain basic to location theory.

Weber begins by classifying all locational factors into general or special factors. General loca-

tional factors are those which apply to all industries without exception, while special locational factors are those affecting only specific industries and are not of general application. As examples he cites such elements as labor and transportation cost as of general application, while such considerations as atmospheric humidity or fresh water supplies are significant only to certain industries, hence are classified as special factors.

Weber further classifies all locational factors as to whether they exert an influence towards a regional distribution of industry or whether they act in such a way as to "agglomerate" or "deglomerate" industry within the regional distribution. The forces tending towards agglomeration or deglomeration are forces interacting between industries to influence their distribution within the region but are independent of the region. An example of an agglomerative factor would be the advantage, in some industries, of plants being located near each other in order to take advantage of specialized service facilities which no one plant could afford. A deglomerative factor would be the high rent resulting from congestion in areas of industrial concentration. Instances of factors influencing regional distribution are mineral resources, wage rates and transportation costs.

A third classification is based on whether a factor is of a natural or technical, or of a social and cultural nature. As examples of social phenomena, Weber cites differences in standards of living and interest rates as factors which have no direct relationship to the natural conditions. It is admitted that this distinction is difficult to apply because a given difference may be due to both types of factors.

From these classifications Weber chooses only the general factors in order to develop a theory of general applicability for all industries. The special factors are not considered. Taking the general factors, Weber subdivides them on the basis of their regional application. The agglomerative and deglomerative factors are set aside, to be taken up in a later section dealing with theory of agglomeration. The distinction between natural and social factors is made only to exclude all purely social and cultural factors.

The general factors of location are ascertained by a simple process. As these factors must by definition be present in any industry, they may be discovered by analyzing any example. As a result,

---

[35] Weber, op. cit.

Weber obtains the following cost elements, and, consequently, possible general locational factors:

(1) Cost of grounds.
(2) Cost of buildings, machines and other fixed capital costs.
(3) Cost of securing materials, power and fuel.
(4) Cost of labor.
(5) Cost of transportation.
(6) Interest rates.
(7) Rate of depreciation on fixed capital.

Of these factors, Weber finds the relative cost of materials and power, including fixed capital, cost of labor and cost of transportation to be of general regional character. The rate of interest, rates of depreciation and cost of land are otherwise classified.

With differences in costs of materials Weber would further simplify the problem by expressing these differences in terms of transportation costs. Cheap material sources are considered as lying nearer to the production point while higher-priced sources are located farther away. In other words, the distance is weighted by the difference in material prices.

This leaves transportation cost and labor cost as the only general regional factors to be considered, with the agglomerating factors to be brought in later. To establish the relative importance of these two factors Weber assumes that all production will be pulled to its most advantageous location relative to transportation cost. This orientation of each plant on transportation cost furnishes the basic locational pattern. Labor costs are then considered to be a force altering the basic pattern, distorting it to conform to labor cost advantages in the region. The agglomerating factors are then added to the problem. As defined, the agglomerative factors serve to distribute industry within the region, being forces interacting between industries independently of the regional setting. They are, then, distorting influences imposed upon the basic pattern established by transportation costs and then modified by labor.

Weber's classification of factors includes those considered significant to the location of Mexican steel. In this case, however, the problem is further simplified by the conditions found relative to costs of materials and labor. These were found to have no significant locational influence in Mexico, leav-

ing costs of transportation as the major factor. Consideration of Weber will therefore be limited to these aspects of his theory.

Before developing the basic transportation orientation Weber makes three specific simplifying assumptions. Firstly, the geographical basis of materials is considered as given. In the case of an industry dependent upon the processing of minerals, as is the Mexican steel industry, this assumption agrees with the facts and will therefore make no difference to the resulting application of the theory to this case. Weber points out, however, that the assumption is less realistic in the case of agricultural raw materials.

Secondly, Weber assumes the location of consumption as a given condition, ignoring for the moment that the labor forces engaged in production are themselves a segment of the market. This also applies to Mexican steel, where the markets for steel are definitely concentrated. Furthermore, these markets are not significantly influenced by labor as a market since the product is not a consumer's good. Whether the assumption is realistic in the case of other industries depends, of course, upon the extent of concentration or dispersion of markets.

Thirdly, Weber assumes labor supplies to be fixed in location and unlimited in amount, with the wage levels given for an industry. While this is not so in Mexico, it will not affect the application of his theory to our problem.

Weber takes weight and distance as the fundamental factors of cost of transportation and arrives at what he calls transport orientation. All other features of this cost are expressed by modifying the basic weight and distance values. Earlier, in considering differences in costs of materials, Weber suggested varying distance proportionately to these cost differences. Now, considering each of the cost elements of transportation, the weight and distance are to be varied similarly.

The first factor in transportation cost to be considered after weight and distance is the type of transportation system and the extent of its use. He asumes a uniform system, namely, railroads. While costs may vary on different parts of the system due to greater or less utilization of the facilities, Weber points out that these variations are usually ignored in making the actual rates. In the event that actual rates reflect these differences in cost, Weber would allow for these differences by assuming distances to be lengthened or shortened in proportion to the different rates. The same solution is applied to the problem of decrease in rates with distance, or long-haul economies. In Weber's words, "Geographical distances should not be measured by their geographic length, but in proportion to the decreasing rate scale."[36] Higher rates on small lots of goods, however, would be expressed by a change in weight rather than a change in distance.

The second factor in transportation costs, in addition to weight and distance, is the nature of the locality influencing the road bed, since it affects costs of construction, maintenance and operation. He points out that these costs could be expressed by changing the distances but that in practice these variations in cost are also ignored in the making of rates. Consequently, he adds the assumption of a flat plain with no physical differentiation.

The third additional factor is the nature of the goods. Some goods require more care or more space than others, thus increasing their costs of transportation. These resulting differences express themselves in different freight rates which would be considered by Weber as increases or decreases in weight.

These modifications of weight and distance would allow, then, a solution for the MTP by mathematical means such as developed by Launhardt. We may check the applicability of these suggestions by reference to the mathematical solution and the mechanical model.

Weber suggests, firstly, that differences in costs for a given material be adjusted by changing the distances these points lie from the production point to the differences in costs. This seems to be untenable. In the first place, we have no basis for determining distances because the location of production is not known and hence can not be adjusted in proportion to material costs.[37] Secondly, the distances of the supply-market points relative to each other may not be changed because it would result in a different locational figure with consequently different results in the solution. These objections would apply to any of Weber's modifications of distances. His attempt to include additional locational factors in the theory by this method must therefore be rejected.

Weber then proposes that, in order to introduce differences in transportation rates as a locational factor, the weighting of the supply-market points be changed in proportion to the differences in rates. This he would apply in the cases of differences in rates on commodities, differences in rates between systems of transportation, or differences in rates resulting from the size of shipment. The result is a change to what Weber terms the "ideal weight."

The ideal weight may be used, under a certain condition, with either of the methods of finding the MTP. The condition is that these differences be uniform with distance. However, a common feature of railroad rates is to decrease with distance, giving rise to savings on long hauls, and it is uncommon for these economies to affect all goods to the same extent. In the important case of unequal rate decreases with distance, then, Weber's suggestion will not apply.

In the Mexican situation, long-haul economies are not uniform for all goods, as may be seen in Figure 4. Therefore, this part of Weber's theory can not contribute to determination of the MTP since this factor of transport cost cannot be included in this case.

Another factor, significant in the Mexican problem, is the influence of the transportation network, which is inadequately treated by Weber. In the analysis of Mexican steel it was noted that the weight-distance minimum point was shifted about 140 km. on account of rail distances and routes, indicating it to be an important feature in an area where the network is sparsely developed. It remained for Palander to bring out its importance, as will be shown later.

Using the mathematical determination of the MTP as a basis for his deductions, Weber presents several principles of location of the MTP. Locations may be divided into those lying at one of the corners of the figure, coinciding with a material or market point, and into those independent of the supply-market points.

The one type, in which the MTP lies at a supply-market point, has been treated earlier. There are two conditions, according to Weber, under which this location will exist.[38] First, it is impossible to construct the weight triangle because one weight is greater than the sum of the others.

[36]*Ibid*, p. 44.
[37]Palander, *op. cit.*, pp. 195-96.
[38]Weber, *op. cit.*, p. 57.

This results in location at the source of the greatest weight.

The second case in which production will locate at a supply-market point is one in which a weight triangle can be constructed, but, if one of the weights is nearly as great as the sum of the others, the location may still be at the corner, depending upon the relative positions of the supply-market points. This may be determined quite readily by constructing the locational circles. If the third corner is included within one of the circles, that corner will be the location of production.

The second type of location of P is the case in which P locates independently of the supply-market points, in which case a weight triangle may be constructed where the weights are somewhat equal.

A special case not covered by the above is found where there are only two supply-market points. This will usually be of the type where one weight is greater than the other and therefore its location will be the place of production. An exception is noted when the weights are equal, in which case Weber contends that production may locate anywhere on the line between the two points. This is true if only the amount of transportation incurred is considered. If we consider the amount of handling necessary at various locations, however, we may see that it is less at either end of the line than at intermediate points. Therefore, minimum points are found only at the terminals.

Weber suggests a measure of the tendency for location at the market or the materials by his "material index" which is the ratio of the weight of materials to product.[39] If the product outweighs the materials, ignoring ubiquities, the material index will be less than one. This would be included in the first case presented above in which one weight is preponderant. If the material index is greater than one, production is not necessarily at the market but may take a location independent of the supply-market points because the location of production depends upon the relative locations and the number and weight of the supply-market points. Thus, if we use the material index, we cannot find an exact point at which we may say that production will find an independent location. However, a material index of several times the weight of the product does indicate a tendency toward the materials and can result in an independent location under the weight-distance assumptions. On the other hand, if one of the supply points is greater than the sum of the other weights, P will locate at this point.

In the Mexican steel industry we find a material index of over four, which shows the industry is not bound to the market. And, as the market is not centrally located with respect to the materials, this index indicates a tendency towards the materials. It does not locate at the source of one of the materials in this case because none of them has a preponderant weight.

Weber also introduces the concept of "locational weight." This does not appear to make any contribution to the theory because it is nothing more than the combined weight of localized materials and the product. Thus its implications are already included in the material index.

Palander, in finding the material index inadequate, has developed a mathematical measure to determine whether production will locate at a supply-market point or independently.[40] It is applicable only to the case of the triangle, but it illustrates the importance of relative location of the supply-market points as well as their relative weights.

Palander's formula gives the limits within which P may be at material or market for the cases where one weight is not preponderant. In these cases, the weight necessary to pull P to A, B or C depends upon the angle formed by the locational triangle at the corner in question. The more obtuse the angle, the less may be the weight necessary to locate P at that corner. This may be shown by Figure 8-K. The maximum weights permissible for P at C may be found by applying the law of cosines to the weight triangle ABO. The angle at C we may call δ, otherwise the terms are the same as used in the discussion of Launhardt. In the figure, the arc AB limits the area for P at C. In this case, then, A and B have the largest weights they may have for market orientation. This condition for P at C may be expressed as

$$c^2 \geq A^2c^2 + B^2c^2 - 2AcBc \cos(180 - \delta)$$

which may be simplified as

$$1 \geq A^2 + B^2 - 2AB \cos \delta$$

[39]*Ibid.*, p. 60.

[40]Palander, *op. cit.*, pp. 155-56.

which puts it into the terms of the original locational triangle. We may learn from this formula that a wide range of weight combinations may result in a location of P at C. As a specific case, should angle δ be 150°, a material index of four would still result in location at C. For angles greater than 150°, the material index may be even higher. The formula may also be applied to the material points.

In this connection Weber also suggests the concept of weight-losing materials in contrast to "pure" materials that contribute their entire weight to the product. This concept has been widely accepted along with Weber's statement that pure materials can never bind production to their deposits.[41] It was left to Palander to point out that it contributes nothing to the theory. If weight must be transported it is irrelevant to this problem whether or not that particular weight goes wholly or partially into the product. The location of P depends only upon the relative weights and their relative location which adequately includes the inferences drawn by Weber relative to pure and weight-losing materials.[42]

Weber's concept of the isodapanes, or lines of equal transportation cost, is a contribution to the study of location that permits wider consideration of the factors of transportation cost than any of the methods discussed so far, though he did not apply it to the determination of the minimum point but used it only to measure the increase of total transportation costs with distance from the MTP. Hereby he was able to determine whether or not production could move advantageously in response to cost differentials in other locational factors, such as labor or power. If, for example, the savings resulting from a change in location caused by lower labor costs were greater than the extra transportation cost incurred, as shown by the isodapanes, then the minimum point would be different from that found on transport costs only.

Palander, recognizing that freight rates should be given more consideration than accorded to them by Weber, used the isodapanes as a method of determining the MTP and found that this method would allow consideration of variations in the rates. The isodapanes will be treated in the succeeding section.

Weber's theory with respect to its application to Mexican steel may now be summarized. We may

accept his fundamental concept of transport-orientation in this case. Moreover, we have here an example of an industry where that factor appears to be the only significant one in determining location since labor and the agglomerative factors are of minor importance. His use of weight and distance as the principal factors of transportation cost may be accepted, also, but we have found that his modifications of these factors, in order to consider other elements of transportation cost, are not applicable. Modification of distance is not possible because we have no knowledge of the distance to be adjusted. The modification of the ideal weight is possible only in the case where freight rates are proportionate to distance, while in Mexico the freight rate structure includes significant long-haul economies.

Weber's use of a single locational figure based upon his assumptions of given material sources and a given market applies very well to our problem. However, it should be recognized that many industries can not be analyzed in this way, either because they draw upon dispersed materials or sell to dispersed markets, or both. Hence, his theory is not a "general" theory but is applicable only to certain industries, or, in a sense, is a "special" theory.

Weber's division of materials into localized materials and ubiquities is valid as shown in our analysis, and has been useful in reducing the number of factors which we have had to consider. His analysis of the role of ubiquities in determining location when they become part of the product also appears to be correct though it is irrelevant to our problem.

The general principles relating to the location of P within the locational polygon or at a supply-market point have also been found correct, both generally and in their application to Mexico. He appears to be in error, though, in the special case of two supply-market points with equal weights. Instead of possible locations anywhere along the line, the minimum points exist only at the terminals.

Weber's material index showing the tendencies for location of P is inadequate because it gives major emphasis to the relative weights of materials and product and does not give sufficient consideration to their relative locations. It has been shown that the two factors are strongly interdependent and that the material index does not express it. The related concept of locational weight does not appear to add to the theory.

---

[41]Weber, op. cit., p. 61.
[42]Palander, op. cit., p. 301.

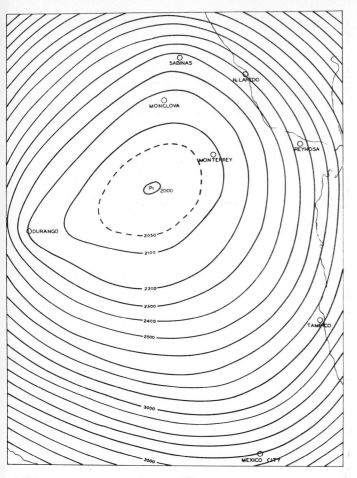

FIGURE 10 Isodapanes Based on Weight and Distance (Values in Ton-Km.).

Weber's analysis of the composition of the material index, based upon division into pure or weight-losing materials, introduces no errors into the theory, but it is beside the point and does not serve a useful purpose. These considerations are adequately treated simply as weights.

Weber's isodapanes, as applied by Palander, have been very useful in our analysis of Mexican steel since they consider the freight rate structure. They will be taken up later.

Palander's Contributions

By necessity we treated part of the work of Palander relating to the MTP in previous discussions. The first of these contributions was the development of Launhardt's concept of possible locations of C on the basis of the pole principle which we applied to Mexican steel. We also mentioned Palander's criticism of the limitations of Weber's material index and his substitution of a mathematical equation to determine the location of P. This permitted exact definition of the conditions for the location of P at C.

We may now consider Palander's development of Weber's concept of the isodapanes in which he covered the factor of variable freight rates in the determination of the MTP.[43]

Isodapanes, or lines of equal total transportation cost, may be determined in several ways. One method is to plot isovectors indicating equal freight cost around each supply-market point. The intersections of these lines then give the total freight cost for each point of intersection. When equal-value intersections are connected by a line, we obtain the isodapanes. In practice it is necessary to develop the isodapanes by plotting the freight costs for two points only. The intersections of these two sets of cost lines are then connected for points of equal cost, resulting in a third set of lines. Another supply-market point may then be added and another set of cost lines obtained. This procedure continues until all supply-market points have been included. The final draft indicates the minimum cost area and the gradation of total transport costs away from the MTP.

Though somewhat empirical, this method has several advantages over the previously-discussed methods of finding the MTP in that it can be applied to situations with more than three supply-market points and, what seems of equal importance, variable freight rates. This is achieved by varying the spacing of the cost lines. Thus the difficult problem of long-haul economies is solved.

The second method of determining isodapanes is by measuring transport cost for numerous points in and around the supply-market polygon. The resulting values may then be isoplethed into isodapanes. This method is useful where only weight and distance are considered. Additional difficulties arise when freight rates are included in the calculations.

Applying the isodapanes to Mexican steel, we may see the effect of this additional factor by comparing Figures 10 and 11. It then becomes evident

---

[43]*Ibid.*, pp. 310ff.

150

that Weber's treatment of freight rates is inadequate and that Palander's emphasis upon them is justified. Figure 10 presents isodapanes based upon weight and distance only, resulting in a minimum area which coincides with MTP P_1 mentioned earlier. In Figure 11 the freight rates are added, still using straight-line distances. The minimum area is thereby shifted to the northeast to include P, Monterrey.

A further effect of the freight rates may be seen from the new pattern assumed by the isodapanes. On the basis of weight and distance only, as in Figure 10, the greatest pull is towards Durango, the source of the greatest weight. Therefore the isodapanes are most widely spaced, or, in other words, the cost gradient is lowest, in that direction. With the inclusion of the rate structure, Mexico City, the major market, exercises a much stronger pull, and the cost gradient is the lowest towards that point. This comes as a result of the high freight rates on the finished product. Conversely, the strong pull of Durango, due to weight, is cancelled by the low freight rates on ore.

These tendencies are also apparent when we introduce an additional factor, the railroad network. Figure 12 shows the ton-km. of transport cost based upon weight and railroad distances, while Figure 13 includes the freight rates. Again the stronger pull of Durango is replaced by Mexico City when the freight rates are considered. Also, the area in which P could be located with only slight increases in cost is smaller in Figure 13.

It may be seen that, in and near the minimum area, distance makes little difference to total costs as movement from the minimum area increases some cost components but decreases others. Beyond the central area costs increase more and more rapidly. In addition, the isodapanes become more concentric with distance from the minimum area, reflecting the smaller proportion of increments to total cost caused by a given change in distance.

As costs change slightly with distance within the minimum area, it is here that other factors such as the transportation network and site factors may exert their greatest influence without appreciably influencing total transport costs.

We may refer to Weber's use of the isodapanes at this point to demonstrate his application of them. Having determined the total transport costs, as in Figure 11, additional locational factors were

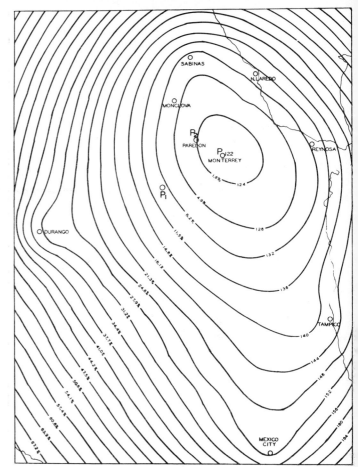

FIGURE 11 Isodapanes Based on Weight, Distance and Freight Rates (Values in Pesos).

then considered by Weber. If a given point presented an advantage in labor costs, for example, reference to the isodapanes would show whether or not this advantage was great enough to create a new minimum point.[44]

In Mexico we could apply this method to the labor factor. If labor were available at some point at lower cost than at Monterrey the isodapanes of Figure 11 would show us the saving necessary from labor to permit a change in the location of production, assuming other production costs to remain the same. In this case where Fundidora labor costs are slightly over 300 pesos per ton of production,[45] the 30 pesos of extra transport costs from Monterrey to Mexico City would have to be

[44]Weber, op. cit., pp. 102-04.
[45]Cia. Fundidora de Fierro y Acero de Monterrey, S. A., Informe Anual 1950, Mexico City, 1951, p. 17.

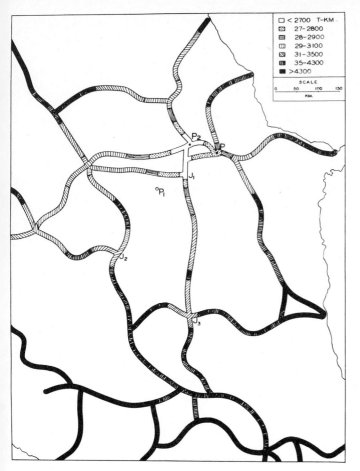

FIGURE 12 Transport Costs Based on Weight and Distance for Locations on the Railroad Network.

counterbalanced by at least a 10 per cent saving in labor in Mexico City. This is not the case in the steel industry, so Monterrey remains the minimum point. In addition, the actual transportation costs for production at Monterrey have been shown to be lower than for the general pattern we have used in the analysis.

There is still another aspect to the consideration of the transportation network as shown in Figure 12. Palander noted in his general considerations that junction points tend to have a significant advantage over other points on the transport network.[46] In Mexico we have the two principal examples of this at Paredon and Monterrey, P_2 and P. At these places junctions occur near the hypothetical minimum points and the junction's advantage makes it then the actual minimum point.

This advantage often results in secondary

points with low transport costs, in addition to the minimum point. Instead of a continual increase in costs away from the minimum point, the junctions may cause a local decrease in costs. Several instances of this may be seen in Figure 12 at the junctions marked J_1, J_2 and J_3. It may be noted that these junctions are all within the supply-market polygon. Junctions beyond the polygon will not show this tendency because all costs are increasing in that area. Within the polygon, however, changes in the location of P will result in a decrease of some costs and an increase of others, thereby allowing these local low points. In general, the more routes entering a junction the greater the possibility that it will create a minimum point. Furthermore, as shown by Palander, if the materials and market lie on difference routes, P will always be a junction, assuming that no one weight is preponderant. Places between junctions will always have higher transport costs than the junctions.

Another feature of junctions, though not applicable to Mexico, is that they often have rate advantages over intermediate points due to competition between the carriers. This would fortify the junction's position and make its effect more pronounced.

Palander made additional contributions relative to the influence of the transport network, bringing out the importance of transshipment points and routes, but they do not apply to our problem.

Palander's contributions applicable to our study have been in the way of improvement upon earlier works. The first of these considered here was the development of Launhardt's pole principle to show the location of P for various locations of C. The second was his substitution of a mathematical formula for Weber's material index, showing the importance of relative location of the supply-market points. The third contribution was the development of Weber's concept of the isodapanes, making it possible to consider variable freight rates in the determination of the MTP. His observations on the role of junctions were a fourth contribution. All of these have been applied and found to agree with the conditions of Mexican steel location.

Conclusion

In this study we have described the steel industry of Mexico, determined its supply and market pattern, and analyzed its location. Location theory applicable to this industry was then dis-

[46]Palander, *op. cit.*, pp. 333-35.

cussed and tested by application to the Mexican situation. We may now summarize our findings.

The Mexican steel industry includes two primary steel plants, three secondary plants of significant size and a number of small secondary producers, producing in all about 400,000 metric tons of crude steel in 1950. This production, covering most types of steel products, satisfies about one-half of the country's steel needs. The large plants are located in the north with Monterrey as the principal center, although Monclova is rapidly attaining equal size.

Material supplies for primary steel were found to be based on essentially the same sources for both plants. There is no significant difference in costs of each material, so that the location of each plant relative to its supplies remained the principle factor giving rise to differences in costs of materials at the plant. Some materials were found to exert little influence upon the location because: (1) they are used in small quantities, (2) they are ubiquities or (3) they are derived from plant operations. Materials remaining significant to location were iron ore, coke, oil and market scrap. Significant supplies for the secondary plants were found to be scrap and fuel or power.

Labor was found to have little influence upon steel industry location in Mexico. There is no surplus skilled labor to attract a plant and unskilled labor here is quite mobile. While wages vary considerably within Mexico, in the steel industry a national union of steelworkers has kept wage rates and employment conditions quite uniform. Wages may be somewhat lower in the south, but the difference is slight. There is no evidence that labor productivity varies significantly from one place to another.

Markets for Mexican steel are concentrated mainly in Mexico City and Monterrey, with only a small percentage of production going to other points. Of total production, about 70 per cent is sold in Mexico City and about 24 per cent in Monterrey. All plants sell on a F. O. B. basis, leaving plant location relative to the market as a significant factor in delivered-to-customer cost. Differences in transportation cost incurred in the assembly of the raw materials and delivery of the product to the market were found to be the major cost variable related to location.

Analysis of the location of the primary plants was first made on the basis of the individual supply-market pattern of each company. Fundidora

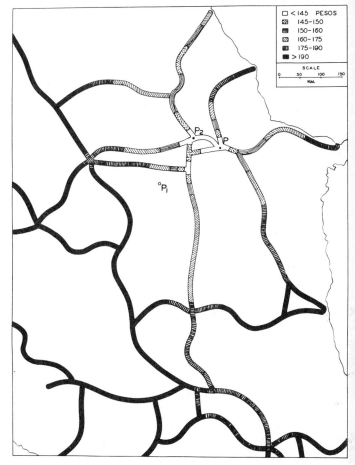

FIGURE 13 Transport Costs Based on Weight, Distance and Freight Rates for Locations on the Railroad Network.

at Monterrey has an advantage over Altos Hornos at Monclova principally because of its location at part of its market, saving freight cost thereby on about one-half of its output. With respect to material supplies, neither plant had a significant advantage. Monterrey's advantage in having natural gas available was largely cancelled by Monclova's nearness to coke.

The supply-market pattern of the individual plants was then combined into a general pattern by using the weighted averages of materials and by substituting the general market for those of the individual plants. This pattern retained all essential features of the individual patterns. Then the industry was analyzed on the basis of weight and distance, to which were added the railroad network and freight rates. With weight and straight-line distance only, the MTP was found to be in north central Mexico on the northern border of Zacatecas. This point was centrally located with respect to the materials, and the market was found to have only a slight effect on its location.

With the introduction of the railroad network, the MTP shifted to Paredón, 140 km. to the northeast, a junction point forming the most direct connection between the materials and the markets. When differential freight rates were considered, however, the MTP moved to Monterrey, the location of part of the market.

APPLICATION OF EXISTING THEORIES

Examination of theory revealed that it may be divided into general theory, concerned with the overall location of economic activities, and special theory, treating the location of individual plants. The aspects of special theory relating to the determination of the MTP were partly applicable to our problem and contributions on this subject were found in the works of Launhardt, Weber and Palander.

All of the above theorists refer to a mechanical device, known as Varignon's frame, by which the MTP may be determined. This was tested and the results found to agree with the empirically-determined MTP. The model can consider only the weight and distance factors, but it is adaptable to problems with any reasonable number of supply-market points.

Launhardt's contribution, the earliest work on industrial location, considered only the factors of weight and distance and offered a geometrical solution to the problem. This was applied to Mexico and found to offer sufficient explanation for the location of the secondary producers. Although Launhardt attempted to apply his solution to problems with more than three supply-market points, he was unsuccessful in doing so. We attempted an application by simplifying the primary steel pattern and, noting that this did not seriously distort the pattern, may have obtained some additional insight into our problem.

Weber's theory of the location of industry was then examined. This work, using the same basic concept as Launhardt, is an attempt to formulate a general theory of industrial location. The basis of the theory, transport orientation, was found applicable to the Mexican steel problem. It is not, however, a general theory but is limited to certain types of industries which agree with the assumptions of fixed materials and markets. While the basic transportation orientation on weight and

distance is acceptable, Weber's modifications of these factors to account for other transport cost elements were found to be inadequate. He did not recognize that distance may not be modified before finding the MTP and the method of treating railroad rates ignored the matter of long-haul economies. The basic principles of orientation deduced from the locational triangle are valid, but his attempt to formulate a material index to indicate the orientation was unsuccessful because the factor of relative location was given insufficient consideration. Weber made a significant contribution in suggesting the concept of the isodapanes.

Palander's contributions relating to the determination of the MTP are in the form of improvements upon the work of Launhardt and Weber. He developed more fully Launhardt's pole principle and brought out its significance in the determination of market areas. His criticism of Weber's material index and substitution of a mathematical formula for it corrected for Weber's inadequate treatment of relative location. Furthermore, he also found that Weber's methods of modifying weight and distance to consider freight rates and transportation routes were inadequate. He therefore successfully developed Weber's concept of the isodapanes to include the freight rate and he also analyzed the effect of routes.

THE LOCATION OF THE MEXICAN STEEL INDUSTRY

As a result of our analysis of the concrete situation and examination of theory of location we have learned that, for the present material supplies and markets the Mexican industry is well located on the whole. The larger primary plant and the secondary plants were all found to be at the MTP. The location of the second primary plant, Altos Hornos, is at some disadvantage compared to Fundidora but, even so, is quite near the minimum area. As long as the industry is based on present material supplies and has Monterrey and Mexico City as its principal markets, the best location, from the viewpoint of transportation costs, will remain in the north.

It may now be of interest to consider, however, changes in location that would result from changed conditions of production or consumption. Mexico is developing industrially and a basic industry such as steel may have to adjust itself to new conditions.

One possibility is that new material supplies

may be developed. In the case of iron ore, many additional small deposits and several large deposits of high-grade ore are known to exist in Mexico. However, we have learned that material, though of large weight, is a comparatively weak locational factor due to its low freight rates. It seems unlikely, therefore, that these resources will become the locations for future steel plants.

While Mexico has a number of coal deposits, the only known deposit of coking coal is that at Sabinas. As coke is used in large quantities and incurs rather high freight costs, it is an important locational consideration and at the moment Mexican steel is somewhat tied to northern locations for this reason. While so little is known about Mexican coal resources that any discussion of them here is purely conjectural, there is an interesting long-run possibility dependent upon the discovery of coking coal in the states of Puebla and Oaxaca. There are numerous coal deposits in this area, many of them only slightly known, among which coking coal could be found. Should it be discovered, it could be combined with ore from the same general area, and oil and gas from Vera Cruz and thus form the basis for a steel plant serving the Mexico markets and probably having reasonably low transportation costs. This would mean a new supply-market pattern based on the resources of this area rather than the north, if we ignore the present inadequate railroad system.

For locations where oil must be used as fuel rather than gas, this material, too, is a significant factor. However, it is available from a number of sources along the east coast, all the way from the United States border to the Isthmus of Tehuantepec, hence alternative supplies would be available, reducing the importance of the present sources as locational factors.

With increased industrialization of Mexico, market scrap will eventually become more plentiful, and, as it accrues principally in the larger cities, this development will bolster the pull of the market for primary steel and also reinforce the present locations of the secondary producers.

Changes in markets will have little effect upon the location of production based upon the present material supply pattern, as we have already noted. Should sizable markets develop along the eastern coast, they would be best served from the center of gravity of the fuels which, due to the present railroad network, may be considered to be Monterrey. Markets in central Mexico, from Puebla

in the east to Guadalajara in the west, would be best served from plants located in the north on a line running approximately from Durango to Monterrey. There is only a remote possibility that Durango could become a center of production because only a small part of west central Mexico would be best served from here, and that part is unlikely to develop a market for steel. For markets in northwestern Mexico Torreón is in an excellent position, being near the Durango-Monterrey line and having a well-developed rail network of which Torreón is the focal point.

Considering the critical shortage of scrap in Mexico and the necessity for its importation, some possibilities exist for additional secondary plants on the east coast, using the Piedras Negras plant as a pattern the MTP of which is the source of scrap. We concluded that this would be the case where a plant obtains all its scrap from a point other than its market. An east coast secondary plant at Vera Cruz, for instance, may be possible on this same pattern. Scrap could be imported by water, a much cheaper form of transportation, and could be processed fairly near the Mexico City market with fuels available in the immediate Vera Cruz area. As pointed out earlier, if plentiful scrap supplies develop within Mexico the position of the secondary plants located at the market would be reinforced. In such a case a plant using imported scrap would probably be at a disadvantage.

Changes in the supply-market pattern could also be brought about by changes in the freight rate structure. If all rates were decreased proportionately, new material supplies would probably become available. If some deposits of ore, for example, at present lie too distant to be economic, a lower freight rate on ore could eliminate this disadvantage if long-haul economies were great enough. Conversely, an increase in all rates could make some deposits now exploited unprofitable. This would result in a contraction of the supply-market pattern and put nearby supplies in a stronger position.

The effect of differential changes in rates on the various materials or the product may be considered as changes in weights, according to Weber. Consequently, a lower rate on a material will reduce its locational attraction, and, conversely, an increase in the rate will make it of greater importance in determining location. If rates are changed only for parts of the transport network the attractiveness of certain possible production points may be lessened or enhanced. A possible example in Mexico would be the introduction of low rates on coke from Sabinas to Durango to encourage use of the returning ore cars. Then points on that line, such as Torreón and Durango, would become more favorable locations for steel production. These possible adjustments have many implications for Mexico where we find a nationalized railroad system and an active program for economic development. They are beyond the scope of this study, however.

Certain technological changes would be additional factors bringing about changes in the location of production. In the steel industry we mean especially those which increase production from a given amount of material. The general effect of this would be a decrease in the attractiveness of materials and an increase in the strength of the market. Another aspect of technological change, possibly of greater significance, is a change in the ratios of one material to another. We have in mind here the changing ratio of ore to coke. Ore, as a rule, is quite efficiently used, but there is much room for improvement in the utilization of coke. In Mexico a significant improvement in this respect is possible, firstly in the production of coke. An improvement in its quality would result in lower consumption of coke. Secondly, the same effect would be produced by more efficient utilization at the furnaces. The result would be a reduction in the pull of the coke supply and a relative increase in the strength of the other supply-market points. The same observation may be made on the utilization of oil.

It has been learned in this study that the Mexican steel industry is well located and location theory appears to be sufficiently developed to offer an explanation for it. How well the theory will apply to the steel industries of other areas or to other industries is a matter for further study.

APPENDIX A

Mathematical Determination of the MTP[1]

1. Let (x_1, y_1), (x_2, y_2), (x_3, y_3), and (x, y) be the coordinates of A, B, C and P, respectively, and let a, b and c be the weights to be moved along the lines AP, BP and CP, respectively. The problem is to minimize the function

$$S = ar + bs + ct$$

[1]This solution was developed by Dr. Gustav Bergman of the Department of Philosophy, State University of Iowa.

with $r = [(x - x_1)^2 + (y - y_1)^2]^{1/2}$ $s = [(x - x_2)^2 + (y - y_2)^{1/2}$, $t = [(x - x_3)^2 + (y - y_3)^2]^{1/2}$. Thus S must be minimized as a function of x and y by putting

$$\frac{\delta S}{\delta x} = 0, \quad \frac{\delta S}{\delta y} = 0.$$

This yields

$$0 = a\frac{x - x_1}{r} + b\frac{x - x_2}{s} + c\frac{x - x_3}{t} \quad (1)$$

$$0 = a\frac{y - y_1}{r} + b\frac{y - y_2}{s} + c\frac{y - y_3}{t} \quad (2)$$

But, as may be seen from Figure 14-A, $a\dfrac{x - x_1}{r}$, $a\dfrac{y - y_1}{r}$; $b\dfrac{x - x_2}{s}$, $b\dfrac{y - y_2}{s}$; $c\dfrac{x - x_3}{t}$, $c\dfrac{y - y_3}{t}$, are,

FIGURE 14 Mathematical Determination of the MTP.

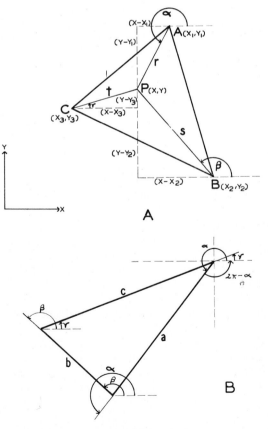

A

B

respectively the x and y components of three forces of the absolute strengths a, b and c which point toward P from A, B and C, respectively. If they are all three inverted so that they issue from P, the relation remains undisturbed. This proves the correctness of the mechanical procedure.

2. Equations (1) and (2) express that the three force vectors of lengths a, b and c form a triangle. As shown in Figure 14-B, the supplementary angles of this triangle are $(\alpha - \beta)$, $(\beta - \gamma)$ and $(2\pi - \alpha + \gamma)$, respectively. This leads to the geometrical construction of P.

3. (a) First we construct the triangle out of a, b and c, thus obtaining the angles $(\alpha - \beta)$, $(\beta - \gamma)$ and $(2\pi - \alpha + \gamma)$, respectively.

   (b) We notice from Figure 14-A that $\measuredangle$ BPA $= \alpha - \beta$. Similarly, of course, $\measuredangle$ CPB $= \beta - \gamma$, and $\measuredangle$ CPA $= 2\pi - \alpha + \gamma$.

   (c) By a familiar theorem of elementary geometry the locus of all the points which subtend a fixed angle to two fixed points forms a circle. This may be easily constructed and P obtained as the point of intersection of these three circles.

Allan Pred

THE CONCENTRATION OF HIGH-VALUE-ADDED MANUFACTURING

Why are some industries spatially concentrated? Why does the nucleation of certain manufactures show a greater proclivity for some areas rather than others? What forces counteract the impetus toward concentration? These questions are not easily answered, nor is it likely that they are reducible to simple unassailable truths; for even as August Lösch, perhaps the most abstract of the location theory titans, remarked: "Concepts like production orientation or transport orientation merely describe a location; they do not explain it. The reasons that actually motivate an entrepreneur explain, to be sure, though they do not always convince; an exact calculation of the most important possiblities would be convincing but extraordinarily difficult and, strictly speaking, impossible."[1]

These broad, intractable questions, however, are not totally unanswerable or insurmountable. A partial solution is feasible if a limited number of industries are studied and no more than admittedly confined generalizations are sought. Here the objective is limited to exploring the degree and kind of geographic concentration which is most characteristic of high-value-added industries.

Background to an Hypothesis

Empirical studies have largely ignored the interrelationships between spatially concentrated industries and value added. This may partially be

ascribed to the fact that scholars have more often than not viewed "industrial concentration" as something synonymous with corporative oligopoly,[2] rather than as the manufacture of a commodity within a geographically limited area. (Only Rosenbluth has chosen explicitly to investigate the connection between corporative and geographical concentration of manufacturing).[3] The dearth of literature concerning the composition of value added may also underlie the absence of empirical studies which attempt to link concentration, or the absence thereof, with this simple economic measurement. This is not to give the illusion that value added has been completely ignored, for its general significance has been commented upon,[4] and it has often been used as a basis for mapping manufacturing[5] and analyzing regional shifts of aggregated industrial groups.[6]

If value added by manufacturing has not been applied to the problem of interpreting industrial concentration, it has generally been considered "the best value measure available for comparing the

Reprinted with the permission of the author and publisher from *Economic Geography*, Vol. 41, No. 2, 1965, pp. 108-32. Dr. Pred is Associate Professor of Geography at the University of California, Berkeley.

[1] August Lösch: *The Economics of Location*, New Haven, 1954, p. 377.

[2] Economists understandably seem more prone than others to use this narrow interpretation of the term. For example, see M. A. Adelman: "The Measurement of Industrial Concentration," *Rev. of Econs. and Statistics*, Vol. 33, 1951, pp. 259-296; Joe S. Bain: "Relation of Profit Rate to Industry Concentration: American Manufacturing, 1936-1940," *Quarterly Journ. of Econs.*, Vol. 65, 1951, pp. 293-324; Edward S. Mason: *Economic Concentration and the Monopoly Problem*, Cambridge, Mass., 1957; Betty Bock: *Concentration Patterns in Manufacturing*, New York, 1959; and Richard Evely and I. M. D. Little: *Concentration in British Industry*, Cambridge, England, 1960.

[3] Gideon Rosenbluth: *Concentration in Canadian Manufacturing*, Princeton, 1957.

[4] Victor Roterus: "Value Added by Manufacture and its Significance," *Virginia Economic Review*, Vol. 1, 1938, pp. 1-3.

[5] For example see Alfred Wright: "Manufacturing Districts of the United States," *Econ. Geog.*, Vol. 14, 1938, pp. 195-200.

[6] Wilbur Zelinsky: "A Method of Measuring Change in the Distribution of Manufacturing Activity, 1939-1947," *Econ. Geog.*, Vol. 38, 1962, pp. 251-269; and Victor R. Fuchs: *Changes in the Location of Manufacturing in the United States Since 1929*, New Haven, 1962.

relative economic importance of manufacturing among industries and geographic areas."[7] *The Census of Manufactures* derives value added "by subtracting the cost of materials, supplies, containers, fuels, purchased electricity and contract work from the value of shipments for products manufactured plus receipts for services rendered. The result of this calculation is then adjusted by the addition of value added by merchandising operations (that is the difference between the sales value and cost of merchandise sold without further manufacture, processing, or assembly) plus the net change in finished goods and work-in-progress inventories between the beginning and end of the year."[8] Accordingly, high-value-added manufacturing can roughly be defined as those industries in which value added forms a high percentage of the value of shipments. Naturally, it should not be inferred that all high-value-added industries have similar cost structures. The relative importance of labor, depreciation, other overhead expenses and profit may vary between industries which are high-value-added to a similar extent.

The Hypothesis and Its Constraints

The absence of empirical inquiries into the relationship between industrial cost structure and degree of spatial concentration is somewhat offset by the work of location theorists. Some of the basic premises and observations of location theory lead to an hypothesis that *the highest-value-added industries in the United States should be markedly concentrated in the so-called "Manufacturing Belt," rather than in other parts of the country.*

Alfred Weber's analysis of internal and external agglomeration economies and their influence on the location of industries greatly emphasized the compressibility of production costs.[9] Weber logically demonstrated that an industry's predilection to concentrate is some function of the difference in magnitude between combined outlays for raw materials and power, and the value of the finished product. To oversimplify: the greater the degree to which the value of a product is determined by its manufacturing costs,[10] the greater the extent to which economies of agglomeration can offset transportation economies at alternative dispersed sites of production, and the greater the likelihood that the particular industry will be geographically concentrated. Because of the contrasting nature of internal and external economies, concentration may express itself in the form of a small number of large establishments, or as a clustering of numerous small establishments.[11] The extent to which any specific industry is concentrated is clearly not a function of the industry's average size of plant.[12] Put in slightly different terms, one may expect high-value-added industries, regardless of average size of plant, to be highly concentrated, because in most instances raw material and distribution costs, and thereby transportation costs, are a secondary element in their cost structure. It is particularly true of industries centralized by external economies that transportation costs are not a critical locational factor.[13]

This line of reasoning provides us with an inkling of the forces which purportedly should lead to a pronouncedly concentrated distribution of the United States' highest-value-added industries, but fails to provide any rationale for an argument that such industries should be centralized in the Manufacturing Belt[14] (Fig. 1). Theoretical

[7]U. S. Bureau of Census, *1961 Annual Survey of Manufactures: General Statistics for Industry Groups and Selected Industries, 1961*, Washington, D.C., 1962, p. 2. At the same time it should be realized that: "No single criterion or single complex of criteria can give a map of total manufactural geography." For further comment see John W. Alexander: "Location of Manufacturing: Methods of Measurement," *Annals. Assn. of Amer. Geogrs.*, Vol. 48, 1958, pp. 20-26.

[8]*1961 Annual Survey of Manufactures, loc. cit.*

[9]Alfred Weber: *Theory of the Location of Industries*, Chicago, 1929, pp. 124-172. A translation with introduction and notes by Carl J. Friedrich of *Über den Standort der Industrien*, Tübingen, 1909.

[10]Weber's translator recognized that the term "Formwert," used to refer to the value created by the industrial or formative process itself, is the equivalent of "value added by manufacture." *Ibid.*, p. 163.

[11]Marshall was aware of this prior to Weber. See Alfred J. Marshall: *Principles of Economics, 8th ed.*, New York, 1948, pp. 265-282; as well as Weber, *loc. cit.*, pp. 127-128; and Edgar M. Hoover: *Location Theory and the Shoe and Leather Industries*, Cambridge, Mass., 1937, pp. 90-91.

[12]P. Sargant Florence: *Investment, Location, and Size of Plant*, Cambridge, England, 1948, pp. 52-53. On the other hand, corporate concentration appears to be strongly correlated to the industry's average size of plant. See Rosenbluth, *loc. cit.*, p. 17.

[13]Robert M. Lichtenberg, *One-Tenth of a Nation* (Cambridge: Harvard University Press, 1960), p. 112.

[14]Sten de Geer's original delimitation of the Manufacturing Belt, based on cities having at least 1000 industrial employees, bears a remarkable resemblance to one delineated for 1958, on the basis of county value added data (Fig. 1). While certain inconsistencies may or may not be discerned in the 1958 version, it should be pointed out that the Manufacturing Belt is an amorphous, continually evolving area which is more an intellectual convenience than an integral region. For a comparison with some of the earlier delimitations of the Manufacturing Belt see Sten de Geer: "The American Manufacturing Belt," *Geografiska Annaler*, Vol. 9, 1927, pp. 233-359; Richard Hartshorne: "A New Map of the Manufacturing Belt of North America," *Econ. Geog.* Vol. 12, 1936, pp. 45-53; *Industrial Location and National Resources*, National Resources Planning Board, Washington, D.C., 1943, p. 12; and Harold M. Mayer: "The American Manufacturing Zone," in *Industrial Cities Excursion Guidebook*, Washington, D.C., 1952, pp. 7-18.

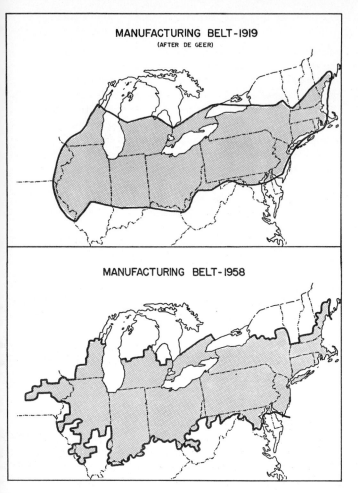

MANUFACTURING BELT-1919
(AFTER DE GEER)

MANUFACTURING BELT-1958

FIGURE 1 The Manufacturing Belt as First Outlined by Sten de Geer and as Delimited for 1958. Related remarks are set forth in Footnote 14.

support may be derived at least partially from the following observation: "Societal development is an historical process. At any given point of time there exists an inherited physical structural framework. Plants have already been erected and are producing. To relocate these plants involves opportunity costs since one would forego the use of facilities forced into obsolescence. Critics of Weber have therefore emphasized the advantages of existing production points as centers of agglomeration, whether they reflect labor or any other form of orientation. As new units of production come into existence, they will tend to gain localization economies by agglomerating around established production points. Thereby they frequently strengthen the gravitational pull of these points."[15] Furthermore, since it

is usually found "that the larger and better established centers play a leading part as germinating grounds for new (related) industries,"[16] a self-perpetuating momentum often characterizes industrial concentrations.[17] It follows, in general, that *high-value-added manufacturing should be concentrated in the traditionally highly populated and industrialized areas of a country,* which, in the case of the United States, means an area coterminous with the Manufacturing Belt. However, the inertial forces encouraging the perpetuation of high-value-added manufacturing in the Manufacturing Belt, or in the older industrial areas of other countries, are not solely economic. The complexly interacting forces of historical accident, local innovation, and precedence cannot be eliminated from any scheme which seeks to relate high-value-addedness and concentration and, at one and the same time, attempts to account for such disparate phenomena as the clustering of typewriter production facilities in upstate New York, of potteries in Staffordshire, England, and of watchmaking in Switzerland's western cantons.[18]

The superficial evidence regarding the total United States industrial structure would seem to indicate that high-value-added industries have remained highly centralized in the Manufacturing Belt. High-value-added industries in the United States are often characterized by a labor force predominantly composed of highly skilled workers, and for such industries "locating outside the established industrial centers involves two difficulties: the firm must find a labor market big enough to provide an adequate number of workers with the necessary aptitudes; and the firm must resign itself to a prolonged training period for a major segment of its labor force."[19] In contrast, American cities located outside the Manufacturing Belt and classified as "manufacturing cities" at one time could be typified as being dominated by industries in

[15]Walter Isard: *Location and Space Economy*, New York,

[16]Carter Goodrich, *et. al.: Migration and Economic Opportunity*, Philadelphia, 1936, p. 334.
[17]Edward L. Ullman: "Regional Development and the Geography of Concentration," *Papers and Proceedings of the Regional Science Association*, Vol. 4, 1958, p. 184.
[18]For a discussion of the locational importance of inertia, local inventiveness, and chance, see such works as Allan Rodgers: "Industrial Inertia—A Major Factor in the Location of the Steel Industry in the United States," *Geogr. Rev.*, Vol. 42, 1952, pp. 56-66; Malcolm Keir: *Industries of America: Manufacturing*, New York, 1928, pp. 120-140; and John W. Alexander: "Manufacturing in the Rock River Valley—Location Factors," *Annals Assn. of Amer. Geogrs.*, Vol. 40, 1950, pp. 237-253.
[19]Martin Segal: *Wages in the Metropolis*, Cambridge, Mass., 1960, p. 20.

which raw material costs were pre-eminent.[20] In addition, between 1929 and 1954, the average mobility of concentrated industries in the United States proved to be considerably less than that of already more scattered industries.[21] Beyond this skimpy support, confirmation of the proposed hypothesis can be attained only by probing the locational patterns of specific industries.

But the danger of misinterpretation or misrepresentation runs high unless two groups of qualifications are explicitly spelled out. Firstly, while the hypothesis contends that high-value-added industries should have highly sporadic rather than nearly ubiquitous distributions, it is not to be implied that the converse is true, i.e., that low-value-added industries should have scattered distributions and cannot occur in a limited number of locations. To avoid this modification would be tantamount to denying the existence of centralizing forces other than that of high-value-addedness. Clearly, this is not the case. Raw material and climatic considerations may precipitate a concentrated distribution, e.g., an extremely low-value-added industry such as tobacco stemming and re-drying is highly localized. Some industries which are not high-value-added are concentrated in the western portion of the Manufacturing Belt so as to minimize transport costs to the national market, e.g., agricultural machinery; while others are nucleated in the South because of the attraction exerted by cheap labor and local amenities, e.g., cotton textiles. It is also feasible for national competition within an industry to result in concentration. It sometimes occurs under conditions of oligopolistic competition that no one company can monopolize any regional market, and hence the threshold of scale economies cannot be realized at any location outside the most populous core of a country.[22]

Secondly, human ecologists and geographers have on occasion pointed to the "forces of diversification" which conflict with the "forces of unification," or to the interaction between centrifugal and centripetal forces,[23] and within this light it is both imperative and logical to identify the forces

which counteract the concentration of high-value-added industries in older manufacturing regions.

Transportation costs are probably the most important factor militating against the hypothesized concentration. It is not always true, as has already been implied, that raw material assembly and product distribution costs are a secondary element in the cost-structure of high-value-added industries. Weber himself recognized that the likelihood of an industry agglomerating was not only contingent upon its value-added characteristics, but was also inversely proportional to the prevailing transport rates and the industry's locational weight[24] (or the total weight of goods to be moved in assembling and distributing one ton of finished product). However, while Weber's concern was appropriately turned to the restrictions imposed by transport costs, it was not properly focused. It is not so much the locational weight of an industry as the nature of its raw materials and products which determine the ultimate role of transportation in permitting or preventing concentration. Loading costs for a ton of fluid and a ton of delicate machinery are not comparable, nor are the handling costs of a ton of sand and a ton of glassware nearly equivalent. (Weber's entire theoretical construct has often been criticized for its neglect of terminal and transshipment costs.) That freight rates apply to finished products in accordance with their value, as well as their sheer weight, is equally apparent. Presumably, then, *high-value-added industries cannot concentrate if: (1) the fragility or perishability of their finished products incurs undue terminal or handling costs; or (2) the value of their products per unit weight is low enough to obviate long-distance hauling.*

In addition, long-range trends in the general level of freight rates for manufactured goods have encouraged the regional decentralization of high and low-value-added industries alike. Concentration has been considerably inhibited by the fact that long-haul rates have increased more rapidly than those for shorter distances. In particular: "The railroads, to meet the growing competition of the truck, have been obligated to refrain from raising short-haul rates, while concentrating their rate increases on the longer-hauls."[25] The distance factor has also been looming ever larger as a deter-

---

[20]Chauncey D. Harris: "A Functional Classification of Cities in the United States," *Geogr. Rev.*, Vol. 33, 1943, p. 91.

[21]Fuchs, *op. cit.*, p. 121.

[22]Ullman, *op. cit.*, p. 187.

[23]For example see G. K. Zipf: *Human Behavior and the Principle of Least Effort*, Cambridge, Mass., 1949, p. 365; and Charles C. Colby: "Centrifugal and Centripetal Forces in Urban Geography," *Annals Assn. of Amer. Geogrs.*, Vol. 23, 1933, pp. 1-20.

[24]Weber, *op. cit.*, pp. 155, 164, and 166.

[25]Raymond Vernon: *Metropolis 1985*, Garden City, 1963, p. 92.

rent to concentration because of the increasing costs of handling and moving finished packaged materials. At the same time, economies in the volume shipment of raw materials have been attracting industries to locations which serve regional rather than national markets.[26] Recent analysis has revealed the "great importance of the transportation cost factor in accounting for differences in concentration" amongst Canadian industries.[27] Similarly, during the last three decades the industries in the New York Metropolitan Region which serve national markets have become more and more typified by industries whose transportation costs are a small proportion of total costs. High-transport-cost industries have been leaving the New York area in order to get closer to their markets.[28] On the other hand, transportation developments have begun partially to counteract the trend toward decentralization, but their possible over-all effect in the future appears unclear. These developments include the spread of coordinated services, such as "piggy-back" and fishy-back," and the growing use of air cargo facilities.[29]

Population growth outside the older manufacturing, or "core," regions of countries also acts in opposition to the concentration of high-value-added industries. Weber was cognizant of the fact that increasing density of population makes possible increasingly larger agglomerations.[30] Presumably, population growth would tend to reinforce the formidable advantages already enjoyed by high-value-added industries localized in traditional manufacturing regions. However, increased levels of concentration, or scale-shifts, may express themselves between any two points on a total output curve, i.e., the creation of production facilities where they did not exist represents an increase in concentration. The implications of this simple obseravtion are perspicuous: population increases in the formerly sparsely settled areas of a country will eventually create regional markets capable of satisfying the scale thresholds of some high-value-added industries. Thus, population growth beyond a certain point should bring about a relative, although rarely an absolute, decline in the importance of high-value-added manufacturing within older industrial areas. The population total necessary to attain scale thresholds will naturally vary from industry to industry; and in some instances continued technical progress, with attendant increases in the optimal scale of operation, will raise the level of the threshold. Thus, inordinate population growth in new areas need not automatically lead to a relative decentralization of any particular high-value-added industry.[31]

Recent trends in the distribution of manufacturing as a whole in both the United States and Canada seem to substantiate the deterrent effect of an expanding population upon concentration. There is a general tendency for comparable industries to be more concentrated in Canada than in the United States, and this is apparently attributable to the enormous difference in population between the two countries.[32] In addition, the disproportionate growth of population on the Pacific Coast and in the Southwest has led to a rate of industrial expansion in those areas which exceeds the national average. The diminishing importance of the eastern portion of the Manufacturing Belt in comparison to the Great Lakes portion of that belt is also at least partially ascribable to differential rates of population growth.[33]

Finally, the standardization of production processes on occasion may also precipitate the decentralization of high-value-added manufacturing. The pronounced concentration of capital, decision-making elites, and research facilities in older industrial areas usually attracts new industries which are still in the experimental stage and incapable of converting to uniform assembly-line production. "But eventually the processes of almost any industry become routinized, through technical and managerial improvements, so that ordinary labor without special training can be used. The normal result is that the industry spreads or moves to other areas, its dispersion from the original centers being sped by the relatively high wages and inflexible conditions that have become established there by the skilled elite."[34]

---

[26]Ullman, *op. cit.*, p. 185. For other pertinent remarks on the effect of transportation costs on industrial centralization see National Resources Planning Board, *op. cit.*, p. 250; and Gunnar Alexandersson: *The Industrial Structure of American Cities*, Lincoln, 1956, p. 13.

[27]Rosenbluth, *op. cit.*, p. 47.

[28]Benjamin Chinitz: *Freight and the Metropolis*, Cambridge, Mass., 1960, pp. 93 and 127.

[29]*Idem.*, and Raymond Vernon: "Changing Forces of Industrial Localization," *Harvard Bus. Rev.*, Vol. 38, 1960, p. 132.

[30]Weber, *op. cit.*, p. 168.

[31]This entire line of reasoning is consistent with Weber's assumption that local agglomeration will occur whenever the minimum scale requirements (threshold) are satisfied.

[32]Rosenbluth, *op. cit.*, pp. 19–20.

[33]Zelinsky, *op. cit.*, p. 126; and Fuchs, *op. cit.*, p. 28.

[34]Edgar M. Hoover, *The Location of Economic Activity* (New York: McGraw-Hill Book Company, Inc., 1948), p. 174.

The Distribution of High-Value-Added Manufacturing in the United States

The 1967 Annual Survey of Manufactures, which lacked detailed areal statistics, revealed that only 23 out of the Standard Industrial Classification's 400-odd four-digit manufacturing industries had a total value-added equivalent to at least 70 per cent of their total value of shipments (Table I).[35] Of these 23 industries no less than 17 had at least an estimated 80 per cent of their 1958 productive activity (as measured by value added) localized within the Manufacturing Belt.[36] By comparison, in 1958, the Manufacturing Belt contained approximately 65.3 per cent of the nation's industrial value added, while only 47.3 of the country's population inhabited the area.[37]

Clearly then, the nation's highest-value-added industries have a distinct tendency to be more concentrated in the Manufacturing Belt than manufacturing as a whole. As a matter of fact, four of the industries — pharmaceuticals, machine tool accessories, safes and vaults, and dressed and dyed furs — had more than 90 per cent of their value added at locations within the Manufacturing Belt.

NONCONFORMING INDUSTRIES

But what of the six industries which were not highly concentrated in the Manufacturing Belt? Certainly, if there is any validity to the hypothesized nucleation of high-value-added industries in older industrial areas, such as the Manufacturing Belt, then the six deviations should be attributable to other than purely random factors. What then are these six exceptions? And what forces, if any, can be identified which counteract the supposed inclination of these industries to be concentrated?

Interestingly, two of the nonconforming in-

dustries can be ranked amongst the most ubiquitously distributed of all industries. The two, newspapers and manufactured ice, are found in just about every city of any size in the United States; although, because of climatic conditions, local production of manufactured ice is particularly high in the southern states and California. The anomalous position of manufactured ice does not arise because economies of large-scale production are not possible. The industry's scattered distribution is easily understood in light of the virtual ubiquitousness of the product's basic raw material, its perishability, and its extremely low value per unit weight.

The decentralized publication of newspapers, however, is not easily explained in solely economic terms. Much of the newsprint used in Atlantic Coast cities is brought in by rail from Canada, just as it is to many inland newspapers.[38] This would seem to indicate that transport costs on raw materials do not prevent concentrated publication. That the high-value character of the industry could permit more centralized production is irrefutably supported by the highly concentrated newspaper production of Japan, the Soviet Union, England, Sweden, and other countries of northern Europe. Further support for this contention may be derived from the success of *Time* and *Newsweek* magazines, which are little more than weekly newspapers, as well as the less spectacular operations of the *Wall Street Journal* and the *Christian Science Monitor.* However, two factors apparently obviate a consolidation of mass newspaper production in this country: one is a federalist tradition which creates interest in news at the state and local levels; the other is the role of American newspapers "as carriers of advertisements in general and especially those of firms with a geographically restricted market."[39]

The metal plating and polishing industry had a high percentage (73.8) of its value added in the Manufacturing Belt in 1958, but fell somewhat short of the arbitrarily selected 80.0 per cent limit which typified most of the highest-value-added industries. Despite its relative concentration in the Manufacturing Belt, the industry is characterized by a near ubiquitous distribution of small plants. In 1958 there were 2646 establishments performing metal plating and polishing functions; none of

---

[35]The nation's highest-value-added industries, according to the 1929 and 1939 Censuses of Manufactures, were identified by Charles A. Bliss in *The Structure of Manufacturing Production,* New York, 1939, pp. 168-178; and by the National Resources Planning Board, *op. cit.,* p. 270.

[36]Estimates were only necessary for those states, or segments thereof, for which no data was given in the *U.S. Census of Manufactures: 1958 Vol. 2, Industry Statistics,* or *Vol. 3, Area Statistics,* Washington, D.C., 1961. Estimates were made by apportioning value added for groups of states according to employment data. In some instances it was necessary to use a supplement to the 1958 Census: *Location of Manufacturing Plants by Industry, County, and Employment Size,* Washington, D.C., 1961. As the estimates never involved more than a minor portion of the total value added for any particular industry, the likely margins of error are small.

[37]*U.S. Census of Manufactures: 1958, Vol. 3, op. cit.;* and U.S. Bureau of the Census, *U.S. Census of Population: 1960, Vol. 1, Number of Inhabitants,* Washington, D.C., 1962.

[38]Chinitz, *op. cit.,* p. 95.

[39]Alexandersson, *op. cit.,* p. 86.

TABLE I General Characteristics of the United States' Highest-Value-Added Industries

S.I.C. number	Industry	Estimated % in the Manufacturing Belt—1958[a]	1961 Value added as a % of shipments	Value added 1961 ($1000)	Value of shipments 1961 ($1000)	Production workers' wages as a % of 1961 value added	All other payroll as a % of 1961 value added	No. of plants 1958
3492	Safes and vaults	96.6	70.8	49,240	69,546	24.8	16.1	33
3992	Furs, dressed and dyed	94.0	79.7	21,598	27,099	50.7	13.3	137
3545	Machine tool accessories	92.8	71.3	474,198	665,467	36.4	21.3	905
2834	Pharmaceutical preparations	91.1	71.6	2,219,227	2,919,568	10.1	14.5	1114
3262	Vitreous china food utensils	89.8	81.9	40,236	49,153	50.1	19.2	29
3421	Cutlery	88.8	73.6	159,740	217,051	23.2	14.3	183
3263	Earthenware food utensils	88.0	74.3	43,227	58,200	60.1	11.6	34
3671	Electron tubes receiving type	87.4	73.6	230,913	313,860	38.1	18.9	85
3544	Special dies and tools	87.3	74.7	876,309	1,173,450	51.9	16.5	5745
3565	Industrial patterns	87.1	80.3	85,457	106,360	57.5	11.6	1174
3229	Pressed and blown glass n.e.c.	87.1	72.7	425,338	584,751	36.2	8.6	140
2794	Electrotyping and stereotyping	86.6	76.8	60,099	78,244	53.6	20.1	226
2789	Bookbinding and related work	86.1	72.5	148,540	204,970	54.6	14.0	972
3572	Typewriters	85.2	72.4	195,834	270,535	34.8	13.1	18
2791	Typesetting	81.4	87.6	178,508	203,665	59.9	14.0	1188
3622	Industrial controls	81.3	70.8	388,269	548,322	27.3	22.2	216
2753	Engraving and plate printing	80.0	73.2	67,328	92,010	55.2	16.8	528
2793	Photoengraving	77.8	82.3	153,801	186,822	54.8	23.3	914
3471	Metal plating and polishing	73.8	72.2	330,903	458,609	48.7	11.9	2646
3259	Scructural clay products n.e.c.	58.4	71.2	107,411	150,080	46.4	12.9	193
2711	Newspapers	55.1	70.1	2,988,881	4,224,793	30.3	27.4	8250
3822	Automatic temperature controls	52.4	77.6	324,568	418,097	28.9	20.0	83
2097	Manufactured ice	28.4	72.9	100,195	137,422	26.8	21.3	1570

[a] Based on value added. See footnote 36.

Sources: *1961 Annual Survey of Manufactures; U. S. Census of Manufactures: 1958, Vol. II Industry Statistics,* and *Vol. III, Area Statistics;* and *Location of Manufacturing Plants by Industry, County, and Employment Size.*

these had more than 250 employees and 2104 of them employed less than 20 individuals. Plants existed in 46 of the 48 contiguous continued states, as well as in Washington, D.C., Charleston, West Virginia, was the only one of 55 S.M.S.A.s which had a 1960 population in excess of 300,000 and which did not have a metal plating and polishing establishment. Most smaller S.M.S.A.s, i.e., between 100,000 and 300,000 population, were also represented by the industry.[40] The industry's Census definition contributes somewhat to a clarification of this distribution: "This industry comprises establishments primarily engaged in all types of electroplating, plating, anodizing and coloring, and finishing of metals and formed products for the trade. Most of the work done in this industry is done on materials belonging to others."[41] Because this industry alters materials belonging to others,

[40]*Location of Manufacturing Plants by Industry, County, and Employment Size, Part 7, op. cit.,* pp. 83-86.
[41]*U.S. Census of Manufactures: 1958, Vol. 2, Part 2, op. cit.,* p. 34 D-3.

it is understandable that its national distribution should be more in accord with the distribution of manufacturing as a whole than is the case with some other high-value-added manufactures. On the other hand, it is perfectly logical that the demand for the services of a metalworking industry should be somewhat higher in the Manufacturing Belt than elsewhere in the country.

A fourth exception, the manufacture of automatic temperature controls, had only about 52.4 per cent of its value added in the Manufacturing Belt in 1958. Significantly, the largest portion of production occurring outside the Manufacturing Belt was concentrated in one location, the Minneapolis-St. Paul S.M.S.A., home of the Minneapolis Honeywell Regulator Company. It may be legitimately argued that such concentration *at a single point* beyond the traditional manufacturing area is the exception which proves the rule. The Honeywell Company began under very modest circumstances in 1885, and was apparently the first producer of heat furnace regulators in the country. Historical accident, and the accumulation of labor and management skills,[42] therefore largely account for a high percentage of this industry being located beyond the confines of the Manufacturing Belt. Furthermore, that more than one-half of the industry is yet found in the Manufacturing Belt perhaps bespeaks the strong affinity of high-value-added manufacturing for older industrial areas.

The fifth irregularity, which had 58.4 per cent of its value added in the Manufacturing Belt, is a catch-all category used by the Census — structural clay products, not elsewhere classified. This industry produces a wide range of goods, the most important of which are clay sewer pipe, drain tile, and terra cotta. The situation in this industry is somewhat analogous to that which has already been observed in the manufactured ice industry. The basic raw material is nearly ubiquitously distributed on a regional scale, if not on a local scale. In addition, most of the industry's products are either of low value per unit weight or incur high transport costs because of their fragility. In either case, the transportability of the products is limited and the tendency toward concentration is impeded. Consequently, the manufacture of clay pipe and tile products is scattered in rough proportion to the distribution of population, and, by inference, the distribution of construction activity.[43]

The sixth nonconforming industry, photoengraving, with 77.8 per cent of its 1958 value added in the Manufacturing Belt, was shy of the 80.0 per cent boundary by an even smaller amount than the metal plating and polishing industry. It would

[42]Availability of skilled labor is considered by some to be the dominant locational determinant of the automatic temperature controls industry. Lichtenberg, op. cit., p. 265.
[43]Alexandersson, op. cit., p. 60; and National Resources Planning Board, op. cit., p. 295.

be fruitless and foolhardy to seek any elaborate explanation for such a minor discrepancy and consequently, mention of the industry will be deferred until four other printing subcontracting industries are considered.

HIGH–VALUE–ADDED INDUSTRIES CONCENTRATED IN THE NEW YORK METROPOLITAN REGION

Obviously, the 17 highest-value-added industries which had 80.0 or more per cent of their 1958 value added in the Manufacturing Belt did not have identical patterns of distribution within that area. Most of the industries had rather localized distributions which evidenced a marked preference for either the Great Lakes or Megalopolitan portions of the Manufacturing Belt, or for a few of the Belt's major S.M.S.A.s.

Four printing subcontracting industries (engraving and plate printing, bookbinding and related work, typesetting, and electrotyping and stereotyping) and the above-mentioned photoengraving industry are all disproportionately concentrated in the New York Metropolitan Region. These industries are also strongly represented in Chicago, and are of varying importance in the Philadelphia, Boston, Detroit, and Cleveland metropolitan areas. In 1958, New York City and its environs accounted for 42.4 per cent of the nation's value added in the engraving and plate printing industry; and that same area had at least 27.4 per cent of the national total in each of the other printing subcontracting trades (Table II and Figs. 2–6).

The concentration of job printing in New York is very much a reflection of the city's position in the national and, in some respects, the world economy. "New York has become more and more of a national center, with increasing numbers of printing consumers coming into the city: advertising agencies (especially those specializing in

TABLE II Value Added in the Printing Subcontracting Industries: Percentages of 1958 U.S. Total

	Total six S.M.S.A.s	N.Y. S.M.S.A.	Chicago S.M.S.A.	Four other S.M.S.A.s[a]	Total Manufacturing Belt
Bookbinding and related work	70.6	41.4	15.1	14.1	86.1
Typesetting	61.5	30.0	15.1	16.4	81.4
Engraving and plate printing	60.9	42.4	7.7	10.8	80.0
Photoengraving	57.0	32.4	13.4	11.2	77.8
Electrotyping and stereotyping	56.0	27.4	15.5	13.1	86.6

[a] Philadelphia, Boston, Detroit, and Cleveland.
Source: U. S. Census of Manufactures: 1958, Vol. III, Area Statistics.

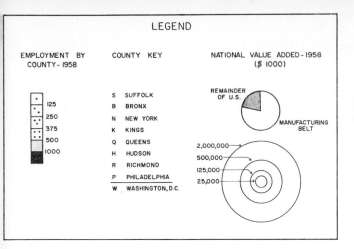

LEGEND

EMPLOYMENT BY COUNTY - 1958

125
250
375
500
1000

COUNTY KEY

S   SUFFOLK
B   BRONX
N   NEW YORK
K   KINGS
Q   QUEENS
H   HUDSON
R   RICHMOND
P   PHILADELPHIA
W   WASHINGTON, D.C.

NATIONAL VALUE ADDED - 1958
($ 1000)

REMAINDER OF U.S.

MANUFACTURING BELT

2,000,000
500,000
125,000
25,000

FIGURE 2   Legend for Maps of County Employment of Individual Industries. Employment is shown for the Manufacturing Belt only. In each case the proportional circle in the upper left-hand corner refers to national value added.

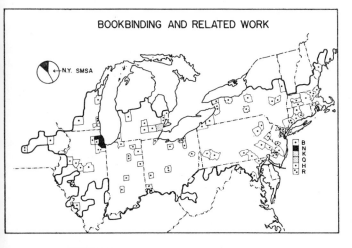

BOOKBINDING AND RELATED WORK

N.Y. SMSA

FIGURE 3

FIGURE 4

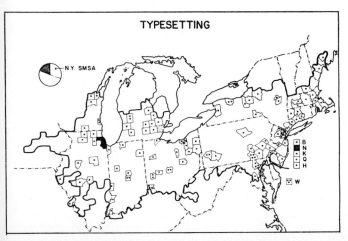

TYPESETTING

N.Y. SMSA

direct-mail and poster campaigns), head offices of corporations, legal firms, foundations, wholesalers, national associations of all sizes and varieties. All these contributors to New York's role as a headquarters city are constant purchasers of printing, much of it work which must be done in close conjunction with the originating office and to a fairly tight schedule."[44] The time pressures and the unstandardized nature of printed products forces the average establishment to remain small, for scale economies in these industries "arise not from the size of the establishment, beyond a relatively small size, but from the average number of copies produced on specific printing jobs."[45]

Printing subcontractors centralized in New York benefit from numerous external economies as well as from the tremendous demand generated in that metropolis. Proximity to paper suppliers eliminates the necessity of maintaining large inventories; the ready availability of repair and maintenance services for printing presses and miscellaneous equipment represents a considerable economy for small and medium-sized firms; and "random fluctuations in labor requirements can be met by drawing on the pool of skilled labor through the institutions maintained by unions and employer associations."[46] The importance of the last named economy is magnified considerably if one realizes the extent to which labor costs dominate the cost structure of these industries (Table I). In addition, postage and rail freight rates further reinforce New York's locational advantages. Much of the printed matter produced in New York is comprised of direct-mail advertising circulars. Postal regulations permit the mailing of bundles which weigh at least 20 pounds, or contain 200 items, throughout the country at a flat third-class rate. This means that there is no distributional cost advantage to be derived by printing the material elsewhere. Similarly, transport costs on raw material are no greater than at most alternative locations since the delivered price of paper is uniform in a broad belt which includes all states east of the Mississippi, except for those south of Tennessee and North Carolina.

The dressed and dyed fur industry is even more remarkably nucleated in the New York Metropolitan Region (Fig. 7). The processing of fur

---

[44]W. Eric Gustafson, "Printing and Publishing," in Max Hall, *edit., Made in New York*, Cambridge, Mass., 1959, p. 150.
[45]*Ibid.*, p. 165.
[46]*Ibid.*, p. 171.

goods in New York is inextricably related to that city's role as a fashion and wholesaling center. The industry, like the various job printing trades, is represented by a large number of small firms whose proximity to one another generates so-called "communication economies." "Tastes and fashions change rapidly in these communications-oriented industries, and to keep abreast of the market in terms of forthcoming fashions and contracts the manufacturers must be constantly on the alert and in touch with current developments. These imperatives require clustering, . . ."[47] For much the same reasons the British fur industry is highly localized in London. Transport costs on fur goods are inconsequential in terms of the value of the items involved, and consequently, New York has usurped a larger portion of the national market as freight transport has become speedier and more efficient.[48]

While the pharmaceutical preparations industry is also inordinately concentrated in the New York Metropolitan Region, as well as in adjacent portions of New Jersey and Pennsylvania (Fig. 8), its presence is not easily explained. Average wage levels in the drug industry are higher in the New York and Philadelphia areas than elsewhere in the country.[49] "Communication economies" and accessibility to scientific research talent are doubtlessly factors which contribute to an explanation of the industry's distribution; but these forces probably are subordinate in importance to those exerted by inertia. The cost structure of drug manufacture (Table I) and the high value of pharmaceuticals in relation to their weight theoretically permit the industry to locate as economically in one area as another.[50] The early start of drug production in New York and Philadelphia has perpetuated the dominance of those centers, although several other cities in the Manufacturing Belt now have a considerable output.

HIGH–VALUE–ADDED INDUSTRIES CONCENTRATED IN OTHER PORTIONS OF THE MANUFACTURING BELT

Unlike the industries discussed above, the manufacture of electron receiving tubes was once largely centered in the vicinity of New York, but has since become somewhat more dispersed (Fig. 9). "The work of inventors like de Forest and

[47]Jean Gottmann: *Megalopolis,* New York, 1961, p. 491.
[48]Chinitz, *op. cit.,* p. 127.
[49]Segal, *op. cit.,* p. 78.
[50]Lichtenberg, *op. cit.,* p. 40.

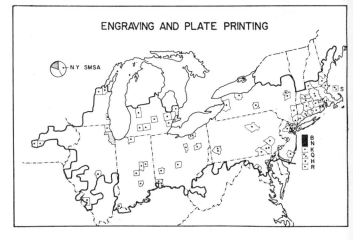

FIGURE 5

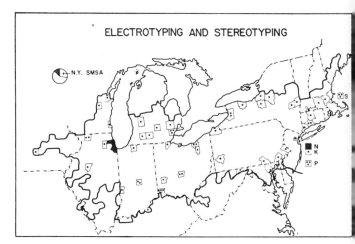

FIGURE 6

FIGURE 7

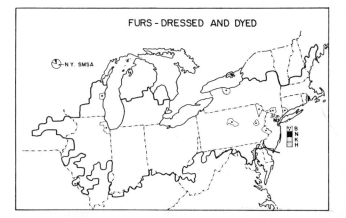

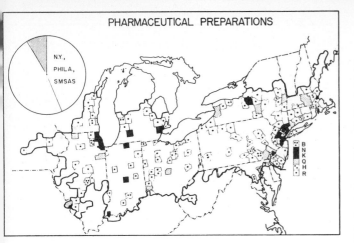

PHARMACEUTICAL PREPARATIONS

N.Y.,
PHILA,
SMSAS

B N K Q H R

FIGURE 8

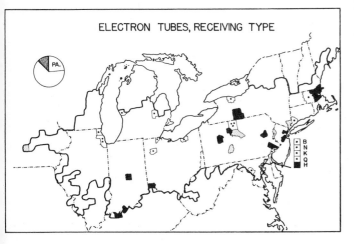

ELECTRON TUBES, RECEIVING TYPE

PA.

B N K Q H

FIGURE 9

FIGURE 10

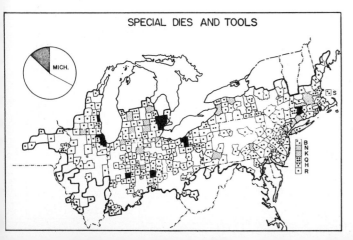

SPECIAL DIES AND TOOLS

MICH.

S

B N K Q H R

Edison, carried on in the New York Metropolitan Region where there was a concentrated market in which to test, manufacture and sell their inventions, helped to establish the Region as of prime importance in the (electronics) industry."[51] As early as 1912 the Western Electric Company was manufacturing tubes in Manhattan. By the 1930s the technology of tube production had been vastly improved upon, and true assembly-line production was feasible. As raw material assembly and product distribution costs were insubstantial, and as plant operations were repetitive and dull but demanding of manual dexterity and alertness, the manufacturers began seeking low-wage areas with surplus female labor. Thus it was, for example, that Emporium, Pennsylvania, became the site of Sylvania's principal receiving tube factory, and Horseheads and Bath, New York, became the locations for expanded production by Westinghouse. Labor conditions also attracted the industry to eastern Massachusetts and Pennsylvania's anthracite mining district.[52] Despite the commencement of production in Alabama and Oklahoma, 87.4 per cent of the industry's value added remained in the Manufacturing Belt in 1958.

The production of special dies and tools, machine tool accessories, and industrial patterns within the Manufacturing Belt is most pronounced in the Great Lakes states, especially around Detroit, Chicago, and Cleveland, although a not inconsiderable percentage of the output remains anchored in New England and the New York Metropolitan Region (Figs. 10–12). In each of these industries the availability of skilled labor is a crucial locational determinant; while, at the same time, wage levels are relatively insignificant in the locational calculus.[53] Despite the fact that the industries are basically insensitive to transport costs, they are very much market oriented, i.e., oriented toward the major centers of automobile and machinery production. Machinery and motor vehicle manufacture began attracting these industries to the Midwest at the end of the nineteenth century, and for the past 60 years the automobile industry has been the largest consumer of machine tools.[54] Since

[51]James M. Hund, "Electronics," in Hall, *op. cit.*, p. 255.
[52]*Ibid.*, pp. 278-287.
[53]This is partly so because: "Interregional or intercity differences in wages of skilled workers are considerably smaller than differences in wages of semiskilled or common labor." Segal, *op. cit.*, p. 21.
[54]See for example Victor S. Clark: *History of Manufactures in the United States*, Vol. 3, New York, 1929, pp. 153-154;

the industries are predominantly composed of small job order shops, concentration of firms at a market location affords sundry external economies. The making of repairs and replacements is greatly facilitated; rush orders are more easily fulfilled within the requisite time; large orders may be subcontracted or the number of employees temporarily expanded; and the diffusion of style changes and technical innovations is hastened. Accessibility to special steels apparently further strengthens the locational advantages of Midwestern industrial cities.

Firms manufacturing motor starters and other electrical controls of industrial machinery are also of greatest frequency in the Great Lakes states. Southeastern Wisconsin alone had 46.5 per cent of the nation's value added in the industrial controls industry in 1958 (Fig. 13). This extreme concentration is again in part associated with the distribution of machinery production, and, in fact, some industrial control equipment is sold in conjunction with motors and other related equipment.[55] However, the market factor should not be exaggerated, particularly in the case of Milwaukee, where much of the industry's output enters international trade,[56] and where the advantages of an early start have been pyramided into a commanding dominance of the industry. (For some time prior to World War I Milwaukee was the center for the production of such diverse items as electrical control systems for elevators, devices to stop and control printing presses, and controls for ore unloaders, drawbridges, stagelights, and revolving battleship turrets.)[57]

The safe and vault industry represents an archetypal example of concentration (Fig. 14). Two Ohio cities, Hamilton and Canton, completely dominate the industry. Almost one-half of the world's safes and bank vaults are made in Hamilton's two factories.[58] Such a localized distribution is to be expected in an industry where sizable production economies are feasible only when operations are performed on a large-scale, and where the market, even at an international level, is of

Robert Gold: *Manufacturing Structure and Pattern of the South Bend–Mishawaka Area,* Chicago, 1954, pp. 113-114; and E. Willard Miller: *A Geography of Manufacturing,* Englewood Cliffs, 1962, pp. 343-345.
    [55]Jules Backman: *The Economics of the Electrical Machinery Industry,* New York, 1962, p. 70.
    [56]Edward Hamming: *The Port of Milwaukee,* Chicago, 1952, p. 62.
    [57]*Gear Shifting by Electricity,* Milwaukee, 1914, p. 31 ff.
    [58]Donald J. Bogue and Calvin L. Beale: *Economic Areas of the United States,* New York, 1961, p. 930.

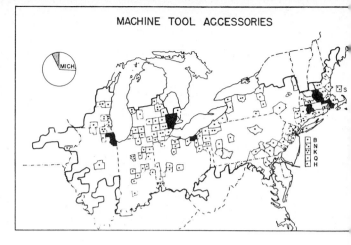

MACHINE TOOL ACCESSORIES

FIGURE 11

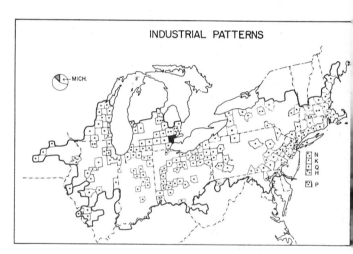

INDUSTRIAL PATTERNS

FIGURE 12

FIGURE 13

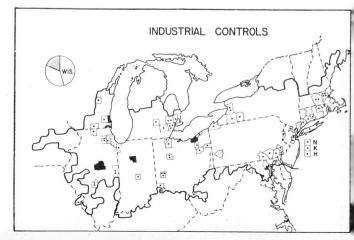

INDUSTRIAL CONTROLS

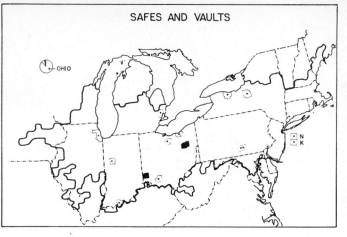

FIGURE 14

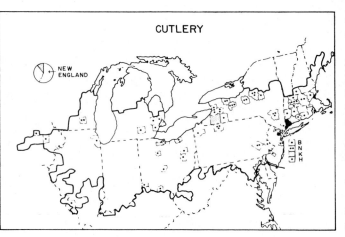

FIGURE 15

FIGURE 16

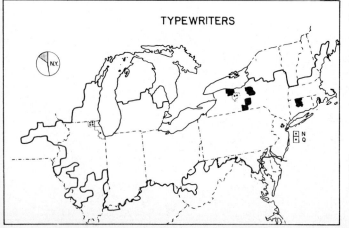

limited dimensions. Hamilton and Canton have the particular advantages of low transport costs to the national market and accessibility to locally produced steel. In view of the high freight rates which must be imposed on the industry's bulky and cumbersome products, the former advantage is of overriding importance.

Two other metal consuming industries, cutlery and typewriter production, are not influenced by transport costs in the same manner. Both manufactures show a distinct preference for upper New York State and southern New England (see Figs. 15 and 16). That these two areas supersede others within the Manufacturing Belt is to a large degree a function of historical inertia, for from a purely economic standpoint these industries are "footloose," i.e., the profitability of their operations is theoretically not greatly influenced by geographic location. In the case of the cutlery industry, labor and managerial skills have been accumulating in such places as Boston and New Haven County for more than a century. Cutlery manufacturing remains concentrated in these early centers, and has not been influenced by the growth of markets farther west, because the cost of the raw materials and of freight upon materials and products is a relatively small fraction of the selling price of the finished goods. The same general comment can be made in regard to the material and transport costs of the typewriter industry. In 1873, C. S. Sholes and his associates successfully completed experiments for the use of automatic machinery and interchangeable parts in the manufacture of typewriters. The willingness of the Remington Corporation—then operating an armory in Ilion, New York—to implement Shole's innovations led to an amassing of skills and a perpetuation of the industry in upstate New York.[59] Production is restricted to a few large establishments because distinctly higher per unit production costs would prevail in factories which operated at even half the optimal plant scale.[60]

The three remaining industries, pressed and blown glass not elsewhere classified, vitreous china food utensils, and earthenware food utensils, are to varying degrees concentrated in western Pennsylvania, Ohio and adjacent portions of West Virginia

[59]Clark, op. cit., Vol. 2, p. 362.
[60]Joe S. Bain: "Economies of Scale, Concentration, and the Condition of Entry in Twenty Manufacturing Industries," American Econ. Rev., Vol. 44, 1954, p. 25. Apparently, the economies of large plant operation provide "a very significant deterrent" to small-scale entry into the typewriter market.

(Figs. 17—19). The pressed and blown glass category includes cheaper glassware for electrical and lighting purposes. The manufacture of cheaper glass products has developed in the upper Ohio River Valley since the mid-nineteenth century because of the coincident location of fuels, i.e., coal and gas, and glass sands.[61] More recently the availability of pipeline gas, and a favorable location with respect to accessibility to the national market, have reinforced the area's early advantages. The pressed and blown glass industry also includes the production of tumblers, goblets and other stemware, as well as ornamental and decorative glassware. The production of these latter commodities, which is greatly dependent upon skilled labor, is most notably centered in Steuben County, New York. Over the long-run, the upper Ohio River Valley has also proved to be well suited to the vitreous and earthenware food utensils industries because of the availability of natural gas and the relative cheapness of national distribution. Production in New Jersey is also of early origin, and is oriented toward imported high-quality clays.

Summary

This cursory treatment of the locational characteristics of 23 industries substantially confirms the hypothesis that high-value-added manufacturing should be concentrated in older industrial regions. But, it is also evident that the mere founding of a high-value-added industry in an area such as the Manufacturing Belt does not guarantee an immobilized and ossified distribution for the future. The resolution of forces which does or does not create a concentrated pattern for specific high-value-added industries can be overwhelmingly and monumentally complex. The self-perpetuating momentum, accumulation of skills, and general transportability of products which favors older areas is counteracted by regional population growth and the attainment of scale thresholds, the standardization of production processes, and the occasional intransportability of products. Historical accident further obfuscates matters; e.g., the typewriter industry in upstate New York substantiates the hypothesis, while the automatic temperature controls industry in Minneapolis does not. Raw

[61]Pearce Davis: *The Development of the American Glass Industry*, Cambridge, Mass., 1949, pp. 43, 74, and 123-125.

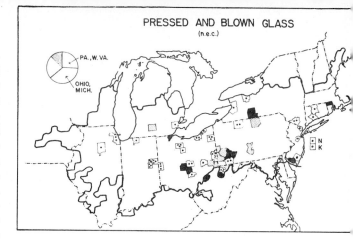

FIGURE 17

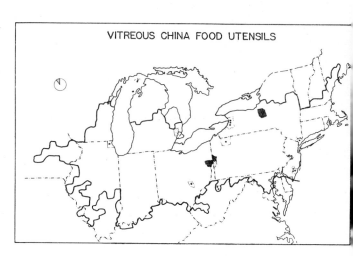

FIGURE 18

FIGURE 19

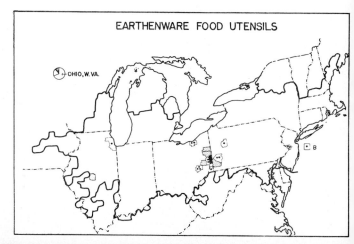

material considerations also exert some influence; e.g., the localization of most pressed and blown glassware production in southwestern Pennsylvania, Ohio, and West Virginia. Further complications arise because the intangibles of political and cultural tradition can precipitate anomalous distributions, as in the case of newspaper publication.

The imperfections of the hypothesis are self-evident, but the constraints placed on it help explain most of the exceptions found in the United States. The hypothesis obviously does not illuminate or clarify the reasons behind the wide variety of distributions within the Manufacturing Belt. Furthermore, since high-value-added characteristics are not the sole inducer of concentrated industrial patterns, it may be legitimately asked whether or not any of the high-value-added industries concentrated in the Manufacturing Belt are in reality centralized by factors completely anathema to those discussed here. A confession of this possibility is merely a reiteration of the labyrinthal intricacies underlying industrial distributions. There is no single touchstone capable of intelligibly and precisely explaining industrial concentration.

Walter Isard and John H. Cumberland

NEW ENGLAND AS A POSSIBLE LOCATION FOR AN INTEGRATED IRON AND STEEL WORKS

Historically the location of iron and steel industries has been crucial in both regional political status and economic welfare. This, plus the fact that in the last century the strategy of iron and steel location has been a highly dynamic one, makes a study of the industry's spatial character both significant and timely.

Considerable speculation has centered upon the possibility of a New England location. Although in the past the various locational factors have effectively ruled out New England as a steel center, their relative strengths have altered greatly. It is relevant to inquire whether the region may now qualify as a potential location for iron and steel production. We first indicate briefly the pertinent locational factors and present some historical background.

Historical Aspects of Location

Iron and steel is primarily a transport-oriented industry. Although the costs of labor, raw materials at the source, power, and other items are significant, the differentials between possible steel producing regions with respect to these items are small compared to differentials in transport costs on raw materials and finished products which these regions incur. To be sure water, site and other conditions may be decisive when it comes to choosing the best site within a given region, but in

this paper we shall emphasize general regional forces.

Historically, the major advances in modern iron and steel technology have resulted in fuel economy. When in the mid-eighteenth century about eight to ten tons of coal were required per ton of pig iron, without question the industry was oriented towards coal sites. It was more economical to move two to three tons of ore to the coal site and the pig to the market than to move coal to the ore site or to the market. As late as the middle of the nineteenth century the pull of coal sites on steel and wrought iron production was still overwhelmingly dominant. For though coal per ton of pig had been cut to two and a half tons, at least as much more was required for converting the pig to steel or wrought iron. However, during the latter half of the nineteenth century, coal lost its dominance, owing to still greater economies in the blast furnace and elsewhere. By 1939 coal requirements had fallen to one and a half tons per ton of finished steel. This remarkable technological achievement explains the attenuation of the pull of coal sites in steel production.

At least two other interrelated factors affected the play of locational forces. One was the increasing use of scrap as a substitute for pig iron in steel production. This has of course been partially responsible for the fall in coal requirements cited above, for less coal is required in the open hearth furnace for melting scrap than in the blast furnace for reducing ore. At the same time this increase in scrap utilization implies the use of less ore. Thus we can easily understand why ore consumed per ton of semifinished iron and steel in the United States fell nearly one-half from 1900 to 1935; from

Reprinted with the permission of the authors and publisher from *Economic Geography*, Vol. 26, No. 4, 1950, pp. 245-59. Dr. Isard is Chairman of the Department of Regional Science at the University of Pennsylvania, Philadelphia; Dr. Cumberland is Professor of Economics at the University of Maryland, College Park.

1.83 tons to less than a ton. However, owing to large recent increases in steel production and other factors, somewhat less scrap and more ore is being used than in 1935.

The use of scrap, therefore, has greatly diminished the pull of both coal and ore sites. But the use of scrap has worked in still another direction. It has increased the attraction of a market location, especially an old established one. In the nineteenth century when relatively little scrap was used, location away from the market necessitated transporting the finished steel to the market. But now location away from the market usually entails the added transportation of scrap to the production site. When, as is often the case, the production site, e.g., Pittsburgh, does generate scrap, but not in sufficient quantity to meet all of its production needs, scrap must be imported. Location at an old established market, such as New England, thus implies a minimum of scrap transportation.

The other development to be considered is also related to fuel economies. In order to utilize blast furnace and coke oven gases and to avoid excessive cooling and reheating of materials, the blast furnaces, open hearths, and converters have had to be increased in size and closely integrated with rolling mills. Thus today an iron and steel market location necessitates a market large enough to absorb the output of a works of the size required to achieve most of the economies of integration.

In sum, considering the facts that (a) in 1939, approximately 1.4 tons of ore and 1.3 tons of coal were required per ton of finished steel, where Lake Superior ores were employed, (b) transport rates on finished steel are significantly higher than on ore and coal, and (c) approximately one-third of a ton of purchased scrap is required on the average per ton of finished steel, it is apparent that the strongest locational pull is that of an established market (where it is of sufficient size), even though the pull of the market is not yet completely dominant.

Present trends toward (1) beneficiation and purification of ores at the mine, permitting lower transport costs; (2) mounting accumulation of scrap in older market areas; (3) technological advances permitting fuel economies both from the use of oxygen and of enriched air in the blast furnace, open hearth, and converter and the use of high pressures; and (4) continuing development of techniques which permit the use of a greater variety of types of coal, thus tending to make coal less localized and more ubiquitous—all point to an increasing relative strength of the market pull.[1]

Transport Costs

Let us examine New England as a potential steel producer. The region has a long established industrial market and generates considerable scrap. A location here would enjoy relatively low transport costs on finished steel in serving the local market and in transporting purchased scrap. The major competing production points will not be located close to both coal and ore, but to just one of these raw materials, or at intermediate junctions. Some will and some will not be within surplus scrap areas. Thus, none of these points, including a New England location, will exhibit a composite pull of overwhelming dominance. The problem is this: Should New England be served by a production point within the market, near coal deposits, near ore deposits, or intermediate between the three? Looking at the historical picture and trends, one is tempted to maintain that since the pull of the market seems to have grown stronger than that of either coal or ore, New England should be served by a New England producer. However, we reserve judgment until we examine in some detail vital aspects of the New England market and of steel production costs.

Table I presents, for several actual and hypothetical production points, data on transport costs on raw materials and finished product for serving Worcester, a major consuming point in New England. Sparrows Point, Buffalo, Bethlehem, Pittsburgh, and Cleveland are existing major production points best located with respect to the New England market. Fall River and New London are hypothetical production points, each of which has been proposed by its respective state as the best production point for serving New England. For a thorough analysis, we must compare the advantages at hypothetical New England points not only with those at the better located existing production

[1]W. Isard, "Some Locational Factors in the Iron and Steel Industry since the Early Nineteenth Century," *Journ. of Polit. Economy*, Vol. LVI, 1948, pp. 203-217; W. Isard and W. M. Capron, "The Future Locational Pattern of Iron and Steel Production in the United States," *Journ. of Polit. Economy*, Vol. LVII, 1949, pp. 118-133.

FIGURE 1 Northeastern United States, Showing Urban Centers Mentioned in Article as well as all Principal Cities.

points, but also with those at the better hypothetical sites outside New England. For this reason we include Trenton, a strategic transport junction with respect to the rich Venezuela ores on the one hand, and the major eastern seaboard market on the other. The United States Steel Corporation has already announced plans to construct an integrated works of two million tons ingot capacity on a Delaware River site immediately below Trenton.

Considering the recent Labrador and Venezuela ore discoveries,[2] it does not seem unreasonable to assume that foreign ore of high quality will be available for New England. We have posited that ore for New England comes by rail and water from Labrador or Venezuela, and coal from West Virginia and east Kentucky by rail to Norfolk and water to New England.

Bearing in mind that the steel industry is transport oriented, that the major cost differentials among various sites involved in serving a given market are transport cost differentials, we see from Table I that New England locations such as Fall River and New London are best suited to serve the Worcester market (provided of course that the size of the New England market is adequate). Their transport costs on Venezuela ore, coal, and finished steel amount to $14.31 and $14.90 respectively, below those for Trenton and Buffalo and well below those for Pittsburgh and Cleveland. Tables II and III showing transport costs of various production points for serving Boston and Providence again testify to the transport advantages of Fall River and New London. Trenton and Buffalo offer the strongest competition.

When, however, we consider the markets of Hartford (Table IV), and especially New Haven (Table V), the transport advantages of Fall River and New London diminish noticeably. For serving

[2]W. M. Goodwin, "Labrador Iron Ore," *Bureau of Mines,* Ottawa, 1949; T. W. Lippert, "Cerro Bolivar," *Journ. of Metals and Min. Eng.,* Vol. 187; B. Packard, "San Isidoro—More Iron Ore in Venezuela," *Iron Age,* Vol. 165, 1950, p. 107.

TABLE I   Transportation Costs on Ore and Coal Required Per Net Ton of Steel and on Finished Products for Selected Actual and Hypothetical Producing Locations Serving

WORCESTER

Location	Transportation Costs On			Total
	Ore	Coal	Finished Products	
Fall River ⌠ Labrador	$4.56	$6.01	$ 5.00	$15.57
⌡ Venezuela	3.68	5.63	5.00	14.31
New London ⌠ Labrador	4.56	5.79	5.80	16.15
⌡ Venezuela	3.68	5.42	5.80	14.90
Pittsburgh	5.55	1.56	15.00	22.11
Cleveland	3.16	3.85	15.00	22.01
Sparrows Point	4.73	4.26	11.60	20.59
Buffalo	3.16	4.27	12.40	19.83
Bethlehem	5.56	5.06	10.20	20.82
Trenton	3.68	4.65	9.60	17.93

Sources: We have based our computations upon the following requirements of coal and ore per ton finished steel: for points using Lake Superior ores, 1.42 tons of ore and 1.32 tons of coal; for points using Labrador ore, 1.36 tons of ore and 1.28 tons of coal; for points using Venezuela ore, 1.23 tons of ore and 1.20 tons of coal; and for Sparrows Point using Chile ore, 1.26 tons of ore and 1.22 tons of coal.   These estimated requirements are based upon: W. A. Haven, "The Manufacture of Pig Iron in America," Journal of the Iron and Steel Institute, Vol. CXLI, 1940, pp. 442—46, 457—58; U. S. Bureau of Mines, Minerals Yearbook, 1940, p. 895; W. Isard and W. M. Capron, "The Future Locational Pattern of Iron and Steel Production in the United States," Journal of Political Economy, Vol. LVII, April 1949, pp. 120—22; and T. W. Lippert, "Cerro Bolivar," Journal of Metals and Mining Engineering, Vol. 187, February 1950, p. 132.
Iron content of Lake Superior, Labrador, Chile and Venezuela ores has been taken at 51.1, 53.4, 57.8 and 59.0 per cent respectively.
Transportation costs on finished products refer to rail movement.   Those on ore and coal to actual production points refer to the existing rail-water routes employed.   Those on ore and coal to hypothetical production points refer to rail-water routes as indicated below or as already indicated in text.   Coal to Trenton is assumed to move by rail.
Domestic ore transportation costs are based upon figures from U. S. General Services Administration, Bureau of Federal Supply, and upon A. H. Hubbell, Engineering and Mining Journal, Vol. 150, April 1949, p. 87.   Ore transportation costs on Labrador ore for New England are based upon our estimates of $2.00 per gross ton for the 360 mile rail haul from Knob Lake, Labrador to the deepwater port at Seven Islands and $1.75 per gross ton from Seven Islands by ship to New England.   With respect to Venezuela ores, we estimate the cost of rail transport from Cerro Bolivar to Barcelona (274 miles) to be $1.35 per gross ton and the cost of water transport from Barcelona to Trenton or New London or Fall River to be $2.00 per gross ton.   The transport cost on Venezuela ore ought not to be markedly different if either of the alternate rail-water routes from Cerro Bolivar to the Gulfo de Paria are developed.   Ore transportation costs to Bethlehem, Pa., are based upon use of Cornwall and Lake Superior ores in the ratio of 1:3 (in rough accord with 1949 consumption).   Ore transportation costs to Sparrows Point are 1939 figures for Chilean ores (U. S. Transportation Investigation and Research Board, "The Economics of Iron and Steel Transportation," Washington, 1945, Tables 26, 33 and 43).   If Sparrows Point shifts to Venezuela ore, deposits of which are controlled by Bethlehem Steel, the relevant figure should be roughly comparable with Trenton's.
Coal rates are from the National Coal Association and are weighted 80—20 between high and low volatile.   Rates on finished products are from the U. S General Services Administration, Bureau of Federal Supply, and from estimates of the Freight Rate Department, New York, New Haven and Hartford Railroad.

New Haven, Trenton's $15.73 is well under Fall River's $17.31 and not too far above New London's $13.90. Clearly Trenton and Bethlehem have strong competitive positions with respect to the southern and western parts of the New England market. But a few qualifications are in order.

Bethlehem, as all other production points utilizing Lake Superior ores, faces rising ore costs owing to the impending depletion of higher-grade open-pit domestic ore sources. Though processes to utilize taconite and intermediate ores may prove feasible, in all probability operating costs for blast furnaces smelting Lake Superior materials will be noticeably higher.[3] In addition, taxes in Minnesota are ad valorem at the rate of 12 per cent whereas agreements with appropriate Canadian

provincial governments indicate taxation and royalty payments at a much more modest rate. Nor is there any precedent for heavy iron ore taxation in South America.[4] Thus it seems likely that at the mine the effective cost (including taxes and royalties) of Labrador or Venezuela ores will be at least as low as and probably lower than the effective cost of Lake Superior ores. (We speak here of effective costs as actual costs per ton of ore adjusted for iron content as well as coke requirements for smelting. Thus our statement is not inconsistent with lower actual per ton costs for Lake Superior ores.) This then would give New England coastal points an advantage over Bethlehem (as well as over other points using Lake Superior ores) not shown in the tables.

[3]W. A. Lloyd, "Iron Ore," Iron Age, Vol. 163, 1949, pp. 229-238.

[4]"Tax Systems of the World, 1950," Commerce Clearing House, Inc., New York, 1950, pp. 75, 401.

TABLE II Transportation Costs on Ore and Coal Required Per Net Ton of Steel and on Finished Products for Selected Actual and Hypothetical Producing Locations Serving

BOSTON

Location	Transportation Costs On			Total
	Ore	Coal	Finished Products	
Fall River ⎰ Labrador	$4.56	$6.01	$ 4.60	$15.17
⎱ Venezuela	3.68	5.63	4.60	13.91
New London ⎰ Labrador	4.56	5.79	6.80	17.15
⎱ Venezuela	3.68	5.42	6.80	15.90
Pittsburgh	5.55	1.56	15.20	22.31
Cleveland	3.16	3.85	15.20	22.21
Sparrows Point	4.73	4.26	12.40	21.39
Buffalo	3.16	4.27	12.60	20.03
Bethlehem	5.56	5.06	10.60	21.22
Trenton	3.68	4.65	10.40	18.73

Source: See Table I.

TABLE III Transportation Costs on Ore and Coal Required Per Net Ton of Steel and on Finished Products for Selected Actual and Hypothetical Producing Locations Serving

PROVIDENCE

Location	Transportation Costs On			Total
	Ore	Coal	Finished Products	
Fall River ⎰ Labrador	$4.56	$6.01	$ 3.60	$14.17
⎱ Venezuela	3.68	5.63	3.60	12.91
New London ⎰ Labrador	4.56	5.79	5.00	15.35
Venezuela	3.68	5.42	5.00	14.10
Pittsburgh	5.55	1.56	15.20	22.31
Cleveland	3.16	3.85	15.20	22.21
Sparrows Point	4.73	4.26	12.20	21.19
Buffalo	3.16	4.27	13.40	20.83
Bethlehem	5.56	5.06	10.40	21.02
Trenton	3.68	4.65	9.60	17.93

Source: See Table I.

Further, part of Bethlehem's advantage is due to low transport cost on near-by Pennsylvania ores, the deposits of which are limited and could not well support expansion at Bethlehem.[5] Moreover, Bethlehem does not produce items which New England normally consumes in large quantities; and Bethlehem's production essentially is and logically ought to be oriented toward the New York City market.

Trenton, on the other hand, would not be confronted by these difficulties. In fact, should New England smelt Labrador ore, perhaps because the pattern of intercompany control of ore resources forces her to, Trenton, in smelting Venezuela ore, might have certain advantages. Venezuela ore, already estimated at well in excess of 1 billion tons, is considerably richer than Labrador ore, though it contains considerably less manganese. In all likelihood, Venezuela ore will require less coke for smelting and be more easily mined owing to more clement climatic conditions. Only

[5] H. M. Mikami, "World Iron-Ore Map," *Economic Geology*, Vol. XXIX, 1944, p. 5.

TABLE IV Transportation Costs on Ore and Coal Required Per Net Ton of Steel and on Finished Products for Selected Actual and Hypothetical Producing Locations Serving

HARTFORD

Location	Transportation Costs On			Total
	Ore	Coal	Finished Products	
Fall River⌠Labrador	$4.56	$6.01	$ 6.80	$17.37
⌡Venezuela	3.68	5.63	6.80	16.11
New London⌠Labrador	4.56	5.79	5.00	15.35
⌡Venezuela	3.68	5.42	5.00	14.10
Pittsburgh	5.55	1.56	14.00	21.11
Cleveland	3.16	3.85	14.40	21.41
Sparrows Point	4.73	4.26	10.60	19.55
Buffalo	3.16	4.27	12.20	19.63
Bethlehem	5.56	5.06	8.60	19.22
Trenton	3.68	4.65	8.40	16.73

Sourc: See Table 1.

TABLE V Transportation Costs on Ore and Coal Required Per Net Ton of Steel and on Finished Products for Selected Actual and Hypothetical Producing Locations Serving

NEW HAVEN

Location	Transportation Costs On			Total
	Ore	Coal	Finished Products	
Fall River⌠Labrador	$4.56	$6.01	$ 8.00	$18.57
⌡Venezuela	3.68	5.63	8.00	17.31
New London⌠Labrador	4.56	5.79	4.80	15.15
⌡Venezuela	3.68	5.42	4.80	13.90
Pittsburgh	5.55	1.56	13.60	20.71
Cleveland	3.16	3.85	14.40	21.41
Sparrows Point	4.73	4.26	10.20	19.19
Buffalo	3.16	4.27	12.20	19.63
Bethlehem	5.56	5.06	8.40	19.02
Trenton	3.68	4.65	7.40	15.73

Source: See Table 1.

a season of six to seven months of open-pit mining can reasonably be expected at Labrador, and the water shipping season will be much shorter than the ten months during which the port of Seven Islands is ice-free.[6] Thus the effective costs of Venezuela ore may be lower than Labrador ore. In addition there would result a decrease in New London's transport cost advantage over Trenton and an increase of Trenton's advantage over Fall River in serving New Haven and more southerly points. In short, the competitive position of Trenton in the lower and western New England market would undoubtedly be strong.

We have used rail rates in computing costs of transport on finished products. The picture is changed only slightly when we consider highway and water movement. Comparative rail and motor carrier rates are presented in Table VI. Motor carrier rates tend, though irregularly so, to be somewhat below rail rates. But only with respect to the Boston, Providence, and Worcester markets does

[6]N. B. Melcher, "Quebec-Labrador as a Future Supply of Iron Ore for the United States," U. S. Bureau of Mines, *Mineral Trade Notes*, October, 1948, pp.8-10.

TABLE VI Comparative Rail and Motor Carrier Rates, Cents Per 100 Lbs.[a]

FROM:	Fall River		New London		Trenton		Sparrows Point		Bethlehem		Buffalo	
	Rail	Highway	Rail	Highway	Rail	Highway	Rail	Highway	Rail	Highway	Rail	Highway
TO:												
Boston	23	23	34	33	52	48	62	84	53	50	63	85
Worcester	25	24	29	28	48	45	58	57	51	48	62	57
Providence	18	19	25	25	48	46	61	57	52	48	67	85
Hartford	34	33	25	22	42	39	53	52	43	42	61	55
New Haven	40	39	24	23	37	36	51	50	42	39	61	57
New York	52	53	44	42	24[c]	28[b]	42	44[b]	29	32[b]	58	55[b]

Sources: Correspondence with U. S. General Services Administration, Bureau of Federal Supply; New York, New Haven and Hartford Railroad Co., Freight Traffic Department; Middle Atlantic States Motor Carrier Conference, Inc.; and the New England Motor Rate Bureau, Inc.
[a] Motor carrier rates from New England points are for a minimum of 20,000 lbs.; and from other points, 23,000 lbs. Rail rates are for a minimum of 40,000 lbs.
[b] New York, Zone 1.
[c] Harlem River.

highway transport offer a greater saving for actual and potential non-New England production points than for potential New England production points.

Owing to expensive port and handling charges, water shipments of steel along the New England coast are relatively negligible. For example, in 1939 coastwise receipts at the Port of Boston amounted to 11,230 tons of iron or steel plates and goods and, in 1947, to 8,803 tons of an approximately comparable category.[7] When we recognize that (1) one of the best points in New England to serve by coastal water shipments should be the Boston area because it is farther from Sparrows Point than any other major New England consumption point upon the seaboard, and (2) according to the *Iron Age* study, consumption of the Boston area comprises one-fifth of New England's, it does not seem that any major domestic movement of steel by water along the New England and Middle Atlantic coasts is to be expected in the near future.

Other Costs

Though differentials among regions with respect to other cost items are usually unimportant, except for scrap, nonetheless it is helpful to touch upon them briefly. The supplies of limestone for a New England steel operation seem to be ample and excellent in quality. For example a broad belt of limestone extends from Vermont through western Massachusetts down into northwestern Connecticut, with a number of deposits in excess of 95 per cent, and reaching as high as 98 per cent, purity.[8] Though deposits are not immediately adjacent to New London and Fall River, this should not impose a major disadvantage.

In regard to coal prices at the mine, a factor which was not considered in the computation of our tables, differentials are minor. The National Coal Association reports a maximum spread of 15 cents per net ton between mine prices of coal in West Virginia and Pennsylvania for low volatile coal and 25 cents for high volatile.

Although labor costs form a high percentage of total costs in iron and steel, labor cost differentials among firms and regions can be ignored as a locational influence. The industry is highly unionized; and the Labor Department has largely accepted union wage scales in setting the minimum wage scale which a company must observe to qualify to sell steel to the government under the Walsh-Healy Public Contracts Act. For example, a laborer in the lowest job classification is paid $1.18½ per hour by all major firms, except in the South, where a differential of 14½c. per hour exists which equalizes effectively the efficiency wages of Southern and other workers.[9]

With respect to land and related factors, our three hypothetical sites are reported to possess ap-

---

[7] *Annual Report of the Office of Engineers, U. S. Army*, 1940 and 1948, "Commercial Statistics," Part 2, p. 80 and p. 40 respectively.

[8] "Limestone—Massachusetts and Connecticut," memorandum of the Department of Industrial Development, New York, New Haven and Hartford Railroad Company.
[9] U. S. Department of Labor, Title 41—Public Contracts, Chap. II, Part 202, p. 1; and "Wage Chronology No. 3: United States Steel Corp., 1937-48," *Monthly Labor Review*, Vol. 68, pp. 194-200.

propriate geological substructures, sufficient flat terrain and adequate potable and industrial water. Existing state and Army engineering plans call for the deepening and improvement of the relevant water channels of these sites, which would permit the development of extensive waterfront facilities. New England's disadvantage for the generation of power and the procurement of fuel oil is already embodied in our assumptions concerning the utilization of coking-oven and blast furnace gases, and in the data in our tables on coal consumption and transport costs.

Taxes are a critical element. Rates vary considerably from state to state as well as from locality to locality within a state. In addition assessments are notoriously arbitrary and without doubt concessions will be offered by various local and state authorities. As of fiscal 1948 local property tax rates were 35 mills for Freetown (Fall River), 35 mills for New London and around a minimum of 30 mills for Bucks County, Pa. (Trenton). Corporate income taxes amounted to roughly 6 per cent for Massachusetts, 3 per cent for Connecticut, and 4 per cent for Pennsylvania which also levied capital stock and franchise taxes of 5 mills.[10] Perusal of these figures, however, gives little insight into what total tax burden might actually be. In light of the factors cited as well as numerous others, any estimate of relative tax burdens must be considered little more than speculation at this point.

Scrap Prices

A vital consideration we cannot ignore is scrap costs. However, the derivation of transport costs on scrap is a complex matter. Unlike other steel raw materials, whose sources may be considered as geographical points for location analysis, scrap is supplied from a large area. The scrap going into a ton of steel may come from several different points at different rates. Thus we have to rely upon analyses of scrap prices. Because of their sensitivity to changing geographic supplies and demands for scrap, the market prices for scrap at various points

reflect not only scrap resources of immediately surrounding areas, but also costs of transportation from surplus areas.

As of March 2, 1950, the price of number 1 heavy melting scrap at Boston was $10.50 to $11.00 below that at Pittsburgh (see Table VII) and considerably lower than the price paid at the major producing points currently supplying New England. Assuming the use of one-third ton of scrap per ton of steel, this would *a priori* imply an advantage of roughly $3.50 for a Boston producing point over Pittsburgh. But this reasoning is fallacious. It is true: (1) that recently around a million tons of scrap has been originating annually in New England on Class I Steam Railways while less than 30 per cent has been terminating;[11] (2) that an integrated works producing a million tons of ingots annually would require roughly 250,000 tons of purchased scrap; and (3) that as scrap prices rise new sources are tapped which tend to become permanent. But any potential production point in New England would not be able to supply its needs from its immediate environs. It would have to import from other points thus incurring the relatively high handling costs on scrap. This might leave a New England production point with a scrap price advantage over points like Pittsburgh of, say, $1.00 per ton of steel, and with some small advantage over interior points like Buffalo and Cleveland (see Table VII). It seems likely that a scrap price advantage over Sparrows Point or Trenton, also within the eastern seaboard surplus area, would at best be slight.

Market

Granted a favorable supply of ore and proximity to local consumers, definite transport cost advantages today appear to favor serving New England steel consumers from a New England mill. This merely reflects the historically increasing strength of the market pull. However, not only supply (cost), but also demand (market) conditions must be considered. To realize maximum economies of integrated large-scale blast furnace, coke oven, open hearth and rolling mill operation, a market must be able to absorb the output of a full-scale

[10]"Facts and Figures on Government Finance: 1948-1949," The Tax Foundation; Pennsylvania, Tax Study Commission, "Report," Parts I and II, February 1949; Tyler and Company, Inc., "Financial Statistics of Massachusetts," Boston, December 1949; State of Connecticut, "Information—Assessment and Collection of Taxes," 1948, Public Document No. 48, Hartford, 1949, p. 24.

[11]U. S. Interstate Commerce Commission, "Tons of Revenue Freight Originated and Tons Terminated in Carloads by Groups of Commodities and by Geographic Areas—Class I Steam Railways," Washington, annually.

TABLE VII   Prices of Number 1 Heavy Melting Scrap (Per Gross Ton)

	July 4, 1949	November 14, 1949	March 2, 1950
Pittsburgh	$21.00	$29.00—$30.00	$31.00
Cleveland	14.50—$15.50	30.00— 30.50	28.00—$28.50
Philadelphia	18.00	25.00	23.50
Detroit	14.50— 15.00	21.00— 22.00[a]	21.00— 22.00[a]
Buffalo	19.00— 19.50	28.00— 28.50	28.00— 28.50
New York	12.50— 13.00[a]	21.00— 22.00[a]	20.50— 21.00[a]
Boston	13.00— 13.50[b]	20.00— 20.50[b]	20.00— 20.50[b]
Birmingham	18.00	25.00	24.00

Source: *Steel*, Vol. 125, July 4, 1949, p. 132; Nov. 14, 1949, p. 144; Vol. 126, March 6, 1950, p. 150.
[a] Broker's buying price, F.O.B. shipping points.
[b] F.O.B. shipping points.

specialized works. How nearly can New England?

The latest and most complete information on New England consumption of steel products is found in a 1948 study by *Iron Age*[12] and in the 1947 *Census of Manufactures*.[13] The more conservative and much more reliable census data are used here, in conjunction with our estimates on items not covered by the census. In Table VIII we have set down in the first row the census figures on consumption of bars and shapes, sheet and strip, structural shapes, plates, other carbon steel, alloy steel, and stainless steel by New England's metal fabricating and producing establishments. The census figure on drawn-wire consumption is not used. New England's production of drawn wire exceeds her consumption. If we used the drawn-wire consumption figure, we would understate New England's consumption of wire-rods which is the pertinent factor in estimating market potential for the output of a New England steel works. We have estimated New England's wire-rod consumption in 1947 at 364,699 tons. This is based on the assumptions that 90 per cent of New England's capacity for wire drawing was utilized in 1947 and that a weight-loss of 5 per cent is incurred in drawing wire.

The census does not provide data on consumption of non-manufacturing industries—such as construction, rail transportation, agriculture, mining and lumbering. Crude estimates of the steel consumed by each of these industries in New England were arrived at by multiplying steel consumed nationally by these industries in 1947[14] by the following percentage figures: for construction, by New England's percentage share of new construction in 1947 (5.07);[15] for rail transport, by the percentage of total United States freight and passenger revenue of Class I railways earned by New England railways (3.74);[16] for agriculture, by New England's percentage of total United States agricultural income payments (1.95);[17] and for mining, quarrying, and lumbering, by the percentage of recorded United States taxable payrolls in these activities originating in New England (0.42).[18]

From our total consumption figures in Table VIII, we must subtract New England production to arrive at an estimate of total consumption of non-New England steel, which *a priori* might be considered the potential market for a new steel works in New England. As of January 1, 1948, New England possessed ingot capacity for producing 170,000 tons of hot rolled strip and for producing 246,500 tons of wire-rod, assuming a weight-loss of 15 per cent from the ingot to the wire-rod.[19] If we posit that New England facilities were operating at 90 per cent of capacity in 1947,

[12]"Steel Consumption in 1948," A report by *Iron Age* to the metalworking industry, New York.
[13]*U. S. Census of Manufactures: 1947*, "Geographic Distribution of Consumption of Metal Mill Shapes and Forms and Castings: 1947" (Preliminary report, Series MC 100-10), Dec. 30, 1949.

[14]American Iron and Steel Institute, *Annual Statistical Report*, 1948, New York, 1949, p. 116.
[15]U. S. Bureau of Foreign and Domestic Commerce, "State Distribution of Construction Activity, 1939-1948," *Construction and Construction Materials*, Statistical Supplement, Washington, D.C., 1949.
[16]I.C.C. Board of Transportation, Economics and Statistics, "Revenue Traffic Statistics of Class I Steam Railways in the United States," Washington, D.C., 1948.
[17]"Survey of Current Business," Vol. 28, August 1948, pp. 15 and 18.
[18]U. S. Department of Commerce, "Business Establishments, Employment and Taxable Pay Rolls, First Quarter 1947, By Industry Groups and By Countries," Washington, D.C., December 1948, Part I, pp. 20, 46, 50, 66, 86 and 98.
[19]American Iron and Steel Institute, "Directory of Iron and Steel Works of the United States and Canada," New York, 1948.

TABLE VIII New England Consumption of Steel, Production of Steel, and Consumption of Non-New England Steel (in Net Tons), 1947[a]

	Bars and Shapes	Sheet and Strip	Structural Shapes	Plates	Wire-rod	Rails and Related Items	Other Carbon Steel	Alloy Steel	Stainless Steel	Total
1. Consumption by metal fabricating and producing establishments; (Census estimates)[b]	273,175	494,171	74,509	99,594			140,447	136,940	12,316	1,231,152
2. Consumption of wire rods by New England wire drawing plants					364,699					364,699
3. Consumption by construction and contractors' product industries	59,279	111,271	107,214	89,175	899	1,151	61,536	*	*	430,525
4. Consumption by New England railroads	15,954	15,606	21,794	34,903		89,115	5,136	*	*	182,508
5. Consumption by agricultural, mining, quarrying and lumbering industries	11,560	7,936	1,144	2,135	117	422	2,164	*	*	25,478
6. Total Consumption	359,968	628,984	204,661	225,807	365,715	90,688	209,283	136,940	12,316	2,234,362
Less New England Production		153,000			221,850					374,850
Total Consumption of Non-New England Steel	359,968	475,984	204,661	225,807	143,865	90,688	209,283	136,940	12,316	1,859,512
U. S. Exports	695,033	488,286	416,694	1,110,862	39,050	1,057,482	399,213	*	*	2,206,692

* Included with carbon steel products.

[a] The figures on consumption and production of the various steel products are calculated on a basis that avoids duplication. No item appearing in one column appears again in a second column as a more finished product.

[b] The estimates of the Iron Age Study, though considerably higher for New England, are not used here. They are based upon a sample from plants employing approximately one-third of the total workers in the metal working industry whereas the Census figures are derived from an actual canvass of all plants. The Census reports consumption for New England as 1.48 million tons and for the U. S. as 43.15 million tons in 1947. Iron Age totals for 1948 are 2.78 million tons and 45.95 million tons respectively. The U. S. totals are fairly close (a difference of 6%). Since total steel production was 84.89 million tons for 1947 and 88.64 million tons in 1948 (a difference of 4%), the Iron Age total for the U. S. is acceptable. However, the discrepancy between the New England figures for the two years is 49% of the larger figure. This is too great to be attributed to different rates of production in two years. It reveals that New England's consumption pattern is sufficiently divergent from that of the rest of the country to throw doubt upon the consumption estimates derived from sampling. The source of error probably lies in the fact that in estimating totals from samples, the assumption was made that consumption is proportionate to number of workers employed, whereas New England employment per ton is higher than in the rest of the country because of the specialized forms produced.

we obtain the figures of 153,000 and 221,850 respectively. New England had no ingot capacity for producing the other steel items listed in Table VIII.

However, the interpretation of the figures on total consumption of non-New England steel as a potential market for a New England steel plant requires several serious qualifications. First, there is no way to account for what may be New England's slice of the export market. Nor is there any basis for estimating what the size of the export market may be in future years. The nature of the export market by product for 1947 is indicated in Table VIII. Although we do not relate any part of the export market (which is largely served from Atlantic seaboard points) to possible New England production, the reader may wish to do so. Columns 1 and 2 of Table I indicate that the comparative cost position for a New London or a Fall River location for such markets is not decidedly favorable, especially if Sparrows Point does come to utilize Venezuela ore. As regards other markets in the United States which can be reached by water shipment—for example, Florida and the Gulf Coast—again New England sites may not be able to compete easily with more southerly points on the Atlantic seaboard. Another very uncertain element in the picture is shipbuilding demand. New England has excellent shipbuilding facilities. If a military program calls for constant replacement of obsolete warships, New England's demand for steel in the future, especially for plates, may be considerably increased.

Second, it is very probable that the New England demand for rails and related products, for alloy and stainless steel, and for each of the diverse products listed in other carbon steel, will be insufficient to warrant the specialized, but large-scale, facilities required in their production. We should restrict our attention to New England's demand for the five categories in the first five columns of Table VIII. The total of New England's consumption of non-New England bars and shapes, sheet and strip, structural shapes, plates, and wire-rod amounts to 1,410,285 tons. This would seem more than enough to absorb the output of an integrated works with a capacity of 1¼ million tons of ingot. However, we must compare the capacity of efficient rolling mills designed to produce the range of products used in New England in each of these five categories with the 1947 New England consumption in each of these five categories. Recent modern sheet and strip mills versatile enough for New England have annual capacities of from 600,000 to 800,00 tons,[20] whereas the comparable figure in Table VIII is 475,984 tons. Modern efficient plate mills range in capacity from 250,000 to 300,000 tons;[21] the figure in Table VIII is 225,807. Information seems to indicate that a structural mill large enough to meet New England's range of demand would have a capacity of from 300,000 to 720,000 tons,[22] which figure contrasts with estimated New England imports of a little over 200,-000 tons in 1947. An efficient bar mill can be as small as 270,000 tons;[23] the relevant figure in Table VIII is 359,968 tons. Rod mills become economical at a capacity of from 150,000 to 250,000 tons;[24] in 1947 New England's net imports are estimated at 143,865 tons. Thus, from these comparisons, it is clear that the total of these first five categories must be used with considerable circumspection. A more detailed study of specific steel items consumed by various industries in terms of the input-output and other techniques is required.[25]

Third, and perhaps most important of all, a tidewater location southwest of New York City possesses tremendous advantages. A works at such a location threatens to pre-empt a large part of the southern New England market and perhaps some of the western New England market. We have already commented upon Trenton's strength for serving New Haven. This would be still greater for serving the large consuming points such as Bridgeport and Norwalk south of New Haven. It should be borne in mind that the *Iron Age* study estimates that the Bridgeport-New Haven-Waterbury area accounts for roughly one-fifth of New England's steel consumption (578,807 tons out of an over-estimated total of 2,870,278).

Also it has been intimated that a New England plant could serve the huge New York City market.[26] Perusal of Table IX casts serious doubt upon this hypothesis. Trenton reaches New York City at a total transport cost of $13.13 per ton; Bethlehem, at $16.42; Sparrows Point, at $17.39; whilst Fall River and New London reach New York City at the relatively high total transport costs of $19.71 and $17.90 respectively. However, it is important to remember that iron and steel producers frequently invade each other's markets (especially during depressions as long as they can cover out-of-pocket costs). We should expect New England's market to be invaded by outsiders even if there did exist a New England plant with definite cost advantages. But then we should expect the New England producer to invade other markets, and the New York City market would be an excellent one to penetrate without incurring high transport costs.

Fourth, the iron and steel industry attaches to itself an agglomeration of other production activities. Arguing from historical experience in the Sparrows Point-Baltimore-Philadelphia area, Neal has estimated that from 1947-1960 a reasonable maximum increase in New England's consumption of carbon-steel sheets, strip, plates, and bars and silicon-steel sheets might be 546,000 tons.[27] This figure, of course, includes normal growth. However, such an estimate based upon past experience in a different region necessarily cannot have much substance. Aside from pursuing detailed location studies of possible ancillary industries and carrying out the extensive computations involved in an input-output analysis, there is no tenable basis for

[20]"The Modern Strip Mill," Association of Iron and Steel Engineers, 1941, p. 5.

[21]J. Anthony, "Plate Mill Modernization at Central Iron and Steel," *Iron Age*, Vol. 164, Nov. 24, 1949, pp. 70-72.

[22]F. M. Gillies and W. E. Dittrich, "Production of Structural Shapes and Rails," *Steel*, Vol. 125, August 22, 1949, pp. 82-96.

[23]*Ibid.*, p. 88.

[24]R. R. Snow, "The Joliet Coarse Rod Mill," paper read before the American Iron and Steel Institute, New York, May 1947.

[25]W. W. Leontief, "The Structure of American Economy, 1919-1929," Cambridge, Mass., 1941.

[26]"Statement by Alfred C. Neal, Vice President and Director of Research, Federal Reserve Bank of Boston, On Behalf of the New England Council Steel Committee," Jan. 26, 1950, Exhibit D.

[27]*Ibid.*, Exhibit D, Chart III.

TABLE IX Transportation Costs on Ore and Coal Required Per Net Ton of Steel and on Finished Products for Selected Actual and Hypothetical Producing Locations Serving

NEW YORK

Location	Transportation Costs On			Total
	Ore	Coal	Finished Products	
Fall River ⎰ Labrador	$4.56	$6.01	$10.40	$20.97
⎱ Venezuela	3.68	5.63	10.40	19.71
New London ⎰ Labrador	4.56	5.79	8.80	19.15
⎱ Venezuela	3.68	5.42	8.80	17.90
Pittsburgh	5.55	1.56	12.40	19.51
Cleveland	3.16	3.85	14.00	21.01
Sparrows Point	4.73	4.26	8.40	17.39
Buffalo	3.16	4.27	11.60	19.03
Bethlehem	5.56	5.06	5.80	16.42
Trenton	3.68	4.65	4.80	13.13

Source: See Table I.

anticipating how much and what kind of agglomeration might ensue.

In sum, the total figures of Table VIII look impressive and we can expect continuous growth and agglomeration. Nonetheless, with the strong possibility of Trenton sharing the southern New England market, we do not have, given the gross classification of products employed by the census and our rough computations, an adequate basis for stating whether or not the market situation is favorable.

Other Critical Factors

In addition to the forces already discussed, several others may prove to be strategic. Both Fall River and New London are contacted directly on only one major railroad. They cannot offer the keen competition among railroads on the basis of services provided which in the past has often been a major consideration in a location decision. The potential threat that United States Steel may develop Trenton as a major steel site and that Bethlehem Steel may expand facilities at Sparrows Point, Bethlehem, Pa., and Buffalo, N. Y., may also operate as a deterrent to sinking a huge investment in a New England plant. Moreover, some believe that many segments of the steel industry lack the type of vigorous entrepreneurship responsive to a dynamic situation. However, alternative pricing policies ought not to affect the feasibility of a New England mill. Neither a basing point nor an f.o.b. mill pricing policy influences long-run costs in serving any given market, which is the crucial matter.[28]

One final consideration may prove critical for the immediate future. Construction costs of steel plants have risen precipitously since World War II. It has been estimated that, on the average, construction costs for steel capacity have risen some 95 per cent from 1939 to 1949.[29] Some steel spokesmen maintain that until steel prices are brought into line with construction costs, development of new locations as an alternative to reinvestment in existing facilities is not feasible. However, should this be true in the short-run, in the longer run worn-out facilities must be entirely replaced even at high construction costs. This implies that if prices are out of line with construction costs today, they will have to be adjusted in the long-run. In any event exploitation of the Labrador and Venezuela ore deposits requires time. Construction of plants predicated upon their use cannot be expected for a few years. Moreover, it is very likely that the transport savings of new Atlantic tidewater locations in serving the Eastern seaboard can permit profitable operation despite depreciation charges on a higher initial investment.

[28] W. Isard and W. M. Capron, op. cit., pp. 131-133.
[29] Testimony by M. W. Reed before the Joint Committee on the Economic Report, Washington, D.C., January 24, 1950.

Conclusion

In conclusion, a New England operation based on Labrador or Venezuela ores would enjoy definite transport cost savings over existing operations in serving the New England market. However, the advantage over the potential site of Trenton disappears as one approaches the southern New England area. Other costs of production are not unfavorable for New England, and there may be some slight advantage as regards the price of scrap.

The size of New England's steel market has been estimated by utilizing the gross census categories of semi-finished steel products and by employing crude methods for including steel consumption by industrial sectors not covered by the census. The total of non-New England steel consumed in New England *per se* seems sufficient to support an integrated works with a capacity of 1¼ million tons of ingot. However, a large number of specialized items comprise this total, many of which, because of limited New England demand, could not be profitably produced in New England. As a consequence, New England's market potential may be somewhat larger than necessary, or may be not quite large enough. In this more or less marginal market situation, (1) much more information on the consumption of specific steel items by specific industries is needed, and (2) more use of input-output and other techniques to estimate growth and agglomeration is required before one can judge whether or not a New England integrated steel works is feasible.

Chauncy D. Harris

THE MARKET AS A FACTOR IN THE LOCALIZATION OF INDUSTRY IN THE UNITED STATES *

Manufacturing in the United States is highly localized as a result of a complex of many factors. In the Manufacturing Belt of the Northeastern United States, which occupies only a twelfth of the country, is concentrated half the entire national market, seventy per cent of the industrial labor force, and the sources of supply of most materials and parts directly used in manufacturing. It should be made clear at the outset that the existence of this historically evolved belt, with its markets, labor force, factories, mines, transportation, and other established facilities, is far more important than the distribution of any particular raw material (such as iron ore) or of fuel (such as coal or petroleum), or of any other single factor such as labor or markets. The interrelationship between growth of this and other manufacturing areas and location of markets has been reciprocal; manufacturing has developed partly in areas or regions of largest markets and in turn the size of these markets has been augmented and other favorable conditions have been developed by the very growth of this industry. It is good to focus attention on man, as the active agent who develops tools, cultures, and technologies to satisfy his wants from whatever natural resources he can find and be able technically or economically to utilize. A coalfield is useless until it falls within the technological capabilities of specific human groups and until it can be utilized in a favorable economic environment. Geographers can learn much from economists with their emphasis on wants and markets and their flexibility in considering alternative resources that can be substituted for one another in the satisfaction of human needs.

Individual industries vary, of course, in their locational requirements both in respect to processing costs and to transfer (transport) costs.[1] The location of some factories is strongly affected by regional differences in processing costs, either of labor (cotton textiles) or of power (aluminum reduction). In order to minimize total transport costs other factories are best located between sources of raw materials and markets. Factories that sharply reduce either the bulk or perishability of the materials in processing minimize total costs by locating near the source of raw materials; such are ore concentrating plants, sugar beet factories, creameries, cheese factories, sawmills, and canneries. These factories constitute only a small and decreasing fraction of manufacturing. Factories greatly increasing either the bulk or perishability of products locate near *local* markets: bread bakeries, ice cream factories, ice works, gas works, bottling plants for soft drinks, building construction, newspaper printing. Such industries, though large in total volume, are ubiquitous and do not contribute substantially to regional differentiation.

Reprinted with the permission of the author and publisher from the *Annals*, Association of American Geographers, Vol. 44, No. 4, 1954, pp. 315-31 and 341-48. Dr. Harris is Professor of Geography at the University of Chicago.

*The author is grateful to John W. Alexander, Colin Clark, Alice Foster, William L. Garrison, Walter Isard, Harold M. Mayer, James J. Parsons, Thomas R. Smith, Edward L. Ullman, and Alfred J. Wright for ideas or suggestions that have been incorporated in this paper.

[1] Edgar M. Hoover, *The Location of Economic Activity.* New York, 1948. Especially Part One, "Locational Preferences and Patterns," pp. 27-141; Richard Hartshorne, "Location as a Factor in Geography," *Annals of the Association of American Geographers*, XVII (1927): 92-99; Robert S. Platt, "A Classification of Manufactures, Exemplified by Puerto Rican Industries," *Annals of the Association of American Geographers*, XVII (1927): 79-91; and H. H. McCarty, "Manufacturing Trends in Iowa," *Iowa Studies in Business*, VIII (July 1930): 1-79.

A large and very significant fraction of manufacturing in the United States is not tied to local raw materials, local markets, or to current regional differences in power or labor costs; this segment, typified by the automobile and agricultural machinery industries, appears to be concentrated in areas having maximum accessibility to national or regional markets for such products. These markets typically are associated with a considerable industrial labor force, with numerous other factories, and with well-developed facilities of many kinds. It is with such markets and associated phenomena that this paper is concerned.

The following questions seem pertinent to an analysis of the role of regional and national markets. Is the importance of the market as a location factor generally increasing or decreasing? Where are the markets? How can accessibility to them be measured? What are their divisions in terms of regions or of specialized activities such as mining, agriculture, or manufacturing? Does recent industrial growth indicate any attraction to markets and their associated phenomena? Such questions might be posed about any area or about the entire world, but the United States has been selected for investigation here. It embodies a widespread and very large market characterized by relatively homogeneous cultural and economic conditions, by a dense and interconnected transport network, by considerable national distribution, and by the absence of major internal trade barriers. Furthermore, comparable statistical materials are available.

Importance of the Market

Economic activities tied to the location of raw materials are waning in relative importance; activities carried on near markets or in intermediate positions are surging upward. In contrast to falling employment in raw-material-oriented primary activities, employment in secondary and tertiary activities is rising rapidly. Primary, secondary, and tertiary as here used refer broadly to the production of raw materials, to the processing of materials, and to the performance of services, and not to basic or service function in the economic support of a given area.[2] Between 1940 and 1950 the number of workers in agriculture in the United States diminished from 8.4 million to 7.1 million or about 15

per cent.[3] During this same period employment in secondary activities grew from 13.5 to 18.6 million or 37 per cent and in tertiary activities from 22.3 to 29.3 million or 31 per cent. These shifts are part of a long-run trend. Between 1820 and 1950 the proportion of persons occupied in primary activities in the United States shrank from 72 to 13 per cent, while that in secondary activities expanded from 12 to 33 per cent, and in tertiary from 15 to 53 per cent.[4] The location of the now dominant secondary and tertiary activities is not tied primarily to the distribution of raw materials, but exhibits a correspondence to the disposition of regional and national markets; yet these very markets are partly an outgrowth of the historical development of these self-same activities.[5]

In the location of manufacturing, as in economic activities in general, the distribution of raw materials is of decreasing weight. Materials undergo many processing stages from the crude raw material to the final product; in general the first stages are near the sources of raw materials, the intermediate stages somewhat footloose in location, and final stages close to the market.[6] Products are becoming more highly fabricated with the result that the initial treatment of raw material is diminishing in relative importance; the automobile is more intricate than the buggy and the mechanical refrigerator than the ice box. Within related industries employment in the final processing segments typically is growing more rapidly than in early or intermediate stages. Between 1939 and 1947, for example, the rate of increase of production workers in the apparel industries (final stage) was nearly five times as high as in textiles, and in machinery

[2] Cf. Richard B. Andrews, "Mechanics of the Urban Economic Base: The problem of Terminology," *Land Economics,* XXIX (August 1953): 266.

[3] *Statistical Abstract of the United States, 1952,* p. 185. During the same period farm output rose 24 per cent (*Agricultural Statistics, 1953,* p. 584).

[4] See Colin Clark, *The Conditions of Economic Progress.* London, 1940. "The Flow of Labour to Tertiary Production," Chapter V, pp. 176-219; *idem., The Economics of 1960.* London, 1942. "The Trend of Secondary and Tertiary Productivity," Chapter III, pp. 22-32; and P. K. Whelpton, "Occupational Groups in the United States 1820-1920," *Journal of the American Statistical Association,* XXI (Sept. 1926): 339-340.

[5] The location of certain of these activities shows an increasing effect of amenity factors (Edward L. Ullman, "Amenities and Regional Growth," abstract in International Geographical Union, XVIIth International Geographical Congress, United States, 1952. Abstracts of Papers, "Publication No. 6." Washington, D.C., 1952. p. 92; full paper in the *Geographical Review,* XLIV (January 1954): 119-132. The importance of the market as a locational factor is recognized in Thomas R. Smith, "Locational Analysis of New Manufacturing Plants in the United States," *Tijdschrift voor Economische en Sociale Geographie,* XLV (February 1954): 46-50.

[6] U. S. National Resources Committee, *Structure of the American Economy, Part I, Basic Characteristics.* Washington, 1939. Chapter IV, "The Structure of Production—Geographical Structure," pp. 33-59.

nearly three times as high as in primary metals.[7]

The production of iron and steel illustrates the decreasing significance of the location of raw materials in manufacturing. In the middle of the eighteenth century each ton of pig iron produced in Britain required about 8 tons of coal and 3 tons of iron ore.[8] In the United States in 1952 for each ton of steel produced, only 1.2 tons of iron ore, 0.9 tons of coal, and 0.6 tons of scrap were consumed.[9] But about half the scrap comes from the market areas (the rest is produced within each plant). Excluding limestone, which is widely distributed, the ratio of the mined raw materials such as coal and iron ore to market-oriented materials such as purchased scrap and produced steel has sunk from 11 to 1 to a low of 1.6 to 1, or only a seventh as high. During this same period transportation and mechanized handling have become more efficient and much cheaper for bulky raw materials. Especially dramatic is the use of pipelines for the transmission of oil and natural gas. In general finished products do not lend themselves to bulk handling, but involve high labor costs in transportation. The truck, however, has benefitted short hauls of finished products.

The production of iron and steel, even though a raw-material-processing industry, exhibits the importance of the market factor.[10] At times the steel industry of Pittsburgh has been considered as "based mostly on the coking coal of the Connellsville district;"[11] it is equally an expression of superb central location amidst the huge markets of the American Manufacturing Belt. Malcolm Keir demonstrated that the iron industry of Pittsburgh arose in relation to the market; iron-using factories, such as rolling mills and plow works, preceded by many decades the production of pig iron in the city.[12] The conspicuous growth of the steel industry has been near markets, as symbolized by the founding of Gary near Chicago half a century ago and the recent construction of the Fairless Steel Works on the Delaware River convenient to New York City; both have low total transport costs by virtue of the cheapness of water carriage of distant ores and the proximity to markets.[13] In spite of the favorable juxtaposition of local coking coal, iron ore, and limestone, Birmingham, Alabama, has remained a small producer. The small size of the Southern markets has been one factor stunting its growth. Duluth near the iron ore deposits of Minnesota has stagnated because of distance from markets.[14] The general world distribution of the iron and steel industry exhibits a congruity with markets rather than with the distribution of coal, iron ore, or any other raw material.

Location of Markets

Population and markets are unevenly distrib-

[7]Production workers in textiles increased 1939-1947 from 1,082 to 1,147 thousands or 6 per cent, in apparel industries from 753 to 973 thousands or 29 per cent; in primary metals from 672 to 1,010 thousands or 50 per cent; in machinery from 784 to 1,883 thousands, or 140 per cent. (U. S. Bureau of the Census, *Census of Manufactures: 1947, Vol. II, Statistics by Industry*. Washington, 1949. p. 22.)

[8]Walter Isard, "Some Locational Factors in the Iron and Steel Industry since the Early Nineteenth Century," *The Journal of Political Economy*, LVI (June 1948): 203-217, citation on p. 204. See also L. Dudley Stamp and Stanley H. Beaver, *The British Isles*. 3rd ed., London, 1941. p. 333.

[9]Production of steel 93 million tons; consumption of iron ore, 112 million tons, of coal (all purposes) 87 million tons (78 for coke), and of scrap 53 million tons (American Iron and Steel Institute, *Annual Statistical Report 1952*. New York, 1953. pp. 7, 15, 18, and 23. In addition fuel oil, natural gas, and purchased electric power supply significant amounts of energy.)

FIGURE 1 Belt with Half the Retail Sales in the United States in 1948. This belt occupies only 8 per cent of the country.

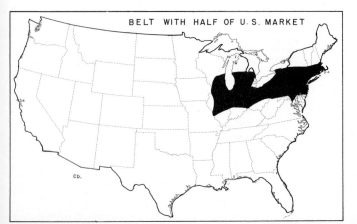

BELT WITH HALF OF U.S. MARKET

[10]Cf. Richard Hartshorne, "The Location of the Iron and Steel Industry," *Economic Geography*, IV (1928): 241-252; and Allan Rodgers, "Industrial Inertia, A Major Factor in the Location of the Steel Industry in the United States," *Geographical Review*, XLII (January, 1952): 56-66.

[11]L. Rodwell Jones and P. W. Bryan, *North America, An Historical, Economic and Regional Geography*. London, 1933. p. 289.

[12]Malcolm Keir, "The Iron and Steel Industry," *Manufacturing Industries in America, Fundamental Economic Factors*, Chapter V. New York, 1920. pp. 142-172, Pittsburgh on pp. 114-116. The opening sentence in this chapter announces Keir's theme, "The story of iron and steel in the United States turns about one central theme, the market for the products."

[13]Walter Isard and William M. Capron, "The Future Locational Pattern of Iron and Steel Production in the United States," *Journal of Political Economy*, LVII (April 1949): 118-133.

[14]Langdon White and George Primmer, "The Iron and Steel Industry of Duluth: A Study in Locational Maladjustment," *Geographical Review*, XXVII (1937): 82-91.

uted over the United States. Many factors contribute to this irregularity: scanty rainfall in the western half, hence less agricultural settlement there; spotty distribution of other resources such as coal, petroleum, metalliferous ores, forests, level land, rich soil, water power; history of settlement, which advanced from the Eastern Seaboard, at which arose the main seaports and urban concentrations; the development of transportation facilities by water (canals, rivers, and the Great Lakes) and by land (road and railroad); the sequence of the rise and spread of modern manufacturing from New England westward into the present Manufacturing Belt; and many other factors.

Population is one measure of the market, but income or retail sales provide more adequate indices. For international comparisons national income serves well. Within the United States sharp regional differences in income level occur. In 1949 the median income per family in New Jersey was $3,670 or more than three times as high as in Mississippi, $1,198.[15] Thus the average family in New Jersey has about three times as much money to spend as the average family in Mississippi. Retail sales approximate the ultimate market for goods sold commercially to consumers. In spite of certain limitations, these sales appear to provide the most valuable single index of the total final market for commercial goods. Fortunately such figures are readily available by counties from the Census of Business, 1948.[16]

Half the retail sales in the United States are made in a small belt in the Northeast, extending from Boston to St. Louis (Fig. 1). A manufacturer distributing to a national market is likely to make about half his sales here. The development of industries in the South or the West has sometimes been considered evidence of a trend toward location near markets. Insofar as such developments represent branch plants to serve regional markets this interpretation is correct. Distribution costs from these areas to the total national market, however, run higher than in most parts of the Manufacturing Belt (Fig. 7).

In terms of total size of market the Northeastern states dominate the entire country. On Figure 2 the area of each state has been made to vary with the size of the retail market in the state.

The country appears to be afflicted with a hospital case of hydrocephalus, in which the head (from Illinois to Massachusetts) has swelled six times normal size to exceed in bulk the rest of the body. The shriveled Southeast hangs limply like the forelegs of a kangaroo. The Mountain States have atrophied and nearly disappeared. The giant New York Metropolitan Area is larger than all the Southern States on the Atlantic south of the Potomac. The Chicago Metropolitan Area takes the measure of Texas. Massachusetts equals the combined Mountain States.

Some states in the Northeast have a density of market several hundred times as high as other states in the West. The United States may be divided into five grades of decreasing intensity of market as follows (Fig. 3): 1) the Eastern Seaboard states extending from Massachusetts to Pennsylvania with very high densities, five to fifteen times the national average; 2) the western half of the Manufacturing Belt from Ohio to Illinois with densities several times the national average; 3) most of the rest of the eastern half of the United States with densities about the national average; 4) the central and southern Great Plains with low densities; and 5) the Mountain States and Dakotas with very low densities, only a twentieth to a fourth the national average.

In order to determine more exactly and quantitatively the relative accessibility of various parts of the United States to the widespread markets, two new measures are proposed in this paper: 1) the

FIGURE 2 A Market View of the United States. The area of each state is proportional to the amount of retail sales in 1948. Sales of important metropolitan areas are indicated by shading. Some, such as New York City and Chicago, extend into more than one state. The Mountain states have been grouped as a single unit east of California.

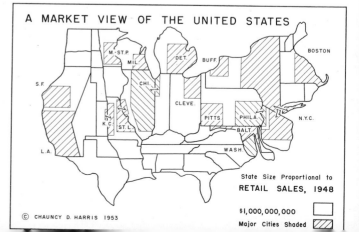

[15]U. S. Bureau of the Census, *County and City Data Book 1952.* Washington, 1953. p. 3, col. 20.
[16]*Ibid.*, col. 67. The 1949 edition giving the same data in column 2 was actually used in the tabulation for this paper.

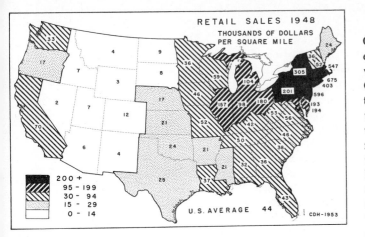

RETAIL SALES 1948
THOUSANDS OF DOLLARS
PER SQUARE MILE

200 +
95 - 199
30 - 94
15 - 29
0 - 14

U.S. AVERAGE   44

CDH-1953

FIGURE 3 Intensity of the American Market as Measured by Density of Retail Sales in 1948 by States.

market potential and 2) the point of lowest transport-cost to market. These will be discussed in turn.

The Market Potential

The term market potential, suggested by Colin Clark, is analogous to that of population potential as proposed and mapped by John Q. Stewart.[17] It is an abstract index of the intensity of possible contact with markets. The concept is derived ultimately from physics, in which similar formulas are used in calculating the strength of a field, whether electrical, magnetic, or gravitational.

The market potential (P) is defined as the summation (Σ) of markets accessible to a point (M) divided by their distances from that point (d).

$$P = \Sigma \left(\frac{M}{d} \right).$$

Two measures need to be selected and tabulated, one of the market and the other of distance.

A good measure of the over-all ultimate market for goods in the United States is provided by the figures for retail sales. These data have been tabulated on a county by county basis to give the values of M in the equation.

With respect to a measure of distance (d), for this purpose transport cost is superior to sheer miles. With the help of Harold M. Mayer, Colin

Clark and I calculated generalized formulas for estimating transportation costs by road, rail or water between any two points in the United States. On the basis of studies in the Chicago area typical terminal and running costs were established and utilized. Thus it was found that local truck delivery within a city costs about $6 per ton and that running costs approximate an additional 4 cents per ton-mile.[18] Trucking costs thus are set at $6 for local delivery, $8 for movements up to 50 miles, $10 for 100 miles, $18 for 300 miles, etc. Beyond this distance railroad transport costs were utilized. These were calculated at $5 per ton rail terminal costs plus 2½ cents per ton-mile, plus truck delivery costs of $6 per ton at destination.[19] The rail rates work out at $22 per ton for 440 miles and $40 for 1160 miles, etc. Total costs per ton-mile decrease with distance because of the lessening proportion of terminal costs in long hauls. Thus the *total* cost including railroad terminal costs, truck delivery costs, and a constant running cost per ton-mile declines from 5 cents per ton-mile for 440 miles to 3½ cents per ton-mile for 1160 miles. For intercoastal water transportation in the United States total terminal costs are estimated at $18 ($6 for terminal ship costs in the port; $6 for truck collection on land, and $6 for delivery by truck at

---

[17]John Q. Stewart, "Empirical Mathematical Rules Concerning the Distribution and Equilibrium of Population," *Geographical Review*, XXXVII (1947): 461-485, esp. 471-482; idem., "Demographic Gravitation: Evidence and Applications," *Sociometry*, XI (1948): 31-58; idem., "A Basis for Social Physics," *Impact of Science on Society*, III (1952): 110-133, esp. 118-122.

[18]These generalized truck cost figures are based on studies by Colin Clark and Harold M. Mayer, checked against a series of rates for specific items. The rates have been analyzed to separate out running costs from terminal costs. For example the rate on barbed wire, nails, and steel sheeting is estimated at 74¢ a hundred pounds for 100 miles, 92¢ for 200 miles, $1.12 for 300 miles (*Montgomery Ward Fall and Winter Catalogue* 1952-1953, p. 1041). The difference in rate between 100 and 200 miles is 18¢, and between 200 and 300 miles is 20¢, an average of 19¢. Multiply this figure for 100 pounds by 20 to get tons or $3.80 per ton for 100 miles or 3.8¢ per ton-mile for running costs. Subtract 19¢ running costs from 74¢ (for 100 miles) to get 55¢ terminal costs per 100 pounds or $11 per ton. For another example, the rates by public carrier for an 8-ton truckload of books from the Midwest Inter-Library Center in Chicago for delivery to the University of Chicago (½ mile) or to Illinois Institute of Technology (4 miles) is $56. (*Midwest Inter-Library Center Newsletter*, February 28, 1953, p. 8) Both may be considered local delivery and the rate works out at $7 per ton. For delivery to the University of Minnesota at Minneapolis the rate is $208, or $26 per ton. Subtract $7 per ton for terminal charges and divide the remaining $19 per ton for running costs by 419 miles to get about 4½¢ per ton-mile for running costs.

[19]By the Illinois Central Railroad the rate on plows by carload lots from Chicago to St. Louis is 78¢ per 100 pounds, to Memphis $1.18, and to New Orleans $1.46. The corresponding figures per ton are $18.50, $28.00, and $34.60. It is 284 miles to St. Louis, 536 to Memphis, and 719 to New Orleans. The difference in rate from Chicago to St. Louis and Memphis is $9.50 per ton (252 miles hence 3.8¢ running costs per ton-mile) and between Memphis and New Orleans is $6.60 per ton (183 miles hence 3.6¢ running costs per ton miles). Taking the figure of 3.6¢ per ton-mile running costs for the 284 miles between St. Louis and Chicago gives a figure of $10.22 for running costs between the two cities; this subtracted from the $18.50 rate leaves just over $8.00 for terminal costs. On this route for this commodity one could use figures of $8.00 per ton terminal and 3.6¢ per ton-mile additional running cost.

destination). The running costs are very low, only ¼ cent per ton-mile. On the other hand the distances by sea may be much greater than by land. Inland waterways have not been included in the calculations.

It should be emphasized that these figures are estimated transport *costs* for simple manufactured goods not actual *rates* for any specific article.[20] Rates for bulk commodities, such as coal, are much lower. Whether a particular product takes a higher or lower rate would not affect the calculations significantly since the distance ratios would remain approximately the same.

To determine the market potential (P) for a given city, one simply makes a summation (Σ) of the market potentials for that city of all counties in the area under consideration (the United States or a major region). The market potential of each county is the retail sales of that county divided by the transport cost of reaching the city for which the market potential is being calculated $\left(\dfrac{M}{d}\right)$.

In making the calculations two assumptions are made: 1) that because the United States is covered by a dense network of highways and railroads, the shortest distances on a map are proportional to actual route miles and therefore it is not necessary to tabulate data for individual routes; and 2) that because of the large number of counties involved figures can be grouped into class intervals. In the actual computations concentric circles are drawn on tracing paper around each selected city representing transport costs of 6 (local county), 8, 10, 12, 14, 18, 22, 30, 40, 50, 60, 70, and 80 dollars. The retail sales of each concentric circle are calculated by simply adding the retail sales of all counties within the band included by that circle and not by a smaller circle. (The county figures are recorded on a base map that can be used over and over again.) The market potential of each band is then calculated by dividing the total sales of the band by the cost of reaching it from the city under consideration. The total market potential for this city is then obtained by adding the market potentials for all the bands or concentric circles. Dots on the maps indicate the cities for

which these detailed calculations were made. On the basis of the values determined for these points, lines of equal market potential are drawn on maps, much as one draws contours or isotherms. For easier comparisons the figures are expressed as percentages of the city with the highest value (Fig. 4).

A fixed volume of retail sales within a city (transport cost $6) provides ten times as much market potential to this center as would the same volume of *total* retail sales in a county 1960 miles away (transport cost $60 by land).

Validity for the concept of market potential as a meaningful index of accessibility to markets would seem to rest on a progressive decline in quantity of goods moved with increasing distance. Market potential appears to gauge the possible spatial interaction between producers and markets, of the likely flow of goods from a point to accessible regions.[21] A number of studies indicate that freight movement as well as many other types of relationships between any two points varies directly with their size and inversely with their distance apart.[22] Actually there is a complex hierarchy of distribution areas from any given city; some products may have national or international distribution, others regional, and many local only. The aggregation of these various distribution areas results in a large volume of local and nearby movement with amounts decreasing with distance, just as in a contour relief model of a hill, all layers are represented at the center, but a decreasing number as one moves outward to the edge. Walter Isard, who has undertaken research on the decrease of shipments with distance, estimates that within the

[20]For a series of maps and graphs showing actual rates for specific commodities as affected by distance see Stuart Daggett and John P. Carter, *The Structure of Transcontinental Railroad Rates.* Publications of the Bureau of Business and Economic Research, University of California, Berkeley, Calif., 1947.

[21]See Edward L. Ullman, "Human Geography and Area Research," *Annals of the Association of American Geographers,* XLIII (March 1953): 54-66; idem., *Maps of State-to-State Rail Freight Movement for 13 States of the United States in 1948,* Office of Naval Research, Contract N50RI-07633, Report No. 3, Harvard University, Cambridge, Mass., 1951 (preliminary); idem., "Advances in Mapping Human Phenomena," reproduced in the same series as Report No. 5; idem., and Walter Isard, *Toward a More Analytical Economic Geography: The Analysis of Flow Phenomena,* Report No. 1, in the same series. For a discussion of the relationship of population and distance in retail trade see: William J. Reilly, "Methods for the Study of Retail Relationships," *University of Texas Bulletin* No. 2944 (Bureau of Business Research, Research Monograph No. 4), November 22, 1929; idem., *The Law of Retail Gravitation,* New York, 1931; P. D. Converse, "New Laws of Retail Gravitation," *Journal of Marketing,* XIV (October 1949): 379-384; and Robert B. Reynolds, "A Test of the Law of Retail Gravitation," *Journal of Marketing,* XVII (January 1953): 273-277.

[22]See George K. Zipf, *Human Behavior and the Principle of Least Effort.* Cambridge, Mass., 1949. "The Factor of Distance," pp. 386-409; and Donald J. Bogue, "Distance from the Metropolis," chapter IV, *The Structure of the Metropolitan Community, A Study of Dominance and Subdominance.* Ann Arbor, Michigan, 1949. pp. 67-78.

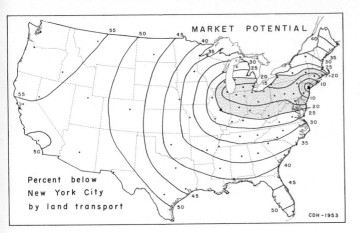

FIGURE 4 Distribution of Market Potential for the United States, Based on Retail Sales in 1948 and on Land Transportation only. The points for which calculations were made are indicated by dots on this and on following similar maps. For method of calculation see the text.

United States the total tonnage of Class I railroad shipments varies inversely with distance raised to roughly the 1.7 power when a straight line is fitted to the data plotted on double log scale.[23] If the exponent were as low as 0, distance would have no effect. If it were as high as 3 (distance cubed), only nearby markets would have much weight. In total shipments utilized by Isard, bulky raw materials loom large. In the calculations of this paper I have used an exponent of 1, which may be approximately correct for manufactured goods. Research needs to be undertaken to calculate the actual values for different types of commodities and for different areas.

Areas of high market potential furnish especially suitable conditions for the development of manufacturing. Industries in which economies of scale are important find in the immense markets a particularly favorable environment. The existence of a large and diversified labor force, the presence of many specialized services, the ease of obtaining components or sub-assemblies nearby, the presence of large industrial markets for new parts and gadgets, the ability to deliver quickly to the markets,

and a host of other factors reinforce the transport advantages.

AREAL DISTRIBUTION OF MARKET POTENTIAL

The market potential for the United States reaches a very high level in a broad belt between Massachusetts and Illinois and attains its maximum at New York City (Fig. 4, which is calculated on the basis of land transportation). The belt of high market potential extending east-west nearly coincides with the Manufacturing Belt. It stretches from Boston on the east to the Mississippi River on the west and from mid-Michigan on the north into Kentucky on the south. One of the interesting features of the westward extension of the area of high potential is the ridge of maximum potential, away from which the level drops sharply both to north and to south (Fig. 5). This ridge extends from New York City westward through Philadelphia, Harrisburg, Altoona, Pittsburgh, Cleveland, Toledo, and South Bend, to Chicago. Omitting the high peak for New York City on the east and the lower peak for Chicago on the west, the ridge is remarkably even, varying less than 2 per cent in height between Altoona on the east and South Bend on the west, and reaching its highest point in this section at Cleveland (Fig. 5). Baltimore (A in Fig. 5) lies south of the ridge and Detroit and Upper New York State (1–5 in Fig. 5), north of it. West of Chicago or east of New York City the market potential falls precipitately; in the 150 miles between Chicago and Rock Island or in the 180 miles between New York City and Boston it declines by a greater amount than anywhere in the 750-mile ridge of high potential between New York City and Chicago.

That the apex of market potential occurs in New York City reflects both the size of the city and its central position within the early settled, densely populated, highly urbanized Atlantic Seaboard extending from Boston on the north to Washington on the south.[24] A compact coastal belt includes Boston, New York City, Philadelphia, Baltimore, and Washington, 5 of the 11 cities in the United States with retail sales of more than 1 billion dollars in 1948 (Fig. 2). It contains 45 other coun-

[23]Walter Isard and Merton J. Peck, "Location Theory and International and Interregional Trade Theory," *Quarterly Journal of Economics*, LXVIII (February 1954): 97-114. cf. Rutledge Vining, "Delimitation of Economic Areas: Statistical Conceptions in the Study of Spatial Structure of an Economc System," *Journal of the American Statistical Association*, XLVIII (March 1953): 44-64, especially charts 2 and 5.

[24]See Jean Gottmann, "La Région Charnière de l'Économie Américaine," *Revue de "La Porte Océane,"* VII (March 1951) No. 71: 9-14 and VII (April 1951) No. 72: 11-20.

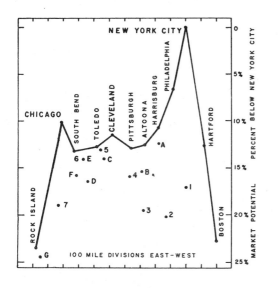

FIGURE 5 Market Potentials for Cities on or near the Ridge of High Potential Between New York City and Chicago. Cities north of the ridge are indicated by numbers: 1. Albany; 2. Syracuse; 3. Buffalo; 4. Erie; 5. Detroit; 6. Battle Creek; and 7. Milwaukee. Cities south of the ridge are identified by letters: A. Baltimore; B. Cumberland, Md.; C. Columbus, Ohio; D. Cincinnati; E. Fort Wayne; F. Indianapolis; and G. St. Louis. Cities are aligned according to position on an east-west axis.

ties with retail sales of more than 100 million dollars each. With a little more than 1 per cent of the area of the country it accounts for nearly one-fourth of the total retail sales.[25] In this diminutive area more retail sales are made than in the 60 per cent of the United States west of the Mississippi River, excluding the Pacific Coast.[26] Another expression of the importance of the large compact market on the Eastern Seaboard is the market potential for the area within 200 miles of various cities. The market potential for New York City of the area within 200 miles only of the city is about eight times as great as for any Southern city within a similar area.[27]

The Southeastern United States is characterized by moderate market potentials. The belt of

[25]38,000 square miles or 1.3 per cent of the area of the United States; $29.9 billion in retail sales in 1948 or 22.9 per cent of the total for the United States.
[26]The eight Mountain States, seven West North Central States, and four West South Central States with an area of 1,798,000 square miles and retail sales of $28.6 billion in 1948.
[27]Knoxville, Tenn., Greensboro, N. C., Atlanta, Ga., and Greenville, S. C., in that order, have the highest market potentials within 200 miles in the South. Houston and Dallas by virtue of their size, have higher potentials within 100 miles, but less intense markets in the intermediate umlands.

highest potential extends east-west and the Atlantic Coastline trends southwesterly. Coastal Georgia lies due south of Ohio, mid-way in the belt. Consequently all points in the Southeast have fair access to all parts of the belt. Greenville, S. C., for example, is closer to both New York City and Chicago than they are to each other.

The eastern corners of the country in Maine and in Florida have low market potentials. All their market support must be derived from a sector of less than a quarter of a circle, whereas inland points may draw sustenance from all directions.

The western areas have very low potentials. A minimum occurs in the Pacific Northwest, which is farther than the Southwest from eastern markets and which also contains a smaller local market.

The market potential rises in Southern California, the only major break in the otherwise persistent and regular decline away from New York City and the ridge of high market potential. The large local market accounts for this rise.

The differential between the market potential of the Eastern Seaboard ports and of Midwestern cities is heightened by the utilization of water transport, where cheaper (Fig. 6). Use of the sea roughly halves the cost of shipment between the Pacific Coast and the Atlantic Seaboard although ocean routes are much longer than land routes. Water transportation gives the Gulf Coast cheaper access to the immense markets of both the east and west coasts. The Pacific Coast potentials, although still lower than those of the East, rise above other parts of the West. By combined land and sea transport the Mountain States form a trough of low potential in contrast to a continuous decline to the

FIGURE 6 Distribution of Market Potential for the United States, by Combined Land and Sea Transport.

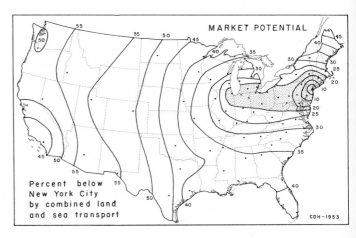

Pacific Coast for land transport. Most of the goods move by rail, but the rates on the coast are lowered by the competition of water transport. The sharp impact of cheap ocean transportation shows more clearly in the second measure of accessibility, the point of lowest transport costs to market.

Comparative Transport Costs to Market

Assume that a manufacturer is to serve an entire market area, is to absorb the costs of shipment, and wishes to locate so as to minimize his freight costs to market or, to use Isard's term, his distance inputs.[28] What will his location be?[29] Here instead of maximizing the summation of sales divided by distance as in market potential, one sets out to ·minimize the summation of sales multiplied by the transport costs, according to the formula.

$$T = \Sigma(Md),$$

where T is total transportation costs to an aggregate of market areas, M is the size of the market in each unit (county in this case), and d is the distance in transport costs from any given city to the market in this unit (county). The same transportation cost figures, assumptions, and methods

[28]Walter Isard, "Distance Inputs and the Space-Economy," *Quarterly Journal of Economics*, LXV (1951): "Part I: The Conceptual Framework," 181-198; "Part II: The Locational Equilibrium of the Firm," 373-399. Isard is concerned with total distance inputs on materials as well as products.
[29]Cf. Leonard C. Yaseen, *Plant Location*. Roslyn, N. Y., 1952. Chapter III "Competitive Advantages in Raw Materials, Sources and Markets," pp. 21-38.

FIGURE 7   Transport Cost to the United States National Market (as measured by retail sales in·1948) by Land Transport Only. For method of calculation see the text.

are utilized as in the calculation of the market potential.

In contrast to market potential, the point of lowest transport costs is only slightly affected by cheap local deliveries and is dominated by expensive distant shipments.[30] For example, the retail sales of the Pacific Coast amount to 11.4 per cent of the total sales for the United States, yet because of their distance account for only 4.6 per cent of the market potential for Chicago, but for 22.0 per cent of the freight cost of serving a national market from Chicago. Market potential presupposes a declining market with distance, whereas the transport cost calculations postulate that the size of the market is unaffected by distance within the area being measured.

AREAL DISTRIBUTION OF COMPARATIVE TRANSPORT COSTS

The area with lowest transport costs to serve the entire United States market by land transportation has an interior position centered on Fort Wayne, Indiana (Fig. 7). It lies within the belt of high sales in the northeastern United States, but in the western part of it because of the small, yet distant, markets west of the Mississippi River. The area with transport costs less than 10 per cent higher than Fort Wayne extends from Harrisburg on the east to St. Louis on the west. Beyond this, transport costs rise regularly in all directions to reach 50 per cent higher costs in eastern Maine or southern Florida and 100 per cent higher costs along the Pacific Coast.

Philadelphia, at the point where the Chicago—New York axis of largest market intercepts the margin of cheap sea carriage, has the lowest transport costs to the national market by combined land and sea movement (Fig. 8). Most parts of the Manufacturing Belt fall within the area with transport costs less than 10 per cent above Philadelphia. This area reaches on the north to Albany and Detroit, on the west to Chicago, and on the south to Cincinnati and Roanoke.

[30]In this it is similar to the "center of population" as calculated by the U. S. Bureau of the Census. See "Center of Population of the United States: 1950," *U. S. Bureau of the Census, Geographic Reports*, No. 2. Washington, September 30, 1951. See also E. E. Sviatlovsky and Walter Crosby Eells, "The Centrographical Method and Regional Analysis," *Geographical Review*, XXVII (April 1937): 240-254.

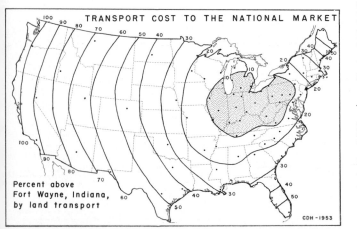

TRANSPORT COST TO THE NATIONAL MARKET

Percent above
Fort Wayne, Indiana,
by land transport

CDH-1953

The Gulf and Pacific coasts are especially benefitted by water transport (cf. Fig. 7 and 8). The Gulf Coast possesses cheap water transport to the Atlantic Seaboard and to the Pacific Coast. Houston, Texas, by land transport has costs 40 per cent above the minimum point, but by combined land and sea only 18 per cent. Nevertheless, it is still higher than points within the Manufacturing Belt, for even by water transport, freight costs are heavy to the belt of high retail sales. San Francisco by land transport has costs 102 per cent above the minimum point, but by combined land and sea only 56 per cent higher. The sharp difference between land and sea costs is probably a major factor in the clustering of the population on the Pacific Coast around the seaports: Los Angeles, San Francisco, Portland, and Seattle. The Mountain States constitute a plateau of highest transport costs by combined land and sea transport—more than 70 per cent above the minimum point.

The large size of the market on the Pacific Coast and its remoteness and consequent high transport cost from other parts of the country encourage the development of an independent market area. James J. Parsons has noted the rise of industries here in response to the Western market.[31] On the basis of the possibility that the Pacific market may become somewhat independent, let us re-examine our figures. Since the area is relatively distant from the eastern United States its removal will not greatly affect figures for market potential, but its separation would sharply reduce the freight bill for many Eastern concerns. The points of lowest transport costs to the national market, excluding the Pacific Coast, have interior locations, whether transport is by land alone or by combined land and sea (Fig. 9). Fort Wayne and Cleveland have the lowest costs. The Gulf Coast, the Atlantic Seaboard, and Florida benefit from sea transport but not enough to offset more central location of interior points.

The Midwestern parts of the Manufacturing Belt combine central position within the belt of high retail sales with fair access to the markets of the South and the West. Points outside this belt have higher transport costs to national markets simply because they have to ship so much into the

[31]James J. Parsons, "California Manufacturing," *Geographical Review*, XXXIX (1949): 240.

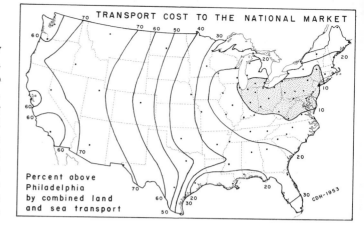

FIGURE 8 Transport Cost to the United States National Market by Combined Land and Sea Transport.

belt. St. Louis, for example, at the western edge of the belt, has a high freight bill because of having to transmit large amounts long distances to the huge markets of the Atlantic Seaboard. Boston, on the other end, has much freight moving long distances into the big markets of the Midwest. Ohio, Indiana, and Pennsylvania in the central part of the belt of high retail sales have the most favorable position for minimizing transport costs to market. The automobile industry is localized in this area. Its development to the north of the center of the area may be due in part to historical circumstances and possibly in part also to the pull of the Canadian market in this direction. Within the Manufacturing Belt, New England with costs 10–20 per cent above those of the central part lies in a dis-

FIGURE 9 Transport Cost to the National Market Excluding the Pacific Coast by Land Transport Only (solid lines) or by Combined Land and Sea Transport (dashed lines where different from lines for land transport only).

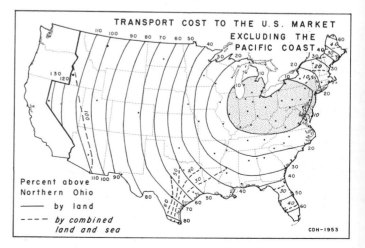

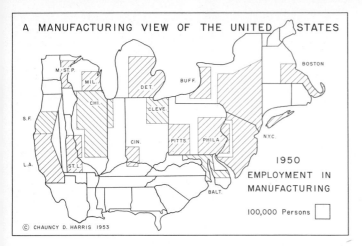

FIGURE 26 A Manufacturing View of the United States. Areas of states are proportional to the number employed in manufacturing in 1950. Employment in important metropolitan areas is indicated by shading. Some, such as New York City and Chicago, extend into more than one state. The Mountain states have been grouped as one unit, and the Prairie states also.

advantageous position for industries in which cost of transportation to market is a significant localizing factor. It is interesting that the shift of textile industries from New England to the South has not significantly altered the transport cost to market. Figure 9 is thought to be a fair approximation of the relative favorableness of various areas for the location of industries to serve the national market (excluding the Pacific Coast), insofar as these industries are transport oriented with respect to market.

Thus far the market has been considered in national terms and for all products taken together.

FIGURE 27 Counties in the United States with More Than 2500 Persons Employed in Manufacturing in 1950. In order not to overemphasize certain large counties in the Western United States, they have been represented by a symbol, the size of typical county.

Counties with more than 2500 employed in manufacturing

Now we turn first to an analysis of regional markets, and secondly to the various segments of the national market. . . .

MANUFACTURING

Manufacturing is more sharply localized than either the total market or agriculture. More than two-thirds of the employment in manufacturing in the United States in 1950 was in the Northeast, east of the Mississippi and north of the Ohio River. In Figure 26 New Jersey is twice as large as Texas. Connecticut is larger than Missouri, and Rhode Island larger than Maine. The Chicago Metropolitan Area surpasses California. New York and Pennsylvania combined exceed in size all the land west of the Mississippi River, or the entire South. The distribution of the manufacturing areas within each state is depicted on Figure 27.

Attention needs to be directed toward manufacturing as the main source of its own materials. An industrialist searching for components for a product may not look directly to the forests, mines, or farms of the country, but rather to other factories. Four-fifths of the industries in the United States utilize materials that have already been processed by other industries.[42] The map of distribution of manufacturing depicts the generalized pattern of the availability of materials, of the treated products of farm, forest, or mine. The automobile industry illustrates clearly the nature of the machinery industries which utilize primarily metals, parts, and subassemblies rather than raw iron ore. G. Ross Henrickson's map of the sources of materials for the Buick automobile factory in Flint, Michigan, shows that these materials come almost entirely from within the Manufacturing Belt.[43] Manuscript maps compiled by Harold M. Mayer and Allen K. Philbrick for the sources of supply for the Studebaker factory in South Bend, Indiana, show similar distribution of sources of materials. A study by Albert L. Hennig of the major industries of Milwaukee revealed that most of their materials came from the western part of the Manufacturing Belt.[44] Bernard H. Schockel found that

[42]U. S. National Resources Planning Board, *Industrial Location and National Resources.* Washington, 1934, p. 3.

[43]G. Ross Henrickson, *Trends in the Geographic Distribution of Suppliers of Some Basically Important Materials used at the Buick Motor Division, Flint, Michigan,* "Institute for Human Adjustment, Horace H. Rackham School of Graduate Studies, University of Michigan." Ann Arbor, 1951. Fig. 7, p. 47.

[44]Albert L. Hennig, "Metal Industries of the Milwaukee Metropolitan Area," unpublished Master's thesis, Department of Geography, University of Chicago, 1953.

the major source of supply for the industries of Evansville also lay in the western part of the Manufacturing Belt.[45]

Borrowing a concept from ecology, one might compare the Manufacturing Belt to a climax (formation), in which machinery factories represent the dominant and most characteristic species, but one that thrives best in the presence of a great many other species which prepare the ground. The concepts of ecology in the study of the complex interrelationships within communities might illuminate some of the foundations for the prosperity of plants, industrial as well as botanical.

New York City is the point of highest manufacturing potential as measured by the summation of employment in manufacturing divided by transport cost (Fig. 28). The city itself has the largest manufacturing employment of any city in the country (6 per cent of the total), but even more important is its central position in the manufacturing area along the Eastern Seaboard (Fig. 26). Nearly 30 per cent of the employment in manufacturing in the United States is within 200 miles of New York City.

A belt of high manufacturing potential extends from New York City westward to Chicago (Fig. 28). Outside the environs of New York City, the potential is astonishingly uniform all the way from Altoona, through Pittsburgh, Cleveland, Toledo, and Detroit, to Chicago. The only variation is a slight rise at Cleveland, just as there was in market potential (Figs. 4 and 5). If there were only a single focus of manufacturing within a country one would not expect such a long and uniform belt of high manufacturing potential. We have observed already that for the agricultural market Northern Illinois occupies a central position. Chicago lies at the point of nearest approach of the Great Lakes to the agricultural heart of America. At Chicago then is the center for many types of activities oriented toward agricultural markets or toward Midwestern or interior markets. Between New York City the dominant port, largest city, and center of highest intensity of manufacturing, and Chicago, the center for the agricultural and interior markets, stretches the belt with highest manufacturing potential. The general decline outward from the Manufacturing Belt is inter-

[45]Bernard H. Schockel, *Manufactural Evansville*, Ph.D. dissertation, Department of Geography, University of Chicago, 1947 (lithoprinted), Table 57, p. 211, Table 27, p. 136, and pp. 170-171.

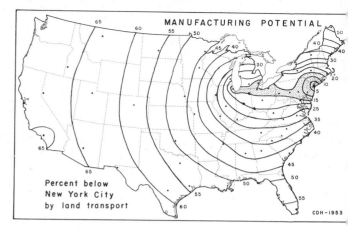

FIGURE 28 Manufacturing Potential 1950 as Measured by the Summation of Employment in Manufacturing Divided by Distance in Transport Cost from Cities Indicated by Dots. Land transport only.

rupted only by a rise in the Los Angeles area.

The point of lowest land transport cost to reach the manufacturing market or manufacturing source of materials lies not on the Eastern Seaboard, but at Cleveland in the interior (Fig. 29). If water transport is taken into account Philadelphia, New York, and Baltimore drop a bit below Cleveland, primarily because of the effect of cheaper transport from these ports to the Pacific Coast (Fig. 30). Manufacturing, unlike farming, has certain peripheral tendencies; these reflect the function of ports in import of raw materials or export of finished products, the historic role of ports as entry ways for ideas, new industries, and industrial labor from across the Atlantic, and the heavy concentrations of urban population in these areas.

FIGURE 29 Transport Cost to the National Manufacturing Market as Measured by Employment in Manufacturing. Land transport only.

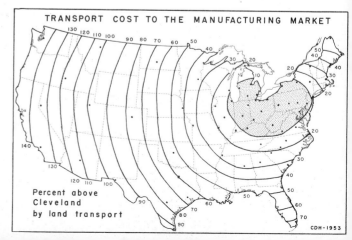

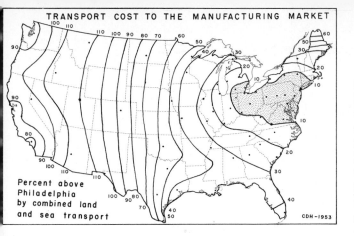

Percent above Philadelphia by combined land and sea transport

CDH-1953

FIGURE 30 Transport Cost to the National Manufacturing Market as Measured by Employment in Manufacturing. Combined land and sea transport.

Recent Growth of Manufacturing

The growth of manufacturing by counties during the years 1939–1947 as mapped by John Alexander reveals that the greatest absolute increases in this period took place in the large cities on the axis of highest market potential: New York City, Philadelphia, Pittsburgh, Cleveland, and Chicago (Fig. 5) or in cities just north of the axis (Detroit, Milwaukee, and Buffalo) or just south of it (St. Louis, Peoria, Indianapolis, Cincinnati, and Dayton).[46] The cities of the South showed only modest development in this period of rapid war-stimulated expansion of the metal and machinery industries.

During the longer period 1914–1947, 60 per cent of the total growth in employment in non-local manufacturing took place in the Manufacturing Belt from New York to Illinois, and another 20 per cent was in the industrial areas of the Southeast and the Pacific Coast (Fig. 31).[47] The remaining 20 per cent was widely scattered. This period spans two world wars, a great depression, and a remarkable development of the machinery industries. In order to make the map a more sensitive index of non-local changes, two types of industries have been excluded: ubiquitous industries, such as baking of bread, and material-oriented industries, such as canning or lumbering.[48]

The distribution of industrial development during the years 1914-1947 reflects many factors.[49] In the Manufacturing Belt accessibility to markets and materials and the presence of skilled labor and extensive facilities have been important. That the increase in industry in the western part of the Manufacturing Belt has been twice as great as in the eastern part (Fig. 31) may reflect the lower land transport costs to market from this part of the belt (Fig. 7) as well as the growth of the automobile and agricultural machinery industries.[50] In the development of the Southeast, low cost of labor was important in the expansion of the textile industry, but availability of labor and the regional market have become more significant recently. The Pacific Coast, particularly California, has witnessed the creation of market-oriented industries to serve the large but isolated regional market. One curious feature is the zone of slight growth both north and west of the Southeastern manufacturing area. Virginia, West Virginia, and Kentucky on the north and Arkansas and Mississippi on the west have had less growth than adjacent states in any direction (Fig. 31). The comparative poverty of the local markets is a probable factor in Mississippi and Arkansas and a possible one in Kentucky and West Virginia. The location of major regional centers near, but outside, Mississippi and Arkansas may also help to account for the low standing of these two states. Other factors that may have played a role in the slight development of manufacturing in West Virginia are unfavorable terrain, poor rail connections to the north and northeast, and economic lag because of the relatively late development of this part of the coal-field. In New England

[46]John Alexander, "Industrial Expansion in the United States 1939-1947," *Economic Geography*, XXVIII (1952): 128-142. Map on p. 130.

[47]Cf. A. J. Wright, "Recent Changes in the Concentration of Manufacturing," *Annals of the Association of American Geographers*, XXXV (1945): 144-166.

[48]The 1914 calculations were made by Colin Clark from the Census of Manufactures for that year. The 1947 calculations are from: U. S. Bureau of the Census, *Census of Manufactures:*

1947, Vol. III. Washington, 1950. Table 4 for each state. A good example of a state markedly affected by such adjustments is South Dakota, in which about 90 per cent of the workers are in material-oriented industries, such as meat packing or stone products, or else in ubiquitous activities, such as bakery products, bottled soft drinks, millwork, or newspaper printing (*ibid.*, p. 564).

[49]For a summary of the numerous important studies in trends in industrial location see Coleman Woodbury and Frank Cliffe, "Industrial Location and Urban Redevelopment," Part II in *The Future of Cities and Urban Redevelopment* (Coleman Woodbury ed.). Chicago, 1953. pp. 104-288. Table I on page 148 gives employment in manufacturing by regions in 1899 and 1947 and shows three areas of greatest increase in relative importance: East North Central, the South, and the Pacific Coast.

[50]For statistics and analyses of shifts in relative importance between 1869 and 1935 for 33 industrial areas, mostly within the Manufacturing Belt, see Glenn E. McLaughlin, *Growth of American Manufacturing Areas, A Comparative Analysis with Special Emphasis on Trends in the Pittsburgh District*, "University of Pittsburgh, Bureau of Business Research Monograph No. 7." Pittsburgh, 1938. For a good survey of factors in the South see McLaughlin and Robock, *op. cit.*

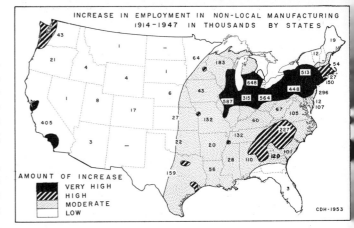

FIGURE 31   Increase in Employment in Non-Local Manufacturing 1914-1947 in Thousands by States. Excluded from the figures of this map are (1) raw-material oriented industries, such as lumbering and the canning of food and (2) ubiquitous industries localized near local markets, such as baking of bread. Calculation made in cooperation with Colin Clark. Generalized areas of amount of increase are based on distribution of total employment on a county basis.

Connecticut accounts for more than half the total growth. The contrast between Connecticut and the rest of New England rests partly on the structure of industry (metals vs. textiles), but may reflect in part also the advantages of Connecticut's greater accessibility to New York with resulting higher market potentials.

The three areas with little or no increase in manufacturing 1914–1947 are all areas remote from the main national markets and therefore areas of low market potential and high transport cost to market: 1) the Mountain States and the Northern Great Plains, 2) Florida, and 3) northern New England (Fig. 31).

Problems for Further Study

Further investigation in some of the aspects of this paper is called for.[51] What effect would the inclusion of Canada have on the maps of market potential and transportation cost? What is the role of overseas markets and how much would their inclusion alter the balance between coastal and interior points? How nearly does the actual freight-rate structure approximate the generalized transport cost bands used in the calculations of this paper? What has been the role of freight-rate territories with their differing rate structures? How much do the Great Lakes, the Ohio and Mississippi rivers, and the Erie Canal alter the freight-rate structure? The actual marketing areas for specific products and for specific regions need examination. In this connection a few case studies of cities outside the Manufacturing Belt, such as Kansas City, Oklahoma City, Dallas, or Houston, might be instructive in recognizing the types of industries and tributary areas of these centers. Analysis of actual distribution patterns for industrial goods (often through wholesaling centers) might contribute to our understanding of the role of regional centers as ports of entry into regions. We need to apply the methods of cultural anthropology to study manufacturing as a phenomenon which has arisen in centers of invention (earlier mainly in England) and spread by specific routes of communication and imitation to New England and the Middle Atlantic States and thence westward toward interior markets and, to a lesser extent, southward.[52] Research on conditions at the time of the rise of some of the American industries would throw light on the genesis and evolution of the Manufacturing Belt, the existence of which is the dominating factor in present-day industrial location in the United States.

[52]Carl O. Sauer was a pioneer among American geographers in the recognition of the significance of this concept in geography. Cf. Robert S. Platt, "Die Entwicklung der Kulturgeographie in Amerika," *Erdkunde,* VI (1952): 261 and R. H. Kinvig, "The Geographer as Humanist," *The Advancement of Science,* XXXVIII (September 1953): preprint p. 4.

[51]For an account of the contributions of American geographers to the study of manufacturing see Chauncy D. Harris, "The Geography of Manufacturing," Chapter 12 in Preston E. James and Clarence F. Jones (eds.), *American Geography, Inventory and Prospect.* Syracuse, N. Y., 1954, pp. 292-309. For a fuller listing of works see *idem.,* "A Bibliography of the Geography of Manufacturing," Department of Geography, University of Chicago, 1952 (mimeographed).

John E. Brush

THE HIERARCHY OF CENTRAL PLACES IN SOUTHWESTERN WISCONSIN

Small towns and villages in agricultural areas of Anglo-America exist mainly because of their function as central places for the exchange of goods and services, each for its local farm trade area. In any given area small centers are closely spaced and more numerous; large centers, offering greater services, are more widely spaced and less numerous. Theoretical consideration must be given to these commonplace facts in view of the need for developing an analytical framework for settlement geography, comparable to the principles of location in industrial geography. If generalizations can be found true of the functions and spacing of trade centers, the significance of regional differences in the hierarchy of these centers can be assessed.

The theoretical principles for anaylzing trade centers derive from two main sources: European geographers and American rural sociologists. Christaller[1] in Germany has presented the most comprehensive theoretical system of analysis, covering centers from the smallest market towns to the largest cities. He was preceded almost 20 years by Galpin,[2] who studied rural communities in New York and Wisconsin. Galpin and the sociologists who have followed him are concerned primarily with the social relationships of farmers with other farmers and with the inhabitants of the trade centers. Christaller and the European geographers influenced by him give their attention to functional

attributes and spatial arrangements of the centers.

Two basic principles derive from the work in Europe and America: (1) trade centers are graded according to population and functional attributes (though the categories recognized are widely divergent and there is no agreement on criteria); and (2) the locational pattern of trade centers is controlled mainly by the radial movement of traffic, which creates circular trade areas and causes centers with equivalent functions to be spaced at approximately equal distances from one another over any uniformly productive and populated territory.

But because there is no such thing as a perfectly uniform territory, many geographers have not received these theories wholeheartedly: the concepts seem too rigid to explain the observable variations in the actual distribution of trade centers. Nearly all geographic studies of trade centers in America emphasize the unique character of particular places, dealing with site and transportation factors.[3] Yet the American Middle West would seem to fulfill the ideal conditions as nearly as

---

Reprinted with the permission of the author and publisher from the *Geographical Review,* Vol. 43, No. 3, 1953, pp. 380-402. Dr. Brush is Professor of Geography at Rutgers—The State University, New Brunswick, New Jersey.

[1]Walter Christaller: Die zentralen Orte in Süddeutschland (Jena, 1933).

[2]C. J. Galpin: The Social Anatomy of an Agricultural Community, *Univ. of Wisconsin Agric. Exper. Sta. Research Bull.* 34, 1915.

[3]Two good examples of the treatment of location of small urban settlements in terms of site and transportation are S. T. Emory: Topography and Towns of the Carolina Piedmont, *Econ. Georgr.,* Vol. 12, 1936, pp. 91-97; and C. M. Davis: The Cities and Towns of the High Plains of Michigan, *Geogr. Rev.,* Vol. 28, 1938, pp. 664-673, C. B. Odell, in "The Functional Pattern of Villages in a Selected Area of the Corn Belt" (Diss. [abridgement], Ph. D., University of Chicago, 1937; University of Chicago Libraries, 1939), describes a small group of Illinois villages but makes little attempt to analyze their location. The best examples of classification of small agricultural trade centers based on functional attributes and population are A. L. Seeman: Communities in the Salt Lake Basin, *Econ. Geogr.,* Vol. 14, 1938, pp. 300-308; and P. W. Picklesimer: Agglomerated Settlements in the New Bright Tobacco Belt, *ibid.,* Vol. 22, 1946, pp. 38-45. The best theoretical statements by American geographers on the problem of location are E. [L.] Ullman: A Theory of Location for Cities, *Amer. Journ. of Sociology,* Vol. 46, 1940-1941, pp. 853-864; and C. D. Harris and E. L. Ullman: The Nature of Cities, *Annals Amer. Acad. of Polit. and Soc. Sci.,* Vol. 242, 1945, pp. 7-17.

possible; one would expect the functional and spatial hierarchy to be developed in the parts of the agricultural interior of the continent where manufacturing and its urbanizing influences are absent.

The present analysis deals with 234 agglomerated settlements in six counties and parts of four other counties of Wisconsin (Fig. 1), west of the American Manufacturing Belt. The settlements are east of the Mississippi River, south of La Crosse, and west of Madison, in the physiographic division known as the Driftless Hill Land,[4] a region with moderate, uniform relief. The limits of the study area are determined not by landforms but by evenness of population distribution and economic dependence on agriculture. In this dairying region the trade centers exist to supply the needs of farm dwellers. Mining of lead and zinc, once a major industry in Grant, Iowa, and Lafayette Counties, is now reduced to a small output. Census figures[5] show that trade and services employ nearly all the nonagricultural workers; the ratio is roughly one worker in "central services" to two in farming. Since the manufacturing is confined to small agricultural and service industries, and since mining is chiefly of historic significance, the functional development and spatial patterns of trade centers are presumably controlled by the requirements of local farm markets.[6]

Criteria of Trade Centers

The usual measure of the importance of a place is its population. The advantage of this measure is that it reduces all the diverse elements in a settlement to a single common denominator. If population is to be used as the criterion of the functional grades of trade centers, there should be gaps or offsets in the progression from small to large centers indicating fundamental distinctions in size groups. However, no clear-cut breaks are

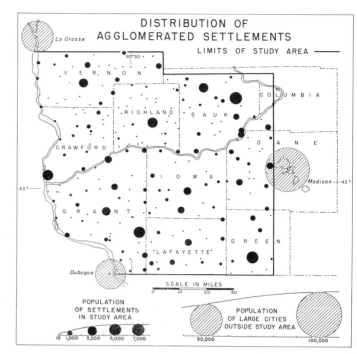

FIGURE 1   Distribution of Agglomerated Settlements. (*Source: 1950 Census data.*)

evident if the agglomerated settlements in southwestern Wisconsin are arranged according to rank in population[7] (Fig. 2); indeed, the smooth curve formed by the progression suggests an exponential relationship of population and rank.

[7]Estimates of the population of unincorporated settlements were obtained from Rand McNally's "Commercial Atlas," New York, Chicago, San Francisco, 1949, and Dun and Bradstreet's "Reference Book for Wisconsin, 1949," New York, 1949. Strong biases are noticeable in the estimates, favoring populations of 10, 15, 25, and their multiples.

FIGURE 2

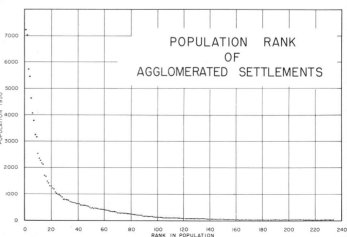

---

[4]G. T. Trewartha and Guy-Harold Smith: Surface Configuration of the Driftless Cuestaform Hill Land, *Annals Assn. of Amer. Geogrs.*, Vol. 31, 1941, pp. 25-45.
[5]Sixteenth Census of the United States, 1940: Population, Vol. 2, Part 7, 1943, Wisconsin Tables 23 and 24.
[6]In a study of hamlets in southwestern Wisconsin, G. T. Trewartha observes that Christaller's "hierarchy of evenly distributed settlements and lines of communication is disturbed by natural factors, locational advantages for manufacturing, and through lines of transportation" (The Unincorporated Hamlet: One Element of the American Settlement Fabric, *Annals Assn. of Amer. Geogrs.*, Vol. 33, 1943, pp. 32-81; reference on p. 57).

There is a rank-size rule[8] for cities by which an exponential constant, empirically determined, permits one to calculate within a small margin of error the number of people to be found in any city if the city's rank is known. The largest settlements in southwestern Wisconsin are too small in proportion to the other settlements to form this kind of progression. The rule is applicable only to a large group of urban settlements in a large country such as the United States or India and to the entire continent of Europe.

The progression from large to small settlements in the study area is observed (Fig. 3) to be geometrically constant[9] from 7000 to about 1000 and from 800 to 200. The trend line breaks between 1000 and 800, showing that the few large settlements with more than 1000 inhabitants are disproportionately larger than the host of small settlements with fewer than 800. But there is no clear offset that permits discrimination between large and small settlements. Population alone does not provide a satisfactory criterion. One suspects

---

[8]J. Q. Stewart: Empirical Mathematical Rules Concerning the Distribution and Equilibrium of Population, *Geogr. Rev.*, Vol. 37, 1947, pp. 461-485. The rule may be tested by plotting the rank-size progression on a graph in which both ordinate and abscissa are logarithmic scales.

[9]The relationship may be expressed in the formula $y = Ae^{Bx}$, where y is the population of a given city, e is the constant determined empirically, x is the rank of a given city, and A and B are parameters determined by the data.

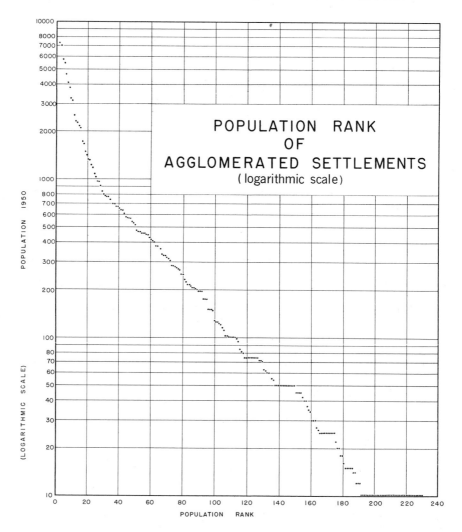

POPULATION RANK
OF
AGGLOMERATED SETTLEMENTS
(logarithmic scale)

POPULATION 1950
(LOGARITHMIC SCALE)

POPULATION RANK

FIGURE 3

that any functional classification of trade centers based exclusively on population is purely arbitrary. The number of inhabitants is the product of a multiplicity of factors besides trade, such as number of family dependents, retired persons, and persons employed outside the settlements.

The status of trade centers is determined by the functions they perform—by the combination, or association, of distinctive sets of functional units. There is, however, no clear-cut break in the progression from large to small settlements in the frequency of any one kind of functional unit; frequency of grocery stores, for example, is a progression from large to small centers similar to the progression of population. By this criterion of function a threefold classification becomes apparent—hamlets, villages, and towns (Table I).

HAMLETS

The smallest agglomerated settlements are hamlets. They serve as trade centers of the most rudimentary sort. In order to be classed as a hamlet,[10] a settlement must consist of at least five residential structures or other buildings used for commercial or cultural purposes clustered within one-quarter of a mile (linear distance), and it must contain at least one but not more than nine retail and service units. Only grocery stores and elementary schools are typical of hamlets; taverns, filling stations, and churches are common. All these commercial and cultural units are also found at roadside locations outside agglomerated settlements, but rarely grouped together.

VILLAGES

In settlements of this class there is a larger commercial nucleus. The criteria, adopted on the basis of empirical evidence, require that a village must have a minimum of 10 retail and service units of all types. Moreover, there must be, in addition to the groceries, taverns, and filling stations found in hamlets, at least four other retail businesses, selling autos, implements, appliances, lumber,

hardware, or livestock feed. Three other essential services, such as auto repair, banking, and telephone exchange or postal delivery, must be provided. Freight transportation by truck is more commonly available than by rail. The public high school is a service provided in more than half of the villages, but rarely in hamlets. As a rule, villages are incorporated for local governmental purposes, but they employ only one or two full-time functionaries.

Villages are incomplete trade centers, and personal and professional services are not well developed. Physicians and dentists are usually found only in large villages (more than 600). Villages lack many features of urban centers, such as motion-picture theaters and other recreational facilities, yet they are significant centers for the goods and services most frequently demanded by rural people.

TOWNS

Settlements of this class are more widely specialized urban centers. Here are provided not only the ordinary goods and services available in smaller centers but also many of the specialized goods and services required by town, village, hamlet, and farm dwellers. In towns there are at least 50 retail units, 30 of which are types other than grocery stores, taverns, and filling stations. The criteria require that towns have banks and weekly newspapers. There must be high schools, and four other professions must be represented—physicians, dentists, veterinarians, and lawyers. In Wisconsin, towns are usually organized as cities of the fourth class, a legal status to which they become eligible upon reaching a population of 1000. Many towns are county seats, but this role is neither necessary for the development of towns nor the dominant feature of any town in the study area.

The multiplicity of functions that gives towns distinction as trade centers is to be attributed to four main causes. First, the mere fact of aggregation of people, forming large local markets, facilitates the development of certain specialized types of retail goods, personal services, and recreational facilities related directly to the concentration of town dwellers and not maintained in smaller centers. Food specialty shops such as meat markets, bakeries, and retail dairies, fuel and ice dealers, news dealers, and gift, radio, and sporting-goods

---

[10]The author adheres to Trewartha's minimal requirements of size and agglomeration. He defines a hamlet as consisting of not fewer than "(1) *four* active residence units, at least two of which are non-farm houses; (2) a total of at least *six* active functional units,—residential, business, social or otherwise; and (3) a total of at least *five* buildings actively used by human beings" (*op. cit.* [see footnote 6, above], p. 37).

TABLE I   Functional Classes of Trade Centers in Southwestern Wisconsin 1949—1950

ASSOCIATED FUNCTIONAL UNITS[a]	44 Hamlets[b] POPULATION Mean, 65 Range, 20-300	73 Villages POPULATION Mean, 481 Range, 115-1415	19 Towns POPULATION Mean, 3324 Range, 1329-7217
Retail trade	Grocery or general store	Tavern Filling station Auto and/or implement dealer Hardware store Appliance store Lumber yard Food store	Food specialty store Restaurant Drugstore Department store Apparel or shoe store Variety (5 & 10 cents) Fuel dealer Florist Furniture store Jewelry store
Wholesale trade	....	....	Livestock buyer Bulk oil distributor
Finance	....	Bank	Insurance agency
Trades and personal service	....	Auto repair shop	Electric repair shop Shoe repair shop Undertaker (mortician) Portrait photographer Barber Beautician Dry cleaner Hotel
Amusements	....	....	Movie theatre Billiard hall Bowling alley Public park
Transportation	....	Livestock trucker Milk trucker Freight truck line	Railroad freight depot Passenger bus line Local dray
Communication	....	Post office Telephone exchange	Weekly newspaper
Utilities	....	....	Water system Sewage system Electric power distribution
Manufacturing	....	Feed mill	Bakery Printing press Dairy processing plant
Professional services	Elementary School	Church High School[c]	High School Physician Dentist Health practitioner Veterinary Lawyer
Government	....	Village	City (4th class)

[a] Sources: Dun and Bradstreet's "Reference Book for Wisconsin, 1949" [see text footnote 7]; telephone directories and business or professional directories. The types of functions listed occur in at least 75 per cent of the centers in each class and are considered to be distinctive of each successively higher class in the hierarchy.

[b] Only hamlets investigated by the author are reported because of the unreliability of published sources.

[c] High schools are found in 70 per cent of the villages.

shops find most of their customers within the towns. Laundries, dry cleaners, and tailor shops depend primarily on town trade; taxis and drays are peculiarly town transport services. Recreational facilities, such as parks, libraries, and golf courses, can be supported because of the concentration of town dwellers, and this concentration also requires greater exercise of governmental powers. Specialized public officers, such as police, street and park maintenance workers, and administration department heads are employed. Water and sewage systems are required.

Second, the larger trade areas of towns, combined with their larger local markets, enable towns to develop additional types of retail trade and services to those in smaller centers, with their smaller trade areas. Many types of retail establishments are located in towns because of the advantage of gaining country as well as town patronage; grocery supermarkets are an example, and drugstores, clothing and department stores, and furniture, florist, and jewelry stores depend on doing a large part of their business with farmers. Financial services, including real estate, insurance, and loan agencies, divide their business equally between farms and the town. Photographers and morticians, barbers and beauticians, and the auto, shoe, and electrical repair shops are supported by both. Movie houses, billiard halls, bowling alleys, and taverns are used by rural and urban people alike. The towns' weekly newspapers circulate widely among farm dwellers; the post offices and telephone exchanges serve them.

The larger populations of towns can support specialized professional services. Changes in medical practice and ease of transport have caused medical services to become more and more centralized. Clinics and hospitals generally exist in towns but not in villages, and dentists, chiropractors, and opticians are concentrated in towns. Legal services are distinctly urban, though many of the lawyers' clients are farm dwellers. Town churches draw much of their membership from the surrounding rural territory, and town high schools similarly draw much of their enrollment from farms round about.

Third, the larger farm markets of towns enable them to offer goods and services solely for farmers that are not obtainable in smaller centers. Dairy and other food-processing plants are attrac-ted to towns, though they use raw materials obtained outside. Wholesaling of livestock, poultry, and cheese is centered in towns; feed mills and veterinarians are found there, though they serve only the needs of farmers. The county agricultural fairs are held on the outskirts of towns. A town is the county seat, though many of the administrative duties of county officers have little to do with town dwellers; the county agricultural agents, home agents, and soil-conservation technicians maintained in county seats by the federal government likewise have nothing to do with town dwellers.

Fourth, the towns attract commercial travelers and develop wholesale distribution because of their concentration of business and population. These functions generally involve relations between towns and trade centers of lower or higher functional orders. Groceries, auto parts, and petroleum products, manufactured elsewhere and brought to the towns, are distributed for sale from retail units located in the towns or in smaller centers nearby. Traveling salesmen make frequent visits to towns because of the concentration of retail business. Hotels, restaurants, and passenger terminals are maintained in towns because of the number of transients. Thus towns display many of the features of economic specialization that are considered to be typically urban in the United States.

Locational Patterns

The classes cannot be determined merely by functional attributes. Fundamentally, it is the spatial relationships of the centers that determine the existence of three discrete classes (Figs. 4[11] and 5). The smaller centers occur in an interlocking locational pattern, as well as in a subordinate functional relationship with the larger centers. The centers closest to towns are hamlets; villages are farther from towns but close to one another. In traveling from villages to towns, one usually passes hamlets. In this respect the locational pattern is in agreement with Christaller's "law of central places."

[11] The method of symbolization employed in Figure 4 was suggested by Hans Carol's map of trade centers in Canton Zurich, Switzerland, reproduced by Hans Boesch in "Die Wirtschaftslandschaften der Erde," Zurich, 1947, p. 202.

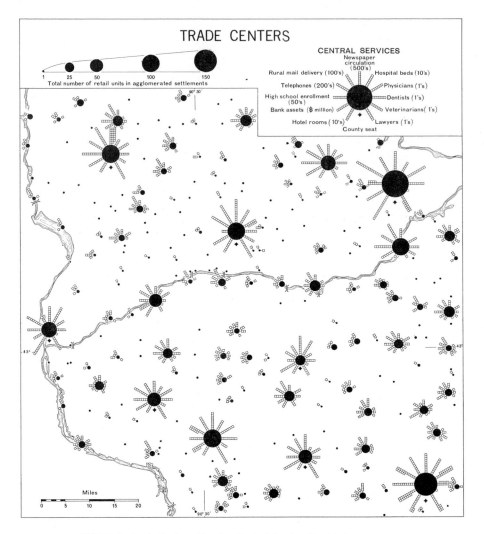

FIGURE 4 Trade Centers, Showing Central Services Provided.

Theoretically, two features of spatial arrangement are to be expected: (1) the average trade area must be a close approximation to a circle, with traffic routes converging toward the center from all parts; and (2) the centers must be regularly spaced in a radial-circular system, the higher-ranking centers falling in a framework of successively larger tributary areas and standing at successively greater distances apart. Geometric laws determine what would seem to be the most efficient manner of serving the inhabitants of any area.[12] Each center has a circular trade area in

contact with the trade areas of six equal-ranking and equidistant centers (Fig. 6). The costs of reaching one center increase progressively outward from the center in all directions up to an economic limit fixed by transport costs and travel time. Hence additional centers of like kind should always develop beyond the reach of any one center. Galpin found that competition existed in a zone of overlap between neighboring centers. Christaller theoretically eliminated overlap by reducing the circles to hexagons, which are the perfect mathematical resolution of adjacent circles covering a plane surface. A rectangular arrangement with each center equidistant from four other centers

_____

[12]C. J. Galpin: Rural Life (New York, 1918), p. 87.

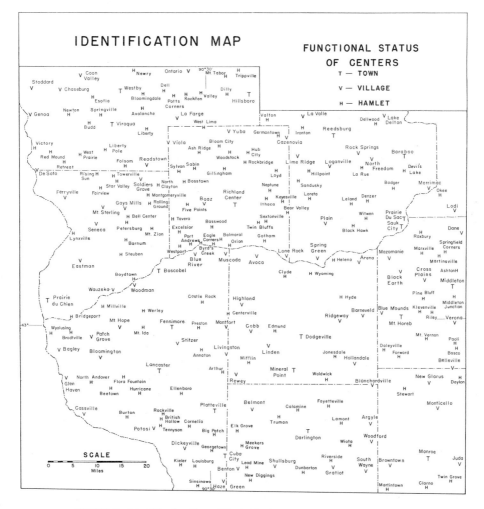

FIGURE 5   Identification Map of Trade Centers.

would result in more overlap and require more centers to serve a given area.

There are several corollaries of the radial-circular, or service, principle, according to Christaller.[13] The area of any higher center, for example a town—C in Figure 6—invades the nearest parts of the areas of the six nearby hamlets—A centers—and supersedes the hamlets' services with services the hamlets do not provide. The villages—B centers —also invade the hamlets' areas, and each A area is divided equally among three higher centers of B or C class. Because the hamlets are spaced no

farther from towns or from villages than they are from one another, they stand at the intersecting boundaries of B and C areas. The mean hamlet area is one-third of a village area and one-ninth of a town area. The distance between centers of each successive class increases by $\sqrt{3}$. These theoretical features of spatial arrangement for providing services (Christaller's *Versorgungsprinzip*) are to be expected throughout the hierarchy, including regional cities and metropolitan centers. Christaller admits the possibility of other influences besides the service principle as expressed in hexagons.[14]

---

[13]A brief statement of Christaller's theory may be found in a paper presented at the International Geographical Congress in 1938, *Comptes Rendus Congr. Internatl. de Géogr., Amsterdam, 1938*, Vol. 2, Sect. IIIa, Leiden, 1938, pp. 123-138.

[14]Christaller's latest statement of general principles is contained in "Das Grundgerüst der räumlichen Ordnung in Europa: Die Systeme der europäischen zentralen Orte," *Frankfurter Geogr. Hefte*, Vol. 24, No. I, 1950, pp. 5-14.

The demands of adminstrative coordination (*Zuordnung*) do not alter the shape of the service area, but the requirements of long-distance transportation (*Verkehr*) cause centers to be aligned along main routes. The tributary areas in this case are elongated figures in which the short axes coincide with the transport route and the long axes extend at right angles. Christaller believes that the influence of transportation makes itself evident only in the development of rows of low-ranking centers on main routes between higher centers. But he discounts the transport principle (*Verkehrsprinzip*) in Germany, where many small centers grew in late medieval times to serve local needs before the influence of long-distance transport became pronounced.

Kolb, an American sociologist who elaborates on Galpin's radial-circular concept, does not concur with Christaller's hexagonal scheme. Kolb[15] observes that the small A areas (Fig 6)—that is, the primary neighborhood or single-service centers —exist near the peripheries of the secondary service areas of the high-ranking C centers. Farther out are found B centers with incomplete services and smaller service areas. A centers are closer to B centers than to C centers, but outside the primary influence of B centers. Both A and B centers are within the larger area of specialized services around C. In other words, not only does the specialized service area of a large center supersede the service areas of lower-ranking centers, but the aggregate of all services provided by the higher center attracts people from a greater distance and reduces the lower centers' areas even in those primary and secondary services in which they duplicate the higher center. This theoretical scheme is in accord with Reilly's "law of retail gravitation"[16] and Tuominen's "proportional range of influence" (*Reichweitenverhältnis*).[17] The pull

exerted by a trade center measured either by its population (Reilly) or by its retail stores (Tuominen) varies directly with the size of the center and decreases outward with increasing distance. The smaller centers are therefore not likely to develop as close to large centers as they are to one another.

Spacing of Centers in Southwestern Wisconsin

The radial-circular concept would seem to be supported in the study area by the fact that the mean distance between centers increases in each successive class (Table II), and intercenter distances approximate the $\sqrt{3}$ rule. If the hamlets in southwestern Wisconsin were perfectly spaced in a hexagonal system, they would be 5.8 miles apart; actually, they occur at a mean distance of 5.5 miles from one another and from the higher functional classes. Villages would be 10.4 miles apart; actually, they occur at a mean distance of 9.9 miles from one another and from towns. Towns would be 20.5 miles apart; they are, on the average, 21.2 miles apart.

However, the radial-circular principle can be only a partial explanation of the observed locational pattern. The tendency of centers to group themselves in rows or clusters is pronounced. Hamlets gravitate to the areas farthest from larger centers at a mean distance of 4.8 miles from other hamlets, 5.6 miles from the nearest villages, and 6.9 miles from the nearest towns. The mean distance between villages grouped in rows or clusters is 6.8 miles, but the distance between villages and the nearest towns is 11.3 miles. Towns grouped in rows or pairs are 12.2 miles apart, but they are on the average 25.8 miles from towns in similar groups. Kolb's observations are borne out by the crowding together of low-ranking centers in the areas farthest from the large centers. The higher centers, however, are drawn more closely toward one another than would be expected from either Kolb's or Christaller's scheme.

The cause of the linear pattern of location in southwestern Wisconsin lies largely in the influence of railroads. Distributing and collecting points on the long-distance lines gave the stimulus re-

[15] J. H. Kolb and E. de S. Brunner: A Study of Rural Society, edited by W. F. Ogburn (3rd edit., Boston, 1946); see especially Chapters 4 and 5, pp. 75-138. On p. 128 is Kolb's graph showing theoretical interrelations of types of service centers in rural areas. This graph first appeared in J. H. Kolb: Service Relations of Town and Country, *Univ. of Wisconsin Agric. Exper. Sta. Research Bull. 58*, 1923, p. 8.

[16] W. J. Reilly: Methods for the Study of Retail Relationships, *Univ. of Texas Bur. of Business Research, Research Monograph No. 4* (*Univ. of Texas Bull. No. 2944*), 1928, p. 26. See also his book "The Law of Retail Gravitation" (New York, 1931).

[17] Oiva Tuominen: Das Einflussgebiet der Stadt Turku im System der Einflussgebiete SW-Finnlands, *Fennia*, Vol. 71, No. 5, Helsinki, 1949, pp. 114-121.

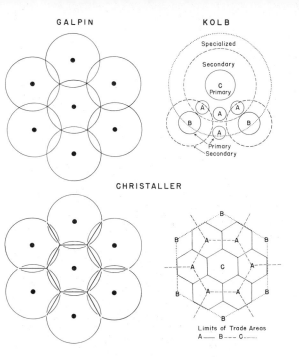

TABLE II Spacing of Trade Centers (In miles)

Intercenter Distances	142 Hamlets	73 Villages	19 Towns
Theoretical distance[a]	5.6	10.0	19.8
Mean measured distance[b]	5.5	9.9	21.2
Range of variation	1.0—12.0	3.5—18.5	7.0—38.0

[a] Calculated according to the formula given by J. A. Barnes and A. H. Robinson: A New Method for the Representation of Dispersed Rural Population, *Geogr. Rev.*, Vol. 30, 1940, pp. 134—137. If the centers are equally spaced in a hexagonal system.

$$D = 1.07 \sqrt{\frac{A}{n}},$$

where D is the distance between the centers, A is the total area within which the centers are dispersed, and n is the number of centers.

[b] The means are simple arithmetic averages of straight-line distances between centers, measured on a base map on the scale of one inch to four miles. Road distances between the centers measured in sample areas indicate that straight-line distances are 15—25 per cent less than road distances. Therefore a correction factor of plus 20 per cent should be applied to the straight-line distances given in the table to obtain approximations of road distances between the trade centers.

FIGURE 6 Theoretical Distribution of Trade Centers.
(*Sources:* C. J. Galpin, 1914, as reproduced by J. H. Kolb and R. A. Polson: Trends in Town-Country Relations, *Univ. of Wisconsin Agric. Exper. Sta. Research Bull.* 117, 1933, p. 30; Kolb, modified from diagram in "Service Relations of Town and Country" [see text footnote 15], p. 8; Christaller, "Die zentralen Orte in Süddeutchland" [see text footnote 1].)

quired for centers to grow into villages or towns. Christaller's *Verkehrsprinzip* was a powerful force in the settlement of this region, where railroad construction followed the arrival of farmers within a few decades. The rail depot was the original site of agglomeration for numerous trade centers. Earlier sites were, in chronological sequence, river landings, lead deposits, county seats, and mill dams. During the period 1830–1880 some early trade centers attained the status of villages or towns without railroads, but few villages, and no towns, were maintained without a rail connection. The incised terrain of ridges and valleys contributed to the development of rows where these terrain features were followed by rail lines. Chains of villages and towns developed in some valleys at series of mill dams, exemplifying what Christaller would call *Pseudoverkehrsorientierung*. Unexplained linear patterns are also displayed by somewhat irregular rows of towns that follow the alignment neither of any continuous ridges nor of any rail lines but run roughly north-south at right angles to the Wisconsin River, parallel to the Mississippi (Figs. 4 and 5).

The more or less scattered distribution of hamlets in the voids between higher centers is accounted for by the dispersion of farm population throughout the area before 1880, when wagon roads were the sole means of access to most of the territory away from the rivers and there were few railroads. Hamlets appeared during the period 1830–1880 at the same types of sites as villages and towns, as well as at churches, stores, taverns, hotels, post offices, and schools. This somewhat random location of rudimentary trade centers occurred at a basic spacing of four to six miles throughout the settled area where no larger centers had developed earlier.

The spatial pattern of agglomerated settlements is the result of site and transport influences during the nineteenth century. Inertia of the settlement pattern is so great that centers have not died out completely, though rural population has decreased. Railroads, once the life lines of trade, have lost nearly all their local traffic, having been replaced by trucks and passenger cars. Hamlets have regressed as trade centers but remain viable as residential settlements, retaining some of their central services. Villages are important, though incomplete, local centers; their functional attributes have changed and even increased in variety, while their population has generally remained stable or increased slightly during the past 40 years. Towns are the only centers that continue to make large gains in population, making relatively and absolutely the greatest gains in new functional units.

Thus the functional status of settlements is dynamic, influenced by economic and technological changes. But their locational pattern remains fixed.

Tributary Areas and Traffic Areas

The map of traffic areas (Fig. 7), derived from the average movement of all vehicular traffic[18] (Fig. 8), is interpreted by the author to represent roughly the map of tributary areas. A traffic area is defined as the area within which the attraction is clearly exerted most strongly by the center near its mid-point. Seldom are there six roads from six villages converging at each town, as Christaller postulates, or six roads from six hamlets converging at each village. Usually there are two or three roads coming into a town or village that bring both local and long-distance traffic; often there are two roads, sometimes three, that bring only local traffic. Lateral roads bearing local traffic join the main-traveled roads in the open country, adding to the streams of traffic that broaden toward towns and villages. Hamlets, even if they are far from main roads and from towns or villages, do not exhibit sufficient traffic convergence to permit delimitation of traffic areas. The boundaries of the tributary areas of towns and villages are traffic divides where few vehicles travel.

Evidence from the field indicates that there can be no precise boundary of trade, or tributary, areas.[19] Every commodity or service has its own particular area, which overlaps similar areas of other centers. If the boundaries of several services are superimposed, they are seldom found to coincide, because some areas are smaller and others larger. However, it is possible to describe generalized, composite, trade areas, though the boundaries become vaguer and the zone of overlap wider.[20]

Since in reality there exists only a nuclear area of absolute dominance near each center,[21] and farther out there are ill-defined boundaries, the analysis of traffic is a satisfactory method of defining tributary areas. The movement of vehicles is a ready measure of the combined economic and cultural influences drawing farmers to the centers in a region where every farm is provided with automobile transport. The mean tributary area is to be derived by apportioning the area of traffic divergence between neighboring centers. A mean line demarcating the relatively greater attraction of one center as opposed to another would lie somewhere in an ill-defined traffic divide.[22]

The map of traffic areas supports conclusions previously reached in regard to spacing of trade centers. Abundant evidence is seen that as a result of linear or clustered location of the centers the tributary areas are seldom circular or hexagonal. They tend to be elongated at right angles to the axes of rows of centers or extended eccentrically from centers in clusters. Village areas exist in belts between the town areas. Many hamlets are situated at the margins of town or village areas or in the traffic divides; some, however, are well within the zones of influence around large centers.

The relationships of the traffic areas of villages and towns (Table III) show clearly that village influence is less extensive than it would be if the true hexagonal system existed. Hamlet areas, actually shrunken or nonexistent, would be theoretically 27.5 square miles. Village areas would be

---

[18]Traffic data were collected during 1948 by the Highway Planning Division of the State Highway Commission of Wisconsin and were made available in a series of county maps indicating the average number of vehicles passing temporary observation points spaced every two or three miles on roads carrying 35 vehicles or more a day. The traffic counts, made on two successive days, are adjusted for seasonal variation so as to be representative for the year. The seasonal index used by the Planning Division as a correction factor is based on data from 11 continuously operating traffic meters in various parts of Wisconsin and from other short-term records. Only two of the permanent observation stations are located in the study area; all other counts here must be regarded as samples.

[19]The results of the author's inquiry among business proprietors in the study area are corroborated by the reports of sociologists for other areas. G. F. Deasy (Sales and Service Industries in Luce County, Michigan, *Econ. Geogr.*, Vol. 26, 1950, pp. 315-324) finds an area of overlap and an area clearly dominated by one center.

[20]Galpin's analysis of community areas was based on the outlines of eight areas: groceries, dry goods, banking, local newspaper, milk marketing, church, high school, and public library. J. F. Thaden outlines composite areas on the basis of six services: hardware, clothing, banking, newspaper, rural mail delivery, and high school (The Lansing Region and Its Tributary Town-Country Communities, *Michigan State College Agric. Exper. Sta. Special Bull.* 302, 1940).

[21]Hans Carol (Das agrargeographische Betrachtungssystem: Ein Beitrag zur landschaftskundlichen Methodik, dargelegt am Beispiel der Karru in Südafrika, *Geographica Helvetica*, Vol. 7, 1952, pp. 17-67) designates this nuclear area as the *Kernzone*; the transitional area bordering it is the *Übergangszone* (pp. 27-28). These concepts are similar to Deasy's "core area" and "zone of competition" (*op. cit.*, p. 322).

[22]The author's experience with the mapping of road turnings at farmstead entrances suggests that if the method were combined with the analysis of traffic flow, it would undoubtedly narrow the traffic divides. The road-turning method has been advocated both by geographers (S. D. Dodge and L. S. Wilson: The Umland of Howell, Livingston County, Michigan, *Papers Michigan Acad. of Sci., Arts and Letters*, Vol. 22 [for 1936], 1937, pp. 355-357) and by sociologists (F. H. Forsyth: The Use of Road Turnings in Community Research, *Rural Sociology*, Vol. 9, 1944, pp. 384-385).

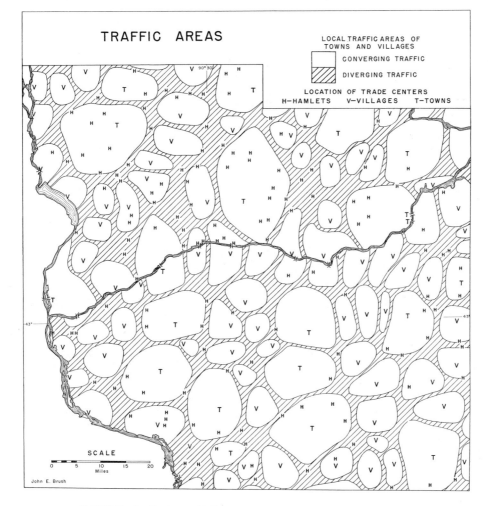

FIGURE 7 Traffic Areas, 1948.
(Source, Figs. 7 and 8: State Highway Commission data.)

three times this, or 82.5 square miles; actually the village mean is only 57 per cent of the theoretical area. Village areas are small not only because of linear spacing but also because of the encroachment of town areas.

According to Christaller's rule, towns should have local tributary areas, or umlands,[23] identical in size with the village areas, within which they provide the same goods and services as villages. Actually, average town areas are four times the theoretical size (Table III)—a fact that substantiates Kolb's observations rather than Christaller's

[23]The author proposes to use "umland" to denote the local tributary area of a village or town; "hinterland" can then be reserved to denote the larger tributary area of a town which extends beyond the town "umland" and includes the village "umland."

TABLE III   Traffic Areas and Population*

Traffic Area	62 Villages	13 Towns
Mean area exclusive of borders (in sq. mi.)	32.2	129.1
Range in size (in sq. mi.)	9.6—76.8	27.2—241.6
Mean population[a]	608	2439
Mean area including borders[b] (in sq. mi.)	47.5	190.5
Mean population	897	3598

* Includes only the trade centers with their entire traffic areas within the limits of the map. Mean population of villages, 486; of towns, 3373.

a The population is calculated from the mean density of farm and hamlet population—18.9 persons to a square mile—in eight of the nine counties in the study area. Dane County is omitted because of the presence of urban-fringe population near the city limits of Madison.

b The border areas comprise 2074.4 sq. miles, or 32.2 percent of the area studied, divided between towns and villages in the same ratio as their traffic areas—47.1 per cent to towns and 52.9 per cent to villages.

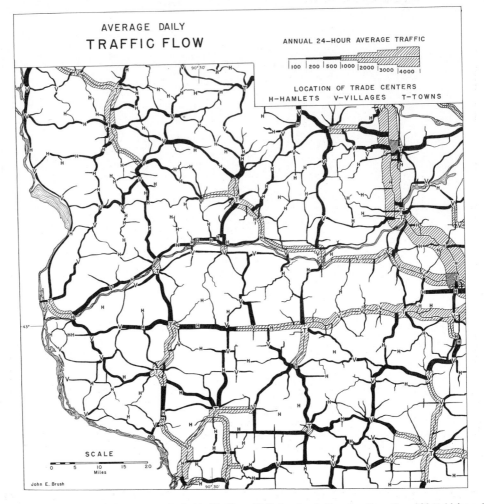

FIGURE 8 Average Daily Traffic Flow, 1948, for Roads Carrying More than 100 Vehicles a Day.

and reflects the much greater attraction exerted by towns, commensurate with their greater assemblage of central services.[24] The mean population of village areas, however, is one-fourth again as great as that of the villages, whereas the mean population of town areas is about one-third less than that of the towns. Towns are disproportionately large in relation to their umland areas.[25]

It must be remembered that the influence of towns extends beyond their umlands to the hamlets at the traffic divides and to the villages and their areas. In the study area as a whole, it can be inferred that four or five villages are subordinate to the average town. Analysis of the traffic flow on the main roads leading from villages to towns suggests that many villages are linked to two towns (Fig. 9); some villages near the three cities outside the study area are linked to these cities instead. The boundaries of these town and city hinterlands are necessarily more diffuse than local umland boundaries. It can be assumed that an average of four villages are dependent on each town in the study area and that each town serves an additional 128.8 square miles of territory peripheral to its local umland area. Towns appear to

---

[24]The same relationship probably exists between European centers and their tributary areas. See the maps in Tuominen, *op. cit.* [see footnoe 17, above], p. 119; F. H. W. Green: Urban Hinterlands in England and Wales: An Analysis of Bus Services, *Geogr. Journ.,* Vol. 116, 1950, pp. 64-88; and Sven Godlund: Bus Services, Hinterlands, and the Location of Urban Settlements in Sweden, Specially in Scania, *Lund Studies in Geogr.,* Ser. B, Human Geography, No. 3, 1951, pp. 14-24.

[25]According to Christaller the population means of **three** successive classes should be in the ratio 1:2:4. The actual means of hamlet, village, and town classes in southwestern Wisconsin are in the ratio 1:8:50.

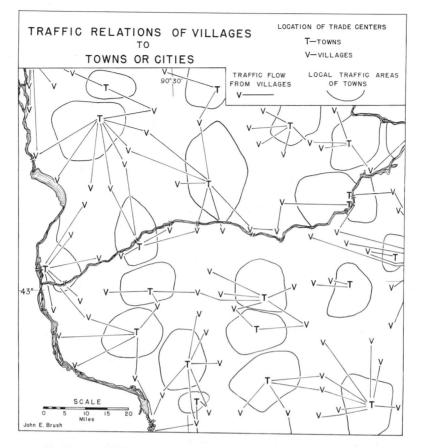

FIGURE 9 Traffic Relations of Villages to Towns or Cities.
(*Source:* State Highway Commission data.)

be disproportionately small, then, in relation to the total population of their larger hinterlands.

Traffic movement along main roads also reveals the attraction exerted by the cities of Madison, Dubuque, and La Crosse, which draw people from all towns and villages in the study area. These cities belong in a higher functional order of trade centers than the towns in the area, and they extend their influence into the town hinterlands, supplementing and superseding the towns in services just as the towns supplement and supersede the villages. When the circulation of vehicles along a main road is graphed as a profile (Fig. 10), the high points are parts of the road with little traffic and the lower points are parts with heavy traffic. The towns appear at lower points than the villages, registering strong local convergence of traffic gradients; the villages appear as small notches along gradients toward towns or cities. The in-

creased traffic density near towns along a road that shows still greater density as it approaches cities can be conceived as analogous[26] to the overflow of interior drainage basins, the higher ones emptying into the lower ones. The highest points on the main roads are the human dividing ridges between the hinterlands of the cities. These city traffic divides in the study area coincide closely with the commonly recognized trade areas of cities based on daily newspaper circulation.

General Laws of Central Places

Is the system of central places in southwest-

---

[26]The analogy comes from Green, *op. cit.* [see footnote 24, above], pp. 76-77, who has mapped similar divides on the basis of frequency and direction of bus services for small urban centers in Great Britain.

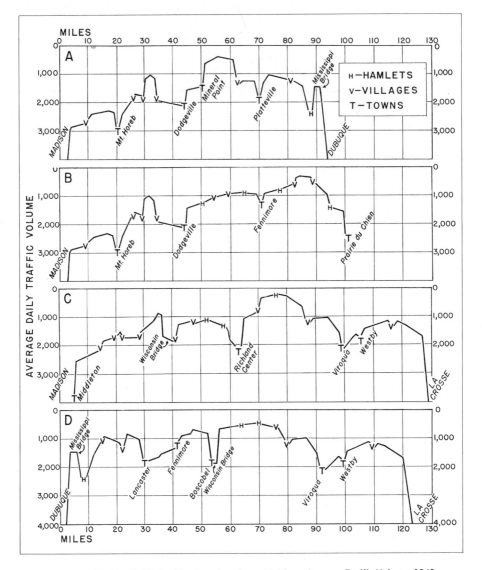

FIGURE 10 Traffic Profiles Based on Annual 24-hour Average Traffic Volume, 1948.
(Source: State Highway Commission data.)

ern Wisconsin a particular case of a general law? Is there a system not as rigid as Christaller's theory that underlies the functional development and spacing of centers in all closely settled regions? Some striking similarities are to be observed in the findings of geographers in Europe.[27] Of course, it is impossible to equate precisely the hierarchy in any one region with the hierarchy in another.[28] Differences in specific attributes of the centers are to be expected because of differences in transportation, economic development, population density, and, above all, the evolution of the social and political organization of the people. Separate and distinct orders of function will probably be found in each of the major cultural realms of the Old World. Uniformity is not to be expected in Anglo-America because of the modifications caused by

---

[27]See also note on pp. 414–416 of *Geographical Review*, [Vol. 43, No. 3, 1953].

[28]Carol, *op. cit.* [see footnote 21, above], holds that there is a universal ranking of centers in seven main grades, ranging from farmstead to world metropolis. Each of the grades may or may not exist in any one region or country.

site attraction, methods of transport, and modes of settlement prevalent during initial periods of settlement. Yet wherever a commercial economy prevails, there may be fundamental spatial factors that cause small centers to grow at more or less regular intervals, and larger centers to grow at greater intervals to serve more than local rudimentary needs for the exchange of goods and services.

The farmstead possesses the lowest degree of centrality, as the seat of farm operations, storage, and residence in the midst of fields. The agricultural village of the Old World and Latin America possesses a similar centrality but in higher degree, because services such as church, school, and agricultural processing are provided. In Anglo-America, where farm villages are generally absent, the same services are relegated to hamlets or the open country.

In closely settled areas of northwestern Europe the threshold of rudimentary trade is apparently reached in urban villages, spaced at 2–4 miles and having several hundred or even a thousand inhabitants.[29] In Wisconsin the lowest level of agglomeration is the hamlet or single-service center, spaced at 2.5–5.5 miles but with fewer than a hundred inhabitants. In areas such as Finland or South Africa the substratum of sparse agricultural settlement gives rise to rudimentary centers at much wider intervals.

The market town, the lowest distinctly developed center in Europe, occurs at intervals of 4–8 miles, has 1000–4000 inhabitants, and provides a much greater variety of services than the lowest well-developed center in Wisconsin—the village or semicomplete center, spaced at 8–10 miles and with 500–900 inhabitants. The most nearly equivalent centers in Finland are 30 miles apart and in South Africa 60 miles apart. All these centers belong, perhaps, in the fifth and lowest distinct order of the hierarchy suggested by both Smailes and Carol.[30]

The centers of the fourth ascending order in the hierarchy are the complete, partly specialized centers designated as towns in Wisconsin. The English town, 10–15 miles from other towns and with more than 5000 population, is equivalent to the *Kreisstadt,* or possibly the *Bezirksstadt,* of Germany, spaced respectively at 13 and 22 miles and with populations of 4000 and 10,000. Towns in Wisconsin have fewer inhabitants but are spaced at somewhat greater distances. In Finland and South Africa fourth-order centers are much farther apart, and larger in population.

Third-order centers, in which are found highly specialized urban services, occur at 35–40-mile intervals in both Wisconsin and Germany but are 60–90 miles apart in Finland. This order and the two higher ones postulated by Smailes and Carol are much less clearly understood.

An interesting field of comparative geographical research is open in the study of central places. Development of regular functional grades and spatial patterns should not be expected where the economic support of the population is chiefly manufacturing or mining, or where large suburban residential and recreational agglomerations occur, as Smailes has shown in England. The relative influence of area for trade as opposed to site for manufacturing or residence has yet to be evaluated.

[29] R. E. Dickinson: The Distribution and Functions of the Smaller Urban Settlements of East Anglia, *Geography,* Vol. 17, 1932, pp. 19-31.

[30] A. E. Smailes: The Urban Mesh of England and Wales, *Inst. of British Geogrs. Publ. No. 11* , 1946, pp. 85-101; Carol, *op. cit.* [see footnote 21, above], pp. 26 and 57-63.

Sven Godlund

TRAFFIC, UMLANDS AND BUILT-UP AREAS—
PROGNOSIS AND RECOMMENDATIONS

... there is a distinct relationship between relative position and function and development as expressed in terms of centrality. The intention now is to endeavor to ally these phenomena to a general spatial localisation and development theory concerning the formation of built-up areas and the methodics of administrative regional divisions using, as a basis, the methodics outlined in the previous chapter and the information gathered concerning the position and function of the built-up areas.

As regards the development of built-up areas, in as far as their centrality is concerned, the deductions made in the foregoing chapter enable us to establish the following hypothesis for the development of built-up areas as expressed in terms of centrality. Fig. 15.[1]

In Fig. 15, A and B are taken to be two well-established δ-places, with an equal centrality rating, and the intermediate regions to contain evenly divided built-up areas with either a low or a zero centrality rating or equal possibilities for the formation of built-up areas. The curves indicate the frequency of the potential or real contacts with the two places in question, A and B. In Fig. 15b an intermediate growth of a group of central places has arisen in the divide zone, i.e., where the influence of the existent δ-places (A and B) is weakest. In Fig. 15c, one built-up area in this group (C)

has developed into a central place with a fairly high centrality rating. In Fig. 15d this place C has grown to the point where it has the same centrality rating as the two older places, A and B. In the intersecting zones between the now established fields of influence two new high-rating central places have begun to emerge (D and E). This process of urbanisation—for purposes of simplicity shown above as an even, successive halving of the distance between equal δ-places—can be expected to progress until the saturation stage has been reached, i.e., until the population's purchasing power and need of central service has been satisfied. In Fig. 15e this saturation stage has been exceeded, e.g., as a result of the growth of bus traffic and the depopulation of the country areas, and the importance of the smaller central places at D and E has begun to diminish as a result of there being insufficient background for a continued expansion of trading facilities.

The picture of the umlands has of necessity been restricted to the current situation (on the basis of traveller data for 1947–53). On the other hand, centrality calculations—at least approximate ones—can be made for a period of years, 1900–1950. Thus, to be able to make a closer study of the dynamics of the formation of the umlands and the built-up areas as per Fig. 15 we require data for the umlands—approximate data at least—for the same period of time as for the centrality information. In consequence, we are faced with the task of establishing a utilizable calculation of the umlands for the period in question.

The total number of arriving and departing bus passengers in a number of δ-places and the centrality of these places as determined by for-

Reprinted with the permission of the author and publisher from "The Function and Growth of Bus Traffic Within the Sphere of Urban Influence," *Lund Studies in Geography,* Series B, No. 18, 1956, pp. 59–72. Dr. Godlund is Professor of Geography in the Geografiska Institution, Göteborgs Universitets, Sweden.

[1] In addition to the work mentioned reference may also be made to, inter alia, *Ajo* (1944), *Firey, Loomis and Beegle* (1950), *Kant* (1946 and 1951), *Kareda* (1938), *Lösch* (1944) and *Reilly* (1929 and 1931).

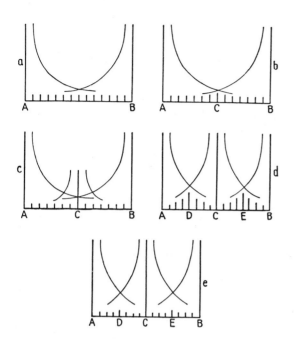

FIGURE 15

is exerted from A and B, can be obtained from the following formula[3]

$$r = \frac{l}{C_A - C_B} \cdot \sqrt{C_A \cdot C_B} \qquad (13)$$

and

$$m = \frac{C_A \cdot l}{C_A - C_B} \qquad (14)$$

If we compare this theoretical umland—"centrality" umland—on the basis of the 1945/1946 C-values with the actual traffic surround based on the passenger statistics for 1947–51—the "bus traffic umland"—we get the following table (28) and Fig. 16 with examples from L- and M-counties.[4]

---

[3] The two formulae can be easily obtained by adopting the following procedure: If in a co-ordination system the origin is placed at the one point (place A) and the other point (B) is chosen as $(l, 0)$, then the condition for equal effect in (x, y) is constant

$$\frac{C_A}{x^2 + y^2} = \frac{C_B}{(l-x)^2 + y^2} \qquad (15)$$

which gives $C_A \cdot (l^2 + x^2 + y^2 - 2 \cdot l \cdot x) = C_B (x^2 + y^2)$ (16)

or $(C_A - C_B) \cdot (x^2 + y^2) - 2 \cdot C_A \cdot l \cdot x + C_A \cdot l^2 = 0$ (17)

or

$$x^2 + y^2 - \frac{2 \cdot C_A \cdot l}{C_A - C_B} \cdot x + \frac{C_A \cdot l^2}{C_A - C_B} = 0 \qquad (18)$$

or

$$\left(x - \frac{C_A \cdot l}{C_A - C_B} \right)^2 + y^2 = \frac{C_A \cdot C_B \cdot l^2}{(C_A - C_B)^2} \qquad (19)$$

which means a circle with radius

$$r = \frac{l}{C_A - C_B} \cdot \sqrt{C_A \cdot C_B} \qquad (13)$$

and the centre point $\quad m = \dfrac{C_A \cdot l}{C_A - C_B} \qquad (14)$

[4] The distances are calculated on the straight line distances between the places and between main point and main point of the business centre of the respective places. The empirical distances are reckoned on the basis of fig. 14, the theoretical (D_t) can be easily calculated from

$$D_t = m - r \qquad (20)$$

For example, $C_{Tomelilla} = 10.6$, $C_{Simrishamn} = 8.5$ while the distance between these two places as the crow flies is 26 km. We thus get

$$r = \frac{26}{10.6 - 8.5} \sqrt{10.6 \cdot 8.5} = 117.6 \qquad (21)$$

$$m = \frac{10.6 \cdot 26}{10.6 - 8.5} = 131.2 \qquad (22)$$

which means that the theoretical umland of Simrishamn has a circular boundary line as opposed to that for Tomelilla where the centre of the circle is 131.2 km from Tomelilla on the extension of the straight line and where the radius in this circle is 117.6 km. The point of intersection, D_t, on the straight connecting line between the places fall at
131.2 — 117.6 km = 13.6 from Tomelilla
This distance, in round figures, will be found in the right-hand column in table 28.

---

mula have been found to conform so well that it is safe to use the formula as a means of determining the centrality. Thus, working on the same lines as Tuominen (1949 p. 114 ff) (distance studies) and Emerson, Aurosseau and Fawcett (1913 p. 136, 1923 p. 273 and 1932 p. 105) (studies of nodal points) we can see whether reasonably good agreements can be obtained between field strengths determined on the basis of the centrality in the δ-place and the surround and the real umlands to these places as determined by means of the data in respect of bus passengers, i.e., between "centrality umland" and "bus traffic umland."

If we assume that the centrality influence of a δ-place decreases with the square of the distance —as is the case with passenger traffic to and from such places . . .—then, if C_A designates the centrality in the one δ-place,[2] A, C_B the centrality in the other δ-place, B, $C_A \geq C_B$, $l \mid A{-}B \mid$ in km, r the radius of the umlands of B and m the distance between the mathematical centre of this umland and A, the boundary of the umland or the isodyne between A and B i.e., the line along an equal effect

---

[2] The centrality has been calculated in accordance with formula (8) in Chapter II. [See Godlund, op. cit., p. 34.]

The figures shown in table 28 and the information given in Fig. 16 show that as a rule there are only very slight differences between empirical and theoretical umland "boundaries." Thus, the theoretical boundary falls within or in the immediate vicinity of the empirical boundary zone. Only in a few cases—one of which is included in table

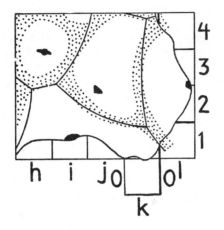

FIGURE 16 The Empirical Umland (bus traffic umland) and the Theoretical Umland (centrality umland) of δ-Places in an Arbitrarily Selected Part of L- and M-Counties. The place in cell i1 is Ystad, that in cell j2 Tomelilla and in cell 12-13 Simrishamn.

28, viz: the relation Malmö–Sjöbo—are there any great differences between these two types of boundary. In these cases, however, the "error" may just as well lie in the calculation of the empirical umland as in the theoretical. In the case mentioned, where the bus traffic umland of Lund is the one that "actually" separates the Malmö and Sjöbo regions, it will be found that if we make allowance for the railway connections and use only the data for the bus traffic, the theoretical boundary is just as well defined as the empirical. The intended application of the method as a means of determining the factors for series of years during the half-century 1900–1950 confirms this.

It is quite obvious from the foregoing that umlands determined in this way for the entire period 1900–1950 are necessarily uncertain and incomplete. As mentioned earlier, the risks of inaccuracies creeping in are large even when determining the centrality. In addition, there is the lack of an earlier "check time point" than that which can be obtained on the basis of the traveller data —which data cannot be considered as being com-

pletely representative for the umlands of all δ-places since they refer only to part of the passenger traffic. However, the reasonably good agreement between firstly the bus traffic umland and secondly the trading umland as related to the general road traffic umland makes it reasonably safe to say that the theoretical umland calculated on the centrality of the δ-places gives, as far as this work is concerned, a reasonably accurate expression for the umland regions of the places in question during the given period.

TABLE 28

RELATION	The Empirical umland boundary zone (traffic divide) falls within the undermentioned distance in km from the first-mentioned place	The theoretical umland limit (the centrality isodyne), D_t, falls at the under-mentioned distance in km from the first-mentioned place
Kristianstad—Åhus	10—12	10
" Tomelilla	30—35	34
" Hörby	20—24	22
" Vinslöv	13—16	11
" Osby	21—32	25
Hälsingborg—Höganäs	14—17	13
" Ängelholm	13—16	14
" Astorp	12—15	12
" Landskrona	14—18	13
Höör—Eslov	7—10	8
" Perstorp	15—17	14
" Tyringe	14—19	13
" Hässleholm	8—13	13
" Hörby	4— 7	6
Malmö—Lund	8—11	10
" Sjöbo	The umlands do not border on each other	33
" Svedala	12—15	13
" Trelleborg	15—19	18
Trelleborg—Svedala	10—14	9
" Skurup	14—18	16
Ystad—Skurup	15—18	14
" Sjöbo	16—19	16
" Tomelilla	8—12	9
Tomelilla—Sjöbo	9—13	10
" Simrishamn	11—14	14

In view of the above it has been considered possible, in this case, to use the theoretical determination of umlands based on the centrality of the δ-places. The umlands so obtained—by virtue of the basic material limited to L- and M-counties and the years 1900, 1910, 1920, 1930/31, 1938/

40 and 1950[5]—are, together with details of the centrality rank of all the built-up areas for the same years, mapped in six figures in the Swedish edition. In this English edition only the maps of 1900, 1930/31 and 1950 are shown (Figs. 17–19).

. . . The next senior places after δ-places, ε- and ζ-places, are clearly grouped in the vicinity of the isodynes between the umlands of the δ-places while the other places of even lower centrality rating, η- and ϑ-places, are distributed over

the entire region or are appreciably nearer the δ-places than the first-mentioned places. The maps also enable us to follow the development of the centrality of the built-up areas in relation to the location. The built-up areas which have grown up into δ-places during the period are without exception situated in the immediate vicinity of the surround boundary between older δ-places. In particular, it seems that those parts of the counties where several isodynes run together—where the distance to existing δ-places are greatest—are regions in which the trend is strong enough to promote the growth of new δ-places. A distinct halving of the distances between δ-places can also be

---

[5]To obtain the "outer" boundary lines the near-lying δ-places in counties K, G and N and their surrounds have been marked on the maps, as have the places of lower centrality in these counties where the boundary lines run. Table 29 is in respect of places in L- and M-counties, of course.

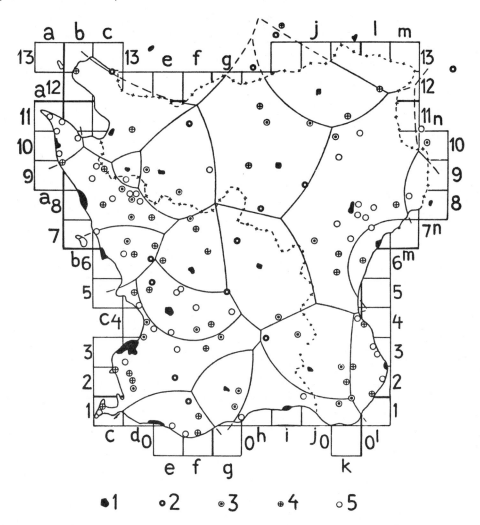

FIGURE 17 Theoretical umlands of δ-places and built-up areas in degrees of centrality in L- and M-Counties in 1900. 1 = δ-place, 2 = ε-place, 3 = ζ-place, 4 = η-place, 5 = ϑ-place. The identification cells are 10 × 10 km.

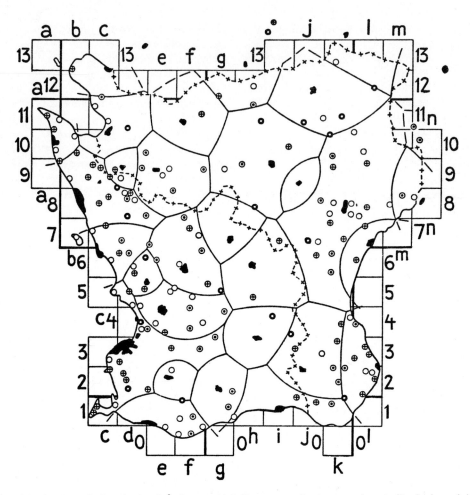

FIGURE 18 Theoretical umlands of δ-places and built-up areas in degrees of centrality in L- and M-Counties in 1930—31. For details of conventional signs see FIGURE 17.

noted. Stagnation or a decrease in the centrality can also be noted in places situated relatively close to those in the development stage. The hypothetical picture of the development of the centrality of built-up areas as shown in Fig. 15 would therefore appear to be confirmed by the actual growth inasfar as this has been registered in the map series for L- and M-counties.

A quantitative appreciation of this course can be obtained if we study the changes during the five approximately 10-year periods represented by the maps with the aid of the zone division of the δ-umlands as used in table 27. We get table 29.

If we compare the number of places showing increased centrality as indicated in table 29 with the corresponding expected division where the increase has been similarly divided over the built-up areas (= the total number of built-up areas in the various zones in 1900, 1910, 1920, 1930/31 and 1938/40 disregarding those places which, as a result of depopulation, have been omitted from one census to the next) we get table 30.

When checking the percentages by means of the X^2-criterion we get a distinct difference ($X^2 = 23.5$, $v = 4$ ∴ $P = 0.0001$).

As will be seen from Figs. 17–19 . . . there is a distinct relationship not only between the present centrality and position of the built-up areas but also between their centrality *growth* and *position* in relation to the superior centra: the greater the

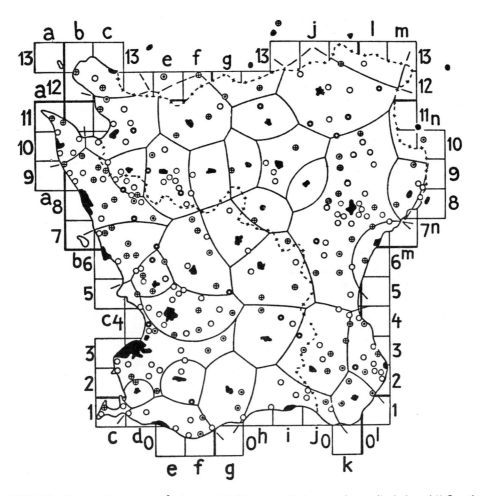

FIGURE 19 Theoretical umlands of δ-places and built-up areas in degrees of centrality in L- and M-Counties in 1950. The largest places are: Malmö (cell d 3), Lund (e 4), Landskrona (c 6), Hälsingborg (b 8), Kristianstad (k 8), Ystad (i 1) and Trelleborg (e 1).

relative distance between a lower centrality place and a δ-place the greater the chance that the place is, or will become, a higher centrality place. And the nearer a place lies to a δ-place the greater the chance that it will become of lesser centrality.

This relationship is so uniform that after examining the maps in Figs. 17–19 we can go as far as to foresee the probable development of the places as far as their centrality is concerned. It is thus probable that Broby (cell k 10, exactly on the isodyne between Kristianstad and Osby and close to its point of union with the isodyne Kristianstad–Hässleholm and Hässleholm–Osby) will become a δ-place, as will Svalöv (or possibly Teckomatorp) where the surrounds to Landskrona, Kävlinge and

Eslöv meet (cell e 7 or e 6). The examples can be reproduced and differentiated. A decrease in centrality can probably be expected in a number of places close to expanding δ-places. Such a reduction may come to be in the case of η-places in cell f 4 (about 10 km east of Lund), η-places in cell d 6 and ζ-places in cell d 7 (about 10 km east of Landskrona).

Knowledge of the indicated conformity with a known rule is important when we wish to explain the development and importance of places. One often emphasizes only the "in situ" conditions, e.g., the natural geographical advantages. Just how one-sided such a method of consideration is becomes obvious against the background of the dy-

TABLE 29

PERIOD	CENTRALITY CHANGES		Number of places of changed centrality in the respective distance zones from the δ-places at the beginning of the period. Distance Zone 1=nearest δ-place					TYPE OF CHANGE DURING PERIOD IN QUESTION
			Zone 1	Zone 2	Zone 3	Zone 4	Zone 5	
From 1900 to 1910	From ε to δ		—	—	—	3	2	Increase 1900—1910
	" ζ " ε		—	1	—	2	5	
	" η " ζ		—	—	2	—	5	
	" ϑ " η		—	—	2	1	7	
	" δ " ε		—	—	—	—	—	Decrease 1900—1910
	" ε " ζ		—	—	—	—	—	
	" ζ " η		—	—	—	—	—	
	" η " ϑ		—	—	—	—	—	
From 1910 to 1920	From ε to δ		—	1*	—	—	—	Increase 1910—1920
	" ζ " ε		—	—	—	—	1	
	" η " ζ		—	—	2	3	—	
	" ϑ " η		1	—	—	1	4	
	" δ " ε		—	—	—	—	—	Decrease 1910—1920
	" ε " ζ		—	—	—	—	—	
	" ζ " η		—	—	—	—	—	
	" η " ϑ		—	—	—	2	—	
From 1920 to 1930/31	From ε to δ		—	—	—	—	1	Increase 1920—1930/31
	" ζ " ε		—	—	1	2	3	
	" η " ζ		—	—	1	5	8	
	" ϑ " η		—	3	4	3	9	
	" δ " ε		—	—	—	—	—	Decrease 1920—1930/31
	" ε " ζ		—	—	—	—	—	
	" ζ " η		—	—	1	—	—	
	" η " ϑ		—	—	—	—	1	
From 1930/31 to 1938/40	From ε to δ		—	—	—	1	1**	Increase 1930/31—1938/40
	" ζ " ε		—	—	2	—	3	
	" η " ζ		—	—	—	2	—	
	" ϑ " η		—	—	—	1	4	
	" δ " ε		—	—	—	—	—	Decrease 1930/31—1938/40
	" ε " ζ		—	—	—	—	—	
	" ζ " η		—	—	—	—	—	
	" η " ϑ		1	4	2	2	1	
From 1938/40 to 1950	From ε to δ		—	—	—	3***	2	Increase 1938/40—1950
	" ζ " ε		—	—	—	—	1	
	" η " ζ		—	—	1	3	3	
	" ϑ " η		—	—	2	3	4	
	" δ " ε		—	—	—	—	—	Decrease 1938/40—1950
	" ε " ζ		—	—	—	—	—	
	" ζ " η		—	—	—	—	—	
	" η " ϑ		1	—	1	—	1	
Number of places showing increase......			1	4	17	33	65	Σ=120
Number of places showing decrease......			2	4	4	4	3	Σ=17

** Arlöv, a suburb of Malmö, is not included in the total.
** From ζ-place to δ-place.
** Of which 1 from ζ-place to δ place

namic process illustrated by the examples from L- and M-counties.

A knowledge of the conformity is also of importance when we consider the practical planning work. The depopulation of the country areas allied with an improved communication service and an increased demand for not only centralised trade and other commercial service but also for general

TABLE 30

ZONE	Number of built-up areas showing an increase in centrality 1900—1950 T_R	Total number of built-up areas 1900, 1910, 1920, 1930/31 and 1930/40 T_p
1	1 (1 %)	50 (7%)
2	4 (3%)	113 (15%)
3	17 (14%)	129 (18%)
4	33 (28%)	160 (22%)
5	65 (54%)	281 (38%)
Σ	120 (100%)	733 (100%)

service institutions such as schools, medical facilities, libraries etc., would seem to make it increasingly necessary to endeavour to develop a somewhat more permanent method of assessment since in view of the large-scale investments involved and the relatively "long life" of such investments, it is important that mistakes resulting from erroneous localisation be avoided as far as possible. In everyday words, it is a question of deciding which areas are a reasonably "safe bet." It should be possible to make higher demands on the accuracy of such estimates than if the basis were confined to simple population data or similar development possibilities. What is probably needed in such cases is a regional study of the conditions.[6] What is the position of the place in question compared with other places? What is the likely development in the other places in the region and to what extent can this development be expected to influence conditions and possibilities in the place in question?

Planning on a regional basis will naturally call for great attention to be paid to the question of communications. The exact "placement" of a central place is to a great extent determined by the traffic conditions—now primarily main road connections—and, furthermore, it is necessary to arrive at an effective, well-operated and economic road system. The centralisation and extension of schools and also the construction of new centralised communal centres has already caused, and will probably cause in the future, problems that can only be solved by regional planning and a co-ordinated system of built-up areas.

A further allied factor in this case is the division of regional adminstration. Motorism—and thus also bus traffic—has, allied with the depopulation of the country areas and the considerable expansion of certain built-up areas, had the effect that an administrative regional regulation, especially of communities and counties, has become a necessity.[7] The principles adopted when making such a revision should, as has been pointed out by Hantos (1932), Meynier (1934), Christaller (1937) and Dickinson (1947), be primarily to endeavour to arrive at an agreement between surround, i.e., spontaneous, functional units and administrative districts both as regards extent and central point ... and at the same time ensuring that there will be a sufficient number of people in the created units. In this respect, as is pointed out by Meynier (1934 p. 131 f), bus traffic can be directed so as to form "bus traffic umlands" and thereby constitute a basis for the division. A county division or other superior division can then be formed by joining such theoretically[8] or empirically[9] formed sub-regions to make super regions, the approximate size of which is determined by, e.g., charting the shortest driving time by car to the existing or contemplated county centre. ...

REFERENCES

Ajo, R., 1944: Der Verkehrsraum von Tampere. Helsinki.

Aurousseau, M., 1923: The Geographical Study of Population Groups. *The Geogr. Review.*

Christaller, W., 1937: Die ländliche Siedlungsweise im Deutschen Reich und ihre Beziehungen zur Gemeindeorganisation. Stuttgart.

Dickinson, R. E., 1947: City, Region, and Regionalism. London.

Emerson, F. V., 1913: A Geographical Interpretation of Missouri, *Geogr. Journ.*

Fawcett, C. B., 1932: Distribution of the Urban Population in Great Britain 1931. *Geogr. Journ.*

Firey, W., Loomis, C. P. and Beegle, J. A., 1950: The Fusion of Urban and Rural. *Highways in our National Life. A Symposium.* Ed. J. Labatut and W. J. Lane. Princeton.

[6] "A knowledge of the reasons for human settlements at different times and places ... is obviously of first-rate importance in the planning of a new town or the major expansion of an old one." Holford 1950 p. vii. One of the principles in such a case can be to attempt to combine the bus lines constituting a traffic area focussed on one or a few central places.

[7] A new division of communal areas in Sweden has been carried out since 1.1.1952 on the basis of SOU 1945:38 and 1945:39, although the viewpoints expressed above concerning the agreements between surrounds and administrative districts were not considered even where they could have been. It is probable that considerable corrections will be required in the near future. Proposals concerning a new county division in Sweden were put forward during the 1953 Riksdag.

[8] E.g. figs. 12—14 in this work [not included in this volume.]

[9] E.g. fig. 19 in this work.

Hantos, G., 1932: Administrative Boundaries and the Nationalization of the Public Administration. Budapest.

Kant, E., 1946: About Internal Migration in Estonia in Connection with Complementary Areas of Estonian Towns. *Swedish Geogr. Yearbook.*

Kant, E., 1951: Umland Studies and Sector Analysis. *Tätorter och omland.* Lund.

Kareda, E., 1938: Tartu ja tema abitsentraalide hulgikaubanduslikud minemialad (The Wholesale Trade Areas of Tartu and its Satellite Centers). *Sem. Univ. Tart. Oecon.-Geogr. nr²².*

Lösch, A., 1944: Die räumliche Ordnung der Wirtschaft. Jena.

Meynier, A., 1934: Les caractères géographiques du réseau d'autobus dans le massif central de la France. *Compte Rendus du Congrès Intern. de Géographie Varsoive 1934. Tome 3, Sec. III.* Varsoive.

Reilly, W. J., 1929: Methods for the Study of Retail Relationships. *Univ. of Texas Bulletin No. 2944.*

Reilly, W. J., 1931: The Law of Retail Gravitation. New York.

Tuominen, O., 1949: Das Einflussgebiet der Stadt Turku im System der Einflussgebiete SW-Finnlands. *Fennia 71,* N:o 5, Helsinki.

Part Three

RESTATEMENTS OF THEORY

Introductory Note

The articles included in this section represent attempts to reformulate location theory within the framework of modern economic and quantitative analysis.[1] The guiding principle for selecting these articles was that the concepts they embody appear relevant in the context of locational analysis in economic geography. Hence, the more purely economic work concerned with general equilibrium analysis in location theory is not represented strongly.[2] Furthermore, these selections are only indicative of the work being done and there are even more recent theoretical contributions on many of the problems.[3]

Perhaps the outstanding characteristic of recent location theory has been the use of activity analysis as the framework within which many of the models have been reformulated. To the extent that the location problem usually has been viewed as one of maximization (i.e., of rent per acre) or minimization (i.e., of transport costs), then the application of linear programming in this context appears quite appropriate.

Garrison, in his three essays, reviews many of the applications of activity analysis and stresses the relevance of this approach for the geographer concerned with studies of location. The first essay discusses six major works on location theory which appeared in the 1950's. Garrison

1The reading of many of these selections will require familiarity with some of the concepts of micro-economic theory. The reader, therefore, might find it useful to consult one of the many standard works on this topic, for example, J. F. Due and Robert W. Clower, *Intermediate Economic Analysis* (Homewood, Illinois: Richard D. Irwin, Inc., 1966).

2For example M. L. Greenhut, *Microeconomics and the Space Economy* (Chicago: Scott Foresman and Company, 1963); A. S. Manne, "Plant Location under Economies-of-Scale—Decentralization and Computation," *Management Science*, Vol. II, No. 2, 1964, pp. 213–35; B. H. Stevens and C. P. Rydell, "Spatial Demand Theory and Monopoly Price Policy," *Papers and Proceedings, Regional Science Association*, Vol. 17, 1966, pp. 195–204.

3For examples on agricultural land-use see T. Takayama and G. G. Judge, "An Interregional Activity Analysis Model for the Agricultural Sector," *Journal of Farm Economics*, Vol. 46, No. 2, 1964, pp. 349–65; similarly on the type of problem considered by Beckmann and Marschak, see L. Lefeber, *Allocation in Space* (Amsterdam: North Holland Publishing Co., 1958).

suggests that these books "show how economic insights can be used to construct patterns which, in turn, may also be interpreted by geographic insights." Although the linear programming model is outlined in Garrison's second essay, it is worth noting that the present book does not include any works which provide either full expository introductions to the field of linear programming or discussions of the mathematical solutions. The student is referred elsewhere for these.[4] Five different problems in spatial analysis, all of which relate to locational questions, are outlined and referenced in this second essay. In the final essay the perspective is broadened to include a discussion of four problems in transportation introduced as "ways of thinking about spatial patterns." Then follows a treatment of interindustry and interregional relationships as they have been analyzed by way of input-output techniques, interregional linear programming, and industrial complex analysis.

Of the topics considered in Garrison's essays, three are given further attention in the remaining articles of this section. One is Dunn's discussion of agricultural locations. The Von Thünen model now is reformulated as a maximization problem for n commodities and a set of unknown prices, demands, boundaries, and supplies. The unique solution for a given set of assumptions "will provide the price of every commodity, the quantity of each commodity that will be produced and consumed, and at the same time will explicitly determine the spatial orientation of production."

An alternative approach to the question of the location of agricultural production is provided by Henderson. The maximization of net farm return is now presented as a linear programming problem involving the allocation of a given amount of cropland among m crops, subject to certain constraints. In the second part of Henderson's study as originally published, there was an empirical application of this model to some U.S. data; this has been omitted in this selection. It is worth noting however, that land allocation studies similar to Henderson's are well represented in the literature of farm economics,[5] and in the final section of this book Wolpert illustrates their applicability in economic geography. These allocation studies usually do not incorporate transportation costs and distance factors explicitly, nor do they refer to the rent-distance relationship which is such a central theme in the work of Von Thünen and Dunn.

The rent-distance relationship reappears in Alonso's article, now with respect to urban land-use. Dunn's marginal rent line becomes both a profit

---

[4] See the statements by Isard in W. Isard, *Methods of Regional Analysis* (New York: John Wiley & Sons, Inc., 1960), Chap. 10, "Interregional Linear Programming," pp. 413–92; R. L. Morrill and W. L. Garrison, "Projections of Interregional Patterns of Trade in Wheat and Flour," *Economic Geography*, Vol. 36, No. 2, 1960, espec. pp. 125–6; M. Yeates, "Hinterland Delimitation: A Distance Minimizing Approach," *The Professional Geographer*, Vol. 15, No. 6, 1963, pp. 7–10; K. Cox, "The Application of Linear Programming to Geographic Problems," *Tijdschrift voor Economische en Sociale Geografie*, Vol. 56, Nov./Dec. 1965, pp. 228–35.

[5] See for example, R. A. King (ed.), *Interregional Competition* (Raleigh, N. C.: Agricultural Policy Institute, 1963); E. O. Heady and A. C. Egbert, "Regional Programming of Efficient Agricultural Production Patterns," *Econometrica*, Vol. 32, No. 3, 1964, pp. 374–86.

curve for urban business and a bid-rent curve for all urban land-use activities. This article presents in capsule form the elements of a location model which is described more fully in Alonso's book.[6]

Beckmann and Marschak's article, which also was reviewed by Garrison, is included here as a more extended illustration of the application of linear programming to the manufacturing location problem. Although the model appears complex it should be noted that it applies to only one firm but with several plants. Beckmann and Marschak make no attempt to interpret the dual variables in their linear programming solution. In contrast, Stevens' article is concerned only with this aspect of the problem. The dual variables in a location-transportation model are interpreted as location rents both at the markets and the production points. Stevens' work supplements the Beckmann-Marschak model and expresses in a linear programming formulation the concept of site-rent which is central to so much of location theory.

The statement by Berry and Barnum draws together several inductively derived generalizations on central place systems. These generalizations are manipulated as mathematical equations to obtain certain higher-order statements concerning elements of the systems.

---

[6]William Alonso, *Location and Land-Use* (Cambridge, Mass.: Harvard University Press, 1964).

William L. Garrison

SPATIAL STRUCTURE OF THE ECONOMY: I, II, III

(Part I)

What determines the spatial arrangement (structure, pattern, or location) of economic activity? Attention has been given to this question recently in books by Isard, Dunn, Greenhut, Ponsard, Lösch, and Boustedt and Ranz, and in a number of articles.[1] These are the subject of this and subsequent review articles.

A cursory examination of this literature reveals that the subject matter of these studies varies widely. A few workers have dealt with the individual decision-maker, e.g., studies of the spatial connections of households; some have dealt with problems of the locations of individual firms; whereas others have approached the question at more aggregated levels. A number of these workers have dealt with the location structures of meaningful aggregates of firms, e.g., the petroleum industry of the United States, and others have dealt with urban, regional, national, and world aggregates of activities.

The four levels of work just discussed merge rather nicely with classifications adopted by writers who orient their work toward significant, theoretical, policy, and/or practical questions. Work on residential site selection, for example, is at the level of the individual decision-maker, work on the selection of factory locations and/or sites for retail business is at the level of the individual firm, and a number of transportation and planning problems fit into the two aggregative classes. Theoretical works on the determinants of spatial patterns are available at each level of subject matter, although theoretical works which attempt to merge geographic patterns with economic equilibrium are largely at the aggregated levels.

The glance at the literature also reveals contrasts in the apparatus through which researchers erect and explore their problems. In recent years growth of the general field of activity analysis, especially linear programming, has had a marked influence upon research. Recent workers have made use of programming; earlier workers structured problems in other ways. This has not been a matter of changing the approach in order to be fashionable. Certain very real benefits may be obtained through the use of these tools. Many prob-

Reprinted with the permission of the author and publisher from the *Annals,* Association of American Geographers, Vol. 49, No. 2, 1959, pp. 232-39; Vol. 49, No. 4, 1959, pp. 471-82; Vol. 50, No. 3, 1960, pp. 357-73. Dr. Garrison is Director, Center for Urban Studies, University of Illinois, Chicago Circle.

[1]Walter Isard, *Location and Space Economy* (Cambridge: Technology Press of the Massachusetts Institue of Technology; New York: John Wiley and Sons, 1956). xiii and 350 pages. Illustrations, index. $8.75.

Edgar S. Dunn, Jr., *The Location of Agricultural Production* (Gainesville: University of Florida Press, 1954). vii and 115 pp. Illustrations, index. Paper, $2.50; cloth, $3.50.

Melvin L. Greenhut, *Plant Location in Theory and Practice: The Economics of Space* (Chapel Hill: The University of North Carolina Press, 1956). xiii and 338 pp. Illustrations, bibliography, index. $7.50.

Claude Ponsard, *Économie et Espace: Essai d'intégration du facteur spatial dans l'analyse économique,* Observation économique, Collection publiée sous la direction de André Piatier, Vol. VIII (Paris: Sedes, 1955). xv and 467 pp. Illustrations, bibliography. 2,000 fr.

August Lösch, *The Economics of Location,* translated from the second revised edition by William H. Woglom with the assistance of Wolfgang F. Stolper (New Haven: Yale University Press, 1954). xxviii and 520 pp. Illustrations, index. $7.50. The German title is *Die raümliche Ordnung der Wirtschaft* (Jena: Gustav Fischer, 1943).

Olaf Boustedt and Herbert Ranz, *Regionale Struktur-und Wirtschaftsforschung, Aufgaben und Methoden* (Bremen: Walter Dorn, 1957). xviii and 218 pp. Bibliography. DM 16.

Two books that might have been reviewed with these works were called to the author's attention too late for inclusion. The first, recommended by Professor Torsten Hägerstrand, is Ejler Alkjaer's *Erhvervslivets Beliggenhedsproblemer* (Kobenhavn: Einar Harcks, 1953). viii and 95 pp. This book would be of special interest to those concerned with problems of the location of retail business. The second, recommended by Professor Brian J. L. Berry, is Hans Ulrich Meyer-Lindermann's *Typologie der Theorien des Industriestandortes* (Bremen: Walter Dorn, 1951). xv and 235 pp.

lems that were intractable ten years ago are now very close to being trivial, and many new problems have been recognized. Programming is newer than the A-bomb. This reviewer agrees with Flood[2] that it is possibly of comparable importance.

In Parts II and III of this review the impact of programming approaches on analysis will be given special attention. Unavoidably, this treatment means dealing with a literature other than that concerned directly with spatial problems, and, since programming is couched in mathematical terms, it also means that certain mathematical statements will be made.

Six Recent Books

Six important books dealing with spatial questions appeared between 1954 and 1957. The English translation of Lösch's *The Economics of Location* appeared in 1954. (Here 1954 is regarded as the date of appearance since the 1943 edition in German has not been generally available in this country.) Dunn's book on agriculture was also published in 1954, and the books by Isard and Greenhut were published in 1956. In 1955 a book by Ponsard was published in France, and the book by Boustedt and Ranz was published in Germany in 1957.

Professor Isard's many publications on spatial problems are well known to geographers, economists, and planners. Core parts of his book, *Location and Space Economy*, are restatements of journal articles published during the late 1940's and early 1950's. In the book these statements are augmented and linked into an integrated view of location process. This presentation accomplishes several things: (1) it provides a summary statement of the results of earlier workers who treated the general location problem, (2) it gives a brief glimpse of some empirical regularities which suggest the existence of spatial order and, thus, processes, (3) it develops the concept of transport inputs, (4) it uses the device of substitution analysis and the concept of transport inputs to add a spatial dimension to economic analysis, and (5) it outlines a statement of the total space economy through a mathematical model and through graph-

ic synthesis. Of these, the overriding accomplishments are placing spatial problems within the substitution analysis framework of traditional economics, and in showing how a landscape can be constructed from theory.

Isard begins by posing the problem, reviewing general works by Lösch, Palander, Predöhl, and others, and then showing certain empirical regularities which are associated with the space economy. These topics are respectively a chapter each, and together they pose the problem for analysis in the book as a whole. The empirical regularities discussed include the rank–size rule and the diminution of interactions with distance.

Isard's analytic discussion begins with his identification of the concept of the transport input —a weight-distance unit—which can be thought of in the same way that capital, labor, and other industry inputs are considered. A cost may be attached to the transport input, and the firm compares these costs with costs associated with other types of inputs and the value of outputs. The location problem becomes the problem of "substitutions" among alternate costs and output revenues; that is, costs and outputs are compared (substituted for one another) until net profits are maximized. This is a major contribution of the book—the location problem is placed in the metric of the transport input and analyzed as a substitution problem.

Isard gives his discussion generality by showing how transport inputs may be considered when selecting among market areas, supply areas, products, alternate transport inputs, and so on. He shows how agglomeration may be treated as a problem in substitution and how agricultural and urban rents may be involved in the substitution process. The relations between location and trade theory are also examined.

Isard's final chapters deal with general situations. In a chapter couched in mathematical terms he sets forth some aspects of a general theory. His final chapter is a graphic integration of his previous analysis. This graphic synthesis serves as a summary and shows the conservative character of Isard's approach. The approach does not yield radical answers; neither does it destroy or downgrade any conclusions which have been available, however intuitive, heretofore.

Dunn has provided a statement for agriculture which emphasizes rent as the determining agent in location decisions. *The Location of Agricultural*

[2]Merrill M. Flood, review of Andrew Vazsonyís, *Scientific Programming in Business and Industry*, in *American Scientist*, Vol. 46 (December, 1958), p. 358A.

Production is the outgrowth of his Ph.D. dissertation written at Harvard in 1951, a time when Isard was at Harvard. Thus it is not surprising that Dunn's approach to agriculture is quite similar to that of Isard. Dunn builds chiefly on Thünen's early study,[3] Lösch's work, and a well-known work of Brinkmann,[4] but he extends his analysis considerably beyond that of these earlier writers. In the first half of his book he develops an explanation for the spatial structure of agriculture, assuming a plain that is homogeneous in natural resources, and that transport structures, population, and certain other variables are not subject to change. The discussion carries through several chapters which set forth the general problem and the manner in which the distance factor influences the spatial distribution of rents and, thus, land-use patterns. The equilibrium of land-use patterns is considered, and finally, general statements are given bearing on the multiple product firm, multiple markets, and the varying production possibilities of land. In the last section of his book Professor Dunn relaxes some of the assumptions used in his static analysis. Processes of change in the regional economy as induced by population shifts are also reviewed in a somewhat general way.

This analysis represents a marked advance over much of the previous work in this field. Dunn's statement is somewhat more incisive than Lösch's, for example, since it contains an explicit distance function which recognizes possibilities for variations in transportation rates among commodities. Dunn's analysis of rent is more direct than Brinkmann's analysis, and his argument is superior to Thünen's in generality and consideration of boundary conditions. On the other hand, Dunn's analysis does not extend very far beyond an analysis of static equilibrium at the industry level. Discussions at the level of the firm and the discussion of dynamic factors are cursory although provocative in places. Perhaps rents could have been more closely connected with flows, and perhaps the analysis of the general ordering of markets and crop areas could have been more penetrating. Nevertheless, there is no question that Dunn's work represents a significant step over and above previous literature.

Greenhut's book, *Plant Location in Theory and in Practice: The Economics of Space,* is aimed at the particular problem of the location of industrial plants and incorporates a set of empirical studies of plant location factors. In these ways, Greenhut's book is somewhat like that of Yaseen,[5] but Greenhut's penetrating attention to the plant location problem led him to consideration of cases of locational interdependence, discriminatory price systems, and like features of imperfect competition that, for the most part, are skimmed over in works written to assist industry decision-makers with location problems. His major contribution is chiefly in his interdependence statements and his attempt to gear the site location of the firm into the theory of the firm.

In the first part of his book Greenhut provides a review of major aspects of location theory and develops a summary statement which is put forward as a tentative location theory. This is followed by a detailed consideration of several profit determinants—transportation and processing costs, product demand, revenue-increasing factors, and "personal factors." He then presents his empirical studies of eight firms, ranging from a DDT manufacturing establishment to a peanut processing plant, and provides some general support for his theory. He emphasizes that in each case only a few of the location determinants were recognized, and he also stresses the "personal factor" in the decision process. In the last portion of the volume, Greenhut reconsiders the theoretical statements of the first two sections and the empirical materials of his third section. This yields a rather brief general statement couched in both verbal and symbolic terms, which is intended as an outline of a theory incorporating the results of his empirical studies.

From the point of view of concepts Greenhut's book is very superior to previous studies which have dealt specifically with the plant location problem from an engineering point of view. On the other hand, he has failed to give us the breadth or originality of Isard's work and anything other than impressionistic notes toward a general theory. This reviewer views Greenhut's empirical studies with considerable skepticism. The author seems aware of the difficulties of empirical work. Perhaps this is the reason why his empirical observations are not

---

[3] Johann Heinrich von Thünen, *Der isolierte Staat in Beziehung auf Landwirtschaft und Nationalökonomie* (Hamburg, 1826).

[4] Theodor Brinkmann, *Economics of the Farm Business,* translated by E. T. Benedict (Berkeley: University of California Press, 1935).

[5] Leonard C. Yaseen, *Plant Location* (New York: Institute for Business Planning, Inc., 1955).

integrated closely into the final portion of the book. The types of cases selected and the analytical methods applied weaken the empirical portion, although some interesting insights are given.

Ponsard's *Économie et Espace* provides a complete and penetrating review of much of the available material in the location field. Although published before either Isard or Greenhut, Ponsard makes extensive reference to the articles of these writers and, essentially, anticipates the appearance of their books. Unlike Greenhut, Isard, or Dunn, Ponsard recognizes some of the work in the geographical literature as well as some of the newer work on efficient transportation flows, spatial equilibrium, and activity analysis (subjects of later parts of this essay). Isard refers to some of these approaches in his footnotes and recognizes their tremendous implications for problems of spatial structure, but both Dunn and Greenhut ignore them.

Ponsard's volume is divided into two "books," four parts, and fourteen sections. The first and larger "book" deals with the micro- and macro-economics of location—roughly, discussions at the level of the individual firm and at levels of aggregations of firms, regional aggregations, and urban aggregations. The second and smaller "book" deals with the equilibrium of the decision-maker, the local community, the state, and the world community. Traditionally, discussions of decision-makers have been at the level of the household (worker-consumer) and the firm. As Ponsard's discussion is somewhat broader than the traditional discussion, it is here that he makes his original contribution.

Ponsard's book claims in the title that it is an integration. This is hardly true. It is an exhaustive recapitulation of works on location, together with some general remarks on large-scale aspects of the problem. As a review of the literature, the book is unequalled. Ponsard gives us a penetrating and complete recapitulation of the available literature, much of which is difficult to come by. Certainly Ponsard's book will be used as a reference many times. Perhaps it is too much to ask for a really thorough integration. Ponsard's original discussion of decision-makers is cursory, but it is a first approach to interesting problems.

August Lösch's volume, *The Economics of Location*, has been widely acclaimed as one of the more important books of the decade. It differs somewhat from others in the field in that it deals with what Lösch thinks a spatially ordered society should be, rather than with an explanation of what exists. Thus, he is concerned chiefly with location as a problem in efficient productions and with constructing location systems yielding efficient production and distribution. The work is divided into four divisions: (1) location problems, (2) economic regions, (3) trade problems, and (4) examples. Lösch makes at least three major contributions.

First, he provides the first general statement of location equilibrium. That is, he has written out a set of equations displaying all locations, boundaries, and production—the location system. The equations are straightforward, but it is not completely clear how this system relates to other portions of Lösch's work. Beckmann has pointed out that the equilibrium conditions contain no explicit reference to the price system and supply and demand relations.[6] He also notes: " . . . it remains somewhat obscure how the various principles interact, fail to conflict with each other, and indeed succeed to produce equilibrium." Isard (pages 44–48) also reviews Lösch's equilibrium system. Isard notes that Lösch fails to treat the relationships between the optimum location for production and consumption and thus limits himself to several major sectors of the basic economy. These objections aside, Lösch's system remains a pioneering first attempt to investigate the existence of a system of spatial arrangements.

Lösch's well-known model of a hexagonal lattice of distribution and production locations is essential to his equilibrium statement and is another major contribution of his volume. The argument by Lösch is well known. He postulates a continuous distribution of population on a homogeneous plain and asks, What will be the distribution of producing places for this population? The answer to this question is achieved by analyzing the possible shapes of regions, location of production points, and possible sizes of market areas. The result is a complex system of hexagons resulting in an ordered arrangement of cities and transportation routes. The idea of a system of cities having hexagon-shaped trading areas is not new, having been presented by W. Christaller some years earlier.[7] Christaller considered several systems on the verbal

[6]Martin Beckmann, "Some Reflections on Lösch's Theory of Location," *Papers and Proceedings,* Regional Science Association, Vol. 1 (1955), pp. N-1 through N-9.
[7]Walther Christaller, *Die zentralen Orte in Süddeutschland* (Jena: Gustav Fischer, 1933).

level, but Lösch spells the derivation of several systems and presents patterns resulting from a rotation of the hexagon systems. Lösch's conditions of general equilibrium discussed previously, such as the notion that areas of supply, production, and sales must be as small as possible, flow directly from this elegant system.

Lösch's third major contribution is his presentation of empirical information. Here is a wealth of otherwise widely scattered information, organized according to the theme of the book with great insight and with illuminating comments. Much of the material is from the United States and will be of interest to workers here for this reason. On the other hand, there is much literature from other places, especially Germany, which may not be known to researchers in the United States and is of interest for that reason. Lösch's attitude toward empirical information is extremely interesting. He rejects the notion of comparing such information with theory to judge if the theory is correct. "No! Comparison now has to be drawn no longer to test the theory, but to test reality! Now it must be determined whether reality is rational." (Page 363.) Elsewhere, however, Lösch states that his empirical data demonstrate how strong are the forces of spatial order. Examples range from locations of production and towns through considerations of market areas and price levels in space. The empirical materials are highly suggestive, but variable in convincingness. Materials on the spacing of towns, for example, seem to tell us only that large towns are farther apart than small towns. Is this evidence of regularity? Is this evidence of "strong forces of order"?

In a review, one can only skim over the major contributions of Lösch and cannot properly reveal the richness of Lösch's discussion. There is much that is original and provocative, such as the notion of price waves to which Lösch gives much attention. So far as this reviewer knows, this is a new idea with Lösch, and it certainly is an idea which should be further explored.

How may the book be summarized? It is relatively complete, since it covers problems of spatial structure from the level of the individual farm (with a glance at households) through regional and international systems. It also considers the problem of spatial equilibrium. It is rich in insight, but it is spotty. In the review of Dunn's book, for example, it was mentioned that Lösch's discussion of agriculture lacks depth because of failure to focus on transportation rates differentiated among products. In another instance, although his system of urban centers and networks of supply areas is elegant and incisive, his assumption of a homogeneous plain begs the question of whether his is even a reasonable first approximation. Also, the discussion of associated transportation routes seems unconvincing. He notes, for example, that the areas around major places should be divided into twelve sectors, six with relatively few settlements, six with many settlements. He then postulates the existence of transportation routes along the edges of the sectors. He nowhere notes how the transportation routes of major systems are interconnected; and by principles noted elsewhere in his book, it is easy to see that the transportation routes should be displaced into the sectors with dense settlements.

Boustedt's and Ranz's *Regionale Strukturund Wirtschaftsforschung, Aufgaben und Methoden* is similar to the other books. It is a direct approach to explanations of patterns of spatial arrangements and it contains a survey, integration, and synthesis of previous ideas. Like the other books it is motivated by ideas flowing from earlier workers. Despite these similarities, it is quite different from the others. In much of the book, the authors are concerned with methods of making regional studies; thus, stress is on operations within a regional framework. Problems are stated and treated as regional problems throughout the book, whereas in other books the regional characteristics of the problems are in most cases rather implicit. A portion of the book deals with economic models and, again, the regional emphasis is very strong. The models discussed are those which are operable at the regional level.

The book is divided into three parts. The first is used to state the objectives of regional research and some general statistical problems in regional work. The second part discusses the role and methods of research on regional structure. The final part covers regional economic research.

The first part is a short statement of the nature of regional science *(Regionalforschung)* and aspects of the statistical requirements of the science. The primary problem of spatial science *(Raumforschung)* is the development of fundamental laws of spatial organization. It covers the totality of all factors and their mutual relations in space. It is synthetic since it uses spatial analysis to summarize the findings of other disciplines (including geography). Its objective is fundamental, and its concept has abstract contents. Its practical application is mostly in planning.

The authors view statistical problems chiefly as problems of obtaining data and combining them into effective summary measures to display some regional characteristics. They stress problems of the sizes of statistical units, data collection, and the like. The authors are not unaware of problems of carrying on with statistics through problem-solving operations and discuss briefly the applicability of tests of significance to regional data, but for the most part the idea of statistics as used in this volume is the idea of obtaining and ordering a mass of data bearing on a problem.

The second part of the book continues the discussion of research on regional structures. It treats problems of delimiting spatial units, using the traditional concepts of homogeneous and functional areas, and then treats problems of arranging spatial units into types. The discussion is well organized and competently given in general statements, as well as well-selected examples. The discussion of homogeneous spatial units ranges from a discussion of physiographic regions through cultural, economic, and agricultural regions. Examples range in location from Brazil and Canada to the Netherlands, and include recent work done in the United States on state economic areas and other systems of economic areas suggested by Bogue. The discussion of functional units is concerned largely with the metropolitan landscape and work on urban agglomerations. The only exception is a short discussion of transportation districts in Germany. For the most part, then, the idea of a functional area is essentially equivalent to the idea of a nodal region. Again, examples are given from many areas, from the Scandinavian countries to the United States.

This discussion of classification problems is quite limited. The general problem is discussed, and types of economic communities, social communities, and cities are treated. Only a few examples are given and, in the case of the types of the cities in the United States where a great deal of the work has been done, the authors' references are rather skimpy. Throughout the book the authors attempt to compare approaches and give judgments as to their value. In the case of the arrangement of spatial units into groups, for example, there is a four-paragraph discussion of the methods of making up typal arrays. Not much can be said in four paragraphs, but the authors are able to stress the increasing importance of the method and certain of its problems. The authors also point out some of the difficulties of using random samples to obtain data for many small areas.

The final section of the book deals with regional economic research and is the largest section. It covers some of the traditional problems of economics on a regional level, including levels of the operation of the economy and money flows. These topics are first discussed in a general way; then, the final part of the section reviews research. There is a brief discussion of problems of regional growth. The larger part of the discussion is based on rather crude models of regional flows and interregional input—output analysis. The latter is treated grossly and uncritically.

The book is extremely well organized, it is easy to read, and the authors have achieved a survey of a large amount of material. The book is advanced in the sense that regional problems are discussed in general and a knowledge of the field is required in order to interpret the general propositions. The book is not statistical in the sense that mathematical symbols and problems appear. Nonetheless, a considerable knowledge of statistical methods of inference is needed in order to interpret certain of the statements. The authors make several incisive comments on random methods of data gathering, for example, and one needs to know what this is about. In another case, the authors comment on variance versus regression models in the delimitation of regions. Since characteristics of such models are not described, acquaintance with them is presumed. It is easy to criticize lack of depth in a book that covers a large amount of material. This reviewer noted especially the rather shallow treatment given to problems of regional grouping and classification in the light of methods available to handle these problems. Much is not covered in the final section on economic models. Even the discussion of input—output analysis is skimpy.

The Six Books

What do these six books represent? Certainly they evidence a continued interest by economists in location problems. Whether they represent, in the span of time they cover, a relatively greater increase in attention to location problems than had previously been the case is a question very difficult to answer. In examining the books, one is quite aware of the long history of interest by economists in location questions.

If there are implications in these books for traditional economics, they probably concern introducing location questions via substitution analysis into analysis of the firm. This is a procedure identified earlier but emphasized strongly for the first time by Isard. Evidence of interest along this line is given by the recent paper by Moses, which criticizes Isard for his failure to consider U-shaped cost curves.[8] Moses shows that this refinement can be made and moves the location problem closer to traditional economic analysis.

Valavanis recognizes Lösch's notions on the arrangement of towns and market and supply areas as a concept of major consequence for economists, but he points out that there is no analogy to this concept in traditional economics.[9] Consequently, it is hard to see how this concept could be embraced by traditional economics. As noted before, this concept is basic to Lösch's general mathematical system and accounts for the set of conditions which Lösch attempts to meet in stating his general system. Will this relatively unfamiliar concept have any notable impact on economics? By definition, it could hardly have an effect on traditional economics.

Economists are not the only ones who have followed this literature with interest. What is its consequence for workers in other fields, such as geography? This reviewer doubts if the books by Dunn, Isard, Ponsard, and Greenhut will excite many in geography. These books are written from the standpoint of economics and have as a major objective the placing of location considerations within the sphere of traditional economics. Books that fly more familiar flags for the geographer are those by Lösch and by Boustedt and Ranz. Certainly Lösch treats many situations for which there are direct analogues in geography. Notably, Lösch's constructs on rural and urban interrelations, economic boundaries, and regional systems all have analogues in geographic work. Boustedt and Ranz emphasize the solution of regional problems for which there also are direct analogues in geography,

but since much of the work in their volume is available in the English-language literature, their contribution is more in terms of providing a one-volume collection than in development of new concepts.

Nevertheless, Isard, Ponsard, Greenhut, and Dunn should not be dismissed too quickly. These writers have attempted to incorporate location decisions within the traditional economics. This is not quite the same thing as saying that they bring geographic insights to the field of economics, and it is certainly not the same thing as saying that they bring economic insights to the field of geography. But each does this: they show how economic insights can be used to construct patterns which, in turn, may also be interpreted by geographic insights. This is especially true of Isard's concluding chapter in which he constructs a landscape using ideas developed in previous chapters of his book; here is the urban and rural scene constructed exclusively from location theory. What is equally important is that this landscape is constructed without violating a single notion from economics or from geography. This is extremely suggestive of the mutual relations between geographic and economic forces. Perhaps a major difference between Isard and Lösch is that Lösch has identified some of these mutual relations in greater degree than Isard, but Lösch has broken in some respects from traditional economics in order to identify these insights.

Must geographers break with or augment some of their traditional insights to embrace economic realities? Could a book be written to bring economic considerations into geography? A book has yet to be written which would do for geography what Isard has attempted for economics. This would require an exposition of economic ideas, rather than an assumption of them, as Isard has done.

Stimulation of Interest

This reviewer is tempted to say that one major result of these works, especially Isard's book, has been the stimulation of new and increased interest in geographic problems from a point of view that uses concepts from both economics and geography. There is a good bit of evidence for this assertion. In 1954, approximately 60 persons attended the business meeting of the Regional Science Associa-

[8]Leon M. Moses, "Location and the Theory of Production," *Quarterly Journal of Economics,* Vol. 72 (February, 1958), pp. 259-72.
[9]Stefan Valavavanis, "Lösch on Location," *American Economic Review,* Vol. 45 (September, 1955), pp. 637-44. [See page 69 of this volume.]

tion in Detroit, and the association was formally organized under that name. There have been annual meetings of the association since that date and the association now has approximately 1200 members. Papers presented at its meetings are published in its *Papers and Proceedings*, and four volumes have appeared. In addition, the Institute of Regional Science at the University of Pennsylvania began publishing the *Journal of Regional Science* in 1958, only the first issue of which is available. These organizations and their publications certainly evidence a strong interest in problems of spatial arrangements. Persons in many professions are members of the Regional Science Association, with economists having the strongest representation. Since meetings of that organization have been with the American Economic Association and like organizations, papers presented are largely by economists. For these reasons, results have been chiefly the bringing of economic insights to bear on problems long of interest to geographers. For the same reasons, the interpretation of results chiefly is in economic terms.

(Part II)

Six important general studies of spatial structure were reviewed in Part I of this essay. Part II, the present discussion, and Part III will review developments since these studies were made. Part II will introduce the programming methods used in many recent works and present five relatively simple problems in spatial structure which have been couched in programming terms. Part III will discuss more general recent studies, general in that they deal with regional aggregations of economic activities. These recent studies individually fall short of the comprehensiveness revealed in the books by Isard, Ponsard, and Lösch, but they extend work on location structures in significant ways.

The ensuing discussion will present materials which may be quite unfamiliar to the reader. For this reason, a reader's guide to the content of the discussion may be valuable, even at the risk of some repetition. The first section of this discussion contains an analysis of a sample problem. It shows how a problem couched verbally may be written algebraically as a linear programming problem. This is an essential idea. The ability to translate problems into the linear programming format is responsible for the wide use of the method in recent research. This part of the essay contains summa-

tion signs and other algebraic symbols. The impatient reader or one who wishes to avoid the algebra might skip directly to the last two paragraphs of the first part of the discussion. These contain a summary of the character of linear programming and references to the literature.

The second section of the discussion shows how five problems have been treated in the linear programming format. This section contains references to the sample problem discussed in the first section of the essay, but if the reader agrees that translation into the linear programming format is possible, much of this section may be read without a detailed reading of the first section. A number of figures appear in this section which provide general statements of the problems treated by means of the linear programming format. These five problems have many counterparts in everyday geographical analysis. These counterparts have not been emphasized in this essay, but the writer hopes that the reader will let his imagination wander as the problems are presented. The final section summarizes the accomplishments represented by the five models and the use of linear programming.

Linear Programming and Problems of Spatial Structure

Work on linear programming and related devices has been of great importance in model building for several purposes. The devices are relatively simple. Their generality has made them particularly relevant to the analysis of spatial systems, and they are used in much current work on spatial structure. Linear programming means just what the term implies. It is concerned with linear relations which take the form $A + B = C$. The term "programming" refers to following a set "program" to obtain a solution to the linear equations.

A sample problem in spatial structure will serve to introduce the programming method and its use in problems of spatial structure. The sample problem might be thought of as a problem in administrative organization; it concerns the location of boundaries of urban tributary areas. Once the problem is written out, it may be seen that it is equivalent to a linear programming problem, that a solution for the linear programming problem is also a solution to the problem in spatial structure.

The objective in this problem is to arrange

the tributary areas of urban centers so that (1) the population of the tributary area of each urban center is proportional to the population of that center and (2) if the distances individuals are from their associated urban centers are summed, the total distance from urban centers is a minimum (Fig. 1). This might be a desideratum, for example, for urban tributary areas of post offices or school districts. It will be necessary to describe components of the problem in greater detail before it can be stated exactly.

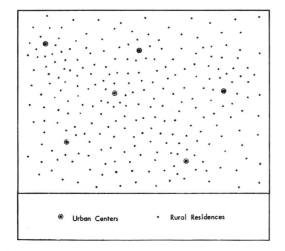

FIGURE 1   How should boundaries be drawn (1) so that the zone around each urban center contains a rural population proportional to the population of the urban center and (2) the sum of the distances from rural residences to assigned urban centers is a minimum?

A study area contains urban centers and rural residences. There are m urban centers, numbered 1, 2, and so on up to m. The rural residences scattered through the rural portion of the area may be numbered 1, 2, and so on up to n. The population of each urban center is known, as is the number of persons residing at each rural residence. Also, the distance from each rural residence to each urban center is known. In stating the problem, it will be convenient for the total population of the urban centers to equal the total population of the rural area. Consider the population of each urban center as an adjusted population. Populations of urban centers have been changed up or down so that total urban population is equal to total rural population, but the percentage distribution of population among urban centers is unchanged.

Recall that part of the objective of this problem is to arrange the tributary areas of urban centers so that the size of the tributary area of each urban center is proportional to the size of that center. Use of adjusted populations described in the paragraph above allows this part of the objective to be stated: the population of each tributary area will be equal to the population of its associated urban center.

In Table 1 urban centers are listed at the column heads and their populations are shown at the bottom of the table. Rural residences are numbered along the left-hand side of the table, and the right-hand column contains the number of persons residing at each residence. Each row in the table shows the distance from a rural residence to each urban center. Thus the upper left hand "cell" of the table contains the distance, d_{11}, from the first residence to the first urban center. The next cell contains the distance from the first residence to the second urban center, etc.; u_1 is the population of urban center 1; r_1 is the population of rural residence number 1. These distances also can be discussed in a general way. For this reason the table notes the distance from the ith residence to the jth urban center. The variable is x_{ij}, the number of persons in the ith rural residence which a boundary assigns to the jth urban center.

TABLE I   Data for the Boundaries Problem

Rural Residences	Urban Centers									
	1	2	3	.	.	.	j	.	.	.	m	
1	d_{11}	d_{12}	d_{13}				d_{1j}				d_{1m}	r_1
2	d_{21}	d_{22}										r_2
3	d_{31}											
.												
.												
.												
i	d_{i1}						d_{ij}				d_{im}	r_i
.												
.												
.												
n	d_{n1}										d_{nm}	r_n
	u_1	u_2		.	.	.	u_j	.	.	.	u_m	

Since the number of persons assigned from the countryside to an urban center is to be equal to the population of that urban center, for urban center 1 the sum of the persons assigned from the rural residences to the first urban center must equal u_1. In general terms,

$$\sum_{i=1}^{n} x_{ij} = u_j \qquad j = 1, \ldots, m$$

where capital sigma is a summation sign, and the subscripts indicate that the summation extends over the n rural places to determine the number of persons assigned to the jth urban center. This is the first general rule.

Another rule stems from the objective of assigning every person at a rural residence to an urban place. Thus, for each residence the number of persons assigned to urban places must be equal to the number of persons within that residence. In algebraic terms, then,

$$\sum_{j=1}^{m} x_{ij} = r_i \qquad i = 1, \ldots, n$$

The fact that there are as many rural dwellers as there are persons in urban centers may be written:

$$\sum_{i=1}^{n} r_i = \sum_{j=1}^{m} u_j$$

Furthermore, since it makes no sense to have negative assignments of persons, there is the additional rule:

$$x_{ij} \geq 0 \qquad \begin{matrix} i = 1, \ldots, n \\ j = 1, \ldots, m \end{matrix}$$

Also, it must be indicated that persons are to be assigned so that the sum over the distances persons are from their associated urban centers is a minimum. Recalling that the number of persons assigned from the ith residence to the jth urban center is x_{ij} and the associated distance is d_{ij}, this objective is:

$$\sum_{i=1}^{n} \sum_{j=1}^{m} d_{ij} x_{ij} = \text{Minimum}$$

Here are two summation signs, since the summation extends over all urban centers and all rural places. Without changing the sense of the problem, the equations may be collected and written:

$$\text{Minimize:} \quad \sum_{i=1}^{n} \sum_{j=1}^{m} d_{ij} x_{ij} = Z$$

Subject to:
$$\sum_{j=1}^{m} -x_{ij} \geq -r_i \quad i = 1, \ldots, n$$

$$\sum_{i=1}^{n} x_{ij} \geq u_j \qquad j = 1, \ldots, m$$

$$x_{ij} \geq 0 \qquad \begin{matrix} j = 1, \ldots, m \\ i = 1, \ldots, n \end{matrix}$$

A typical linear programming problem is written in the form shown below:

$$\text{Minimize:} \quad p_1 x_1 + p_2 x_2 + \ldots + p_n x_n = Z$$

$$\text{Subject to:} \quad a_{11} x_1 + a_{12} x_2 + \ldots + a_{1n} x_n \geq c_1$$

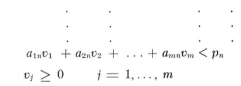

$$a_{m1} x_1 + a_{m2} x_2 + \ldots + a_{mn} x_n \geq c_m$$

$$x_i \geq 0 \qquad i = 1, \ldots, n$$

The form of these equations is exactly the same as the equations of the sample problem given previously (in the sample problem $a_{ij} = 1$ or 0). Thus, the sample problem is equivalent to a linear programming problem. Since linear programming problems can be solved, the sample problem also can be solved. Also, it is known that if a solution exists for the linear programming problem given in the form above, then a solution exists for the problem identified by the set of equations written below:

$$\text{Maximize:} \quad v_1 c_1 + v_2 c_2 + \ldots + v_m c_m = Z$$

$$\text{Subject to:} \quad a_{11} v_1 + a_{21} v_2 + \ldots + a_{m1} v_m < p_1$$

$$a_{1n} v_1 + a_{2n} v_2 + \ldots + a_{mn} v_m < p_n$$

$$v_j \geq 0 \qquad j = 1, \ldots, m$$

In this problem the unknowns are the v's and the constants are the same as those that appeared in the previous problem, although rearranged. The metric of the v's is determined by the metrics of the constants. The maximum value found in the second problem is exactly the same as the minimum value found for the first problem. The minimization problem is regarded as the *primal* problem, and the maximization problem is regarded as the *dual* of the primal problem. (Or, if chief interest had been in the maximization problem, the minimization problem would have been regarded as its dual.)

Knowledge that the sample problem is equivalent to a linear programming problem gives an operational method of finding a solution, as well as the information that there is an associated dual problem. The dual may be easier to compute than the primal problem, and be of interest for that matter. The dual may be of conceptual interest, since it formalizes a companion problem to the one of chief interest. It also supplies sets of numbers bearing on the problem since a set of unknowns is associated with the dual. The review will refer frequently to the practicability of computing the programming problems and the existence of the dual to a primal formulation. Additional notions about the dual problem will be introduced where they are needed.

Briefly, the linear programming format fits a situation where some quantity is to be maximized or minimized, subject to a set of rules or restraints. That quantity which is to be minimized or maximized is expressed in a single linear equation, the objective function. The rules or restraints are written down as a series of linear equations, a set of inequalities. Each linear programming problem has a companion problem, known as a dual. If the primal problem is a maximization problem, the dual problem is a minimization problem, and vice versa.

The literature on linear programming is voluminous, although linear programming methods have been available for only a few years. In the mathematical literature, an especially good advanced treatment is in a set of notes by A. W. Tucker,[1] and introductory treatments also are available.[2] Economists have been quick to seize upon

linear programming. Dorfman, Samuelson, and Solow have recently published an excellent book showing the wide applicability of linear programming in economics.[3] Linear programming papers also have appeared in the engineering literature, as well as in recent issues of the journals *Operations Research* and *Management Science*.

Five Problems of Spatial Structure

Five problems of spatial analysis, each of increasing complexity, are discussed below. The first is one in which everything is given except commodity flows. The following problems treat more complex situations ultimately including several raw materials, plant locations and markets; indivisibilities of plants; and interdependence of locations. Even at this degree of complexity, though, the analysis is relatively simple, since these problems do not extend to regional complexes of industries. As mentioned before, these more complicated situations are postponed to Part III of this essay.

1. The Transportation Problem

Given (1) supplying centers with known surpluses, (2) receiving places with known demands, and (3) connecting transportation routes with known transport costs, what is the least-cost method of moving surpluses to receiving places (Fig. 2)? This is known as the transportation problem.[4]

---

[1]A. W. Tucker, *Game Theory and Programming*, National Science Foundation, Summer Mathematics Institute Notes (Stillwater: Dept. of Mathematics, Oklahoma A. and M. College, 1955). A more advanced treatment of the basic mathematics is available in H. W. Kuhn and A. W. Tucker (eds.), *Linear Inequalities and Related Systems*, Annals of Mathematical Studies No. 38 (Princeton, N.J.: Princeton Univ. Press, 1956) and in Nos. 24 and 28 of this series. For a summary statement see A. W. Tucker's remarks on linear and nonlinear programming in "Symposium on Modern Techniques for Extremum Problems," *Operations Research*, Vol. 5 (1957), pp. 244-57. For bibliographies on linear programming see: F. Virginia Rohde, "Bibliography on Linear Programming," *Operations Research*, Vol. 5 (1957), pp. 45-62, and Harvey M. Wagner, "A Supplementary Bibliography on Linear Programming," *Operations Research*, Vol. 5 (1957), pp. 555-63.

[2]John C. Kemeny, J. Laurie Snell, and Gerald L. Thompson, *Introduction to Finite Mathematics* (Englewood Cliffs: Prentice-Hall, Inc., 1957), pp. 249-306.

[3]Robert Dorfman, Paul A. Samuelson, and Robert M. Solow, *Linear Programming and Economic Analysis* (New York: McGraw-Hill Book Company, Inc., 1958). A good expository paper is Alexander Henderson and Robert Schlaifer, "Mathematical Programming," *Harvard Business Review*, Vol. 32 (May-June, 1954), pp. 73-100. A basic reference is T. C. Koopmans (ed.), *Activity Analysis of Production and Allocation*, Cowles Commission Monograph 13 (New York: Wiley, 1951).

[4]The problem is sometimes called the Hitchcock-Koopmans transportation problem since it was independently developed by these workers. T. C. Koopmans, "Optimum Utilization of the Transportation System," *Econometrica*, Vol. 17, Supplement (July, 1949), pp. 136-46. Frank L. Hitchcock, "The Distribution of a Product from Several Sources to Numerous Localities," *Journal of Mathematical Physics*, Vol. 20 (1941), pp. 224-30. Fels points out that the Soviet mathematician L. V. Kantorovich stated the problem in 1939. Eberhard M. Fels, "Some Soviet Statistical Books of 1957," *Journal of the American Statistical Association*, Vol. 54 (March, 1959), p. 17. Marble has listed 70 references to the transportation and related problems. Duane F. Marble, "The Transportation Problem—A Bibliography" (mimeographed), Dept. of Geography, University of Washington, June 1957. For computational methods see: Edward H. Bowman and Robert B. Fetter, *Analysis for Production Management* (Homewood: Richard B. Irwin, 1957), H. S. Houthakker, "On the Numerical Solution of the Transportation Problem," *Operations Research*, Vol. 3 (1955), pp. 210-14, or Milton M. Snodgrass and Charles E. French, "Simplified Presentation of 'Transportation Problem Procedure' in Linear Programming," *Journal of Farm Economics*, Vol. 39 (1957), pp. 40-51. Comments on the use of the transportation problem for plant location decisions are in Maurice Fulton and L. Clinton Hoch, "Transportation Factors Affecting Locational Decisions," *Economic Geography*, Vol. 35 (1959), pp. 58-59.

It is not complex because it involves only movements along transportation routes, supplies available, amounts demanded, and transportation costs. But even if it is not complex, solution of a large problem may not be obvious. This transportation problem is identical in character to the sample problem discussed earlier. There, urban centers were points of demand, the rural residences were points of supply; these were connected over a transportation route, and it was desired to achieve the linking of urban centers with rural residences in the most efficient way, i.e., so that the least total distance would be travelled between urban centers and rural residences.

An interesting recent study using the transportation problem has appeared in a monograph by James M. Henderson, *The Efficiency of the Coal Industry, an Application of Linear Programming.*[5] Henderson divided the United States into fourteen districts, eleven of which produce significant amounts of coal, but since costs vary between underground and surface mining, Henderson identifies these activities separately and treats twenty-two coal-supplying areas. Since all fourteen of the districts consume coal, there are fourteen places to be supplied.

What is the efficient pattern of interregional coal trade? Henderson answered this question via three solutions of the transportation problem, one for 1947, another for 1949, and another for 1951. How efficiently does the coal industry perform? This question was answered by comparing the solutions of the transportation problem with actual patterns of coal flows. Since flows which vary from those displayed by the model presumably are less efficient than the theoretical flows, variations from the model are regarded as imperfections.

Henderson points out that the pattern of flows determined by the model is that which would exist under conditions of perfect competition. The reader may refer to the dual of the sample problem discussed earlier. For Henderson's problem the unknowns of the dual problem, the v_i's, would be in a price metric, since the vector $(p_1 p_2 \ldots, p_n)$ is in units of interregional transportation cost and the a_{ij}'s $= 1$ or 0. Values of the v_i's are relative

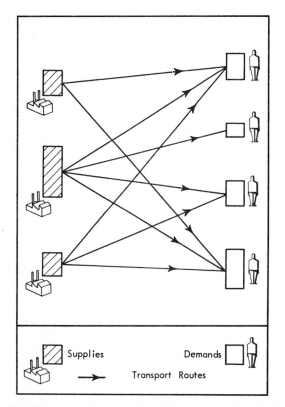

FIGURE 2 How Can Supplies be Moved to the Points of Demand at Minimum Transport Cost? Unit cost of transportation on each route and supplies and demands are known.

prices in exporting and receiving regions. Entrepreneurs acting in terms of these "efficiency" or "comparative advantage" prices would solve the dual problem. Since the dual of this problem is the problem in coal flows, the problem in coal flows would have been solved.

A transportation problem with twenty-two sources and fourteen receiving places presents no particular computational difficulties. As is ably discussed by Henderson, the chief problem for the analyst is the arrangement of the data so that the transportation problem format is meaningful.

Treating the data may not be simple, however, if there are large numbers of shipping and receiving places. In the case of wholesale drug centers and pharmacies, for example, in the United States or in a large region in the United States, so many shipping and receiving places would be involved that some approximations might be essential. Marcello Vidale[6] has provided a graphical

[5]James M. Henderson, *The Efficiency of the Coal Industry, An Application of Linear Programming* (Cambridge: Harvard Univ. Press, 1958). xii and 146 pp. Tables, bibliography. $4.50; "A Short-run Model for the Coal Industry," and "Efficiency and Pricing in the Coal Industry," *Review of Economics and Statistics*, Vol. 37 (1955), pp. 336-46, and Vol. 38 (1956), pp. 50-60.

[6]M. L. Vidale, "A Graphical Solution for the Transportation Problem," *Operations Research*, Vol. 4 (1956), pp. 193-203.

solution of the problem for cases such as this. Vidale utilizes transportation cost maps, difference maps (maps showing cost differentials for shipping products from two sources), and consumption maps. A promising topological configuration of market areas is selected, and boundaries are displaced until a solution is found (Fig. 3). If the solution cannot be found, another topological configuration for market areas is selected, and boundaries are displaced in search of a solution. The selection of topologically promising market areas and boundary displacements continues until the solution is found. Vidale states that once the difference and consumption maps are available, a market division with from five to seven sources and over a thousand consuming centers could be performed in a few hours.

2. Spatial Price Equilibrium

The spatial price equilibrium problem, like the transportation problem, is concerned with flows between regions, but both amounts to be shipped and received and regional prices are to be determined by the model, in addition to the orientation of flows. In the problem the locations of transportation routes and supplying and receiving points, as well as transportation costs, are known. It is desired to find the amount shipped along transportation routes under a least-cost program, subject, of

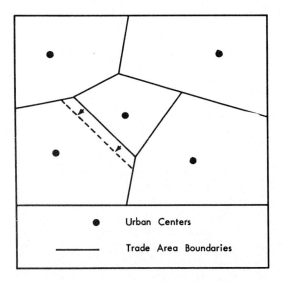

FIGURE 3 Vidale's Problem is Solved by Systematic Displacement of Trade Area Boundaries.

course, to conditions that supplies be shipped and demands be met. Supplies and demands are functions of price, and these relationships also are known. A simple example will serve as an illustration.

Suppose A is a surplus region and B is a deficit region, and the transportation cost between these regions is 50 cents per unit shipped. A has 100 units and B has 25 units and the prices respectively are \$1.00 and \$2.50 per unit. How much will be shipped between A and B? This is an easy question to answer: A will ship to B until the price in A rises and that in B falls and prices in the regions are separated by transportation costs. If prices were to shift further, then A could not ship to B and overcome the transportation cost of 50 cents per unit. How rapidly will the prices shift? This depends on the relations between price and supply. If this relationship is given by $P = 300 - 2Q$, then after A ships 25 units to B the price at A is \$1.50 per unit and that at B is \$2.00 per unit. The amount shipped and prices are determined.

The spatial price equilibrium problem is sometimes described as the Enke-Samuelson problem since the problem was first investigated by Enke using an analogue,[7] and Samuelson showed how Enke's problem could be stated as a linear programming problem.[8] Fox and Fox and Taeuber have worked out trade movements for livestock feeds,[9][10] Judge has produced a study of the movement of eggs,[11] and Morrill has made a study of the movement of wheat and flour.[12] These are cases in which supply and deficit regions are separated over large areas and movements are interregional in scope.

Morrill also has studied market areas for physicians' services using the spatial price equilibrium

[7]Stephen Enke, "Equilibrium Among Spatially Separated Markets: Solution by Electric Analogues," *Econometrica*, Vol. 19 (1951), pp. 40-48.

[8]Paul A. Samuelson, "Spatial Price Equilibrium and Linear Programming," *American Economic Review*, Vol. 42 (1952), pp. 283-303.

[9]Karl A. Fox, "A Spatial Equilibrium Model of the Livestock-Feed Economy of the United States," *Econometrica*, Vol. 21 (1953), pp. 547-66.

[10]Karl A. Fox and Richard C. Taeuber, "Spatial Equilibrium Models of the Livestock-Feed Economy," *American Economic Review*, Vol. 40 (1955), pp. 584-608.

[11]George G. Judge, *Competitive Position of the Connecticut Poultry Industry—A Spatial Equilibrium Model for Eggs* (Bull. 318, Storrs Agri. Expt. Station, 1956).

[12]Richard L. Morrill, "An Experimental Study of Trade in Wheat and Flour in the United States," unpublished M.A. thesis, Dept. of Geography, University of Washington, 1957. Also, Richard L. Morrill and William L. Garrison, "Projections of Interregional Patterns of Trade in Wheat and Flour," *Economic Geography*, [Vol. 36 (1960), pp. 166-26.]

model (Fig. 4).[13] This is an arrangement similar to Vidale's problem and the sample problem discussed earlier. Morrill's work varies in scale from interregional movements on a national level to movements in Seattle, Washington. Judge and Wallace have written on the computation of price equilibrium models,[14] and Orr has noted some of the relationships between theories of location and transportation rates and the spatial price equilibrium model.[15]

3. Determining both Locations and Flows

The location of the shipping point may also be one of the unknowns to be determined. For example, how can one determine the location of a set of warehouses? If the locations of customers are known, where should warehouses be located in order to minimize the cost of distributing goods from customers to the warehouse? Wester and Kantner and Brink and de Cani have suggested methods applicable to the case when customer demands are known and the capacity of each warehouse as well as its location is to be found.[16, 17] In the Wester and Kantner scheme the analyst selects starting positions and capacities for the warehouses and then allocates customers using the transportation model. Next, each warehouse is located optimally relative to its customers by computations equivalent to those used by Weber (Fig. 5).[18] Finally, capacities are reassigned among ware-

[13]Published in William L. Garrison, Brian J. L. Berry, Duane F. Marble, John Nystuen, and Richard Morrill, *Studies of Highway Development and Geographic Change* (Seattle: University of Washington Press, 1959). For an expository discussion of this problem and related problems see, William L. Garrison, "Three Highway Impact Problems," forthcoming in a *Bulletin* of the Highway Research Board (Washington, NAS-NRC, 1959).

[14]George G. Judge and T. D. Wallace, "Estimation of Spatial Price Equilibrium Models," *Journal of Farm Economics,* Vol. 40 (Nov. 1958), pp. 801-20.

[15]Earle W. Orr, "A Synthesis of Theories of Location, of Transportation Rates, and of Spatial Price Equilibrium," *Papers and Proceedings,* Regional Science Association, Vol. 3 (1957), pp. 61-73. For an application see William L. Garrison and Duane F. Marble, "Analysis of Highway Networks: A Linear Programming Formulation," Highway Research Board, *Proceedings,* Vol. 37 (1958), pp. 1-17.

[16]Leon Wester and Harold H. Kantner, "Optimal Location-Allocation," paper read at the Boston Meeting, Operations Research Society of America, 1958 (mimeographed; Chicago: Armour Research Foundation of Illinois Institute of Technology, 1958).

[17]Edward L. Brink and John S. de Cani, "An Analogue Solution of the Generalized Transportation Problem with Specific Application to Marketing Location," *Proceedings of the First International Conference on Operational Research* (Baltimore: Operations Reseach Society of America, 1957), pp. 123-36.

[18]Alfred Weber, *Ueber den Standort der Industrien* (Tübingen, 1909), translated by C. J. Friedrich as *Alfred Weber's Theory of the Location of Industry* (Chicago: Univ. of Chicago Press, 1929).

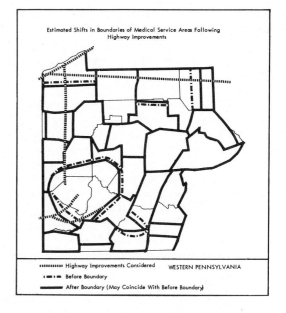

FIGURE 4 Morrill Postulated a Decrease in Highway Transportation Costs. He then solved the spatial price equilibrium problem for the distribution of medical services and associated trade areas.

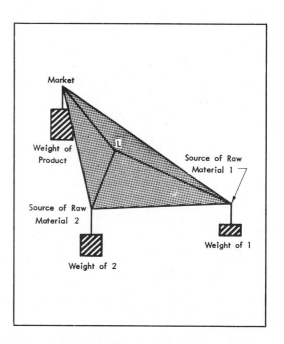

FIGURE 5 After Markets are Assigned to Warehouses Using the Transportation Problem, Wester and Kantner shift warehouse locations using a method equivalent to Weber's force table analogue.

houses according to the rule that each customer is to be served from the closest warehouse. These three steps are repeated, and, since each step reduces total transportation cost, the computations converge toward the optimal spacing of warehouses within customer tributary areas. The Brink and de Cani scheme uses an analogue computer to solve essentially the same problem.

Baumol and Wolfe have considered problems in which warehouses are intermediate between factories and ultimate consumers and it is desired to minimize the total delivery cost—delivery from the factory to the warehouse, within-warehouse cost, and delivery from the warehouse to the ultimate consumer (Fig. 6).[19] This problem is very

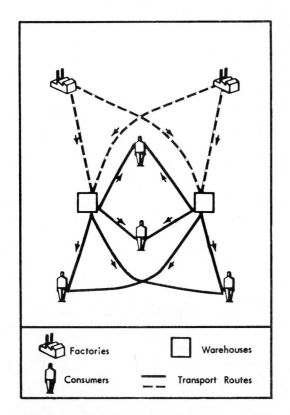

FIGURE 6 Goods are Shipped from Factories Through Warehouses to Customers. Given transportation cost on each route, warehouse costs, and supplies and demands, what pattern of shipments meets demands at least cost?

Factories · Warehouses · Consumers · Transport Routes

similar to the transportation problem since transportation costs may be considered to be the aggregate costs of a flow from a factory through a specific warehouse (including inventory cost) to an ultimate consumer. On the other hand, the problem may become complex if the unit inventory cost within warehouses is a function of the number of units passing through the warehouses.[20] In this situation, the cost function becomes nonlinear, and computation becomes difficult. Baumol and Wolfe have suggested an iterative technique for this problem, and they have supplied an illustrative small-scale computation.

Walter Fisher has treated an even more general problem.[21] Fisher imagines a situation in which the amount demanded by customers will depend on the delivery cost—the higher the delivery cost the less will be demanded. Also, the greater the number of warehouses the greater the unit cost of warehousing. There are two things appealing about Fisher's problem: (1) it is more general than other statements of the problem; and (2) Fisher treats the problem from the formal point of view of aggregation problems, i.e., he recognizes the problem of spatial aggregation as part of a larger and more general aggregation problem. In special cases the computation of Fisher's problem would be straightforward, but no method of computation is given for the general problem.

4. Raw Materials, Plants, and Markets

Goldman has discussed the problem of the efficient transportation of several goods when one good may be hauled as a backhaul from another good.[22] He proposes that one island has coal, another has iron ore, another has limestone, and each demands steel products. He then asks where production should be located and thus flows oriented, so that steel is available in the desired amounts at the least transportation cost (Fig. 7). This obviously is a complex problem, since the location of production on any one island would make available empty bottoms for shipping raw materials and fin-

[19]William J. Baumol and Philip Wolfe, "A Warehouse-Location Problem," *Operations Research*, Vol. 6 (1958), pp. 252-63. A similar problem is treated in Kenneth S. Kretschmer, *On the Warehouse Location Problem* (Computation and Data Processing Center, University of Pittsburgh, 1958). Processed, 8 pp.

[20]Generally, large warehouses are more efficient than small warehouses because the use of many warehouses increases bookkeeping and other administrative costs, and may increase the amount of inventory to be held against the flow of shipments.

[21]Walter D. Fisher, "Economic Aggregation as Minimum Distance," paper read at the Detroit Meeting, Econometric Society, 1956, abstract in *Econometrica*, Vol. 25 (1957), p. 363.

[22]Thomas A. Goldman, "Efficient Transportation and Industrial Location," *Papers and Proceedings*, Regional Science Association, Vol. 4 (1958), pp. 91-106.

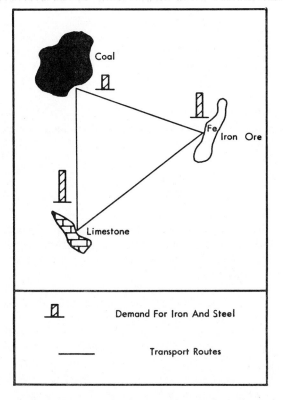

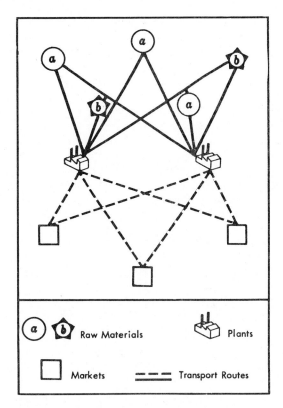

FIGURE 7   Where Should Iron and Steel Capacity be Located in order to Meet Demands for Iron and Steel at Least Cost? Availability of "backhaul" cargo space affects the minimum cost solution.

FIGURE 8   There are Several Raw Materials, Factories, and Markets. What flow pattern will meet market demands at minimum cost, without violating capacity limitations on factories and raw materials?

ished products from that island. Although Goldman's problem is written in terms of production technology and cost which does not vary between islands, the model could be readily adapted to include these variations and should be applicable to the analysis of industrial combines such as the Southern Urals-Kuznetsk iron and steel developments.

Beckmann and Marschak have provided a model of raw material flows from production sites to manufacturing plants and finished product flows from manufacturing plants to markets (Fig. 8).[23] This model complements Goldman's, since it stresses aspects of the problem other than backhauls. The following are given: (1) several raw materials and a number of sources of each raw

material, (2) several processing plants, and (3) a number of final markets. Limitations on production at each raw material site and on plant capacity restrict the amount of final product that can be sold at the final market. Costs of transportation and raw material and finished product prices are given. The objective is to select those raw material and finished product flows which will maximize net revenue. Gross product is obtained by multiplying the price obtained in each market by the number of units delivered. From this, cost of resources and transportation must be subtracted to obtain net revenue. In addition to the restraints on capacity noted earlier, the problem includes the condition that finished products shipped from each plant may not be greater in amount than that permitted by the inputs of raw materials. Again, this is a linear model which can be stated in a linear programming problem and for which an optimum solution can be obtained.

[23] Martin J. Beckmann and Thomas Marschak, "An Activity Analysis Approach to Location Theory," *Proceedings,* Second Symposium in Linear Programming (Washington: National Bureau of Standards, 1955), pp. 331-79. Revised version published in *Kyklos,* Vol. 8 (1955), pp. 125-43. [See page 287 of this volume.]

5. Indivisibilities and Interdependence

Koopmans and Beckmann have investigated problems of assigning n manufacturing plants to n locations in such a way as to maximize the combined profits of the plants.[24] This problem is of interest from the point of view of location questions, and also bears on a broader set of problems known as "assignment problems" (e.g., assigning workers to machines so as to maximize production). Indivisibilities are stressed since there is no possibility of assigning parts of plants to locations. Also, interdependence is stressed since the assignment of one plant may affect the profitabilities of plants assigned to other locations (Fig. 9).

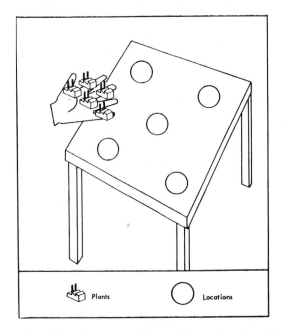

FIGURE 9 Five Plants are to be Assigned to Five Locations. There are 5•4•3•2•1 = 120 ways this may be done. In the linear assignment problem the profitability of one plant at a location is not affected by the location of other plants, but the profitability of a given plant varies from location to location. The problem is to select from the 120 different location patterns that pattern which maximizes the combined profitabilities of the plants.

There are two parts to the analysis. The first ignores the possibility of interdependence of profits and stresses indivisibilities. This is termed the "linear assignment problem," and it can be formulated as a problem in permutation matrices, or linear programming, or as a zero-sum two-person game. The profitability of plant k at location i is a_{ki} $(k;i = 1, \ldots, n)$, a_{ki} is independent of the location of other plants. Feasible assignments are represented by permutation matrices, $P = (p_{ki})$, each row and column of which contain a single element 1 and zeros elsewhere. The problem is to find a permutation matrix $\hat{P} = (\hat{p}_{ki})$ such that $\sum_{k,i} a_{ki}p_{ki} \leq \sum_{k,i} a_{ki}\hat{p}_{ki}$. This problem is mathematically trivial since there are $n!$ permutation matrices and the answer may be found by inspection (Fig. 10). However, since for more than a handful of plants and locations $n!$ would be so large that evaluation of each permutation matrix would not be feasible, the permutation matrix approach does not yield a practicable computation method.

The linear programming problem is formed by ignoring the indivisibility of plants and imagining that fraction x_{ki} of the kth plant may be assigned to the ith location. The linear programming problem is to choose x_{ki} so as to maximize:

$$\sum_{k,i} x_{ki}a_{ki}; \text{ subject to: } \sum_{k} x_{ki} = 1; 0 \leq x_{ki} \leq 1.$$

It is then shown that the solution of this problem is the solution of the linear assignment problem. Although fractions of plants are imagined, only whole plants are assigned in the optimum solution. Koopmans and Beckmann also present a note on a zero-sum two-person game which Von Neumann has shown to be equivalent to the linear assignment problem.

When transportation between plants is considered, the profitability at one plant becomes dependent upon the location of other plants. The a_{ki} become "semi-net revenues" from which shipping cost must be subtracted. Koopmans and Beckmann describe this as a quadratic assignment problem since elements of the permutation matrix enter into the transportation cost term more than once. The solution of this problem in terms of permutation matrices would be extremely difficult.

The associated linear programming problem formulated by allowing fractional assignments is shown to be one which cannot be a solution to the problem in permutation matrices. Consequently,

[24]Tjalling C. Koopmans and Martin Beckmann, "Assignment Problems and the Location of Economic Activities, *Econometrica*, Vol. 25 (Jan., 1957), pp. 53–76.

Locations

	1	2	3	4	5
A	17	14	18	20	19
B	21	16	19	22	15
C	18	24	20	16	19
D	19	15	21	17	23
E	24	19	16	18	20

Profitability Matrix for Five Plants and Five Locations

Example Permutation Matrix

Locations

	1	2	3	4	5
A	0	1	0	0	0
B	1	0	0	0	0
C	0	0	0	0	1
D	0	0	0	1	0
E	0	0	1	0	0

Plant A is Assigned to Location 2, B to 1, C to 5, D to 4, E to 3.

FIGURE 10 Examples of Profitability and Permutation Matrices

linear programming does not offer a computation method for this problem. Also, Koopmans and Beckmann reach certain conclusions regarding the price system and the location system. These will be noted shortly.

Accomplishments

Although the models are restricted in scope and do not provide a complete location theory, they represent marked operational and conceptual progress. They also present some obvious liabilities. One of these is that they are couched in terms of a spatial system consisting of points and lines; another is that they deal with "instant-in-time" or static situations.

The transportation problem serves as a case in point. Supplying areas and receiving places are treated as points which are connected by lines. In Henderson's treatment of the coal industry, for example, the coal-producing areas were treated as if all production in a given area was located at a given point. That point was connected with each market, with the markets also treated as points, by transportation routes which were lines.[25] When the transportation problem was applied to the sample problem, the objective was to find boundaries. The boundaries were not really found, of course. Individuals at points (rural residences) were "shipped" to other points (urban centers). The solution of the problem finds the connections but does not draw the boundaries. Except for cases where peculiarities of shipping cost occasion overlapping of trade areas, it would be a simple matter to draw boundaries enclosing connected points. But boundaries around points may be drawn in many configurations. If there were added requirements, such as the requirement that the total length of boundaries be a minimum, then some unsolved problems might arise.

The models are static in that certain things are taken as given, such as the location of transportation routes or the availability of plant capacity. Even in the spatial price equilibrium model, where the amounts to be supplied and amounts demanded are not given, the locations of production, consumption, and transportation routes, and supply and demand functions are given. Thus these models cut across the location structure at an instant in time. Much significant work has been done with dynamic models, but most dynamic questions remain obscure in this field as elsewhere.

Part I of this review noted that one achievement in the recent literature has been establish-

[25]For an example of treatment of continuous space see Martin Beckmann, "A Continuous Model of Transportation," *Econometrica*, Vol. 20 (1952), pp. 643-60.

ment of location patterns using concepts from location theory (see especially Isard's final chapter). The five problems just discussed also accomplish this. They provide patterns of flows and locations; in short, location systems. Goldman's treatment of backhauls, together with the Beckmann and Marschak model, for example, lays out the location system in terms of interdependence of commodity flows on the transportation system. This is a real accomplishment over previous statements in the tradition of Weber, which emphasize weights of goods hauled and weight-losing (or -gaining) characteristics of manufacturing.

It was also mentioned in Part I of this discussion that an accomplishment of Isard's book was the treatment of transport input within the context of the economist's substitution analysis. Linear programming models also allow economic analysis. The transportation problem, for example, has as its dual a problem in price differences between originating and receiving areas. The objective function of the dual problem maximizes the difference between regional prices. Other equations of the dual problem specify price differences that must exist for flows to occur. Indeed, the transportation problem may be thought of as a problem in regional price structures (the dual) or as a problem in commodity flows (the primal). In the spatial price equilibrium problem, information from the dual is used to determine regional prices and, thus, amounts supplied and demanded. In Henderson's problem, information from the dual was used to suggest pricing systems in the coal industry. In the Koopmans and Beckmann linear assignment problem, the authors discussed the character of the dual in great detail. They note that the market will produce rents which solve the dual and thus cause an optimal assignment of plants. A linear programming formulation will not solve the Koopmans and Beckmann quadratic assignment problem (viz., when both indivisibilities and interdependence are considered); so the authors are pessimistic about the ability of the market system to sustain an optimal assignment of plants to locations.[26]

Other remarks could be made regarding the duals of problems discussed earlier, but it is most important to emphasize that problems couched in linear programming terms display the price interdependences associated with the location system in a manner which was not possible before.

Utilization of linear programming models has given an operational character to problems of location structure. This is not to say that all the problems discussed can be readily solved, for nonlinear problems generally present computational difficulties. Koopmans' and Beckmann's quadratic assignment problem, for example, defies computation, as does Fisher's problem. However, in certain cases, such as that of Baumol's model, nonlinear problems can be solved.

The size of the problem might prove a limiting feature to some of the models. Vidale's graphic methods suggest one way of treating problems which are very large. The word "very" really should be capitalized. This writer knows of one problem which involved an equation system with 1,555 columns and 195 rows.[27] Since it was possible to do some computing with this model, all models smaller than this may be characterized as computable. The real operational problem is fitting a viable research question within a programming format.

(Part III)

Publications Reviewed:

Industrial Complex Analysis and Regional Development, by Walter Isard, Eugene W. Schooler, and Thomas Vietorisz. Cambridge: Technology Press of the Massachusetts Institute of Technology; New York: John Wiley and Sons, Inc., 1959. xvii and 294 pp. $8.75.

Location Factors in the Petrochemical Industry, by Walter Isard and Eugene W. Schooler. Washington: U.S. Department of Commerce, 1955. vi and 102 pp. $3.00.

The Location of the Synthetic-Fiber Industry, by Joseph Airov. Cambridge: Technology Press of the Massachusetts Institute of Technology; New York: John Wiley and Sons, Inc., 1959. xii and 203 pp. $9.75.

Allocation in Space, by Louis Lefeber. Amsterdam: North-Holland Publishing Company, 1958. xv and 151 pp. 17 guilders.

Part I of this essay reviewed certain general approaches to an understanding of the spatial structure of the economy by summarizing and

---

[26]For elaboration of the significance of this point see Charles M. Tiebout, "Location Theory, Empirical Evidence, and Economic Evolution," *Papers and Proceedings,* Regional Science Association, Vol. 3 (1957), pp. 74-86.

[27]Thomas A. Marschak, "A Spatial Model of U.S. Petroleum Refining," U.S. Air Force, Project RAND; Research Memorandum, RM-2205, June, 1958.

comparing six recent books on the subject (see *Annals*, Vol. 49 [1959] pp. 232-9). Part II of this essay presented one of the new tools, programming, in the kitbag of the analyst and reviewed five rather restricted problems of flows and locations (see *Annals*, Vol. 49 [1959], pp. 471-82). Part III, the present and final part of the essay, will present certain recent trends in regional analysis. We will be concerned with interrelations of economic activities within and among regions. Certain problems related to those discussed in Part II of this essay will receive cursory treatment before these regional problems are discussed. Several persons who commented on Part II of this essay expressed interest in additional problems at this level of generality; so the main threads of Part II of this essay will be pursued a bit further.

A note on the character of the essay may be useful. The essay has undertaken the hopelessly large task of capsulizing and commenting upon recent developments which assist in the analysis of the spatial structure of the economy. Excepting the books which were reviewed in Part I of this essay, recent additions to the literature have been articles or specialized monographs. Because it would be tedious and often repetitive to treat these works one at a time, certain problems were singled out for discussion in Part II of this essay and the organization around problems will be continued through Part III.

It also is proper to mention that this essay does not treat large blocks of recent materials which are pertinent to the study of the spatial structure of the economy. Some of these are omitted because they are either well known or readily available to workers in geography. They include Professor Edward Ullman's studies of commodity flows and other studies of the geography of transportation. Dr. William Warntz's studies of potentials, studies of resource evaluation and of central place theory, and the bulk of the work on migration, circulation, and diffusion at the Royal University of Lund. Statistical problems of data collection, organization, and model verification are also deliberately omitted from the essay. This important subject is too large for inclusion here.

As mentioned before, five rather restrictive problems were discussed in Part II of this essay. Four more problems will be capsulized very briefly here, and major attention will be devoted to a tenth problem. As mentioned before, this is the analysis of interrelated economic activities and consequent

regional interrelations. The several subtitles used when this problem is discussed—*Input-Output, Industrial Complex Analysis*, etc.—are alternate methods of treating this problem.

Four Additional Problems

The reader will recall the transportation problem discussed in Part II of this essay. This problem treats the pattern of flows over a network, with amounts to be shipped and received and costs of transportation given. This problem was augmented through a series of problems which dealt with location patterns of production and consumption and of plants or warehouses on the transportation network, subject to various resource, plant capacity, and demand constraints. Problems briefly identified below also may be thought of as extensions from problems in the transportation format. But instead of considering locational patterns such as those just mentioned, chief attention will be given to patterns of flows on the networks, subject to various constraining characteristics of networks.

1. The Transshipment Problem

This problem includes two considerations: one is finding the least-cost routes between places; the other is allocating shipments to routes so that total transportation costs are at a minimum. The term "transshipment" is used where a shipment moves from one place to another via an intermediate place. Alex Orden has found a very simple method of solving the transshipment problem.[1] Orden introduces artificial stockpiles at transshipment places. These greatly reduce the complexity of the problem and permit its treatment within a simple programming format.

Some expository discussion may clarify the problem. Suppose the transportation network has only direct routes between places. If this is the case, minimum cost routes between places are immediately known and the problem of assigning flows between places may be solved quickly by use of the transportation problem. But this may not be the case in some problems. A transportation network may offer a large number of alternate routes between places and the best solution of the problem may require shipping via intermediate places. In Figure 1, for example, one may ship from B to D

---

[1] Alex Orden, "The Transshipment Problem," *Management Science*, Vol. 2 (April, 1956), pp. 227-85.

either directly or via place C. The lowest cost solution would be via C. Some inspection will reveal that the cheapest route from E to C is via A and D. Here two transshipments are required. In a simple system like that in Figure 1 it is easy to locate least-cost routes. In more complex systems, such as the highway network of the United States, a lengthy inspection of alternate routes would be required to find least-cost routes. It is in cases such as this that Orden's solution of the problem is useful.

2. The Traveling Salesman[2]

The traveling salesman problem may be presented by asking how a salesman could begin at a city in one state, visit specified cities in 47 other states, and return to the origin in a manner that the shortest route is followed. One might begin at Albany, New York, for example. There are 47 remaining cities; so there are 47 choices for the first move. Select the next city and go there. The next choice is from among 48-2 cities (Fig. 2). It is easy to see that this problem involves (48-1)! choices, constrained by the condition that the tour end at the starting point. The problem is of much wider application than the finding of optimal salesmen's tours, of course.

In a sense this is a trivial problem. Note that there is a finite number of choices, so that all one

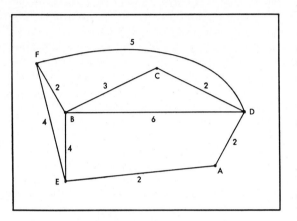

FIGURE 1   Routes and Costs. Least-cost route from B to D is via C. From E to C the least-cost is via A and D.

[2]Merrill M. Flood, "The Traveling Salesman Problem," *Operations Research*, Vol. 4 (February, 1956), pp. 61-75; George Dantzig, R. Fulkerson, and S. Johnson, "Solution of a Large-Scale Traveling-Salesman Problem," *Journal of the Operations Research Society of America*, Vol. 2 (November, 1954), pp. 393-410; and "On a Linear-Programming, Combinatorial Approach to the Traveling-Salesman Problem," *Operations Research*, Vol. 7 (January-February, 1959), pp. 58-66.

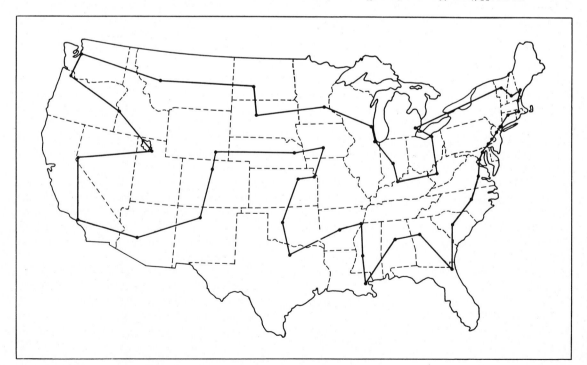

FIGURE 2   Optimal Tour Among 48 Cities. After Flood, p. 70.

needs to do is to list all alternates and select the shortest tour among these alternates. From a practical point, though, this observation is not very helpful. Even in the rather simple case of a tour among 48 cities, there are (48-1)! or millions of alternates from which to select. The problem is not that of knowing how to find the solution. The problem is that of knowing how to find the solution easily. Most work has been done toward finding characteristics of optimum solutions (one of the few things known is that the optimum tour does not cross its own path) and in finding efficient computational algorithms (computing routines) for finding shortest tours.

3. Max–Flow Min–Cut

There is a well-known max-flow min-cut theorem which states that the maximum flow on a network is equal to the minimum cut. This requires some explanation. Imagine a network with a source and destination, connected by routes and nodes of varying capacity (Fig. 3). How much can flow in a unit of time between the sources and the destinations? Assuming an unlimited supply of goods to be shipped and unlimited demand, the flow is constrained by the capacity of the network. But how do we find the limiting capacity? We must look for "cuts," or bottlenecks, in the network.

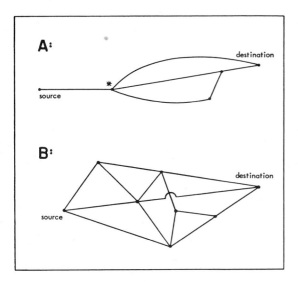

FIGURE 3   Two Networks. It would be easy to determine the capacity of network A. Ability to compute min-cuts and max-flows assists the analysis of more complex networks, such as B.

Technically, a cut is a collection of directed routes and intersections through which passes every route from source of destination. The notion of a cut is illustrated by Figure 3A: clearly the maximum flow from the source to the destination cannot be greater than the capacity of the node marked with the asterisk.

Dantzig and Fulkerson have developed a linear programming solution of the max-cut min-flow theorem.[3] The maximization side of the problem is the max-flow. The restraining equations locate the min-cut and the dual problem gives its capacity. Besides giving an extremely clear statement of the theorem, linear programming gives an efficient method of computing maximum flows and locating minimum cuts. This computational ease is important. In a complicated network, such as that in Figure 3B, it is by no means immediately apparent what the flow capacity of the network is nor where the minimum cut lies.

4. Design of Networks

A review of the literature will reveal that most analyses of communications systems are restricted to single links or intersections of networks. That is, design or use of a road is considered more or less in isolation from the network as a whole, or a railroad addition is considered in isolation from the network. The larger problem of the layout and use of an entire network is interesting for its own sake, and it may have practical values in underdeveloped areas or in the development of new networks in developed areas (e.g., the interstate highway system). Also, general models enable one to ask whether restricted objectives and decisions about parts of communications systems are consistent with objectives and decisions about entire networks. Works on the over-all characteristics of systems may be divided roughly into two types: (1) those that consider the routes and nodes of communications networks as given and involve decisions about increase (or decrease) of the capacity of individual routes or nodes, and (2) those that consider a network built from scratch or nearly so.

Kalaba and Juncosa[4] have written on the design and utilization of such networks as telephone

[3] G. B. Dantzig and D. R. Fulkerson, "On the Max-Flow Min-Cut Theorem of Networks," *Papers on Linear Inequalities and Related Systems* (Annals of Mathematics Studies, No. 38), H. W. Kuhn and A. W. Tucker, editors, 1956, pp. 215-21.
[4] R. E. Kalaba and M. L. Juncosa, "Optimal Design and Utilization of Communication Networks," *Management Science*, Vol. 3 (October, 1956), pp. 33-44.

systems. Here the problem is that of meeting some desired performance standard by increasing the capacity of switching points (nodes) and routes (lines) between switching points. Capacity costs are considered to be the only significant costs and the problem is to select from among alternative capacity costs that minimal investment which meets the desired level of performance. This problem may be handled nicely in linear programming format, as may certain of the problems stated by Quandt.[5]

Quandt considers improvements in a network to provide capacity demanded by traffic at minimal cost. Quandt is able to formulate realistic programming problems in the rather restricted case when the total budget available for improvements is determined from outside the problem, say by the action of the legislature. When this is done, the dual programming problem gives an interpretation of interest rates and of the relative values of improvements at various places in the network. Quandt considers a transshipment case and the case where links between nodes may be added to the network. In this case combinatorial problems appear and computation may be difficult.

Quandt's and Kalaba's and Juncosa's models apply in cases such as highway or long-line telephone links in the U. S. where the basic outline of the pattern is shown. But even in such cases these models may not be completely applicable. Long-line telephone networks are gradually being replaced by microwave communication systems. Here one starts from scratch. New nodes (intersections or switching stations) may be created, as may links between these nodes.

Principles for the design of new networks have been treated recently by Beckmann[6] and Vadnal.[7] Beckmann considers cases of varying complexity. If the network is to be constructed to connect given nodes, the problem is that of choosing links and perhaps new nodes from among a

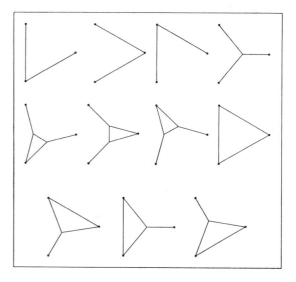

FIGURE 4 Configurations of a Network Joining Three Points. The first three configurations in the first row are special cases of the fourth configuration. After Beckmann.

large number of possible configurations. If three nodes are given, then a number of configurations of connecting links are possible, and some involve the creation of new intersections (Fig. 4).

Individual configurations may be analyzed without difficulty. But if it is necessary to choose among configurations and if this choice includes a large number of alternates, then analysis may be quite difficult. Suppose there are seven points, for example. There are many configurations to choose among. One set might be all those configurations presented by possibilities of joining three points in one subset of the network, four points in another, and then joining the two sub-networks. The large number of combinations possible leaves problems such as this fairly open, except in special cases.[8]

Beckmann considers a number of other cases, including the case of a continuously distributed population. He properly emphasizes that his models may be difficult to compute. However, if they are augmented by insight, judgment, and experience from outside the problem, they provide principles which may assist in the design of networks.

[5]Richard E. Quandt, "Models of Transportation and Optimal Network Construction," *Journal of Regional Science*, Vol. 2 (Spring, 1960), pp. 27-45. Another paper on this topic is D. R. Fulkerson, "Increasing the Capacity of a Network: The Parametric Budget Problem," *Management Science*, Vol. 5 (July, 1959), pp. 472-83.

[6]Martin Beckmann, "Principles of Optimum Location for Transportation Networks," [in W. L. Garrison and D. F. Marble, eds., *Quantitative Geography; Part I: Economic and Cultural Topics*, Studies in Geography, No. 13. (Evanston: Northwestern University Press, 1967, pp. 95-119).] Also, Martin Beckmann, "A Continuous Model of Transportation," *Econometrica*, Vol. 20 (October, 1952), pp. 643-60.

[7]A. Vadnal, "The Location of the Communication Network in a Circle" (paper given at the European Economic Congress, Bilbao, 1958).

[8]One exception is the special case of finding a route of minimum length. See William Miehle, "Link-Length Minimization in Networks," *Operations Research*, Vol. 6 (March-April, 1958), pp. 232-43.

Vadnal treats the problem of the optimum pattern of a communications network within an economic area having the shape of a circle, with the network to provide transportation to the center of the circle. Vadnal shows how variations in the pattern of radials and circumferential routes will follow from different relations between over-the-road and capacity costs. Vadnal's model presents operational difficulties, but like Beckmann's it provides general principles which may be augmented by analytic devices and insight and is useful in understanding the layout of some types of transportation systems—urban freeways being a good example.

The problems described above are somewhat less than briefly capsulized. Nonetheless, the descriptions should give a glimpse of some systematic work on properties of some simple spatial patterns. This writer must again appeal to the reader's imagination. These four problems have many counterparts in everyday geographic analysis; they are ways of thinking about spatial patterns. The min-cut of a highway network and of the distributaries of a river are but two instances of a network property.

At this point we turn attention to the analysis of interrelated economic activities and consequent within- and among-region relationships.

Interindustry and Interregional Relationships

Regional interrelations may be thought of as stemming from two conditions: (1) Uneven distribution of resources. Some regions are rich in resources and some are poor. Provided that demands for goods and services do not correspond with the distribution of resources, regions will be dependent upon each other for markets for their products and for sources of things that they consume. (2) A set of technical interrelations reflecting the technical state-of-the-arts. For example, the production of pig iron requires iron ore and coal, among other things. If pig iron is produced in one region and iron ore and coal are available only in other regions, then regional interrelations arise due to unequal resource distribution. But the unequal resource distribution results from raw material requirements of the industry which are a matter of the technical state-of-the-arts. Certain

other interrelationships may be noted. Iron ore production may require coal. To produce the coal used to produce the iron ore used to produce the pig iron may require iron. So iron outputs flow to the coal-producing region and extra coal must be shipped to produce this iron. The chain of technical interrelations never ends.

What has just been said is hardly new. What is new is that attempts have been made to attack problems of interdependences rather explicitly. Technical interrelations have been attacked at several levels. The level of generality represented by input-output is perhaps the one that has received the greatest amount of interest in recent years.

INPUT–OUTPUT

Suppose some information is available on interindustry interdependences. It will be convenient for the moment to think of industries lumped together at a point, so that there is no companion problem of interregional relations based on inter-industry relations and differences in regional supplies and demands. It would then be possible to write down the interindustry flows or interrelations for n industries in a system of simple equations (1):

$$x_{11} + x_{12} + \ldots + x_{1n} + C_1 = X_1$$
$$x_{21} + x_{22} + \ldots + x_{2n} + C_2 = X_2 \qquad (1)$$
$$\vdots \qquad \vdots \qquad \vdots$$
$$x_{n1} + x_{n2} + \ldots + x_{nn} + C_n = X_n$$

This shows flows. C_i is the flow to final consumption from the ith industry and X_i is the total production of the industry. Reading across the row represented by the first equation, for example, indicates that the total output of industry 1 is equal to the amount produced for final consumption, C_1, plus amount used up by other industries, such as the amount x_{12} which industry 1 ships to industry 2. The amount of its own product that industry 1 consumes is indicated by x_{11}.

The first equation shows the disposition of the products of industry 1, the *outputs*. The first column shows the *inputs* to industry 1. Industry 1 uses an amount x_{11} of its own product, an amount x_{21} of the products of industry 2, and so on. In general, x_{ij} is the output of the ith industry that goes to the jth industry and is, at the same time, the input to the jth industry from the ith industry.

No statement has been made regarding the units of the data. There is some flexibility available, but in practice entries are made in monetary units.

For the unit of time and level of output for which they are collected, data of this sort give a useful picture of the complex of interindustry flows in an economy. Arranged in the form of equations (1) the data are of limited use as an analytic device for the study of changes. However, coefficients (Leontief input-output coefficients) may be computed from the data and the equations arranged into an analytic device as follows:

$$a_{ij} = \frac{x_{ij}}{X_j} \quad \text{or} \quad X_j a_{ij} = x_{ij} \qquad (2)$$

Economists have much to say about these coefficients. Their computation requires rather rigid assumptions about economies of scale. But this is another topic. The assumption does allow the equations of (1) to be written as equations (3) by carrying out the substitution defined by equation (2):

$$X_1 a_{11} + X_2 a_{12} + \ldots + X_n a_{1n} + C_1 = X_1$$
$$\vdots$$
$$X_1 a_{n1} + X_2 a_{n2} + \ldots + X_n a_{nn} + C_n = X_n$$

or

$$(1 - a_{11})X_1 - a_{12}X_2 - \ldots - a_{1n}X_n = C_1$$
$$\vdots \qquad \vdots \qquad (3)$$
$$-a_{n1}X_1 - a_{n2}X_2 - \ldots + (1 - a_{nn})X_n = C_n$$

Equations (3) represent the economy in a manner susceptible to analytic work. A point that is very often of interest is how the economy would react given a new set of final demands, the C's. Such questions may be answered from equations (3). The a's of equations (3) are known numbers as are the C's. There are n X_i's which are unknown and there are n equations. In this case it would be expected that the n equations can be solved for the n unknowns by algebraic methods. Once the X_i's are known they can be converted back into the x_{ij}'s of equation (1) via equation (2).

Several interesting problems have been attacked using the notions described very briefly above. A word of caution about this brief description is warranted before going on to some of these. This is a very brief sketch of a subject on which

books have been written.[9] While the brief sketch will suffice for the purposes of this review, the reader should note that this essay has passed over problems of industry definition, obtaining data, what happens if the C's are also unknowns, inclusion of households and imports and exports, and other topics. It would be wise to consult standard sources before using these notes beyond the context of this essay.

1. Single Region Studies

No one has set down material for a world input-output study, but several studies have been done for nations and a number have been done for smaller areas. Actually, these studies might be thought of as two-region studies. In almost every case the demands, indicated as C's in equations (1) and (3), are given from outside the model. Some of these demands originate within the region and others originate from the rest of the world. The two regions are not exclusive areas, of course.

The first large-scale study was the 1947 interindustry study of the U. S. economy.[10] Interindustry flow information was obtained and a final table prepared for about 200 industries. There were smaller studies of the economy prior to the 1947 study and small-scale studies of other nations have been done since the 1947 U. S. study.[11]

The flow data from these studies are of great value. They give a glimpse of a structure of industry within nations. Also, enough information has

[9]A bibliography of input-output studies is available in Vera Riley and Robert L. Allen, *Interindustry Economic Studies: A Comprehensive Bibliography on Interindustry Research* (Baltimore: John Hopkins University Press, 1955). Two basic books are Wassily W. Leontief, *The Structure of the American Economy 1919-1939* (New York: Oxford University Press, 1951), and Wassily W. Leontief et al., *Studies in the Structure of the American Economy* (New York: Oxford University Press, 1953). Good statements of the nature of input-output analysis are given in Robert Dorfman "The Nature and Significance of Input-Output," *Review of Economics and Statistics*, Vol. 36 (May, 1954), pp. 121-33, and Hollis B. Chenery and Paul G. Clark, *Interindustry Analysis* (New York: John Wiley and Sons, 1959).

[10]W. Duane Evans and Marvin Hoffenberg, "The Interindustry Relations Study for 1947," *Review of Economics and Statistics*, Vol. 34 (May, 1952), pp. 97-142. Bureau of Labor Statistics, U. S. Department of Labor, *General Explanations of the 200 Sector Tables: The 1947 Interindustry Relations Study*, March, 1953.

[11]A number of these are discussed in Tibor Barna (ed.), *The Structural Interdependence of the Economy* (New York: John Wiley and Sons, ca. 1955). Additional references are in Richard Stone, *Social Accounts at the Regional Level: A Survey* (Cambridge: Department of Economics, April, 1960), mimeographed, and Hollis B. Chenery and Tsunehiko Watanabe, "International Comparisons of the Structure of Production," *Econometrica*, Vol. 26 (October, 1958), pp. 487-521.

been developed to allow comparisons of inter-industry structures from nation to nation.[12] The national studies also provide methods of studying the reactions of national economies to demands made upon their productive capacity. Subject to uncertainties regarding the stability of the input-output coefficients, it is possible to postulate different levels and structures of demands and examine resulting interindustry gross outputs and changes in interindustry requirements.

Studies have been done for areas smaller than nations. These include regions, states, and urban areas. There is available, for example, a study of Utah versus the rest of the world.[13] Regional studies may be made simply to identify the structure of regional activities or as a basis for speculating on the effect of the growth of demands outside the region on industries within the region. Questions of the following sort may be treated. It is known that the economy of the Pacific Northwest is closely related to the growth of California. The export of electricity from the Pacific Northwest, and perhaps even water at some future date, might assist in the growth of California. This induced growth of California would, through a series of inter-industry relations, affect the structure and character of growth in the Northwest. But how much? An input-output analysis would assist in studying this induced growth.

A number of studies have been made for urban areas. On occasion input-output coefficients for the national economy have been used as if they applied directly to the urban area. On other occasions, new input-output coefficients have been

computed for the subject urban area. In both cases, it is possible to see some of the interrelations between the urban area and the nation. When new input-output coefficients are developed, it is possible to see some of the differences in structure between the urban economy and the national economy. These differences may be great.[14]

2. Multiregion Studies

A number of interesting studies have been made using input-output tables recognizing several regions.[15] Output of all commodities is divided up among regions and industries within regions and the same is done for inputs. A regional input-output table for a nation, for example, permits the study of between-region flows resulting from interindustry interdependences and growth or decline in regions resulting from changes in demand. Strategy in table construction may vary greatly. Leontief has suggested dividing industry into national and local categories and studying regional reaction to changes in the outputs of national industries.[16] More complex models are required for the study of interregional relationships and national reaction to changes in regional output.[17] Regional studies might also differ greatly in level of regional or industry aggregation.

In addition to problems of industry classification, assumptions regarding input-output coeffi-

---

[12]Chenery and Watanabe, *op. cit.*

[13]Frederick T. Moore and James W. Petersen, "Regional Analysis: An Interindustry Model of Utah," *Review of Economics and Statistics,* Vol. 37 (November, 1955), pp. 368-83. Other studies are Werner Z. Hirsch, "An Application of Area Input-Output Analysis," *Papers and Proceedings,* Regional Science Association, Vol. 5 (1959), pp. 79-92, and "Interindustry Relations of a Metropolitan Area," *Review of Economics and Statistics,* Vol. 41 (November, 1959), pp. 360-9; Irving Hoch, "A Comparison of Alternative Inter-Industry Forecasts for the Chicago Region," *Papers and Proceedings,* Regional Science Association, Vol. 5 (1959), pp. 217-35 and *Forecasting Economic Activity in the Chicago Region: A Progress Report* and *Final Report* (Chicago Area Transportation Study, 1957 and 1959); Guy Freutel "The Eighth District Balance of Trade," *Monthly Review,* Federal Reserve Bank of St. Louis, Vol. 34 (June, 1952), pp. 69-78; *A Regional Interindustry Study of Maryland* (Bureau of Business Research, University of Maryland, 1954); C. D. Kirksey, *An Interindustry Study of the Sabine-Neches Area of Texas* (Bureau of Business Research, University of Texas, 1959); and Roland Artle, *Studies in the Structure of the Stockholm Economy* (Stockholm: Stockholm School of Economics, Business Research Institute, 1959). Several more fugitive references are given in Stone, *op. cit.*

[14]See the tables in Hirsch, *op. cit.,* and Hoch, *op. cit.*

[15]Walter Isard, "Interregional and Regional Input-Output Analysis: A Model of a Space-Economy," *Review of Economics and Statistics,* Vol. 33 (November, 1951), pp. 318-28, and "Regional Commodity Balances and Interregional Commodity Flows," *American Economic Review,* Vol. 43 (May, 1953), pp. 167-80; Walter Isard and Robert A. Kavesh, "Economic Structural Interrelations of Metropolitan Regions," *American Journal of Sociology,* Vol. 60 (September, 1954), pp. 152-76; Walter Isard and Robert E. Kuenne, "The Impact of Steel Upon the Greater New York-Philadelphia Industrial Region: A Study in Agglomeration Projection," *Review of Economics and Statistics,* Vol. 35 (November, 1953), pp. 289-301; Hollis B. Chenery, "Interregional and International Input-Output Analysis," chapter in *The Structural Interdependence of the Economy, op. cit.,* pp. 339-56; Robert A. Kavesh and James B. Jones, "Differential Regional Impacts of Federal Expenditures: An Application of the Input-Output Matrix to Federal Fiscal Policy," *Papers and Proceedings, Regional Science Association,* Vol. 2 (1956), pp. 152-67; Leon N. Moses, "The Stability of Interregional Trading Patterns and Input-Output Analysis," *American Economic Review,* Vol. 45 (December, 1955), pp. 803-32; and Hollis B. Chenery, Paul G. Clark, and Vera Cao Pinna, *The Structure and Growth of the Italian Economy* (Rome: U.S. Mutual Security Agency, 1953), pp. 97-130.

Some of these studies (Isard and Kuenne, and Kavesh and Jones) might be classed with those in note 13. These are two-region models where chief attention is given to one of the regions.

[16]Leontief, *Studies in the Structure of the American Economy, op. cit.,* pp. 93-115.

[17]For example, Isard, "Interregional and Regional Input-Output Analysis . . ," *op. cit.*

cients, and so on, recognized earlier, regional input-output studies are characterized by several distinct problems of their own. One is the sheer size of the undertaking. A 50-industry ten-region input-output model of the United States would require a matrix of input-output coefficients 500 × 500, or obtaining data for some 250,000 coefficients. Another computational problem is that for the same degree of industry identification, a multiregion model involves many more equations than a single-region model. With the advent of large computers this problem is becoming manageable.

It may or may not be difficult to assume that input-output coefficients are invariant for different levels of production. If the range of final outputs for which an input-output system is studied does not vary greatly from the level at which the input-output coefficients were computed, then the assumption of invariancy would not be difficult to make. In interregional input-output a similar sort of assumption must be made regarding the invariance of regional trading patterns. One might have, for example, a set of interregional input-output coefficients obtained for a given level of production and consequent interregional relations. The level of final demand changes. This might well change interregional trading paths. One region may not buy from another at a particular level of output but as demands increase, flows may begin between the two regions. Moses has indicated ways of attacking this problem directly by showing clearly how interregional input-output coefficients are derivable from sets of interindustry relations and sets of interregional trade coefficients.[18] Moses' arrangement makes practicable the study of interregional trading paths apart from interindustry coefficients and vice versa.

An examination of the several studies that are available will reveal that interregional input-output provides a very flexible method of approach. Investigators may start with somewhat different purposes, different types of data, and different problems. The exact form of the model may then be chosen to reflect the purposes and resources available. Identification of industry sectors, and handling of capital formation and exports and imports may all be varied to suit the problem at hand.

3. A Migration Model

A good example of applying a format developed for one problem to another is provided by Lövgren's use of an input-output arrangement in studying migration between districts in Sweden.[19] The study also provides a sample problem in input-output and may clarify some of the points above. Lövgren observes that migration involves a complex series of circulations. In Sweden, for example, it has been observed that migration from various districts to Stockholm is associated with a complex set of in- and out-migrations among districts (Fig. 5).

Such migration flows may be set down in the input-output format and coefficients computed. Lövgren has provided fictitious coefficients for a multi-region system (Table 1) and a solution to the proposition that 100 persons migrate from region 3 to region 4 (Table 2). The structure of migration currents is such that 132 persons leave region 3, 32 bound for regions other than region 4. At the same time, 80 persons moved into region 3 from regions 1 and 2.

These results were obtained in the following manner: First, observe that migration relations of Figure 5 may be expressed in equations (4):

$$X_1 - x_{21} - x_{31} = 0$$
$$- x_{12} + X_2 - x_{32} = 0 \qquad (4)$$
$$- x_{13} - x_{23} + X_3 = 0$$

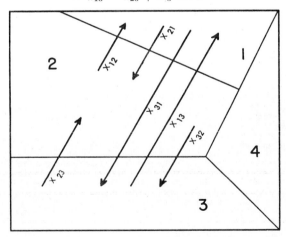

FIGURE 5 Migration Currents Between Three Areas. After Lövgren, p. 161.

[19]Esse Lövgren, "Mutual Relations between Migration Fields: A Circulation Analysis," *Proceedings*, Symposium on Migration in Sweden (Lund Studies in Geography, Ser. B. Human Geography, No. 13, 1957), pp. 159-69.

[18]Moses, *op. cit.*

The first equation states, for example, that total out-migration from region 1, X_1, minus the out-migration from region 1 to region 2, x_{21}, minus the out-migration from region 1 to region 3, x_{31}, is equal to 0. Migration coefficients were defined using equation (5)

$$a_{ik} = \frac{x_{ik}}{X_i} \qquad (5)$$

yielding equations (6).

$$\begin{aligned} X_1 - a_{21}X_2 - a_{31}X_3 &= 0 \\ -a_{12}X_1 + X_2 - a_{32}X_3 &= 0 \qquad (6) \\ -a_{13}X_1 - a_{23}X_2 + X_3 &= 0 \end{aligned}$$

Lövgren's proposition was that 100 persons migrate from region 3 to region 4. Placing this information together with the fictitious coefficients of Table 1 in equations (6) achieves equations (7).

$$\begin{aligned} X_1 - 0.2X_2 - 0.3X_3 &= 0 \\ -0.4X_1 + X_2 - 0.3X_3 &= 0 \qquad (7) \\ -0.5X_1 - 0.1X_2 + X_3 &= 100 \end{aligned}$$

Solution of these equations for the X's and applying the migration coefficients of Table 1 and relation (5) yields the results in Table 2.

TABLE 1   Fictitious Migration Coefficients[1]

Out-migration from—	In-migration to region—		
	1	2	3
1	—	0.2	0.3
2	0.4	—	0.3
3	0.5	0.1	—

[1] From Lovgren, p. 161.

TABLE 2   Migration Between Areas 1, 2, and 3 if 100 Persons Migrate from Area 3 to Area 4[1]

Out-migration from—	In-migration to region—				Total out-migration
	1	2	3	4	
1	—	12	40	0	52
2	21	—	40	0	61
3	26	6	—	100	132

[1] From Lovgren, p. 162.

This is an extremely simple example of a one-industry (say, labor) three-region model. (Again, one might term this a four-region model. Three regions are specifically identified. The fourth region plays a role analogous to final demand in the ordinary input-output format.) It should be noted that this operation is somewhat more uncertain than the ordinary input-output operation. A great deal has been said elsewhere regarding the assumptions underlying the computation of input-output when coefficients are computed for industry flows. Similar analyses have not been made for the computation of migration coefficients.

Lövgren has worked with a ten-region model of Sweden and studied the effect of flows to an additional region, Stockholm, on migration among the ten regions. In Sweden data are available for a comparison of migration coefficients from year to year and Lövgren has done such comparative work. Although this work is very exploratory, Lövgren concludes that this type of circulation analysis is superior to more traditional methods.

INTERREGIONAL LINEAR PROGRAMMING

Input-output is an established analytic procedure for studying single areas, and interregional input-output is well on its way to acceptance as a standard method of analysis. Interregional linear programming is following hard on the heels of input-output techniques and, indeed, shows promise of eclipsing input-output analysis. A linear programming model may be constructed from an input-output model without too much difficulty, and the results of the linear programming analysis are quite a bit richer than those of an input-output analysis.

The reader will recall that the typical linear programming problem involves something to be maximized or minimized and a set of constraining equations. Equations (3) may be turned into a set of constraining inequalities simply by substituting inequalities for the equalities. In the first equation, for example, the left-hand side might be required to be greater than or equal to the final demand from that industry, C_1. This would assure that the total amount produced, X_1, minus the amounts shipped to other industries would be at least equal to and could be greater than the amount demanded. If one of the equations in the set of equations (3) referred to the use of labor, the inequality would run the other way. That is, one would require that the amount of labor used in various industries not exceed the total amount available. The input-output equations of (3) could be augmented by a whole series of equations requiring that the drawdown of various resources not be greater than the amount of each resource available.

The remarks above accomplish the transformation of an input-output format into a linear programming format, except for deciding what is to be maximized or minimized and this requires distinguishing between intermediate and final products. The variables X_i refer to gross production. One might want to maximize the sum of these values weighted by their prices. But a more likely problem would require that the value of net output be maximized. That is, treat the C_i's as variables and maximize their sum when weighted by their prices.

Problems may be written several ways to accomplish the latter objective. In general, the constraining equations would display interindustry relationships, require that resources used in production processes not exceed those available, and require that net output of certain or all commodities reach some minimum level(s). Two sorts of variables might be recognized: intermediate and final commodities. In some cases a commodity may appear as a resource, an intermediate commodity, and as a final commodity. Coal is an example of such a commodity.

This adds up to the observation that the researcher's choice is very wide in the formulation of an interregional linear programming problem as well as in the formulation of interregional input-output problems.[20] Not only does one have wide choices of industry classifications and constraints, but opportunity for choice extends to the objective function which expresses what is to be maximized or minimized. It was remarked before that one possibility is to maximize the value of the final goods produced. Prices would be determined outside the model and the amounts of radios, automobiles, etc., would be chosen according to the

rule that the mix of maximum value be produced. Because prices are tied in some manner to quantities, it may seem somewhat artificial to take prices as given regardless of quantities. Beckmann and Marschak handle this by couching an interregional linear programming problem in terms of vector maximization, i.e., to characterize that set of vectors that satisfies the constraints so that each vector in the set is larger with respect to some component than another vector in the set only if it is smaller with respect to a different component.[21] Another way to handle this problem is to set down some artificial prices based on interregional price differences resulting from interregional transport costs and explore solutions using these prices. An even more general approach would require enlarging the problem to include finding the amount and location of all production and consumption and all prices.

General interregional linear programming is more on the horizon than it is an accomplished fact. Two restricted empirical studies are available in the literature, however.

1. Petroleum Refining

Marschak has made an interregional programming study of the petroleum refining industry, based on an earlier study by Manne.[22] Marschak broke down Manne's national model into four regions—Gulf, Midwest, East, and West—and introduced transportation activities within and between regions. Manne's model contained 105 equations. In order to represent technology in each of the four regions without using 420 equations, Marschak reduced Manne's model to 39 equations. The 39 equations in each of four regions together with equations covering transportation gave 195 equations in Marschak's model. There were 1,555 variables in the regional problem.

Marschak did some computing with his model. Data for 1952-53 were placed in the model and the final product mix maximized. Marschak found that nearly as much could be produced

[20]For examples of model construction see: Walter Isard, "Interregional Linear Programming: An Elementary Presentation and a General Model," *Journal of Regional Science*, Vol. 1 (Summer, 1958), pp. 1-59; Benjamin H. Stevens, "An Interregional Linear Programming Model," *Journal of Regional Science*, Vol. 1 (Summer, 1958), pp. 60-98; Benjamin H. Stevens and Robert E. Coughlin, "A Note on Inter-Areal Linear Programming for a Metropolitan Region," *Journal of Regional Science*, Vol. 1 (Spring, 1959), pp. 75-83; and Edward B. Berman, "A Spatial and Dynamic Growth Model," *Papers and Proceedings*, Regional Science Association, Vol. 5 (1959), pp. 143-150.

[21]Martin J. Beckmann and Thomas Marschak, "An Activity Analysis Approach to Location Theory," *Proceedings*, Second Symposium in Linear Programming (Washington: National Bureau of Standards, 1955), p. 367.

[22]Thomas A. Marschak, "A Spatial Model of U. S. Petroleum Refining," U. S. Air Force, Project RAND, Research Memorandum, RM-2205, June 1958, and A. S. Manne, "A Linear Programming Model of the U. S. Petroleum Refining Industry," *Econometrica*, Vol. 26 (January, 1958), pp. 67-106.

without interregional shipments of intermediates as could be produced with interregional shipments. Particular attention was focused on the effect of transportation bottlenecks on production. As would be expected, Marschak found that with efficient use of transportation there is a great excess of tank cars and tankers. When the amount of tanker shipping space available is arbitrarily reduced, tank car and pipeline transportation is substituted for tankers and at the one hundred tanker level all tank car and pipeline capacity is used. The availability of transportation also affects the productive capacity of the industry (Figure 6).

Marschak emphasized that his model is highly exploratory and that there may be some errors in the transportation coefficients used. He does stress, however, that his model solves problems which may not be solved by "back-of-the-envelope" calculations.

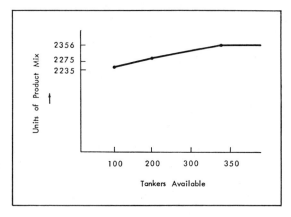

FIGURE 6 Output and Tankers. An increase in the number of tankers (standardized on type T-2 tanker) available increases the capacity of the petroleum refining industry. After Marschak, p. 84.

2. Land Utilization

Henderson has proposed two models of the utilization of agricultural land and has done empirical work with one of these. One is an extension of the model used in Henderson's study of coal flows discussed in Part II of this essay.[23] This problem differs from the transportation problem used for the study of coal flows, however, in that there are several commodities and that the costs of delivery to be minimized include both transportation

---

[23]James M. Henderson, *The Efficiency of the Coal Industry* (Cambridge: Harvard University Press, 1958), pp. 133-7.

costs and cultivation costs. Since there are several crops, there are sets of demand requirements for each crop. Each region has capacity restrictions on the amount of land available.

In Henderson's second model, interregional flows are not treated directly.[24] The farmer's decision problem is taken to be the choice of land utilization. The farmer selects a land utilization pattern which maximizes his expected net revenue, the difference between the prices he expects to receive for his crops and his costs. The farmer's utilization of land is constrained by his inability to use more land for his crops than is available on the farm, and by his short-run "stickiness." Henderson states that farmers do not make drastic changes in land utilization from year to year; instead their changes are rather gradual. Also, government-imposed acreage allotments fix maximum allotments for certain types of crops. "Stickiness" is introduced into the programming format by constraining the amounts of land devoted to individual crops within limits close to traditional limits or within limits imposed by acreage allotments.

Henderson implemented the model in two cases for the 1955 crop year. Instead of considering individual farms, regions were used as decision-making units, and each region was treated as if it were a farm. In one case 160 separate areas were recognized, of which 23 were areas where irrigation farming was important. The irrigation farming areas overlapped 28 of the total areas. A smaller model was also developed. This recognized 43 dry-farming areas plus 12 irrigation-farming areas. In this case, the 12 irrigation-farming areas were coexistent with 12 of the 43 dry-farming areas. Both the 160 and the 55 region models were operated using data on 11 field crops. Altogether, these 11 field crops accounted for two-thirds of the value of all United States' field crops. It was necessary to have knowledge of cost and expected prices,

---

[24]James M. Henderson, "The Utilization of Agricultural Land: A Regional Approach," *Papers and Proceedings*, Regional Science Association, Vol. 3 (1957), pp. 99-117, and "The Utilization of Agricultural Land: A Theoretical and Empirical Inquiry," *Review of Economics and Statistics*, Vol. 41 (August, 1959), pp. 242-59. [See page 281 of this volume.] Other studies of agriculture include Robert Koch and Milton M. Snodgrass, "Linear Programming Applied to Location and Product Flow Determination in the Tomato Processing Industry," *Papers and Proceedings*, Regional Science Association, Vol. 5 (1959), pp. 151-62, and Milton M. Snodgrass and Charles E. French, *Linear Programming Approach to the Study of Interregional Competition in Dairying* (Lafayette, Indiana: Purdue University Agricultural Experiment Station, 1958). For a method of studying land utilization in urban areas see Stevens and Coughlin, *op. cit.*

acreage allotments, expected yields and so on, in order to implement the model. These data were developed from a variety of standard sources, and coefficients which constrained the range of selectable amounts of acreage were calculated.

Results for each region were computed separately; so the results from each model represented the composite of 160 or 55 separate computations. The results of Henderson's computations were compared with "naïve" estimates produced by using 1954 data as the estimate of 1955 conditions. The results were also compared with land utilization estimates prepared by the Crop Reporting Board of the U.S. Department of Agriculture. The large regional model was better than the small and both models seemed better than naïve estimates. Crop Reporting Board estimates were better than those produced by Henderson's small model, but apparently not as good as those of his large model. It is difficult to compare the efficacy of one estimating device versus another, especially where the devices are prepared in different formats. In this case the comparison seems to have been arranged so as to favor the Crop Reporting Board estimates. Had a more even comparison been possible, the superiority of Henderson's large model might well have been more marked.

INDUSTRIAL COMPLEX ANALYSIS

Industrial complex analysis is a term used by Isard.[25] It refers to the analysis of a complex of industries within which interindustry relations may be clearly recognized and to the use of a variety of analytic tools. Much research in this field could be termed industrial complex analysis, if a catholic interpretation is given the term, because much research requires use of several analytic devices and reduction of a problem to an industry (complex). For example, Part II of this essay discussed Wester and Kantner's combining of a transportation-type problem with the Weberian location problem and a simple allocation problem to find locations for

warehouses.[26] Also, Henderson's land-use problem discussed above utilized both a linear programming formulation and certain simple calculations to determine limits within which land uses might change.

This essay does not attempt to cover all the analytic tools for making an industrial complex analysis. The range of available tools include simple cost accounting, potential models, localization indices, and other widely used techniques. As mentioned before, these topics have been omitted from the present essay although some are subjects of interesting current research. Our attention will be limited to two recent examples of industrial complex analysis.

1. Petroleum Refining, Petrochemical, and Synthetic Fibers in Puerto Rico

The refining-petrochemical-synthetic fiber complexes were the subject of a recent industrial complex analysis by Isard, Schooler, and Vietorisz.[27] The authors present some of the technical interrelations of these truly complex industries in the flow-sheet showing how over 50 products emerge, mostly through a series of intermediate products, from the raw materials, natural gas and crude oil (pp. 30–31). These products range from gasoline through plastics to fertilizer. In many cases, of course, still other industries, such as the textile industry, use these end products as their raw material.

The purpose of the analysis was the evaluation of regional advantages of Puerto Rico for the industry. This required recognition of variations in cost from place to place in the mix of capital, labor, and other inputs used by the industries, as well as variations in prices received for the finished products over the range of alternative product mixes. Also, it was necessary to trace economies of scale resulting from variations in sizes of manufacturing plants and other types of economies.

---

[25]No doubt the term is not original with Isard. For a discussion of industrial complex analysis see Walter Isard and Thomas Vietorisz, "Industrial Complex Analysis and Regional Development," *Papers and Proceedings*, Regional Science Association, Vol. 1 (1955), pp. U1–U17, and Walter Isard and Eugene W. Schooler, "Industrial Complex Analysis, Agglomeration Economies and Regional Development," *Journal of Regional Science*, Vol. 1 (Spring, 1959), pp. 19–33.

[26]Leon Wester and Harold H. Kantner, "Optimal Location-Allocation," paper read at the Boston Meeting, Operations Research Society of America, 1958 (Chicago: Armour Research Foundation of Illinois Institute of Technology, mimeographed, 1958).

[27]Walter Isard, Eugene W. Schooler and Thomas Vietorisz, *Industrial Complex Analysis and Regional Development* (Cambridge: Technology Press of the Massachusetts Institute of Technology; New York: John Wiley and Sons, Inc., 1959), and Walter Isard and Eugene W. Schooler, *Location Factors in the Petrochemical Industry* (Washington: U. S. Department of Commerce, 1955). Chief reference is to the former.

Reviewing works where the authors deal with so many considerations is truly the reviewer's despair. There are so many facets to such a study that it is practically impossible to cover them adequately without reproducing the whole work. Roughly this is what was done: Different production programs or industrial complexes were considered for location in Puerto Rico. These considerations sifted the feasible production programs down to a handful, and detailed analysis of all the costs of each of these programs was then undertaken. The end result of this detailed analysis is a recognition of alternative production patterns which could be defined as efficient for Puerto Rico. It was concluded that Puerto Rico has advantages over all other areas for certain types of refining-petrochemical-synthetic fiber production systems. In particular, local advantage was found for a complex comprising the production of dacron A, petroleum refinery fertilizer production, and an associated synthetic fiber plant. Compatible technical processes, low labor costs, and the fertilizer market in Puerto Rico combine to provide the advantage for this complex.

2. Synthetic Fibers

Airov has studied the locational advantages in several regions for the synthetic-fiber industry.[28] He began by projecting demands for synthetic fibers; he then examined alternative location choices for the investment needed to meet the demands. The industry complex splits several ways in locational choices. Choices may be made between raw material producing areas for investment in expanded raw material production; chemical intermediate and end product fiber production require choices between raw material and market locations. There are also choices involving size of plant, product mix, etc.

The hydrocarbon and chemical raw materials of the industry are effectively limited to the Texas-Gulf Coast area and the West Virginia area; markets are in the textile manufacturing areas of New England, the Middle Atlantic, and the South. Airov's detailed analyses of costs lead to the conclusion that most of the intermediate capacity will

be located in the Texas-Gulf Coast area with exception of the production of nylon salts, much of which will be produced in the textile region of the South. Lowest cost for synthetic fiber production as an end product is found in the market regions, especially the South and Puerto Rico.

There are many things that may be said for industrial complex analysis. It is no-holds-barred analysis stressing interrelations between variables and using all analytic resources available. It is hard to see how anything could be done better. Intuition plays a role, of course, but seems reasonably well confined to the efficient formulation of the problem and selection of tools. Reliance on intuition is minimized in places where it might lead to errors, such as in choosing levels of activities within a complex.

GENERAL SPATIAL EQUILIBRIUM

Nearly everything that has been discussed to this point in this essay is often subjected to the criticism that the analyses are overly restricted and use models which do not reveal the Kantian "essence" of things. The latter criticism is inappropriate. More to the point is the comment that the models are restricted, certain things are taken as given and fixed and the problem is limited to a few variables. Although it is proper to question whether a variable is determined within the problem or is taken as given, this does not mean that models using fixed elements are of no value. Indeed, it is hard to see how one could do work of any sort with systems where everything conceivably related to the problem is subject to change. There are advantages in recognizing explicitly just what variables are being studied and which are not. The alternative is to attempt to study a completely variable system, which in practice means looking at variables one at a time or otherwise constraining the study, perhaps unknowingly.

There is one other comment about the models which is appropriate. How does one know that *in toto* the considerations of the model or the broad system represented by the model represent some workable system? Is the model internally contradictory or does it, however imperfectly it is formulated, resolve the problem to which it is addressed? Does it have a solution? Is the character of the solution consistent with the processes which the

[28]Joseph Airov, *The Location of the Synthetic-Fiber Industry* (Cambridge: Technology Press of the Massachusetts Institute of Technology; New York: John Wiley and Sons, Inc., 1959).

model displays (e.g., the market in a competitive economy)? Knowing whether or not equilibrium exists in a system and recognizing conditions under which it might exist, throw a great deal of light on the consistency and completeness of the statements that go into the model.

Equilibrium in economic models has been a subject of continued study, building on Walras' treatment of equilibrium. The Walras-like equilibrium systems treat a world without spatial properties. Questions of flows of commodities among regions, prices of transportation services, comparative advantage, choice of location, urbanization, and the like all lie outside these systems. In other words, the problems treated by the spatially-oriented models discussed in this essay lie for the most part outside the classical considerations of economic equilibrium.[29]

Interest in equilibrium in models that stress locational characteristics emerged with the gradual development of location theory. Lösch raised the question of the existence of a solution for his location system, as noted in Part I of this review. The few pages in which Lösch discusses this problem present a succinct summary of just what Lösch did and did not accomplish.[30] The existence of an equilibrium solution to Lösch's model is an open question. Lösch claims that he presents a complete system inasmuch as there are as many variables in the system as there are equations; so there is a solution. But this counting of equations and variables is not enough to guarantee a meaningful solution.

Isard considered both partial and full equilibrium in his *Location and Space Economy*. As was the case in Lösch's volume, Isard's comments on equilibrium, especially those in his mathematical chapter, are a succinct statement of his system.[31] Actually Isard does not claim his system is completely general. It seems to this reviewer that it neglects the demand and price sides of a completely general problem.

Recent works have dealt with general models which are related to the models discussed previously in this part of this essay.

McKenzie has treated the special case of comparative advantage in international trade models.[32] Comparative advantage as it has been classically treated has been a rather restricted notion. Several countries trade. According to the principle of comparative advantage some activities are suppressed and others stressed with each nation, the result being patterns of specialization which are efficient on an international scale. Is this true? McKenzie has generalized the comparative advantage principle so that it indeed covers many countries and many kinds of activities, and has shown that competition and free trade will lead to an efficient overall pattern of production within the concepts and variables specified by the model. While McKenzie's work is interesting and some of his findings and approaches are very pertinent to the construction of equilibrium models, his is not quite the same as any one of the problems revealed by the previous models. Transportation costs and patterns, which were eliminated from McKenzie's work, are very much at the heart of the models in the preceding discussion.

Lefeber has recently published a monograph on the topic of general spatial equilibrium analysis.[33] The problem is divided into several parts. Transportation is stressed throughout the analysis and the method of treatment of transportation is discussed early in the first part of the discussion. The remainder of the first part treats the location of production. Both the classical approach and programming formulations are presented. The second part of the discussion merges distribution and production and treats their mutual equilibrium. The final part of the discussion merges the choice of industrial locations with the analysis of production and distribution. Programming methods are

[29]A good introduction to the equilibrium problem is Walter Isard's "General Interregional Equilibrium," *Papers and Proceedings*, Regional Science Association, Vol. 3 (1957), pp. 35-60. Walter Isard and David J. Ostroff have placed current equilibrium problems in economics in a regional context in "Existence of a Competitive Interregional Equilibrium," *Papers and Proceedings*, Regional Science Association, Vol. 4, (1958), pp. 49-76, and "General Interregional Equilibrium," *Journal of Regional Science*, Vol. 2 (Spring, 1960), pp. 67-74.

[30]August Lösch, *The Economics of Location*, translated from the second revised edition by William H. Woglom with the assistance of Wolfgang F. Stolper (New Haven: Yale University Press, 1954), pp. 92-100.

[31]Walter Isard, *Location and Space Economy* (Cambridge: Technology Press of the Massachusetts Institute of Technology; New York: John Wiley and Sons, 1956), pp. 221-53.

[32]Lionel W. McKenzie, "Specialization and Efficiency in World Production," *Review of Economic Studies*, Vol. 21 (1953-4), pp. 765-80, and "On Equilibrium in Graham's Model of World Trade and Other World Systems," *Econometrica*, Vol. 22 (April, 1954), pp. 147-61. Also, T. M. Whitin, "Classical Theory, Graham's Theory and Linear Programming," *Quarterly Journal of Economics*, Vol. 67 (November, 1953), pp. 520-44.

[33]Louis Lefeber, *Allocation in Space* (Amsterdam: North-Holland Publishing Company, 1958). Also, "General Equilibrium Analysis of Production, Transportation and the Choice of Industrial Location," *Papers and Proceedings*, Regional Science Association, Vol. 4 (1958), pp. 77-86.

used widely through Parts II and III of the discussion. Lefeber's discussion is liberally augmented by miniature numerical examples and by expository introductions and summaries. The final chapter covers a series of related topics including notes on investment problems, treatment of transportable and nontransportable factors, and so on. The appendix gives a short statement of the complete system.

Equilibrium in models is a fascinating subject. But it is a highly technical subject and it is not easy to give a bird's eye view of studies and their accomplishments. As mentioned before, the studies provide succinct summaries of general systems. Also, the studies show the conditions under which economic systems are solved by market mechanisms. It is easy to see how partial spatial equilibrium is achieved.[34] General spatial equilibrium, such as that analyzed by Lefeber, requires consideration of many industries and regions, and equilibrium considerations are more complex. Equilibrium is an open problem when indivisibilities of locations and productive processes are features of the system.[35]

Summary and Forecast

This essay began by summarizing a half-dozen books written or published in the early 1950's. Each of these books relied heavily upon a long but relatively small stream of interest in location problems on the part of economists. Each work added to concept and practice in the analysis of location problems. Relatively speaking, the books were long on conceptual implications and short on implications for analysis.

The materials appearing in the literature more recently stand in marked contrast to these benchmark books. Recent additions to the literature have been more specialized, excepting Lefeber's general volume. Also, they have been rich in both concept and in implications for analysis. There are two overriding concepts from those articles and monographs that have been discussed. First is the concept of the location system as a *combina-tion of interrelated activities* at different places. Some activities are suppressed and others are carried on at a variety of levels according to constraints of resource availability, capacities of man-made facilities, technical interrelations, and so on. Second, the concept of the location system as a system of activities makes clear the role of market forces, rents, and so on, on the one hand, and the physical patterns of flows and production on the other. This is achieved through the concept of duality, using notions from activity analysis. This allows one to enlarge the concept—we may think of the location system as a pattern of *efficient* combinations of activities at different places. The word "efficient" arises from the economic pressures operating on the problem: something is maximized or minimized.

The richer the concept the greater is the challenge to implement it. Implementation has been emphasized over and over again in the latter portions of this essay. These portions of the essay have demonstrated that the researcher has a large number of building blocks from which to tailor a device to implement his study of a problem. The approaches that have been mentioned here, together with other well-known approaches and appropriate statistical and data-processing tools, give a power to analysis that is immeasurably greater than what has been available before.

Lest it may seem that we are claiming too much, it might be wise to remark that these developments are what one would expect. The growth of the sciences in the past few years has been so rapid that explosion is to be expected. Paralysis and stagnation are unexpected.

What of the next decade? Apart from the obvious forecast of continued rapid development of this area of knowledge, this writer will make two predictions based on two needs. There is good evidence that the tools of analysis have rapidly outstripped their raw material. An analysis of regional growth and development in the United States using a fine-grained interregional linear programming model is conceptually practicable, and with the rapid advance in computer technology would be physically practicable in the near future. But where are the raw materials for such an analysis; where are the data? Our analytic devices have outstripped the data to feed them. This need will direct more attention to developing new data sources and improving the data already available.

[34]Equilibrium of a single industry. See the discussion of spatial price equilibrium in Part II of this essay.
[35]This is the Koopmans and Beckmann problem discussed in Part II of this essay. See Tjalling C. Koopmans and Martin Beckmann, "Assignment Problems and the Location of Economic Activities," *Econometrica*, Vol. 25 (January, 1957), pp. 53-76.

There is another major need. Nowhere is there a single summary volume bringing together the methods of analysis developed in the last few years and described in part in the latter portions of this essay.[36] Such a volume would have great pedagogical value and would be a must for the analyst's bookshelf. It is not difficult to forecast that this need will be met in the very near future.

When this essay was in final draft I had the privilege of seeing the galley proofs of Professor Walter Isard's new book, *Methods of Regional Analysis*.[37] The topics covered in this essay, and more, are covered in this new volume. This field owes much to Walter Isard. Through his research, his organizational energies, and his ability to interest students and others, he deserves much of the credit for recent accomplishments in regional analysis. His *Methods of Regional Analysis* promises to be another major contribution.

[36]This is not completely true. See Claude Ponsard, *Économie et Espace: Essai d'intégration du facteur spatial dans l'analyse économique*, Observation économique, Collection publiée sous la direction de André Piatier, Vol. VIII (Paris: Sedes, 1955), and Olaf Boustedt and Herbert Ranz, *Regionale Strukturund Wirtschaftsforschung, Aufgaben und Methoden* (Bremen: Walter Dorn, 1957) reviewed in Part I of this essay.

[37] . . . Regional Science Series (Cambridge: Technology Press of the Massachusetts Institute of Technology; New York: John Wiley & Sons, [1960]).

Edgar S. Dunn, Jr.

THE EQUILIBRIUM OF LAND-USE PATTERNS IN AGRICULTURE

Starting with Thünen, a number of writers have presented systems for describing the spatial equilibrium of agricultural production. All of these schemes have been deficient or incomplete in one respect or another. The purpose of this article is to integrate and extend the disparate elements of such a location theory.

An effort will be made to define an explicit distance-rent function. Using this function, location will be pictured as a result of the rational maximization process. In the conventional statement of the firm equilibrium profit is maximized. In the equilibrium statement that follows, it is rent arising from the advantage of position that is maximized. The solution is worked out in a multiple-product economy and, in the process, the conditions that give rise to zonal production and the conditions for entry are made explicit. The whole space system is enlarged at the end with the consideration of demand and the mutually interdependent price system. There follows an attempt to illustrate and summarize the nature of the space-price equilibrium under simplified conditions and by means of simple equations. No effort is made to introduce modifying and complicating factors into the analysis.

Definition of Terms

The lead of Thünen is followed by recognizing that the controlling factor in the determination of land-use is land rent. That form of land-use which provides the greatest rent will make the highest bid for the land and hence displace all others. The following formula expresses as a function of distance the additions to total land rent made by each new unit of the land devoted to the cultivation of a single commodity as the distance from the market is increased.[1]

$$R = E(p - a) - Efk \qquad (1)$$

The variables are classified as follows:

Dependent Variable

R = rent per unit of land

Independent Variable

k = distance

Constants or Parameters

E = yield per unit of land

p = market price per unit of commodity[2]

a = production cost per unit of commodity

f = transport rate per unit of distance for each commodity.

This explicit statement of a distance-rent function brings several points to our attention. The present analysis conceives of the *industry* as the

---

Reprinted with the permission of the author and publisher from the *Southern Economic Journal*, Vol. 21, No. 2, 1955, pp. 173-87. Dr. Dunn is Research Associate with Resources for the Future, Inc., Washington, D. C.

[1] If the previous theorists in the field of agricultural location have been guilty of a common weakness it is their failure to develop an explicit distance function.

[2] Under conditions of competition p will naturally be considered as a parameter by the groups of firms that make up each industry.

maximizing unit.[3, 4] This does not mean that the traditional firm equilibrium is unimportant. It merely means that it is subordinated in order to simplify the statement and highlight the essential characteristics of the space-price equilibrium. Nor does it mean that rent maximization conceived and described on an industry level is inconsistent with profit maximization on the firm level. It is the effort of competing firms to maximize profits that establishes the level of rent for any given land use.

In order to subordinate the substitution problems characteristic of the firm equilibrium, it is necessary to make certain simplifying assumptions. (1) *We assume perfect mobility and divisibility of all factors other than land (i.e., returns to scale are constant).* (2) *We assume undifferentiated resources over space so that yield (E) is everywhere the same.* (3) *The supply of factors is adequate for all production and is available at constant prices.* These three assumptions make it possible to assume that the cost of production per unit (a) is constant at any distance from the market. We recognize, of course, that E, a and f typically bear some functional relationship to distance in a realistic case. To analyse the character of this relationship necessitates a detailed analysis of the theory of the firm. Thus it is simpler at the outset to consider them as parameters. The essential character of the spatial orientation of products on an industry level is not significantly modified by this simplification.

It is worth emphasizing that in the statement that follows the hypothetical production unit (the industry) is concerned with maximizing rent and not profits. It is because of this factor that the present system considers space or distance explicitly. The production problem is not one of adjusting output to a marginal revenue line, but one of adjusting the spatial location of production to a marginal rent line. Rent in this case cannot be stated as a function of output. Rather it must be expressed as a function of distance from the market. Hence the explicit consideration of space.

With the marginal rent function written in the form of equation 1 and with the assumptions implicit in the designation of the parameters, it becomes plain that the formula describes a linear functional relationship between the two variables, distance and rent. This is graphically presented in Figure 1.

The R-intercept tells us that a unit of land producing at the market will derive a rent equal to the yield times the net receipts per unit. The slope reveals that, as we leave the market the maximum addition to total land rent per unit of land, $E(p - a)$, is diminished for each unit of distance at a rate equal to the product of the yield and freight rate. The rent is entirely absorbed at the k-intercept where

$$k = \frac{p - a}{f}$$

Location as a Result of the Rational Maximization Process

The motive force which lies behind the determination of production location in agriculture is the same as that which lies behind the equilibrium of all economic forces—namely, the maximization of economic return. In the equilibrium statement that follows rent arising from the advantage of position is maximized.

MAXIMIZATION SOLUTION FOR ONE PRODUCT

Consider the mechanics of the solution portrayed in Figure 1. We see that the sloping rent line which has been plotted may be interpreted as a marginal rent line for an industry producing this product. For any value of k it tells the rent that will be derived from the infinitesimal unit of land at that distance from the market. Thus, as the industry expands its production by placing into cultivation more distant land (i.e., as we increase the value of k), this line tells us the amount that will be added to total rent by each successive unit of

---

[3] In this paper the term *industry* is used primarily to designate a level of aggregation that abstracts from the substitution problems of the firm. More specifically, it is a group of firms (or farms) producing a single farm product, or, later, a group of firms producing a similar combination of farm products by a similar process.

[4] In so far as there has been developed for agriculture an articulate theory of location, it has been almost exclusively on an industry level of analysis as distinct from the theory of the firm. This may be due in part to the fact that this level of analysis shows some promise for handling a range of problems that is considered significant for social policy. Attention is instinctively focused upon the competition of production systems for the use of the land. More important is the fact that this amount of aggregation of the variables offers an attractive degree of theoretical simplification. At the outset we intend to maintain this convention.

land—in short, the marginal increment.[5] In this case the variable plotted along the horizontal axis is distance, not output, and we ignore for the moment the influence of the correlated output upon price. Since rent is expressed net of production costs, we recognize the horizontal base line (*Ok*, Figure 1) to be the marginal cost line. The solution that maximizes economic gain is where marginal rent equals marginal cost $\left(\text{i.e., where } k = \dfrac{p-a}{f} \right)$

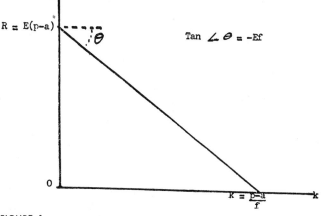

FIGURE 1

MAXIMIZATION SOLUTION FOR TWO PRODUCTS

Equilibrium Conditions

Extend the same kind of solution to the case where there are two industries producing two products. Such a case is presented in Figure 2.

Consider first the maximization problem of industry I.

The marginal rent of this industry is represented by *AB*. However, industry II can produce over the same region at a marginal rent represented by *CD*. Since the increment of rent for each unit of land for industry I is greater than for industry II near the market, industry I will produce near the market. However, the rent yielding potential of industry II over the same area represents an alternative use of the land. This alternative can be thought of as an opportunity cost for industry I. Thus, we see that *CD* is a new constraint for industry I (in contrast to $R = 0$ in the one-product case). Industry I will consequently extend its production spatially until its marginal rent equals marginal (opportunity) cost, both expressed as a function of distance. This determines the spatial limit of product I at *E* in Figure 2.

The equilibrium solution for industry II presents a new problem. Since industry II has been outbid for the use of the land near the market, it

has two margins to consider. Spatial location in our scheme is measured in terms of radial distance from the market. There is in this case, therefore, both an inner and outer limit to establish. In Figure 2 both industry I and industry II can produce with profit over the area *OB*. (We speak of areas because we are really concerned with the entire ring determined by these radial distances.) Over part of this area industry II yields the larger return. It will extend its production toward the market until its marginal rent, *CD*, equals *AB*—which now represents marginal cost for industry II. The limit of this extension is *E* and this establishes the inner limit of production of product II. The outer limit for industry II duplicates the equilibrium for the one-product case. It is established where marginal rent, *CD*, equals marginal cost—i.e., the base line *Ok*.

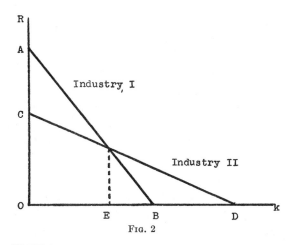

FIG. 2

FIGURE 2

---

[5] An acute observer might point out that the formula given for marginal rent is the derivative of the area under the curve in Figure 1. Since production will be extended in every direction away from the market, the *total* rent derived from the production of any crop must equal, not the area under the curve but the volume of a solid cone of revolution. The true marginal rent, therefore, will be the derivative of this volume and not of the aforementioned area. The first derivative of this function, however, corresponds to equation 1 multiplied by a factor of proportionality, $2\pi k$. Since this factor makes the marginal rent function a quadratic and since it is always divided out in the important operations like determining product boundaries and equilibrium conditions, we have chosen to use the simpler form. It can be demonstrated mathematically to give the same results.

Conditions for Ring Formation

Before we consider more than two products or industries, let us examine the conditions that are necessary for rings to be established in the two-product case. Since these marginal rent lines are, under the present assumptions, linear distance functions, an examination of these functions should give us some information.

If we examine Figure 3a we can readily make one generalization. In order for ring formation to develop, the marginal rent functions must cross. One way of expressing this condition is to say that one industry must have a steeper negative slope $(-E_1f_1 < -E_2f_2)$ at the same time that its R-intercept is greater than the R-intercept of the second industry $[E_1(p_1 - a_1) > E_2(p_2 - a_2)]$.[6] By the same token, Figure 3b reveals that if an industry has a smaller negative slope when its R-intercept is greater, or has a larger negative slope when its R-intercept is smaller, no ring formation will result. In the former case the industry will be dominant, and in the latter case the industry will be excluded. In short, the rent functions must cross in the positive quadrant.

These conditions for ring formation reveal the logic of crop transition in its simplest form. At the market one industry (industry I in Figure 3a) will yield a greater rent return than the other and will be produced there to the exclusion of the other. However, the superiority of product I is lost with distance because the freight charges (E_1f_1) reduce this superior rent yield more rapidly per unit distance than is the case for product II. If this does not happen (as in Figure 3b) then product I dominates the entire area.

Summary statements about the logic of crop transition seem to have been the favorite sport of earlier writers in the field. For example, it is an often cited Thünen generalization that products whose transport costs are high relative to value will be produced closest to the market.[7] Even if we assume that transport rates are identical so that transport costs are proportional to weight and volume, it does not follow that the product for which

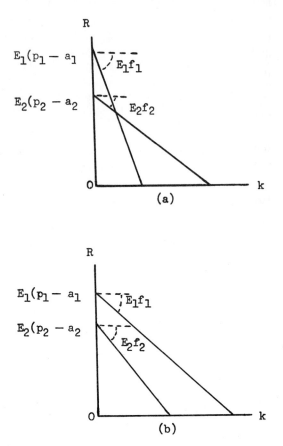

FIGURE 3

the transport cost forms the largest percentage of value will be located closest to the market. Examine Figure 3a. It cannot be established that the transport cost should form a larger percentage of the net value at the market for product I than for product II. Further, when one takes into account the change in transport costs over distance we see that they may form varying percentages of the net market value depending upon the distance from the market.

Again, Brinkman and Lösch both claim that products with the highest yield per acre would be produced closest to the market.[8] It is plain from the previous exposition that a product with high market price and transport rate might occupy the

---

[6] Or, conversely, one industry must have a smaller negative slope at the same time that its R-intercept is smaller than the R-intercept of the second industry. This amounts to the same thing since it depends on the order in which the industries are numbered.

[7] Johann Heinrich von Thünen, *Recherches sur l'influence que le prix des grains la richesse du sol et les impots excerent sur les systems de culture*, translated from German by M. Jules Laverriere (Paris: Guillaumin et Cie, Libraries, 1851), p. 2.

[8] Theodor Brinkmann, *Economics of the Farm Business*, English edition translated by Elizabeth Benedict (Berkeley: University of California Press, 1935), p. 89. August Lösch, *Die raumliche Ordnung der Wirtschaft* (second edition, Jena: Verlag Gustav Fisher, 1944), p. 29.

favored market position even though its yield in terms of transport units was less than some other product.

MULTIPLE PRODUCT SOLUTION

Equilibrium Conditions

Consider next the equilibrium solution for any number of products or industries. The technical conditions of production and the state of our knowledge establish a large number of products or agricultural industries that are technically, if not economically, feasible. These we shall designate $I_1, I_2, \cdots I_n$. Each of these industries has a marginal rent function of the type we have been discussing, $R_1, R_2, \cdots R_n$. We number these industries in the order of the decreasing slopes of their marginal rent functions.

It is a simple matter to make a generalized statement about the spatial equilibrium for any industry. Take I_3 in Figure 4 to represent any industry, I_r. This industry will extend its production toward the market as long as it has an advantage over the best alternative (in this case I_2). This establishes the inner boundary which we designate as k_{ri} (rth industry, inner limit). At the same time it extends its production away from the market as long as its marginal rent is higher than marginal

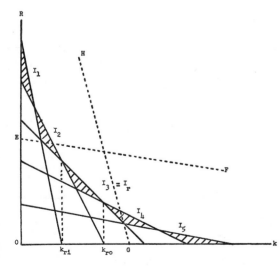

FIGURE 4

opportunity cost (in this case I_4). This establishes the outer limit, k_{ro}. On the strength of this we can make a summary statement. The spatial equilibrium of an industry is established when

$$R_r = R_{r-1} \text{ (establishes } k_{ri})$$
$$R_r = R_{r+1} \text{ (establishes } k_{ro}) \tag{2}$$

This includes all possible cases, for when $R_r = R_1$, $k_{ri} = 0$. Also when $R_r = R_n$, $R_{r+1} = 0$ and k_{ro} is readily established.

Conditions for Entry

The above conditions, however, describe the equilibrium process only for an industry that finds it profitable to produce. There are certain additional conditions that must be fulfilled before any industry, I_r, can establish its existence in competition with the rest.

In the two-product case we do not describe the conditions necessary for either industry to be assured of its existence. The reason is obvious. When the conditions for ring formation are met, the production of both industries is assured. We need two conditions to establish ring formation; one to assure that the marginal rent functions will cross, and another to assure that the intersection will occur in the positive quadrant. Once we consider a multiple-product case we practically guarantee the existence of ring formations.[9] However, to establish the existence of ring formation in the multiple-product case does not assure that any one industry can establish its existence in competition with the rest. It is necessary for us to develop additional conditions that will, if satisfied, assure that a particular industry will produce.

An investigation reveals that two conditions are necessary. First, the value of k for $R_r = R_{r-1}$ must be smaller than the value of k for an intersection of R_r with any of the industries with a smaller slope. This condition assures that I_r will not be excluded by the competition of any of the industries that come after it in the order of diminishing slopes. Second, the value of k for $R_r = R_{r+1}$ must be greater than the value of k for the intersection of R_r with any of the industries with a

---

[9] Out of "n" possible cases any two may not fulfill the conditions above, but it is highly improbable that there will not be some combination among these that will satisfy these conditions. Lösch classifies the values of the variables that result in ring formation in the two-product case. He concludes that zonal production arrangements will be a special case. In so doing he overlooks precisely the point made in this note. Lösch, *op. cit.*, ch. 5.

greater slope. This condition assures that I_r will not be excluded by the competition of any of the industries that come before it in the order of diminishing slopes.

Consideration of Demand and the Mutually Interdependent Price System

MARKET EQUILIBRIUM IN THE ONE–PRODUCT CASE

The maximization procedure we have been discussing for the industry shows that the spatial extent of production is inevitably determined by the process of maximizing rent. We can explain the essential elements by considering the simple one-product case depicted in Figure 1. In this case both the radial extent of production $\left(\dfrac{p - a}{f}\right)$ and the total area of cultivation $\left[\pi\left(\dfrac{p - a}{f}\right)^2\right]$ are explicitly determined. Also the total supplied to the market at a given price is determinate and equals $\left[E\pi\left(\dfrac{p - a}{f}\right)^2\right]$.

All of this is based on the assumption (as has all of the discussion up to this point) that the price (p) is a given and constant quantity. Once we take into account the influence of demand upon the space equilibrium, however, such a simplification is no longer admissible. Even though the industry considers price as a parameter in the maximization of rent, price is certainly variable in the market. Once price is considered to be variable we see that as the price (p) increases so does the spatial extent of production $\left(\text{i.e., } \dfrac{p - a}{f}\right)$ which gives the greatest return, and with it the area of production and supply. Thus, we have a positively sloping supply curve for the commodity, and with each supply is a determinate spatial location of production. If we face this with a negatively sloping demand curve in the central market, there must be an equilibrium price for which the spatial location of production is consistent. This reveals the essential character of the space-price equilibrium.

MARKET EQUILIBRIUM IN MULTIPLE–PRODUCT CASE

The space-price equilibrium works itself out in a similar manner for the multiple-product case.

Consider any industry (I_r) depicted by the marginal rent line AB in Figure 5. In this case as in the one-product case the total area producing product r is explicitly determined but is now the area of a ring instead of a circle. Thus,

$$A = \pi(k_{ro}^2 - k_{ri}^2).$$

By the same token at a given price the total amount of the product supplied to the market is determined and equal to $E\pi(k_{ro}^2 - k_{ri}^2)$. Again, if the price (p_r) increases, so does the spatial extent of production which gives the greatest return and with it the area of production and supply. We see this graphically portrayed in Figure 5 in terms of the shift from AB to $A'B'$. The increase in p_r does not change the slope of the marginal rent line $(-Ef)$ but serves to increase the R-intercept $E_r(p_r - a_r)$ and thus produce a vertical shift. The boundaries for I_r are seen to be farther apart. This establishes once again a positive slope for the supply curve. When faced with the negative market demand for the product of I_r, an equilibrium price is established.

However, the derivation of a supply curve for I_r as a function of p_r takes place in a different setting from that described in the simple case. In the general case, when the price of r increases the boundaries $(k_{ri}$ and $k_{ro})$ are moved farther apart. The production area (and hence supply) of both I_{r-1} and I_{r+1} is immediately diminished. This is true because the inner boundary of I_r is the same as the outer boundary for I_{r-1} and the outer boundary of I_r is the same as the inner boundary for I_{r+1} and the outer boundary of I_r is the same as the inner boundary of I_{r+k}. If the supplies of both I_{r-1} and I_{r+1} are in equilibrium with their prices before the increase in p_r, this equilibrium will be destroyed. Since the demand for the products of these two industries will be large relative to the reduced supply, their prices will rise. This will cause vertical shifts in CD and EF (Figure 5) similar to that depicted by $A'B'$. This will serve to increase the supply of the products of I_{r-1} and I_{r+1} until equilibrium has been reestablished for these two industries. However, the values of k_{ri} and k_{ro} are changed once again, and the production of I_r is restricted. We can go on in this fashion but this is sufficient to establish the most important point. The spatial orientation of any agricultural industry, and hence its supply, is determined not only by its own equilibrium price, but by the equilibrium price of all other industries as well.

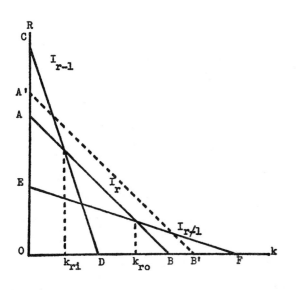

FIGURE 5

There is no simple way, therefore, of describing this spatial equilibrium for any one industry. The orientation of them all must be simultaneously determined, and the only way to handle the solution is by means of a system of equations.

Summary: General Equilibrium Statement of the Space Economy for Agriculture

There seems to be a serious question in the minds of many concerning the utility of mathematical formulae in describing the complicated relationship of pricing. I am convinced that they can serve a useful function in giving a "birdseye view" of the complicated interrelated nature of the space-price equilibrium. There follows an attempt to illustrate and summarize the nature of the space-price equilibrium under simplified conditions and by means of simple equations. No effort is made to introduce modifying and complicating factors into the analysis.

There are two conditions of equilibrium. (1) All individuals and industries in the economic society base their maximum positions upon equilibrium price. In short, they regard prices as constant parameters independent of their influence. (2) The equilibrium prices are determined by the condition that the demand for each commodity must equal its supply. Lange calls the first of these

conditions the *subjective* condition of equilibrium and the latter the *objective* condition.[10]

Subjective Conditions of Equilibrium

The subjective condition of equilibrium is carried out in part by the actions of individual consumers attempting to maximize their utility. The equilibrium process for the consumer is so well known that there is no need to elaborate upon it here. Suffice it to say that the consumers maximize the total utility derived from their income by spending it so that the marginal utility of a unit is equal for all commodities. This involves the usual assumptions about the possibility of ordering consumer utilities and the independence of consumer choice. Through this process, with incomes and prices given, the demand for consumer goods is determined. This part of the equilibrium process can be represented by equations 3.

$$D_1 = F_1(Y_1, Y_2, \ldots Y_s; p_1, p_2, \ldots p_n)$$

$$\cdots \qquad (3)$$

$$D_n = F_n(Y_1, Y_2, \ldots Y_s; p_1, p_2, \ldots p_n)$$

$Y_1, Y_2, \ldots Y_s$ represent the income of the s individuals in the economic system. $D_1, D_2 \ldots D_n$, and $p_1, p_2, \ldots p_n$ represent the aggregate demand and the prices of the n commodities it is possible to produce. This system of equations states that the demand for each good is a function of consumer incomes and the prices of all goods. Implicit in this system of functional equations is the entire equilibrium process of the household. The presentation of this set of equations forces us to point out two additional simplifying assumptions.[11] Since we are concerned with the spatial equilibrium for agriculture alone, (4) *we include in our system only agricultural commodities.* In short, we assume the economy to be completely agrarian. The inconsistencies that result from this assumption are obvious, but it facilitates a brief exposition of the equilibrium process. (5) *We assume $Y_1, Y_2, \ldots Y_s$ to be known constants.* No attempt is made in this analysis to describe the relationship between income and the ownership of and the demand for productive factors.

[10]Oskar Lange and F. M. Taylor, *On the Economic Theory of Socialism,* edited by B. E. Lippencott (Minneapolis: University of Minnesota Press, 1938), p. 65.
[11]The first three assumptions were made explicit in the definition of terms.

271

$$k_{1o} = \varphi_1(E_1, a_1, f_1, p_1; E_2, a_2, f_2, p_2; \ldots E_n, a_n, f_n, p_n)$$

$$(4)$$

$$k_{no} = \varphi_n(E_1, a_1, f_1, p_1; E_2, a_2, f_2, p_2; \ldots E_n, a_n, f_n, p_n)$$

The effort of each producing industry to maximize revenue represents the second aspect of the subjective condition for equilibrium. It is at this point that the general equilibrium statement of the space economy for agriculture differs markedly from the typical general equilibrium statement. This distinction was made in some detail in the definition of terms.

The details of the production (i.e., spatial) equilibrium for each industry have been carefully worked out earlier in the paper. We content ourselves here to recall that each industry maximizes its rent by expanding in both directions (i.e., both toward and away from the market) until its marginal rent equals its marginal opportunity costs. This process establishes the spatial limits of production for the industry, k_{ri} and k_{ro}. We recall further that these limits are determined by the marginal rent function of the industry in question and the marginal rent functions of those industries restricting its extension on either side. The two latter functions serve as opportunity cost restraints for the industry in question. We also see that, when we allow for the influence of demand and variable market price, the k_{ri}'s and k_{ro}'s are, in reality, determined by the marginal rent functions of all industries. This part of the equilibrium process, therefore, can be represented by the equations 4 [see above]. This set of equations expresses the outer limit of each industry (k_{ro}) as a function of the marginal rent functions *for all industries*. We can also set up a similar sea of equations for the inner limits for each industry. However, this would be redundant for the inner boundary of one industry is the same as the outer boundary of the one which joins it nearest the market. Thus, once all the outer boundaries are determined, we know all of the inner boundaries.

E, a, and f in the above equations are all constants. This makes explicit the sixth simplifying assumption. (6) *The transport rate is constant over time and space.* It should also be pointed out that in order for equations 4 to be valid *we must assume*

(7) *that the industries are ordered around a single market.*

Earlier in the paper we pointed out that the supply of a product is determined once the spatial boundaries for that product are determined. Equations 5 express this relationship.

$$S_1 = E_1\pi(k_{1o}{}^2 - k_{1i}{}^2)$$

$$(5)$$

$$S_n = E_n\pi(k_{no}{}^2 - k_{ni}{}^2)$$

In order for this relationship to be expressed in so simple a form, *it is necessary to assume* (8) *that we have an undifferentiated transport network* so that the market rent function of each industry is the same in all directions away from the market.

Objective Conditions

We come at last to the objective conditions of equilibrium. It is necessary for the supply of a commodity to equal the demand. This is the market equilibrium condition. Thus,

$$D_1 = S_1, D_2 = S_2, \ldots D_n = S_n. \qquad (6)$$

Solution of the System

The four sets of equations (3-6) form a complete system. A careful inspection of these equations show that there are 4_n unknown variables in the system. These are:

Variables		Number of Unknowns
prices	$(p_1 \ldots p_n)$	n
demand	$(D_1 \ldots D_n)$	n
boundary	$(k_{1o} \ldots k_{1n})$	n
supply	$(S_1 \ldots S_n)$	n
		—
		$4n$

There are n equations in each of the four sets giving $4n$ equations. When solved simultaneously this system, given the present assumptions, will yield a unique solution. This solution will provide the price of every commodity, the quantity of each commodity that will be produced and consumed, and *at the same time* will explicitly determine the spatial orientation of production.[12]

One thing further needs to be pointed out. Conceptually we have included in the *n* product all products that are technically feasible, given the state of the arts. We know that all of these need not establish their existence in competition with the rest. However, this presents no problem. If any one industry or product does not fulfill the conditions for entry outlined previously, this in effect removes four unknowns and four equations from the system. They exert no influence upon the equilibrium solution. However, these possibilities always remain. If at any time the character of demand and/or technology changes, it is possible for these industries to enter the system.

This, then, is the general equilibrium statement of the space economy for agriculture. It is highly simplified, but it is adequate to illustrate that the location of agriculture is a part of the equilibrium process resulting from the exercise of the rational economic motive. We hope that it has served to synthesize and extend the elements of a location theory for agriculture.

In our exposition of the general equilibrium system there are listed eight limiting assumptions. (There are really more, not emphasized, that are common to all economic equilibrium systems—spatial or otherwise.) It is the removal of these limiting assumptions that will raise legitimate questions about the generality and utility of the concept of rings or zones and about the reality of a unique solution.

We regret that space will not allow a discussion of the modifying influence of taking some of these factors into account—such things as differentiated resources and transport systems, the reality of curvilinear and discontinuous distance-rent functions, and the results of considering the firm equilibrium.[13] This is out of the question. However, we would like to suggest the consequences for location analysis of considering the joint-cost character of farm production on the level of the firm.[14]

When this is done one realizes that it is an unnecessary simplification to assume that an agricultural ring or zone is engaged in the production of a single product. Any one ring or zone of agricultural production may be devoted to any number of products in combination. Further, the same crop may appear in several successive zones. This fact has been a source of confusion. It has led many to conclude that, in a realistic situation, the Thünen rings do not exist. This is not true. For example, one cost interrelationship may call for the production of A, B and C jointly. An alternative cost interrelationship may result in the joint production of A, B and D. The production of A, B, and C will yield one marginal rent line on an industry level, and the production of A, B, and D will yield another. As the distance from the market increases a point is reached where the rent line for *ABC* falls below the rent line for *ABD*. When this takes place *ABD* as a system replaces *ABC*. Throughout the area encompassed by these two zones both A and B will be produced, sometimes with C and sometimes with D. To the uninitiated it may appear that there is nothing left of the zonal

---

[12]The solution presented is similar to that made familiar by Hicks and others (following Walras). Since the demand and supply functions are homogeneous in the prices, the solution is homogeneous of the zero degree. Hence, there is one less than 4*n* independent functions. (If the values of all but one of the functions are known, the value of that one follows.) In the usual procedure, therefore, one of the *n* goods is taken as a *numeraire*, as Walrus calls it. The prices of all other goods are expressed in terms of the price of the *numeraire*. The solution is in terms of 4*n* − 1 ratios, the relative prices.

It should be pointed out, however, that the conventional solution is not mathematically correct. We become involved in the attempt to find a common solution for two sets of incompatible equations. The assumption of fixed incomes in the demand equations is incompatible with the assumption of the maximization of rent revenue in the supply equations. (These variable rents represent incomes for consumers.)

Two approaches can be taken in removing this incompatibility. We can introduce a new set of equations that will specify how the social product is distributed. A second alternative is available that allows us to avoid complicating the analysis further. We can assume that the government owns all productive factors and produces according to our maximization criteria. It takes all of the social product and pays to individuals money incomes that are specified in amount. If we make this assumption we can make our system of functions consistent and retain them without alteration. Since, in effect, the *numeraire* is now extraneous to the system, the demand functions become homogeneous in both incomes and prices. There are now 4*n* independent functions, and each solution will give absolute money prices for all *n* commodities.

I am indebted to Dr. Cecil Phipps of the Mathematics Department at the University of Florida for this bit of enlightenment relative to the mathematics of the solution.

[13]If the reader is interested in a detailed account of the consequences of these factors for the location of agricultural production, see Edgar S. Dunn, Jr., *The Equilibrium of Land-Use Patterns in Agriculture* (Gainesville: University of Florida Press, 1954).

[14]We would like to emphasize that to dip into the theory of the firm to consider the reality of multiple-product production is not intended at this point to unleash all of the variability over space of yield (*E*) and cost of production (*a*). We are considering the modifications of one aspect of the firm equilibrium alone—namely, joint-cost and multiple-products.

pattern of arrangement attributed to Thünen. However, the analysis is not altered in any essential respect. When the combination of products which forms any one system is altered by the addition of a new product or the replacement of an old, a new ring or zone is established.[15] Once we recognize that farming takes place in systems, the analysis is complicated in two ways: (1) the rent yield and the marginal distance rent lines are based upon the total operation and not the production of one product; (2) the total number of possible rings or zones is greatly increased. The number of rings is no longer limited to the number of feasible products but to the number of possible combinations of these products in systems. These are important differences and they change the whole complexion of the location analysis for agriculture. However, the basic principles that describe the equilibrium of the space economy remain unaltered.

Two closing comments are in order. This kind of descriptive analysis is certainly not an opera-

tional model. An exercise of this sort must find its utility as a framework of reference in identifying important variables and important interrelationships in tackling any specific research problem. It may particularly serve the latter. Research in the field of farm economics and regional analysis needs sorely to take account of these interrelationships. As a single example, in developing a prognosis for the citrus industry in Florida, how important it is to be aware of the competition for the use of the land it faces from a growing cattle industry.

Lastly, this descriptive system is particularly lacking in that it does not take into account industrial production and its interrelationship with agriculture, nor does it take into account the influence of multiple markets. Isard has a recent article in which he develops a mathematical analysis that is completely general in the sense that it handles all forms of production and considers market areas and supply areas as well. His unifying principle implies the various existing location theories and must be considered a core element of a general theory of location.[16]

---

[15]Many interesting results may be identified with irregular transformation functions of various types. Large changes in local prices may bring about very little change if the transformation function is sharply curved. A wavy transformation function may bring about abrupt and discontinuous change in the product mix with a small change in local prices. In another case we might find recurrence of a production system at different distances from the market.

---

[16]Walter Isard, "A General Location Principle of an Optimum Space Economy," *Econometrica*, Vol. 20, No. 3, July 1952, pp. 406-430.

William Alonso

A THEORY OF THE URBAN LAND MARKET

The early theory of rent and location concerned itself primarily with agricultural land. This was quite natural, for Ricardo and Malthus lived in an agricultural society. The foundations of the formal spatial analysis of agricultural rent and location are found in the work of J. von Thünen, who said, without going into detail, that the urban land market operated under the same principles.[1] As cities grew in importance, relatively little attention was paid to the theory of urban rents. Even the great Marshall provided interesting but only random insights, and no explicit theory of the urban land market and urban locations was developed.

Since the beginning of the twentieth century there has been considerable interest in the urban land market in America. R. M. Hurd[2] in 1903 and R. Haig[3] in the twenties tried to create a theory of urban land by following von Thünen. However, their approach copied the form rather than the logic of agricultural theory, and the resulting theory can be shown to be insufficient on its own premises. In particular, the theory failed to consider residences, which constitute the preponderant land use in urban areas.

Yet there are interesting problems that a theory of urban land must consider. There is, for instance, a paradox in American cities: the poor live near the center, on expensive land, and the rich on the periphery, on cheap land. On the logical side, there are also aspects of great interest, but which increase the difficulty of the analysis. When a purchaser acquires land, he acquires two goods (land and location) in only one transaction, and only one payment is made for the combination. He could buy the same quantity of land at another location, or he could buy more, or less land at the same location. In the analysis, one encounters, as well, a negative good (distance) with positive costs (commuting costs); or, conversely, a positive good (accessibility) with negative costs (savings in commuting). In comparison with agriculture, the urban case presents another difficulty. In agriculture, the location is extensive: many square miles may be devoted to one crop. In the urban case the site tends to be much smaller, and the location may be regarded as a dimensionless point rather than an area. Yet the thousands or millions of dimensionless points which constitute the city, when taken together, cover extensive areas. How can these dimensionless points be aggregated into two-dimensional space?

Here I will present a non-mathematical overview, without trying to give it full precision, of the long and rather complex mathematical analysis which constitutes a formal theory of the urban land market.[4] It is a static model in which change is introduced by comparative statics. And it is an economic model: it speaks of economic men, and it goes without saying that real men and social groups have needs, emotions, and desires which are not considered here. This analysis uses con-

Reprinted with the permission of the author and publisher from *Papers and Proceedings, Regional Science Association,* Vol. 6, 1960, pp. 149-57. Dr. Alonso is Professor of Regional Planning at the University of California, Berkeley.

[1] Johann Heinrich von Thunen, *Der isolietre Staat in Beziehung auf Landwirtshcaft und Nationalökonomie,* 1st. Vol., 1826, 3rd. Vol. and New Edition, 1863.

[2] Richard M. Hurd, *Principles of City Land Values,* (New York: The Record and Guide, 1903).

[3] Robert M. Haig, "Toward an Understanding of the Metropolis," *Quarterly Journal of Economics,* XL:3, (May 1926). [See page 44 of this volume.]; and *Regional Survey of New York and Its Environs,* (New York: New York City Plan Commission, 1927).

[4] The full development of the theory is presented in my *Location and Land Use,* (Cambridge: Harvard University Press, 1964).

cepts which fit with agricultural rent theory in such a way that urban and rural land uses may be considered at the same time, in terms of a single theory. Therefore, we must examine first a very simplified model of the agricultural land market.

Agricultural Model

In this model, the farmers are grouped around a single market, where they sell their products. If the product is wheat, and the produce of one acre of wheat sells for $100 at the market while the costs of production are $50 per acre, a farmer growing wheat at the market would make a profit of $50 per acre. But if he is producing at some distance—say, 5 miles—and it costs him $5 per mile to ship an acre's product, his transport costs will be $25 per acre. His profits will be equal to value minus production costs minus shipping charges: $100 - 50 - 25 = \$25$. This relation may be shown diagrammatically (see Figure 1). At the market, the farmer's profits are $50, and 5 miles out, $25; at intermediate distance, he will receive intermediate profits. Finally, at a distance of 10 miles from the market, his production costs plus shipping charges will just equal the value of his produce at the market. At distances greater than 10 miles, the farmer would operate at a loss.

In this model, the profits derived by the farmers are tied directly to their location. If the functions of farmer and landowner are viewed as separate, farmers will bid rents for land according to the profitability of the location. The profits of the farmer will therefore be shared with the landowner through rent payments. As farmers bid against each other for the more profitable locations, until farmers' profits are everywhere the same ("normal" profits), what we have called profits becomes rent. Thus, the curve in Figure 1, which we derived as a farmers' profit curve, once we distinguish between the roles of the farmer and the landowner, becomes a bid rent function, representing the price or rent per acre that farmers will be willing to pay for land at the different locations.

We have shown that the slope of the rent curve will be fixed by the transport costs on the produce. The level of the curve will be set by the price of the produce at the market. Examine Figure 2. The lower curve is that of Figure 1, where the price of wheat is $100 at the market, and production costs are $50. If demand increases, and the

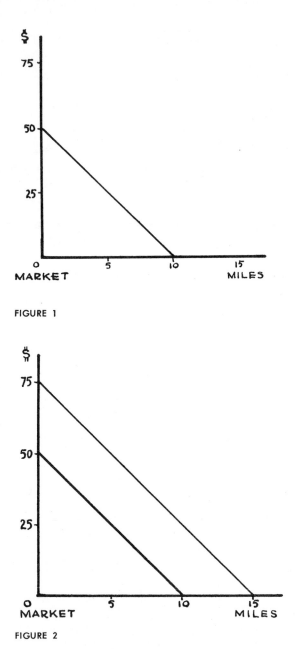

FIGURE 1

FIGURE 2

price of wheat at the market rises to $125 (while production and transport costs remain constant), profits or bid rent at the market will be $75; at 5 miles, $50; $25 at 10 miles, and zero at 15 miles. Thus, each bid rent curve is a function of rent vs. distance, but there is a family of such curves, the level of any one determined by the price of the produce at the market, higher prices setting higher curves.

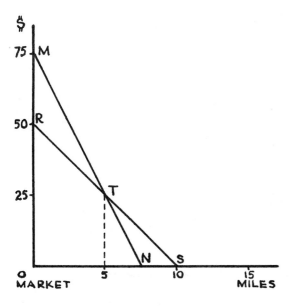

FIGURE 3

Consider now the production of peas. Assume that the price at the market of one acre's production of peas is $150, the costs of production are $75, and the transport costs per mile are $10 These conditions will yield curve MN in Figure 3, where bid rent by pea farmers at the market is $75 per acre, 5 miles from the market $25, and zero at 7.5 miles. Curve RS represents bid rents by wheat farmers, at a price of $100 for wheat. It will be seen that pea farmers can bid higher rents in the range of 0 to 5 miles from the market; farther out, wheat farmers can bid higher rents. Therefore, pea farming will take place in the ring from 0 to 5 miles from the market, and wheat farming will take place in the ring from 5 to 10 miles. Segments MT of the bid rent curve of pea farming and TS of wheat farming will be the effective rents, while segments RT and TN represent unsuccessful bids.

The price of the product is determined by the supply-demand relations at the market. If the region between zero and 5 miles produces too many peas, the price of the product will drop, and a lower bid rent curve for pea farming will come into effect, so that pea farming will be practiced to some distance less than 5 miles.

Abstracting this view of the agricultural land market, we have that:

(1) land uses determine land values, through competitive bidding among farmers;

(2) land values distribute land uses, according to their ability to pay;

(3) the steeper curves capture the central locations. (This point is a simplified one for simple, well-behaved curves.)

Abstracting the process now *from* agriculture, we have:

(1) for each user of land (e.g., wheat farmer) a family of bid rent functions is derived, such that the user is indifferent as to his location along any *one* of these functions (because the farmer, who is the decision-maker in this case, finds that profits are everywhere the same, i.e., normal, as long as he remains on one curve);

(2) the equilibrium rent at any location is found by comparing the bids of the various potential users and choosing the highest;

(3) equilibrium quantities of land are found by selecting the proper bid rent curve for each user (in the agricultural case, the curve which equates supply and demand for the produce).

Business

We shall now consider the urban businessman, who, we shall assume, makes his decisions so as to maximize profits. A bid rent curve for the businessman, then, will be one along which profits are everywhere the same: the decision-maker will be indifferent as to his location along such a curve.

Profit may be defined as the remainder from the volume of business after operating costs and land costs have been deducted. Since in most cases the volume of business of a firm as well as its operating costs will vary with its location, the rate of change of the bid rent curve will bear no simple relation to transport costs (as it did in agriculture). The rate of change of the total bid rent for a firm, where profits are constant by definition, will be equal to the rate of change in the volume of business minus the rate of change in operating costs. Therefore the slope of the bid rent curve, the values of which are in terms of dollars per unit of land, will be equal to the rate of change in the volume of business minus the rate of change in operating costs, divided by the area occupied by the establishment.

A different level of profits would yield a different bid rent curve. The higher the bid rent curve, the lower the profits, since land is more expensive. There will be a highest curve, where profits will be zero. At higher land rents the firm could only operate at a loss.

Thus we have, as in the case of the farmer, a family of bid rent curves, along the path of any one of which the decision-maker—in this case, the businessman—is indifferent. Whereas in the case of the farmer the level of the curve is determined by the price of the produce, while profits are in all cases "normal," i.e., the same, in the case of the urban firm, the level of the curve is determined by the level of the profits, and the price of its products may be regarded for our purposes as constant.

Residential

The household differs from the farmer and the urban firm in that satisfaction rather than profits is the relevant criterion of optimal location. A consumer, given his income and his pattern of tastes, will seek to balance the costs and bother of commuting against the advantages of cheaper land with increasing distance from the center of the city and the satisfaction of more space for living. When the individual consumer faces a given pattern of land costs, his equilibrium location and the size of his site will be in terms of the marginal changes of these variables.

The bid rent curves of the individual will be such that, for any given curve, the individual will be equally satisfied at every location at the price set by the curve. Along any bid rent curve, the price the individual will bid for land will decrease with distance from the center at a rate just sufficient to produce an income effect which will balance to his satisfaction the increased costs of commuting and the bother of a long trip. This slope may be expressed quite precisely in mathematical terms, but it is a complex expression, the exact interpretation of which is beyond the scope of this paper.

Just as different prices of the produce set different levels for the bid rent curves of the farmer, and different levels of profit for the urban firm, different levels of satisfaction correspond to the various levels of the family of bid rent curves of the individual household. The higher curves obviously yield less satisfaction because a higher price is implied, so that, at any given location, the individual will be able to afford less land and other goods.

Individual Equilibrium

It is obvious that families of bid rent curves are in many respects similar to indifference curve mappings. However, they differ in some important ways. Indifference curves map a path of indifference (equal satisfaction) between combinations of quantities of two goods. Bid rent functions map an indifference path between the price of one good (land) and quantities of another and strange type of good, distance from the center of the city. Whereas indifference curves refer only to tastes and not to budget, in the case of households, bid rent functions are derived both from budget and taste considerations. In the case of the urban firm, they might be termed isoprofit curves. A more superficial difference is that, whereas the higher indifference curves are the preferred ones, it is the lower bid rent curves that yield greater profits or satisfaction. However, bid rent curves may be used in a manner analogous to that of indifference curves to find the equilibrium location and land price for the resident or the urban firm.

Assume you have been given a bid rent mapping of a land use, whether business or residential (curves $brc_{1, 2, 3}$, etc., in Figure 4). Superimpose on the same diagram the actual structure of land prices in the city (curve SS). The decision-maker will wish to reach the lowest possible bid rent curve. Therefore, he will choose that point at which the curve of actual prices (SS) will be tangent to the lowest of the bid rent curves with which it comes in contact (brc_2). At this point will be the equilibrium location (L) and the equilibrium land rent (R) for this user of land. If he is a businessman, he will have maximized profits; if he is a resident, he will have maximized satisfaction.

Note that to the left of this point of equilibrium (toward the center of the city) the curve of actual prices is steeper than the bid rent curve; to the right of this point (away from the center) it is less steep. This is another aspect of the rule we noted in the agricultural model: the land uses with steeper bid rent curves capture the central locations.

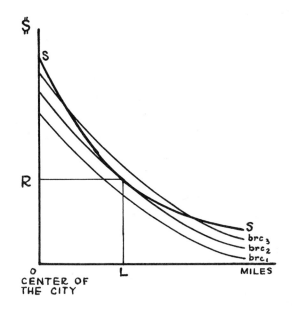

FIGURE 4

Market Equilibrium

We now have, conceptually, families of bid rent curves for all three types of land uses. We also know that the steeper curves will occupy the more central locations. Therefore, if the curves of the various users are ranked by steepness, they will also be ranked in terms of their accessibility from the center of the city in the final solution. Thus, if the curves of the business firm are steeper than those of residences, and the residential curves steeper than the agricultural, there will be business at the center of the city, surrounded by residences, and these will be surrounded by agriculture.

This reasoning applies as well within land use groupings. For instance, it can be shown that, given two individuals of similar tastes, both of whom prefer living at low densities, if their incomes differ, the bid rent curves of the wealthier will be flatter than those of the man of lower income. Therefore, the poor will tend to central locations on expensive land and the rich to cheaper land on the periphery. The reason for this is not that the poor have greater purchasing power, but rather that they have steeper bid rent curves. This stems from the fact that, at any given location, the poor can buy less land than

the rich, and since only a small quantity of land is involved, changes in its price are not as important for the poor as the costs and inconvenience of commuting. The rich, on the other hand, buy greater quantities of land, and are consequently affected by changes in its price to a greater degree. In other words, because of variations in density among different levels of income, accessibility behaves as an inferior good.

Thus far, through ranking the bid rent curves by steepness, we have found the relative rankings of prices and locations, but not the actual prices, locations, or densities. It will be remembered that in the agricultural case equilibrium levels were brought about by changes in the price of the products, until the amount of land devoted to each crop was in agreement with the demand for that crop.

For urban land this process is more complex. The determination of densities (or their inverse, lot size) and locations must be found simultaneously with the resulting price structure. Very briefly, the method consists of assuming a price of land at the center of the city, and determining the prices at all other locations by the competitive bidding of the potential users of land in relation to this price. The highest bid captures each location, and each bid is related to a most preferred alternative through the use of bid rent curves. This most preferred alternative is the marginal combination of price and location for that particular land use. The quantities of land occupied by the land users are determined by these prices. The locations are determined by assigning to each successive user of land the location available nearest the center of the city after the assignment of land quantities to the higher and more central bidders.

Since initially the price at the center of the city was assumed, the resulting set of prices, locations, and densities may be in error. A series of iterations will yield the correct solution. In some cases, the solution may be found by a set of simultaneous equations rather than by the chain of steps which has just been outlined.

The model presented in this paper corresponds to the simplest case: a single-center city, on a featureless plain, with transportation in all directions. However, the reasoning can be extended to cities with several centers (shopping, office, manufacturing, etc.), with structured road patterns, and other realistic complications. The theory

279

can also be made to shed light on the effects of economic development, changes in income structure, zoning regulations, taxation policies, and other. At this stage, the model is purely theoretical; however, it is hoped that it may provide a logical structure for econometric models which may be useful for prediction.

James M. Henderson

THE UTILIZATION OF AGRICULTURAL LAND:
A THEORETICAL AND EMPIRICAL INQUIRY

For purposes of economic analysis, two important characteristics of agricultural land are its heterogeneity and the possibility of its use for the production of alternative outputs. One or both of these characteristics are frequently recognized in theoretical studies of land utilization. David Ricardo and his followers used the heterogeneity of land as a cornerstone in their theoretical analysis, but ignored the possibility of alternative uses. Later, Jevons and other economists extended the theory to encompass both characteristics.

With the increasing application of linear programming methods, alternative land uses, and occasionally land heterogeneity, are being emphasized in empirical studies of land utilization for individual farms and small groups of farms. However, empirical studies of land utilization for the economy as a whole are seldom, if ever, constructed with an explicit recognition of these two important characteristics of agricultural land. These studies are either formulated without an explicit theoretical framework, or built around a statistical version of the neo-classical demand and supply analysis.

This paper is aimed at the development of a theoretical analysis based upon maximizing behavior which can be empirically implemented and will generate numerical predictions of short-run land utilization patterns for the economy as a whole. Particular emphasis is placed upon land heterogeneity and alternative uses. New methods are developed for the study of agricultural supply relations. Factors such as technological change and input substitution, which are of great importance for a long-run analysis, are largely ignored in the present short-run formulation.

The analysis is developed within the institutional framework of agriculture as practiced in the United States. Land utilization decisions are made by a large number of farmers, each of whom possesses a relatively small parcel of land. Generally, we may assume that farmers act independently, i.e., the decisions of each are unaffected by those of the others. The decisions of different farmers are similar only insofar as the factors conditioning their decisions are similar. The dissimilarity of conditioning factors, however, is of particular importance. National land utilization patterns are the result of decisions made by individual farmers who possess different types of land and are subject to a diversity of other conditioning factors.

A mass of existing data has been brought together for the purpose of using the theoretical analysis to make predictions of the land utilization patterns of individual decision-making units for the 1955 crop year. Each decision-making unit is assumed to allocate its land among alternative uses in such a way as to maximize its expected return,

Reprinted by permission of the author and publishers from J. M. Henderson, REVIEW OF ECONOMICS AND STATISTICS, *Cambridge, Mass.: Harvard University Press,* Copyright, 1959, by the President and Fellows of Harvard College. Dr. Henderson is Professor of Economics at the University of Minnesota, Minneapolis.

This paper contains some of the results of a general study of natural resource utilization being undertaken as a part of the research program of the Harvard Economic Research Project. The author is indebted to the members of the staff of the project for aid in the preparation of this paper. He owes a particular debt of gratitude to the staff members who aided in the arduous task of gathering and rectifying the data. Mrs. Virginia McK. Nail provided expert help in all phases of this task. Jan Basch, Richard H. Day, Barbara King, and Ronald J. Wonnacott each made substantial contributions in one or more of its phases. An earlier version of the theoretical part of this paper was presented at a joint meeting of the Econometric Society and the Regional Science Association in Cleveland in December 1956, and was reproduced in *Papers and Proceedings* of the Regional Science Association, Vol. III.

subject to a number of technical and institutional constraints. Limited linearity assumptions are postulated, and the decision problem of each unit is expressed as a linear programming problem. Predictions of national and state allocation patterns are obtained by aggregating the patterns predicted for individual decision-making units.

The present analysis is both *descriptive* and *recursive*. It is descriptive rather than normative in that the question asked is *what will be done* rather than *what should be done*. In this respect it differs from other current applications of linear programming to agriculture, which are intended to determine how individual farmers should allocate their land. It is recursive in that the values of the variables for a particular crop year are determined from data for preceding crop year.

The Theory

Assume for the moment that each individual farmer is a separate decision-making unit and that all domestic cropland is distributed among n farmers. Each farmer is assumed to hold a fixed number of acres of cropland of a given type, but different farmers may hold cropland of different types. The decision problem of each farmer at the beginning of a crop year is to determine how much of his land to devote to the cultivation of each of m alternative crops which will mature and be sold at a subsequent date within the crop year. The decisions of the farmers are independent, and a description of the decision problem of an arbitrarily selected farmer, the ith, is sufficient to describe the decision problems of all the farmers.

THE FRAMEWORK FOR DECISION–MAKING

The ith farmer's land utilization pattern is given by a set of values for the acreages for each of the m crops, which are assumed to be grown separately. His choice of land utilization patterns is limited by the rather obvious constraint that he cannot devote more land than he possesses to the cultivation of crops:

$$\sum_{j=1}^{m} x_{ij} \leqq a_i \qquad (1)$$

where x_{ij} is the number of acres he devotes to the jth crop and a_i is the number of acres of cropland which he possesses. Relation (1) is expressed as

a weak inequality, since the farmer has the option of leaving some of his cropland unused.

The farmer's land utilization decisions are conditioned by a number of economic, technical, institutional, and sociological factors. Factors such as costs, prices, and yields are, at least in principle, easily quantified. Factors such as lack of knowledge, uncertainty, and lethargy defy direct quantification. Indirect methods must be employed to allow for factors that cannot be observed.

Many of these factors are reflected in the farmer's reluctance to make large changes in an established land utilization pattern. A wide variation would require the purchase of new equipment and entrance into lines of production on a large scale in which the farmer has limited experience. Change always involves effort, and frequently the effort required is proportionate to the size of the change. The farmer is also reluctant to shift a large proportion of his acreage to the crop which promises the largest return since he derives a number of benefits from diversity which are not recognized in the calculation of his expected return for a single year. Diversity means that he is able to practice advantageous crop rotation and labor distribution programs and to reduce the variance of his expected return if his fortunes do not depend upon a single crop.

In accordance with these observations, the farmer's land allocation pattern is not assumed to be computed anew for each crop year. His land allocation decisions for the current crop year are described in terms of deviations from the allocation pattern which he established in the proceeding crop year. Specifically, his acreage plantings for each crop are assumed to be constrained by maximum and minimum limits which indicate his desire for diversity and reluctance to depart from an established pattern:

$$(1 - \beta_{ij,\,min})\, x_{ij}^{*} \leqq x_{ij} \leqq (1 + \beta_{ij,\,max})\, x_{ij}^{*}$$
$$(j = 1, \ldots, m) \qquad (2)$$

where x_{ij}^{*} is the acreage which the ith farmer devoted to the jth crop in the preceding crop year, and $\beta_{ij,\,min}$ and $\beta_{ij,\,max}$ are respectively the minimum and maximum proportions by which he is willing to deviate from his established pattern. The β coefficients are assumed to be constants for the determination of the farmer's current land utilization pattern.

The $2m$ β coefficients for the ith farmer provide an indirect description of the immeasurable constraints to which he is subject. The coefficients may differ in value for each of the n farmers, but it is possible to derive general conditions to which every set of coefficients must conform.

First, assume that the farmer's total available cropland equals the sum of his base-year acreages for the m crops:

$$a_i = \sum_{j=1}^{m} \overset{*}{x}_{ij}. \qquad (3)$$

An increase in the acreage of one crop, therefore, implies a corresponding decrease in the acreage of one or more of the other crops.

Each of the maximum limits considered separately must be attainable in order to be meaningful. The values of the β coefficients, therefore, must be such that the maximum potential increase for each crop is not greater than the sum of the maximum potential decreases for the other crops:

$$\beta_{ij,\,max}\, \overset{*}{x}_{ij} \leqq \sum_{\substack{k=1 \\ k \neq i}}^{m} \beta_{ik,\,min}\, \overset{*}{x}_{ik} \quad (j=1,\ldots,m). \quad (4)$$

If (4) did not hold for one of the crops, it would not be possible to set the acreage for that crop equal to its maximum limit and at the same time satisfy all of the constraints given by (2).

Each of the maximum potential acreage declines must also be attainable. Therefore,

$$\beta_{ij,\,min}\, \overset{*}{x}_{ij} \leqq \sum_{\substack{k=1 \\ k \neq j}}^{m} \beta_{ik,\,max}\, \overset{*}{x}_{ik} \quad (j=1,\ldots,m). \quad (5)$$

The $2m$ relations given by (4) and (5) do not describe the farmer's behavior, but merely serve to define feasible sets of values for the nonnegative β coefficients.

Generally, a farmer who devoted a high proportion of his base-year acreage to the jth crop will assign a lower value to $\beta_{ij,\,max}$ than a farmer who devoted a smaller proportion of his base-year acreage to the jth crop. The same value for $\beta_{ij,\,max}$ would imply that the first farmer was willing to make a greater proportionate reduction of his acreage devoted to other crops than the second. If the first farmer devoted 60 to 100 acres to the jth crop, a $\beta_{ij,\,max}$ coefficient of 0.2 implies that he is willing to shift a maximum of 12 acres from other crops to the jth. This represents a 30 per cent re-

duction in the base-year acreage for the other crops. If the second farmer devoted 20 of 100 acres to the jth crop, the same coefficient implies that he is willing to shift a maximum of 4 acres. This represents only 5 per cent of his base-year acreage for the other crops.

Using a similar argument, it appears likely that the farmer with the substantially higher proportion of his base-year acreage devoted to the ith crop will also assign a lower value to $\beta_{ij,\,min}$. The same value would imply that the first was willing to increase his plantings of other crops by a much higher proportion than the second.

The receipt of governmental price supports for a number of crops, such as wheat, cotton, and rice, is contingent upon the farmer's compliance with governmentally-imposed acreage allotments which place maximum limits upon the acreage he can devote to these crops. Let the crops be numbered so that the first w are the ones which are subject to acreage allotments. The effects of the acreage allotments can be expressed by weak inequalities:

$$x_{ij} \leqq \bar{a}_{ij} \quad (j=1,\ldots,w) \qquad (6)$$

where $\bar{a}_{ij}$ is the ith farmer's acreage allotment for the jth crop.

Relations (2) and (6) both give maximum limits for each of the first w crops. Obviously, both cannot hold unless by chance they happen to be equal. In each case the smaller of the two limits is assumed to be effective. An acreage allotment can force a farmer to consider a smaller increase than he would in the absence of the allotment, but he is always free to consider a smaller increase than the allotment allows.

Acreage allotments are sometimes intended to reduce the acreages devoted to a crop below the levels of the preceding year, i.e., $\bar{a}_{ij} < \overset{*}{x}_{ij}$ for some j. The restriction may be so severe that the allotments are less than the minimum acreages given by (2). In this case the maximum limit equals the acreage allotment, and it is convenient to define the minimum limit as

$$\bar{a}_{ij} - 1 \leqq x_{ij} \quad \text{if} \quad \bar{a}_{ij} \leqq (1-\beta_{ij,\,min})\, \overset{*}{x}_{ij}. \quad (7)$$

The reason for making the minimum slightly less than the maximum will become obvious when the per-acre rents associated with the acreage allotments are computed.

COSTS AND RETURNS

It is assumed that the farmer's costs can be separated into three mutually exclusive categories: (a) costs of planting, cultivating, and harvesting the m crops; (b) costs of his other agricultural enterprises; and (c) general costs which are necessary for the existence and maintenance of the farm but are invariant with respect to the choice of a cropland utilization pattern. The interest cost of the farmer's investment for his land, whether a real or an opportunity cost, is included in the third category. The amount of this cost is a historical datum not necessarily related to current conditions. The market value of a farm is determined by capitalizing current and expected profits gross of this interest cost. Assuming that the farm will remain in existence during the short-run period under consideration, only the costs in the first category are relevant for the determination of the farmer's current cropland utilization pattern.

The m crops are assumed to be produced independently, and each farmer is assumed to incur a constant per-acre cost for each crop within the range defined by his maximum and minimum constraints. The total Category (a) costs for the ith farmer are denoted by v_i and are a linear function of his crop acreages:

$$v_i = \sum_{j=1}^{m} c_{ij} x_{ij} \tag{8}$$

where c_{ij} is his constant per-acre cost for the jth crop. Given the assumption of inter-farm land heterogeneity, the per-acre costs will most likely be different for different farms.

The farmer's revenue from an acre of land devoted to the jth crop equals the price he receives for the jth crop multiplied by its per-acre yield. His total revenue from all m crops, denoted by u_i, is the sum of his per-acre revenues multiplied by the appropriate acreages:

$$u_i = \sum_{j=1}^{m} (p_{ij} y_{ij})\, x_{ij} \tag{9}$$

where p_{ij} is his farm price for the jth crop expressed in dollars per physical unit of output, and y_{ij} is his yield expressed in physical units of output per acre. Neither prices nor yields are known with certainty at the time the farmer must make his land allocation decisions, and his decisions are based upon his expectations of their values. His total revenue,

therefore, is an expected rather than a certain value. Single-valued price and yield expectations are used for the construction of (9). However, their joint variances are among the factors which determine the farmer's maximum and minimum acreage constraints.

The farmer's expected net return from the m crops, denoted by π_i, is the difference between his expected revenues (9) and costs (8), and may be expressed as a linear function of his acreages:

$$\pi_i = \sum_{j=1}^{m} z_{ij} x_{ij} \tag{10}$$

where $z_{ij} = p_{ij} y_{ij} - c_{ij}$ is his expected per-acre return from the jth crop. Working within the framework of the constraints given by (1), (2), (6), and (7), it is postulated that the farmer will select a cropland utilization pattern, i.e., values for x_{ij} ($j = 1, \ldots, m$), which maximizes his expected net return.

The farmer's expected net return differs from his expected accounting profit. To obtain expected accounting profit from expected net return from cropland one must add expected net return from other enterprises and deduct general costs, including all interest costs on land investment which are paid by the farmer.

THE PROGRAMMING PROBLEM

The farmer's decision problem can be expressed as a linear programming problem. He desires to select a land utilization pattern which maximizes (10) subject to the following linear constraints:

$$\sum_{j=1}^{m} x_{ij} \leq a_i, \tag{11}$$

$$x_{ij} \leq a_{ij,\,\mathrm{max}} \quad (j = 1, \ldots, m), \tag{12}$$

$$-x_{ij} \leq -a_{ij,\,\mathrm{min}} \quad (j = 1, \ldots, m), \tag{13}$$

and

$$x_{ij} \geq 0 \quad (j = 1, \ldots, m), \tag{14}$$

where $a_{ij,\,\mathrm{max}}$ is the appropriate maximum acreage chosen from (2) or (6), and $a_{ij,\,\mathrm{min}}$ is the appropriate minimum acreage chosen from (2) or (7). Both sides of the minimum acreage constraints have been multiplied by -1 and the direction of the inequalities reversed. The constraints (14) are a mathematical statement of the obvious fact that it is impossible for the farmer to devote a negative acreage to any of the crops. Ignoring (14), the programming problem contains m variables and $(2m + 1)$ constraints.

CROPLAND RENTS

Linear programming problems always come in related pairs. Given one of the problems, the other, its dual, can be derived from it by applying formal rules.[1] The problems have distinct sets of variables, but both contain the same constants, though their arrangement differs. The variables of each problem are equal in number and related to the constraints of the other. The dual for the land allocation problem with m variables and $(2m+1)$ constraints contains $(2m+1)$ variables and m constraints.

Let the variable of the dual of the land allocation problem which is associated with the general acreage constraint (11) be denoted by r_i, the variables associated with the maximum acreage constraints (12) by $r_{ij, \max}$ and the variables associated with the minimum acreage constraints (13) by $r_{ij, \min}$. The dual of the land allocation problem is to select a set of values for its $(2m+1)$ variables which minimizes

$$p_i = a_i r_i + \sum_{j=1}^{m} a_{ij, \max} r_{ij, \max} - \sum_{j=1}^{m} a_{ij, \min} r_{ij, \min} \quad (15)$$

subject to

$$r_i + r_{ij, \max} - r_{ij, \min} \geqq z_{ij} \ (j = 1, \ldots, m) \quad (16)$$

and

$$r_i, r_{ij, \max}, r_{ij, \min} \geqq 0. \quad (17)$$

A basic theorem of dual systems states that the minimum value of p_i equals the maximum value of π_i. If the farmer solves either of the programming problems, its optimum solution will imply the optimum solution of the other. Since we have postulated that the farmer maximizes π_i, the objective function (15) is not of particular significance for our purposes, but its variables are.

The dual problem was derived by applying general rules which are applicable to all programming systems, but there are no general rules which allow an interpretation of its variables. This task must be performed separately for each specfic programming system. However, in economic appli-

cations the dual of a production or allocation problem with output or associated variables is generally a valuation problem with price or rent variables. In the present system the dual variable r_i is interpreted as the general per-acre rent for the ith farmer's cropland, and the variables $r_{ij, \max}$ and $r_{ij, \min}$ are interpreted as his specific pre-acre rents with respect to his maximum and minimum limits for the jth crop.

The per-acre rents reflect the marginal values of the farmer's acreage constraints. His general pre-acre rent is the amount by which his expected return would increase if his cropland were increased by one acre with his maximum and minimum limits remaining unchanged. The rent $r_{ij, \max}$ is the increased return which he would obtain if his maximum limit for the jth crop were increased by one acre with the other constraints remaining unchanged. Finally, the rent $r_{ij, \min}$ is the amount of increased return if the minimum limit for the jth crop were reduced by one acre.

The formal properties of dual systems allow a further exploration into the nature of the cropland rents. An important duality theorem states that the kth variable of one problem vanishes in its optimum solution if the strict inequality holds for the kth relation in the optimum solution of the other. Applying this theorem to the variables of the valuation problem and the relations of the allocation problem,

$$r_i = 0 \text{ if } \sum_{j=1}^{m} x_{ij} < a_{i,} \quad (18)$$

and

$$r_{ij, \max} = 0 \text{ if } x_{ij} < a_{ij, \max} \quad (19)$$

$$r_{ij, \min} = 0 \text{ if } - x_{ij} < - a_{ij, \min}. \quad (20)$$

Clearly, if the farmer is leaving a portion of his cropland unused, an additional acre would not allow him to increase his expected return. Similarly, an increase of an ineffective maximum or decrease of an ineffective minimum limit would not allow him to increase his return. Since $a_{ij, \max} > a_{ij, \min}$, the maximum and minimum limits for the jth crop cannot both be effective; therefore, at least one of the specific per-acre rents for each crop must equal zero.

Since the minimum acreage limits for each crop are positive, the optimal acreage for each crop must also be positive. Therefore, in an optimum solution the strict equality holds for all m of the relations of the valuation system given in (16);

[1] The reader who is unfamiliar with the elementary properties of dual programming systems is referred to R. Dorfman, P. A. Samuelson, and R. M. Solow, *Linear Programming and Economic Analysis* (New York, 1958), ch. 3.

the net per-acre rent for each crop equals its expected per-acre return. Relations (16) become a system of m equations in $(2m+1)$ variables. Generally, the inequality will hold for $(m+1)$ of the constraints in the optimum solution of the allocation problem, and relations (18) through (20) can be used to reduce the relations of the valuation problem to an easily solved system of m equations in m variables.

Martin Beckmann and Thomas Marschak

AN ACTIVITY ANALYSIS APPROACH TO LOCATION THEORY

. . .

Our discussion of the allocation problem confronting the firm with branch plants parallels in several ways the substitution analysis of location developed by Predöhl[9], Furlan[10], and on a more sophisticated level by Isard[11]. In substitution analysis transportation is treated in the same way as commodity inputs, and the theory of optimal factor combination, as developed for smooth transformation functions, is applied. In our approach, too, an analysis of substitution among production locations, among material deposits, and among markets will be central. But we shall not make the strong assumption that the transformation functions involved are everywhere differentiable. It will be shown that the substitution equations, although derived from comparisons "in the small," are sufficient to determine an optimum "in the large."

A criticism that may be levelled against almost all existing location theories is that though conducted at the industry level they do not refer explicitly to a price mechanism but instead try to cut through the complicated interdependence that only a simultaneously determined price system can adequately represent. A notable exception is Palander's treatise[12] on location in which the "isotime"

(iso-price curve) approach was developed to be taken up again by Lösch. For this reason, Koopmans' papers on the transportation problem[13], which obtained a system of prices at locations having a requirement or availability of a transportable commodity, proved to be important. Some of his ideas were further developed in papers by Samuelson[14], Enke[15], and one of the authors[16] on the spatial equilibrium of prices in a one-commodity market.

A transportation or spatial price equilibrium model, however, is not yet "location theory," for the precise reason that in location theory the local or regional supply and demand functions that are assumed given in such models must be explained from underlying data—the technology and locations of plants, and the locations of resource deposits, labor pools, and consumption centers. A complete long-run analysis would not stop there but would in turn explain what caused plant concentrations, and how labor sources and markets developed—would explain, in short, the distribution of human and man-made resources given the distribution of natural (but non-human) resources. But the powers of theory are limited. There are many incompletely understood relationships even in the short run and it is to these that we shall turn in an attempt to show how linear activity analysis, which has proved a useful tool in the study of other economic problems of the short run, may be applied to the problems of location.

Reprinted with the permission of the authors and publisher from *Kyklos*, Vol. 8, 1955, pp. 128-41. Professor Dr. Martin Beckmann is Director of the Institut für Ökonometrie und Unternehmensforschung at the University of Bonn; Dr. Marschak is Associate Professor in the Graduate School of Business, University of California, Berkeley.

[9]A. Predöhl, Das Standortproblem in der Wirtschaftstheorie, *Weltwirtschaftliches Archiv*, Vol. 21 (1925), p. 294-321.

[10]V. Furlan, Die Standortprobleme in der Volks- und Weltwirtschaftslehre, *Weltwirtschaftliches Archiv*, Vol. 2 (1913).

[11]W. Isard, "A General Location Principle of an Optimum Space-Economy", *Econometrica*, Vol. 20 (July 1952), p. 406-430.

[12]T. Palander, *Beiträge zur Standorttheorie*, Uppsala 1935, Almqvist and Wiksells.

[13]T. C. Koopmans, "Optimum Utilization of the Transportation System", *Econometrica*, Vol. 17, Supplement (July 1949), p. 136-146.

[14]P. Samuelson, "Spatial Price Equilibrium and Linear Programming", *American Economic Review*, Vol. 42 (June 1952), p. 283-303.

[15]S. Enke, "Equilibrium among Spatially Separated Markets: Solution by Electric Analogue", *Econometrica*, Vol. 19 (January 1951), p. 40-47.

[16]M. Beckmann, "A Continuous Model of Transportation", *Econometrica*, Vol. 20 (October 1952), p. 643-660.

The Allocation Problem for a Firm

In this section we consider a firm composed of branch plants which obtain their inputs from "resource deposits" and sell their outputs at "markets." At first an unrealistically simple and incomplete description of the firm is given and then assumptions about the firm's goals and the technology and market conditions which it faces are gradually added. The question to be answered at each stage is the following: What can be said about the firm's location decisions—its production program at each plant location, how much of each input is obtained from each resource deposit for use in each plant, and how much of each output from each plant is sold in each market?

1. Let a firm which produces a single commodity possess a number of branch plants which require a fixed overhead outlay no matter what the scale of output. Suppose the firm is to decide on its production and sales program. We assume that the technology is such that apart from fixed plant all inputs are in constant proportion to output and that their ratio is independent of the location. To begin with, let the price of inputs be the same at all resources deposits and the price of outputs the same at all markets.

Then the profitability of any level of output at any location depends on transportation cost only. There exists a critical value of transportation cost that renders production at a location just profitable. If transportation cost is less than this, part of the revenue may be regarded as "rent" on plant. Rent per unit of output is then a measure of the profitability of a plant location.

Nothing can be said under these simple conditions about the scale of operations. Only a simple question can be answered: where is production definitely unprofitable and where might it be profitable?

So long as prices for resources are the same at all "resource deposits" there is no problem of choice among the sources of supply. If transport cost is proportional to distance it is always the geographically nearest location where an input can be obtained at lowest cost; and if market prices are the same, each plant delivers to the nearest market location.

2. Now let product prices to the firm be different at different markets and resource prices different at different deposits. Moreover, let transport cost per unit distance vary with distance shipped. Then the resource deposit which is nearest for any production location is replaced by the one which is "cheapest"—the one for which the resource can be brought to the production site for the least total cost per unit; and the nearest market is replaced by the "most lucrative" market—the one for which the net revenue (net of transport cost) from the sale of a unit product is the largest.

3. So far we have not made precise the allocation problem of the firm. We now specify that its goal is profit maximization.

4. Suppose that the firm makes the decision about what plants to run and is faced with an overall restriction on its operating budget, which puts a limit on *total* expenditure for inputs and transportation. Then it is obviously the plant with the highest ratio of profit per unit of output to the sum per unit output of transportation and input costs which alone will be run.

Alternatively, let availability restrictions on some critical item (with negligible transportation cost) limit the total output of all plants. Then, of course, the plant with the highest profit per unit of product is chosen to produce the entire output.

5. Next, let the production capacity of each plant be specified. So long as no other restrictions enter, as in 1-3, this merely determines the scale of operations in plants where production is profitable. With over-all restrictions present, the set of plants operated consists of those with the highest profit-to-cost or profit-to-output ratio which still satisfy the over-all limitation.

6. Let capacity limitations i.e., upper bounds on the amounts which can be obtained from the deposit per unit of time now be imposed on the resource deposit[17]. We assume now that these deposits are owned by the firm but that the firm pays a price for a unit of resource—namely, its cost of extraction—which may differ at different deposits.

Then a plant may find it profitable to obtain resources also from other deposits as soon as the capacity limit(s) of its cheapest source(s) is (are) reached. How far it should go in its search for materials is clearly indicated by the marginal cost principal: sales price in the most lucrative market must cover the cost of supply from the dearest sources that are resorted to (plus cost of transporta-

---

[17]Resource deposits may occur at plant locations; labor, for example, may be such a "localized" resource.

tion to market); the tapping of additional, increasingly dear, sources is pushed to the point where this cost can no longer be covered for any untapped source. The marginal cost of production, it will be noted, is here a step function which jumps whenever the capacity limit of some supply deposit is reached and remains constant between such jumps.

7. For an integrated firm, the supply problem is more complex, however, than the point of view of the individual plant suggests. Consumption of a resource from a deposit with short supply by a plant for which that deposit is "cheapest" may take place at an opportunity cost to other plants which use the same resource deposit. As a result it may be more profitable (to the firm) for the given plant to shift to the use of some other resource deposit if such a shift adds less to its costs per unit of its output than it subtracts from the costs of other plants who now use the resource it has liberated.

The deposits from which a given plant obtains its supplies of a resource tend to be embedded in an area—the supply area—whose extension and shape is determined by the transportation cost structure and the location of rival plants. If the cost of transport per unit distance decreases with distance then it is possible that the supply area of some plant properly encloses that of another one. (In other words, the supply area may not be simply connected[18].)

It may also be profitable to shift supplies at certain deposits from one plant to other plants without providing compensating supplies from different deposits. This amounts to a shift of production into plants of higher profitability.

If supplies of only one resource are limited, the supply from a given deposit should always go to that plant where it gives rise to the highest profit (revenue less processing costs and costs of *all* other inputs and transportation). If several resources are in short supply, the profits which are jointly attributable to the marginal shipments to a plant from deposits whose capacity limits are reached must equal or exceed the profits attributable to any distribution of these marginal shipments among other plants.

8. A more elegant description of these substitution relations is based on the introduction—in *addition* to the "external" market prices for prod-

ucts and extraction costs for resources—of prices *internal* to the firm. These are prices on (1) resources at deposits, and (2) resources at plant locations.

The internal price of a resource at a deposit equals the opportunity cost of earmarking for use in a plant a unit of the resource at the deposit. The internal price of the same resource at a plant location equals transportation cost from that deposit where this opportunity cost is smallest plus this smallest opportunity cost. Later the internal price of a resource at a deposit will be considered a "rent" imputed to the deposit per unit of the resource used.

Even without explicit reference to these interpretations the internal prices may be defined formally as follows. The difference of internal resource prices between plant and deposit does not exceed transportation cost and equals it when shipments are actually taking place. The (external) price of product at the most lucrative market less transportation cost to the market must not exceed the cost of production in terms of internal resource prices at plant. Price and cost are equal whenever production is actually carried out. The internal price of a resource at a deposit is greater than or equal to the (external) f.o.b. price (the cost of extraction) at resource deposits and equal to it if the capacity limit of that deposit is not reached.

It is not obvious that these conditions are in fact all that is needed to determine the system of internal prices of outputs and flows. That these internal prices with the required properties do exist is also in need of rigorous proof which will be given in the subsequent mathematical section.

9. The allocation of markets to plants within the firm does not raise any comparable problems as long as any market can absorb all that is delivered to it at a given price. Each plant will realize its maximum profit by delivering to its most lucrative market (or if there are several, to any one of them) and this will maximize profits of the firm. Of course, one given market may be most lucrative for, and therefore served by, several plants.

10. Now suppose however, that the firm cannot determine product sales freely in each market, but is constrained to a fixed program. We may imagine that a system of maximum sales quotas and of (external) prices has been imposed by a monopolistic combination (e.g., an international cartel). Now to maximize profit, the firm still supplies each

---

[18]The theoretical analysis of market and supply areas is facilitated by a continuous model of transportation and location. Cf. Beckmann, *op. cit.*

market from that plant which can supply the market in question at the smallest opportunity cost and it fills each quota up to the point where opportunity cost becomes equal to revenue per unit, or it exhausts the quota if this cost remains below the revenue. It may be profitable now for one plant to deliver to several markets of unequal lucrativity. The most lucrative one then gives rise to an "external" profit which may be imputed as "rent" to the quota at that market and the less lucrative ones give rise to smaller (possibly zero) rents.

Again recourse may be had to internal prices but now, in addition, internal product prices need to be introduced. The internal product price at a plant equals the (external) product price at a market that is most lucrative after subtracting quota rent per unit product, minus the transportation cost from the plant to that market. Formally, we may again define the internal prices as accounting prices which permit at most zero ("internal") profits on production and transportation. If they are resource prices, they are equal to the (external) f.o.b. resource price at deposits whenever the deposit capacity is not reached, and are not lower otherwise. If they are product prices, they are equal to the (external) market price if the quota is not filled and are not higher otherwise. The existence of such prices and the sufficiency for profit maximization in the firm of the criteria furnished by these prices is capable of mathematical proof. (See Mathematical Section.)

11. If in addition plant capacity is limited, opportunity cost is still more complex. The new limitation gives rise to one more rent, in each plant as located, per unit of output. This is to be added into the internal price of product at plant and renders it greater than or equal to its previous value, and equal if plant capacity is not reached.

The role of rent in the cost accounting of the firm is one of allocating the total profit to what might be called its sources: the resource deposits of favorable location and low f.o.b. cost, the quotas in lucrative markets, and the plants at advantageous locations. These rents have significance for long run decisions as well: a comparison of rent with the cost of capacity expansion indicates the profitability of (small scale) investments not exceeding critical magnitude (beyond which the pattern of rents would be changed).

12. If a choice now exists between several production processes in a plant, that process will be selected for which total cost is minimal in terms of internal prices of inputs. This amounts to a substitution of resource inputs at relatively low internal cost for more expensive ones. The situation is more complex if capacity does not assume the simple form of a ceiling on output, but of a limitation on the use of various pieces of fixed equipment. The problem becomes one of tailoring the production program to the plant facilities. As in the general theory of production we may assume that several processes may be run independently of each other in one plant. More precisely, this means that input ratios in one process are independent of the level of total output emerging from any other process. In general, it will now be a mixture of processes that is most advantageous, because application of the most lucrative process alone at its maximum level would leave certain facilities underutilized. The best combination is again characterized by zero profitability in terms of certain internal prices. With each piece of equipment which limits the capacity of plant is now associated an internal rent which is positive only when this capacity limit is effective. A set of such rents exists which together with the internal prices of other inputs will permit nonnegative profits only, and permit zero profits on each process used in the optimal combination.

13. Finally, let us admit joint production. Again the process "levels" have to be chosen, where the level of any process may be defined arbitrarily as the amount of some one output emerging. The price relations we have described remain substantially the same. The only new possibility is that it may not pay to ship a by-product to markets but is more profitable to dispose of it locally at zero price (or at a cost).

14. Our discussion has been concerned with the allocation of supply sources and plant capacities to outputs, given the sales price or sales program. Such allocation problems arise regardless of the organizational structure of the product market. We have shown how the level of sales in each market by a firm is determined if the price is regarded as fixed or if, in addition, sales are limited by quotas. The determination of the sales policy in less extreme cases raises questions of monopolistic pricing policy which we prefer to avoid. In these cases allocation and sales problems cannot be disentangled in theory or practice; if (external) price in each market changes as the amount sold by the firm changes, the firm must know both the

marginal revenue and the marginal cost of each product in each market in order to attain its goal of maximizing profit. For a given combination of product sales at markets, however, a "suboptimization" problem—determining the internal production decisions which minimize cost—arises. To this problem an analysis such as the preceding one, involving internal resource and product prices and rents on plants at locations, is still applicable.

Implications for the Industry

If the industry is made up of several firms with branch plants each owning its supply deposits and, possibly, each with market quotas, an allocation which minimizes the cost to each firm of its deliveries to markets does not insure that the cost of providing the various markets with product has been minimized for the industry as a whole. An indication of this is that the internal prices of each firm, if quoted openly as market prices for purchases and sales of (limited quantities of) resources and products, might still permit arbitrage at a profit.

The allocation of resources in a firm with branch plants resembles that of an industry under competitive conditions. We permit the price determination problem, which is identical with the allocation problem, to become somewhat unusual in order to carry the analogy with the firm as far as possible. Let the demand for a product facing the industry in a given market location as well as the supply of resources at each deposit be perfectly elastic up to a point and thereafter be perfectly inelastic. Let all plants be rented to the firms operating them and assume that all resources are traded in competitive deposit markets. Then the previous internal prices are now market prices, profits (after paying rents) are zero for each firm; plant locations afford rents, and resource f.o.b. prices contain an element of rent reflecting the locational advantage of a deposit. The market price of product is either at or below the level at which the schedule is perfectly elastic, and can be below that level only if the saturation point of this market is reached.

The transition from the profit maximizing decisions of the firm to the competitive equilibrium of the industry described thus introduces no further analytical problems. In the absence of competition methods of a different nature from the ones we have used are needed in order to find the equilibrium allocation of resources in the industry.

Derivation of the Price Theorem[19]

(MATHEMATICAL SECTION)

We now derive formally the internal price conditions described in Section 2 which solve the allocation problem for a profit-maximizing firm with branch plants.

We shall treat here only the case in which limitations exist on the availability of resources at various deposits and on the output capacity of plants. After the principle has been established the generalizations provide no difficulties.

Let a firm be able to sell any amount of its unique product in market locations k at prices p_k. We assume that it controls a number of supply points of inputs or resources m, which yield maximum amounts of q_i^m per unit of time, no materials being brought from or sold to the outside. The f.o.b. price (extraction cost) of resource m at deposit i is denoted by p_i^m and is not necessarily the same for all i. The firm possesses a number of plants each at a different location. The plant at location j has output capacity c_j. All inputs are assumed proportional to output with the input coefficients a^m (the amount of input m required per unit output) the same everywhere. Let x_{ij}^m denote the flow of m from deposit i to plant location j, and let t_{ij}, t_{jk} denote transportation costs from i to j and j to k, respectively, per weight unit; all commodities are measured in weight units.

We are interested in the quotas of sales x_{jk} allotted to plant j in market k and the levels of production $\sum_k x_{jk}$ of plant j which will maximize profit to the firm. Under the present assumptions profit equals

1. $$P = \sum_{j,k} p_k x_{jk} - \sum_{i,j,m} p_j^m x_{ij}^m - \sum_{j,k} t_{jk} x_{jk} - \sum_{i,j,m} t_{ij} x_i^m$$
$$= \sum_{j,k} (p_k - t_{jk}) x_{jk} - \sum_{i,j,m} (p_i^m + t_{ij}) x_{ij}^m,$$

where the first term denotes net revenue from sales after transportation cost, and the second term is the gross procurement cost of inputs.

---

[19]The non-mathematical reader may turn directly to the *Conclusion* on p. 292.

The flows are related and constrained in various ways. First, receipts of materials at plant j must be at least equal to the input requirements:

2. $a^m \Sigma_k x_{jk} - \Sigma_i x^m_{ij} \leqq 0.$

Next shipments from a material deposit must not exceed its yield capacity:

3. $\Sigma_j x^m_{ij} \leqq q^m_i$

Finally, output must not exceed the plant's capacity:

4. $\Sigma_k x_{ik} \leqq c_j.$

In addition, we have the requirement that all the flows and productions levels be non-negative:

5. $x^m_{ij} \geqq 0. \; x_{jk} \geqq 0.$

The problem of maximizing a linear form of non-negative variables (such as 1.) subject to linear equations and inequalities (such as 2.–4.) as constraints is known as a linear programming problem.[20] Its unknowns here include the production levels and sales quotas of the plants and the flows of inputs from deposits to plant locations.

For any activity analysis problem it is possible, without actually computing, to characterize the solution in terms of a set of equations and inequalities known as the efficiency conditions.[21] We shall discuss these with reference to the present problem.

The efficiency conditions of activity analysis, though formulated for problems of choice among production activities, are a general set of conditions that must be fulfilled by any solution to a linear programming problem.

Theorem: Necessary and sufficient for $x = (x_k)$ to be a solution of

$$\text{Max } \Sigma_{x \; k=1}^{K} b_k x_k$$

subject to the constraints

1a. $\quad x_k \geqq 0 \qquad k = 1, \ldots K$

2a. $\quad \Sigma_{k=1}^{K} a_{nk} x_k \leqq c_n \quad n = 1, \ldots N$

is the existence of some set of numbers v_n such that

3a. $\quad \Sigma_{n=1}^{N} v_n a_{nk} \geqq b_k$ and "=" if $x_k > 0 \; k=1, .. \, K$

4a. $\quad v_n \geqq 0$ and "=" if $\Sigma_{k=1}^{K} a_{nk} x_k < c_n \; n=1, .. \, N$

The "efficiency conditions" (3a. and 4a.), together with the original constraints (1a.) and (2a.) are also sufficient (in addition to being necessary as stated before) for x to be a maximizing solution.

Let us denote the v-components associated with the inequalities 2., 3. and 4. by v^m_j, v^m_i and v_j, respectively. Then, as a consequence of 3a., when profits are maximized

6. $p^m_i + v^m_i + t_{ij} \geqq v^m_j \quad$ and "=" if $x^m_{ij} > 0$

7. $v_j + \Sigma_m a^m v^m_j \geqq p_k - t_{jk}$ and "=" if $x_{jk} > 0$

And because of 4a. the non-negative numbers v^m_j, v^m_i and v^k_i vanish respectively whenever in the associated inequalities the "$<$" sign applies.

In order to interpret (6.) let us tentatively identify v^m_j with the internal price of resoure m at plant j, and v^m_i with an internal rent on the deposit of resoure m at i. The sum $p^m_i + v^m_i$ then denotes the internal price or opportunity cost of resource m at deposit location i. (6.) therefore expresses a profitability condition for transportation of m from deposit i to plant j. In (7.) v_j now obviously represents an internal rent on plant per unit output. For then the left hand side of (7.) denotes the unit cost of production at plant j, and the right hand side the unit revenue. It is seen from the last sentence of the preceding paragraph, that both v^m_i and v_j have a property we have required of rents: they are zero if the relevant capacity is not reached.

This completes the proof (based on the indicated theorem of activity analysis) that in order for the required maximum to be attained it is necessary *and sufficient* that there exist internal resource prices, $p^m_i + v^m_i$ and v^m_j and internal plant rents v_j with the properties stated verbally in section 2.

Conclusion

We have seen that in a short run approach some of the peculiar difficulties that beset location

---

[20]Following the terminological suggestions of Koopmans the analysis of such linear programming problems that arise from resolving production into its constituent activities, as in the previous section, is called (linear) activity analysis.

[21]Cf. Koopmans, *op. cit.*, p. 86, theorem, 5. 6.

theory may be skirted and recourse may be had to the price theoretical methods of allocation and equilibrium analysis which activity analysis provides. This sheds light on the geographical distribution of observed prices and clarifies the role of internal or accounting prices as guides to allocation. Substitution takes the form of a variation of processes and of supply and market points. Because of short run rigidities in plant and market capacities there may not be freedom of substitution in all directions: the profit maxima occur at the edges of the possibility set, mathematically speaking, and this necessitates efficiency conditions in terms of marginal inequalities as well as equations.

But the resulting conditions of allocative optimization and equilibrium are intuitive: possible profits must not be positive and must equal zero in efficient activities. These are conditions that hold "in the small" and may be verified independent of each other. At the same time they are sufficient conditions, and this, it may be noted, is due to the fact that, in spite of discontinuities in the substitution relations, the law of decreasing returns to substitution is maintained. Details may be found in the theory of activity analysis on which this approach has been based.

Benjamin H. Stevens

LINEAR PROGRAMMING AND LOCATION RENT†

1. Introduction

Several recent papers discuss the application of linear programming techniques and models to problems in the location of economic activity. The papers by Beckmann [1], Berman [3], Isard [13], Lefeber [17], Samuelson [21], and Stevens [23] emphasizes the use of linear programming models to set forth the basic production, trade, and price relationships of a multi-location economy. Fox [7], Henderson [10], Judge [15], Morrill [19], and Snodgrass [22] are concerned with applications to empirical problems of spatial price equilibrium and distribution patterns for particular commodities. Moses [20] uses input-output coefficients and carload-waybill data to determine optimum levels of production and trade for a three-region breakdown of the U.S.

In almost every case the authors of these studies examine the dual variables in the "classical" linear programming manner. Shadow prices on capacities are interpreted as the marginal values of increasing those capacities; shadow prices on commodities are shown to be equal to marginal costs of production and/or to marginal revenue productivity; and the relationships between shadow prices in one location, transport costs to a sec-

ond location, and shadow prices in the second location are carefully spelled out.

However, there has been surprisingly little recognition of the relationship between dual prices in multi-location linear programming and the classical theory of location rent. Even in the standard work on the economics of linear programming, the opportunity to give a location rent interpretation to the dual of the "transportation" model is passed up in favor of a location advantage and value interpretation which indicates the structure of spatial price equilibrium without explaining its close connection with the theory of rent. This is particularly surprising in view of the fact that elsewhere the authors refer repeatedly to the general theory of scarcity rent.[1]

It is true that both Beckmann [1] and Stevens [23] make a partial location rent interpretation of certain of the dual variables produced in their models. However, in the former a somewhat restricted view is taken of the rent concept while in the latter there arise problems in separating differential location rent from overall scarcity rent. By combining the production and location problems these authors achieve generality at the cost of expositional simplicity. The location rent concept is entangled in the general argument about resource allocation among locations, and the important location rent implications of the dual are never made entirely clear.

The purpose of the present paper is to make up for these apparent deficiencies in the existing linear programming literature. At the same time, it is hoped that location and rent theory will gain from even closer association with the straightforward models and applicable methods of linear programming.

Reprinted with the permission of the author and publisher from the *Journal of Regional Science*, Vol. 3, No. 2, pp. 15-26. Dr. Stevens is Professor of Regional Science at the University of Pennsylvania, Philadelphia.

†This paper was done, in part, under a Ford Foundation Faculty Research Fellowship and this support is gratefully acknowledged. The conclusions, opinions, and views expressed are the writer's own, however, and are not necessarily those of the Ford Foundation. The writer is also grateful to the National Science Foundation, the Regional Science Research Institute, and Resources for the Future Inc. for support during the completion of the paper. The helpful comments and criticisms of William J. Baumol, Edwin von Boventer, William L. Garrison, and Duane F. Marble made possible substantial improvements from an earlier draft of the paper.

[1]Cf. Dorfman [5], esp. Chapter 5.

2. *The Transportation Problem*

The "transportation problem" of linear programming provides the simplest framework for the present discussion. It is often expressed as the problem of distributing a homogeneous commodity from several spatially separated sources (such as warehouses) to several spatially separated consumers in such a way as to minimize total transport costs.

We are given a homogeneous commodity and:

C_i = the capacity in units of the commodity of the warehouse at i ($i = 1, 2, \cdots, m$);

D_j = total demand for the commodity by consumers at j ($j = 1, 2, \cdots, n$);

t_{ij} = cost of shipping a unit of the commodity from i to j.

The problem is to find those

X_{ij} = the amount of the commodity shipped from i to j $\begin{array}{l}(i = 1, 2, \cdots, m) \\ (j = 1, 2, \cdots, n)\end{array}$

That minimize:

(2.1) $\quad Z = \sum\limits_{i=1}^{m} \sum\limits_{j=1}^{n} t_{ij} X_{ij}$, which is total transportation costs,

Subject to:

(2.2) $\quad \sum\limits_{i=1}^{m} X_{ij} \geq D_j$ ($j = 1, 2, \ldots, n$) which require that all demands be fulfilled; and:

(2.3) $\quad -\sum\limits_{j=1}^{n} X_{ij} \geq -C_i$ ($i = 1, 2, \ldots, m$) which prevent capacities from being exceeded; and finally:

(2.4) $\quad X_{ij} \geq 0$ $\begin{array}{l}(i = 1, 2, \cdots, m) \\ (j = 1, 2, \cdots, n)\end{array}$ since negative shipments are not allowed.

If we also specify:

(2.5) $\quad \sum\limits_{i=1}^{m} C_i = \sum\limits_{j=1}^{n} D_j$, total supply exactly equals total demand,

we can turn constraints (2.2-2.3) into equalities and use any of the usual methods for solving limited linear programs of this kind. The structure of the primal transportation problem and solution

methods for it are relatively common knowledge and require no further discussion here.[2]

The structure of the dual to the transportation problem is also simple but less well known. For the dual it is necessary to specify two new sets of variables:

u_i = the shadow price on (warehouse) capacity at i ($i = 1, 2, \cdots, m$): and

v_j = the shadow price on demand at j ($j = 1, 2, \cdots, n$).

The dual problem is to maximize:

(2.6) $\quad Z' = \sum\limits_{j=1}^{n} D_j v_j + \sum\limits_{i=1}^{m} - C_i u_i$

Subject to:

(2.7) $\quad v_j - u_i \leq t_{ij}$ $\begin{array}{l}(i = 1, 2, \cdots, m) \\ (j = 1, 2, \cdots, n)\end{array}$[3]

Notice that no verbal interpretation has been made of (2.6) or (2.7) or of the term "shadow price." It is the purpose of this paper to provide such an interpretation, one which will emphasize the close connection between the dual and the classical theory of location rent.

3. *Basic Interpretation of the Dual*

We start with the best current interpretation and call u_i the value of the commodity F.O.B. the source i, and v_j its value delivered at consumer j. In value terms, then, constraints (2.7) express the requirement that the value differential between origin and destination cannot exceed the transport costs involved in making the shipment from warehouse to consumer.[4] This is *like* the usual conditions of spatial price equilibrium, but it is somewhat strange to speak in value terms. Why not, then, speak in terms of prices? We have nowhere mentioned production costs and, in fact, have no

---

[2]Cf. Dorfman [5], Garvin [8], Gass [9], Vajda [25], or any other standard work on linear programming.

[3]Even if (2.5) is used to make constraints (2.2-2.3) into equalities, the dual constraints (2.7) must be expressed as potential inequalities, at least until the optimal solution is known. The mathematical reasons for this are discussed in Garvin [8]. The economic reasons will become clear below. Note also that we have placed no sign restrictions on the u's and v's. Garvin [8] and Bennion [2] explain the possibility of negative values for dual variables which correspond to constraints requiring strict equality. We will see below that the possible existence of negative shadow prices in no way affects the argument to be made.

[4]Dorfman [5, p 124].

way in which to determine "price" in the usual sense. But let us assume a price, p, which expresses production costs (including normal profits) and call this the base price of the commodity at all locations. Notice that we can incorporate this base price into constraints (2.7) by rewriting them as:

$$(3.1) \quad (v_j + p) - (u_i + p) \leq t_{ij} \quad \begin{array}{l} (i = 1, 2, \cdots, m) \\ (j = 1, 2, \cdots, n) \end{array}$$

without, in fact, altering the constraints. Since the base price also appears as both a positive and a negative in the objective function (2.6) the value of the latter will likewise be unaffected.[5]

We may now speak of $(u_i + p)$ as the F.O.B. price at i and $(v_j + p)$ as the delivered price at j. Constraints (3.1) express the usual conditions of spatial price equilibrium.

Let us concentrate first on delivered price to see how it is determined. Clearly the delivered price at each location is the result of a spatial competition among the various suppliers of the good. There is also competition among consumption points trying to obtain limited available supplies of the good. But we begin by assuming away this latter problem by considering a case with only a single consumption location.

In Figure 1, DD' is the perfectly inelastic demand for D_j units posited for location j. The supply curve SS' *at location j* is a composite of the supplies available from four warehouses: e, f, g, and h. If we assume an equal F.O.B. price, p, at all warehouses, the delivered supply price from the "nearest" warehouse e is $OE = p + t_{ej}$ and C_e is the amount which can be supplied at this price. Similarly the supply price from f is $OF = p + t_{fj}$ and so on. Observe that SS' is a step function. This is because once the supply of a nearer warehouse is used up, the delivered price must rise enough to cover the *extra* transportation charges incurred in drawing upon a warehouse farther away.

Clearly, in this simple example, $(v_j + p) = OG =$ the equilibrium delivered price at j. OG also equals the delivered price on the commodity shipped from the warehouse at g, or $(p + t_{gj})$. If

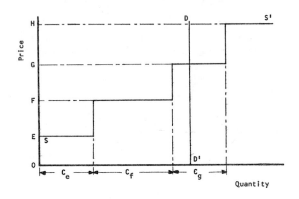

FIGURE 1   Demand and Supply Curves for a Transportation Problem With a Single Consumption Location.

we substitute $(p + t_{gj})$ for $(v_j + p)$ in constraints (3.1) and recall that for shipments actually made, the corresponding dual constraints must be equalities, we find:[6]

$$(3.2) \quad \begin{aligned} v_j &= t_{gj} \\ u_g &= v_j - t_{gj} = 0 \\ u_f &= v_j - t_{fj} = t_{gj} - t_{fj} \\ u_e &= v_j - t_{ej} = t_{gj} - t_{ej} \end{aligned}$$

Equations (3.2) provide us with a means of determining the values of the u's for the three supplying warehouses in terms of known constant transportation costs. But what do the u's mean? They are, in fact, location rents within the classical meaning of the term. For notice that the equilibrium delivered price is established by the delivered price from the "farthest" warehouse actually supplying the consumers at j. This farthest warehouse g earns zero rent. Closer warehouses f and e receive differential location rents equal exactly to the amounts saved on transportation on units sup-

---

[5]This would be true, of course, only as long as we assume (2.5). For if we do not assume equality of total supply and total demand, we cannot be sure that:

$$\sum_{i=1}^{m} C_i p = \sum_{j=1}^{n} D_j p.$$

---

[6]Notice that we have made the sum of the supplies from the four warehouses greater than the demand at j. The purpose was to point up, even in this simple problem, the possibility of warehouses which are unable to compete at a particular consumption point. Shipments are not made from warehouse h because $u_h - v_j < t_{hj}$. Furthermore in this simple case, $u_h = 0$.

This would not necessarily be true if there were alternative consumption locations which might be supplied by h. But even in the latter case, the inequality above would hold if h were not at least a potential supplier of j at equilibrium prices. This is a requirement of both duality theory and the theory of spatial price equilibrium. For further discussion see Samuelson [21].

plied by them as opposed to units supplied by g.[7]

It is important to keep in mind that the u_i are the correct rents only on marginal units of capacity at each warehouse location. A small capacity at a high-rent location such as e could earn the same location rent, u, per unit as is earned by the original C_e. But suppose that enough units of capacity were added at e to allow the demand at j to be fulfilled by e and f alone, eliminating g from competition. In this case, we would have:

$$
\begin{aligned}
u_g &= 0 \\
v_j &= t_{fj} \\
u_f &= v_j - t_{fj} = 0 \\
u_e &= v_j - t_{ej} = t_{fj} - t_{ej}
\end{aligned}
$$
(3.3)

A comparison of equations (3.2) and (3.3) shows that, as expected, the elimination of g from the market at j reduced the location rents at e and f. The original location rents would be correct over a *range* of capacities at e and f, at least in this case. But suppose that g had been supplying only one unit to j. Then the total capacity at e and f could be increased only by less than one unit if rents were to remain unaffected.

Now suppose a marginal unit of warehouse capacity were established at the highest-rent location of all, the market itself. A warehouse at j would incur no transportation cost in supplying demand at j. Therefore, by the argument of (3.2), u_j for such a warehouse would be:

(3.4) $\qquad u_j = v_j - t_{jj} = v_j - 0 = v_j$

In other words, the dual supplies a direct measure of location rent per unit on marginal warehouse capacity established at market. We can and will interpret the v_j as just such location rents.

It is important to reiterate that the v_j, like the u_i, are rents on marginal units only. For suppose, as an extreme example, that enough warehouse capacity were established at j to supply the total

demand of j. Then no transport costs at all would be incurred, and the location rents would all be zero. As theory tells us, and as equations (3.2-3.4) emphasize, the existence of transport costs is basic to the existence of location rents.

As already suggested, the location rents would be smaller if total transport costs were lower. But total transport costs are a function of both the distance of each consumption location from its supplying warehouse(s) and the consumption demand. If demand at a location were reduced enough, the location could be supplied completely by "nearby" warehouses and the level of the location rents would fall. The effect would be the same as that achieved by making substantial increases in the capacities of nearby warehouses. Referring again to Figure 1, if demand were reduced until DD' fell in the range C_f, e and f would provide all the necessary supply and the location rent levels would be in accordance with equations (3.2).[8]

The relationship between the level of demand and the level of location rents provides an economic rationale for the necessary mathematical relationship between the D_j and the v_j. The rents u_i on the scarce capacities C_i are expected in linear programs and can be interpreted quite naturally. But the rents v_j on demands D_j do not appear to submit to such natural interpretation and create something of a problem in the usual discussions of the dual to the transportation problem. The location rent concept avoids this problem, however. Once the dual is thought of as a location rent system the v_j become merely another set of such rents, not really different in kind from the u_i themselves.

The location rent v_j at the consumption loca-

[7]It is interesting here to quote Marshall [18, p. 441], who writes, "If . . . two producers have equal facilities in all respects, except that one has more convenient situation than the other and can buy or sell in the same markets with less cost of carriage, his differential advantage . . . is the aggregate of the excess charges for cost of carriage to which his rival is put; . . . this becomes the situation value of his site."

The term "situation value" used by Marshall means exactly the same thing as our term "location rent." It appears that Marshall does not use the latter term because he wishes to avoid confusion among the various causes (fertility differences, location, etc.) of "rent" to land. For further discussion of location rent, see Hoover [12, Ch. 1].

[8]Throughout the discussion it has been emphasized that the location rents are rents per unit of commodity or commodity capacity. It is tempting to tie the discussion even more closely to classical theory by transforming rents per unit commodity into rents per unit of land. If there were a one-to-one correspondence between commodity units and land units, this might be possible. But it might also be misleading. Warehouse capacity for a particular commodity is a specialized resource which may be scarce at a location relative to effective demand at that location. But land is a more general resource which becomes an input to all types of warehousing as well as other economic activities. It would be a mistake, therefore, to attempt to establish location rents on land on the basis of anything less than a full scale location model for all land-using activities. In such a model it might be found that for an equilibrium rent system part of what we have been calling scarcity rent would actually be rent on scarce capacity and part would be rent on land. In order to keep the exposition simple, therefore, we deal only with the rents to "locations" in the supply of a particular commodity. A discussion of a system with both "scarcity" and "land" rents can be found in Stevens [23].

tion is earned, indirectly, by outlying warehouses at a rate discounted by transport costs as indicated by equations (3.2). In this case there is a complete location rent "surface" for the three origins and the one destination. The rent-surface concept becomes much more meaningful when there are several consumption points and many warehouses, however. A full discussion is thus postponed to the next section of the paper where multi-destination models are presented.

First, however, we are still faced with the problem of interpreting the dual objective function (2.6). To do this we posit a set of purely competitive traders who distribute the good in question. This means that the traders buy the commodity at the warehouses, ship it to the consumption point, and resell it to consumers there. The unit profit w_{ij} of a trader on a transaction between i and j is:

(3.5) $w_{ij} = (v_j + p) - (u_i + p) - t_{ij}$ or delivered price minus the sum of F.O.B. price plus transport costs.

Be eliminating the p's we obtain:

(3.5a) $$w_{ij} = v_j - u_i - t_{ij}$$

Now we know that the traders will attempt to maximize profits individually. But in our purely competitive, though spatial, world this can be measured as joint profit maximization of all traders on all transaction taken together. We should then consider the traders' total profits:

(3.6)
$$W = \sum_i \sum_j w_{ij} X_{ij} = \sum_j \sum_i X_{ij} v_j - \sum_i \sum_j X_{ij} u_i - \sum_i \sum_j X_{ij} t_{ij}$$

By (2.2), (2.3), and (2.5) we have $\sum_j X_{ij} = C_i$ and $\sum_i X_{ij} = D_j$ for all i, j. If we substitute these expressions in (2.10), we can rewrite it as:

(3.6a) $W = (\sum_j D_j v_j - \sum_i C_i u_i) - \sum_i \sum_j X_{ij} t_{ij}$

The two terms in the parenthesis on the right-hand side of (3.6a) are equal to Z' which is the dual objective function (2.6). The last term of (3.6a) is equal to Z which is the primal objective function (2.1). Then the maximization of W is accomplished by maximizing the difference between Z' and Z subject to both the primal and dual constraints. But by a fundamental theorem in

linear programming, this will be accomplished by simultaneously maximizing Z' and minimizing Z. The maximum of Z' will turn out to be equal the minimum of Z so that the traders will, in fact, make zero profits. Nevertheless, their attempt to profit from trade will lead to optimal solutions for both the primal and dual problems.

The rationale for the minimization of transport costs in the primal was obvious. The attempt to maximize profits from trade is a reasonable objective for the trader group. No further explanation or interpretation of the dual objective function (2.6) is therefore necessary. We attempt to maximize (2.6) merely because it is consistent with the attempt to maximize (3.6a) and minimize (2.1).

The traders' profitless condition is also consistent with spatial price equilibrium. For suppose that somewhere short of an optimal solution a trader noticed a price spread greater than transport costs. He would then enter trade and continue until supply-demand conditions would force the delivered price down and the F.O.B. price up until the spread exactly equalled transport costs. He cannot stop short of this point and pocket profits; the rules of linear programming prevent this. But so does economic theory if traders are truly competitive. There will always be the marginal trader attempting to extract the last little bit of profit from a miniscule price spread and he will spoil the game for everyone else. There might not be much demand for the job of trader in a linear programming world. But it need not concern us that the traders chase ephemeral profits and eventually become victims of unfilled expectations; at least they do not lose anything.[9]

4. Location Rent Surfaces

With the basic concepts established, we may now interpret the dual of our transportation problem in full. First, we extend our graphic presentation to several warehouses and consumption

---

[9]The use of traders to force price equilibrium was introduced by Isard and Ostroff [14]. The viewpoint of these authors was somewhat different, but the results obtained were virtually the same: the attempt of traders to maximize profits leads to a minimization of the transport costs necessary to support the spatial equilibrium system, to profitless price relationships on shipments actually made, and to unprofitable price relationships on all other possible shipments.

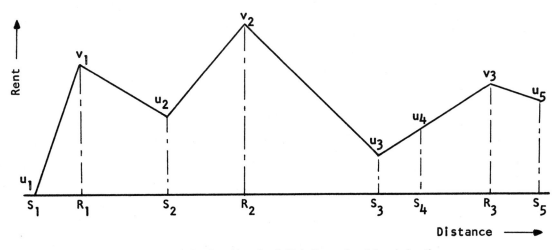

FIGURE 2 Location Rents and Transport Gradient Lines for Multiple Demand and Supply Locations.

locations in accordance with (2.1-2.7). Figure 2 provides an example for five warehouses and three consumers located along a line.

Notice that in Figure 2 the base line is also assumed to be the base price line for equal production cost p. Thus the heights of the vertical lines are the direct measure of location rents at both warehouses and consumption locations. Furthermore, sloping "transport gradient" lines have been used to connect warehouses S_i with the consumption locations R_j which they serve. As drawn, these gradients imply that delivered price rises at a constant rate per unit distance as one leaves a particular warehouse in a given direction. This would further imply constant transport costs per unit distance over any line segment in a given direction. Alternative transport cost assumptions such as zone rates or decreasing rates over longer distances would of course be possible, but only fixed unit rates for any warehouse-consumer pair are consistent with the requirement of constant t_{ij} in the linear programming formulation.

In the linear program we are given only the cost of moving a unit of the commodity from point to point; transport *rates* per unit distance are not defined. If they were defined they might yield smooth, or even straight, transport gradient lines. Since they are not, the transport gradients in Figure 2 should technically be replaced by discontinuous jumps equal to the t_{ij} for each origin-destination pair much as in Figure 1. As long as it is understood that the smooth gradiants are merely

an assumption, however, they turn out to be a rather useful fiction. In particular, they allow us to discuss what would happen to new warehouses or consumer locations entering the system in between established points.

Several other features of the figure require comment. First notice that warehouse S_1 is the only one which earns zero rent while consumers at R_2 and R_3 are served completely by warehouses earning non-zero rents. This is not inconsistent with our previous statements on the generation of rents, however. The warehouse at S_1 is the marginal supplier, not only to R_1, but to the whole interconnected *system* of consumption points. Rent u_5 arises because S_5 supplies R_3 which is also supplied by S_3 which also supplies R_2 which is also served by S_2 which supplies R_1, which finally, receives supplies from S_1 with $u_1 = 0$. The whole structure of rents depends on the existence of a zero rent on some warehouse location. But if there is complete interconnection there need be only one such location. It is only because of the competition for the supplies available from S_3 that rent arises at this point. For suppose S_3 supplied R_3 only. Then u_3 would drop to zero, and u_4, v_3, and u_5 would be cut by the same amount. The case of S_2 is a little more complicated, however. If S_2 were to supply R_1 only, u_2 would depend on the zero rent paid at S_1 and would remain at the level shown in the figure. If S_2 *supplied* R_2 only and S_3 also continued to supply R_2, then u_2 would fall until u_3 was equal to zero. S_3 would then provide the zero-rent margin for both R_2 and R_3. Finally, if S_2 supplied R_2 only and S_3 supplied R_3 only, both u_2 and u_3 would be zero.

Whatever the rent and supply structure is, it must be consistent with the maximization of (2.6), the minimization of (2.1) and the fulfillment of constraints (2.2)-(2.7). In the interconnected system of Figure 2, it is extremely easy to compute rents at every point. For example, $u_3 = v_2 - t_{32}$, $v_2 = u_2 + t_{22}$, $u_2 = v_1 - t_{12}$, $v_1 = u_1 + t_{11}$ so that $u_3 = u_1 + t_{11} - t_{12} + t_{22} - t_{32}$.[10] Fortunately, most distribution problems demonstrate this interconnectivity. But even where there is an optimal solution with disconnected groups of warehouses and consumers, rents are easy to compute once the zero-rent points are known.

It is possible to generalize the foregoing by introducing the concept of the rent surface. Figure 2 of course provides a highly restricted example of such surface. But if warehouses and consumers were distributed over areas rather than along lines, and warehouses were connected to the consumers they supply by transport gradient lines, the basic structure of such a surface would be established. The completion of the surface would require merely the assumption that a marginal producer could supply a miniscule quantity or a marginal consumer buy a miniscule quantity at any intermediate point at a price established by the surface at that point. In the simplified case of Figure 2, S_4 is an example of such a point if we assume that it supplies only a small fraction of the demands at R_3.

It is important to bear in mind that the rent surface for the typical transportation problem will not be a series of intersecting "tents" such as those found in Von Thünen [24], Hoover [12], and Dunn [6]. Rather they will be a series of intersecting lines, often with slope discontinuities at points where transport rates change. Again referring to our figure, u_4 could have been substantially higher or lower than the line joining u_3 and v_3 if the per-unit-distance transport rate were different to the right and left of S_4. But the major difference from the "tent" structure is due to the discreteness of location in manageable transportation problems of the type being discussed. The usual tent surfaces arise only when transport costs are a linear function of distance and when suppliers are spatially extensive and more or less uniformly distributed. Farmers and the suppliers of certain basic commodities appear to provide the only examples of such extensive and numerous areas of supply.

5. Conclusions

Our discussion was limited to the transportation problem for expositional purposes only. As already suggested, much of the foregoing can be (and to some extent has been) applied to more general linear programming models of location, production, and trade. It seems appropriate to generalize even further and suggest that location theory and location rent theory are mutually dual. This would not be a particularly original or even useful suggestion were it not for the confusions that exist, particularly in the location theory literature, concerning the existence, meaning, and implications of location rent. If it were made clear that location and distribution theory and the theory of rent are really just two different ways of looking at the same phenomena, much of this confusion might be avoided.

The fact that rents arise when transport costs are incurred tends to take spatial economics out of the main stream of the economics of pure competition and place it in the less well-defined areas of monopolistic competition. But if the monopoly rents in location models are due to location *alone*, many of the assumptions and conclusions of pure competition remain valid. In particular, if all consumers can draw upon large numbers of suppliers and transport inputs are competitively priced, the classical theory of pure competition is directly

---

[10]And also, for example, $u_2 - v_3 < t_{23}$. There will be many relationships of this latter kind appearing in the dual to every transportation problem. For m warehouses and n consumers, there will generally be $m + n$ shipments in the solution of the primal and $mn - m - n$ price spread inequalities in the dual together with $m + n - 1$ price spread equalities corresponding to the $m + n$ shipments being made. The fact that there is one less dual equation than potentially non-zero dual variables allows us to set one variable arbitrarily equal to zero. We ordinarily pick one of the u_i since we know that some supplying warehouse must have a zero location rent. On the basis of this arbitrary selection the system of rents may, as previously suggested, contain some negative values. It is then perfectly permissible to take the lowest rent value, set it equal to zero, and recompute all other rents in terms of this one. This is legitimate because the dual sets only relative, not absolute, rent values. Since in any practical problem no supplying location would command a negative rent, and since at least one location must command a zero rent, this adjustment procedure merely allows us to reproduce a realistic rent structure by shifting the level of the rent surface without altering its shape. For further discussion see Dorfman, [5. p. 125].

applicable. The natural monopoly of site[11] is not nearly as difficult to handle in theory or in practice in location analysis as the problems of input substitution over space[12] or external economies due to locational agglomeration.[13]

REFERENCES

[1] Beckmann, M. and T. Marschak, "An Activity Analysis Approach to Location Theory," *Kyklos*, 8 Fasc. 2, (1955), pp. 125-141. [page 287 of this volume.]

[2] Bennion, E. G. *Elementary Mathematics of Linear Programming and Game Theory*, East Lansing, Mich.: Michigan State University Press, 1960.

[3] Berman, E. B., "A Spatial and Dynamic Growth Model," *Papers and Proceedings of the Regional Science Association*, 5, (1959), pp. 143–150.

[4] Chamberlin, E. H., *The Theory of Monopolistic Competition*, Cambridge, Mass.: Harvard University Press, 1933.

[5] Dorfman, R., P. A. Samuelson and R. M. Solow, *Linear Programming and Economic Analysis*, New York: McGraw-Hill, 1958.

[6] Dunn, E. S., Jr., *The Location of Agricultural Production*, Gainesville, Fla.: University of Florida Press, 1954.

[7] Fox, A., "A Spatial Equilibrium Model of the Livestock Feed Economy in the U.S.," *Econometrica*, 21, (1953), pp. 547–566.

[8] Garvin, W. W., *Introduction to Linear Programming*, New York: McGraw-Hill, 1960.

[9] Gass, S. I. *Linear Programming, Methods and Applications*, New York: McGraw-Hill 1958.

[10] Henderson, J. M., "A Short-Run Model for the Coal Industry," *Review of Economics and Statistics*, 37, (1955), pp. 224-230, and "Efficiency and Pricing in the Coal Industry," *op. cit.*, Vol. 37, (1955), pp. 50-60.

[11] Hitchcock, F. L., "The Distribution of a Product from Several Sources to Numerous Localities," *Journal of Mathematics and Physics*, 20, (1941), pp. 224-230.

[12] Hoover, E. M., *Location Theory and the Shoe and Leather Industries*, Cambridge, Mass.: Harvard University Press, 1937.

[13] Isard, W., "Interregional Linear Programming: An Elementary Presentation and a General Model," *Journal of Regional Science*, 1, (1958), pp. 1-59.

[14] Isard, W., and D. J. Ostroff, "General Interregional Equilibrium," *Journal of Regional Science*, 2, (1960), pp. 67-74.

[15] Judge, G. G., "Competition Position of the Connecticut Poultry Industry-A Spatial Equilibrium Model for Eggs," *Bulletin 318*, Storrs Agricultural Experiment Station, University of Connecticut, January, 1956.

[16] Koopmans, T. C., "Optimum Utilization of the Transportation System," *Proceedings of the International Statistical Conference*, Washington, D. C., 5, (1947), (Reprinted as Supplement to *Econometrica*, 17, 1949).

[17] Lefeber, L., *Allocation in Space, Production, Transport and Industrial Location*, Amsterdam, Neth.: North Holland Publishing Co., 1958.

[18] Marshall, A., *Principles of Economics*, (Seventh Edn.), London: Macmillan, 1916.

[19] Morrill, R. L., "A Model of Interregional Movement," *Proceedings of the XIXth International Geographical Congress*, Stockholm, 1960.

[20] Moses, L. N., "A General Equilibrium Model of Production, Interregional Trade, and Location of Industry," *Review of Economics and Statistics*, 42, (1960).

[21] Samuelson, P. A. "Spatial Price Equilibrium and Linear Programming," *American Economic Review*, 42, (1952), pp. 283-303.

[22] Snodgrass, M. M., and C. E. French, *Linear Programming Approach to Interregional Competition in Dairying*. Agricultural Experiment Station, Purdue University, 1958.

[23] Stevens, B. H., "An Interregional Linear Programming Model," *Journal of Regional Science*, 1, (1958), pp. 60-98.

[24] von Thünen, J. H., *Der Isolierte Staat in Beziehung auf Landwirtschaft und Nationalokonomie*, Hamburg, 1826.

[25] Vajda, S., *Readings in Linear Programming*, London: Pitman, 1958.

[26] Weber, A., *Theory of the Location of Industries*, transl. Carl J. Friedrich, Chicago, 1929.

---

[11]Cf. Chamberlin [4] for further discussion.
[12]Cf. Lefeber [17] for extensive analysis of this problem.
[13]Cf. Hoover [12], or Weber [26].

Brian J. L. Berry and H. Gardiner Barnum

AGGREGATE RELATIONS AND ELEMENTAL COMPONENTS OF CENTRAL PLACE SYSTEMS†

Recently completed studies of central place systems permit us to summarize the fundamental characteristics of these systems in a compact set of equations.[1] The equations, empirically derived, but theoretically meaningful, reveal that both a continuum of places and a classic central place hierarchy are to be found in any region. If a small relatively homogeneous subregion is studied, the existence of a hierarchy of urban centers is most apparent, as for example in the case of the centers indicated in Figure 1 and described in Table 1. However, even in the area depicted some variability exists from place to place.[2] If, on the other hand, much larger areas are studied, the heterogeneity is greater and inter- and intra-area differences combine to create a continuum. For example, a scatter diagram utilizing data for a nine-county area including the counties shown in Figure 1, with population of central places plotted on the ordinate and number of retail, service, and other establishments on the abscissa is linear and continuous, and the correlation of population and establishments is 0.98. Greater homoscedasticity is ensured by transformation of both variables to common logarithms. After transformation, the correlation is 0.96, with the regression of population on establishments having the form: Log population $= -163 + 17.64$ (Log establ.). As is noted below, an interrelated series of such functional relationships appears to be universal throughout central place systems.

Principal components analysis of incidence matrices of central functions in central places permits the isolation of the continuous and hierarchical aspects of central place systems and identification of the levels of the hierarchy. This paper reports on one such analysis in detail. It is the first study, we believe, to isolate and measure the relative significance of the continuum and the hierarchy in a central place system. Questions have been raised about the value of components analysis in regional science, and particularly about the "interpretation" of components. This paper attempts to answer some of these questions.

Basic Features of a Central Place System

A system of central places develops in a region to serve the consumers living in that region with the goods and services they require. If the region is an extensive rural area, then the central places which develop to serve the rural residents are hamlets, villages, towns and cities. Consumers requiring service also live within these urban centers however, and in the intra-urban case, neighborhood, community and other business centers constitute the central place system.[3]

Reprinted with the permission of the authors and publisher from the *Journal of Regional Science*, Vol. 4, No. 1, 1962, pp. 35–42. Dr. Berry is Professor of Geography at the University of Chicago; Dr. Barnum is Assistant Professor of Geography at the University of Vermont.

†Thanks are expressed to the Geography Branch, U. S. Office of Naval Research, for support under Contract NONR 2121-18, Project NR 389-126.

[1]The studies began with a review of the literature, reported in Berry and Pred [6]. Results of empirical investigations undertaken subsequently are drawn together in Berry [3].

[2]For further details concerning the Iowa study area refer to Berry, Barnum and Tennant [4].

[3]But not specialized localizations such as automobile row, or the variety of commercial ribbons, for which different locational processes must be postulated.

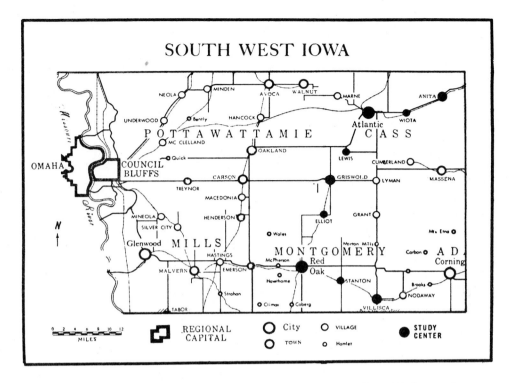

FIGURE 1 Study Centers Located Beyond the 30-mile Sphere of Influence of Omaha Council Bluffs east of the Missouri are arranged in a city-village-town-city . . . Hierarchy along U.S. highways.

TABLE I Characteristics of Market Centers in Southwest Iowa, 1960

TYPE OF CENTER	CENTRAL PLACE	POPULATION	NUMBER OF	
			BUSINESS TYPES	ESTABLISHMENTS
City	Red Oak	6,421	90	312
	Atlantic	6,890	92	411
Town	Griswold	1,207	50	102
	Anita	1,273	50	84
	Villisca	1,690	43	90
	Oakland	1,340	49	97
Village	Lewis	501	24	43
	Elliott	459	26	42
	Stanton	514	21	28

To describe the basic relationships which characterize a central place system we need definitions of several variables:

P_c The population of a central place, or more generally, the number of people supported by those activities of the place that serve people residing outside that place.

P_{ex} The population of the trade area served by a central place.

$P_t = P_c + P_{ex}$ The total population served by a central place (obviously for business centers serving only urban residents within a city $P_t = P_{ex}$, for such a business center does not support a readily denumerable population P_c in the same sense as a village, town, or city serving surrounding rural areas).

303

D_m The maximum distance that consumers travel to a central place of a given size.[4]

A The area of trade served.

Q_{ex} Population density of the outlying trade area served by a central place.

Q_t Gross population density of the entire area served by a center, outlying and the center itself.

C The number of central functions performed by a central place (i.e. the number of separate types of business).

E The number of establishments located in a central place.

F The number of "functional units" in a center. In larger centers this will, in general, be the same as E, but in smaller centers it will exceed E because such combinations as, for example, gas station and general store in the same establishment in hamlets are recorded separately.

f Reads "some function of" and in the context below will equal πD_m if rural densities are uniform and a transport surface obtains.

Log Common base ten logarithms are used.

Three *equalities* should also be defined:

(E.1) $$A = f(D_m)$$

(E.2) $$P_{ex} = AQ_{ex} = f(D_m)Q_{ex}$$

and since the area of a central place makes a negligible contribution to the size of A

(E.3) $$P_t = AQ_t = f(D_m)Q_t$$

We can now write the system of *structural equations* as:

(1) $$Log\ P_c = a_1 + b_1 C$$

(2) $$Log\ F = a_2 + b_2 C$$

(3) $$Log\ F = \left(\frac{b_1 a_2 - a_1 b_2}{b_1}\right) + \frac{b_2}{b_1}\ Log\ P_c$$

or (3.1) $$Log\ F = a_3 + b_3\ Log\ P_c$$

(4) $$Log\ D_m = a_4 + b_4 C$$

with the *implications* that:

(5) $$Log\ P_{ex} = Log\ Q_{ex} + Log\ [f\{Log^{-1}(a_4 + b_4 C)\}]$$

(6) $$Log\ A = Log\ [f\{Log^{-1}(a_4 - b_4 a_1 b_1^{-1})\ P_c^{b_4/b_1}\}]$$

(7) $$Log\ P_t = Log\ Q_t \\ + Log\ [f\{Log^{-1}(a_4 - b_4 a_1 b_1^{-1})\ P_c^{b_4/b_1}\}]$$

Equation (1) is a simple statement about the relationship between the population of a central place and the basic activities of that place: Population of a center displays a log-linear pattern of association with the number of different central functions performed by the center. Elsewhere, we have shown number of central functions to be an accurate index of the "centrality" (or information content) of a place, and thus, the drawing power of that place.[5] A given number of basic functions performed for surrounding areas supports a given number of jobs, and, adding the workers' families, people. Allowing for secondary effects, the population residing in the center follows as a natural consequence. Since the relationship is log-linear, the population multiplier works in such a way that for each new central function added, population increases by a constant percentage of its previous size.[6]

Secondary effects are expressed in equation (2), which shows the number of functional units to increase by a constant percentage of the previous total for each central function added. Available data reveal that b_2 and b_1 are not significantly different;[7] hence, number of functional units increases linearly as the urban population increases, see (3) and (3.1). This means that multiplication of establishments of the same kind is in direct response to growing demands within the urban center.[8]

Equation (1) may, in practice, only be applied to central places serving surrounding rural areas. However, (2) and (3) apply in both the

---

[4] This is defined operationally as the upper asymptote of the logistic curve that describes the cumulative distribution of consumers with increasing distance from a central place.

[5] Berry, Barnum, and Tennant [4].
[6] *Ibid.*, for a further discussion of this condition of "macroscopic negentropy."
[7] *Ibid.*
[8] Several other implications follow: (1) as new functions are added at the top (i.e., as "higher order" functions are added), it is the lower order functions which duplicate; (2) the duplication of lower order establishments is accompanied by development of secondary or nonbasic business centers subsidiary to the CBD, which contains the basic central functions. Thus we also find $BC = a_5 + b_5\ P_c$ or $BC = a_6 + b_5$, where BC is the number of business centers located within a city.

urban and the rural cases, so that there is no doubt that (1) would also apply within the city if total population supported by jobs in any business center could be estimated.

Residuals suggesting "population excess" will be found from (1) in regions where certain urban centers perform specialized economic activities, especially of a primary and secondary kind. Such cases indicate clearly that a good fit to (1) is to be expected where urban places are fundamentally market and service centers for surrounding regions. On the other hand, we should expect (3) to provide a good fit in all cases, including those where large residuals from (1) are to be found. This indeed appears to be the case.[9]

Equation (4) implies a limit: that there is a maximum distance which consumers travel to a center of any particular size. This limit has been called elsewhere "the range of a good."[10] Whether the limit reflects the "outer range" (maximum distance a consumer is willing to travel in the absence of alternatives) or the "real range" (beyond which the consumer will travel to a competing alternative) is not critical. What is important is that the centrality of a center at the same time determines and is constrained by the size of the surrounding area which is served.

The trade area served is some function of maximum distance consumers will travel (E.1). Similarly area multiplied by population density gives total population residing in the trade area (E.2). It should immediately be apparent that trade area population is a function of densities and size of center (5). Hence, trade area increases as the population of centers increases exponentially (6), and increases in total population served depend upon densities and the exponential increase in urban population (7).

That (7) is valid depends upon (E.1), (E.3), (1) and (4). Figure 2 shows how (E.3) applies in four different cases of gross densities in the United States, one urban, one suburban, one in the corn belt, and one in the wheatlands.[11] The two most fundamental structural equations are thus (1) and (4), which respectively relate population and functions of centers, and trade area and these same functions. In any area, since trade area increases as numbers of functions increase, there must be fewer larger centers with larger trade areas; the larger trade areas in turn imply wider spacing. This is as it should be, since central place theory concerns the size, spacing, and functions of urban centers.[12]

Three empirically derived inequalities complement the system of structural equations:

$$(8) \qquad Log \, A_{villages} < 10.4 - 2.67 \, Log \, P$$

$$(9) \qquad Log \, A_{towns} < 9.3 - 2.067 \, Log \, P$$

$$(10) \qquad Log \, A_{cities} < 22.25 - 4.75 \, Log \, P$$

Just as the first six equations described a variety of continuous functional relationships, so these three inequalities identify discontinuities resulting from the existence of an urban hierarchy.[13]

The major implication of classical central place theory is that of a hierarchy of central places. Inequalities (8)-(10) identify certain upper limits of area and population served at any gross population density; these limits are expressions of the maximum size of centers at any level of the hierarchy, given the local "environmental constraint" of population density, or distribution of consumers to be served. Figure 3 enables one to visualize the implications: as population densities diminish, centers of any rank serve larger areas, but fewer people, hence becoming simpler in function.[14]

But what is the justification for (8)-(10)? In Figure 3 the corn belt (S. W. Iowa) cases have been plotted with order in the hierarchy identified (village, town, city, regional capital — see also Table 1 and Figure 1). Similar plots for each other area enabled the upper bounds (8)-(10) to be placed in Figure 3 with remarkable precision: only a straight-edge was required.[15] Inequalities (8)-(10) express the result.

In each case the identification of the levels of the hierarchy and the allocation of centers to

[9]See Berry, Barnum, and Tennant [4] for examples.
[10]See for example Barnum [1].
[11]Berry [3] contains the basic studies.

[12]Berry and Pred [6].
[13]The three inequalities also apply to streetcorner (convenience), neighborhood, and community centers within cities, respectively, thereby revealing real consistency between the urban and rural cases. For a further discussion of this point, refer to Tennant [15].
[14]Tennant [15] provides a theoretical rationale, couched in terms of the interaction between conditions of entry of firms and distances consumers are willing to travel. Note that Figure 3 adds two more cases: the extensive rangelands, and the "dispersed city" wherein the first possibilities for locational specialization exist.
[15]A subsequent set of least squares fits produced identical limits, with each r^2 exceeding 0.98.

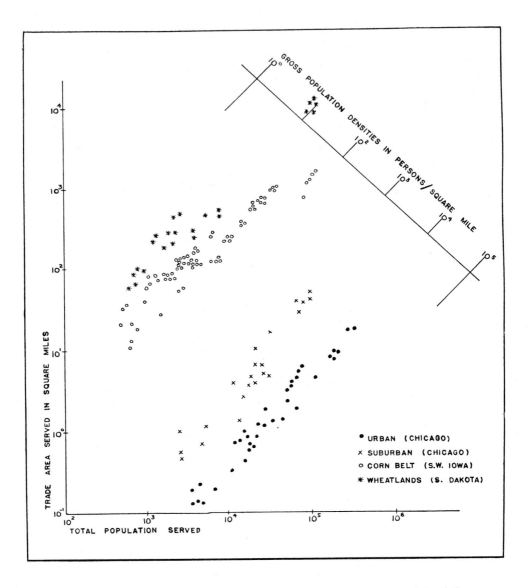

FIGURE 2 Four Examples of the Relationship Between Trade Area, Population Served, and Population Densities.

these levels was accomplished by a principal components analysis of an incidence matrix recording the presence or absence of central functions in central places. Separate analyses were completed for every area. Yet when the results were plotted in Figure 3, the consistency expressed by (8)-(10) resulted. Apparently, then, consistent patterns of variation of central place systems are to be found, not only in terms of the relationships expressed by equations (1), (4) and their implications, but also in terms of the discontinuities of a hierarchy (8), (9) and (10).[16]

---

[16]Note also that the consistency transcends urban, suburban and rural differences. For further light on the discontinuities at the urban and suburban levels, see Tennant [15].

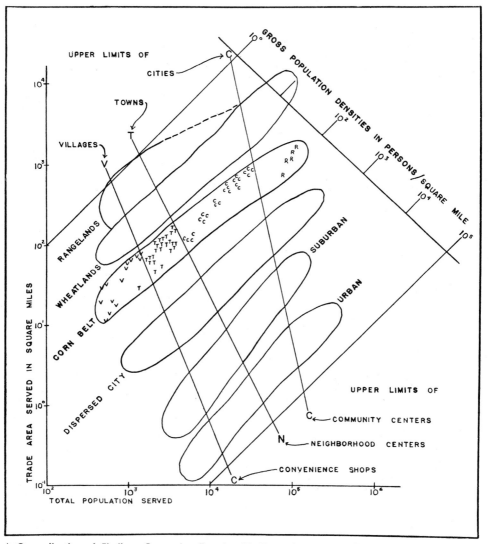

FIGURE 3 A Generalization of Findings Concerning Equation (E. 3), as they were earlier presented in Figure 2, with inequalities (8)—(10) also depicted. Villages, towns, cities and the regional capital are identified in the corn belt example of S.W. Iowa, to illustrate how the inequalities were derived. The classification of centers is based upon a direct factor analysis of an incidence matrix. For further details concerning the data, see Berry (3).

REFERENCES

[1] Barnum, H. G. *The Range of Goods in a Rural Area.* Unpublished M. A. thesis, University of Chicago, 1961.

[3] Berry, B. J. L. *Market Centers and Retail Distribution.* Englewood Cliffs, N. J.: Prentice-Hall, forthcoming.

[4] Berry, B. J. L., H. G. Barnum, and R. J. Tennant. "Retail Location and Consumer Behavior," *Papers and Proceedings,* Regional Science Association, 8, (1962).

[6] Berry, B. J. L., and A. Pred. *Central Place Studies. A Bibliography of Theory and Applications.* Philadelphia: Regional Science Research Institute, 1961.

[15] Tennant, R. J. *Shopping Patterns of Urban Residents.* Unpublished M.A. thesis, University of Chicago, 1962.

Part Four

NEW APPROACHES IN EMPIRICAL ANALYSIS

Introductory Note

Each of the articles in this section is concerned with a familiar geographic problem situation. Wolpert and Gould discuss spatial variations in agricultural phenomena. Casetti is concerned with the location of steel plants and associated transportation flow patterns. The industrial structure of a large metropolitan area is examined by Karaska, while Berry and his associates present a statistical analysis of a central place system in southwestern Iowa. Finally, Morrill traces the evolution of an urban settlement pattern through time.

In all of these studies however, there is a decidedly new approach to these familiar problems. In his analysis of farming in middle Sweden, Wolpert is concerned with the deviations between the spatial pattern of actual labor productivity and the pattern that would result if all farmers behaved in a rational economic manner seeking to optimize their returns. This ideal economic pattern is established by a linear programming solution and the deviations are explained in terms of the risk perceptions, values, and information levels of the farmers. Gould considers some questions of land-utilization in central Ghana within the framework of game theory. The farmers are seen as competing against nature with different payoffs resulting from alternative cropping strategies. A similar analysis is presented for cattle traders.

Casetti employs a linear programming model to determine an optimum location for a new steel mill in eastern Canada. His study is an empirical application of the model developed by Goldman which was reviewed in Garrison's second essay in Part Three. The input-output model which is a powerful tool of economic analysis is being used increasingly in locational and regional analysis. Isard and his associates initiated much of this work,[1] but it has been developed also by other scholars.[2] The study by Karaska included here describes a recent input-output analysis of the industrial structure of the Philadelphia metropolitan area. The relevance of this approach for locational analysis is noted by Karaska.

The study by Berry, Barnum, and Tennant is illustrative of some of the recent empirical work on central place systems. The relationships between different urban phenomena which are established by way of regression analysis and multivariate techniques, specifically direct factor analysis, are used to verify that a hierarchy of central places and urban functions does exist. This hierarchy is discussed further in map analysis of consumer shopping and travel behavior.

A Monte Carlo procedure is employed by Morrill in his attempt to simulate the development of the spatial distribution of towns in Sweden. The model in this case is a probabilistic one and in this respect it differs from the more deterministic approach characteristic of the earlier work on urban systems.

Morrill's contention that location patterns incorporate a considerable random element is also implicit in the studies of Wolpert and Gould. In the former, the spatial diffusion of information among farmers is viewed as a random process and is simulated. Consideration is given also to the element of risk in the decision-making process and the consequent necessity for weighing the probabilities of occurrence of different outcomes. The game theory model used by Gould is not a probabilistic one, but the farmers are seen as choosing among alternative strategies, the payoffs for which "depend upon an unpredictable environment about which Man has only highly probabilitistic notions based upon past experience."

These probabilistic notions about spatial behavior have still to be incorporated into location theory, and this appears as one of the research frontiers in current locational analysis. There are a number of others. The whole realm of behavioral analysis appears virtually untapped by location theorists. Attempts to use nonlinear programming frameworks have only begun recently and there is still much to be accomplished.[3] The modeling of the complex patterns of interaction and interrelationships between land use and transportation is being given widespread attention in the context of urban and regional planning, but progress is slow.[4] On the empirical side also, a great deal of work remains to be done in testing

---

[1] See W. Isard, *Methods of Regional Analysis* (New York: John Wiley & Sons, Inc., 1960), Chap. 8, "Interregional and Regional Input-Output Techniques," pp. 309-374.

[2] For example R. Artle, *The Structure of the Stockholm Economy* (Ithaca: Cornell University Press, 1965); W. Z. Hirsch, "An Application of Area Input-Output Analysis," *Papers and Proceedings*, Regional Science Association, Vol. 5, 1959, pp. 79-92; R. L. Allen and D. A. Watson, *The Structure of the Oregon Economy: An Input/Output Study* (Eugene, Oregon: Bureau of Business and Economic Research, University of Oregon, 1965).

[3] See for example T. Takayama and G. G. Judge, "Equilibrium Among Spatially Separated Markets: A Reformation," *Econometrica*, Vol. 32, No. 4, 1964, pp. 510-24.

[4] See the papers in "Land Use Forecasting Concepts," *Highway Research Record*, No. 126, 1966.

existing theories and in making operational many of the concepts they embody. It is hoped that the studies included in this final section might suggest some ways to pursue this empirical analysis; while at the same time indicate the range of interests and approaches that the economic geographer brings to locational analysis.

Julian Wolpert

THE DECISION PROCESS IN A SPATIAL CONTEXT[1]

Behavioral and social scientists to an increasing degree have begun to question the value of theory predicated upon the existence of an omniscient and single-directed rational being, such as Economic Man, as relevant to man's behavior. Alongside classical normative theory, behavioral concepts and generalizations have been proposed, some of which offer promise of wide applicability. One such system of behavioral concepts, the principle of bounded rationality,[2] has been selected to assist in this analysis of variations in economic behavior. Extended to the spatial dimension, these concepts have relevance in the interpretation of the behavior of the population under study, a sample of Middle Sweden's farmers.

As usually stated, the concept Economic Man is a normative one, an invention descriptive only of the types of decisions which would or should be made under the assumptions of economic rationality. As a rational being, Economic Man is free from the multiplicity of goals and imperfect knowledge which introduce complexity into our own decision behavior. Economic Man has a single profit goal, omniscient powers of perception, reasoning, and computation, and is blessed with perfect predictive abilities. For these reasons his

behavior may be studied in a controlled environment, his strategies may be anticipated, and the outcome of his actions can be known with perfect surety. Economic Man organizes himself and his activities in space so as to optimize utility.

The assumptions implicit in the Economic Man concept, perfect knowledge of alternative courses of action and their consequences and the single desire to optimize utility or productivity, must be relaxed in a behavioral analysis. Similarly, they must be relaxed in the analysis of a geographic region. Allowance must be made for man's finite abilities to perceive and store information, to compute optimal solutions, and to predict the outcome of future events, even if profit were his only goal. More likely, however, his goals are multidimensional and optimization is not a relevant criterion.

An essential first step in this investigation, therefore, involves establishing that the sample population does not behave as Economic Man and does not achieve the fruits of his rational actions, i.e., optimum productivity from a given set of resources. Measurements may be applied to determine to what degree the normative assumptions err in their characterization of actual behavior. A second objective is to demonstrate that the decision process has a spatial dimension, that some of the elements affecting decision behavior may be expected to differ spatially among a population. The overall objective, of course, is to be able to substitute a workable spatial and behavioral model of the decision process for the untenable structure of classical theory.

There is little about the theoretical framework or approach used in this analysis which is not equally applicable to the decision process of the firm in manufacturing, or in any situation in which

Reprinted with the permission of the author and publisher from the *Annals*, Association of American Geographers, Vol. 54, No. 4, 1964, pp. 537-58. Dr. Wolpert is Associate Professor in the Department of Regional Science at the University of Pennsylvania, Philadelphia.

[1] This paper is a partial report of research undertaken at Uppsala University and the Royal Agricultural College in Sweden under the sponsorship of the Foreign Field Research Program of the NAS–NRC and the Social Science Research Council. A more complete description of procedures and findings may be found in the author's Ph.D. dissertation, "Decision-Making in Middle Sweden's Farming—A Spatial Behavioral Analysis," University of Wisconsin (1963), available from University Microfilms, Ann Arbor, Michigan.

[2] See, for example, H. A. Simon, "A Behavioral Model of Rational Choice," *Quarterly Journal of Economics*, Vol. 69 (1952), pp. 99-118.

it is suspected that decision behavior is affected by factors which vary spatially. A farming population was selected for study because the results and consequences of its decision behavior are more easily observable on the landscape. Unlike large-scale manufacturing, the decision making in farming is dispersed spatially among many producers. The diffusion of market and technical information to a dispersed group of producers may be expected to reveal a greater degree of distributional unevenness and lag than would be the case with urban-concentrated firms. The dependence of farming upon physical conditions such as the stability of patterns of weather, for example, creates a source of uncertainty for producers which clearly has a spatial dimension. Lastly, farmers' decision behavior may be expected to reflect a wider range of goals with respect to profit and security, from market orientation to pure self-sufficiency. Competitive forces in most other economic sectors act more quickly in driving out nonmaximizing producers.

The individual farmer, just as the industrial manager, must periodically make decisions with respect to the allocation of available resources among alternative uses. The farmer, functioning as a manager, must periodically decide how his land, labor, and capital will be used, what will be the crop—livestock combinations, the investments in machinery, and the other operating necessities. His goals with respect to income may vary anywhere from mere survival to optimization. The information available to the farmer most likely does not include all of the relevant facts about costs and technology, and it cannot include knowledge of future events which will affect the consequences of his decisions. Within this environment of uncertainty, the farmer must make choices and must bear the burden of outcomes. All farmers are faced with similar problems but actual decisions vary because farmers have different goals, different levels of knowledge, and vary in their aversion to risk and uncertainty. These differences and variations have a spatial dimension and are not randomly distributed among the population.

The Sample Population

Rapid changes are taking place in Sweden's agriculture and the focus of this dynamism is centered especially in the more urbanized and in-

dustrialized central portions of the country. Here, ten per cent of the farms have been abandoned since 1956, and the survivors have been steadily moving in the direction of greater farming specialization and intensification. Although the tempo of change is very rapid, the recent events have been documented with characteristic Swedish thoroughness, a factor of significance for both the normative and behavioral analyses.

The portion of Sweden included within Middle Sweden as defined for this investigation corresponds approximately to the zone known as Mellansverige but has been confined to the full eight central counties (Fig. 1). The essential criterion used to delimit the counties to be included was based upon balancing the desire for diversity of farming situations with the need for restricting the coverage to manageable proportions for field investigation. Consequent upon the selection process the area, to which we shall refer as Middle Sweden, includes a significant amount of diversity among its 68,000 farmers. The area is also sufficiently limited so that by means of an appropriately designed sample the major dimensions of surface variation could be observed. The names of the eight counties are indicated in Figure 1 along with the abbreviated letter designation used by the Swedish Central Bureau of Statistics. The letters B, C, D, E, R, S, T, and U are used to refer to the separate counties.

In this analysis, the areal surface of Middle Sweden's farming is the population. The purpose of the sample design is to survey the spatial properties of the decision behavior of Middle Sweden's farming population. To carry out this objective, a systematic sample was designed. Forty-five sampling units of 211 square kilometers (81.4 square miles) were selected from a hexagonal network

FIGURE 1 The Sample Area, Middle Sweden, and its Counties.

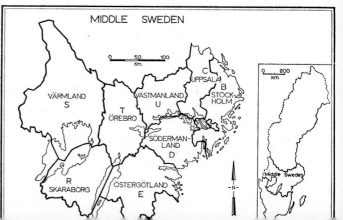

and constitute a twelve per cent sample of: 1) the surface of Middle Sweden, 2) its arable land and, 3) farmers. The sample population consists of a variety of farm situation types in terms of size, economy, site, and settlement characteristics.

The Normative and Behavioral Analyses

In a behavioral analysis, allowance is provided for the entire continuum of human responses from optimization to that minimum of adaptation which may be essential for survival.[3] Economic Man has a position at one extreme of the continuum. His position is predetermined in any situation in which the existence of an optimum may be demonstrated. The existence of a continuum provides an opportunity to explore the problem of determining the relative position of individuals on its scale.

The format of matched comparison serves as a suitable analytic framework for our discussion of the decision process. The decision behavior of the population under study is compared with that of the matched control. Economic Man, who has the same supply of resources but is equipped with the necessary knowledge and foreknowledge to achieve his goal of optimization. The factors of interest are the individual's goals or objectives and his level of knowledge which may be observed by means of a matching variable.

Performance levels in farming may be assessed according to a wide variety of criteria, only two of which were utilized in this analysis, organization and technology. Farm organization refers to the group of management decisions involving allocation of available resources among alternative activities. We shall define technology as the level of knowledge and application of crop and husbandry procedures. Finite farm resources of land, labor, capital, and building facilities must somehow be combined to produce desired outputs at a given level of technology.[4] For each farm situation, with its finite set of resources, there exists, in addition to the actual organization and technology followed by the individual farmer, an optimum counterpart which may be determined. Emphasis is reserved here for the gap between the organization of resources on the actual farms, their technology, and the optimum technologic level and organization of the same resources, as measured by the differences in resulting labor productivity.[5] The productivity which the individual receives is matched with the optimum returns which the same resources would yield to Economic Man through optimum organization and technology. The degree to which the departures are clustered spatially is a reflection of the systematic distribution of factors affecting decision behavior. The focus is reserved here for these spatial attributes of the decision process.

Three spatial distributions are involved with respect to labor productivity, that resulting from: 1) the actual technology and organization of farm resources; 2) the optimum or potential technology and organization of the same resources; and 3) the gap between the actual and potential distributions. The optimum or potential productivity values were determined by means of a linear programming analysis[6] for seventeen representative farm situations, and values interpolated for the remaining 533 farms of a systematic subsample (the JEU sample)[7] through regression estimation.[8] Linear programming, a mathematical technique permitting simultaneous consideration of many possible alternative organizational plans, specifies the most profitable plan consistent with available

---

[3]H. A. Simon, "Some Strategic Considerations in the Construction of Social Science Models," Chapter 8 in Paul F. Lazarsfeld (Ed.), *Mathematical Thinking in the Social Sciences* (Glencoe: Free Press, 1954).

[4]Capital, as employed in this study, refers to working capital, assets in liquid or semiliquid form (which can be translated into liquid assets within one crop season), e.g., cash on hand, value of livestock, and crops planted. The working capital values are calculated by subtracting from total assets the real estate value of farm property, buildings, and long-term inventory items such as machinery and tools. Therefore, working capital measures the assets available to the farmer for direct use in enterprise selection.

[5]Labor productivity refers to net labor returns to the farm family per equivalent man-hour after a deduction of five per cent interest return on investment. Optimum technical levels were determined from estimates of potential regional yield levels for crops and milk as reported in: *Proceedings of the 1960 Agricultural Investigation* (Uppsala: Department of Agricultural Economics, Royal Agricultural College, March 3, 1962). To achieve the potential yields, the farmer would find it necessary to fertilize according to a plan based upon a soil survey of his arable land, and selective breeding and proper feed mixture for dairy cattle would be necessary as well.

[6]Further details of the linear programming model and findings may be found in the author's Ph.D. dissertation, *op. cit.,* Appendix III, and in the mimeographed reports of Professor Lennart Hjelm and his assistants at the Royal Agricultural College, Uppsala. Details of the techniques of linear programming as applied to agriculture are discussed in: E. O. Heady and W. Candler, *Linear Programming Methods* (Ames, Iowa: The Iowa State University Press, 1958).

[7]The sampling design followed the format of "multiphase sampling," wherein information collected in each phase is used for stratification in the next phase, and there is opportunity provided for feedback of sampling quality control. In this investigation, Agricultural Census cards (1956) for the 68,000 farmers of Middle Sweden provided information to permit a twelve per cent systematic sample of 8,000 farmers and a check

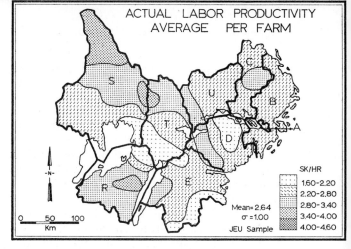

FIGURE 2

resources and the input—output relationship for the alterative enterprises. The range of possible enterprises included various crop and livestock combinations as well as foresty and afforestation of arable and pastureland, off-farm employment, and off-farm investment. The linear programming procedure involves balancing the alternative enterprises according to their relative contribution to net returns and their use of the finite supply of resources. The solution is in terms of the productivity or labor income which would result from the single most profitable combination of enterprises that is within the resource limitations, i.e., the potential productivity which the individual farmer could attain if his goal were optimization and his knowledge perfect.

The surface of actual productivity (Fig. 2) reflects the consequences of the outcome of the technology and organization followed by the subsample farmers during the 1956-1959 period.[9] Given their finite supply of resources, their individual goals, and their levels of knowledge and foreknowledge, the actual productivity reflects the net return to their labor. Even in the zones of highest average productivity, as in R and northern S. the values fall considerably short of parity level with industrial workers' earnings.

The surface of potential productivity (Fig. 3) represents the theoretical limits of labor income with the present distribution of resources, i.e., the distribution of income if farm organization and technology were optimal. Any further increase in

productivity would require additional resources. The major determinant of the potential levels is the ratio of the supply of capital to land and labor resources. Where the ratios are low, as in southern T, the poor structural balance limits labor productivity. The potential levels are highest in the northerly zone of Middle Sweden and in R where 4.00 Swedish Kroner (U.S. $0.80) an hour may be earned within present resource limitations. The distribution of potential productivity is closely related to the structural variations in Middle Sweden's farms. Well-structured farms, in terms of the capital ratio, have higher potential levels because the need is not so great to organize resources so as to consume excess labor. When it is considered that the potential values indicated represent the optimum that may be achieved in the short run, it must be concluded that labor income on the sample farms is severely restricted, to an extent which varies spatially, by present structure and shortages of capital resources. This limit or ceiling appears especially noteworthy when one

FIGURE 3

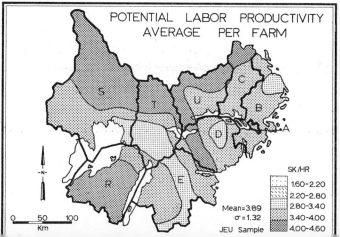

for representativeness. The 8,000 sample permitted further stratification into 550, with checks also provided for referring to the larger sample and parent population. For purposes of the linear programming analysis, the 550 JEU farms were stratified into seventeen groupings in terms of input-output relationships and resource categories, with tests designed also to check the effectiveness of the groupings and the interpolation procedure, the results of which form the basis for Map 3. The JEU farms participate in a government-financed, long-term study of farm economics which is sponsored by the Royal Board of Agricult ure in Stockholm. The farms are selected according to a plan which aims for representativeness regionally as well as in terms of type of farming, level of technology, and other conditions. Of the participating farms, 550 are located within the forty-five sample units in Middle Sweden, and they had taken part in the study continuously from 1956 to 1960. The 550 subsample farms (to which we refer as the JEU sample) are aggregated by the forty-five sample units to simplify the cartographic presentation of distributions. The distributions are based, therefore, upon a one per cent sample biased toward the better farmers, it is suspected, because of their practice of maintaining bookkeeping records.

[8]The regression interpolation was accomplished by means of the RGR Multiple Regression Program for the Control Data Corp. 1604 Computer, Social Systems Research Institute, University of Wisconsin.

[9]The four-year period, 1956-1959, rather typical in terms of weather and market fluctuations, was used as the base for both the optimum and actual productivity calculations.

considers that nowhere in Middle Sweden do even these potential values approach parity with the general income level in Sweden. The variations in the distribution are an indication of the varying degree of structural or resource maladjustment. Potential is merely a measure of available farm resources equated in terms of their income-producing possibilities. Clearly, income on Middle Sweden's farms is restricted by shortages of labor-conserving capital.

Imposed upon the structural maladjustment is the additional gap between the income that is realized and the potential income. We have combined the two distributions into a single ratio of actual to potential income (Fig. 4) to illustrate the extent and the variations in the gap from place to place. The sample population attains a lower productivity than their resources permit. The surface, to which we shall refer as the Productivity Index or PI surface, represents essentially the human element in farming, the consequences of the decision behavior of Middle Sweden's farmers with the resource differences removed. The gap as it varies spatially reflects the departure of the decision behavior of our sample population from that of Economic Man and the degree to which the normative assumptions of optimization, and perfect knowledge must be relaxed in the behavioral analysis. The presence of variations in the PI surface leads one to suspect that there are significant spatial variations in the goals and knowledge levels of the population, and that the decision process has a spatial dimension.

FIGURE 4

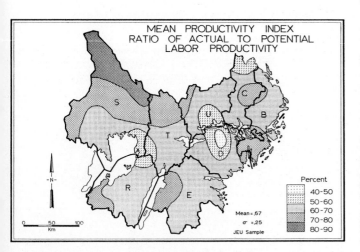

MEAN PRODUCTIVITY INDEX
RATIO OF ACTUAL TO POTENTIAL
LABOR PRODUCTIVITY

Percent
40-50
50-60
60-70
70-80
80-90

Mean = .67
σ = .25
JEU Sample

For convenience, the PI surface may be stratified into reasonably homogeneous regions. An analysis of variance test of the distribution of PI values suggested the presence of five separate core areas with more or less distinct boundaries, suitable for a fivefold regional breakdown of the PI surface (Fig. 5).[10] The regional means vary from 58.6 to 72.9 per cent (Region 5 as opposed to Region 1) but as one may infer from the standard deviations, the intraregional differences between farms are considerable.

The regions with the highest average values of PI (Regions 1 and 2) are as different in terms of physical environment, farm structure and organization, and locational situation as is possible within Middle Sweden. Region 2 is an island of intensive farming and dense agricultural settlement. Region 1 is very sparsely settled with agriculture confined to areas where there occur outcrops of nonmorainal soils, such as silty clays and light sands in the narrow river valleys and lakeshores. Similarly, with respect to the other regions, the rank order does not appear to be justifiable from the point of view of physical resources. These have been held largely constant or removed in the calculation of the PI values, so that the variation between the farmers themselves might be perceived and examined as a nonrandom but systematic distribution in the spatial dimension.

The five regions are delineated by the single criterion of PI value. This ratio, however, is a composite index reflecting nearness to or departure from economic rationality. Thus, although the regionalization classifies areas according to a single dependent variable, we know that the classification extends to the explanatory variables also. In Regions 1 and 2, for example, not only are the average PI values relatively higher but because they are higher, then, of necessity, one would expect to find decision behavior more closely approaching that of Economic Man. We would expect to find that resources are more knowledgeably combined

[10]The objective in the regionalization was to minimize the ratio of variance within contiguous regions to that between regions by grouping the forty-five sample units. Although the distributions reflected in Figures 2, 3, and 4 represent the mean values for the 550 farms aggregated by the forty-five sample zones, the regionalization in Figure 5 is based upon the distribution of variance within the sample zones as well. Thus the regionalization in Figure 5 is based upon the 550 individual values and differs from the distribution represented in Figure 4, which has been constructed on the basis of the forty-five sample means. After a fivefold division of the surface, there was relatively little reduction of ratio values to be gained through further subdivision.

and integrated so as to achieve higher profits. On the other hand, the lower average values of PI in Regions 4 and 5 would be an indication that decision behavior was less directed toward maximum profits, and that farm organization and technology were hampered to a relatively greater extent by imperfect knowledge. Thus, the regions reflect a degree of internal homogeneity with respect to the dependent variable, the PI values, as well as the independent variables, knowledge, and goals. The variance between regions reflects also differences with respect to both dependent and independent variables.

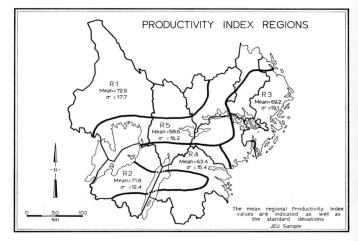

FIGURE 5

Goal Orientation

"Comparison now has to be drawn no longer to test the theory, but to test reality."[11] The evidence presented would seem to suggest that reality is arational.[12] The hypothesis which was examined proposed that Middle Sweden's farmers do not achieve profit maximization and that productivity is not limited only by the amount and combination of resources. Testing of the hypothesis for a sample population revealed that the average farmer achieved only two-thirds of the potential productivity which his resources would allow. With productivity not at the optimum level, then it may be assumed that one or both of the prerequisites for economic rationality (perfect knowledge and optimizing behavior) are absent.

The alternative concepts of the "optimizer" and the "satisficer"[13] are a central issue in this investigation in terms of their respective value as explanatory guides to the goal orientation of our sample population. To a certain extent the optimizer concept has been introduced into economic geography by the tacit assumption that men organize themselves, their production, and their consumption in space so as to maximize utility or revenue. Whenever the analyst projects his knowledge of the best or most efficient location of economic activities into an explanation of the actual distribution of phenomena and finds correspondence, he assumes, even though tacitly, that man is

rational and that his objective reality corresponds with the subjective reality of the actor being observed.

Whereas the profit motive is present in every production decision in the sense that producers may be expected not to seek losses, maximization may not be so universal. The controversy between the Rationalists and their critics revolves more around the possible shortcomings of theory based upon the assumption of maximization than on the importance of the profit motive in economic decisions.[14]

Simon and others attack the Rationalists' position that the decision maker ranks all sets of possible alternatives from the most preferred to the least preferred in terms of consequences and then selects the specific alternative which leads to the preferred set of consequences:

Most human decision-making whether individual or organizational, is concerned with the discovery and selection of satisfactory alternatives; only in exceptional cases is it concerned with the discovery and selection of optimal alternatives.[15] To optimize requires processes several orders of magnitude more complex than those required to satisfice.[16]

The appeal of the satisficer concept or the principle of bounded rationality is clear. Based upon sound empirical investigations by social psychologists of actual economic behavior, it requires

[11]August Lösch, *The Economics of Location* (New Haven: Yale University Press, 1959), p. 363.

[12]The term arational is used to refer to situations outside the sphere in which rational distinctions or judgments may apply, as distinguished from irrational.

[13]H. A. Simon, *Models of Man* (New York: John Wiley & Sons, 1957), pp. 196-200.

[14]D. C. McClelland, *The Achieving Society* (Princeton: Van Nostrand Company, 1961), pp. 14-15.

[15]J. G. March and H. A. Simon, *Organizations* (New York: John Wiley & Sons, 1958), p. 141.

[16]March and Simon, *op. cit.*, p. 140.

nothing which is beyond the capacity of the human organism. The decision maker merely classifies the various alternatives in his subjective environment as to their expected outcomes, whether satisfactory or unsatisfactory. If the elements of the set of satisfactory outcomes can be ranked, then the least satisfactory outcome of this set may be referred to as the level-of-aspiration adopted by the decision maker for that problem. His search is complete and the action is taken. The theory suggests that aspiration levels tend to adjust to the attainable, to past achievement levels, and to levels achieved by other individuals with whom he compares himself.[17]

To some extent, the departures reflected in the PI surface may be attributable to the irrelevancy of the optimization yardstick employed in its construction. There is greater justification for regarding the satisficer concept as more descriptively accurate of the goal orientation of Middle Sweden's farmers than the optimizing criterion. The sample population is more concerned with alternatives which are good enough than in finding optimum solutions. The objective optimum solutions, as revealed by the linear programming analysis, are not perceived by the decision makers, who appear instead to have aspiration levels which they have a reasonable expectation of achieving, such as reasonable profits.

The satisficer model is not easily verifiable, for there is no simple way of determining the aspiration levels of individuals. Regional variations do exist, in the degree to which the farmers are commercially oriented, which are expressed by their lags in shifting with market changes. It may be argued, however, that the lag in response is attributable not to any lack of motivation but may be traced rather to imperfect knowledge which obviates the possibility of maximization. It is debatable, therefore, as to whether we have an optimizing population with imperfect knowledge or a population with goals other than pure profit maximization. Certainly, the distinction matters little and to some extent is arbitrary, for goal orientation and level of knowledge are typically causally interrelated. Limited investigation of this argument revealed that non-economic considerations appear also to influence the decision behavior of the sample population, especially with respect to work preferences.

Knowledge Situation

The assumption of omniscience implicit in the concept of Economic Man is not tenable with respect to the decision environment of Middle Sweden's farmers. Limited to finite ability to reason and compute, to perceive alternatives, and to realize goals, optimization may not be expected. The variations in the PI surface partially reflect these limitations as well as the effects of the uneven flow of information upon which the effectiveness of decisions is based. Information about prices, production methods, and technological changes diffuses through spatial channels which discriminate between producers and create variations in knowledge situations. The emphasis given here to the communication process and the flow of information reflects the conviction that the individual's experience alone is insufficient to carry on productive agriculture. Productivity as a concept may be considered as an innovation diffused from group values.

Unlike the industrial firms who undertake the search for information on their own, the farm firm is usually somewhat isolated from the source of communicable information. The farmer is largely reliant for the information he needs upon the efficiency of a communication system which he is seldom able to control. The information comes to him largely without expense, in contrast to the situation of the industrial firm, but the lag in the transfer from expert to user is considerably greater, and perception and acceptance of the information are hardly automatic.

To a very great extent, information about recommended farm practices, new agricultural machinery, new seed varieties, expected costs, and market prices originate for Middle Sweden's farmers among institutions in the Stockholm—Uppsala area.[18] Although information is disseminated in a rapid and reasonably efficient manner, the communication process affects farmers unequally and this unevenness is significant spatially.

The diffusion process proceeds by steps, from the experts in the core zone of Stockholm—Uppsala

---

[17]March and Simon, *op. cit.*, pp. 182-83.

[18]The diffusion of information process which is described in this section is an inductive and extremely concise statement generalized from interviews with the sample farmers and the agricultural extension administrators. A description of the analysis and the simulation design which was used to predict the velocity of information flow may be found in the author's Ph.D. dissertation, *op. cit.*

to the disseminating organizations' central offices, then to the local county offices which are situated typically in the county's leading city. This initial process takes place rather rapidly without significant differences from one county to another in Middle Sweden. The transmission then proceeds in stepwise fashion, directed at first to the larger farmers and those situated within the major agricultural districts of each county. An intracounty diffusion process is set in motion which involves filtering and imitation through the farmers' ranks so that considerable lag intervenes until small farmers who are isolated are made aware of new information. Farm size, membership in the farmers' organizations, and location with respect to other farmers all apparently influence the network of communication over the surface. The uneven spatial distribution of farmers according to farm size, membership, and proximity to other farmers is proposed as the primary determinants of the uneven flow of information and the variations in knowledge levels. These governing rules for the communication process may be incorporated within a simulation model in order to estimate stochastically the spatial variations in the supply of information at a given time.

The demand for information may be considered as well as the spatial supply process by assuming, for example, that in the areas of highest potential productivity (Fig. 3) the innovation of rationality would have started earliest, developed fastest, and be least restricted by a ceiling.[19] The communication stream would be fastest in the areas of highest potential productivity (responding to the greater demand for information) and the spatial lag would be greatest where the relative advantages of shifting in the direction of rationality were least (where there is less demand for information). The distribution of opportunities, as revealed by the surface of potential productivity, is suggested as the major determinant governing the demand for information.

It is not sufficient, therefore, merely to substitute the behavioral concepts of finite ability to perceive and absorb information for the untenable assumption of omniscience in characterizing the knowledge situation of Middle Sweden's farmers.

Spatial biases exist in the communication channels which enable farmers in some areas to receive information more rapidly and thus to have access to larger funds of knowledge upon which to base their decisions.

The Environment of Uncertainty

In the discussion of communication channels, it had been assumed that knowledge was essentially available to be disseminated and that knowledge levels were dependent upon the intensity of diffusion. The decision maker is limited further, however, to *ex ante* information and must bear the consequences for the gap in his knowledge about future events.

In addition to the objective uncertainty which occurs because of unpredictable change and variations, notice must be taken also of the uncertainty apparent to individual decision makers which may be considerably different. The uncertainty environment to which the decision maker reacts is dependent not only upon the inherent instability of phenomena but upon the state of knowledge concerning this instability. Uncertainty has a spatial dimension, therefore, not only because the inherent stability of phenomena may differ from place to place, but also because communication channels diffuse information unevenly in space, and because perception varies.

The farmers of Middle Sweden must make decisions in an uncertain environment. These decisions appear with respect to crop and livestock combinations, production techniques, and other practices which affect farm income and survival. The consequences of their decisions during the 1956 to 1959 period are reflected in their productivity distribution for those years (Fig. 2). Most likely, with *ex post* information, their decision behavior would have been significantly different.

Five types of potential sources of objective uncertainty may be identified which are relevant for Middle Sweden's farmers.[20] Uncertainty may be introduced through instability in: 1) personal factors, e.g., farmers' health and ability to work;

---

[19]For a review of this approach, see: Zvi Griliches, "Hybrid Corn: An Exploration in the Economics of Technological Change," *Econometrica*, Vol. 25 (1957), pp. 501-22.

[20]These potential sources of uncertainty are discussed in: O. L. Walker, *et al.*, *Application of Game Theory Models to Decisions on Farm Practices and Resource Use* (Ames, Iowa: Iowa State University, Agricultural Experiment Station Bulletin 488, 1960).

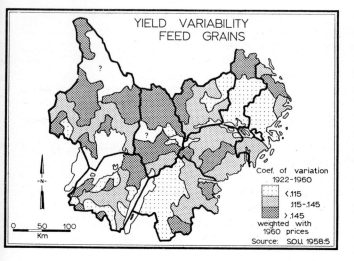

FIGURE 6 The yield variability of feed grains. (Data drawn from *Permanent skördeskadeskydd* [Permanent Protection against Crop Damage], Statens offentliga utredningar 1958:5, Ministry of Agriculture, Stockholm.)

2) institutional arrangements, e.g., government policy, landlord—tenant relationships; 3) technological changes; 4) market structure; 5) physical factors, e.g., weather, blight, and other environmental variables. These potential sources of uncertainty have been reduced systematically, however, through social insurance, legal tenant contracts, and long-term government price policies

FIGURE 7 The yield variability of winter bread grains. (Data drawn from *Permanent skördeskadeskydd* [Permanent Protection against Crop Damage], Statens offentliga utredningar 1958:5, Ministry of Agriculture, Stockholm.)

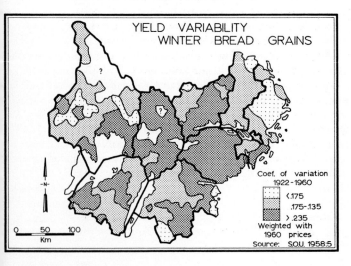

in the agricultural sector. Only yield variability arising from weather uncertainty remains as the most significant unknown in the planning environment of Middle Sweden's farmers, and its impact is spatially differentiated. Climatological records for the past are an insufficient tool for predicting weather accurately enough to insure optimal selection from among cropping alternatives. Wide and irregular fluctuations of output occur in Middle Sweden's farming which cannot be controlled or predicted. Resources are committed and expended at the beginning of a crop season when output is uncertain and will not be known for months. The period under investigation, 1956 to 1960, was, in aggregate, quite normal for Middle Sweden. Some farmers had ideal weather and good yields but for many others, the cost of uncertainty was wasted effort, expenditures and unstable income.

Coefficients of yield variations $(\frac{\sigma}{M} \cdot 100)$ have been determined for feed grains (barley, oats, and mixed grains) and winter bread grains (wheat and rye), to illustrate their respective degree of variability during the period 1921 to 1960[21] (Figs. 6 and 7). The fact that little correlation exists between the yield variability of the different crops may be used to advantage by farmers in deciding upon suitable crop combination and rotational systems. Reducing uncertainty through diversification and complementarity are strategies that are extensively followed by Middle Sweden's farmers. In addition, the correspondence is generally very high between yield variability and crop emphasis. In the areas of relatively higher risk for feed grains, emphasis is shifted to crops subject to comparatively less local variability, as hay.

The separate coefficients of variation for the crop groups have been combined into one measure and weighted by prices (1960), average yields, and the acreage devoted to the individual crops (Figs. 8 and 9). The average percentage departure in crop revenue that may be expected each year may be interpreted from Figure 8. In the high risk zone in the northeast coastal area, for example, total crop revenue may be expected each year to

[21]Data were derived from the primary tables of: Ministry of Agriculture, *Permanent skördeskadeskydd* (Permanent Protection Against Crop Damage), S.O.U. 1958:5 (Stockholm, 1958), and the yield variability tables maintained by the Agricultural Division of the Central Bureau of Statistics, Stockholm.

depart by ± twenty-five per cent from the average. Immediately to the north, the average variation is only ± fifteen per cent. The difference may be traced to several causes. The areas differ little in terms of variability for individual crops but in the high risk area a greater proportion of the acreage is devoted to higher risk crops and average yields are higher. The risk is relatively lower in the northwest because yields are normally low for most crops and much of the arable land is planted in lower risk hay. If greater emphasis were given to winter grains, a much higher degree of variability could be expected.

A relatively similar distribution pattern results when the expected variability is translated into a measure of average revenue departure per hectare of arable land (Fig. 9). In the central plains area of *E*, farmers may expect a normal variation of ± 150 Swedish Kroner per hectare (U.S. $12.00 per acre) each year. An average farm there with thirty hectares of arable land (seventy-four acres) should anticipate that revenue from crops will vary an average of U.S. $900 yearly from the long-term average unless broad diversification is followed. The revenue per hectare varies less in most other areas of Middle Sweden, for less emphasis is given to wheat, oleiferous plants, and other risky crops. The typical farmers in *E* appear to prefer cultivating the more lucrative crops despite the risk. Greater stability in income is apparently considered more desirable by those in central *S*.

The uncertainty resulting from unpredictable weather variations is an extremely significant factor in Middle Sweden's agriculture. Even with the present pattern of diversification, farmers must expect their revenue from crops to vary between fifteen and twenty-five per cent from the average. The factor that appears to account to the greatest extent for the spatial variations in this distribution is the emphasis given to individual crops and combinations in the rotation plan, the environment of uncertainty which the individual decision makers determine for themselves.

Spatial inequalities exist at any given time in the extent of foreknowledge possessed by the farmers of Middle Sweden, owing in part to the inequalities in information diffusion. Foresight is more easily achieved in areas subject to less unpredictable change but knowledge of the methods which are available to reduce its amplitude plays

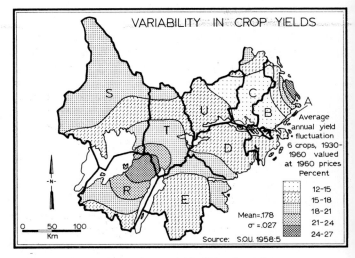

FIGURE 8 The variability of crop yields. (Data drawn from Permanent skördeskadeskydd [Permanent Protection against Crop Damage], Statens offentliga utredningar 1958:5, Ministry of Agriculture, Stockholm.)

a significant role as well. The communication channels which disseminate information bring news about the technical and economic measures which may lead to greater control over the unknowns. Therefore, we may expect to find that, in the areas of more intense interaction and communication, farmers are better acquainted with the risks involved with alternative enterprises and the means

FIGURE 9 The variability of crop yields—deducted value per hectare. (Data shown from Permanent skördeskadeskydd [Permanent Protection against Crop Damage], Statens offentliga utredningar 1958:5, Ministry of Agriculture, Stockholm.)

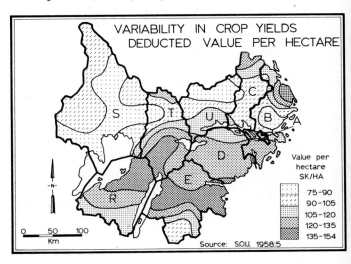

323

by which uncertainty may be reduced to acceptable risk levels.

The presence of uncertainty eliminates the possibility of profit maximization. Even if the intention is to optimize, imperfect knowledge prevents its realization. The existence of risk and uncertainty about the consequences of alternative courses of action makes it necessary for the decision maker to consider not only the desirability of outcomes but also their probability of occurrence. Courses of action must be determined, the outcomes of which are both sufficiently certain and desirable to satisfy the decision maker. The quest for income stability is apparently at least as important to Middle Sweden's farmers as the pure profit motive. We are aware that in a behavioral investigation the assumption of perfect knowledge must give way to a knowledge continuum. Similarly, recognizing that individuals vary in their aversion to risk and uncertainty, the mechanical optimizer must now yield to a utility continuum.

Attitudes toward risk and uncertainty are not easily observable. Theoretically it should be possible to analyze the cropping and other decisions made by Middle Sweden's farmers and determine their respective positions on the continuum scale. This type of evidence is revealing but hardly sufficient alone. Instead, we shall attempt an indirect procedure by analyzing factors which are hypothesized as causally related to position along the continuum.

Research by social psychologists and others has revealed that certain personal and situational characteristics are related to individuals' attitudes toward risk aversion.[22] Age, for example, has been found to be a particularly important variable. It has been consistently confirmed in these investigations that older people tend to a greater extent to select courses of action which involve lower degrees of risk. In Middle Sweden, a selective migration has all but emptied certain rural areas of young farmers. Therefore, one would expect, if position on the utility continuum were dependent purely upon the age distribution of farmers, that a very definite regional hierarchy on the continuum scale could be expected. This is the sense in which the existence of spatial variations in goal structure is implied. Aspiration levels are difficult to measure

and assess but their major dimensions may be perceived through knowledge of factors which affect their formulation.

Factors other than age play decisive roles in the satisficing scale and several have spatial distributions which are nonrandom. Equity position influences the ability to take chances and still survive. Size of family may be expected to influence attitudes toward stability and security. Farmers who are located in areas subject to periodically destructive weather conditions, such as early frost, might tend to select those alternatives which minimize risk. Other factors undoubtedly affect the type of compromise which farmers select, such as amount of available working capital, farm scale, opportunities for efficient diversification or shifting, the time preference in consumption, institutional restrictions in the capital and marketing systems, the time sequence of poor years in the past, and personal atitudes toward conservatism or gambling.[23] Some farmers require a certain income to insure the survival of their farm, and they accept the risks necessary to achieve this level. For others who may be considering a change of occupation, nothing less than income parity with nonfarm workers is sufficient. Thus, although income goals themselves may not be revealed through simple measurement, some aspects of their distribution among Middle Sweden's farmers may be revealed through analysis of the distribution of some of the factors mentioned above.

Various alternatives are available to farmers who wish to temper their desire for profit with a measure of security. When uncertainty may be reduced to definite risk probability, maximization at least of expected income is possible. Techniques have been determined for calculating maximum income at various risk levels. Even when absolute uncertainty is present and goals are defined in terms of maximum—minimum incomes or other security levels, it is still possible to specify procedures for selecting the best means for realizing these goals.

The risk-programming and game-theory procedures are still normative and are inadequate to characterize the response of Middle Sweden's

---

[22]Walker, op. cit.

[23]For a discussion of these and other factors, see: *Proceedings from the Research Conference on Risk and Uncertainty in Agriculture* (Fargo: North Dakota Agricultural Experiment Station Bulletin 400, 1955).

farmers to uncertainty.[24] For our purposes, the satisficer type of approach appears more appropriate. The farmers of Middle Sweden do not necessarily select the best course of action for realizing their goals with respect to profit and security but follow a process of adaptation based upon the feedback of information. It is proposed that the farmers arrive at some normal production program for their farm enterprises based upon their subjective knowledge of alternative courses of action with respect to technology and selection of enterprises, their resource position, their aspiration levels, and the pressures and restrictions imposed by institutions. This normal pattern is maintained as long as returns remain within a range which is satisfactory to the farmer. When a crisis occurs, the farmer is jarred out of the previous pattern and shifts in a direction so that, once again, a satisfactory outcome may be expected. The normal production program pattern need not be a static one, for normal growth and expansion may be anticipated and readjustment might require long-term-change.[25]

The established programs include some provision for stability of income which may be inferred from the distribution of crop rotation patterns and crop and livestock combinations. There are various means which farmers have at their disposal to achieve stability despite the uncertainty of their environment. The creation of credit institutions, crop insurance, and marketing agreements have had an important impact, but our major concern is with the measures used by individual decision makers.

Farmers, as other decision makers, may postpone the making of decisions until further information is available. Some of the farmers delay entering into new lines of production until prices appear to be stabilized over a period of time. Many decisions in farming cannot be postponed beyond a very limited date, such as planting or harvesting dates. The retailer and manufacturer may rely upon the constant feedback of information and may make relatively short-run decisions. Farmers must commit large proportions of their resources at one time and have little opportunity of shifting crops, for example, when more weather information becomes available.

The more common means used to avert or diminish risk and uncertainty involve diversification, shifting, and flexibility. Maintaining a cash or semiliquid reserve with which to meet sudden emergencies allows for a degree of flexibility but only at the expense of profits in the short run. Shifting may involve transference from a risky crop to one which gives more stable yields, or the farmer may leave farming entirely and shift to a more certain occupation. Through diversification, a combination of enterprises may be selected which reduces the risks that may be associated with specialization.[26] Diversification may succeed in reducing the total variability in returns to a level which is less than the variability of the separate enterprises.

Specialization, even in dairying, is accompanied by considerable risks, and in hay production the risk is much higher, but when the two enterprises are combined, the total income variation is considerably less than either alone (Table 1). Similarly, the lucrative production of rape seed may be undertaken at a comparatively low risk level when combined, for example, with wheat and

TABLE I Diversification and Income Variability

Enterprise	Income variation as a percentage of gross income
Milk cows	21
Hay	51
Hay and feed grains	30
Milk cows and hay	14
Milk cows, hay, and feed grains	13
Rape seed	47
Wheat	38
Potatoes	42
Rape seed and wheat	30
Wheat and potatoes	33
Rape seed, wheat, and potatoes	23

Source: L. Hjelm, *Specialization as a Way of Increasing Efficiency in Agriculture* (Uppsala: Dept. of Agric. Econ., Royal Agricultural College, 1962, Mimeographed).

[24]See, for example, A. M. M. McFarquhar, "Rational Decision-making and Risk in Farm Planning—An Application of Quadratic Programming in British Arable Farming," *Journal of Agricultural Economics*, Vol. 14 (1961), pp. 552-63, and Ulf Renborg, *Studies on the Planning Environment of the Agricultural Firm* (Stockholm: Almqvist & Wiksell, 1962).

[25]R. M. Cyert and J. G. March, *A Behavioral Theory of the Firm* (Englewood Cliffs, New Jersey: Prentice-Hall, 1963), pp. 99-101.

[26]L. Hjelm, *Specialization as a Way of Increasing Efficiency in Agriculture* (Uppsala, Sweden: Department of Agricultural Economics, Royal Agricultural College, 1962, Mimeographed).

potato cultivation. By means of diversification, farmers may balance potential profits against potential risk to find a suitable combination of enterprises. Diversification, as with respect to the other measures, may bring about a greater level of stability but at the expense of efficiency or profit. Uncertainty and risk have a cost which detracts from opportunities.

The departures reflected in the PI surface, as well as the spatial variations, may be partly understood through knowledge of the uncertainty-environment to which Middle Sweden's farmers react, and through the means they have created to provide a controlled environment of relative stability.

Indicators of Knowledge and Goals

Essentially, the groups of components which determine the income or productivity of the sample population have been accounted for: 1) the set of farm resources which define the potential or limits of productivity; 2) the goals which define the selection from alternative courses of action according to the desirability of their expected outcome; 3) the knowledge which defines the awareness and perception of alternatives and their consequences; 4) the inherent instability of the farm situation which is defined by the uncertainty of its environment. These components acting in combination account for the variations in the PI surface.

The objective in the empirical analysis is to uncover some of the major indicators of goals and knowledge, measures by which these factors may be perceived. Factors such as age, education and training, technical knowledge, equity ratio, and tenancy may perhaps all be related to the farmers' attainment levels but it was strongly suspected that resource flexibility largely explains the differences between farmers. Earlier it had been proposed that the most critial element in defining the potential productivity was the balance between resources, especially with respect to capital. The greater is the ratio of working capital to the supply of land and labor resources, the higher is the potential productivity which the farmer can receive. Conceivably, the supply of working capital not only defines the productivity which is possible in the short run but also materially affects how

closely actual productivity approaches the optimum on the sample farms.

A supply of working capital permits the farmer to remain flexible, to survive short-term income fluctuations, and to shift rapidly between enterprises. Working capital is invested in such items as fertilizer, seed, and concentrated fodder, any of which may be substituted for quantities of farm land and labor.

A multiple linear regression model was formulated to reflect the proposed hypothesis relating capital intensity to the Productivity Index values. The equation includes the PI values as the dependent variable and five independent variables which reflect the quantity of farm resources:

$$Y_c = a_{y \cdot 12345} + b_{y1 \cdot 2345}X_1 + b_{y2 \cdot 1345}X_2 + \ldots + b_{y5 \cdot 1234}X_5 + E$$

where $Y =$ the Productivity Index, the ratio of actual to optimum productivity, measured in per cent

$X_1 =$ arable land, hectares

$X_2 =$ forest land, hectares

$X_3 =$ capital, Swedish Kroner in hundreds

$X_4 =$ labor supply, hours in hundreds

$X_5 =$ Calculated optimum productivity, Swedish Kroner per man-hour.

Arable and forest land and labor are expected to exert a negative influence on the Productivity Index when considered alone and capital to exert a strong positive influence. The fifth independent variable is the optimum productivity calculation for each farm which was derived from the linear programming solutions and which occurs as the denominator of the PI ratio. The optimum value has been included because it represents a suitable estimate of the overall balance between resources for each farm as well as reflecting, perhaps, the demand for information. The objective of the regression model was to estimate the relative effectiveness of resource combinations as indicators of the farmers' knowledge levels and income goals.

COMPOSITE ANALYSIS

The equation was estimated initially for all 550 sample farms, the sample surface of Middle Sweden, considered as one unit. The coefficients of simple correlation, partial correlation, and multiple correlation are indicated in Table 2, along

TABLE 2 Results of Correlation and Regression Analysis: Composite for Middle Sweden

COEFFICIENTS OF SIMPLE CORRELATION							REGRESSION COEFFICIENTS AND THEIR STANDARD ERRORS			
	Y	X_1	X_2	X_3	X_4	X_5		Variable	Coef.	Stnd. Error
Y PI Value	—	−0.23	−0.06	0.54	−0.05	0.30	Step 1	X_3	0.63	0.04
X_1 Arable land		—	−0.05	0.44	0.05	0.11	Step 2	X_1	−1.39	0.07
X_2 Forest land			—	0.07	0.04	0.01		X_3	0.94	0.04
X_3 Capital				—	0.14	0.05	Step 3	X_1	−1.47	0.06
X_4 Labor					—	−0.08		X_3	0.94	0.03
X_5 PO Value						—		X_5	0.59	0.05
							Step 4	X_1	−1.51	0.06
COEFFICIENTS OF PARTIAL CORRELATION								X_2	−0.12	0.02
$X_{y1 \cdot 2345} = -0.57$			$X_{y4 \cdot 1235} = -0.07$					X_3	0.96	0.03
$X_{y2 \cdot 1345} = -0.15$			$X_{y5 \cdot 1234} = 0.50$					X_5	0.59	0.04
$X_{y3 \cdot 1245} = 0.74$							Step 5	X_1	−1.52	0.06
								X_2	−0.14	0.02
COEFFICIENTS OF MULTIPLE CORRELATION AND DETERMINATION								X_3	0.99	0.03
$(r_{y3} = 0.54)$			$(r^2 = 0.29)$					X_4	−0.09	0.06
$R_{y13} = 0.76$			$R^2 = 0.58$					X_5	0.63	0.04
$R_{y135} = 0.82$			$R^2 = 0.67$							
$R_{y1235} = 0.84$			$R^2 = 0.70$				$Y_c = 46.55 - 1.52X_1 - 0.14X_2 + 0.99X_3$			
$R_{y12345} = 0.85$			$R^2 = 0.72$				$-0.09X_4 + 0.63X_5 + E$			

Source: Values calculated from JEU sample farm data.

with the stepwise regression[27] coefficients and their standard errors. The hypothesis relating variations in the PI surface to the supply of capital is strongly supported. With the interrelated effects of the other variables removed, the coefficient for capital rises from 0.54 (the simple coefficient, r_{y3}) to 0.74 (the partial coefficient, $r_{y3 \cdot 1245}$). With respect to arable land, forest land, and labor supply, the coefficients indicate negative association with the dependent variable.

The stepwise procedure is illustrated with respect to the regression coefficients. In step 1, the capital variable, X_3 was introduced because it had the largest partial correlation coefficient (0.74) of the five independent variables. At that point, the regression coefficient was 0.63 (indicating that with the addition of 100 Swedish Kroner [$20] of working capital, the average increase in the Productivity Index is 0.63 per cent per man-hour).

In step 2 the arable land variable, X_1, enters as the next most significant variable ($r_{y1 \cdot 2345} = -0.57$). Its entering regression coefficient is −1.39

and this variable is significant at the ninety-nine per cent level also. With the inter-relationship between arable land and capital allowed for, the addition of one hectare of arable land (2.471 acres) has the average effect of lowering the Productivity Index by 1.39 per cent. Note how the coefficient for capital rises to 0.94 when the observed relationship between arable land and capital is held constant. From the two regression coefficients, it may be seen that with the addition of one hectare of arable land, 148 Swedish Kroner ($30) of capital (i.e., 1.39/0.94 × 100) must be added to maintain the same Productivity Index value. In the final step, after all the variables have been entered, the coefficient for arable land has become more negative and that of capital, more positive.

The analysis has indicated, empirically for the sample farms, the very significant association of working capital to the Productivity Index. Unless resources of arable land, forest land, and labor are accompanied by considerable amounts of capital, actual productivity falls far short of the potential productivity which the resources permit. The farmers who maintain a balance of resources which includes a relatively high ratio of capital to other resources come closer to realizing the potential for their farms.

[27]The stepwise regression computations were performed with the BIMD 09 computer program (BIMD Computer Programs Manual, Division of Biostatistics, University of California, Los Angeles, 1961) on a CDC 1604 computer (Numerical Analysis Laboratory, University of Wisconsin, Madison).

REGIONAL ANALYSIS

Passing on from the general view of the sample surface to the analysis for the five regions (Fig. 5), significant contrasts in the coefficients may be noticed.[28] In Table 3, the coefficients determined by estimation of the separate regional equations are indicated.

In Region 1, the north and northwestern section of Middle Sweden where the average sample farm has only seventeen hectares of arable land but forty-three hectares of land in forest, the net effect of capital is more critical in defining how closely actual productivity approaches the potential levels than in any of the other regions. The explanation for the generally high levels of attainment in this region may be understood through the prevailing tendency toward flexibility by maintaining relatively large amounts of liquid or semi-liquid assets relative to the supply of arable land and labor.

On the farms of Region 2, the supply of capital per farm is larger than in the other regions of Middle Sweden and this factor apparently accounts for the relatively higher Productivity Index

[28]The covariance assumptions with respect to parallelism of the separate regression surfaces and nonsignificant differences in variance between regions were not fulfilled.

values achieved here. Region 2 is confined largely to the fertile plains areas of E and R, yet the average performance level in terms of productivity was no higher here than in the zone of forest farms of Region 1. As has been indicated, the contrast between the two regions in resources and farm situations is about as great as may be found within Middle Sweden. The Region 2 farms have typically the most productive soils, the highest yields, and relatively the largest supplies of working capital. The farms in Region 1 and in Region 2 are similar to the extent that in both types of farm situations a balance between resources has been achieved which is relatively more conducive to productive farm operation than in the other regions of Middle Sweden.

Capital levels are lower in Region 3 even though average acreages of arable land are higher and considerable additional labor is available. These factors contribute to the explanation of why lower levels of productivity are achieved here. Agriculture is less intensive, less capital is available for fertilization, yields are lower, and less productive use is made of the labor supply.

The regression results reveal a similar situation in Region 4, which includes the more forested zones fringing Region 2. Capital is in short supply and the ratio of the supply of capital to the acreage

TABLE 3 Results of Correlation and Regression Analysis: Regional Coefficients

SIMPLE CORRELATION WITH THE PI VALUES (Y)

Variable	X_1	X_2	X_3	X_4	X_5
Region 1	−0.35	−0.01	0.56	−0.31	0.16
Region 2	−0.11	−0.03	0.70	−0.08	0.27
Region 3	−0.20	−0.17	0.66	−0.05	0.10
Region 4	−0.23	−0.02	0.34	0.03	0.47
Region 5	−0.40	−0.35	0.35	0.04	0.52
Composite	−0.23	−0.06	0.54	−0.05	0.30

PARTIAL CORRELATION WITH THE PI VALUES (Y)

Variable	X_1	X_2	X_3	X_4	X_5
Region 1	−0.83	−0.72	0.91	−0.48	0.72
Region 2	−0.68	−0.72	0.85	0.09	0.42
Region 3	−0.83	−0.12	0.90	−0.45	0.61
Region 4	−0.81	−0.34	0.82	0.00	0.72
Region 5	−0.77	−0.35	0.75	−0.19	0.77
Composite	−0.57	−0.15	0.74	−0.07	0.50

REGRESSION COEFFICIENTS

Variable	X_1	X_2	X_3	X_4	X_5
Region 1	−1.66*	−0.16*	1.06*	−0.42*	0.66*
Region 2	−1.37*	−0.21*	0.97*	0.12	0.40*
Region 3	−1.90*	0.07	1.30*	−0.82*	0.78*
Region 4	−1.76*	−0.14*	0.97*	0.00	1.00*
Region 5	−1.28*	−0.15*	0.93*	−0.22†	1.11*
Composite	−1.52*	−0.14*	0.99*	−0.09	0.63*

COEFFICIENTS OF MULTIPLE CORRELATION AND DETERMINATION

	R_{y12345}	R^2_{y12345}
Region 1	0.94	0.89
Region 2	0.86	0.75
Region 3	0.91	0.83
Region 4	0.88	0.77
Region 5	0.89	0.80
Composite	0.85	0.72

* Significant at the ninety-nine per cent level.
† Significant at the ninety-five per cent level.
Source: Values calculated from JEU sample farm data.

of arable land is the most critical factor in defining how closely actual productivity approaches the optimum levels.

Region 5, representing the central zone of Middle Sweden, includes the farms which achieved the lowest PI values on the average. The ratio of capital to resources of arable and forest land is lowest here, and this factor accounts to a considerable extent for the lower productivity levels. Long-term investments, as in land, buildings, and equipment reach their highest level in this region and the interest on this invested capital consumes, therefore, a large proportion of gross revenue, leaving little for labor income.

The regression and correlation analyses indicated that a large proportion of the variations in the PI surface may be accounted for by the variations in capital intensity on Middle Sweden's farms. Together, the five resource variables accounted for seventy-two per cent of the variation in PI values with all the sample farms considered together, and varied between seventy-five and eighty-nine per cent of variance explained in the separate regional analyses. The critical need for capital is apparently so strong as to overshadow the effect of socioeconomic variables. Capital largely defines the productivity which is possible on the sample farms, and defines the actual productivity which is achieved as well.

REEXAMINATION OF THE REGRESSION MODEL

To an extent which still remains unknown, a portion of the interregional differences in the Productivity Index may be explained by the differences in capital supply and intensity between the farms in the different regions. To determine whether significant differences still remain between regions, a further test was made by estimating the regression equation again, this time, however, with four dummy regional variables included as X_6, X_7, X_8, and X_9 representing Regions 1, 2, 3, and 4, respectively.[29] Estimation of the new equation gave the following results:

[29]The procedure involved the addition of four regional variables (R_1, R_2, R_3, and R_4) to the equation. All observations in Region 1 are assigned the value *one* for variable R_1 and all the farms in Regions 2, 3, 4, and 5 are assigned a *zero* for that variable. Similarly, all observations in Region 2 are assigned a *one* for variable R_2 and all farms in Regions 1, 3, 4, and 5 are assigned a *zero* for that variable. The same process was carried out for variables R_3 and R_4. In the case of the farms in Region 5, no separate variable is devised to indicate the presence of

$$Y = 47.51 - 1.48\overset{**}{X_1} - 0.14\overset{**}{X_2} + 0.99\overset{**}{X_3} -$$

$$0.09X_4 + 0.63\overset{**}{X_5} + 2.80X_6 - 3.31X_7 +$$

$$4.47\overset{*}{X_8} - 3.90\overset{*}{X_9} + E$$

$** =$ significant at ninety-nine per cent level
$* =$ significant at ninety-five per cent level

and partial correlation coefficients for the regional variables:

$r_{y6.12\ldots9} = +0.06$		Region 1
$r_{y7.12\ldots9} = -0.08$		Region 2
$r_{y8.12\ldots9} = +0.10$		Region 3
$r_{y9.12\ldots8} = -0.09$		Region 4

and a coefficient of multiple determination $(R^2) = 0.75$

As may be noted from the solutions, two of the regional variables emerged as significantly related to the dependent variable (at the ninety-five per cent level of significance). The farms of Regions 3 and 4 are significantly different from those in Region 5 in a respect not accounted for by the other independent variables. In addition, Regions 1 and 3 are significantly different from Regions 2 and 4. For reasons which are unknown, the presence of a farm in Region 1 is an indication that the average Productivity Index is 2.80 per cent above that of the average farm in Region 5 with, of course, all other factors held constant. In Region 2 the net effect is 3.31 per cent lower than Region 5, and so on. Following through with this procedure, it appears that an unknown variable or group of variables is responsible for the interregional differences and accounts for the ranking in terms of net addition to the PI value in the order: Region 3, Region 1, Region 5, Region 2, Region 4. This is the rank order of the regression coefficients for the dummy regional variables. The ranking provides a supplementary guide in the selection of new independent variables which may explain the residual differences between the regions and account for the rank order.

farms in this region. For further information about the use of "dummy" variables, see: D. B. Suits, "Use of Dummy Variables in Regression Equations," *Journal of the American Statistical Association*, Vol. 52 (1957), pp. 548-51, and J. Johnston, *Econometric Methods* (New York: McGraw-Hill Book Company, 1963), pp. 187-92.

Reexamination of factors suspected to account for the residual regional effect noted above indicated the strong possibility that yield variability, mentioned earlier, would provide the solution. The spatial distribution of normal variability in yields (Fig. 6) corresponds closely with the residual variance of the final equation and it was determined that little intercorrelation exists between this risk variable and the resource variables included within the equation.

Solution of the regression equation for the entire sample surface with the added variable had the anticipated result that the dummy variable became nonsignificant. Yield variability did account for the regional effect and it should be added that with the inclusion of this variable, the same proportion of variance was explained, i.e., $R^2 = 0.73$. The other regression coefficients remained unchanged with the addition of the risk variable. Yield variability is negatively associated with the Productivity Index.

To a large extent, the variability between regions in the PI scale was accounted for by the six variables included within the revised equation. The regression equations for the regions provide descriptions of the relations between the dependent variable and the five independent variables when the subsets of relatively more homogeneous farms are examined separately. We have said very little thus far about the internal homogeneity of the five regions, however, and our analysis may not be considered complete until a check has been made. In each of the five regions, therefore, the $Y-Y_c$ residuals from the respective regional equations were plotted for the individual farms in the forty-five sample areas.[30]

In terms of the distribution of residuals for the farms within the sample areas, autocorrelation was still present. In some of the sample units, the majority of farms still had residuals that were predominantly positive or predominantly negative. The most obvious characteristic of the distribution of the positive and negative sample units was their location with respect to the core of their respective region. The farms in the fringe sample units most often had residual PI values which were transi-tional between the values at the core of their region and that of the neighboring region. It was proposed, therefore, that the autocorrelation of residuals on the surface may be attributed partially to the lack of complete homogeneity within the regions, especially with respect to the differences between core and fringe sections. It had not been expected that the boundaries between the regions would be abrupt, and these findings tended to verify the contention that the change in relationship between the variables over the surface is transitional. A further test of the regression equations with a new independent variable designed to measure distance from the regional core zone confirmed the observation about the clustering and the spatial autocorrelation was accounted for. A subsequent plot of the new residuals revealed no systematic spatial clustering. It may be concluded, therefore, that the variations in the PI surface have been accounted for empirically by the six independent variables plus the distance factor.

The objective of the empirical analysis was to pinpoint and isolate indicators of the knowledge level and goal orientation of Middle Sweden's farmers. Based upon the contention that, whereas the variations in the PI surface are logically (according to the model) attributable to variations in farmer's level of knowledge and goals with respect to income, these factors are sufficiently elusive and difficult to measure that more concrete variables would be desirable as indicators. The empirical analysis has indicated preeminence of capital intensity as a guide to understanding the spatial variations in farming technology and organization.[31]

Summary

It has been necessary to relax all of the assumptions of economic rationality in order to interpret the spatial variations in the labor productivity achieved by Middle Sweden's farmers. As a group, the sample population does not achieve profit maximization, nor are its goals directed solely to that objective. Perfect knowledge is denied by the existence of unpredictable change and lag in the

---

[30]The objective of this procedure was to test for spatial autocorrelation, to determine the extent to which the residual variance was clustered spatially. Plotting the residuals permits us to observe the applicability of the single regional equation in describing the relationship between variables uniformly over the surface in that region.

[31]Rationality in farming is, thus, a cumulative learning process. Most essential is the accumulation of a capital surplus from year to year which is plowed back into current production rather than invested in land, building facilities, and equipment.

communication and perception of information. The decision behavior reflects not only the objective alternatives which are available, but also man's awareness of these alternatives and the consequences of their outcomes, his degree of aversion to risk uncertainty, and his system of values.

The concept of the spatial satisficer appears more descriptively accurate of the behavioral pattern of the sample population than the normative concept of Economic Man. The individual is adaptively or intendedly rational rather than omnisciently rational. Alternatives are considered which are conspicuous (i.e., about which he has received information). To avoid uncertainty, he attempts to emphasize short-run reactions to information feedback and to arrange a negotiated environment.[32]

If the distribution of the individual farmers is considered and allowances are made for spatial lags in the communication process, variations in

aspiration levels, in the inherent instability of planning environments, and in attitudes toward the avoidance of risk, then the spatial variations in farming activities, productivity, and income may be more clearly understood.

The framework of matched comparison between Middle Sweden's farmers and Economic Man was designed with several purposes in mind. The initial objective was to demonstrate the inappropriateness of the rational model in explaining the variations in productivity. A secondary purpose was to locate regions of "maladjustment" or "disequilibrium" where resource restrictions or organizational and technical gaps limit the attainment of income parity. The primary emphasis, however, has been devoted to the third objective, to substitute for economic rationality and its assumptions of optimizing behavior and omniscience, a more descriptive behavioral theory which allows for a range of decisions behavior and spatial variations in decision environments.

---

[32]Cyert and March, *op. cit.*, pp. 99-127.

Peter R. Gould

MAN AGAINST HIS ENVIRONMENT:
A GAME-THEORETIC FRAMEWORK

Without cataloging the many and various definitions of human geography by professional geographers over the past few decades, it is safe to say
that most have included the words *Man* and *Environment*. Traditionally, geographers have had a
deep intellectual curiosity and concern for the face
of the earth and the way it provides, in a larger
sense, a home for mankind. Much of what we see
upon the surface of the earth is the work of Man,
and is the result of a variety of decisions that men
have made as individuals or groups. Unfortunately, we have all too often lacked, or failed to
consider, conceptual frameworks of theory in
which to examine Man's relationship to his environment, the manner in which he weighs the alternatives presented, and the rationality of his choices
once they have been made. Underlining a belief
that such theoretical structures are desirable, and
that they sometimes enable us to see old and oft-
examined things with new eyes, this paper attempts to draw the attention of geographers to the
Theory of Games as a conceptual framework and
tool of research in human geography.[1] Upon its

initial and formal appearance in 1944,[2] a reviewer
stated: "Posterity may regard this . . . as one of
the major scientific achievements of the first half
of the twentieth century," and although the social
sciences have been relatively slow in considering
the Theory of Games, compared to the widespread
application of all forms of decision theory throughout engineering, business, and statistics, its increasing use in our sister disciplines of economics,
anthropology, and sociology indicates a sure trend,
fulfilling the extravagant praise heaped upon it at
an earlier date.

The Theory of Games, despite its immediate
connotation of amusements of a frivolous kind, is
an imposing structure dealing, in essence, with the
question of making rational decisions in the face
of uncertain conditions by choosing certain strategies to outwit an opponent, or, at the very least,
to maintain a position superior to others. Of course,
we do not have to think in terms of two opponents
sitting over a chessboard; we may, as geographers,
think in terms of competition for locations whose
value depends upon the locational choices of
others;[3] or, perhaps more usefully, in terms of man
choosing certain strategies to overcome or outwit

Reprinted with the permission of the author and publisher
from the *Annals,* Association of American Geographers, Vol. 53,
No. 3, 1963, pp. 290-297. Dr. Gould is Associate Professor of
Geography at the Pennsylvania State University, University
Park.

[1]References to Game Theory in geographic literature are
almost nonexistent. What few references there are usually appear
as peripheral points to a larger discussion on linear-programming
solutions, for example: William L. Garrison, "Spatial Structure
of the Economy II," *Annals,* Association of American Geographers, Vol. 49, No. 4 (December, 1959), pp. 480-81. [Re-
printed on page 000 of this volume.] It should be noted, parenthetically, that much of the mathematics used in Game Theory
is the same as that used in linear programming, and one of the
hopeful things about the new ways of looking at old problems
is that a common mathematics underlies many of the same
theoretical structures. In terms of efficiency, a key made from
a little modern algebra may often open many doors.

[2]The basic work, now revised, is John von Neumann and
Oskar Morgenstern, *Theory of Games and Economic Behavior*
(Princeton: Princeton University Press, 1953). Excellent intro-
ductions are J. D. Williams, *The Compleat Stratgyst* (New
York: McGraw-Hill Book Co., 1954); Anatol Rapoport, *Fights,
Games and Decisions* (Ann Arbor: University of Michigan Press,
1961); while a complete critique and survey is R. Duncan Luce
and Howard Raiffa, *Games and Decisions* (New York: John
Wiley and Sons, Inc., 1958).

[3]W. L. Garrison, *Annals,* Association of American Geographers, Vol. 49, pp. 480-81, reviewing Tjalling C. Koopmans
and Martin Beckmann, "Assignment Problems and the Location
of Economic Activities," *Econometrica,* Vol. 25 (January,
1957), pp. 53-76.

his environment. A good example of the latter is a Jamaican fishing village,[4] where the captains of the fishing canoes can set all their fishing pots close to the shore, all of them out to sea, or set a proportion in each area. Those canoes setting pots close to the shore have few pot losses, but the quality of the fish is poor so that the market price is low, particularly when the deep-water pots have a good day and drive the price of poor fish down still further. On the other hand, those who set their pots out to sea catch much better fish, but every now and then a current runs in an unpredictable fashion, battering the pots and sinking the floats, so that pot losses are higher. Thus, the village has three choices, to set all the pots in, all the pots out, or some in and some out, while the environment has two strategies, current or no-current. Game Theory has successfully predicted the best choice of strategies and the proportion each should be used, a proportion very close to that arrived at by the villagers over a long period of trial and error.

Man continually finds himself in situations where a number of different choices or strategies may be available to wrest a living from his environment. Indeed, without soaring to those stratospheric heights of philosophical, or even metaphysical, discussion, to which all discourse in the social and physical sciences ultimately leads, let it be said that to be Man rather than Animal is, in part, to be able to recognize a variety of alternatives, and in a *rationale* manner, reasoning from those little rocks of knowledge that stick up above the vast sea of uncertainty, choose strategies to win the basic struggle for survival. The perception that alternatives exist, and the recognition that their specific value, or utility, for a given time and place may depend upon an unpredictable environment, about which Man has only highly probabilistic notions based upon past experience, is clearly central to any discussion of man–environment relationships within a game theoretic framework. Thus, growing concomitantly with, and, indeed, embedded in, the Theory of Games, is a theory of utility intuitively raised, axiomatically

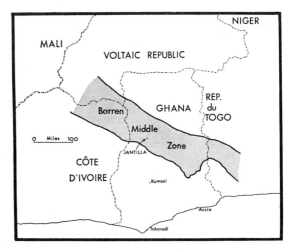

FIGURE 1   The Barren Middle Zone of Ghana of Low Population Density and Extreme Variability of Rainfall.

treated, and experimentally tested in the real world.[5]

The Barren Middle Zone of Ghana (Fig. 1), a belt which, for environmental and historical reasons, has a very low population density, has one of the severest agricultural climates in West Africa,[6] with heavy precipitation followed by the extreme aridity of the Harmatten, which sweeps south from the Sahara. A further problem is that the high degree of variability of the precipitation makes it difficult for the farmers to plan effectively.[7]

Let us assume that the farmers of Jantilla, a small village in Western Ghana, may use the land to grow the following crops, each with different degrees of resistance to dry conditions, as their main staple food: yams, cassava, maize, millet, and hill rice.[8] In Game Theory terms the cultivation of these crops represents five strategies. In the

[4]William Davenport, "Jamaican Fishing: A Game Theory Analysis," *Yale University Publications in Anthropology*, No. 59 (1960); an excellent case study drawn from detailed anthropological field work which provided the basis for assigning actual monetary values to the various choices presented to the village as a whole.

[5]The barbarous treatment of utility theory by those who fail, or refuse, to see the difference between a man declaring a preference because of the supposedly existing greater utility, rather than assigning a higher utility to a man's preference after it has been declared, did much damage at one time in the field of economics. The latter must always be kept in mind to avoid confusion; see Luce and Raiffa, *op. cit.*, p. 22.

[6]Walter Manshard, "Land Use Patterns and Agricultural Migration in Central Ghana," *Tijdschrift voor Economishe en Sociale Geografie* (September, 1961), p. 225.

[7]H. O. Walker, *Weather and Climate of Ghana*, Ghana Meteorological Department, Departmental Note No. 5 (Accra, 1957), p. 37, map (mimeographed).

[8]Manshard, "Land Use Patterns . . .," pp. 226-29. See also Thomas T. Poleman, *The Food Economies of Urban Middle Africa* (Stanford: Food Research Institute, 1961).

same terms, and to simplify this initial example, let us make the somewhat unrealistic assumption that the environment has only two strategies; dry years and wet years. These strategies may be put into matrix form (Fig. 2), called the payoff matrix, and represent a two-person-five-strategy-zero-sum game, in which the values in the boxes represent the average yields of the crops under varying conditions, perhaps in calorific or other nutritional terms. For example, if the farmers of Jantilla choose

to grow only yams, they will obtain a yield of eighty-two under wet year conditions, but the yield will drop to eleven if the environment does its worst. It should be noted that the values in the boxes have been chosen simply to provide an example of Game Theory, but this, in turn, emphasizes the close relationship of these methods to direct field work, for only in this way can we obtain these critical subcensus data. In a very real sense, our tools are outrunning our efforts to gather the necessary materials. We might also note, parenthetically, that extreme accuracy of data, while always desirable, is not essential in order to use Game Theory as a tool, since it can be shown that payoff matrices subjected to a fairly high degree of random shock by injecting random error terms still give useful approximations and insights upon solution.[9]

			ENVIRONMENT MOISTURE CHOICES	
			Wet Years	Dry Years
		Yams	82	11
FARMERS	CROP	Maize	61	49
OF	CHOICE	Cassava	12	38
JANTILLA		Millet	43	32
		Hill rice	30	71

FIGURE 2 Payoff Matrix for Two-Person-Five-Strategy-Zero-Sum Game; Crop Choices Against Moisture Choices.

FIGURE 3 Graphical Solution to Assign Critical Pair of Strategies in Two-Person-Five Strategy-Zero-Sum Game.

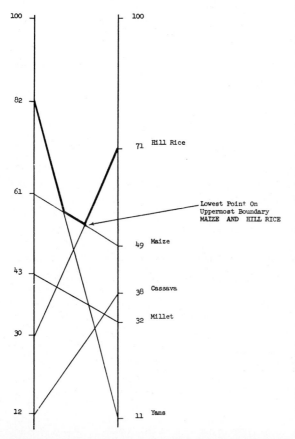

A payoff matrix in which one opponent has only two strategies can always be reduced to a two-by-two game which is the solution for the complete game, in this case a five-by-two. We may, if time is no object, and we like dull, tedious work, take every pair of rows in turn and solve them for the maximum payoff to the farmers; but, fortunately, we also have a graphical solution which will point to the critical pair at once (Fig. 3). If we draw two scales from zero to one hundred, plot the values of each of the farmer's strategies on alternate axes, and connect the points, then the lowest point on the uppermost boundary will indicate which crops the farmers should grow to maximize their chances of filling their bellies.[10] Now we can take this pair of strategies, maize and hill rice (Fig. 4), and by calculating the difference between each pair of values and assigning it, regardless of sign, to the alternate strategy, we can find the proportion each strategy should be used. Thus, maize should be grown 77.4 per cent of the time and hill rice 22.6 per cent of the time, and if this is done the farmers can assure themselves the maximum return or payoff over the long run of fifty-four.

These proportions immediately raise the question as to how the solution should be interpreted. Should the farmers plant maize 77.4 per cent of

[9]In linear-programming terms this would follow from the notion that the boundary conditions would have to change quite drastically, in most cases, in order for there to be a change in the mini-max point which would alter, in turn, the choice of strategies (see Fig. 3).

[10]This is simply the graphical solution to the basic linear-programming problem. The values, and the resulting slopes, have been deliberately exaggerated for the purposes of illustration.

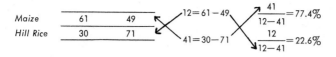

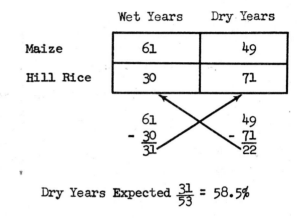

FIGURE 4   Solution of Two-By-Two Payoff Matrix to Achieve Most Efficient Choice of Crop Proportions.

the years and hill rice for the remaining 22.6 per cent, mixing the years in a random fashion;[11] or, should they plant these proportions each year? As Game Theory provides a conceptual framework for problems where choices are made repeatedly, rather than those involving choices of the unique, once-in-history variety, the cold-blooded answer is that *over the long haul* it makes no difference. However, when men have experienced famine and have looked into the glazed eyes of their swollen-bellied children, the long run view becomes somewhat meaningless. Thus, we may conclude that the farmers will hold strongly to the short-term view and will plant the proportions *each year* since the truly catastrophic case of hill rice and wet year could not then occur.

It is interesting to note, simply as an aside, that solving this two-by-two matrix vertically tells us that over the long run we may expect dry years 58.5 per cent of the time (Fig. 5), if we assume the environment to be a totally vindictive opposing player trying to minimize the farmers' returns.

The solution of this little game raises some interesting questions for the geographer. Does the land-use pattern approach the ideal? And if not, why not? If the land-use pattern does not approach the ideal, does this imply a conscious departure on the part of the people, or does their-less-than-ideal use of the land reflect only the best estimate they can make with the knowledge available to them, rather than any degree of irrationality? Do the farmers display rational behavior in our Western sense of the term despite all the warnings of the anthropologists about the illusory concept of economic man in Africa? If one were in an advisory position, would this help to make decisions regarding the improvement of agriculture practices? If the solution exceeds the basic calorific requirements of the people, is it worth gambling and de-

FIGURE 5   Vertical Solution of the Two-By-Two Payoff Matrix to Yield Proportion of Dry Years Expected.

creasing the proportion of one or both crops to achieve a better variety of foods—if this is desired by the people? How far can they gamble and decrease these proportions if inexpensive, but efficient, storage facilities are available, either to hold the surpluses of one year to allay the belt-tightening "hungry season" of the next, or to sell in the markets of the south when prices are high? Thus, the usefulness of the tool is not so much the solving of the basic problem, but the host of questions it raises for further research.

A further example from Ghana will make this clear (Fig. 6). For centuries the people living south of the great Niger arc have raised cattle and have driven them along the old cattle trails to the markets of Ghana.[12] The driving of cattle is a chancy business because, while Man can overcome cattle diseases such as rinderpest with modern veterinary medicines, he cannot yet predict the very dry years in this area of high rainfall variability through which the cattle have to be driven to market. Let us assume that the northern cattle

---

[11]For a discussion on the necessity of a random mix of strategies see R. B. Braithwaite, *Scientific Explanation: A Study of the Function of Theory, Probability and Law in Science* (Cambridge: The University Press, 1955), pp. 236-39.

[12]Peter R. Gould, *The Development of the Transportation Pattern in Ghana* (Evanston: Northwestern University Studies in Geography, No. 5, 1961), p. 137.

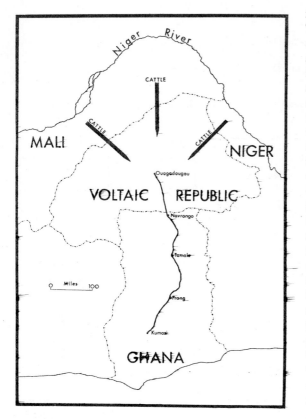

FIGURE 6 Areas of Cattle Production and Main Route to Traditional Cattle Markets.

traders of the Voltaic Republic, Mali, and Niger have the choice of selling their cattle in five markets: Ouagadougou, Navrongo, Tamale, Prang, and Kumasi. Each market thus represents a strategy and the traders may choose any one, or a mixture, of these in which to sell their animals. Let us further assume that Nature, or the environment, also has five strategies ranging from years with

intensely dry conditions to unusually wet years. Thus, the strategies available to the cattle traders and the environment form a two-person-five-zero-sum game and may be represented by a five-by-five matrix which indicates, for example, the average price of an animal in various markets under different conditions (Fig. 7). The matrix indicates that a trader may gamble upon the season being a very wet one, in which case he would drive all his animals to Kumasi; but, if he guessed wrong, and the season was a less than average one, cattle would die or lose a great deal of weight on the way and he would get much less in Kumasi than if he had sold them in another market such as Ouagadougou.[13] This, of course, is a deliberate simplification, for we are not taking into account the possibility of varying demands, the question of alternative local supplies at some of the markets, nor the probability of Ghanaian consumers substituting one source of protein for another, for example, fresh fish from the coast or dried Niger perch.[14] It might be possible to gather data to fill payoff matrices for other suppliers, but the situation would become much more difficult since we would be in the realm of non-zero-sum games that are, both conceptually and computationally, much more complex.[15]

---

[13]It has been suggested by Professor William Garrison that this problem might be readily handled in a practical sense by a standard linear-programming approach; a suggestion that would confirm Luce's and Raiffa's evocative comment on the Theory of Games that ". . . one can often discover a natural linear programming problem lurking in the background," *op. cit.*, p. 18.

[14]Peter Garlick, "The French Trade de Nouveau," *Economic Bulletin of the Department of Economics, University of Ghana* (mimeographed), p. 19.

[15]Zero-sum games are so called because upon choosing a particular strategy one competitor's gain (+) becomes the opponent's loss (−), the gain and loss summing to zero. Non-zero-sum games are those cases where an alteration in strategic choice *may* raise or lower the payoff for both players. Two-person-non-zero-sum games can be handled using the notion of imaginary side payments. N-person-non-zero-sum games may best be described as computationally miserable.

ENVIRONMENT AVAILABLE MOISTURE CHOICES

			Very Wet	Above Average	Average	Below Average	Intense Drought
		Ouagadougou	15	20	30	40	50
CATTLE	MARKETS	Navrongo	20	15	15	20	5
TRADERS		Tamale	40	30	20	15	10
		Prang	60	50	40	20	15
		Kumasi	80	70	40	25	10

FIGURE 7 Payoff Matrix in Two-Person-ı ve-By-Five-Zero-Sum Game; Market Choice Against Available Moisture Choices.

ENVIRONMENT AVAILABLE MOISTURE CHOICES

							1	2	3	4	....	59	60	Total
		Ouagadougou	15	20	30	40	50	15	65	115*	165*	....	2,060	2,110*	32
		Navrongo	20	15	15	20	5	20	25	30	40	....	870	875	0
CATTLE	MARKETS	Tamale	40	30	20	15	10	40	50	60	70	....	2,045	2,055	0
TRADERS		Prang	60	50	40	20	15	60	75	90	105	....	1,875	1,890	0
		Kumasi	80	70	40	25	10	80*	90*	100	110	....	2,065	2,075	28
			15*	20	30	40	50								
			95	90	70	65	60*								
			175	160	110	90	70*								

	Ouagadougou	32	$\frac{32}{60} = 53.4\%$
	Kumasi	28	$\frac{28}{60} = 46.6\%$

2,190 2,250 1,880 1,845 1,830
etc.

FIGURE 8 Solution by Iteration of Payoff Matrix.

Given the above strategies, what are the best markets the cattle traders can choose, and what are the best proportions?—"best" in the sense that over the long run the traders selling certain proportions of their cattle in these markets will get the maximum payoff. The solution of a five-by-five matrix in a zero-sum game is not as easy as the case where one opponent has two, or even three, choices. We do have, however, ways of choosing the strategies and *estimating* the proportions that should be used, the estimation being based upon a relatively simple iteration which converges upon the solution and which may be carried to any degree of required accuracy (Fig. 8). In the above example, the iteration has been carried out sixty times, and by counting the number of asterisks in each row of a market, which mark the maximum figure in each column of the estimating process, we can calculate that the traders should sell thirty-two sixtieths, or 53.4 per cent, of their cattle in Ouagadougou and then drive the remainder right through Navrongo, Tamale, and Prang to the Kumasi market (Fig. 9).

Let us pose the question, now, of what might happen if a really strong transportation link were forged between Tamale and Navrongo, such as the remaking and tarring of a road, so that upon arrival at the Voltaic–Ghanaian border cattle would no longer have to make their way on the hoof, but could be driven in trucks to the southern markets arriving in much better condition even in the very driest of seasons (Fig. 10). The payoff matrix would obviously change, and we might expect very much higher prices to prevail in Tamale, Prang, and Kumasi for the fat, sleek animals, rather

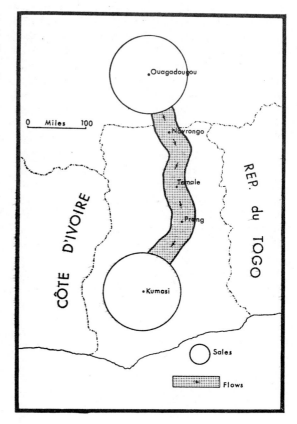

FIGURE 9 Proportional Sales and Flows of Cattle Prior to Road Improvements and Trucking.

than the bags-of-bones that often stumbled into these markets in former years. Again, the payoff matrix can be solved using the iterative method

337

ENVIRONMENT AVAILABLE MOISTURE CHOICES

			Very Wet	Above Average	Average	Below Average	Intense Drought
CATTLE TRADERS	MARKETS	Ouagadougou	15	20	30	40	50
		Navrongo	20	15	15	20	5
		Tamale	80	80	70	70	80
		Prang	100	100	90	80	70
		Kumasi	130	130	120	90	60

FIGURE 10 New Payoff Matrix Indicating Price Changes in Markets as a Result of New Road Link Between Tamale and Navrongo.

160 times on this occasion (Fig. 11), to produce completely different choices and proportions from the previous example. Now it is no longer worthwhile for the traders to sell cattle in the Ouagadougou or Navrongo markets, but sell instead 62.5 per cent in Tamale, 25 per cent in Prang, and 12.5 per cent in Kumasi. Thus, an improved road link, a visible sign on the landscape of a technological improvement, changes Man's perception and evaluation of the same choices available to him before, and as a result changes the patterns of flows and sales (Fig. 12). Now the flow has increased over the northern portion of the route, and it has become desirable to sell portions of the herds in the Tamale and Prang markets, the increases at these markets coming from former sales at Ouagadougou and Kumasi. Again, solving the payoff matrix points up some interesting questions for the geographer. First, it raises the whole question of estimating the effects of improving a transportation link—what will the flows be before and after? Can we obtain payoff values from one part of West Africa and use them to estimate changes of flows in other parts? Secondly, the question, again: how close does the behavior of the cattle traders approach that required to obtain the maximum payoff over the long run? Thirdly, what would be the effect of increasing the speed of communication so that cattle traders who started early in the season could inform others on the trail to the north about the conditions they find? And, finally, we should note the way an improved transportation link in effect extends the influence of one or more markets over others as the effect of distance is broken down allowing the demands of one center to impinge upon another.

By taking two examples from the traditional economy of Ghana, this paper has tried to point out the possible utility of the Theory of Games as a tool of research and as a conceptual framework in human and economic geography. That such frameworks are needed is evident, for without these broad conceptual constructions in which to place our facts and observations it becomes an almost impossible task to raise and tackle, in a meaningful and lasting fashion, questions of Man's equilibrium with his environment, his perceptions and judgments about it, and the rules by which he reacts at different points in time and space? The work of Man is all around us upon the face of our

ENVIRONMENT: AVAILABLE MOISTURE CHOICES

							1	2	3	4	160	Total
Ouagadougou	15	20	30	40	50	50	100	150	190	.....	0
Navrongo	20	15	15	20	5	5	10	15	35	.....	0
Tamale	80	80	70	70	80	80*	160*	240*	310*	.....	100
Prang	100	100	90	80	70	70	140	210	290	.....	40
Kumasi	130	130	120	90	60	60	120	180	270	.....	20
	130	130	120	90	60*						
	210	210	190	160	140*						

Tamale $\frac{100}{160} = 62.5\%$

Prang $\frac{40}{160} = 25.0\%$

Kumasi $\frac{20}{160} = 12.5\%$

etc.

FIGURE 11 Solution by Iteration of New Payoff Matrix.

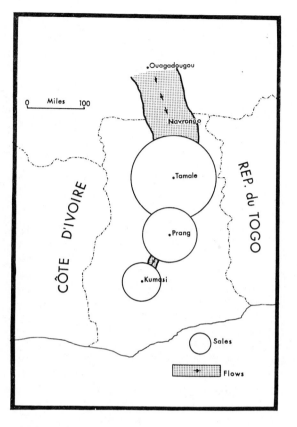

FIGURE 12 Proportional Sales and Flows of Cattle After
Road Improvements and Trucking.

earth, and is the result of men perceiving a variety of alternatives, subsequently limiting the range of choices according to their idea of what is useful and good, and *deciding* upon certain strategies to gain those ends. Thus, the whole body of decision theory, of which the Theory of Games is but one part, has an increasingly important role to play. Perhaps, in the same way that information theory has illuminated old problems of central-place structure, linear-programming solutions have helped our understanding of shifting flows and boundaries, and the theory of queues is throwing light upon problems ranging from those of the Ice Age to those of livestock production, the Theory of Games may also have a role to play.

Emilio Casetti [1]

OPTIMAL LOCATION OF STEEL MILLS SERVING THE
QUEBEC AND SOUTHERN ONTARIO STEEL MARKET

This study is an attempt to analyze the impact upon the optimal location of the steel mills supplying the Canadian market of (1) the flow of iron ore from Seven Islands through the St. Lawrence Seaway to the steel centres around the Great Lakes, and (2) the increase of steel consumption in Canada. These two matters are examined with particular consideration of the possible establishment of new steel capacity in the St. Lawrence area. It is a limited, approximate investigation based on linear programming techniques and does not aim at results of the type required for policy-making or for managerial decisions. However, such results could be arrived at by extending the research through a relaxation of simplifying assumptions and through the use of more fine-grained and up-to-date data than were available to the author. The study is somewhere in the middle of a continuum having at its extremes an investigation of a managerial type and a purely theoretical analysis of the locational influence of transportation flows.

Background Considerations

Speculations on the inauguration of primary iron and steel production in Montreal or in Seven Islands, the rail terminus on the St. Lawrence of the iron mines of Central Quebec, have recently become increasingly frequent.[2] This interest is partly a response to certain non-economic factors, but it is also solidly based on the changes since 1945 in the value of the St. Lawrence area as a possible location of steel plants.

War-time depletion of the high grade ores in the Mesabi and the development of important ore deposits in Labrador and Venezuela suggested at first that mid-western steel producing areas would experience serious competitive difficulties with respect to areas nearer the iron ore sources.[3] The Atlantic and Gulf coast areas appeared to be in a more favourable position to take advantage of the new situation because of their locations close to the large centres of consumption.[4] In addition, the Labrador and Venezuela ores could be transported to the Atlantic coast by large, economic carriers more easily than by the smaller carriers serving midwest centres through the St. Lawrence. Such considerations may well have influenced the United States Steel Company, in the building of its large integrated steel mill on a tide-water site near Philadelphia, Pennsylvania. Expansion of the east coast market played an important role here too. By this time the St. Lawrence area appeared better suited than before the war as a possible location of new steel capacity, but it was still rated second to the coastal locations. Table I gives a comparison of transport costs.

Reprinted with the permission of the author and publisher from the *Canadian Geographer,* Vol. X, No. 1, 1966, pp. 27-39. Dr. Casetti is Associate Professor of Geography at The Ohio State University, Columbus.

[1]The author is inedbted to Professors A. Charnes, W. L. Garrison, and D. Marble, Northwestern University, and to Professor D. Kerr, University of Toronto, for their help, advice, and criticism. The errors are the author's.

[2]Kerr, D., "The Geography of the Canadian Iron and Steel Industry," *Econ. Geog.,* XXXV (1959), 151-63.

[3]Barloon, M., "Steel: The Great Retreat," *Harpers Magazine,* no. 195 (Aug. 1947), 145-55; *Hearings before the Sub-Committee of the Committee on Foreign Relations,* U.S. Senate, 83rd Congress, 1st sess., on S. 589 April 14-May 21, 1953, pp. 25-26, 123-33.

[4]Lippert, T. W., "Cerro Bolivar," *Mining Engineering,* no. 187 (1950), 183.

TABLE I   Cost of Principal Ores Delivered to Representative Consuming Centres in the United States, 1953-54

Ore Source	Natural iron content (percentage)	Cost per gross ton* (dollars)			Cost per Unit† (cents)		
		Lake Erie	Pittsburgh	East coast	Lake Erie	Pittsburgh	East coast
Mesabi	51.5						
Production cost		6.43	8.55		12.5	16.6	
Market price		9.90	12.02		19.2	23.3	
Taconite	63.5						
Production cost		7.77	9.89		12.2	15.6	
Labrador	54.0						
Production cost		7.19	9.31		13.3	17.2	
Venezuela (U.S. Steel)	58.0						
Production cost			9.11	6.30		15.7	10.9
Market price			12.11	9.30		20.9	16.0

Source: P. G. Craig, "Location Factors in the Development of Steel Centers," *Papers and Proc. Regional Sci. Assoc.*, III (1957), p. 257.
* All estimates include freight charges to the indicated destination.
† These estimates are derived by dividing the gross ton costs by the percentage of natural iron content.

The early post-war outlook was substantially changed by improvements in taconite technology and by the opening of the St. Lawrence Seaway. New techniques of beneficiation of low-grade ores kept mines in the Lake Superior area competitive, and have made the locational disadvantages of the midwest with respect to the east and Gulf coast steel centres much less than anticipated.[5] Moreover, the opening of the St. Lawrence Seaway made the Great Lakes area accessible to middle-sized ocean carriers, thus reducing the ore transportation cost from Seven Islands to Lake Erie, and tending to make the transportation of ore via the St. Lawrence less costly than via Philadelphia (or Baltimore) and thence inland by rail.[6] The opening of the Seaway has also increased the advantage of the Canadian areas extending from Seven Islands to Hamilton as potential locations for new steel mills partly because the transportation costs of Quebec ore have decreased, and partly because a flow of this ore has been generated to the United States iron and steel centres around the lakes, in turn necessarily decreasing transportation costs on shipments from the Great Lakes down the St. Lawrence. In addition, after World War II, Canadian steel consumption increased considerably, as indicated indirectly by data on the Gross National Product in Canada, which is correlated with steel consumption (Table II), and directly by the data in Table III which shows the apparent per capita consumption of crude steel.

Flow of Ore

The flow of ore from Seven Islands to the Great Lakes affects the optimal location of steel plants serving the Canadian market because of the sensitivity of the industry to transportation costs. The southwestward flow of ore generates a transportational imbalance resulting in low costs of transportation for commodities moving in the opposite direction.[7] If ships transporting ore from Seven Islands do not return empty, the costs of moving

[5]Table I shows that in 1953-54 the cost of ore on iron unit basis was lowest on the east coast, but that taconite and Labrador ore were not substantially more expensive in the Great Lakes centres than was Venezuelan ore on the east coast. Pittsburgh and other inland centres have always experienced higher costs so that the exhaustion of higher grade ores in the Mesabi Range did not change their position, except that ore became available from three or four sources at approximately equal costs.

[6]The study, *The Impact of the St. Lawrence Seaway on the Montreal Area* (Montreal, 1958), p. 72, estimated rates for moving iron ore from Seven Islands to Ashtabula both before and after the opening of the seaway. The difference is approximately sixty cents per long ton. If the approximate data in Table I are corrected by this amount, the cost of Labrador ore per iron unit at Lake Erie and Pittsburgh becomes respectively 12.2 and 16.1 (instead of 13.3 and 17.2).

[7]This imbalance seems to have generated a change in grain transportation patterns. Kerr remarks that, "by 1963, direct shipments of grain had dropped to less than 40 per cent of the total and trans-shipments at lower St. Lawrence ports had become dominant. A flow pattern has developed on the lower St. Lawrence River by which many of the large lake freighters, having unloaded a cargo of grain return upbound with iron ore from Sept-Isles or Port Cartier." ("The St. Lawrence Seaway and Trade on the Great Lakes," *Can. Geog.* VIII, 4 (1964), 189.

TABLE II Gross National Product in Canada (constant (1949) dollars)

Year	G.N.P.
1930	8,679
1935	7,678
1940	10,911
1945	15,552
1950	17,471
1955	21,920
1960	25,849
1963	29,380

Source: D.B.S., *Canada Year Book 1965* (Ottawa, 1965), p. 1009.

TABLE III Apparent per Capita Consumption of Crude Steel in Canada

Year (average of)	Pounds of steel
1936—38	333
1951—53	789

Source: L. Morgan, "The Canadian Primary Iron and Steel Industry," in *Royal Commission on Canada's Economic Prospects, Report* 1956 p. 68.

the ships from Seven Islands to the Great Lakes and back will be imputed both to the transportation of iron ore and to that of the commodities carried on the return trip. If the ships do return empty, then the ore must bear the two-directional transportational costs. Exactly how costs are divided depends on the institutional framework of the industry. Two instances illustrate tendencies which might be codified into institutional frameworks. If a single company owns steel mills, carriers, and products transported on the return trip, transportation costs might not be divided and the non-empty return trip will decrease the over-all average transportation costs. If, instead, the steel mills, carriers, and merchandise belong to different companies, the total cost will be divided through the mechanism of demand and supply, the elasticity of the demand for transportation being the critical element in the determination of the respective freight rates for iron ore and other products.

If it is supposed that insufficient effective demand exists for transportation in the northeastward direction between Ashtabula and Seven Islands, it is possible that this availability of backhaul space might influence the location of economic activities requiring northbound transportation. For example, a company controlling steel mills and carriers might be interested in starting such activities in order to decrease its over-all transportation costs. If carriers were owned by separate concerns, low shipping rates could be asked for transportation along the route from the Great Lakes to Seven Islands, and in turn these might stimulate the development of new economic activities. Consequently, the flow of ore would actually encourage not only the establishment or expansion of steel mills, but also economic activities requiring transportation in a direction opposite to the flow of iron ore.

It is unlikely that the huge transportation imbalance created by the flow of iron ore supplied by a major mining centre to major steel districts can be entirely restored by the development of activities other than steel production, because of the sheer order of magnitude of the shipments involved. This fact explains why large transportation imbalances have historically favoured the growth of the steel industry. The development of the steel centres on Lake Erie, for instance, has been associated with the low freight rates because "coal is brought as return freight in the cars which carry iron ore from the Lake Erie ports to the Pittsburgh furnaces."[8] Zimmermann calls the lower lake ports from Toledo to Erie "secondary" steel centres "because the presence of steel is in part a reflection or secondary effect of primary forces operating in the Pittsburgh district."[9] In other words, the Pittsburgh district generated a transportation imbalance that made coal cheaper and stimulated the development of steel production.

A transportation imbalance favouring steel mills need not be due to iron ore shipments. Rodwell Jones, in calling attention to the development of the steel industry in Duluth at the head of Lake Superior, remarks that there "coal can be obtained at lower freight rates than at Chicago." This fact is based, he continues, "on the fact that coal moving to Duluth does so as a fill cargo on the return trip of iron and wheat ships moving from the head of Lake Superior to the Erie ports, a position comparable in its effects on the price of the coal, to that of the coal which moved in pre-war days to Italy in ships going to the Black Sea to load wheat

[8]Colby, C. C., and E. A. Foster, *Economic Geography: Industries and Resources in the Commercial World* (Boston, 1947), p. 322.

[9]Zimmermann, E. W., *World Resources and Industries* (New York, 1950), p. 663.

from South Russia and Rumania."[10] It could be added that cheap coal from England was one of the factors that made possible the beginning and early development of the modern steel industry in Italy.[11]

Expansion of Consumption

The increase in Canadian steel consumption is relevant to the optimal location of steel mills (1) because markets have become an increasingly important factor in the location of steel production, (2) because, within limits, steel plants are sensitive to economies of scale, and (3) because market expansion may offset "locational inertia." Inertia has been recognized as a major factor in the location of the steel industry.[12] Its influence, however, is not the same when consumption grows as when it is stable (or decreases). The disinvestment of the heavy capital immobilized in steel plants is very costly. When the steel market is stable a plant will be relocated only in the very improbable case that the advantage of a new location more than compensates for costs of starting a new plant and of disinvesting the capital immobilized in the old one. When, instead, the steel market is increasing and the steel producing capacity is to be increased, new capacity will be added in old locations only if the advantages of the new locations are less than the advantages provided by the investments accumulated in the old locations. The growth of steel consumption in Canada tends to make the locational pattern of steel production for the Canadian

market more responsive to changes in optimal locations of plants.

The increasing importance of markets as a locational factor in the iron and steel industry, as contrasted to sources of raw materials, has been repeatedly emphasized.[13] The increasing role played by market location has been attributed mainly (1) to technological improvements that have made it possible to produce steel with less ore and coal, but also (2) to the increasing dependence of steel plants on scrap iron, which is generated mostly in consuming areas, and (3) to the existence of differential freight rates, much higher for finished products than for raw materials. It should be emphasized that this study stresses variables relating to point 1 above. Points 2 and 3 are not included, so the results represent only an approximation of the relative importance of market and raw material orientation in influencing the location of iron and steel centres.

Simplifications and Assumptions

In order to sharpen the analysis, it is necessary to simplify some aspects of the problem. With respect to iron ore, it will be assumed that Canadian ore used by the United States markets is moved from Seven Islands to Ashtabula, and that the eastern Canadian steel market is concentrated in Hamilton and Montreal. Actually, iron ore moves from the mines at Knob Lake to several destinations on and near the Great Lakes, and steel consumers in eastern Canada are scattered along the St. Lawrence and the northern shores of Lakes Ontario and Erie reaching as far north as Quebec City and as far south as Windsor.

Industrial locations are referred to as "optimal" when they involve minimum processing and transportation costs. In the present context, processing costs will be assumed equal for all possible locations, leaving only variations in transportation costs to be considered. This simplification is consistent with the widely accepted notion that the steel industry is transport-oriented, as opposed to other industries, the aluminum industry for instance, which are process-oriented.[14] The simpli-

[10]Jones, L. L. R., *North America: An Historical and Regional Geography* (London, 1954), p. 288. See also, Smith, J. R., *Industrial and Commercial Geography* (New York, 1913), p. 360.

[11]A theoretical formulation of the dependence of what Zimmerman calls "secondary" development of the steel industry on patterns of traffic flows is given in Hoover, E. M., *The Location of Economic Activity* (New York, 1948), p. 43. "The relative freight ratio of ore and coal depends partly on the predominant direction of traffic flow. A region producing little else but ore or coal is likely to have an excess of outbound tonnage, which provides the basis for a low backhaul rate on inbound shipment of the other material and encourages metallurgical developments in such regions. On the other hand, coal-producing areas usually attract a variety of industries on the basis of cheap fuel supply, and a highly industrialized area usually exports a smaller tonnage than it imports (because manufactured products are less bulky per unit of value than most food and raw materials.) In that case, no backhaul concessions can be expected. However, industrialized areas provide a local market for iron and steel and a local supply for furnace, scrap, both factors that encourage further expansion of metallurgical activities."

[12]Rodgers, A., "Industrial Inertia: A Major Factor in the Location of the Steel Industry in the U.S.," *Geog. Rev.*, XLII (1952), 55-66.

[13]See, for example, Craig, P. G., "Location Factors in the Development of Steel Centers," *Papers and Proc. Regional Sci. Assoc.*, III (1957), 249-65.

[14]*Ibid.*, p. 250.

fication neglects the difference in production costs between old and new plants, differences of "economies of scales," as well as differences in infrastructures and facilities associated with the presence of a well-established steel industry.

The possible locations for steel plants are restricted, by an additional simplifying assumption, to Seven Islands, Montreal, Hamilton, and Ashtabula. (The fictional steel production in Ashtabula is taken here to symbolize the steel products sent from any of the midwest steel districts to the Canadian consumers scattered between Seven Islands and Windsor.) Furthermore, it is assumed that these plants use coal and ore from Ashtabula and Seven Islands respectively.

The cost of moving empty ships is assumed equal to that of moving ships at full cargo. This simplification is not unrealistic because the differences involved in the two situations are due more to the delays for loading and unloading than to per mile costs.[15] It is therefore implied that transporting coal to Seven Islands is not significantly more costly than moving empty carriers to Seven Islands. Hence, because the cost of transporting iron ore is minimal at Seven Islands, it follows that Seven Islands itself involves minimum aggregate raw material transportation costs.

The Canadian steel market is assumed to be concentrated in Hamilton and Montreal. Therefore, the market factor in this study forces the optimal location(s) to be as close as possible to Hamilton and Montreal. It can be concluded that within the framework of this study the optimal location(s) of the steel mills will be determined as points corresponding to the equilibrium of a force that pulls towards Seven Islands with two other forces pulling towards Hamilton and Montreal.

Linear Programming Formulation

The problem of the optimal economic location of steel plants supplying the St. Lawrence area can be formulated as follows: to determine the patterns of steel production, steel transportation, raw material transportation, and empty carrier movement that both involve minimum costs and satisfy

---

[15]*The Impact of the St. Lawrence Seaway on the Montreal Area*, p. 124ff.

the steel requirements of the Canadian markets as well as the ore requirements of the United States markets. This type of problem involving the selection of a set of variables (pattern of steel production, and so forth) that reduce a cost function to a minimum, subject to a set of constraints (steel requirements to be met, and so forth), can be formulated as a linear programme.

VARIABLES

The structural variables of the problem are divided into five sets (Ashtabula, Hamilton, Montreal, and Seven Islands will be henceforth indicated by their respective initials, A, H, M, S):

(1) Variables indicating the amount of steel production at A, H, M, S. These will be denoted by X_{1A}, X_{1H}, X_{1M}, and X_{1S} respectively.

(2) Variables indicating the amount of steel shipped from a steel producing centre to a steel consuming centre.

(3) Variables indicating the amount of coal shipped from A to the other permissible destinations.

(4) Variables indicating the amount of ore shipped from S to the other permissible destinations.

(5) Variables indicating the movement of empty ships between any two possible destinations.

The variables indicating a shipment or a movement of any empty carrier are denoted by an X with three subscripts. The first subscript is a number corresponding to one of the sets of variables defined above. The other two subscripts are letters indicating, respectively, the places of origin and of destination of the trip. For instance, X_{2AH} is the variable corresponding to the shipment of steel from Ashtabula to Hamilton; X_{5SA} is the variable corresponding to an empty (light) trip from Seven Islands to Ashtabula.

CONSTRAINTS

The constraints of the problem are divided into:

(1) Market constraints, which insure that all the steel production in A and S is shipped to the markets in H and M, and that the latter receive an amount of steel greater than, or equal to, their requirements.

(2) Raw material constraints, which insure that A receives all the ore required by the midwest steel districts, and that the four centres, A, H, M, and S, receive coal and ore corresponding to their levels of activity.

(3) Empty shipments constraints, which force the programme to yield a pattern of optimal round trips, not just of optimal raw material and steel shipments. These constraints ensure that the ships are available when and where they are needed.

In the functional of the linear programming model the variables indicating shipments (including empty shipments) are associated with non-zero costs. Steel production variables are given zero costs.

The constraints are listed in Table IV. The first ten constraints and the first sixteen variables (reading from the left across the top of the table) are similar to constraints and variables appearing in interregional linear programming models of activity analysis.[16] The a_{ij}'s are input coefficients, say, tons of coal required per ton of steel produced. Negative coefficients correspond to inputs, the positive coefficients to outputs. Constraints associated with final and with intermediate commodities are respectively of the form $\Sigma_j a_{ij} x_j \geq b_i$ and $\Sigma_j a_{ij} x_j = 0$. Constraints corresponding to primary commodities (of the form $\Sigma a_{ij} x_j < b_i$) do not appear in the model because coal and iron ore are assumed to be available in unlimited quantity.

The last three constraints are designed to insure that the ships return to their ports of origin.[17] They were developed using the following reasoning: ship movements from A to H, from H to M, and from M to S can be represented by three linearly independent vectors:

$$AH = \begin{bmatrix} 1 \\ 0 \\ 0 \end{bmatrix}, \quad HM = \begin{bmatrix} 0 \\ 1 \\ 0 \end{bmatrix}, \quad MS = \begin{bmatrix} 0 \\ 0 \\ 1 \end{bmatrix}.$$

Any other admissible ship movements may be

[16]Koopmans, T. C., "Analysis of Production as an Efficient Combination of Activities," in Koopmans, T. C. (ed.), *Activity Analysis of Production and Allocation* (New York, 1951), p. 33ff; Charnes, A., and W. W. Cooper, *Management Models and Industrial Application of Linear Programming*, Vol. I (New York, 1961), p. 292; Isard W., *Methods of Regional Analysis*, (New York, 1960), p. 444ff; Isard, W., "Interregional Linear Programming: An Elementary Presentation and a General Model" *J. Regional Sci.*, I (1958), 1-59; and Stevens, B. H., "An Interregional Linear Programming Model," *ibid.*, 60-98.

[17]Cf. Goldman, T. A., "Efficient Transportation and Industrial Location," *Papers and Proc. Regional Sci. Assoc.*, IV (1958), 91-106.

expressed as a linear combination of AH, HM, and MS. For instance, trips from H to A, from A to S, and from S to H can be represented as follows:

$$HA = \begin{bmatrix} -1 \\ 0 \\ 0 \end{bmatrix},$$

$$AS = AH + HM + MS = \begin{bmatrix} 1 \\ 1 \\ 1 \end{bmatrix},$$

$$SH = SM + MH = \begin{bmatrix} 0 \\ -1 \\ -1 \end{bmatrix}.$$

Consider a system of equations of the following form:

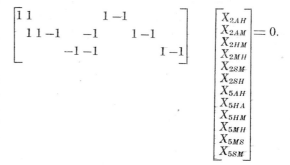

Variables having 2 as a first subscript correspond to steel shipments, the others correspond to movements of empty ships. It is evident by inspection that if some of the variables of type X_{2ij} have non-zero values, and if they do not involve a two-way trip, the system of equations is satisfied only by appropriate non-zero values of the X_{5ij} variables; that is, the system of equations is satisfied only if the ship movements for the transportation of steel are associated with return trips to ports of origin. The matrix of the coefficients of the system of equations is obtained by associating each of the variables with column vectors, the derivation of which was described above. The method applied in this example was employed in order to obtain the last three constraints appearing in the model. That is to say, each variable measuring a shipment or a movement of an empty ship was associated with a vector expressing the trip as a linear com-

TABLE IV Linear Programming Model: Constraints

STEEL PRODUCTION				STEEL SHIPMENTS						ORE SHIPMENTS		
X_{1A}	X_{1H}	X_{1M}	X_{1S}	X_{2AH}	X_{2AM}	X_{2HM}	X_{2MH}	X_{2SM}	X_{2SH}	X_{3SM}	X_{3SH}	X_{3SA}
1				−1	−1							
	1			1		−1	1		1			
		1			1	1	−1	1				
			1					−1	−1			
−a_1												1
	−a_1										1	
		−a_1								1		
	−a_2											
		−a_2										
			−a_2									
				1	1							−1
				1		1	−1		−1		−1	−1
								−1	−1	−1	−1	−1

TABLE V Linear Programming Model*

STEEL PRODUCTION				STEEL SHIPMENTS						ORE SHIPMENTS		
X_{1A}	X_{1H}	X_{1M}	X_{1S}	X_{2AH}	X_{2AM}	X_{2HM}	X_{2MH}	X_{2SM}	X_{2SH}	X_{3SM}	X_{3SH}	X_{3SA}
0	0	0	0	4.3	8.5	5.5	5.5	5.1	9.7	5.1	9.7	12.0
1				−1	−1							
	1			1		−1	1		1			
		1			1	1	−1	1				
			1					−1	−1			
−1.85												1
	−1.85										1	
		−1.85								1		
	−1.28											
		−1.28										
			−1.28									
				1	1							−1
				1		1	−1		−1		−1	−1
								−1	−1	−1	−1	−1

* Cost coefficients listed under respective variables.
† Alternate b values: 100, 50, 0.

bination of the three elementary trips AH, HM, and MS. Some of the variables corresponding to movements of empty ships may be expressed as linear combinations of AH, HM, and MS but they were nevertheless introduced into the problem because they are associated with costs which are not equivalent combinations of the costs of AH, HM, and MS. For instance, the cost of SA is not equal to the sum of costs of SM, MH, and HA. The cost of a trip from, say, New York to London is not equal to the cost of a trip from New York to Montreal and then from Montreal to London.

MODEL TESTED

Table V shows the linear programming model that was run. The coefficients indicating the average amount of coal and iron required for the production of one ton of steel (a_1 and a_2 of Table IV) are based upon data published by Craig.[18]

The steel consumption in Quebec and in southern Ontario were estimated to be 1.0 and 2.3 million tons (1953 data).[19] Costs were calculated under the assumption that any trip between any two possible points is made by an ocean vessel which has a full cargo capacity of 8,600 long tons and was constructed in 1955 at a cost of 2.2 million dollars.[20] (See Table VI for calculation of costs per trip.)

[18]Craig, "Location Factors," p. 258.
[19]Morgan, L., "The Canadian Primary Iron and Steel Industry," in ROYAL COMMISSION ON CANADA'S ECONOMIC PROSPECTS, Report (Ottawa, 1956), pp. 74-75.
[20]The costs are based on estimates published in The Impact of the St. Lawrence Seaway on the Montreal Area, pp. 29ff.,

TABLE IV (cont.)

COAL SHIPMENTS			EMPTY SHIPMENTS												
X_{4AH}	X_{4AM}	X_{4AS}	X_{4AH}	X_{5HA}	X_{5AM}	X_{5MA}	X_{5AS}	X_{5SA}	X_{5HM}	X_{5MH}	X_{5HS}	X_{5SH}	X_{5MS}	X_{5SM}	
															$=0$
															$\geqslant b_1$
															$\geqslant b_2$
															$=0$
															$\geqslant b_3$
1															$=0$
	1														$=0$
		1													$=0$
1	1	1	1	-1	1	-1	1	-1							$=0$
	1	1			1	-1	1	-1	1	-1	1	-1			$=0$
		1					1	-1			1	-1	1	-1	$=0$

TABLE V (cont.)

COAL SHIPMENT			EMPTY SHIPMENTS												
X_{4AH}	X_{4AM}	X_{4AS}	X_{5AH}	X_{5HA}	X_{5AM}	X_{5MA}	X_{5AS}	X_{5SA}	X_{5HM}	X_{5MH}	X_{5HS}	X_{5SH}	X_{5MS}	X_{5SM}	
4.3	8.5	11.2	2.4	2.4	6.6	6.8	9.2	10.1	4.6	4.6	7.8	7.8	3.2	3.2	
															$=0$
															$\geqslant 270$
															$\geqslant 120$
															$=0$
															$\geqslant 320\dagger$
															$=0$
1															$=0$
	1														$=0$
			1												$=0$
1	1	1	1	-1	1	-1	1	-1							$=0$
	1	1			1	-1	1	-1	1	-1	1	-1			$=0$
		1					1	-1			1	-1	1	-1	$=0$

106ff. The estimates rest on the following assumptions: (1) The life span of the vessel is twenty years over which the ship would depreciate at a constant rate from its 1955 purchase price to zero; the annual depreciation is therefore 5 per cent of the purchase price. (2) The purchase of the vessel was financed entirely by borrowed money repayable in annual instalments of constant size over twenty years at an annual interest rate of 5 per cent on the amount outstanding; the resulting average annual interest payment was 2.5 per cent of the vessel's original price. (3) The required profit was fixed at 10 per cent of the capital invested in the trip; thus the annual average profit over twenty years was 5 per cent of the vessel's purchase price. The costs per trip were based on a cost per day running of $1,719, and on a cost per day in port of $1,307, and on an estimate of the time running and time in port required for any type of trip. The costs in port included any cost (wages, provision, stores, sundry, insurance, administration, repairs and maintenance, depreciation, interest, required profits) except fuel. The voyage times in hours were based on data given in *ibid.*, p. 107. The time in ports was increased by twenty-five hours of "loading and unloading" for any non-empty trip. For any trip a total of $300 for port dues and pilot was added, and for the trips involving the use of the canals betwen Montreal and Lake Erie an estimated toll of $1,000 was added to the cost. (The total estimated costs per trip are shown in Table VI.)

TABLE VI Costs per Trip* (in thousands of dollars)

Trip	Full cargo	Light trip
Ashtabula—Hamilton	4.3	2.4
Hamilton—Ashtabula	4.3	2.4
Ashtabula—Montreal	8.5	6.6
Montreal—Ashtabula	8.7	6.8
Ashtabula—Seven Islands	11.2	9.2
Seven Islands—Ashtabula	12.0	10.1
Hamilton—Montreal	5.5	4.6
Montreal—Hamilton	5.5	4.6
Hamilton—Seven Islands	9.7	7.8
Seven Islands—Hamilton	9.7	7.8
Montreal—Seven Islands	5.1	3.2
Seven Islands—Montreal	5.1	3.2

* Costs calculated for ocean vessel class no. 2.

TABLE VII A. Non-zero Variables in the Solutions of the Linear Programming Problem at Four Different Flow Levels (data in shiploads of 8,600 long tons each)

Ore flow	Steel production		Steel shipments			Ore shipments	Coal shipments	Empty shipments		
	X_{1A}	X_{1S}	X_{2AH}	X_{2SM}	X_{2SM}	X_{3SA}	X_{4AS}	X_{5HA}	X_{5HS}	X_{5MS}
320	—	390	—	120	270	320	507	190	83	119
100	64	326	64	120	206	218	424	270	—	120
50	86	303	87	120	183	211	294	270	—	120
0	110	280	110	120	160	204	264	270	—	120

B. Costs at Four Different Flow Levels (in millions of dollars)

Ore flow	Total costs*	Ore flow costs†	Steel costs[a]
320	14.23	7.00	7.23
100	11.28	2.21	9.07
50	10.74	1.10	9.64
0	10.19	0	10.19

* Total costs of each optimal solution.

† Total costs of shipping the number of shiploads of iron ore indicated in the first column from Seven Islands to Ashtabula and of moving the ships back to Seven Islands.

[a] The steel costs are equal to the total costs minus the ore flow costs. The steel costs are the raw materials and steel transportation costs involved in supplying the Canadian market if all the advantages obtained by partial avoidance of empty return trips are passed to the producers for the Canadian market.

The linear programming problem was solved for different levels of flow of ore from S to A; namely, (1) for the 1956 flow, estimated at 2.76 million long tons, (2) for 0.86 million long tons, (3) for 0.43, and (4) for no ore shipments. The latter three flow levels are purely arbitary and were used for studying change in the optimal patterns if the flow of ore decreased and disappeared. Flows higher than the 1956 estimate were not assumed because they would not have changed the optimal pattern of locations and shipments obtained from the 1956 flows. An ore flow of 2.76 million tons is extremely low in comparison to the flow of 8.06 million tons in 1963,[21] or in comparison to the flow to be expected for the future. Labrador ore shipments have been estimated at 30 million long tons in 1970,[22] a very large part of which can be expected to pass through the St. Lawrence.

The data in tons for ore and for steel consumptions in H and M, were divided by 8,600 long tons, the cargo capacity of an ocean vessel class no. 2, so that shiploads were the units used in the computations. The costs also refer to shipment units of 8,600 long tons of steel ore or coal, or to the

"light" trip of an ocean vessel class no. 2. Therefore, in the solution of the linear programming problem the non-zero variables of type X_{1i} indicate a production of X_{1i} shiploads of steel , that is, of X_{1i} times 8,600 tons of steel at place i; X_{hij} times 8,600 is the tons of h (steel, coal, ore, or nothing) moved from i to j.

Results

The optimal solutions of the linear programming problem corresponding to flows of 320, 100, 50, and 0 shiploads of ore from S to A are shown in Table VIIA. In the first solution, based on 320 shiploads, all the steel production for the Quebec and southern Ontario markets is concentrated in Seven Islands. When smaller flows are used, the steel production is divided between Seven Islands and Ashtabula, with Seven Islands contributing the largest share of the total, even at zero flow. In all the solutions, the Quebec market is dependent on Seven Islands. The larger the flow of ore to the United States the more the southern Ontario market is dependent upon steel production at Seven Islands. In none of the solutions was steel production located at Montreal or Hamilton.

[21]*Traffic Report of the St. Lawrence Seaway* (1963), p. 23.
[22]*The Impact of the St. Lawrence Seaway on the Montreal Area*, p. 74.

If the total cost of shipping ore from Seven Islands to Ashtabula and returning the ship to Seven Islands is subtracted from the total cost of the programme, in effect all the advantages obtained by partial avoidance of empty return trips would be passed to the producers for the Quebec and southern Ontario markets. In this case, these markets could be supplied with the steel they require at transportation costs varying between $7.23 million when the ore flow is 320 shiploads, and $10.19 million at zero flow (see Table VIIB). The difference between the two figures measures the saving associated with the flow of iron ore from S to A.

Any comparison between the results shown in Table VII and the actual location of steel production in Canada requires caution because the model used here is simplified and does not include several variables which might affect the actual solution. However, the model does take into consideration the flow of ore to the United States from Seven Islands—a drastically new situation with respect to that within which steel production was developed at Hamilton. In all the optimal solutions in Table VII the raw materials and the raw material flows show a locational influence much stronger than the markets.

Optimal location of steel production for the Quebec and southern Ontario markets was established within the problem at Seven Islands, on the basis of iron ore flows to the United States market up to 2.76 million tons. This amount is much smaller than the present and the future flow through the St. Lawrence. Consequently, forces encouraging the development of steel production in the upper St. Lawrence may be more powerful than would appear from this study.

Conclusion

This study is focused basically on the locational influence of raw materials' flows. It was carried out by selecting an area in which such flows had acquired a particular importance and by building a model which incorporated relevant empirical features. The investigation confirms the usefulness of linear programming techniques for exploring models made of an interconnected complex of theoretical premises and of structural features which correspond to different levels of abstraction from concrete situations. The locational importance of iron ore flows along the St. Lawrence is apparent from the results obtained. The study should be considered only as an exploratory example of a research approach which can be useful in formulating policies and decisions on the establishment of new large-scale steel capacity in the St. Lawrence area.

Gerald J. Karaska

INTERINDUSTRY RELATIONS IN THE PHILADELPHIA ECONOMY

Recent national concern with an undesirably high level of defense expenditures, the uneven geographic distribution of federal research and development awards, and the outcries by communities when defense cutbacks or contract cancelations threaten their economic stability, has motivated the Federal government to encourage research as to the effects of its procurement programs upon geographic areas.

The economic repercussions of federal expenditures may be analyzed in the framework of impact analysis. As an economic problem, the regional effects of changes in levels of federal expenditures may be viewed as the impacts of changes in certain levels of final demand, the so-called multiplier effect.

Several techniques are commonly used to generate a multiplier. The basic-nonbasic approach, certain econometric models, and input-output analysis have all found favor in regional impact studies, and all have been debated for their advantages and disadvantages. Like all models of a complex phenomenon, however, none has found widespread acceptance. One desirable attribute of an input-output approach is its detailed description of the linkages between all sectors of the economy. Put another way, input-output has great utility in outlining the specific repercussions of changes in consumption.

There are, of course, many problems to which impact analyses can be directed. Previous studies have analyzed the impacts of new bridges,[1] new industries,[2] and economic development programs.[3] The expressed concern of a current Philadelphia input-output study is to analyze the impacts of cutbacks in defense expenditures, on the one hand, and on the other, to help evaluate the effects of concomitant, governmental offset policies. Another implicit goal of the study is to provide basic data which would help to orient local industrial development plans. Together with other analytical techniques, investigations of interindustry relationships should furnish valuable information on those industrial linkages, identified by their internal and external flows of goods, which serve as the principal source of income generation for the region.

In addition to the well-known difficulties with input-output analyses (these largely reflect several restrictive assumptions) regional models have been hampered by a lack of extensive and reliable data. Previous regional input-output studies have been forced to use either national information, or adopt highly generalized measurement techniques, or make educated guesses of the regional attributes to be employed in a national model. Although numerous nations have compiled input-output tables, and many with great detail, only a few attempts have been made to construct a table at

[1]E. Uyemura, *Shikoku Interindustry Relations: The SETO Great Bridge Project* (Kagawa University, 1962) (mimeographed).

[2]Walter Isard and Robert E. Kuenne, "The Impact of Steel upon the Greater New York-Philadelphia Industrial Region," *Review of Economics and Statistics,* XXXV (November 1953), pp. 289-301.

[3]Wassily Leontief, "The Structure of Development," *Scientific American* (September 1963), pp. 105-124. John G. D. Carden and F. B. Whittington, Jr., *Studies in the Economic Structure of the State of Mississippi* (Jackson: Mississippi Industrial and Technological Research Commission, 1964), Vols. 1 and 2.

Reprinted with the permission of the author and publisher from *The East Lakes Geographer*, Vol. 2, 1966, pp. 80-96. Dr. Karaska is Associate Professor of Geography at Syracuse University.

*Support of the National Aeronautics and Space Administration is gratefully acknowledged.

the metropolitan level.[4] Where attempted, these nonetheless, have sacrificed detail for the facility or ease in manipulating the final matrix in order to trace some impacts of change. Indeed, frequent reference is made to the marginal gain of detail for the expensive data gathering and computation procedures.

The term input-output really designates two separate concepts: first, the descriptive model or matrix, and second, the manipulation of this matrix or the impact analysis. The matrix is a table in which industries or economic sectors appear as both rows and columns in identical sequence. An entry in each cell of the table indicates the relationship between the respective row and column. This relationship may be measured in monetary values or weight units, or may be expressed as a numerical coefficient. For manufacturing industries this coefficient is usually referred to as the technological coefficient, and expresses the amount of each input or purchase per total output of an industry; hence, the term input-output coefficient. A very basic assumption of impact analysis is that this input-output coefficient is comparable for all firms in any industrial category, and is stable for these industries for any scale of operation and for short periods of time.

The most frequent matrix appearing in the literature is a regional model which designates the total array of industrial relationships irrespective of the geographic source of supply and destination of demand. The utility of this nationally balanced model for metropolitan impact studies is obviously restricted. A better model for such a region is an inter-regional model which would distinguish the local from the non-local sources of supply and destinations of demand, and, hence, distinguish the local impacts from the national impacts. Figure 1 illustrates an inter-regional model as a set of matrices: the local matrix, the import matrix, and the export matrix. For any industry, inputs would be designated as being supplied from local industries A, B, C, . . . ,N, and from non-local industries A', B', C', . . . ,N'. The outputs of any industry would also be represented

as flowing to local industries A, B, C, . . . ,N, and to non-local industries A', B', C', . . . ,N'. A common variation of this model is one which collapses the import matrix into a single row and the export matrix into a single column.

The pertinent qualities of the Philadelphia study will be (1) extensive detail in a single, nationally-balanced matrix, and (2) a set of matrices describing the inter-regional and intra-regional flows of goods and services. The manufacturing portion of the Philadelphia economy will be represented by 370 sectors at the four-digit level of the Standard Industrial Classification (SIC). It is intended that the remaining sectors of the Philadelphia economy will be treated in similar detail. Basic data have been gathered to represent wholesale trade by 20 to 25 sectors, retail trade by approximately 25 sectors, and the construction industry by six sectors. For the remainder of the economy, information is currently being collected for similar detail in order to complement sufficiently the more basic sectors.

Data and information for the Philadelphia study were obtained from three principal sources: interviews with local businesses; published and unpublished reports from state and federal agencies; and from local governmental sources, chiefly the Penn-Jersey Transportation Study. The local interviews were, by far, the most important source of data. For the manufacturing sectors, the interview contacts were made with approximately 3,000 firms over a period of 15 months. Of these, returns from 912 firms with detailed information were used to compute technological coefficients. In addition, less detailed information was utilized from 255 firms. Table 1 shows the extent of this survey coverage for the manufacturing sectors and permits some estimate of the reliability of the final results.

The goal of the survey was to produce information from firms which totalled at least 25 per cent of the employment in each four-digit SIC category. Data were requested for 1959. The sampling procedure was to rank by employment-size all firms in each four-digit category. The next step was to select for interview all those firms with greater than 200 employees. In situations where this first selection did not cover at least 25 per cent of the employment in each category, the largest firms were then selected to total the 25 per cent criterion. The response rate in terms of completed,

[4]Werner Z. Hirsch, "Interindustry Relations of a Metropolitan Area," *Review of Economics and Statistics*, XLI (November 1959), pp. 360-369. W. L. Hansen, R. T. Robson, and C. M. Tiebout, *Markets for California Products* (Sacramento: State of California Economic Development Agency, 1961). Upjohn Institute, *The Kalamazoo County Economy*, Kalamazoo, Michigan, April 1960.

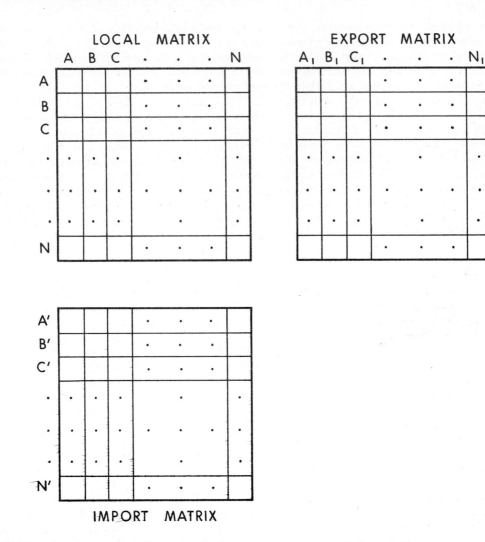

FIGURE 1 Hypothetical Interregional and Interindustry Model for Metropolitan Region.

returned questionnaires averaged about 35 per cent of the initial selection. On the basis of the responses, the next step was to select the largest firms from the remaining list of firms under 200 employees until the 25 per cent criterion was again reached. Depending upon the subsequent responses, this last procedure was repeated several times.

The final stage was the selection of a large number of the remaining small firms in most SIC categories. These were interviewed with a much shortened questionnaire. Since the original sample was biased with large firms, the intent here was to procure information from the vast number of smaller firms in the region. The new questionnaire was shortened so as to ask only selected, strategic questions which were suggested by earlier responses.

In summary the sampling procedure might be described as almost a complete inquiry of firms with greater than 50 employees; of course, not all of these responded with data.

Both questionnaires were designed to be completed by responsible management after being delivered by university personnel. The earlier, longer questionnaire asked for accurate figures from company records, whereas the shorter questionnaire was employed to facilitate estimates by management.

This sampling procedure was greatly ex-

TABLE I Number of Firms and Employees for Philadelphia S.M.S.A. Manufacturing, Survey Sample and Regional Estimates

SIC	SURVEY DATA USED								1959 REGIONAL ESTIMATES		PER CENT SURVEY COVERAGE	
	Incomplete Questionnaire		Complete Questionnaire		Total Questionnaire		Other Sources	Total				
	Empl (1)	Estab (2)	Empl (3)	Estab (4)	Empl (5)	Estab (6)	Estab (7)	Estab (8)	Empl (9)	Estab (10)	Empl (5)÷(9)	Estab (6)÷(10)
20	2,777	21	20,544	59	23,321	80	15	95	52,664	771	44.28	10.38
21	....	..	7	1	7	1	3	4	4,408	20	.16	5.00
22	1,603	25	8,086	71	9,689	96	9	105	37,125	490	16.10	19.59
23	3,181	34	15,502	90	18,683	124	5	129	58,310	1008	32.04	12.30
24	260	6	813	16	1,073	22	3	25	3,178	199	33.76	11.06
25	254	5	2,552	34	2,806	39	3	42	7,159	267	39.20	14.61
26	1,727	11	8,813	33	10,540	44	1	45	21,892	233	48.14	18.88
27	952	18	17,494	57	18,446	75	2	77	41,104	997	44.88	7.52
28	12,724	19	7,424	45	20,148	64	11	75	33,955	422	59.34	15.17
29	....	..	11,477	12	11,477	12	1	13	15,802	51	72.63	23.53
30	3,348	5	4,415	17	7,763	22	3	25	12,773	151	60.78	14.57
31	52	2	2,238	22	2,290	24	1	25	6,352	108	36.05	22.22
32	2,475	13	5,717	51	8,192	64	10	74	14,507	326	56.47	19.63
33	8,884	10	14,297	40	23,181	50	8	58	37,032	203	62.60	24.63
34	1,826	27	14,325	92	16,151	114	4	123	43,807	932	36.87	12.77
35	1,125	21	29,910	118	31,035	139	7	146	47,927	790	64.75	17.59
36	7,360	18	31,103	47	38,463	65	13	78	56,434	329	68.15	19.73
37	1,987	6	35,264	19	37,251	25	6	31	42,113	108	88.45	23.15
38	2,073	10	5,652	29	7,725	39	1	40	13,692	156	56.42	25.00
39	590	4	2,535	59	3,125	63	7	70	10,369	436	30.14	14.45
Total	53,198	255	238,168	912	291,366	1167	113	1280	560,603	7997	51.97	14.59

pedited by the availability of detailed industrial directories compiled by the Pennsylvania Department of Internal Affairs.[5] The directories listed firms by the four-digit SIC code and included addresses and employment-size for each firm. In addition, the same State agency provided both published and unpublished data on wages, value of production, and value-added for all four-digit SIC categories.

Whereas the basic survey provided most of the information for the technological coefficients, extensive reference was made to the 1958 input-output table for the United States being compiled by the Office of Business Economics, U.S. Department of Commerce. In instances where responses to the local survey were limited, national values were used as "dummy" entries, particularly so as to comply with the disclosure rule.[6] These national values largely account for the entries in column (7) of Table 1.

When the interview stage was completed or closed, the next step involved the computation of technological coefficients and total dollar flows or control totals. The principal sources for establishing control totals were the Pennsylvania Department of Internal Affairs, the local Bureau of Employment Security, and the Federal Census of Manufacturers.

The validity of an input-output analysis can be discerned, in part, if a measure of the variance of the technological coefficients is given. If the matrix is to be used in an impact analysis, the obvious question of representativeness of the coefficients becomes of paramount importance. To this end, it is desirable to illustrate, through a sample, some of the variations in the coefficients among Philadelphia industries and firms. Table 2 shows technological coefficients for 11 firms representing the fluid milk industry in Philadelphia. Seven of these firms provided detailed information on their manufacturing operations and four firms provided only limited data. These 11 firms of varying size of operation served as the basis for the Philadelphia technological coefficients. In Table 2 the columns report the ratio of dollar purchases from each industry listed on the left to the total value of produc-

[5] 1962 Industrial Directory, Pennsylvania, Department of Internal Affairs, (Harrisburg: Bureau Publications 1962).

[6] National values for coefficients for each four-digit SIC industry were taken from U.S. Bureau of the Census, Census of Manufactures: 1958 (Washington, D.C.: U.S. Government Printing Office, 1961), Table 3 and Table 7, and, ibid., Selected Materials Consumed (MC 58(1)-7, Supplement) (Washington, D.C.: U.S. Government Printing Office, 1963).

TABLE 2 Input-Output Coefficients for Eleven Philadelphia Fluid Milk Firms

INDUSTRY PRODUCING		Firm A	Firm B	Firm C	Firm D	Firm E	Firm F	Firm G	Firm H	Firm I	Firm J	Firm K	Phila.	Nat'l.
SIC	Name													
0132	Dairy Farms	.5532	.4708	.4599	.5022	.3531	.4637	.5910					.5047	.4634
0133	Poultry Farms	.0179			.0144	.0129							.0081	
2021	Butter	.0133			.0311	.0160							.0082	
2022	Cheese												.0057	.0044
2026	Milk		.0309	.1074									.0162	
2033	Fruit	.0227		.0132	.0143								.0105	
2087	Flavoring	.0256		.0382									.0014	
2654	Sanitary Containers			.0677			.0254	.0274					.0164	.0835
	Miscellaneous					.1360	.1349						.0153	.0631
	Total Materials	.6501	.5018	.6864	.5620	.5181	.6239	.6184	.5076	.5917	.6093	.5732	.5866	.6164
	Wages	.2103	.1603	.1647	.2775	.2489	.2795	.2679					.2005	.1568
	Power	.0043	.0072	.0061	.0087	.0156	.0066	.0195					.0063	.0094
	Other	.1353	.3307	.1428	.1518	.2174	.0900	.0942						
	Total	1.0000	1.0000	1.0000	1.0000	1.0000	1.0000	1.0000					1.0000	1.0000

tion for each firm. The last two columns show the aggregated Philadelphia coefficients and the respective coefficients for the entire United States as reported by the 1958 Census of Manufactures.[7] The relative comparability of production technology for these firms and the industry can be observed, especially for the Dairy Farms row, the Total Material Purchases row, the Wages row, and the Power row. The most apparent variations among these firms involved the minor purchases, and reflect differences in purchases from similar or related industries. That is, variations in the degree to which some firms purchase materials to be further processed and sold as secondary products, for example, eggs, butter, cheese, etc. It is important to note in Table 2 the limited detail (industry purchases) available from published governmental sources.

The question of reliability of the regional, Philadelphia coefficients can be further evaluated, in a limited sense, by their comparison with other coefficients. Unfortunately, only the national coefficients offer a reasonable basis for comparison.[8] Table 3 shows the input-output coefficients for the four Philadelphia industries in the Dairy Products Industrial Group and the respective national coefficients. This table reveals the regional technology of the dairy products industries, and also indicates that in some cases the regional varia-

tions can be quite significant, as with the butter industry.

As indicated earlier, the more valuable characteristics of a regional table are the relationships between the local industries and the non-local industries because regional impact analysis must identify and assess the local repercussions of economic changes. As an example of the nature of the regional and extra-regional relationships, Table 4 shows two sets of input-output coefficients for the Meat Products Industries, one denoting the local purchases and another denoting the non-local purchases or imports. This table reveals the relatively small volume of local purchases and the great dependence on outside industries. Perhaps this is to be expected for a metropolitan area in the case of the agricultral purchases, but Table 4 suggests that there is importation of products which might be available from local sources. All of the industries listed to the left in Table 4 have representative firms in the region.

These differences between the intra-regional and inter-regional purchases are important considerations in industrial development and of great pertinence to location theory. American industry may be characterized by its high degree of specialization and product differentiation. Most manufactured items are available in many different grades and varieties, and each of these different items are manufactured by separate firms to gain certain economic advantages in terms of agglom-

---

[7] Ibid.
[8] Ibid.

TABLE 3 Comparison of Philadelphia and National Input-Output Coefficients for the Dairy Products Industries

		Butter SIC 2021		Cheese SIC 2022		Ice Cream SIC 2024		Fluid Milk SIC 2026	
INDUSTRY PRODUCING		Phila.	U.S.	Phila.	U.S.	Phila.	U.S.	Phila.	U.S.
SIC	Name								
0132	Dairy Farms							.5047	.4634
0133	Poultry Farms	.1588						.0081	
2021	Butter	.6649						.0082	
2022	Cheese	.0280			.1294			.0057	.0044
2026	Fluid Milk		.6242	.5519	.5277	.2782	.1457	.0162	
2033	Fruit							.0105	
2062	Sugar Refining					.0423	.0265		
2087	Flavoring					.0823	.0662	.0014	
2499	Wood Prods.					.0001			
2649	Boxes					.0005			
2654	Sanit. Cont'rs.					.0716		.0164	.0835
2819	Ind. Inorg. Chem.					.0004			
	Miscellaneous	.0496	.1328		.1151	.0011	.2604	.0153	.0651
	Total Materials	.9012	.7570	.5519	.7722	.4767	.4988	.5866	.6164
	Wages	.0327	.0413	.1410	.0722	.1521	.1617	.2005	.1568
	Power	.0012	.0014	.0209	.0115	.0120	.0115	.0063	.0094
	Other	.0649	.2003	.2862	.1441	.3592	.3280	.2066	.2174
	Total	1.0000	1.0000	1.0000	1.0000	1.0000	1.0000	1.0000	1.0000

TABLE 4 Comparison of Local and Import Coefficients for Material Purchases by Philadelphia Meat Products Industries

		Meat Packing SIC 2011		Sausage and Other Prepared Meat SIC 2013		Poultry SIC 2015	
INDUSTRY PRODUCING		Local	Import	Local	Import	Local	Import
SIC	Name						
0133	Poultry Farms					.0565	.7422
0143	General Farms	.0174	.6900				
2011	Meat Packing	.0089	.0808	.0125	.4389		
2013	Sausage and Meats			.0661	.2650		
2211	Cotton Fabrics			.0000	.0015		
2643	Bags					.0056	.0056
2649	Convert. Paper					.0023	.0024
2651	Boxes	.0036	.0041	.0077	.0055		
2819	Ind. Inorg. Chem.	.0001	.0017				
2899	Chemicals n.e.c.			.0010	.0010		
	Total Materials	.0300	.7766	.0874	.7067	.0644	.7502
		3.7 Per Cent Local		11.0 Per Cent Local		7.9 Per Cent Local	

eration or scale economies. These advantages have been noted in the literature as cheapness, variety, and flexibility of supply.[9] American industry has developed to the point where it has become economically imperative for most firms to have access to an assured and wide range of cheap products. The distance input of traditional location theory finds expression in terms of communication, and its parameters are measured by speed, efficiency, and convenience.

The large metropolitan agglomerations of people have become synonymous with large, diversified, industrial bases in which the juxtaposition of a large pool of resources becomes an important locational factor. The location of industry thus may be partly explained by the economic advantages accrued through external, agglomeration economies, or Hoover's *urbanization economies*.[10] This interdependence of industry in a metropolitan area can be neatly portrayed by the input-output matrix, and together with other techniques could also permit a better understanding of the urbanization, agglomeration economies.

Inspection of a detailed national input-output table reveals a clustering of clumping of entries in the cells of the matrix, evidence of the industrial complex whereby products move in several stages from raw material to final consumption. While industrial linkages are quite apparent at the national level, the nature and extent of the local linkages are not at all clear. To this end it would be instructive to investigate the characteristics of the linkages in the Philadelphia region.

The following discussion will describe the interindustry relationships of one industrial complex. The intent here is to show the degree to which one industry is dependent upon both local and non-local industries, and, in an overly simplified approach, suggest the pertinence of the role of urbanization economies. The data to be subsequently presented show that industries in the Philadelphia Region purchase a large number and variety of products from local sources; however, these local purchases do not constitute a large proportion of the total inputs. The industries discussed are shown to be dependent upon a single, outside source of supply which constitutes the largest dollar purchase—the basic raw material—and also dependent upon the procurement of numerous, small purchases from local sources. The thesis offered is that a large, metropolitan area provides the diversified industrial base to furnish industries a quick and efficient source of supply.

The following analysis is in no way a test for the urbanization economies, but is rather an indication of a direction which research pertinent to this problem might be pursued. Further, the following results are only significant as indicated by the size of the sample. An articulate test for the urbanization economies must await more extensive research.

The Paper and Paper Products industrial complex is common to many regions, and it is sufficiently specialized in product differentiation to offer a meaningful example. The linkages in the Paper Industry are from raw material to pulp production, to paper and paperboard manufacture, to converted paper and converted paperboard products, to consuming industry, to final consumption. In the Philadelphia Region there are numerous firms representing all stages in the Paper Industry complex, except pulp manufacture. The question of existing linkages then focuses upon the flows of paper from local paper mills to the local converted-paper industries, and the flows of board from the local paperboard mills to the local, converted-paperboard industries.

Table 5 shows technological coefficients for local and non-local purchases of some Philadelphia paper mills. With pulp being the chief input, and since there are no pulp mills in the region, the local purchases of Philadelphia's paper mills are seen to be insignificant. Note that only 4.4 per cent of total purchases were local.

Looking next at the purchases of the converted paper industries in Table 6, the local purchases are again seen to be insignificant. Although there is considerable production of local paper (as seen in the previous table), local paper converters purchase most of their paper from mills outside the region. On the basis of the sample for the Philadelphia study, while Philadelphia paper mills produce $136 million worth of paper, Philadelphia paper converting firms purchase $68 million worth of paper, only $5 million of which are local purchases. The comparison of the local and import coefficients in Table 6 illustrate the importance of this extra-local dependence, see for example the comparison

[9] Edgar M. Hoover, *Spatial Economics: The Partial-Equilibrium Approach* (Occasional Paper, No. 2, Pittsburgh: Center for Regional Economic Studies, May 29, 1964), p. 8.

[10] Edgar M. Hoover, *Location Theory and the Shoe and Leather Industries* (Cambridge: Harvard University Press, 1937), p. 91.

TABLE 5 Comparison of Local and Import Coefficients for Material Purchases by Philadelphia Paper Mills

INDUSTRY PRODUCING		SIC 2621	
		Local	Import
SIC	Name		
2611	Pulp	....	.2542
2621	Paper	.0018	.0056
2643	Bags	....	.0331
2651	Folding Boxes	.0099	.0149
2655	Fiber Cans	....	.0051
2753	Engraving	....	.0009
2812	Alkalies	.0017	.0018
2816	Inorg. Pigments	.0008	.0015
2899	Chemicals n.e.c.	....	.0026
Miscellaneous		.0008	.0060
Total Materials		.0151	.3257

Per Cent Local Purchases of Total Purchases	4.4 Per Cent
Sample Firms	2
Sample Dollars	109,345
Total Dollars Philadelphia	136,099

of Paper purchases (SIC 2621) and Total Materials purchases.

Table 6 also describes the variability among the different industries in the paper-converting category, namely SIC 264. Through symbols, Table 6 shows that:

(1) most industries purchase little or no local paper,

(2) most industries purchase many products from local sources,

(3) all industries purchase local ink

(4) most industries purchase local glue, and,

(5) most industries purchase converted paper products from local sources.

Turning to the linkages in another part of the Paper Industry—the flow of goods from paperboard mills to paperboard converters—Table 7 compares the local and import coefficients for the paperboard mills. It may be seen in Table 7 that the board mills are much more dependent upon local sources of supply. Thirty-seven per cent of the value of all material purchases come from local industries. The principal input to the paperboard mills is seen to be waste paper, the largest portion of which is supplied from local sources. The sec-

TABLE 6 Comparison of Local and Import Coefficients for Material Purchases by Philadelphia Converted Paper and Paperboard Industries

Industry Producing		SIC 264		SIC 2641	SIC 2642	SIC 2643	SIC 2645	SIC 2649
		Local	Import					
SIC	Name							
2211	Cotton Cloth	.0001	.0031				O	
2281	Yarn and Thread	..	.0011					O
2298	Twine	..	.0012					..
2499	Wood Prods. n.e.c.	..	.0008				..	
2621	Paper	.0490	.3291	O	O	O	..	O
2631	Paperboard	.0086	.0001		X	X	O	
2641	Coated Paper	..	.0053				..	..
2651	Folding Boxes	.0035	..		X	X		
2652	Set-Up Boxes	.0026	..				X	X
2653	Corrugated Boxes	.0012	..				X	X
2655	Fiber Cans	.0001	..	X				
2753	Engraving	.0012	..	X	X			
2793	Photoengraving	.0002	..				X	
2815	Dyes and Pigments	.0006	.0012	O				
2819	Ind. Inorg. Chems.	.0006	.0054	O				
2821	Plastics	.0096	.0002			X		..
2891	Glue	.0044	.0028		..	X	X	X
2893	Ink	.0118	..	X	X	X	X	X
3069	Fab. Rubber Prods.	..	.0356	..				
3079	Misc. Plastics	.0001	..				X	

X = Completely Local Purchases
O = Some Local Purchases
.. = No Local Purchases

TABLE 6 (cont.)

Industry Producing	SIC 264 Local	SIC 264 Import	SIC 2641	SIC 2642	SIC 2643	SIC 2645	SIC 2649
3315 Steel Wire	..	.0008					..
3461 Metal Stampings	..	.0002					..
3554 Paper Machinery	..	.0002				..	
3955 Carbon Paper	..	.0004					..
3964 Needles, Pins, etc.	..	.0002		..			
Miscellaneous	.0084	.0072	O	O	X	X	O
Total Materials	.0997	.4086					
Sample Firms			3	3	2	3	2
Sample Dollars			6,623	8,492	5,371	1,586	3,168
Total Dollars Phila.			42,944	9,841	23,012	6,045	52,071

X = Completely Local Purchases
O = Some Local Purchases
.. = No Local Purchases

ond most important material input is imported pulp, while other inputs represent both local and imported purchases.

Table 8 describes the interindustry relations for the industries in the Converted Paperboard category, that is, the paperboard containers and boxes. As in the preceding tables, the largest volume of material purchases is imported to these Philadelphia industries. Table 8 shows that the major inputs to the region's paperboard converters are paper and paperboard, and that the bulk of both of these commodities is imported. This is in spite of significant local production of paper and paperboard. On another point, Table 8 shows that these converters also make many small purchases from a variety of local industries. Many of the individual converted paperboard industries purchase their supply of some commodities completely from local sources.

As a summary of the preceding discussion, Table 9 is presented. This table is essentially a set of matrices describing the relationships between the paper industries, namely Philadelphia paper industries and the rest of the United States. In Table 9 one may compare the magnitudes of the local and import coefficients, and observe the volume of local and export sales. This table also reveals several pertinent properties of the linkages of the Paper Industry in Philadelphia:

(1) Most of the purchases of Philadelphia's converted paper and converted board industries are paper and paperboard which are imported from outside mills. For example, the converters (SIC 2621) purchase $10 million worth of local paper

TABLE 7 Comparison of Local and Import Coefficients for Material Purchases by Philadelphia Paper Mills

INDUSTRY PRODUCING		SIC 2631 Local	SIC 2631 Import
SIC	Name		
2611	Pulp	....	.1073
2631	Paperboard	....	.0616
2819	Ind. Inorg. Chem.	.0033	.0300
2891	Glue	.0003	.0045
2893	Ink	.0050	.0076
4941	Water	.0041	....
9926	Waste Paper	.1535	.0889
	Miscellaneous	.0035	....
	Total Materials	.1699	.2948
Per Cent Local Purchases of Total Purchases		36.56 Per Cent	
Sample Firms		3	
Sample Dollars		39,372	
Total Dollars Philadelphia		74,835	

TABLE 8 Comparison of Local and Import Coefficients for Material Purchases by Philadelphia Paperboard Containers and Boxes Industries

		SIC 265		SIC 2651	SIC 2652	SIC 2653	SIC 2654	SIC 2655
INDUSTRY PRODUCING		Local	Import					
SIC	Name							
2046	Starch	..	.0039			..		
2298	Twine	.0001	.0003			O		
2621	Paper	.0055	.1643	O	O	..	..	
2631	Paperboard	.0138	.2870	O	O	O	..	..
2641	Coated Paper	..	.0078			..	..	..
2645	Die Cut Pap. & Bd.	.0010	.0002	O				..
2649	Paper & Board nec.	.0007	..					X
2653	Corrugated Boxes	.0072	.0037	X			O	
2654	Sanit. Contrs.	..	.0001				..	
2753	Engraving	.0027	..	X		X		
2819	Ind. Inorg. Chems.	..	.0013			..		
2821	Plastics	.0003	..	X				
2891	Glue	.0089	.0033	O	X	O	O	
2893	Ink	.0064	.0054	O		O	X	
2911	Petrol. Refining	.0002	.0004				O	..
3351	Copper Wire	.0001	.0004			O		
3352	Aluminum Wire	..	.0002					..
	Miscellaneous	.0581	.0006		X	O		
	Total Materials	.1042	.4797					
	Sample Firms			3	2	5	2	2
	Sample Dollars			7,198	2,543	37,813	7,768	983
	Total Dollars Phila.			41,742	13,861	98,406	15,092	7,861

X = Complete Local Purchases
O = Some Local Purchases
.. = No Local Purchases

and $59 million of non-local paper, notwithstanding local paper production of $136 million. Further, the converters (SIC 2631) purchase $5 million of local paperboard and $53 million of non-local paperboard, in spite of local paperboard production of $75 million.

(2) Although most of the converted paper and paperboard products are destined for a whole host of other industries, some production goes to the Paper Industry in general. Table 9 shows that even in these instances the Philadelphia paper firms purchase a substantial proportion of their converted paper and converted paperboard from outside sources. Only in those industries shown

with a star does local converted paper and local converted paperboard appear a credit balance to the region.

The preceding tables also suggest interesting information on the locational pulls of the Paper Industry. The paper mills are not raw material-oriented, since pulp, the major raw material, is imported; nor are the paper mills market-oriented, since the local paper converters purchase only a small proportion of the total local paper supply.

The same note may be made for the paper and paperboard converters. These firms were seen as not raw material-oriented since the major raw materials, paper and paperboard, were imported;

TABLE 9 Local and Import Coefficients and Dollar Flows for Philadelphia Paper Industries

INDUSTRY PURCHASING

Industry Producing	SIC 2621	SIC 2631	SIC 2641	SIC 2642	SIC 2643	SIC 2645	SIC 2649	SIC 2651	SIC 2652	SIC 2653	SIC 2654	SIC 2655	Total Local Sales to Paper Inds. $000[a]	Exports of Phila. Paper Ind. to Rest of Phila. and Rest of World $000[a]	Total Sales $000	Per Cent Sales Local
Local																
2621	.00185	.11370		.05514	.00112	.....	.03613	.00779	.09899	.....	.....		9,847	126,252	136,099	
2631	.....			.00294	.01109	.08098		.02338	.17607	.00418	.....	.....	4,598	70,237	74,835	
2641														47,944	47,944	19%
2642														9,841	9,841	76%
2643	.....							.00820						23,012	23,012	19%
2645												.03822	342*	5,703	6,045	41%
2649	.00990			.00359	.00876								300*	51,771	52,071	49%
2651						.01370	.01602	.04168					1,583	40,159	41,742	21%
2652						.00478	.00566					.01360	916*	12,945	13,861	34%
2653													2,269*	96,137	98,406	74%
2654														15,092	15,092	
2655			.00020										10	7,851	7,861	30%

Import

Industry Producing	SIC 2621	SIC 2631	SIC 2641	SIC 2642	SIC 2643	SIC 2645	SIC 2649	SIC 2651	SIC 2652	SIC 2653	SIC 2654	SIC 2655	Total Import Purchases $000[a]
2621	.0056			.21397	.46199	.02427	.14741	.03118	.08327	.22784	.02599		58,873
2631		.0616		.....	.....	.00193		.31248	.06277	.24434	.55572	.20067	52,545
2641						.08551	.00467			.00660		.19112	2,907
2642													0
2643	.0331							.00180					4,505
2645													75
2649				.....	.....								0
2651	.0149							.00231					2,028
2652				.....		.....					.02482		0
2653						.....	.....				.00037		471
2654													6
2655	.0051		.....										694

[a]Sum of respective row.

and, Table 9 suggests that the paper and board converters are not strictly local market-oriented since the survey reveals that their sales are not completely local. Only two of the nine converted paper and converted board industries sell more than 50 per cent of their products to local industries.

The Paper Industry requires many different sources of supply, and, in turn, supplies many different paper converters, who supply many different industries. The great degree of specialization in manufacturing and the highly differentiated flows of commodities require a more refined articulation of location theory.

Input-output or interindustry analysis is one technique for evaluating the effects of changes in the industrial structure of a metropolitan economy. The detailed input-output study of the Philadelphia economy has been designed to measure the impacts upon the local economy of changes in the present level of national military expenditures.

Whereas the Philadelphia input-output table may also be used to measure impacts of other changes in regional structure, the table additionally presents a vast array of data and information describing locational characteristics of Philadelphia industry. One locational factor which may now be better understood is the role of certain external, agglomeration economies in influencing location in a large metropolitan complex. Information from the Philadelphia input-output table can be used to analyze the attractions for industries to locate close to one another so as to be assured of an inexpensive, efficient, and flexible supply of goods and services. Because of the advanced state of the nation's industry, goods and services flow in highly articulated linkages. The transport input of traditional location theory may be evaluated in terms of economies associated with the linkages between industries and the total community. The input-output matrix provides a useful framework to structure this analysis.

Brian J. L. Berry, H. Gardiner Barnum, and Robert J. Tennant

RETAIL LOCATION AND CONSUMER BEHAVIOR

A review of the literature recently published in the volume, *Central Place Studies: A Bibliography of Theory and Application*[1], pieces together what appear to be the basic features of central place systems. "Piecing" and "what appear to be" need emphasis, however, for none of the works reviewed provides evidence relating to all facets of the central place system, including the size and spacing of central places, locational patterns and groups of retail activities, consumer travel behavior, systems of trade areas, and their interdependencies. Such evidence is provided in this paper.

The present study is one of five[2] in which identical analyses were undertaken. It was the purpose of the over-all body of research to examine not only the interdependencies among the various aspects of central place systems, but also how these aspects and interdependencies vary from place to place. A report on the larger study is now being prepared, and will be published elsewhere[3]. Here we will simply relate the findings of investigations in southwestern Iowa.

Some will object that the findings are not novel. This is inevitable in a study of this kind. But it is hoped that the ways in which many kinds of data are marshalled to provide a variety of related perspectives of the central place system may be useful. If any fresh viewpoints are provided, they relate to differences in findings that result from varying scales of analysis, to the validity and deficiencies of such ideal networks as the $k=4$, to the existence of ranges and thresholds, and to uses of information theory in clarifying the meaning of the term "centrality."

The Study Area

Southwestern Iowa exemplifies the homogeneity that has made the American midwest a classic laboratory for central place studies[4]. In the nine-county study area depicted in Figure 1 rural population densities[5] are 15.5 persons per square mile, except in Pottawattamie County which has 20.4 persons per square mile, reflecting increasing density within the immediate sphere of influence of Omaha and Council Bluffs, and Adams County with only 12.7 persons per square mile. Adams is the poorest of the nine counties. Whereas at least 60 per cent of the farms in the other counties sold products valued in excess of $5,000 in 1959-60, barely 53 per cent of the farms in Adams County did so.

The land is occupied by highly productive farms, cropping corn, small grains, hay and pasture, and fattening cattle or raising hogs. Average

Reprinted with the permission of the authors and publisher from *Papers and Proceedings, Regional Science Association*, Vol. 9, 1962, pp. 65-102. Dr. Berry is Professor of Geography at the University of Chicago; Dr. Barnum is Assistant Professor of Geography at the University of Vermont; Dr. Tennant is Assistant Professor of Geography at York Univerity, Toronto.

[1]Brian J. L. Berry and Allen Pred, *Central Place Studies: A Bibliography of Theory and Applications*. Philadelphia: Regional Science Research Institute, 1961. [See page 65 of this volume.]

[2]These five are, in decreasing order of population density and intensity of occupance: an urban case, part of the City of Chicago; a suburb and satellite case, the southern lobe of the Chicago metropolitan area; an intensive agricultural case, part of the corn belt of southwestern Iowa; an extensive agricultural area, in northeastern South Dakota; a rangeland case, in southwestern South Dakota, also including parks, recreational areas, and mining communities.

[3]In a book which is entitled [*The Geography of Market Centers and Retail Distribution*. Englewood Cliffs: Prentice Hall, 1967.]

[4]See the studies by Lösch and Brush, for example.

[5]Rural is defined in the U.S. Census of Population as "other rural territory."

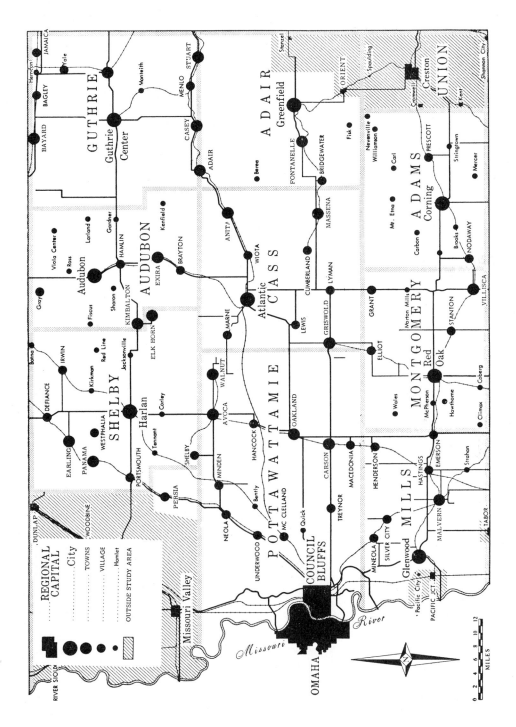

FIGURE 1   The Study Area.

farm size is 190-200 acres. Over the past decades farm sizes have increased and the number of farms has declined, however. For example, in Montgomery County in 1945 there were 1,642 farms with an average size of 163 acres, but in 1955 there were only 1,397 farms averaging 188 acres. In the eastern part of Pottawattamie County, fifteen farms have been abandoned on the average each year since 1945 according to the county agricultural agent.

These changes in agriculture have been accompanied by a decline of rural population. Montgomery County had 9,934 rural residents in 1940, 9,159 in 1950, and only 8,046 in 1960. Between 1950 and 1960 the average decline of rural population was 12 per cent in the area. Adams County declined most (14.7%), a change accelerated by reductions in the activity of the several small coal mines. Pottawattamie showed no decline, though, because increasing suburban population around Council Bluffs balanced rural declines further east.

Just as rural populations declined, so did the populations of all towns except the county seats, which increased in population slightly. The only county seat to lose residents was Corning, in Adams County. Thus, as the numbers of rural residents have fallen, so have the populations of the smaller rural service centers. That these declines have been followed by closures of retail establishments is well illustrated, in any trip through the area, by the number of store buildings that are either abandoned or used for other purposes.

Sources of Data

During the summer of 1960 a field crew[6] spent four weeks in the area collecting data, which consisted of:

(a) An inventory of establishments performing central functions in the nine-county area (for a list of the eighty most ubiquitous of the functions recognized see Table III). Compilation of this inventory involved constructing maps showing the location of every building in which central functions were performed and noting the functions.

(b) Maps of trade areas for 76 selected establishments located in a sample of 20 central places. These maps were based upon a combina-

tion of interviews with customers and use of charge account, check-cashing, and delivery lists. Customers were asked about origins and destinations of their trips, type of transport used, and all establishments visited or to be visited on the trip in addition to the store at which the interview was made.

(c) Interviews in the homes of some 150 rural families and 170 families residing in central places[7], within the "intensive" study area depicted in Figure 10. The respondents were asked questions relating to place and frequency of shopping for groceries, clothing, furniture, gasoline, and appliances, and for obtaining banking, dry cleaning and barber or beauty services. Of interest were the center or centers used to obtain most of these goods and services, other centers visited, whether or not mail order, telephone, delivery, etc. were relied upon, and the means of transportation utilized.

Fortunately, the 1960 Census of Population was taken shortly before the summer's field work began, so that comparable population data were available.

It is upon these data that the analysis is based. In the following pages we will first summarize the empirical regularities that emerged in the study, in an attempted logical sequence, and then speculate about some of their theoretical implications.

Empirical Regularities

CITY–SIZE RELATIONSHIPS

One expects larger central places to have more central functions supporting the larger populations, more establishments, larger trade areas encompassing more people, and more business districts and shopping centers to serve their own populations[8].

---

[7]Consisting of a 10 per cent random areal sample of rural families and families residing in centers with less than 150 households, an 8 per cent sample of families in centers with 150-450 households, 6 per cent in 450-2000, 4 per cent in 2000-5000, and 1 per cent of families residing in centers with over 5000 households.

[8]For a review of the relevant evidence, see Berry and Pred, *op. cit.*

The following operational definitions are used in this study:
firm: a unit of organization.
establishment: a store performing one or more central functions.
central function: a type of activity, such as drug store, church, or veterinarian, regardless of size.
functional unit: the part of a store performing a single function, in the event that more than one function is performed by the store.

---

[6]Under the direction of Prof. John D. Nystuen, this crew comprised R. J. Tennant, H. G. Barnum, K. Pataki, D. Czamanske, and J. Welker.

That such generalizations hold in Iowa is indicated in Table I. Relevant pairwise correlations are extremely high. There are linear relationships between population, number of functional units and number of business districts, and log-linear relationships between the above variables and number of central functions. Regression equations are included in the Table[9].

Figs. 2 and 3 illustrate the linear and log-linear patterns. In Fig. 2 there are two deviants which

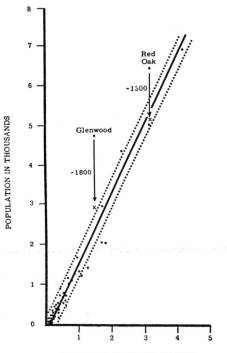

FIGURE 2 Relationship Between Population and Functional Units. Regression is P $=$ 17.6F — 162.7.

point up the importance of service functions for towns in the area. These are the only places in the study that have part of their population supported

by activities other than tertiary central functions. As a result, they have, apparently, excess population if the population is compared with the numbers of central functions they perform[10]. All other places are exclusively central places and do not have such an excess. Approximate adjustments can be made to clarify this point (these are *not* used in any subsequent analysis).

The first deviant, Glenwood, has the Iowa State Institution for the Feeble-Minded, with 1,800 inmates. Note the position of the city in Fig. 2 if its population is reduced by that 1,800. The second deviant, Red Oak, has three small manufacturing plants employing a total of 332 male and 444 female workers[11]. Assume that only the male employees are heads of households. Except for the manufacturing activity, the households would probably not be located in Red Oak. Now postulate four persons per household; this indicates an excess population of 1,300. Subtract 1,300 from Red Oak's population in Fig. 2 and note the result: the same as subtracting 1,800 from that of Glenwood.

In Fig. 3 two distinct regions are evident. The first includes the log-linear relationship between population and central functions for centers with ten functions or more, and the second is an equipossible area including centers lying in the range of 1 to 8 functions and having less than 100 population. The centers in this lower range are the hamlets, once the basic element in the American settlement fabric, but now in the final stages of decline. Because of the decline and lack of size-relationships, hamlets were excluded from the analysis reported in Table I.

Fig. 4 records the relationship between numbers of functional units and numbers of central functions. Again, the break in slope associated with hamlets appears, but thereafter log-linearity is not maintained over the whole curve. Instead, it appears as if several regimes may exist, each with its own log-linearity. Further evidence concerning these regimes is presented below.

---

business district: a group of spatially contiguous establishments less than 300 feet from each other, and *either* separated from other establishments by more than 300 feet at the periphery *or*, if in a continuous shoestring of business, falling into "peaks" or "ribbons" of land values (this latter aspect of definition, together with analyses of land values and their relations to the locational structure of business and to pedestrian counts will be explored in detail in the larger study). An isolated store is counted as a single-establishment district.

[9]Note the similarity of these results and those obtained by Thomas. Edwin N. Thomas, "Comments on the Functional Bases for Small Iowa Towns," *Iowa Business Digest*, Winter 1960, pp. 10-16.

[10]For other examples of such deviations caused by non-central functions see Thomas, *op. cit.* and Brian J. L. Berry, "The Impact of Expanding Metropolitan Communities upon the Central Place Hierarchy," *Annals,* the Association of American Geographers, 50 (1960), pp. 112-16.

[11]National Carbon Company, making Eveready Batteries—135 males, 315 females, of whom 12 males and 41 females are rural commuters; Wilson Concrete Company, making prestressed concrete—100 males, 6 females; Thos. D. Murphy Company, making art calendars, pencils, etc.—97 males and 123 females.

However, Red Oak only has 13 dealers in farm equipment and supplies, etc., in contrast Atlantic's 34, a fact attributable to the farmers' coop in Red Oak, which dominates the farmer supply business. Taking account of this means a 20 unit shift of Red Oak's position on the abscissa of Figure 2.

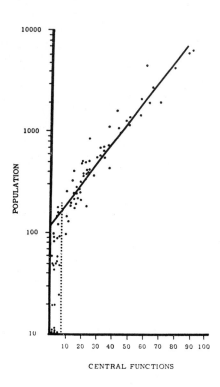

FIGURE 3   Relationship Between Population and Central Functions. Note the log-linearity, with LP = 0.02 CF + 2.095, when decaying hamlets are disregarded.

TABLE I   Selected Size Relationships*

		Correlations					
		P	LP	F	LF	CF	BD
P	Population of Center	$\times$	—	0.979	—	0.890	0.872
LP	Log. of Population		$\times$	—	0.958	0.953	—
F	No. of Functional Units			$\times$	—	0.929	0.881
LF	Log. of Functional Units				$\times$	0.976	—
CF	No. of Central Functions					$\times$	—
BD	No. of Business Districts						$\times$

Regressions

(1) $P = 17.64F - 162.7$

(2) $LP = 1.24LF + 0.731$

(3) $LP = 0.02CF + 2.095$

(4) $LF = 0.018CF + 1.045$

(5) $BD = 0.00548P + 3.09$

* For all central places of village level and above (i.e., with nine or more functional units), see text and Fig. 3.

In Fig. 5 it is clear that there is a close relationship between the dimensions of trade areas and the outlying populations served by centers.

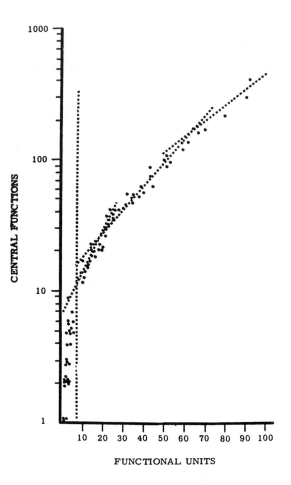

FIGURE 4   Several Regions Appear to Characterize the Relationship Between Central Functions and Functional Units.

This reflects not simply the uniformity of rural population distribution, but also the constancy of the ratio between population of central places and number of dispersed rural residents served, for larger centers serve both farmers and residents of other centers and their "outlying" or "external" populations include the populations of these other centers.

If total population served is considered, the relationship is maintained, as in Fig. 6, but there are once again separate regimes within the over-all pattern which call for explanation. Each regime has upper and lower limits, and the several regimes are arranged in stepwise sequence in the curve.

Figs. 5 and 6 contain points for every trade area developed in the study. For any trade area,

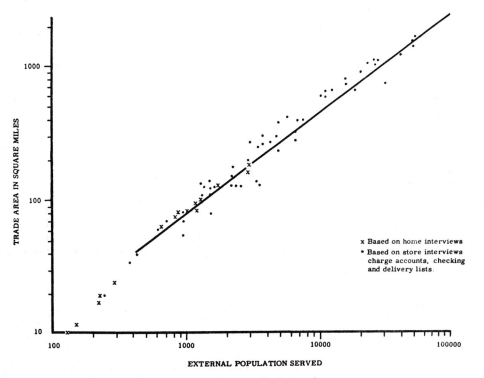

FIGURE 5 External Population Served Increases Evenly as Trade Area Increases.
r = 0.986, and LA = 0.795 LEP — 0.4. Different methods of estimating trade areas give the same results.

an appropriate external population served may be derived from Fig. 5 and a total population from Fig. 6. The total population less the external population equals the population of the central place serving the trade area in question.

Entry of Central Functions

Such strong size regularities are evident that it is possible to construct a table in which the order of entry of central functions into central places is recorded, using the first principal component developed in a direct factor analysis[12] This method of analysis begins with an incidence matrix in which the rows are central places and the columns are central functions. Cells are coded 1 if the func-

tion is present in the center, and 0 otherwise. Direct factor analysis of such an incidence matrix yields pairs of principal components which summarize the underlying dimensions of variation of centers and functions in the matrix. To each pair of components corresponds the same eigenvalue or characteristic root of the incidence matrix. This root reveals the amount of total incidence accounted for by the pair.

Use of such a method with the Iowa data yielded the characteristic roots recorded in Table II. Fifty-nine per cent of the total incidence was extracted by the first pair of components. Of this pair, the column component ranked the central places in order, by number of central functions performed, and the row component provided an order of entry sequence for the central functions. Table III records this order of entry for the eighty most ubiquitous functions. For any number of functions present in a town, Table III will indicate which functions they are most likely to be, and equations (3) and (4) in Table I will provide corresponding urban populations and total number

---

[12]D. E. Saunders, *Practical Methods in the Direct Factor Analysis of Psychological Score Matrices.* Ann Arbor: University of Microfilms, 1950, and Brian J. L. Berry, "Grouping and Regionalizing: An Approach to the Problem Using Multivariate Analysis," *Proceedings,* NAS-NRC Conference on Mathematics in Geographical Research, New York: Atherton Press, in press. Both present these methods of analysis mathematically; hence the mathematical formulation will not be presented here.

of establishments. Only one function, the general store, was shown to be a typical by component one, because stores of this type are found in the smaller centers and then drop out.

Grouping of Functions

Only 60 per cent of the total incidence was accounted for by the pair of order-of-entry com-

TABLE II   Results of Direct Factor Analysis of Iowa Incidence Matrix

	Amount	Per cent
Accounted for by first component	698.500	59.45
second	100.714	8.57
third	30.035	2.58
fourth	30.706	2.61
fifth	25.925	2.21
sixth	21.969	1.87
seventh	18.174	1.55
eighth	16.770	1.43
	942.493	80.27
Total incidence	1175	

TABLE III   Order of Entry of Central Functions

Score on Component	Central Function	Study I.D. Number
5.5-6.0	Gas and Service Station	60
	Automobile Repair	73
	Restaurant	32
5.0-5.5	Bar	95
	Grocery	2
	Farm Materials (Feed-Seed etc.)	144
4.5-5.0	Church	142
	Farm Implements	110
	Farm Sales, incl. Elevator	145
4.0-4.5	Building Materials, Lumber	87
	Barber	8
	Hardware	7
	Post Office	43
	Bank, Savings and Loan	39-40
	Appliances	47
	Local Government Facility	146
3.5-4.0	Meeting Hall	112
	Oil Fuel, Bulk Station	89
	Furniture	48
	Beauty	9
3.0-3.5	Insurance	31
	Variety	11
	Other Building Services	90
	Drug	4
	Specialized Auto Repair	74-77
	Indoor Amusements (Billiards etc.)	104
	Self Service Laundry	28
	Lawyer	45

(TABLE III   continued)

Score on Component	Central Function	Study I.D. Number
2.5-3.0	Doctor	60
	New Auto Sales	71
	Real Estate	29
	Newspaper	128
	Shoe Repair	96
	Drive-In Eating Place	67
	Cleaners and Laundry (Operator)	6
	Used Auto Sales	72
2.0-2.5	Plumbing	85
	Movies	98
	Auto Accessories	85
	Other Medical	64
	Veterinarian	65
	Food Locker	92
	Women's Clothing	23-5
	Supermarket	10
	Dentist	61
	Hotel	93
	Jewelry	44
1.5-2.0	Extensive Amusement (Putting Greens, etc.)	101-3
	Liquor	132
	Men's Clothing	19-22
	Men and Women's Clothing	18
	Radio TV Sales and Service	46
	Funeral	108
	Shoes	35-8
	Motel	68
	Blacksmith, Sheet Metal	141
	Fixit	91
1.0-1.5	Florist	33
	Bakery	13
	Bus, Taxi Station	122
	Coal Yard	88
	Telegraph Office	117
	Telephone Answering Service	118
	Job Printing	106
1.0-1.5	Gifts	50
	Loan	30
	Photographs	55
	Private Warehouse	139
	Commercial Garage	83
	Pay Bills, Currency Exchange	41
0.5-1.0	Movers and Haulers	138
	Candy	133
	Music and Records	53
	Children's Clothing	27
	Electrical Repair	86
	Building and Construction Contractor	131
	County Government	147
	Mission	97
	Second Hand	54
	Monument Sales	109
	Sporting Goods	42
	Dairy	12
	Auto Wrecking	80

ponents. The next two pairs of components, derived by a continuation of the direct factor analysis, accounted for some 11 per cent of the incidences. These two pairs indicated the presence of *groups* of central places characterized by *groups* of central functions. Thus, in addition to the smooth order-of-entry and size-of-center pattern depicted by the first pair of components, certain discontinuities were also indicated. This is the same as in Fig. 6, where identifiable regimes nest within an over-all pattern. The factor analysis therefore confirms the presence of both an over-all pattern and separate regimes.

The first grouping indicated was of *cities,* all of which had more than 55 central functions. Table IV lists the group of functions associated with these cities. All are county seats, provide specialized services, and have central shopping districts whose major attractions include clothing and shoe stores.

A second grouping was of centers with from 28 to 50 central functions. These are the *towns.* Their characteristic central functions are noted in Table V. Such centers may have a general-line clothing store, but the main attractions remain much simpler than those of the cities.

The group of centers with between 10 and 25 functions are the *villages.* Table VI records the groups of village functions, all of a basic convenience character.

Later pairs of components showed the groups of functions to be arranged in a *hierarchy.* The fourth pair, for example, identified cities as a group, and associated with them the group of village functions, showing that cities also perform village-level functions.

The over-all pattern revealed by the factor analysis is thus one of general size relations, but with discontinuities associated with groups of centers and functions arranged in a hierarchy. These

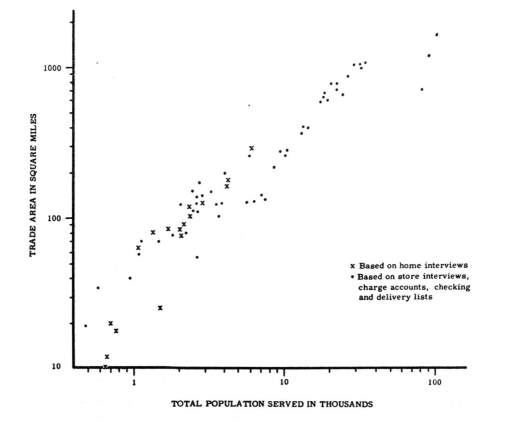

FIGURE 6   Relationship Between Trade Area and Total Population Served.

TABLE IV   The Group of City-Level Functions

Women's Clothing
Men's Clothing
Shoes
Jewelry
Florist
Supermarket
Bakery
Liquor Stores
Other Medical Practice (e.g., Optometrists, Chiropractors)
Lawyer
Hotel
Motel
County Government
Newspaper Publisher
Office of Labor Union
Sales of New Autos
Sales of Used Autos
Specialized Auto Repairs
Auto Wrecking
Cleaners and Laundry (Operator)
Self-Service Laundry
Shoe Repair
Plumbing
Fixit
Movies
Indoor Amusements (Billiards, etc.)
Drive-In Eating Place

TABLE V   Town-Level Functions

Furniture
Appliances
Variety
General Clothing
Drug
Bank
Insurance
Real Estate
Telephone Exchange
Cleaners
Doctor
Dentist
Building Services
Building Materials
Radio-TV Sales and Service
Movers and Haulers
Funeral Home
Veterinarian
Auto Accessories
Farmers' Cooperatives

TABLE VI   Village-Level Functions

Gas and Service Station
Auto Repair
Bar
Restaurant
Grocery
Post Office
Local Government Facility
Church
Meeting Hall
Hardware
Farm Materials
Farm Sales
Farm Implements
Oil Fuel Bulk Station
Barber
Beauty

central places arranged in a hierarchy, and set within the broader frame of city size regularities that appears at the aggregative level[13].

A Hierarchy of Central Places

If we pass from the aggregative to a more elemental level of inquiry, the hierarchy becomes the dominant pattern. What appear, in the aggregate, to be continuous city-size regularities are seen to be the results of the superimposition of local variabilities on the hierarchy.

Figure 9 shows the elemental or "intensive" study area selected for the more microscopic analysis. Note the progressions: moving outwards from the city of Red Oak we encounter a circle of villages—Emerson, Elliott, and Stanton. Moving north and east, next come towns—Griswold and Villisca. Moving north again, next comes another village, Lewis, and then the city of Atlantic. East from Atlantic are the village of Wiota and the town of Anita. The step-like pattern is illustrated in Fig. 10.

Accompanying Fig. 10 is a table which reveals the regularity of the populations, central functions, and functional units of each class of center. Note the villages with populations of 501, 459 and 514 for example, and with 24, 26, and 21 central functions. Similarly the towns have 1,207, 1,273, 1,690, and 1,340 people, and 50, 50, 43, and 49 central functions. The jumps from villages to towns and

discontinuities help explain some of the problems raised by the earlier figures. Figs. 7 and 8 are repetitions of Figs. 4 and 6, but with the city-town-village hierarchy indicated. The patterns produced by the factor analysis provide very logical interpretations of the various regimes appearing in the graphs. The different regimes are of orders of

[13]That the trade areas constructed from home interviews, and those constructed from either interviewing customers in the store, or using charge account, check cashing or delivery lists are consistent is illustrated also in Figs. 4 and 6. Crossed points are those based upon home interviews, uncrossed the rest. The points all fall very neatly within the appropriate regime.

from towns to cities are the steps of the hierarchy.

But at any of the levels perfect uniformity does not obtain. Populations, numbers of central functions, and numbers of functional units vary. When a large enough area is taken, such variations are enough to provide the appearance of continuous linear relationships between, say, logarithm of population and number of central functions, even though the underlying spatial pattern is that of a hierarchy.

The Hierarchy in Consumer Travel Behavior

The hierarchy is also manifested in consumer shopping and travel behavior for central goods and services. Figures 11-17 show trade centers visited for the bulk of food purchases, barber-beauty services, banking facilities, dry cleaning, furniture, appliances and clothing, in the intensive study area. The sample contains 150 rural families and 170 families residing in the central places. Food and barber-beauty exemplify village-level functions; banking, dry-cleaning, furniture and appliances are of town-level, and clothing is a city-level activity.

Note the pattern of shopping for food and for barber or beauty services. Villages, towns and cities have rural trade areas. Moreover, the higher the rank of a center, the larger is its rural trade area. Urban residents patronize the town in which they reside almost exclusively. Within the smaller central places (Lewis and Griswold), the shopping trips of the urban residents focus on single business centers. However, inside cities (Atlantic) several business districts serve neighborhood areas.

The next two maps show the pattern of shopping for town-level convenience services. Note how the villages drop out of the picture in the dry cleaning map (one or two hang on in the case of banking, having small branch banks from cities like Red Oak). The rural trade areas of the towns, such as Griswold, remain much the same as with the village-level functions, but trade areas of cities expand, to engulf the rural trade areas of the villages and the villages themselves. Note how Emerson and Elliott link to Red Oak, and Lewis links to Atlantic, with the town to Griswold remaining relatively independent.

Banking and dry cleaning are convenience-type services obtained reasonably frequently. The next two maps, of shopping trips for furniture and

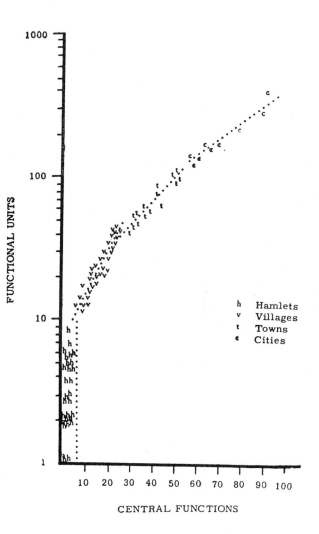

FIGURE 7 Classes of Central Places Have Different Regimes.

appliances, relate to "comparison shopping" commodities obtained less frequently. The Red Oak-Griswold-Atlantic pattern remains essentially similar to that for dry cleaning, because furniture and appliances are town-level functions. However, the pull of the metropolis of Omaha-Council Bluffs exerts itself in the west, and Oakland and Carson fall within the sphere of influence of the metropolis. The variety of goods offered in the metropolis is enough to overcome the pressures of distance for local shopping at the town level, to a radius of 30 miles and more. Further than that, however, the first-choice shopping pattern remains unchanged, although many respondents said they would sometimes go to the metropolis for these kinds of goods.

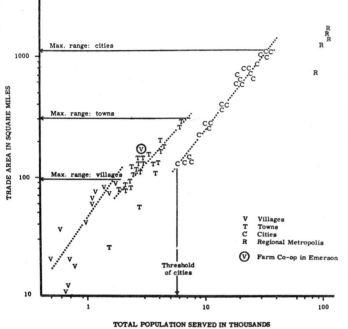

FIGURE 8 Trade Area and Population Served, by Class of Center. For villages LA = 1.37 LTP — 2.5, and r = 0.986. For towns LA = 1.06 LTP — 1.6 and r = 0.86. For cities LA = 1.28 LTP — 2.7 and r = 0.986.

FIGURE 9 Home Interviews Were Made in the Shaded Area.

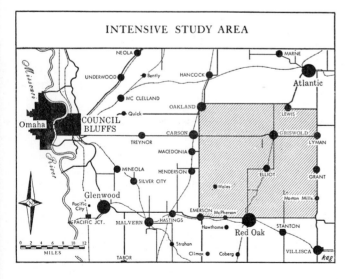

The final map is of a city-level function, sale of clothing. Trade areas of the towns vanish (except for items like work clothes), and the cities extend their trade areas into the territory dominated by the towns for the lower order goods. The western part of the study area focuses upon the metropolis, as in the previous cases of furniture and appliances. Most people in the area say they go to the metropolis to buy clothing at some time. Note how size of rural trade areas is still related to rank of center: that of the metropolis is greater than those of Atlantic and Red Oak, which are approximately of the same size. Note also that Atlantic's residents now all make their shopping trips to a single business center within that city.

If we turn back to Fig. 8, we find that the maximum radius of trade areas for cities is about 18 miles. This is presumably the radius of a city trade area for its city-level functions. Two circles with this radius of 18 miles are drawn centered on Red Oak and Atlantic in Fig. 11. The trade area of Griswold falls entirely within the area of overlap of the circles. The boundary between the two clothing trade areas in Fig. 17 would similarly be delimited by a bisection of that overlap zone. Note how Griswold is, thereby, tied to Atlantic, a fact verified by the urban shoppers' trip patterns. The minimum radius of 6 or 7 miles for the trade areas of cities in Fig. 8 delineates the monopolistic zone within which no center competes with the city. Beyond 6 miles villages like Lewis can command small trade areas for low order goods.

In Fig. 18 a second component is added to Fig. 8, that of trade areas for each level of functions. See how the pattern of increasing trade area with size of center emerges, and also how the discontinuities created by the hierarchy appear.

These discontinuities reflect the spatial arrangement of the hierarchy, and also the spatial patterns of competition between centers, capture of the smaller by the larger, and consequent "nesting" of smaller trade areas within those of larger centers. Fig. 19 illustrates such features of successive dominance and capture.

FACTORS AFFECTING DISTANCE TRAVELLED BY RURAL RESIDENTS

The foregoing considerations naturally raise the question of the factors that influence distance travelled by rural residents to central places for different kinds of goods and services. Several ideas may be tested: for example, that the maximum distance a farmer is willing to travel for any particular central function increases with (a) the number of other shopping opportunities that may be satisfied in the center from which the bulk of the good or service is purchased (the center of first choice); (b) diminution in the frequency of trips; (c) the tendency to recognize and use larger centers such as the metropolis, indicating mobility; and (d) if the phone or mail are used and the good or service is delivered; and will decrease with (a) frictions imposed by poor quality roads; and (b) proximity to, and increasing size of, the alternative center "also visited" to obtain the good (the center of "second choice"), although again affected by the quality of roads to the center of second choice.

Ten regression analysis were completed to evaluate the above notions[14] in the cases of food, gasoline purchased when in the car, gasoline delivered to the farm, barber and beauty service, banking (two problems, differing in that frequency data were missing in one), dry cleaning, furniture, appliances, and clothing. Results are listed in Table VII. The dependent variable is, in each regression, distance travelled to center of first choice (with logarithmic transformation).

In every case number of shopping opportunities in the center of first choice is significant (number of opportunities was interpreted as number of central functions). That this should be the case is not surprising, in view of Figs. 11-17 and Fig. 18. Frequency is significant for convenience items; the consistent negative signs indicate variations in the right direction. Per cent of distance travelled over paved roads is also significant for most items, and the positive signs indicate that shorter trips involve relatively more travel over unpaved roads. Alternative opportunities are related to first choice distance only for food and gas. Also, as more unpaved road has to be traversed to the second choice center, length of trip to the first choice for food shopping increases. As would be expected, with gas delivery there are significant relationships between length of trip and use of the telephone. Distance to the metropolis is significant

[14]For a longer discussion see H. Gardiner Barnum, *The Range of Goods in a Rural Area.* M.A. Thesis, University of Chicago, 1961.

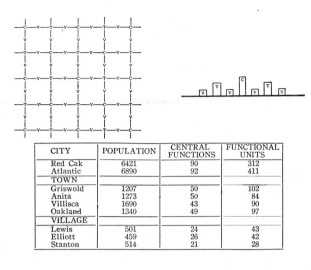

CITY	POPULATION	CENTRAL FUNCTIONS	FUNCTIONAL UNITS
Red Oak	6421	90	312
Atlantic	6890	92	411
TOWN			
Griswold	1207	50	102
Anita	1273	50	84
Villisca	1690	43	90
Oakland	1340	49	97
VILLAGE			
Lewis	501	24	43
Elliott	459	26	42
Stanton	514	21	28

FIGURE 10 The Hierarchy.

in gas purchase, obtaining barber or beauty services, and in the cases of furniture and appliances (see Figs. 15 and 16).

The coefficients of determination are unimpressive, varying from only 0.19 and 0.20 in the cases of gas delivery and furniture to 0.55 and 0.57 for food and clothing. One reason is to be seen in Figs. 11 through 17: people travel short distances to adjacent large centers as well as to small centers, but longer distances only to larger centers. Scatter diagrams of distance against size of center are thus approximately triangular (Figs. 20 and 21), and correlations are lowered by the tendency for shopping at nearest neighbor.

While alternative choices are of little significance in the selection of first choice center, some interesting collinearities appear between the distance to second choice center, number of shopping opportunities in that center, and per cent of distance which must be travelled over paved roads (Table VIII). One reason is to be seen in Figures 22 and 23. Note how the triangularity of the preceding pair of figures has disappeared. Second choice shopping is either to a closer smaller center or to a more distant larger one than the center of first choice. Accordingly, the correlations between size and distance are high. Once again, as the length of trip increases, so shorter trips have

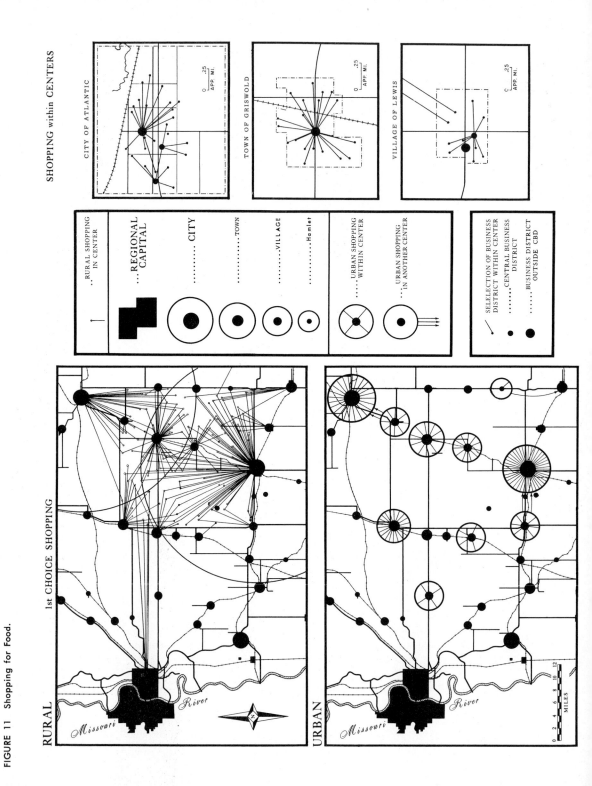

FIGURE 11 Shopping for Food.

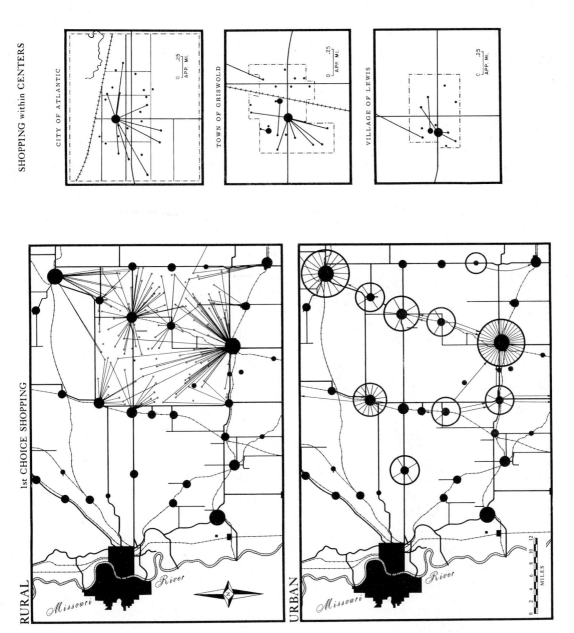

SHOPPING within CENTERS

CITY OF ATLANTIC

0   .25
APP. MI.

TOWN OF GRISWOLD

0   .25
APP. MI.

VILLAGE OF LEWIS

0   .25
APP. MI.

1st CHOICE SHOPPING

RURAL

Missouri River

N

URBAN

Missouri River

0 2 4 6 8 10 12
MILES

FIGURE 12   Obtaining Barber Service.

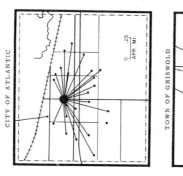
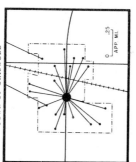
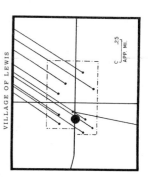

SHOPPING within CENTERS

CITY OF ATLANTIC

TOWN OF GRISWOLD

VILLAGE OF LEWIS

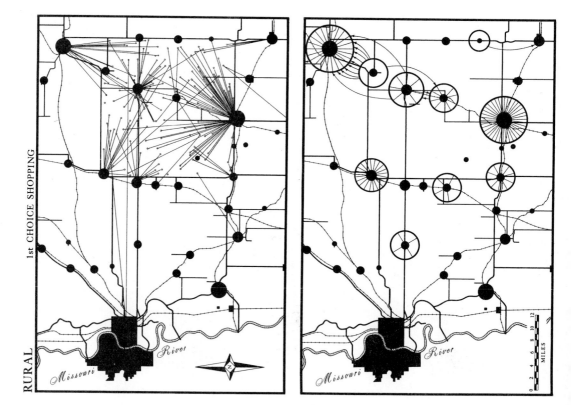

1st CHOICE SHOPPING

RURAL

FIGURE 13   Obtaining Banking Service.

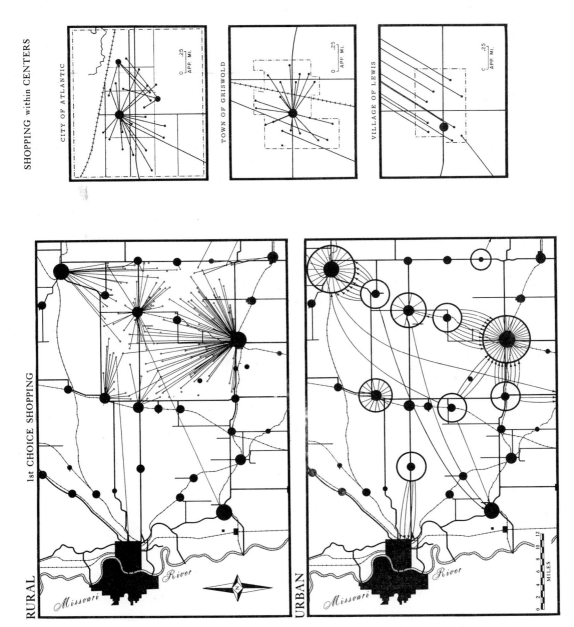

FIGURE 14 Dry Cleaning.

FIGURE 15 Shopping for Furniture.

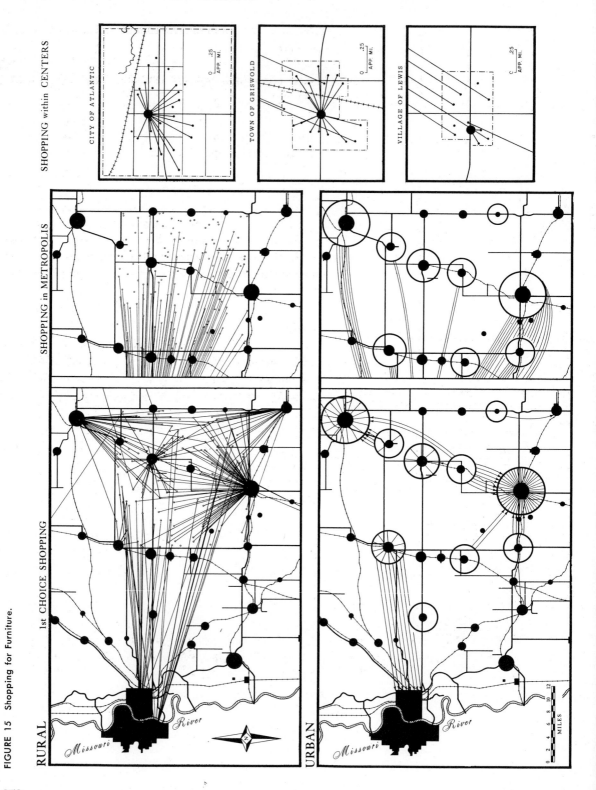

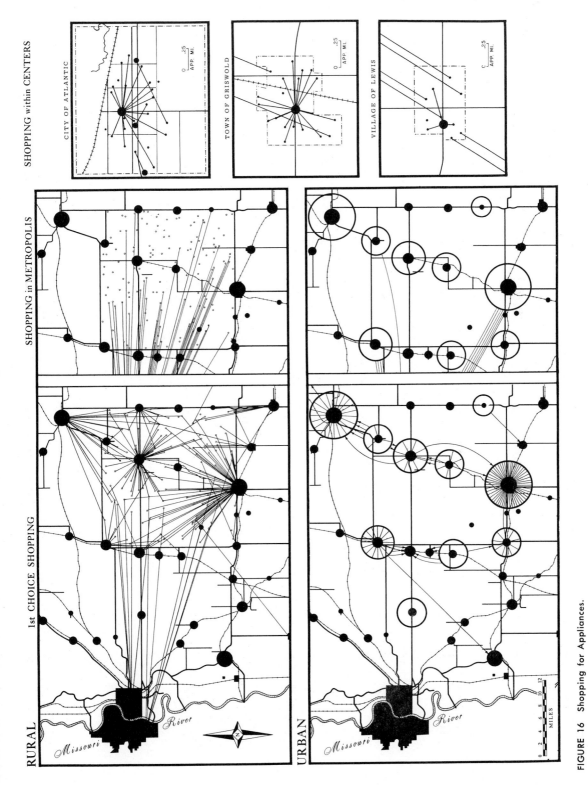

FIGURE 16 Shopping for Appliances.

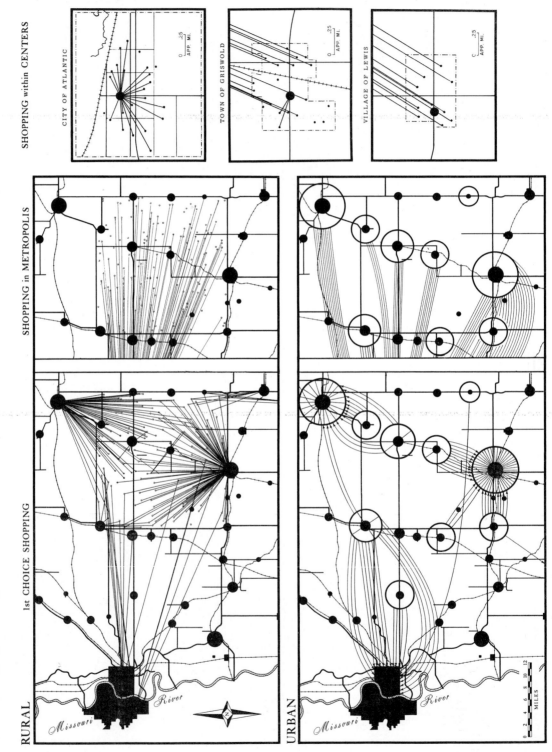

FIGURE 17 Shopping for Clothing.

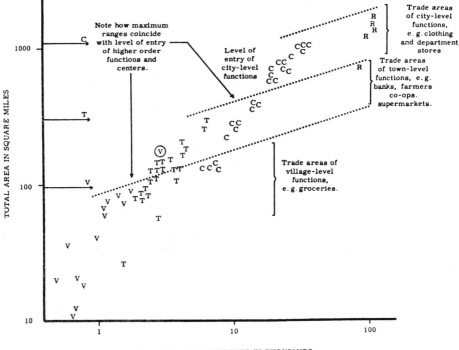

FIGURE 18 Running Across the Regimes for Centers, and Defining the Functional Steps of the Hierarchy, are the Trade Areas for Central Functions of Each Class.

greater proportions of their length over unpaved roads. Second choice behavior is consistent with the first, allowing for the fact that the first choices have seem made.

Interesting patterns also are revealed in out-of-town shopping by urban residents[15]. The out-of-town choice for any good is always the nearest center of next higher order than the center of residence. Thus, in the case of the village-level good, food, residents choose their own center first, but out-of-town shopping for food mimics first choice behavior of town level. Similarly, for clothing, residents of Atlantic and Red Oak look to the metropolis, providing a picture of an even higher level of spatial organization than that of the city. Out-of-town and alternative-choice shopping is, for urban residents, consistently of higher order than that of first choice.

FIGURE 19 The "Nestling" Process.

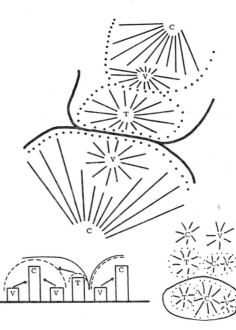

Village-level trade areas

Town-level trade areas

City-level trade areas

---

[15]These points are elaborated in Robert J. Tennant, *Shopping Patterns of Urban Residents*, M.A. Thesis, University of Chicago, 1962.

TABLE VII Regression Analyses of Factors Affecting Distance Travelled by Farmers for Ten Goods

INDEPENDENT VARIABLE	REGRESSION COEFFICIENTS AND STANDARD ERROR IN ANALYSES OF TRAVEL FOR:									
	Food	Gas Purchased	Gas Delivered	Barber & Beauty	Bank (1)	Bank (2)	Dry Cleaning	Furniture	Appliances[c]	Clothing
number of central functions in center of first choice	.0061* (.0008)	.056* (.0001)	.002 (.009)	.004* (.0008)	.004* (.001)	.006* (.001)	.006* (.0008)	.004* (.001)	.005* (.001)	.0072* (.0007)
log. of frequency of trip to first choice	−.55* (.10)	—	—	−.006* (.003)	−.15* (.069)	—	−.019 (.063)	—	—	−.024 (.044)
square root of % of distance over paved road	.043* (.013)	.047* (.012)	.032* (.012)	.018 (.011)	.054 (.018)	−.0002 (.028)	.049* (.014)	.003 (.036)	.045 (.029)	.047* (.013)
no. of central function in second choice center	.18*[b] (.075)	−.007* (.002)	—	.001 (.002)	−.14[b] (.36)	−.061[b] (.052)	−.007 (.006)	.003 (.002)	−.001 (.002)	.0002 (.001)
log. of distance to second choice center	.0027 (.09)	.43 (.22)	—	.15 (.21)	−.096 (.67)	.0021 (.0015)	.30 (.55)	−.26 (.48)	.22 (.29)	−.084 (.12)
square root of % of distance to second choice over paved road	−.023* (.011)	.019 (.015)	—	.008 (.02)	.043 (.087)	.74 (.66)	.034 (.031)	−.008 (.052)	.03 (.027)	.021 (.011)
telephone used? (binary)	—	—	.11* (.05)	—	—	—	—	—	.17 (.11)	—
mail order used? (binary)	—	—	—	—	—	—	—	.041 (.29)	.24 (.24)	.011 (−.028)
ever visit metropolis? (binary)	−.086 (.088)	—	—	—	—	—	—	.041 (.10)	.16 (.11)	−.0065 (−.031)
distance to the metropolis (Omaha)	−.0006 (.0022)	.006* (.003)	.004 (.003)	.007* (.002)	.004 (.003)	.002 (.0063)	.001 (.002)	.028* (.006)	.018* (.005)	−.0015 (.019)
intercept	.44	.30	.24	−.07	.21	.56	−.078	−.79	−1.03	.093
standard error	.21	.24	.20	.23	.23	.24	.22	.49	.47	.16
coeff. of determination	.55	.51	.19	.33	.34	.36	.46	.20	.25	.57

* Significant at .05 level, using t test, two-tailed.
a Log. transform not used.
b Log. transform.
c And their service.

TABLE VIII Second Choice Correlations

TYPE OF FUNCTION	BETWEEN		
	Distance[a] and Number of Functions	Distance[a] and % Roads Paved	Number of Functions and % Roads Paved[b]
Food	.90	.94	.85
Gasoline Purchase	.93	.82	.90
Barber-Beauty	.95	.91	.96
Bank (1)	.98	.98	.99
Bank (2)	.88	.99	.83
Dry Cleaning	.98	.90	.94
Furniture	.95	.91	.98
Appliances	.92	.82	.94
Clothing	.96	.91	.96

a Logarithmic transformation.
b Square root transformation.

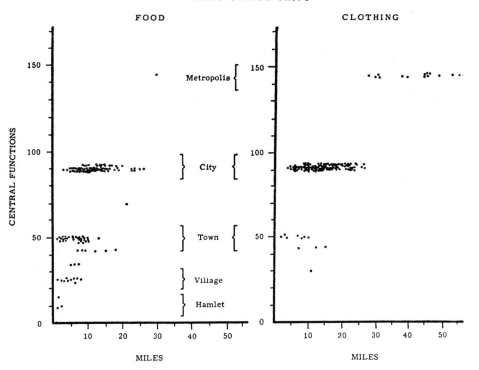

FIGURE 20—21   Distance Travelled to First Choice Center is Related to Size of Center.

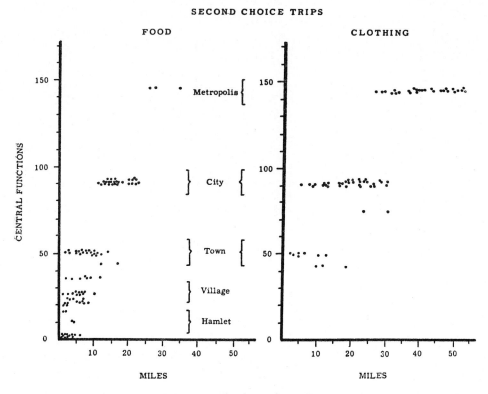

FIGURE 22—23   Second Choice is Either a Smaller Closer Center (Food) or a Larger More Distant Center (Food and Clothing).

Richard L. Morrill

THE DEVELOPMENT OF SPATIAL DISTRIBUTIONS
OF TOWNS IN SWEDEN:
AN HISTORICAL-PREDICTIVE APPROACH[1]

The city or town is now the home of the majority of the population of the more developed countries, but the rise of a modern urban culture has been rapid and rather recent. This phenomenon fascinates scholars in many fields. In geography, attention has centered on three aspects of urbanization: the general nature of urbanization,[2] the detailed analysis of cities, and, within the framework of central place theory,[3] explanation of the size and location of places.

This paper attempts a rather general approach to the development of the spatial distribution of towns. The approach recognizes that urbanization involves more than the location of central place activities; much urban support derives, of course, from activities that do not depend on a local hinterland. Furthermore, the development of urbanization takes place through time, and condi-

tions are constantly changing. For this study an experimental model has been developed in which a pattern of town distribution gradually emerges. The predictive model, of course, rests upon such general knowledge about the process of urbanization as has been accumulated over the years. For verification, the model was applied to a study area in Sweden. The objective of the paper is to develop a theory out of the study of real patterns, the test of which is whether the actual patterns could have been reproduced by the suggested theory.

The discussion that follows is in four parts: first, a discussion of the major factors which must be taken into account in the study of urbanization; second, a tentative description of the process of urbanization; third, a review of the application of the model to a study area in Sweden; and finally, a summary of the suggested model of urban development.

The Problem of Urbanization and Migration

The distribution of towns in any region (implying their location *and* size) is the result of a long and complex interplay of forces. At the very least, any study which proposes to explain the origins of such patterns must take into account these major factors: (1) the economic and social conditions which permit and/or encourage concentration of economic activities in towns and cities; (2) the spatial or geographic conditions which influence the spacing and size of towns; (3)

Reprinted with the permission of the author and publisher from the *Annals*, Association of American Geographers, Vol. 53, No. 1, 1963, pp. 1-14. Dr. Morrill is Associate Professor of Geography at the University of Washington, Seattle.

[1] This paper is a partial report of research carried out at the University of Lund in Sweden under a grant from the National Science Foundation, Office of Social Sciences. Professor Torsten Hägerstrand was most generous in his aid to this research. A detailed presentation of methods, historical background, and findings is in preparation and will be published in *Series B, Lund Studies in Human Geography* (1963).

[2] A. E. Smailes, *The Geography of Towns* (London: Hutchinson's University Library, 1953), pp. 7-83. Harold M. Mayer and Clyde F. Kohn (eds.), *Reading in Urban Geography* (Chicago: University of Chicago Press, 1959): Kingsley Davis, "The Origin and Growth of Urbanization in the World," pp. 59-68, and Robert L. Dickinson, "The Growth of the Historical City," pp. 69-84. Paul K. Hatt and Albert J. Reiss, *Cities and Society* (Glencoe: Free Press, 1957), pp. 64-222.

[3] For an annotated summary of central place work, see Brian J. L. Berry and Allan Pred, *Central Place Studies*, Bibliography Series No. 1 (Philadelphia: Regional Science Research Institute, 1961). [See page 65 of this volume.]

the fact that such development takes place gradually over time; and (4) recognition that there is an element of uncertainty or indeterminancy in all behavior.

The economic aspects of urbanization have been actively studied and have yielded information concerning the rate and direction of economic expansion, economies of agglomeration for activities in cities, threshold conditions for successful entry of activities, and the importance of technological change on the utilization of resources, natural and human. These data influence the kinds, scale, and spatial extent and grouping of activities and hence play a major role in the location and sizes of towns.

The spatial analysis of distributions of towns comprises three aspects: central place theory asks how large an area is necessary to support towns, what is an efficient spacing of settlements, if there is an hierarchy of settlements. Central place activities can be considered as those which serve a local market. The under-lying assumption is that man makes some effort at organizing his activities over space in an efficient manner. Central place theory seeks to ascertain what is the most efficient division of space, given an array of functions.

In contrast, industrial location theory treats the spatial distribution of activities which serve regional or national markets and which depend on a complex of resources, transport connections, labor supplies, etc. These are nevertheless of even greater importance than central place activities as support for urban populations. A realistic model of urbanization cannot ignore one or the other. An example of their mutual dependence is the emergence of an irregular central place net upon a mining-industrial complex or an agricultural base.

The spatial process of the development of rural land uses, especially in agricultural and forest locations, provides a close link between the natural environment and human settlement. However, for purposes of this study, the effects of rural land use are subsumed through the location of central place and other activities which the rural land uses and population support.

The growth of cities based upon the location and concentration of activities implies migration. Migration is the process in space through which the redistribution of population occurs. In the early stages of urbanization, almost the entire population of the new cities must have migrated from rural life. The pertinent spatial questions concern migration distances, types of migrants, and motivations of migrants.

These spatial processes of central place location, industrial location, rural land use, and migration give rise to the observed distribution of settlement—a scatter of towns, a few larger ones, many smaller ones, and a transportation network linking the towns and cities. Together they specify the spatial dimension of urbanization.

The important role of the element of time is suggested by the very word, development. It is not possible to study a spatial process in isolation.[4] The present settlement pattern is the result of a long interplay of forces. The historical dimension is of crucial importance to the study of urban development for three reasons. (1) technologies change; (2) the characteristics of the urban population and physical plant are constantly being modified; (3) locational decisions are made at a point in time, after which social and economic conditions may radically change. Established locations possess great inertia; once decided upon, removal is difficult. An efficient decision at one time may be rendered obsolete well within the lifetime of the facility. Previous locations, later seen as good or bad, must powerfully influence future locations. One must therefore ask whether the fact of growth in time supports or alters central place or industrial location conceptions as presently formulated.

Central place theory has undergone significant development in recent years. A contention of this paper is that a further improvement can be realized through consideration of time as well as space, that is by requiring the locational concepts of central place theory to operate in an historical context. The gradual unfolding of distributions of towns over a long period of changing economic and social conditions helps account for the discrepancies found between theoretical and observed patterns.[5]

One reason for developing a model which operates in time is that our evaluation of space changes with technological improvement, for example, with transportation innovation. However, even if this were not true, the fact that growth as

[4]See also J. M. Blaut, "Space and Process," *The Professional Geographer*, Vol. XII, No. 4 (1961), pp. 3-5.

[5]For other discussions of these discrepancies see *Papers and Proceedings*, Lund Symposium on Urban Geography, International Geographical Congress, Lund, 1960. (Lund: 1963).

such is a process of change requires an expanded central place theory. Places do not suddenly change functional level, but gradually add new activities. Hinterlands expand and contract. Commercialization and urbanization began in certain areas and slowly spread.[6] Under conditions of a moving frontier of settlement the effect of time is even more apparent.[7] The off-center gateway city is a case in point. Thus, at any one time the perfect equilibrium that static theory suggests can never exist in fact.

The development of spatial distributions of towns then, takes place over time within a changing economic and social setting and is subject to changing conditions influencing location. A theory or model could now be devised which would determine in a strict economic or geometric manner all locational decisions. Our knowledge of the real world, however, requires us to admit the operation of another dimension to the problem—randomness. In other words, locational decisions are subject to errors or uncertainties which we cannot specify or wish away. Human decisions are rarely perfect. People may not know a correct decision or be able to distinguish between almost equally good alternatives. Generally, in a period of time, there are many more possible locations for plants, or destinations for migrants, than plants to establish or persons to move. Some kind of random decision, like coin-tossing, is required to decide in the face of such uncertainty. Finally, theories are simplifications and usually deal only with the major variables. Many small forces, whose net effect may often be considered random, also exist. Real patterns of activities and towns will be approximations growing out of many less than perfect decisions. If real patterns are to be understood, theory must incorporate this uncertainty.

The Development of Distribution of Towns

The development of an urban pattern is a growth process involving the location of central place activities, that is, those which serve a local

hinterland, non-central place activities, for example much manufacturing and transportation which have a non-local market, and migration, which provides many of the people for the growing towns.

CENTRAL PLACE ACTIVITIES

The basic notion in central place theory is that those activities which serve a surrounding population vary widely in the minimum population, purchasing power, or threshold, needed for their support.[8] Functional groupings of activities with similar thresholds, that is levels of urban function, are recognizable for a given time. A central place of the lowest level emerges, or an existing central place rises in importance, as it is able to satisfy these basic conditions: to dominate a hinterland with a population at least equal to the minimum needed, all parts of which are closer to the new central place than to any other existing central place. This becomes possible as density of population increases, or as increasing wealth (as from industrialization and commercialization) of the society enables the same population to support a greater volume and variety of activities. Locations midway between existing centers are most likely to become new centers, since they will be the first to be able to secure an adequate hinterland.[9] Under perfect conditions, an hexagonal pattern of places would emerge (if there were only central place activities.)

However, imagine an elongated area, which at a point in time is just able to support two central places. As wealth increases, the minimum threshold falls, and these two places enjoy "excess markets" until a new central place emerges.[10] Many specific locations can be expected to try to become a new center. There may exist one "best" location, but there may be several which satisfy the conditions of a sufficient hinterland. Which succeeds in winning out over its rivals is, in historical fact, found to depend on much more than geometry (a midway position). The presence or absence of manufacturing and mining activities and transportation facilities, entrepreneurial skill, and an

[6]Torsten Hägerstrand, *Innovationsförloppet ur korologisk synpunkt* (Lund: 1953). For a summary see "Propagation of Innovation Waves," *Lund Studies in Geography*, Series B, No. 4 (1952).

[7]In Richard L. Morrill, "Simulation of Central Place Patterns over Time," *op. cit.*, Lund Symposium in Urban Geography, 1960, this aspect is treated in some detail.

[8]B. J. L. Berry, and W. L. Garrison, "A Note on Central Place Theory and the Range of a Good," *Economic Geography*, Vol. 34 (1958), pp. 304-11.

[9]Sven Godlund, "The Function and Growth of Bus Traffic Within the Sphere of Urban Influence," *Lund Studies in Geography*, Series B, No. 18 (1956). [See page 216 of this volume.]

[10]B. J. L. Berry, and W. L. Garrison, *op. cit.*

element of chance, as well as the present population and its characteristics may be decisive, and these factors must be incorporated into an adequate theory.

NON–CENTRAL PLACE ACTIVITIES

Non-central place activities, typified by much manufacturing and by many transport routes, do not depend upon carving out local hinterlands. Many locations, whether a central place, or close or far from one, may compete for such activities. The probability of an area obtaining investments and employment varies with population (labor force) and its characteristics, size of existing settlements, the nature and extent of already existing activities (both urban and rural), transport position, and, of course, natural resources.

A complete theory would include an industrial location analysis for each possible addition of every type. Since the purpose of this study is to understand general distributions of towns and not specific industrial patterns, the location of manufacturers is treated at a secondary level. That is, if we take all the specific plant location decisions for a year, and look at them as a "set of plants or investments" to be allocated without concern for type, it is found that a random assignment (with restricted choice), taking into account the greater attraction of skilled labor pools, good transport, etc., will closely approximate the real pattern of location. A valuable simplification of model, a substitution of partial analysis, is thus permitted.

MIGRATION

Migration is of fundamental importance to the development of the human landscape. Although it is a process in space, it has not been widely studied by geographers. International migration has been extensively studied, pratically by historians and demographers. Although there are often similarities in motivation between internal and international population movements, the latter involve political problems normally absent in more local movement. The displacement of persons as a result of political change has been reviewed recently by Velikonja.[11] Migration has been studied

in three ways: (1) Migration to and from a state or country may be analyzed.[12] Such studies reveal factors which both encourage and restrict movements. Hence, they provide hypotheses to be tested for inclusion in a study of migration. (2) A common approach is a detailed socio-economic survey of regional or national migration or redistribution of population.[13] Such surveys often provide statistical tests of many notions about migration; for example, that there is a relation between migration volume and distance.[14] (3) Another group has provided models of migration.[15] Some of these are deterministic, that is, the migrant's destination is determined by economic or distance conditions;[16] and others are probabilistic, that is, involve individual choice.[17] Recently the importance of indi-

---

[12]For example, J. Fraser Hart, "Migration and Population Change in Indiana," *Proceedings,* Indiana Academy of Science (Indianapolis: 1957), pp. 195-203. Walter M. Kollmorgen, and George Jenks, "A Geographic Study of Population and Settlement Changes in Sherman County, Kansas," *Transactions* of the Kansas Academy of Science (Lawrence: 1951), pp. 449-94. Richard L. Morrill, "Regional Growth and Net Migration," *University of Washington Business Review,* Vol. 21 (1962), pp. 5-13. Warren S. Thompson, "Migration within Ohio, A Study of Redistribution of Population," *Scripps Foundation Studies in Population Distribution,* No. 3 (Oxford, Ohio: Scripps Foundation for Research in Population Problems, Miami University, 1951).

[13]Donald J. Bogue, et al., "Streams of Migration between Subregions," *Scripps Foundation Studies in Population Distribution,* No. 5 (Oxford, Ohio: Scripps Foundation for Research in Population Problems, Miami University, 1953). *Migration in Sweden,* A Symposium. Lund Studies in Human Geography, Series B, No. 13 (University of Lund, 1957). *Population Redistribution and Economic Growth,* Simon Kuznets and D. S. Thomas, eds. (Philadelphia: American Philosophical Society, 1959). Warren C. Thornthwaite, *Internal Migration in the United States,* Bulletin 1, Study of Population Redistribution (Philadelphia: University of Pennsylvania Press, 1934).

[14]Esse Lövgren, "The Geographic Mobility of Labor," *Geografiska Annaler,* Vol. 38 (1956), pp. 344-94. Phillip Nelson, "Migration, Real Income, and Information," *Journal of Regional Science,* Vol. 1, No. 2 (1959), pp. 43-74. Larry A. Sjaastad, "The Relationship betwen Migration and Income in the United States," *Papers of the Regional Science Association,* Vol. 6 (1960), pp. 37-64.

[15]For a summary of migration models see: Walter Isard, "Migration Estimation," Chapter 3, *Methods of Regional Analysis* (New York: John Wiley & Sons, 1960). Richard L. Morrill, "The Development of Models of Migration and the Role of Electronic Processing Machines," International Symposium in the Human Sciences: The Measure of Human Displacement (Monaco, May 1962).

[16]Esse Lövgren, "Mutual Relations Between Migration Fields," in *Migration in Sweden, op. cit.* (1957), pp. 159-69. S. A. Stouffer, "Intervening Opportunities: A Theory Relating Mobility and Distance," *American Sociological Review,* Vol. 5 (1940). G. K. Zipf, *Human Behavior and the Principle of Least Effort* (Cambridge: Harvard University Press, 1949), pp. 386-415.

[17]T. Hägerstrand, "Migration and Area," *Migration in Sweden, op. cit.* (1957), pp. 126-52. R. Porter, "Approach to Migration Through its Mechanism" *Geografiska Annaler,* Vol. 38 (1956), pp. 317-43. Daniel Price, "A Mathematical Model of Migration Suitable for Simulation on an Electric Computer," *Proceedings,* International Population Conference (Wien: 1959), pp. 665-73.

---

[11]Joseph Velikonja, "Postwar Population Movements in Europe," *Annals,* Association of American Geographers, Vol. 48 (December, 1958), pp. 458-71.

vidual social contact has been stressed.[18]

The migration involved in the development of town distributions is primarily an internal circulation between rural and rural, rural and urban, and urban and urban locations. Throughout the period of urbanization the net effect of such movements generally has been the transfer or rural population to urban locations. Migration is normally an individual or family movement which seems to depend on three major controls: (1) Distance between the origin and possible destinations. As the distance from his origin increases, an individual is likely to have contact with a smaller and smaller proportion of available opportunities. The effect of distance as a barrier to migration changes over time, primarily with improvements in transportation and communication. Intervening opportunities may modify the role of distance. (2) The differential attractiveness of areas, both those of present residence, and those of possible destinations. The most important attraction is the greater economic opportunity in more urban and/or wealthier areas, but climate and other amenities play an increasing role. (3) Information, in the sense that migrants must know about an opportunity in order to move to it. Frequently people migrate to areas to which friends and relatives have previously moved.

These factors are brought together into a "simulation" model, a kind of probability model. It is necessary to state here that simulation refers to an experimental procedure of restricted choice which identifies a process—here urbanization and migration—and generates patterns which are similar to actual ones. Before the model procedure is outlined, however, the application of the model to a study area in Sweden will be presented. The model can then be seen in terms of a practical example.

Application of the Model

In this study the simulation model takes as a starting point the population pattern at a particular time. Then, for a selected later time period, assigns, i.e., chooses by means or random numbers, locations for new transport links (out of many possible ones), assigns locations for manufacturing or other non-central place activities, and assigns locations for central place activities. Each stage depends on the previous stage. These assignments of activities change the attractiveness of areas; i.e., the anticipated urban population creates new opportunities. The model then assigns, or chooses paths for migrants, between all areas, in reflection of the altered opportunities. A new population structure results and the entire process is repeated in another time period. A flow-diagram illustrates this process.

Pattern at time→ 1	Assign new→ transport links	Assign new→ manu- factures	Assign new→ central places	Pattern at time 1 modified by urban population anticipated from above assignments ↓
repeat for new pattern next time←at time 2 ← period		assign migrants between areas		

DATA SOURCES

Sweden is a valuable area in which to conduct social studies, since rather accurate and detailed census statistics date from about 1750. These include most changes of property and residence. The Census of Population is complete from 1750 for very small areas which have remained extraordinarily stable over the entire period. Data on details of migration are available, although use of parish church records is required. Data on the industrial structure of places with a population as small as 50 are available.[19] The information on conditions in 1850 was taken from regional maps and histories of the period.

THE STUDY AREA

The particular study area was chosen for its simplicity and convenience. The boundaries generally enclose functional units. The area is restricted in size and population and contains no large cities or ports. Nevertheless it is a regional microcosm of the national urban pattern, and in fact of the urban pattern of any developed country. The same reasons for urbanization apply; the same kinds of economic activities are carried on; the same spatial forces which tend to produce an efficient pattern of towns are present. The distinctive geographic conditions of the area have con-

[18]Hägerstrand, *op. cit.* (1957), pp. 27-158. Benjamin Luebke, and J. F. Hart, "Migration from a Southern Appalachian Community," *Land Economics*, Vol. 34 (1958), pp. 44-53.

[19]*Tätortsregister*: Jönköping och Kronobergs Del., ed. Sven Dahl. (Stockholm: Geografiska Institution vid Handekshögskolan [Community Register]).

tributed to a distinctive distribution of towns, to be sure, if one wishes to emphasize individuality.

HISTORICAL SURVEY

The study area, situated in southern Sweden, is traversed by the main north-south railway and highway (Fig. 1). The population of about 270,-000 has a density of less than 50 per square mile, which is low by European standards. The area lacks much good farmland; most of the land is forested. Although the wood industry (in all forms) is the most important, the area is one of a great diversity of small industries. Industrialization did not begin until 1865 and was not really significant before 1880. By 1960, however, manufacturing supported over 40 per cent of the population, whereas agriculture and forestry supported but 30 per cent. In contrast to the United States, here one finds small factories scattered in towns and villages. Most famous are probably the glass

factories, e.g., those at Orrefors and Kosta.

Figure 2 depicts the contemporary scene. Dominance of north-south transportation routes is evident. A fairly wide sprinkling of urban-type settlements occurs; their distribution closely reflects the railway pattern. The objective of this research was to trace the development of this distribution to discover the conditions which produced it, and to express them in a model which would produce a similar distribution.

As recently as 1850 urban development was extremely limited. Pressure on the land was great, and very large-scale migration to America was just beginning. Emigration reached its peak between 1870 and 1890. The distribution (about 1850) of parish churches, principal roads, inns, and mills is given in Figure 3. The population was rather evenly distributed. Only the local capital and three small regional towns provided a framework for the later urban development.

Construction of the main north-south railway (Stockholm-Malmö) by 1865 provided the impetus for beginning industrialization. The route chosen was a straightened version of an old high road, but it deliberately by-passed principal towns. However a connection was built to the local capital the next year. This first line has always maintained its dominance; hence many of the station villages created in the construction period have become important small industrial and commercial centers. The central place pattern was distorted by the railway—i.e., attracted partially to it. By 1880, fifteen years after the first railway, about twenty non-agricultural villages had developed, and the earlier towns grew rapidly. Some of the manufac-

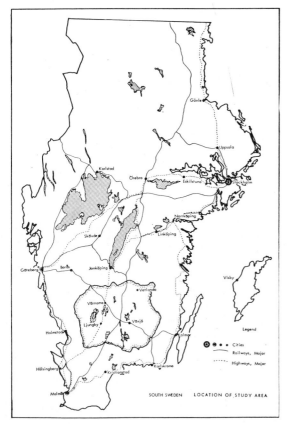

FIGURE 1

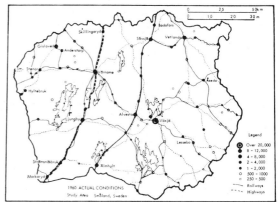

FIGURE 2

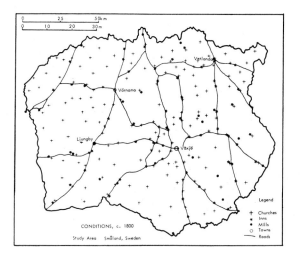

FIGURE 3

turing development was in anticipation of a rail-road. Perhaps only eight of these villages had any significant central place functions. A large-scale movement of population had begun to the towns and new station villages from the overcrowded countryside.

The period 1880-1900 was one of net population loss from migration, but the towns and villages continued to gain population. These settlements frequently developed out of stations on the new railways. Village growth was at the expense of rural areas of their own and neighboring parishes (Fig. 4). By 1900 there were about thirty-five towns and villages, most of which were growing very rapidly. Many railway lines were built. The

motivation for some seems to have been to connect the new towns to the main north-south railway, but for others the motivation was to connect more important outside places.

The urban situation in 1910 is shown in Figure 5. Although the population at this time could support about eighteen basic central places, only fourteen had developed.[20] This discrepancy was simply the result of the spacing of earlier centers, which at this point in time were far enough apart to give many of them excess markets, but not far enough to permit new centers between. (See also Figure 13a and b). Similarly, there could be six higher-level centers, but the location of the four original towns prevented the growth of additional centers. Here is one example, to be found again and again in this study, of how an earlier decision in time prevents the most efficient location patterns and why it is necessary to include the historical dimension in the theory.

From 1900 to 1940 the population remained stable. Gains by natural increase were offset by net migration loss out of the area. Within the area, industrialization and urbanization proceeded rapidly. From 1940 to 1960 the population increased slightly as better opportunities within the area slowed down migration losses to other parts of the

[20]The number of places that could be supported by a population at a given level can be determined from marketing data. If these are unavailable, the ideal maximum number of places may be estimated from the actual distribution by measuring the amount of excess markets.

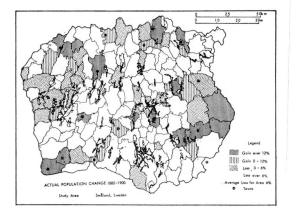

FIGURE 4

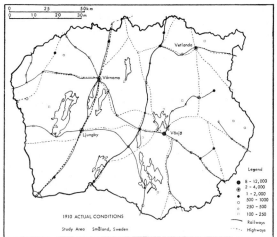

FIGURE 5

country. The urban patterns had now proliferated to the many centers shown on Figure 2.

Several empirical "runs" of the model were made. Two trial simulations were made for 1810–1820 and 1820–1840. Since no urbanization was occurring, the model simply assigned internal migration between parishes. The results were adequate but suffered from lack of consideration of outside factors. Two other simulations using actual data were made. For the period 1860–1880 migration was simulated between parishes as before, but parishes through which the railway passed or in which it was known that some manufacturing was developing were weighted in accordance with employment anticipated by such investment. Differential growth of parishes was induced in the light of this predicted urbanization. For 1960–1980 a predictive simulation was made in which areas were weighted by their urban population. Some of the detailed migration from selected areas is shown in Figure 6. These results were quite satisfactory and correlate with recent events and expected changes.[21]

The main set of simulations, however, was a united series for 1860 to 1960. Each simulation located new activities, which in turn changed the attractiveness of areas and induced a pattern of population gains and losses from migration. Beginning with actual 1860 data and the presence of the four towns (Fig. 3), the only other outside infor-

mation used was the net growth or loss of the region in twenty-year intervals,[22] the volume of activities that the population could support and the total demand for transportation, manufacturing, etc. All railways, manufacturing, and central place activities were randomly assigned. The location of the assigned centers often coincided with the actual ones. In some cases this was random coincidence. In other cases the coincidence reflected the strong advantage of the area relative to already existing centers or a favored transport position. The choice of location for railroads was often quite restricted, and in several cases the routes coincided, at least in part.

The one-hundred year simulation produced a dynamic distribution of urban places and currents of migration to support the urbanization. Distributions may be compared both from generation to generation and as end-products. Since it was not intended to try to reproduce the actual pattern, comparison must be more indirect. Some results are shown in Figure 6-9. The simulated and actual distributions for 1910 are shown on Figures 5 and 7. The distributions for 1960 are shown on Figures 2 and 8.

The objective of the study was to discover and utilize the major locational forces channeling urban development and migration. If this were achieved, the following characteristics of actual development should be matched by the simulated development: (1) The set of urban places should exhibit a certain range of sizes, yet maintain a

[21]Kunglige Arbetsmarknadsstyrelsen, *Lokaliseringutredning För Kronobergs Län* [Location analysis] (Stockholm: 1959).

[22]Shorter time periods would be preferable. The twenty-year interval was accepted for reasons of time and manpower.

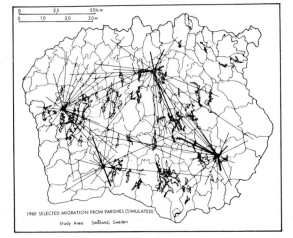

1960 SELECTED MIGRATION FROM PARISHES (SIMULATED)

Study Area   Småland, Sweden

FIGURE 6

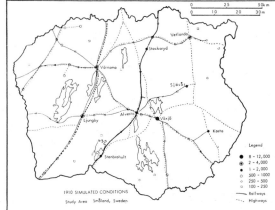

1910 SIMULATED CONDITIONS

Study Area   Småland, Sweden

Legend
● 8 - 12,000
◉ 2 - 4,000
◎ 1 - 2,000
○ 500 - 1000
○ 250 - 500
□ 100 - 250
—— Railways
---- Highways

FIGURE 7

spatial hierarchy. This was achieved very closely (e.g., Figs. 2 and 8). (2) The spatial distribution should have a certain set of distances between places. The distribution was close, but there was slight tendency for the simulated towns to be more regularly spaced. The actual distortion resulting from historical change and from locations of manufacturers and railways was even greater than predicted. (3) Early location decisions, railways, towns, and manufactures, should have strong and lasting effects on later locations. The model reproduced this process well. The extent to which the original towns, both in reality and in the model, restricted and channeled the ultimate development of the current distribution was striking. Although there were great changes in the fortunes of places and much redistribution of population, such changes were not chaotic. The present distribution can be seen as the growth of the old distribution into new conditions. (4) Migration patterns should have a characteristic distribution of distances and directions. The simulation correctly matched the typical distance traveled by migrants, but the failure to take into account the strong dependence of migration on previous movements resulted in a more regular migration field over time than actually occurred. This failure can be easily corrected. (5) A net flow of migrants, of certain volumes and directions, from rural to urban locations should occur. This was achieved. (6) Certain numbers and kinds of areas should gain or lose and by similar volumes. Again the patterns are similar (Figs. 4 and 9), but the simulation is somewhat too regu-

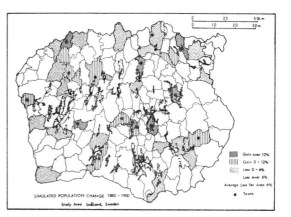

FIGURE 9

lar. Too few parishes lost. The problem here seems to be the omission from the model of significant variations in local birth and death rates.

In sum, the model results can be considered realistic from the point of view of distribution, that is, similarity in spatial structure; and from the point of view of process, or a reasonable recognition and treatment of the pertinent forces. Deviations resulted in the main from oversimplified assumptions rather than from a mistaken approach.

This example of the use of the simulation approach seems to indicate that the technique is applicable to a wide range of problems that involve the development of a spatial pattern over time. Their application to problems of innovation and the spread of techniques and ideas has been well demonstrated.[23] From culture to culture, area to area, and time to time, the exact nature of the forces to be built into a model may differ. In one kind of frontier settlement, for example, it may be best to locate as far as possible from another settler.[24] In another case grouping may be required for protection. Most of the controls over location and migration, however, are more universal. Distance is always a barrier and, when crossed by a route, an opportunity. Only the importance attached to it may vary. There seems to be much historical and predictive research that might utilize such methods: the spread of the frontier, the future development of urban patterns, and the spatial growth of

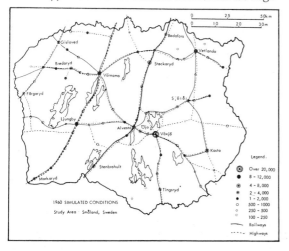

FIGURE 8

[23]Hägerstrand, op. cit. (1953). Professor F. Pitts, University of Oregon, is now completing a dual study of the spread of hand tractors and the disappearance of horses in Japan.
[24]Erik Bylund, Kolonisering av Pite Lappmark (Uppsala: Almquist and Wiksell, 1959).

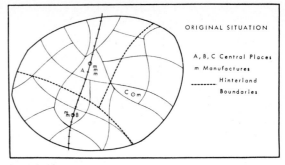

FIGURE 10

the metropolis. The simulation technique, however, is not to be used for it own sake. It is useful only as its provides an operational framework for explanations of behavior in space.

The Simulation Model

The preceding example indicated the general nature of the model—a model which operates as a process through time and which involves locational choice restricted by many regularizing forces. More formally, this simulation model is a system represented by a sampling procedure (random numbers) which satisfies the same probability laws (for example, the probability of migrating various distances).[25] Probability models are often used when it is necessary to evaluate an otherwise indeterminate solution. Rather than various factors converging to a unique solution, a range of possibilities occurs. Certain possibilities, for example locations for an activity, are more likely choices than others and can be given higher probabilities of being selected. The final choice is random, i.e., given by random numbers. The procedure is also called the "Monte Carlo" or "model sampling" method. In this technique, choice ultimately depends on previous decisions and their results. The growth of a distribution of urban centers and the migration to support such growth can logically be treated in such a model. There are only a limited number of new plants, stores, or migrants, but many places compete for them. In addition, an individual decision cannot be isolated from the historical stream of decisions.

A simulation model, however, does not abandon all to chance. Many forces tend to determine a solution, but there is always an element of choice. We cannot reproduce the real world exactly, but we may hope to generate distributions which resemble those of the real world.

Let us demarcate a study region, divide it into component areas, and choose time periods. Figure 10, for example, depicts a possible situation at the beginning of a simulation process. Necessary supporting information is collected: net growth rates for the chosen time period; the demand for new

transportation; the amount of new economic activities of whatever sort that can be supported; and the propensity to migrate.

STEP 1: ASSIGNMENT OF TRANSPORT ROUTES

a. Each demanded link (Fig. 11, the link to C) has several specific possible routes. These are to be evaluated. Eligibility requirements may be included, for example, a rule that a possible route may be only a certain degree longer than the shortest possible route.

b. To choose a particular route for a demanded link it is necessary to determine the probabilities of the various alternative routes. These probabilities will vary according to distance of the route, population (especially urban) of the areas traversed, and costs of construction.

c. A specific route is chosen by means of random numbers as shown in the example (Fig. 11). These probabilities may be taken to mean in this case the relative lobbying strength of the proponents of the three alternatives. Which group would prevail is uncertain. Resorting to a random number solves the problem, after the probabilities are summed in a form useful for matching against random numbers.

The assignment of transport routes is important to the process of urban development, both because of directly added non-agricultural em-

[25]C. W. Churchman, R. L. Ackoff, and E. L. Arnoff, *Introduction to Operations Research* (New York: John Wiley and Sons, 1957).

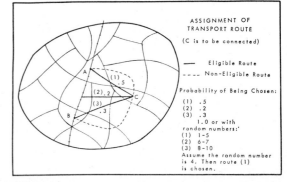

FIGURE 11

ployment, and because of the enhanced attractiveness of the served areas for other economic activities.

STEP 2: ASSIGNMENT OF NON-CENTRAL PLACE ACTIVITIES

a. The demand for new activities is a function of population, income, resources, etc. The number of new plants for the entire area and their contribution to urban support is given from economic analysis.

b. Eligibility of areas. All areas may be considered eligible, or restrictions may be imposed. For example, an activity may be able to locate in a place (area) if costs of assembling and/or processing do not exceed some maximum level, and if the local labor force equals at least some level. Many areas might be rejected at once owing to excess cost or lack of labor (Fig. 12a).

c. Probability of areas for receiving manufactures. Even if eligible, areas will vary widely in their attractiveness to industry. The probability of locating in a particular area will depend on characteristics of the local rural and urban population, on the transport facilities existing previously or just assigned (Step 1), on the cost of assembling materials and processing, and on the volume and kind of activities already present. This step is simply the application of industrial location concepts, but rather than a unique location being found, for every plant of each type, this model recognizes a choice for plants in general among several locations. The best locations, of course, have the highest probability of being chosen. Figure 12a shows how transport facilities and existing towns influence the probabilities.

d. Random assignment of plants: To assign

a limited number of plants among many possible locations, random numbers may be used. To do this, it is necessary to convert the basic probabilities (Fig. 12a) into useful form. In Figure 12b, the equivalent tally of numbers, to be matched against random numbers, replaces the basic probabilities. For example, the probability of area 5 to receive plants is .07. This is the range .04 through .10 if we add the probabilities cumulatively. The equivalent discrete numbers are 4-10. Then random numbers, as many as there are plants to be assigned, are matched against the tally. This process is illustrated in Figure 12b.

STEP 3: ASSIGNMENT OF CENTRAL PLACE ACTIVITIES

This process is one of determining which areas, out of many competing ones, will succeed in carving out a local hinterland, as the economy is able to support greater volume and more levels of activities. The probabilities of areas receiving central place activities (to become central places) depends also on present and anticipated transportation and manufacturing activities.

a. Find the maximum possible number of central places of a given level that could be supported by the population in the new time period. This is simply the total population divided by the minimum threshold needed.

b. Before any possible new central places can be evaluated, minimum hinterlands around already existing central places at that level must be withdrawn from eligibility (Fig. 13a).

c. Any hinterland, new or old, must satisfy these conditions: (1) The hinterland must contain at least the minimum threshold population. (2) The hinterland must contain no area which is actually closer to another existing center. (3) The hinterland must be "integral," that is contain no

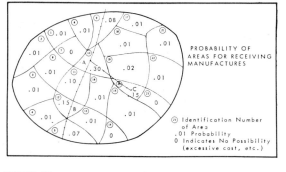

PROBABILITY OF
AREAS FOR RECEIVING
MANUFACTURES

ⓐ Identification Number
   of Area
.01 Probability
0 Indicates No Possibility
(excessive cost, etc.)

FIGURE 12a

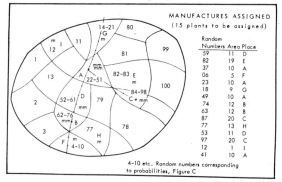

MANUFACTURES ASSIGNED
(15 plants to be assigned)

Random Numbers	Area	Place
59	11	D
82	19	E
37	10	A
06	5	F
23	10	A
18	9	G
49	10	A
74	12	B
63	12	B
87	20	C
77	13	H
53	11	D
97	20	C
12	1	I
41	10	A

4-10 etc. Random numbers corresponding
to probabilities, Figure C

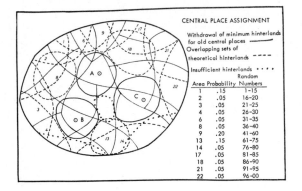

FIGURE 13a

areas farther away than some closer available intervening areas. This does not imply a circular hinterland, since a hinterland may contain areas farther away in one direction than some areas which are closer to older central places in another direction; that is, the "gateway" hinterland may occur (Fig. 13a).

d. The sum of areas around the old central places (areas enclosed by solid lines, Fig. 13a) constitute the withdrawn territory. All the remaining territory from which the new central places and their hinterlands must come is obtained by subtraction.

e. All possible theoretical hinterlands are now found. These must come out of the eligible territory and satisfy the restrictions of c. However, since they are theoretical, not actual, their hinterlands may have many elements in common. In Figure 13a are marked thirteen such hinterlands, from which the actual ones will be chosen.

f. Relative attractiveness of possible central places. Some areas can be expected to have a better chance to succeed in becoming central places than do others. This evaluation depends upon population, especially any urban population resulting from earlier assignment of manufacturing activities, and on transport position. These probabilities are treated as before (Fig. 13a).

g. Which places actually become central places is determined by a priority given by random numbers. The first random number selects the first central place and minimum actual hinterland. When the first is selected, many others may be eliminated from consideration, since in contrast to theoretical hinterlands, actual hinterlands must be mutually exclusive. All the possible central places

contained in the first chosen hinterland or which have elements in common with it are now eliminated. For example in Figure 13b, the first number, 92, selects area 21 (place J). This at once eliminates the possibility of central places in areas 17, 18, and 22.

h. In similar fashion new central places and hinterlands are chosen until there are no more possible hinterlands from which to choose.

i. There will now remain some areas, or parts thereof, which were not in the minimum hinterlands, but from which no additional hinterlands could be formed (for example, the space between the minimum hinterlands of the old central places, Fig. 13a). These are simply assigned to the nearest central place.

j. The process is repeated for higher levels of central places, except that, to be eligible, a place must already be a central place of the next lower order (as from a previous time period).

STEP 4: MIGRATION

While the underlying basis for population redistribution is the creation of differential opportunities (as assigned in the previous steps), the actual population shifts are brought about by migration. The model process is one of assigning migrants between areas.

a. The propensity to migrate, or expected volume of migration from each source area, is a function of population and its characteristics (such as rural and urban components, age structure, race, education), employment conditions, resource depletion, and normal rates of turnover in job, residence, etc.

b. The probability of migration between two areas: The most important factors affecting the destination of migrants from any one area to another are (1) the *distance* between areas, as a

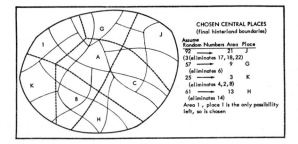

FIGURE 13b

measure of the decreasing probability of contact, (2) the differential *attractiveness* of the area, and (3) previous migration (as a key to contacts via relatives and friends).

c. Relative attractiveness is an index which takes into account those factors tending toward regular net gains or losses. During the basic process of industrialization, commercialization, and urbanization which is studied here, this attractiveness is almost entirely a function of differential economic opportunities. Therefore, it is reasonable to weight more heavily those areas with present or anticipated urban population (as a result of opportunities created in the assignment of activities above (see Fig. 14a). The correct weight for such opportunities must be empirically determined and statistically tested.

d. The basic migration relation between any two areas, that is the probability that a migrant will choose that path, is of the simple inverse distance type (Fig. 14b). The probability varies directly with relative attractiveness of the possible destination and inversely with some function of its distance. The relative strength of distance as a barrier is expected to vary with the state of technology at the time or in the area and perhaps for rural and urban migrants.

e. The sum of probabilities of migrating from one area to all its possible destinations is made to sum to 1 (for probability purposes) and converted into useful form as before. A typical pattern of such probabilities is shown in Figure 14b. There is such a set of probabilities for all source areas.

f. Random numbers, equal to the number of migrants from an area, are matched against its "migration probability field" (Fig. 14b). The random numbers select specific paths (Fig. 14d). The process is repeated for all other areas.

g. Results of migration assignment may be printed out (presumably from machine storage) in entirety (each migrant's source and destination) summarized into the total number of migrants from each area to every other area, or further summed into the total number of migrants to and from an area (Fig. 14c). From the latter, the net gain or loss due to internal migration is easily found.

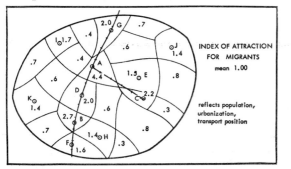

FIGURE 14a

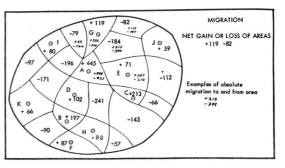

FIGURE 14c

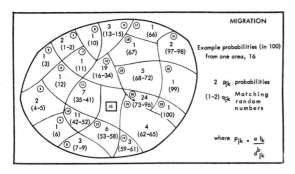

FIGURE 14b

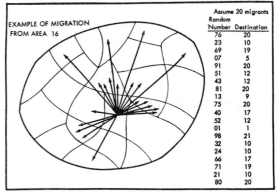

FIGURE 14d

h. At this point the results of the assignment of activities and of migrants can be summarized, and the net population, including its rural and urban components, can be totalled. This sets the stage for repetition of the entire process for another time period. The results of one simulation in a period of time at once alter the population structure and require the computation of whole new sets of probabilities. The computations become enormous. For migration alone, in the present study using 155 areas, there are 155×155 or 24,025, possible migration paths and probabilities, to be recomputed entirely for each time period. The entire migration process was therefore programmed for computer.

The above outline of a particular model illustrates two useful properties of the simulation technique: (1) the fact that no particular mathematical sophistication is required and; (2) the great flexibility of the model. Simulation is a sampling procedure. The "rules" of this sampling may be altered and realtered until the best possible results are obtained. For this present study, the evaluation suggests the inclusion of additional rules, e.g., for migration. In this experimental manner, it is possible gradually to expand and improve our understanding of spatial patterns.

INDEX

PRINTED IN U.S.A.